The signals of the century
Proclaim the things that are to be —

The rise of woman to her place,

The coming of a nobler race.

Angela Morgan
Today

WELTHY HONSINGER FISHER

SIGNALS OF A CENTURY

WELTHY
HONSINGER FISHER

SIGNALS OF A CENTURY

*The Life and Learning of an American
Educator, Literacy Pioneer and Independent Reformer
in China and India
1879 – 1980*

161 927 754

SALLY SWENSON

1988

Permission to use and quote from materials in the Fisher papers in the Special Collection of Twentieth Century Personalities, Mugar Memorial Library, Boston University, is gratefully acknowledged.

Cover by Ove Design.
Cover photos by S. Swenson.
Designed by C.M. Whittaker & Associates.
Printed and bound in Canada by
Love Printing Service Ltd., Ottawa.

Canadian Cataloguing in Publication Data

Swenson, Sally
    Welthy Honsinger Fisher : signals of a century : the life
    and learning of an American educator, literacy pioneer and
    independent reformer in India and China, 1879–1980.

    Includes index.
    Bibliography: p.
    1. Fisher, Welthy Honsinger. 2. Educators — Biography.
I. Title.
LA2317.F48S94 1988   370'.92'4   C88-090430-5
ISBN 0-9693684-0-2

To Welthy's friends —

past, present and future

CONTENTS

PREFACE

Welthy Honsinger Fisher lived the world as one place, her life spanning a century of its history, people and places. Her experience was so varied, one could legitimately write about her from many angles . . . the missionary, the pioneer of literacy, the liberated woman, the world citizen, the China years, the India years, the conquest of aging . . . yet miss her magnitude. With peers for comparison, was there any category where she belonged? Did it make sense to even begin looking at her that way?

When my association with Welthy began I was thirty-five and acutely aware of the need to grow and reach out into the world. Welthy's life offered the best example I could imagine for such learning. I wanted to know everything about her, to discover how a very mature widow came to embark on her seemingly impossible task of eliminating illiteracy in India, why she dared to try, how she leapt over the limitations of people, policies and organizations, striving for a more understanding world until death claimed her at one hundred and one.

How could a woman live so buoyantly, always breathless for more? Where did that unshatterable confidence come from? Was she really liberated though married to a bishop? Why did she begin the most significant work of her life at seventy-three? Why had she chosen India, and earlier China, for the long incubation periods of her growth?

How could she laugh when she knew better than most the world's deep problems? Was making friends really worth the significance she gave it? Why did so many love her in spite of her impatience and sometimes autocratic manner? Was Welthy an early model of the emerging world citizen? And most importantly, for my own personal search, what was she really like behind the public persona—surely she must have a fatal flaw?

She was magnetic and she knew it. That awareness of her strength caught attention to the commanding presence and sparkling personality —the "charisma" usually associated with entertainers and politicians. Was it acceptable in a humanitarian? I wondered if she ever used her power recklessly, harming others.

Why literacy? She had been called a pioneer on the battlefront of human development for nurturing an educational movement towards full literacy in India. Could one woman actually have had such an effect on an ancient society beset with basic problems? Her advanced age, a relentlessly cruel climate and repeated bone fractures would surely prevent even the toughest of the species from achieving such success. What was the source of her motivation and endurance? Was her strategy for literacy appropriate to the need?

Was her planting of a House of Prayer for All People in the heart of India not in direct contradiction to her deeply rooted Christianity . . . she who had been a missionary, a bishop's wife, the foremost Methodist woman speaker in America in the 1940's and author of several clearly Christian books?

This woman had bridged the age from hewers of wood and drawers of water to jet travel and global living, from nuclear family to nuclear world, and from the optimism that anything is possible to the deep pessimism of a disillusioned America. Yet she was obviously thrilled to be alive, full of love and laughter. Why?

Her timing — or luck — was exquisite. She was there in China at the active centre of the great Christian missionary movement at the turn of the century amid the beginnings of revolution; she was there in Europe during the first World War; she was present in India during the early stirrings of the freedom movement; and when the United Nations emerged after World War II to lay the foundations for world cooperation, Welthy mingled with world thinkers and writers, making New York her base. Was all that by chance or design? And why then did it take her five years after India finally won independence to find her place there among Americans eager to help their sister democracy?

Was she prophetic? Ideas that are just beginning to find acceptance in the late 1980's, such as government, education, and religion from within the country receiving aid, and the importance of an active female voice in society, were Welthy's premise fifty years earlier. Did she know she was ahead of her times? If so, how did she handle the rejection and ridicule our society accords to visionaries? How did she keep her eye on the twenty-first century?

Would American feminists see her as one of their own, though her long lonely action was focused on the villages of India, removed from direct political action? In her efforts to empower women, was her determination to work with men strategically wise? Was Welthy consciously feminist?

The questions grew larger and more complex, leading me more surely into the deep productive waters of Welthy Fisher's life. For a year or more after her death I mourned. When I went back over my diary notes of our fourteen years together, the almost careless clues she tossed out leapt off the pages at me. Don't complicate life, they were saying . . . at its fullest, life is simple, we *are* free, we have life. Thus armed, I began to write about Welthy's life.

* * *

My purpose has been to write about Welthy's reason for living and her power to love and delight in life. This is not primarily about literacy and educational methods, nor do I attempt to assess Welthy's influence on Indian or Chinese education, nor to evaluate Literacy House, World Education or World Literacy of Canada as they are now operating.

Neither do I place Welthy within a historical context in the orderly ranking we have been conditioned to crave, as if life were orderly. I think there is no convenient slot to contain Welthy's life. For a woman to create an open space and move into it is freedom we have difficulty associating with female. I know, because in the beginning years I often wished Welthy could be like everyone else, so that I would have less to do. It takes time to develop the kind of power Welthy had; it takes time to comprehend it.

Welthy's goal was not perfection, but pathways to the possible that individuals could approach. I have concentrated on the human values she applied to critical situations and have not attempted to judge, objectify or quantify her achievements. How could I? I was no absentee author looking on her from a cool distance.

What there is in quantity, however, is a steady accumulation of evidence by a wide variety of people in different countries as to the impact Welthy had on their lives and thinking. I consider this necessary testimony to the love and respect Welthy aroused, which was the key to her success, and to counter any skepticism due to my closeness to her. I have tried to pay attention to those things Welthy told me had made an impression on her, and to keep my own prides and prejudices to a minimum, or relegated to the endnotes.

I have included the organizational struggles Welthy endured because they are part of the early history of development and represent part of the darkness from which she constantly struggled to emerge. They are difficult reading, as are the many names that are foreign to the different nationalities involved. One editor even complained about all the Indian names. Welthy had more than new names to learn in the intercultural living and working of her days and it is important to present to people in the various cultures she bridged what was happening in these seemingly separate spaces.

Welthy Honsinger Fisher was a strong foremother to the second wave of the women's movement. The steps and struggles she endured to advance her dream of a world where women's values are in place, as they are now being defined, preceded many of the concepts we are slowly learning to accept today. Pioneering alone on the plains of northern India, she carved out those steps on which modern feminists are building. My years with Welthy coincided exactly with the start of the second wave . . . coincidence or complicity?

As she considered her steps of literacy crudely carved, I feel free to offer these building blocks of her life in this elemental form. If they were too polished and refined they would not be the truth.

* * *

Welthy was seen by some to have taken on the most impossible task in seeking to overcome illiteracy in India; in attempting to write about her, mine is surely the next most impossible. If Welthy seems elusive, she was – to boundaries. If her story seems too much, it is – by the prevailing measure. She began living the world at the start of the century, learned earlier than most what is and what is not important, and acted on that awareness. We are not accustomed to women striking out on their own, especially older women, and the conditioning of both sexes still wants to put her back in her place. But Welthy really did all she said she did, and much more. Should I conceal that out of a misguided sense of feminine modesty? The strength of her presence and personality may seem a problem – or a possibility, depending on one's approach to life.

If I took on her whole, abundant life would I be overwhelmed to the point of paralysis? I knew I could never capture that whole and was frequently overwhelmed by her size and my emotions. Whenever I was looking too narrowly I had to put the work aside for intervals, to grow back into it. If it appears to lack focus, look again through a wider lens.

This could well have been a book of names. It is impossible to include all the people involved in the creation of Literacy House. Many made significant contributions that belong in the history of Literacy House itself, and many who felt close to Welthy will not be found here. To them I apologize. I felt it was important to include as much direct quotation from Welthy as possible, to see her life from her own expressed purpose.

I know now that women have been largely written out of the history we inherited, how they have been swept aside by the conventional measure of quantifiable, external achievement. When I began writing I did not know this, but along the way my learning increased and you will find Welthy becoming more human in the latter part of the book as I grew into my role. I could go on making improvements and rewrite the early part, but the time has come to let this go as it is, for what it is. As

Welthy so often said: "I did the best I could with the brains I had at the time."

* * *

At the outset I realized Welthy's mature life had progressed in several significant fourteen year cycles; her years with Fred Fisher, 1924-38; the wandering widow, 1938-52; building Literacy House, 1952-66; her years with me, 1966-80.

For the early years of Welthy's life there was not much material to draw on, mostly her own recollections to me. The quality of her romance and marriage to Fred Fisher is based largely on letters he wrote to her. Very few of her letters to him exist, and I'm not sure why, though she mentioned some may have burned in a fire, as did all her letters from China to her mother.

Fred was an ardent student of the great minds of the western world, distilling and absorbing the essence of their thought as he prepared sermon and lecture notes. Welthy caught that attitude from him and expanded it into eastern thought, women's lives and the post-war world, carrying her bag of quotations as some carry photographs of their children as identity. They nourished her through the dark years as she prodded beyond their meaning and created her own. The words may be flowery but the ideas are not. Nor has her own language been modernized to the moment, as if history began today, for fear of losing the unique flavour she brought to expression and her perception of reality and morality.

Chapter Seven — Exquisite Loneliness — is the heart of the book, covering the long years it took for a very experienced woman to come to grips with the total change in her life — widowhood, a world at war, the atomic bomb and her own "divine discontent." It has taken me fourteen years since I first thought of this book to come to grips with my own sense of loss after Welthy's death and the changed circumstances of my own life and the world.

Because Welthy was repeatedly asked the same serious question why and how she chose at the end of her life to work in India for literacy, and because her autobiography does not deal with this in depth, I have taken it as the central question. Had she not taken those fourteen years wandering in the wilderness she could never have brought herself to the intellectual clarity, spiritual certainty and individual integrity that enabled her bold action for the remainder of her life.

The emotions, the restless travel and study, the painful confusion and bursts of clarity, and the search for companionship of those deep, dark years drawing down into her essence are tremendously important to understanding the woman who emerged. It took that long for her thought and feeling to reach that point of integrity where her dream became authentic action. We do not really like to know about this side of a woman's reality—it makes us feel uncomfortable and we would prefer to sweep it under the rug—but I consider it essential understanding.

* * *

My diary notes of our fourteen years, taped conversations with Welthy, her friends and colleagues, and the large Fisher Collection at Boston University provide the enormous base on which this book has been built. It is more chronicle than conventional biography, written not for the hurried reader but for questing spirits willing to ride through the rough spots to understand the climate in which Welthy kept growing. You might consider it an inclusive, preliminary gleaning.

Hundreds of articles have been written about Welthy but no biography exists covering the scope of her life. Her autobiography, which concentrates on her early years in China, ends where her major work in India began, and does not reveal the difficulties and controversies she encountered. Colleen Kelly has elucidated Welthy's educational philosophy in the most comprehensive work existing on her but could not go beyond the form and scope of a doctoral thesis.

My credentials are short on the side of literary skills and historical analysis, but strong on direct knowledge and experience of Welthy's life. There is no guesswork here, no need to substitute dramatic imagination for the truth. I have tried to present Welthy front and centre, where she belongs, and to keep myself where I belong, in the last part of her life.

I confess to having flirted with the fantasy of a popular book. What author does not? You see, it is easy to paint an appealing image and interest people in Welthy's wonderful warmth and work. My file of possible titles is a good reminder of flights of fancy. Urged on by well-meaning friends, I laboured in some confusion for a long time as that image floated in and out of my mind.

Others, by their silence, counselled caution. I knew Welthy too well to toss her off clothed as public performer only. I knew in agonizing detail all the ground-breaking thought and work that underpinned her character, forming the solid base on which she could soar to those appealing heights. It would be wrong to present her life in a you-can-do-it-too way that suggests we can all achieve those heights without telling the depth of creation behind.

This manuscript has been consistently rejected by American commercial publishers for its length, limited reading audience and my approach. The press at Welthy's alma mater was the swiftest and sharpest in that. Welthy's life raises more of the right questions than the sure answers our age demands. I knew that it was time once again to take my clue from

Welthy, and finally understood the need to publish this myself. If I err on the side of over-affirmation of Welthy's significance, I do so with awareness of how easily an old woman's work can be dismissed.

* * *

This is essentially a love story. It could not really be otherwise and be true to Welthy's life. Love blinds? If I learned anything from her it is that the absence of love blinds. At best, this book is an invitation to discover Welthy, in the hope of touching open minds and hearts to new possibilities.

ACKNOWLEDGEMENTS

Writing a book such as this is a major test of the friendship of all those far and near who have endured with me through the years and kept me on course. Their vital interest has meant more than they might imagine.

In the beginning there were my longtime friend Pamela McDougall Mayer and my cousin Corinne Scott who led me to Welthy Fisher's doorstep at Literacy House in 1962. I owe the next beginning to Beatrice Pitney Lamb who challenged me in 1974 with her conclusion that Welthy was unbiographable.

It took many runs at several major collections, whose librarians I thank: Yale University Divinity School Library; the Methodist Historical Library in Boston; the World Division, Board of Global Missions of the United Methodist Church in New York; The Schlesinger Library at Radcliffe College; the Ottawa and Stittsville Public Libraries; and most particularly the Muggar Memorial Library of Boston University, whose Archives of Twentieth Century Personalities house the Fisher Collection. Dr. Howard Gotlieb, Margaret Goostray and their staff could not have been more accommodating over a long period of time.

When I first sat down at the empty page, two angels appeared to offer encouragement in the form of a grant from the Canada Council and the wisest counsel from Maurice Nichol of Toronto, who somehow sensed my groping need. To both I express unending gratitude for taking my hand at a critical time.

My very special appreciation goes out to the staff and board of Literacy House in India, and to E.C. Shaw and A.R. Siddiqi, Dr. T.A. Koshy and Mushtaq Ahmed, for their particular cooperation; to Colleen Kelly whose own work on Welthy Fisher has underpinned mine; and to Lael Wertenbaker, that veteran of the written word, for her sane and salty reactions to this evolving manuscript.

To all those particular family members and friends of Welthy's who have repeatedly given their comments and advice, whether or not I followed it, I am forever grateful for going the distance with me. It is hazardous to try to name them all, but let me begin with Helen Krayer Schwartz, L.V. (Mike) Honsinger, Ernest Lauh, Marjorie Haggerty Stokes,

Martha and Tom Keehn, Litta Roberson Hutchinson, Maria Schroeder van-Gogh, Marijke Geertsema, Lisa Sergio and Dr. Marion Edman. And from the seeming remoteness of China, Talitha Gerlach and Rewi Alley brought the constant living connection I needed.

Susan McMaster came along with editorial skills to rescue me when I was awash with wordiness and authorial intrusions, and her strong interest in the story has given clearer shape to the manuscript and to my thinking. For additional editorial assistance I thank Lillian Rukas, who brought her own keen perspective to further enhance the text. Anita McClellan has provided astute assessment and valuable advice as to the publishing prospects of the manuscript.

From her own unique experience of living and writing Christine Burton has expanded my horizons and understanding as I returned to each revision of the manuscript. Oonagh Berry, Dr. James Draper, Valerie Fitzgerald, Selma Freedman, Ellen Frye, Rev. Philip Gentile, Alex Inglis, Jean Elliott Johnson, Judy Lascelles, Andrea Madan, Connie McCallum, Andrew McClure, Ann McDougall, Pamela McDougall Mayer, Dr. Frank Morgan, Dr. Gladys Neale, Virginia Schmedes, Bryan Wannop, Carolyn and Colin Whittaker, and Jonathan Williams have all taken an active interest, in various ways at different stages, in seeing this book published, for which I thank them each.

To my brother, Robert Swenson, my appreciation of his enthusiasm and increasing understanding of this production process and its effect on one's sociability. Catherine O'Keefe, who has been part of the Welthy Fisher story in my life for twenty-six years, has stood the test of friendship most nobly by listening endlessly, proofreading, and reacting with cautious approval or pregnant silence, providing a solidarity for which I am much indebted.

Throughout the fourteen years from the inception of this book, the strongest and surest support has of course been Welthy Fisher herself, whose love of her life and willingness to share it remain miraculous.

ABBREVIATIONS

Abbreviations for frequently cited sources:

D   Diaries of Welthy Fisher.

CW   Fred Fisher, "The Man That Changed the World."

FBF   Welthy Fisher, "Frederick Bohn Fisher; World Citizen."

HB   Welthy Fisher, "Handbook for Ministers' Wives."

MG   Welthy Fisher, "Beyond the Moongate."

PS   Fred Fisher, "Personology."

SBM   Fred Fisher, "That Strange Little Brown Man Gandhi."

SR   Fred Fisher, "India's Silent Revolution."

T   Tape recordings of Welthy Fisher.

TLC   Welthy Fisher, "To Light a Candle."

TW   Welthy Fisher, "Top of the World."

Abbreviations for frequently cited institutions:

AID   U.S. Agency for International Development

IAEA   Indian Adult Education Association

ILB   India Literacy Board governing Literacy House

LH   Literacy House, Lucknow, India

WE   World Education Inc., New York

WLC   World Literacy of Canada, Inc., Toronto

PART ONE

BORN WELTHY

ONE

THE METHODIST ON LIBERTY STREET

S he sat quietly in an upright armchair, her long legs resting on a stuffed Persian footstool, in the serenity of her Southbury, Connecticut condominium home. She was ninety-four then, nearly blind, somewhat forgetful of detail, but still with her handsome, regal bearing and the welcoming arms that reached out in elated greeting to each of her many visitors.

There was time now to savour countless friendships and honours, to regret things undone, to reminisce and reflect on a near-century of vital contact with the world's places and people, and certainly time to feel the arthritic ache in every once broken bone.

We had lived, worked and travelled together for eight years then, past all pretense in our affinity. We were extraordinarily close, though I was fifty-two years younger with vastly different background and experience.

Suddenly I asked her:

"What's the best thing that ever happened to you?"

I might have expected an anecdote about a major event in India or China, where her life's main drama unfolded, or a bit of wisdom from the ages of her living. She might have spoken of the great influences that shaped her—Fred Fisher, Gandhi or any of the other leading personalities she had known. Instead, the answer was pure Welthy—spontaneous, essential. Her whole body quickened, arms leapt up, eyes sparkled:

"Getting born!" she sang out.

* * *

ROME, NEW YORK, 1879

Whether she was a Hunsikker, Hundsitter, Hendsinger, Hunsinger, Honsinger or Hans der Singer, as she liked to think, Welthy was pleased with her Dutch/German ancestry. Of all Abram Honsinger's eleven children, this last one named Welthy seemed destined to live up to her inheritance of ancestry, history, geography and name. Her roots were deeply planted in upstate New York, where the screech of the locomotive whistle and the booming of canal barges brought the world together at Rome, on the western end of the Mohawk Valley, the "fiery crucible in which American liberty was forged".[1] From the start she absorbed every aspect of her environment with unusual curiosity.

She was a fifth generation Honsinger in America, starting with her great great grandfather, Johannes Michael who came with his brother from Utrecht to Rhinebeck, New York, early in the eighteenth century. As staunch Lutherans they sought freedom to conduct their iron business in New Amsterdam but found they could not do business with the young colonists on the scale they wanted, and so headed north to deal with the British. Thinking they had reached Canada, they settled at Alburg and found to their surprise when the boundary line went through that they were residents of the Green Mountain state of Vermont. That happenstance of nationality gave Welthy an early international flavour. For one of her ancestors who succeeded in crossing the line, Welthy reserved special scorn, referring to "that Tory who fled to Canada rather than have anything to do with the ragtag and bobtail revolutionaries under George Washington. I had always been ashamed of him" (TLC, 72). The little cemetery in Alburg bears witness to the first three generations of Honsingers, whose sons and daughters moved westward with other early Vermonters to become the builders of America.

Abram, youngest of five sons in a family of nine children, started an iron forge and manufacturing industry in the hamlet of Peasleville in Clinton County, New York, employing many French Canadians. A deeply religious man, he built a small chapel for his workers wherever he went. When the nearby dam on which he depended for power was swept away in the great "freshet", or cloudburst of 1856, Abram was penniless. Undaunted, he worked as a farm labourer to save enough money for a small carriage shop at Chazy on Lake Champlain. When some of his brothers went south to Saratoga in 1868, he settled in Rome, its northern twin, seeking new opportunity for his growing family.

Soon after the mother of his first six children died, he married Welthy Blakesley Sanford from nearby Camden, fathering another family of five, whose lives varied considerably in longevity: the first son died in infancy, the second son Fred lived to seventy, the first daughter Mabel to forty-nine, and Mina to fifty-nine. Abram's last, most beloved child, Welthy Blakesley Honsinger, survived every member of her immediate family for thirty-seven years. It was as if his love rewarded her with long life.

Abram was fifty-five and his wife forty when Welthy was born, daughter of their maturity, which she believed gave her a headstart. Every doctor who ever examined her knew that she arrived in this world with exceptional genes, born Welthy indeed. The Pronouncing Parallel Bible duly recorded her birth on September 18th, 1879[2] in the house at 41 Court Street just a few blocks from the old Indian portage.

By then, all but one of her step brothers and sisters had grown up and left home, leaving an experienced father freer to raise and enjoy his new young brood. A youngest son himself, he had a special feeling for his own youngest, often joking over her mother's reluctance to have another child. He claimed that Welthy's slightly elongated right earlobe resulted from pulling her mother's ear while making love to her. Welthy adored him for declaring her his child of love, even if his joke created an unintended distance from her mother, who accepted Abram's passion for Welthy calmly. It took years for Welthy to bridge that seeming distance and feel close to her reserved mother.

If Welthy got humour and love from her father, it was her mother's side, the Blakesleys, that produced her name and a sense of action. "They moved — they managed," said Welthy. Her great grandmother was the daughter of Temperance, but a later Blakesley had graduated to Experience, and by 1767 the name Welthy first appeared, the 'a' being dropped somewhere along the Puritan way. She made a game of her name; it was different, giving her a distinct sense of identity as a young girl. Had her parents named her Patience, this book might never have been written.

From England there were Dunbars, Baileys, Sanfords and Blakesleys — Blacklys, Blacksleys, Blakeslees or Blatchleys. The first to reach Massachusetts on the Hopewell in 1635 was Thomas Blakesley, who went to Hartford and Branford before settling in Guilford as a planter and later a merchant. His descendants lived in the Waterbury area of Connecticut, where the Blakesley annual sleigh ride became a tradition, promoting the family iron-working business, and where Welthy would finally settle as an eighth generation American.

The first Blakesley to be born in the wilderness area of Oneida county in New York was Welthy's grandmother, wife of an austere, aristocratic landholder in Camden named Melankthon Sanford, who lived on tenaciously to ninety-one. Their two daughters, Elmina and Welthy Blakesley Sanford, became lonely and frustrated after their mother's death when Melankthon chose for his second wife a woman who disliked children, and had none. Elmina remained at home, a spinster, but her sister had managed to get away to boarding school and then taught school before marrying Abram. Welthy grew up aware of her mother's lifelong regret at Melankthon's unwillingness to send her to college, not for a lack of money but a stubborn refusal to permit such freedom to a daughter. Visits to grandfather Sanford's farm were short and rare, Welthy recalled sadly, reflecting on her mother's unfulfilled early life.

Abram had gravitated to Rome where the great natural dam at the portage had held back glacial waters, protecting the valley and forcing other outlets for the water. The surrounding fertile fields of the valley shaped the policies and characters of the Iroquois Indians and early set-tlers; as the land itself held firm, so the later inhabitants were to stand firm.[3]

Rome was the watershed of New York State, the gateway between the Hudson, St. Lawrence and Ohio Valleys, bringing the Atlantic to the Great Lakes and beyond, accessible from all points by waterways and natural land passages.   Scotch, Irish, German and Dutch sought and won freedom from political tyranny there. Geographically and economically Rome held American history in its hand and formed a basic building block in Welthy's character as it unfolded to her.

That she should have sprung from the largest city in the United States, a distinction Rome's seventy-two square miles held until other centres expanded, explains part of her immense pride in being a Roman. With only twelve thousand inhabitants in 1879, there was plenty of space in which to grow and explore. Three railroads and the Erie Canal converged in that growing manufacturing centre. It was a lively playground for children, with movement to the world beyond in all directions by every means of transportation. Still somewhat of a rough and tumble canal town, full of adventurers, it called for a certain ingenuity on the part of curious children trying to escape a mother's protective eye.

Rome Iron Works, which Abram managed, was its first incorporated enterprise, founded in 1866 to manufacture iron according to a new process, primarily for the railroads. The Company survived the depression and unrest of 1873, but by the time Welthy was born, the substitution of steel for iron rails had forced its closing. With the arrival of commercial telephone and the demand for cable, Rome changed from Canal Town into Copper City.[4]

At fifty-four, Abram Honsinger did not make the transition. He started over again with the iron-working he knew best, establishing his own carriage and blacksmith shop near his home. Just after Welthy was born he built a fine brick shop across from the house and concentrated on carriage repairs and shoeing of horses, providing a most adequate living for his family. Welthy had no complaints about a father who was so available to his children, and who was more drawn to his church and home life than his business. To her, he had his priorities straight. For her careful, hard-pressed mother, however, a little extra income would have been more than welcome.

Welthy's earliest memory was being placed in the centre of the living room floor by Abram whenever guests came, to give her first dramatic performance in the skilled art of buttoning and unbuttoning her little shoes. As many adoring fathers do, Abram put his daughter on centre stage, with a pride and certainty she could never forget.

As she recalled ninety years later, "My father mothered me. I can remember being in his arms cradled and loved, but not in my mother's — odd. He claimed me." She was the sunlight of his late day, a beam reflected back to her with a wonder she never lost. All the later influences of her life were to expand and reinforce that unshatterable early bonding. He was the great stabilizing force whenever she was in doubt or indecision, simply because he loved her and she knew it.

Abram Walker Honsinger was six feet two inches tall, straight as a West-pointer, a giant to the little girl on the floor. Growing to his height would take a lifetime. But when she matured, Welthy was the tallest of his girls. Her fair-haired sisters looked more like their mother and were closer to her. Welthy, or "Babe" as they all called her, whose dark brown hair kept its colour till the last decade of her life, had her father's face. "He was so happy I looked like him — and everything about me. I was in his lap. I belonged to him." What was the best thing about her father? "He loved us." How did she know? "He wanted me with him all the time."

* * *

The three girls slept in one room in two beds, in a house with no electricity or running water. Welthy often resented her mother's discipline, but there were no cross words. A wise woman, their mother knew how to woo her children and make it fun for them to do her bidding. She trained them to "Wake up, Jump up," and the girls would sing back in unison: "Who took me from my warm, warm bed and put me on that cold, cold, pot? My mother!"

She would prod them to get on with their ablutions.

"We've washed as far as possible," the girls would shout back.

"Well, let's wash possible, then."

Though they had a maid, all the children had regular duties. "Mother had everything planned. I liked that. I knew what I had to do. Everybody had something. It was fair. Mine was to empty the slops, sweep the rooms and polish the kitchen stove. Fred shovelled coal and snow. Mabel and Mina had to cook." Conditioned to escaping the latter task, Welthy managed to do so most of her life, by fair means or foul, while developing expertise in the fine art of polishing.

She also had to keep the kerosene lamps clean and filled, stealing away to the woodshed frequently to play with several generations of white rats. Consuela Vanderbilt, the family cat so named by Mabel, completed the household. Abram loved that cat, and would get up before dawn each morning to let it in; her mother tolerated it amiably.

When it came time to put up the preserves each year, Abram organized his children into a cooperative peeling and chopping effort set to the rhythm of favourite songs, saving their mother's energy and teaching them that working together could be fun. Saturday nights they all sat down to a steaming pot of baked beans, in good Bostonian fashion. Otherwise, said Welthy, "I was brought up on tinned corn", an exaggeration to convey her sense of the immense cornfields surrounding Rome. Before exams, however, there was always fish to nourish their brains.

1885

At six, Welthy began her formal schooling at Rome's Liberty Street grammar school. Her real education had begun much earlier, around the fireplace, where Abram taught his children their prayers and all took turns reading from the Bible. They never missed a morning of prayers for any reason; if they were going early to the country, they got up an extra hour earlier for prayers. It was Abram's voice they heard praying. Their tiny, blonde mother was always silent in her prayers. She was the one who placed "the three greatest books in the world – the Bible, the dictionary and the atlas" on the big round table in the living room, and when any question came up at the dinner table, the children were sent to find the answer in the big books. Welthy grew up with learning as natural a habit as eating.

Life for the Court Street Honsingers centered around the First Methodist Episcopal Church a few blocks away, newly built in the revivalist atmosphere of the Independence centennial celebrations. Methodism of the day was a flourishing mix of evangelism and education, the circuit riders carrying small libraries of their publications throughout the country. Adapting to the changing frontier and the needs of a young nation, its mobile, forward thrust caught all the Honsingers in its sweep.

When Welthy was introduced to the Church, its authoritarian structure was giving way to a more democratic involvement of laymen, Abram one of the keenest. The emphasis was on the central teaching of Jesus, as distinct from biblical teaching about him. Individual responsibility and accountability to God, with each the master of his or her own spiritual fate was the message Welthy heard clearly, and saw daily in her father and mother.

Abram built a summer house in the Methodist campground at Trenton Falls and installed the entire family there for the season. Swimming in the creek, climbing the big trees, taking long walks in the woods, singing by the campfire at night, the family grew freely, together. Welthy loved the spirit of those traditional camp meetings, where untrained frontier preachers spoke extemporaneously, doing their reading and thinking in the saddle as they travelled between camps. Even the bishops were mobile. Welthy caught the attitude in the air – learning, movement, responsibility, resilience and community, all woven into song and prayer during summers of significance.

Welthy's first glimpse of a greater God beyond the God of Methodism came the year her father's two grandsons by her step-sister drowned while skating on thin ice. Abram told his family in moving terms of his efforts to console his daughter and the enlightening experience of praying with the Catholic family she had married into. Praying to the same God with the Catholic priests, their deepest need was met. Until then Catholics had been complete strangers to him.

* * *

By 1887 the Rome City Street Railroad proudly opened with nearly seven miles of track for horse-drawn streetcars. After that, the greatest treat was "putting on our little hats" for a Sunday afternoon ride on the open streetcars. Watching the great barges pass through the locks of the canal, so slowly, laden with bricks or trees and with whole families living on them, the children wondered where they were going and what they were doing. And why didn't their children have to be in school? On special holidays, Rome resounded to the percussion of German immigrant bands parading through the streets, their thrilling big drums compelling everyone to come along.

NELLIE BLY

At ten, Welthy's second idol came into view, the amazing Nellie Bly, pioneering star reporter whose sensational round-the-world race astonished the nation. "She stood straight and tall and thin, in a proper, checkered Inverness travelling coat, a small felt hat with a saucy quill, carrying one Gladstone bag," said Welthy. "I immediately became Nellie Bly."

A million people entered the guessing contest to determine Nellie's travelling time, and newspapers ran daily articles of her travels by ship, train, rickshaw, sampan, horse and burro. At the end of seventy-two days she completed her journey by special train from San Francisco to New York, and was greeted by brass bands and fireworks. The world was listening as her journalist's voice demanded reforms in factories, asylums and politics, always focusing on the poor treatment of women.[5] If she could do all that at twenty-two, what couldn't Welthy Honsinger do in a world she was just beginning to imagine?

Nellie was determined to make her life an adventure after years of ill health, by breaking beyond the teaching and nursing professions, crusading for greater freedom where she saw oppression, all with charm enough to disarm critics and foes. Those visions of drama, speed, action and purpose captivated Welthy completely. She read every detail.

"Mother" she said, "I'm Nellie Bly. I'm going around the world. Imagine seeing all the different people and riding on all those oceans!"

The *Rome Daily Sentinel* carried Welthy's first articles on Nellie Bly and the wonderful things women can do. From then on Welthy was an avid reader of newspapers, church journals, the *New York Christian Advocate*, whatever she could find. Encouraged by her mother to read all she could, Welthy began to discover the world. It was no longer Rome.

COUSIN DEE

An even more intriguing personality appeared in Welthy's life, the legendary Cousin Dee — Anna Dorinda Blakesley Barnes, her mother's first cousin. Cousin Dee's father, Henry Blakesley, had sent her to Paris to study with private tutors, as befitted a young Victorian lady from St. Louis. When "finished", she had come back and married Demus Barnes of Brooklyn, a wealthy widower and former Congressman who made a fortune out of Drake's Plantation Bitters (Castoria), and became a leading public figure, patron of the arts, philanthropist and publisher.

To the Roman Honsingers the story was mythical, from his log cabin beginnings to his mansion on West Fifty-Seventh Street in Manhattan which he bought for a hundred and sixty thousand dollars to please his society-loving wife, their cousin.

Welthy's mother once went to New York to see Cousin Dee in her fine mansion and came back with astonishing tales of another world where she experienced the extravagance of one man waiting on three women at luncheon. When Cousin Dee returned the visit, Welthy was startled when she announced she wanted to soak her feet. Imagine! And in the daytime! She could not be more different from Nellie Bly. Welthy was fascinated.

"After that Mother taught me I could do things too. When father told us his bills were too big at the dry goods store, he talked it over with Mother and told us he would pay any amount if we made our own clothes. So I became very ambitious — more than the others. I got a prize at the county fair for sewing — *I did — at the county fair!* Mother taught me. She'd do anything that was essential. I shall never forget I made a lace-edged blouse on her good old sewing machine."

The only spanking Welthy ever got was for dropping and ruining her mother's plaster of Paris hat forms that enabled her to earn enough money making hats to pay for a maid. Housework was never her mother's preference. As Welthy ran about delivering hats and collecting payments she developed a healthy respect for the fine art of doing business, and doing it quickly so there was time for play.

1890

Within the Methodist Church the establishment of the Epworth League for young people, as an extension of Sunday School, and outside the inter-church Student Volunteer Movement, had broad appeal for serious young people. Welthy's mother saw to it that all her children got to church on time, went to the Sunday evening devotional meetings and took part in the many different activities of the League.

"We learned to appear before the public and speak, and to lead meetings. Mother taught us we could do it. Fred was Presiding Officer of the League. Before that we belonged to the junior league. That's where we met people and had little lovers."

Welthy developed a good sense of herself, personally and socially, during those school years. To her, being a Methodist meant being able to get up on your feet and speak well, having lots of friends and playing a part in the community.

"I shall never forget one party, a poverty social. We all went in like farmers — it was written up in the paper and a photographer took my picture five different times. I wore something quite dramatic," said Welthy of her first impression of life in the limelight.

On Sundays the Honsinger sisters took communion together — the three graces, or the three disgraces, as Mabel joked — and were recognized as dedicated Christians. Welthy's Sunday School teacher was certain a literary life lay ahead and named her 'Pansy' after a well-known writer, thereby probably nipping a writing career in the bud. Welthy was not Pansy, nor was she ever able to confine her expansive self to the written word, despite her recurring desire to write. She wanted action.

And she looked for guidance in other places than the church, such as "Peck's Bad Boy" which she read furtively in the back row of the eighth grade. None of the other girls had even heard of it, but Welthy read about a boy who went round at night, drank, played cards, had a shotgun, killed snakes and did all sorts of other things, not all of which had appeal for her. But she told the other girls there were more things they could be doing, the way the boys did. In the end, however, discretion prevailed and she carefully discarded the book, keeping her thoughts to herself. She was in the good graces of her teacher, who was also the school principal, and decided to remain so. The restless yearnings could be contained for now.

1893

Brother Fred, or Fritz as she called him, brought great excitement to Welthy's life when he and a friend went alone by train to the 1893 Chicago World's Fair. The World Parliament of Religions was held in conjunction with the Fair and it was the first time Americans had been exposed publicly to eastern spiritualism, the first suggestion that Hindus and Buddhists were not quite the heathens portrayed by missionaries, that there might be something to learn from them.

The boys heard Swami Vivekananda from India, who told the assembled crowds that holiness, purity, and charity were not the exclusive possessions of any religion, that each one had produced men and women of the most exalted character who had something important to teach. Each must assimilate the spirit of the others and yet preserve his own individuality. The world came to Rome in lectures they prepared on a rotating wooden roller. "It was beyond and outside what anyone in our house had heard before—even my father. Did I admire Fritz!"

Fritz's descriptions of all he had seen and heard whetted Welthy's appetite. She plied him for more as they fished together in Oneida and talked about their dreams of the future. Fritz wanted to study languages and literature, but Abram had other plans for him. A son must have a proper profession, preferably medicine, possibly the ministry. Apparently Abram saw no connection between his own spiritual preoccupation and the world of literature and art.

One morning, a determined Fritz announced his intention. Abram raved against it. "I shall never forget this terrible thing going on between my father and my brother, the shouting. I ran from the room. It ended of course because my father said he wouldn't send him anywhere unless it was medicine. So it was medicine. I thought it was wicked and awful. I wept. I never spoke to father about it, and mother didn't hear the fight, nor would she argue with father." Welthy was in her early teens when that distressing scene took place, unable to understand her father's severity, too shocked to talk about it with anyone, and full of sympathy for Fritz as he headed out reluctantly into the world of medicine.

*   *   *

Welthy's school friends were mostly daughters of Rome's wealthier families—Adams, Stevens, Kingsley, Comstock, Hazleton—but her closest companion was Mabel, four years her senior. Mina was always reading girls' stories, not nearly active enough for tomboy Welthy. "I slid down the longest hill the boys did and knew all the dangerous things. No boy could jump father than I," she claimed. When one of the girls at school became pregnant, it was Mabel who told Welthy the facts of life, later confirmed by her mother. As for joining her fellow students working in the corn factories during summers, Mother said no, her daughters could work at home, helping with gardening, canning and cleaning.

For Methodists, music was always dominant, at home and in the church, a great restorative force reaching beyond the intellect and offering a natural fortress against pessimism. Father, Mabel, Mina and Welthy would sing quartets around the old square piano on rainy Sunday afternoons. "I had to be able to sing. Father's sister Polly had such a beautiful voice — he was always talking about it. I was Polly."

From her earliest days in high school at Rome Free Academy, Welthy sang solos, though she was untrained. She loved being loved for her singing, even at funerals when asked, and she went to hospitals regularly to sing at bedside communion with her church choir-mates.

Singing was in itself tremendous physical exercise for Welthy, a health — sustaining expansion of the lungs enhanced by the deep breathing exercises she did with Mabel. Fascinated by their Swedish gym instructress at school, the new exercises she showed them, and her knowledge of health, the girls were thrilled to have contact with someone from another part of the world who spoke French and German and had new ideas. They followed Bernarr McFadden's plan of fasting one day a week, drinking only orange juice. Every day they walked miles together, and they talked, always talked about their hopes for life.

They were keen piano players, Welthy learning by ear over several winters when bronchitis had kept her home from school, before her burst of physical fitness. "Mother decided to keep me indoors, not in bed, so I wouldn't be out sliding with the boys. She put a piece of cold pork on my chest and took my temperature all the time. She taught me my lessons, math and all. You know, she kept the household accounts and taught me too. I looked up to her." Her mother was becoming someone Welthy could admire as well as obey.

At the neighbourhood outdoor skating rink, it was Welthy who collected the money to put a victrola in the old heated streetcar. Skating gave her freedom and speed; skating to music made her ecstatic. Her long full skirt swirling swiftly ahead of her, she was having the time of her life.

Once she caught the attention of Marshall Morris, he could not take his eyes off her for the next two years as they skated and went to church socials together. "Everyone knew we were young lovers," she said, though they were chaste by modern standards. Her self-confidence took on a new lustre with Marshall's attention. He was always gazing at her. What did he see, she wondered?

Before that she had felt like an ugly duckling beside her tiny, pretty blonde sisters, and took comfort whenever anyone prophesied great things for her. Vanity tricked her into wearing shoes too small for her long feet, leaving her with a badly bent large toe. Mabel was the one who had lots of beaus, and Welthy could hardly compete. One boy who hung around their house infuriated Welthy by saying her voice sounded like a Negro's. She was doubly enraged by the racial slur, since she had made friends with the only black girl in her class because they both loved music. Defending her mezzo soprano voice, she said: "I kept the quality up into the high C. I didn't change to a little trill up there."

At school Welthy was thoroughly Romanized as she learned that the American flag was first unfurled in battle during the British siege right there at Fort Stanwix in 1777, and the pledge to the flag, recited by all American school-children, was composed by a fellow Roman, Francis Bellamy. Her home valley, where Indian fought Indian, French and Indian fought British, and Americans battled British, had been the pivot on which the fate of the War of Independence largely turned.[6]

The commitment to freedom that Welthy inherited sprang from that very ground, symbolized for all by a woman holding a torch in her raised right hand proclaiming "Liberty Enlightening The World" on the eastern shore of the continent. That Statue of Liberty given by France to America was installed and dedicated in 1886, during Welthy's early school years. From representing liberty the statue grew to stand for the innocence, idealism and vitality of the new world – a symbol of pride for all Americans and one Welthy took to heart.

Her father's shop and her school were both on Liberty Street. George Washington himself bought land in the area, and it was he who advised a rich Irish business entrepreneur to buy the two thousand acres that became the heart of Rome, then named Lynchville after him. Welthy always wondered why it should not have been named to honour the central fact of its history – Deowainsta – literally setting down the boat, or the Carrying Place, as the great portage was known.

* * *

All of these impressions of history, the wider world, love, heroes, music, skating, friends and unusual relatives had their effect on Welthy, but none could match the influence of her father. From her early teens, every Tuesday and Thursday night she walked proudly beside Abram to the church, neighbours setting their watches by his punctuality. She was the only young person present at Class Meetings, group sessions where older men and women of all circumstances were encouraged to express their deepest concerns – forerunner of today's mutual support groups.

"I just sat there gazing, listening – what experiences – I wasn't one of them. They all stood up one after the other and told their stories – what religion meant to them – some of them suffered greatly, physically, or with a loss of families – how kneeling all night they succeeded in getting over the hill." It was unusual exposure to adult life for a young girl.

When Abram spoke to the Class, as he did frequently in his beautiful deep voice, he told of his conversion not long after his father's death. At a camp meeting in Vermont a rough and ready lad was so changed that his hindering speech impediment vanished and life seemed to open up before him.

"He saw a great light that seemed to speak to him to change his ways. He said the whole world looked different, the sun looked different, the beauty of the flowers was different, everything took on a new light. It must have been whirring in his mind for a long time — suddenly it came to him. At nineteen he absolutely was a new man. He wanted to follow Christ, to be a religious man, not a church leader. He could stand up and give this experience every day of his life. He was a new man for the rest of his life."

From the depth of Abram's personality, and from his mystical belief that God was everywhere, Welthy received her unshakable religious sense. Abram was also an important influence in church and city life, class leader for twenty-five years, several as a church trustee, and latterly a Republican city alderman. He frequently entertained the Presiding Elder of the church, Mr. Reynolds, and the extra Sunday preachers in their home. In both private and public life he set the example of leadership that shaped Welthy's sense of herself.

When her mother finally bought a whole new set of China dishes for such occasions, Welthy thought it was marvelous to see everything matching for the first time. Sitting round the table they discussed what missionaries did and the support they needed. Abram wanted to give as much as possible for mission work, but his household manager felt he gave too much.

HIGH SCHOOL GRADUATION

In June 1896, the *Rome Daily Sentinel*, in its account of graduation day exercises of the Rome Free Academy, reported: "Miss Welthy Blakesley Honsinger, the recitation honorist, rendered a recitation entitled 'Through Grandfather's Spectacles'. Miss Honsinger made an excellent appearance. Her enunciation was very clear and distinct and her gestures were very appropriate. The audience insisted on her reappearance."

Concentrating on languages, she had completed four years of high school in three, her mother's careful tuition showing. Language and communication she loved; world history was dull except for those parts she learned through stories in Latin and German.

Welthy had already distinguished herself in winning the twenty dollar gold prize in the Declamation Contest in the Rome Opera House. "Imagine, in the Opera House!" she exclaimed at ninety, still savouring that first thrill of giving her dramatic interpretation of Will Carlton's 'Negro Funeral.' "I chose it myself. We all thought the other girl would win — the teacher was her aunt and chose her piece, which she recited from memory, copying every tone. I put the coffin right in front of the audience — here's your wonderful friend, he's gone, but here's your other pretty children, don't be giving all your love to this fellow here, give them some love."

When it was all over, the principal asked Welthy what she planned to do with this power she had over an audience. She burst through the door at home with the news of her prize to a father too nervous to attend. "He couldn't bear it if I lost." Abram's pride was her real reward, as he shared her discovery of the power to communicate feelings and ideas of her own.

Welthy put the twenty dollars into her college fund along with the money she had chosen instead of the traditional grammar school graduation watch. Between her mother and herself there was no question but that she would go to university. And when Abram told Mr. Reynolds of her high school achievements, the result was an Epworth League scholarship that would pay Welthy's full tuition at college.

She would soon be leaving home, endowed with an innate sense of her own abilities, unusual recognition and encouragement, a profound impression of the spiritual life, and her father's hand firmly in hers. "I got all kinds of things from him. Self respect — standing up — be what you are — facing the people. I loved to hear him talk. He was a natural speaker — yes, rather an actor."

As her sixteenth year ended, Welthy had already received her inheritance, that real wealth of being carefully and lovingly taught in the home, enhanced by the community. Running out to meet life, she was exceptionally well prepared to play the role that was to be hers alone.

TWO

WHICH SONG TO SING?

SYRACUSE, NEW YORK, 1896

With a mother determined that her three daughters would have the higher education denied her, each one had strong support and careful guidance in shaping the independent futures of her choice. A father's love and inspiration was one blessing, but add a mother's powerful practicality to the advantage and one may appreciate why Welthy so often said: "With my upbringing, how could I do otherwise?"

Mabel had gone to Utica to study music, and Mina to Albany Normal College. Welthy was now setting off to Syracuse University, where Fritz was well along in the medical school, reluctantly. When Welthy arrived as a freshman, Fritz gallantly took "Babe" under his protective wing, explaining everything and introducing her to his friends, showing himself to her in a new and stronger light. He was happy to have her go places with him, even when courting Evalina Vernon, whose family invited Welthy for frequent dinners, enjoying her wide-eyed enthusiasm. To test her curiosity, Fritz urged Welthy to join him in observing an operation at the medical school, which she did gamely, but once was enough to cure her of any interest in medicine. What she still did share deeply was his attraction to the artistry and sensitivity of language and literature, learned in the religious atmosphere in their home, and now available to Fred only through Welthy.

From millinery savings, her mother paid Welthy's room and board at the Pi Phi sorority house, and in return, Welthy moved about Syracuse on foot, walking miles and miles wherever she had to go. Walking helped to work off her anger at one Marshall Morris, who had gone to the University two years ahead of her and fallen in love with a fellow student.

Welthy was stunned to discover he intended to marry her rival, so certain had she been that one day she would marry her handsome skating partner. It was difficult to accept, but she quickly said to herself: "All right, brother, just go with her. I'm here for study." She never confided that romantic defeat to anyone but Mabel, and to me years later. Had Welthy won her adolescent hero, she would have been a lawyer's widow at an early age.

Her life could be filled in other ways, Welthy decided, and turned with a vengeance to a burst of various activities at that Methodist college, singing in the choir at the First Church, playing basketball and studying dramatics. She took in sewing, getting up a little earlier than the others to fit it into her crowded days, and soon developed her fashion sense to the point where she had several Syracuse ladies as steady customers.

Active and easy to get along with, she had plenty of friends — her closest friend, Grace Huff from Rome, Grace Sheffield from Geneva, Louise Winfield, Wilbur Boyd, Lara Wightman, Leora Sherwood, and many others whose children and grandchildren remember hearing tales of Welthy at Syracuse. What she lost in Marshall Morris she found in a full round of parties, dances, games and long discussions with friends, and was by no means a wallflower.

In fact, she spread herself so thinly in the first year that her marks in optional subjects — chemistry and geometry — were consistently "D". A strategic shift to pedagogy and logic improved her sophomore average to "B", with "A"s in her special interests — elocution, German and Latin. German came easily, taught imaginatively by Professor E. Kraus, who frequently invited her home for family dinners and became a lasting friend.

Another challenge from the opposite sex contributed to Welthy's disillusionment, one she handled without equivocation. The director who had invited her to join the church choir offered her free singing lessons at the university music department, which he headed. Proud and grateful to be singing solos in the best church choir in the city, she accepted.

One evening he insisted on walking her home to the sorority house after class, and while Welthy was chattering along merrily, he suddenly put his arms around her. "He was a married man, my word. I just threw him off. I wasn't going to be trotted around by him. I left that choir with a snap of my fingers and never went to that musical place again. That was my gift to the church — singing in the choir. We were brought up to do something for the church."

Welthy's music study came to an abrupt end, by her choice. At eighteen she had learned a serious lesson that led her to find appropriate ways to express her exuberant energy without inviting compromise.

She began teaching Sunday School at the orphan asylum early Sunday mornings, walking the long distance back and forth across town before the church service. Her class of pre-teens was lively and stimulating. "I liked them. They wrote little letters to me. They liked me and I liked them. If you like children they love you, you know." She captivated them with her own dramatic interpretation of biblical stories, citing one as an example: "The beggar heard that the rich man often gave money to the poor, so he went and sat outside the rich man's gate and put out his hands. When the rich man came out, he shouted 'Go away. Get out of my sight!' Soon he was dying, and all he could see was the beggar holding out his hands, and he hadn't put anything in them."

Welthy asked the orphans: "What things have we to put in beggars' hands? Could we do a little sewing for them if they were in rags? Button up their shoes? Give them some soap to wash their feet if they didn't have any?" In order to help herself, she tried to instill in the children a sense of the needs of others and practical ways to help them. The response she got assured her that even though orphaned they could understand and feel need, and would be able to help the new little ones coming in to the orphanage. It restored her own faith in herself and in others.

Up on the top floor of the sorority house Welthy experimented with secret cigarette smoking. It must have muddled her head because the theme she submitted to the debating society was roundly rejected. Welthy was not a debater and never could adopt the necessary aggressive stance of confrontation, an act not in her repertoire.

But as a forward on the university women's basketball team, which she captained, Welthy was formidable. In their smart white jackets and skirts, the team played neighbour teams in upstate New York, their defence players shouting: "Watch out for that big white lummox!" With Welthy's long arms and legs, her one hundred and fifty-five pounds, her five-foot-nine frame leaping and bouncing down the court, goaded by insults from the opposition and cheers from her side, she was a star performer.

ROME, 1898

Towards the end of her sophomore year, as Easter approached, Abram Honsinger succumbed to pernicious anemia that could not be treated by the doctor Fred brought. He had been declining for eight years since an attack of the grippe, had ceased working six months earlier, and was bedridden the last few months.

Welthy rushed home to a house full of people. "I didn't want to see anybody or talk to anybody. I loved my father and knew him as well as anybody in the world. I didn't want to talk to any of them." Suddenly all the idealism and hope of her life was gone; no one else could fully understand her or replace Abram's love. She wanted to turn away from everyone.

Reverend Greenfield sought her out where she was scrubbing and polishing furiously in the kitchen to burn off her grieving energy. Seeing a towering, lonely creature enduring her suffering with such laborious work, he exclaimed what a good missionary she would make. That was the last thing Welthy wanted to hear, the least consoling. "I glared at him," she recalled vividly, and for a long time that horrid image of the missionary he conjured up remained with her.

For the first time, Welthy was filled with deep uncertainty about life and the future. She wasn't herself anymore. All her assumptions were gone, and the lovelight from his eyes would no more shine on her. It would take six years to find enough meaning to lead her out of sorrow.

That summer, Welthy and her mother worked industriously wallpapering the house and painting the woodwork to make it ready for boarders, as the family income was considerably lowered. "I secretly admired her, and bought her a blue velvet bonnet that looked lovely on her white hair." Mother and daughter grew in understanding as they worked their way out of grief together, silently, each taking new measure of the other. Ever after, Welthy wrote to her mother daily as long as she lived.

SYRACUSE, 1899

Fritz rented a house on Marshall Street, hired a cook and ran it as a student boarding house to pay his way in medical school. To cut back on her expenses, Welthy gave up the sorority house and found a nearby room down the street so she could take her meals at Fritz's house. Admiring his resourcefulness, she increased her extra-curricular efforts to stay afloat at college, drew closer to Fritz and began concentrating more seriously on her studies. She hit her stride academically, keeping a high average, topped off with "A" for her senior year thesis, enabling her to graduate with honours in 1900.

Of all the missionaries who came to that Methodist university to speak to the students, only one ever appealed to Welthy. The rest fitted the image Reverend Greenfield had inadvertently cast upon her. For years her knowledge of the outside world had come chiefly from the drab and dreary looking missionaries who spoke in the church on trips home. Even so, for women at that time, missions offered one of the main avenues out into the world. Though Welthy was interested, she could not catch the spirit that moved these women to such remote service. She definitely did not want to be like them. But Ruth Sites was beautiful to look at, well dressed and spoke with a natural charm of the wonderful things young Americans could do in China in schools and colleges to bring the world closer together.

Welthy wanted to learn more and get acquainted with this appealing woman, but held back out of timidity and fear of being caught up in the mission world. When she did push herself forward she found a missionary she truly admired and respected. Ruth Sites said that it was a great moment for American students to share their experiences of Christian living by going to other countries, speaking the languages of the peoples, and feeling their ambitions. To Welthy she was the "dream of a personality who could do it. To us it was like *drinking fresh water* that those

who knew the rest of the world would share that knowledge with us."
Welthy's negative image of missionaries began to improve.

1900

Launched into the twentieth century on graduation, Welthy was becoming more aware of the world beyond. British supremacy ruled the
world, but American battleships were also on the move, the U.S.S. Maine
having been hit by a mysterious explosion in Havana Harbour. "Remember the Maine. To hell with Spain" was the slogan whipped up for U.S.
armed intervention in the Cuban independence struggle.

The Philippines declared their independence from Spain, yet the islands were ceded to the United States, resulting in war. As Admiral Dewey
arrived to take over the Philippines, he was cheered on by the intense
young men and women in deep discussion at the Pi Phi House, Welthy
prominent in the discussions. "We thought it was wonderful that Dewey
was saving the Philippines from Spain, who were treating them so badly."
And for the next sixty years she refused to set foot in Spain, even if a
flight routing that way was more direct.

Senator Beveridge proclaimed from the U.S. Senate that "the power
that rules the Pacific is the power that rules the world. The Pacific is the
ocean of commerce and the future. With the Philippines, that power is
and will forever be the American Republic."[1] Powerful stuff. Welthy did
not hear the impending imperialism. Instead, she heard of a future with
cooperating hands across the great Pacific. Her eyes began to face west,
towards the Orient on the distant shore.

News was coming through sketchily about the Boxer Rebellion in China
where missionaries were being taunted for demanding indemnities.
Even Mark Twain joined in the attack. Missionary reports in general
were very negative about the Chinese character, a people considered
unpredictable tabletableand potentially dangerous, with talk of "the yellow peril" common in the United States. Americans knew that a woman
sat on the Imperial Throne and had issued an Edict that all foreigners
be slaughtered.

The wave of fanaticism in the air at the end of the nineteenth century,
and her own father's prediction that the world would come to an end
in the year 2000, had little impact on Welthy at twenty-one. She was ready
for action, like other Americans of her era, brimming over with energy
and optimism. There was nothing they could not do if they made the
effort. Look at the automobile! The first commercially successful
American car, a three cylinder Oldsmobile, was unveiled at the first
automobile show in 1900. And the Kodak Box Brownie camera was in-

troduced, selling for one dollar. Everything was theirs to be done. Everything was possible.

* * *

That same year, an idealistic young man from Muncie, Indiana heard Bishop Thoburn of India speak compellingly to a Student Volunteer Convention in Toronto, and his future life came into focus.

* * *

Welthy set out on her first formal teaching job, a chaotically informal, classic example of learning by doing. She had been offered a position near Albany, but was so determined to get the musical training she missed at college that she jumped at the opportunity of teaching at Rosebud College in Garnerville, New York. It was forty-five minutes from Manhattan, offered six hundred dollars a year,—the same as high schools—was run by wealthy trustees, and she could live nearby in Haverstraw in the big Kaemmerlen house of Welthy's step-family overlooking the Hudson River. Mabel soon took a position as a kindergarden teacher in Nyack, to be near Welthy.

For two years Welthy walked two and a half miles each way along the railroad tracks to the one-room establishment, so ambitiously named Rosebud College, where she was responsible for thirty-five children in eight grades. "I learned to teach," she said. She was on her own. Her short optional course in education at Syracuse was no preparation for this bedlam.

"Well, let's begin," thought Welthy. They would have to get acquainted and start to like each other. She had already learned at Syracuse what made a good teacher by watching her professors closely. The subjects they were enthusiastic about were the ones she liked. "Those who poured their personality into their subjects and made them their own — they were believable and made me want to learn. The textbook teachers did not arouse me. Their attitude said it all."

"Each one had strong points in that little schoolhouse. I learned to understand and deal with different levels of ability and interest, and to respect the variety. I couldn't help liking all the children and showing it. They liked me in return and wanted to live up to my expectations. Discipline and motivation never were real problems." Welthy had discovered the secret of making difficult children want to behave. She corralled them as allies in a cooperative teaching-learning adventure that included the lowest and the littlest. Organization and management came easily as she put the classes in separate areas to study, bringing each class up front in turn for its lessons. The older boys took turns keeping the fire burning. Everyone brought their lunch and sat around like a large extended family at noon, Welthy loving almost every moment with her new companions.   Using laughter and song as her teaching aids, Welthy discovered that she was a natural teacher.

JIMMY

One incident stood out sharply in her memory. It was the first realization of her ability to handle a crisis with a symbolic, spontaneous act — a sign of leadership. She was thrust into controversy with one of the three trustees of the school, a wealthy southerner who lived next door on a large estate. Welthy was a frequent guest in his home. His two daughters enjoyed her piano playing and singing, and his house was often filled with their music.

Convinced that one or some of the schoolchildren had stolen cherries from his orchard, the trustee rounded up the entire school outside the building during Welthy's absence at noon and was lecturing them noisily. Welthy arrived on the scene protesting his presumption that all were guilty, and his failure to inform her first. She noticed one student missing, the only black child in the school.

"Where's Jimmy?" she asked.

"I dismissed the nigger and was warning these others," replied the trustee.

Welthy flew off down the road after the terrified lad, and dropped to her knees in the dust as she caught him to her. Sobbing, he denied stealing cherries and refused to return to school.

"If you won't go back, then neither will I", she said, taking his hand. "You're as much a part of the school as I am." (TLC, 11.)

In the few minutes it took to walk back to the astonished crowd, Welthy found the courage to tell the trustee clearly and calmly that she would not return to school unless Jimmy Burley returned. Everyone went back to school. The trustee's daughters were especially pleased that Welthy had stood up to their father, and Welthy was proud to have stood up to her employer on a matter of human decency. Her instinctive identification with Jimmy was as much a revelation to herself as to the onlookers.

* * *

The happy life in the busy Kaemmerlen household and two years of strenuous teaching experience were not enough to satisfy Welthy. She had time for a few piano lessons, but Welthy wanted to sing and needed a voice teacher. Reaching for the top, Welthy was drawn to the new musical mecca of Carnegie Hall in New York. When she found Madame E. H. Canfield there, her singing began in earnest during the great German period of opera, Wagner prevailing.   It was not long before Madame's encouragement, and her own stimulation from the pursuit of her chosen career made Welthy want to plant her feet in Manhattan. With her natural mezzo soprano voice she was already being paid to sing at funerals.

NEW JERSEY, 1903

She found a new position closer to the city and was rapidly promoted to head of the German and French department in Englewood High School in New Jersey. Tall, athletic and animated, her physically commanding presence won the respect of students. And the principal showed her respect for Welthy by asking her to sit in on some of her own classes to discourage the students from clowning around and mimicking the principal's foreign accent. She knew they would behave properly in front of Welthy, not out of fear but of respect for her confident bearing. And the students knew that Welthy liked them and was on their side. She couldn't help showing it.

Madame Canfield arranged for her to join the quartet of a Presbyterian Church in nearby Tenafly that sang twice on Sundays and at frequent concerts, allowing her to earn enough money to pay for the expensive voice lessons. She also took on the extra task of developing the school choir and preparing it to sing at commencement exercises — her first effort at musical directing. Meanwhile, in keeping with the Honsinger musical tradition, Mabel was playing the organ at ice cream socials, accompanying an accordion.

The fabulous Cousin Dee was there in New York in her elegant new home on East 65th Street, having married William H. Bliss, after her first husband died and left her with many millions. To Welthy she remained largely a mystery in those years, though they had some contact. Had that patroness of music discovered Welthy as she was then, determined to sing, a great operatic career might have been shaped. As it was, Cousin Dee knew little about Welthy's ambitions and Welthy was still in awe of the grand lady.

MARY HILL

Because of her knowledge of German and French, Welthy was asked to teach English to European immigrant workers in a special night-school programme at the school. One day in the middle of that adult education class, the door at the back of the room burst open and a voice shouted: "Does you all teach readin' and writin'?"

Without hesitation or formality, Welthy said yes, and invited Mary Hill, the illiterate daughter of a slave, to join the class. Whatever the regulations were, and regardless of the level of the class, Welthy decided to include Mary and find a way to bring her along. It meant extra coaching as she taught her to read phonetically, teaching that continued for several years after Welthy left Englewood.

Later Mary worked as a maid in a Westfield, New Jersey household with a young daughter, Helen Linn, who referred to herself as a by-product of Welthy's first experiment in adult literacy education. Mary Hill always held up the standards of a mythical "Miss Honsinger" to Helen. "Miss Honsinger wouldn't like that!" she would warn. Mary became a community stalwart and at her funeral in 1941 there were no less than six clergymen, which gave Welthy a rewarding sense of pride in helping her black friend use her strengths, aware of the powerful effect reading and writing could have on a single life.

EUROPE, 1904

Welthy made her first trip abroad at twenty-five. Using her savings, and borrowing two hundred dollars, she made her plans to spend the summer exploring music possibilities in France. A special fifty dollar rate for the sixteen day trip across the Atlantic by freighter was arranged by a student's father, who owned the steamship company and felt gratitude to Welthy for influencing him to shift his children from private to public school. Welthy's mother was glad she was using the borrowed money to put something in her mind, where no one could take it from her — a message that was not lost on Welthy.

Her companion, Bertha (Berr) Deyo, was a fellow teacher at Englewood, a Cornell graduate. "She was brilliant. I was absorbed by her knowledge. She knew history. I didn't. I was listening to her all the time. She was intellectual, not very handsome, but you forgot about all that. Lots of fun." As the windows of the world were opening for the girls, so were the eager arms of two French doctors who were the only other passengers on the freighter full of MacCormick reaper machines. "We watched the sunset and the moon with them and learned a lot about France — never a kiss," recalled the well brought up Welthy, admitting that it had been difficult to go back to their cabins at night. Temptation was there, but their puritan chastity remained intact.

Paris was a surprise to Welthy in many ways. Compared with New York, so crowded with great waves of immigrants, Paris was clean, and quiet, with ruffles and lace trimmings everywhere. Her observations were quite limited, for if she had looked far beyond the broad, well-planned avenues she would have found the crowded quarters of the poor. The girls were much more interested in meeting French students, however, and were amazed at their political knowledge, so much more than their own.

Rooming "topside" in a pension at 13 Le Grand Chaumiere in the Latin Quarter, where speaking French at the table was *de rigueur*, they provided entertainment for everyone with Welthy's occasional lapses of memory and Berr's empty slate of vocabulary. When Welthy encountered serious digestive problems, it was a French doctor who introduced her to the lifelong custom of smothering her food in cayenne pepper, to the horror of anyone observing. Was that the great health secret of her longevity?

They studied French, of course, but for Welthy the main purpose of the four months in Europe was to explore the possibility of studying opera there. She met some teachers and very soon realized their fees were far beyond anything she would ever be able to afford, no matter how much English teaching she did on the side. Already in debt, she reluctantly gave up that idea, and even though the operas she had studied — Faust, Samson and Delila — were "heavenly" to her, decided she would have to settle for nights of listening to the opera from the topmost seats.

Anxious to improve her French and German accents, Welthy was keen to move about and talk with people. They visited Bordeaux, Heidelberg, and Munich. At Strasbourg they had a letter of introduction to a French Admiral's family, and were astonished to find them speaking perfect English, not so foreign after all. In Utrecht, home of Welthy's paternal ancestors, they saw a mass wedding underway. An austere, thundering preacher was scolding the brides, quickly arousing Welthy's concern for the low position of women there. In London, Berr gravitated to the British Museum; Welthy learned more from the omnibus drivers.

On the return voyage across the Atlantic, their ship hit an iceberg. Welthy heard the full gamut of human sins confessed by her fellow passengers, men and women who had not prayed in years, on their knees in lifebelts, as they vowed to sin no more, if only their lives were spared. "Oh God, if you let me live through this I will never leave him again, I promise," murmured a voice nearby. These confessions were far more than anything she had heard at the church class meetings back in Rome. Was everyone so disturbed about the way they had lived, she wondered?

* * *

That same summer of 1904 the young man from Muncie, Indiana also passed through London, en route to his mission post. Too young to be ordained in 1900, he had received an "Exhorter's Licence", after offering himself for service in India. In a moving, informal laying on of hands Bishop Thoburn had prayed and said: "I set you apart for India." Feeling exalted, the young apprentice clergyman had sung to himself: "I'll go where you want me to go, dear Lord, over mountain or plain or sea.

I'll say what you want me to say, dear Lord, I'll be what you want me to be."

In fact, as he and his childhood sweetheart bride left London on a Pacific & Orient ship, the first harsh realities hit them. The British colonials aboard would not even deign to speak to them, and furthermore, they considered all Indians inferior. Did they all think they were Rudyard Kipling, he wondered, but tried to understand their imperious attitude by remembering the constructive achievements of the British in opening up Indian communication networks of roads, rails and canals. Americans, he discovered, were considered crude and meddling by their worldly wise British cousins.

When he reached his mission post at Agra, none other than the masterful Kipling himself was in the city. Eager to better understand these British, he rushed to Kipling's hotel to find the famous face covered in shaving cream but ready to extend a warm welcome. They had a rousing talk and Kipling wrote out his poem "The Pioneers" for his new young friend, whom he met several times again and presented with a walking stick. Charmed as he was, the young man was in no danger of becoming an Anglophile.

* * *

New York had a treat in store for Welthy; the new subway system had just opened, carrying her speedily back and forth to the opera every week. She could only afford to sit in the top rows. Mabel was teaching in the city, and Welthy shared her apartment on West 148th Street, commuting one and a half hours each way by ferry across the Hudson River to her job in Englewood. Other friends joined them in the apartment from time to time, and sister Mina soon came down also. The "three graces" were upright young ladies, their social life still centering largely around church activities. Welthy and Mabel introduced Mina to her future husband, Arthur Limouze, a young Presbyterian minister in the limited circle of their friends.

Welthy's voice had developed to the point where she was given solos occasionally with a large chorus at Carnegie Hall, inspired by her singing idol, Edythe Walker, a fellow Roman, who lived and sang in Europe. When Edythe Walker finally came back to sing in the States she told reporters, to Welthy's great shock, that she had stayed away because there was no culture in America. "I could hear my father's prayers," protested Welthy. When Miss Walker's concerts received bad press reviews in her native land, Welthy was even more shocked by the harsh judgment of the critics. "Am I going to give my life to entertaining a fickle public?" she asked herself. Would she be satisfied letting critics be her judge, their pronouncements controlling her career?

PARLA FOSTER

A new friend played a prominent role in Welthy's shifting interests in those indecisive years, in the person of Parla Foster from Portchester, New York (whom she discreetly referred to as 'Tom' in her autobiography). Properly introduced by his teacher aunt, he was unlike anyone Welthy had ever known before. He worked on Wall Street and would call up and say he had made a hundred dollars that day, inviting her to come down and help him spend it. For someone who had always been meticulously careful with money, it was recklessly appealing to even think of using money with such abandon. "We'd go and have a wonderful dinner, sometimes to the theatre, but he wouldn't go to the opera with me. He was very tall, lots of fun. We went to big dances at the Armouries. I loved it — everything with rhythm." But when she went home to Rome in the summers, she did not see Parla at all, and did not tell her mother about him, certain she would not approve of such frivolous pursuits.

In Rome she took walks, read books, dieted and thought. Grandfather Sanford died at ninety-one, willing everything to his second wife and nothing to his daughters, one a widow, the other a spinster. Welthy's mother and aunt were now living together on West Thomas Street, leaving Welthy free to pursue her interests, though she always continued sending money home to her mother. She was not made to feel, nor was she inclined to think, she should stay home to care for them.

Teaching, singing, dancing, and sailing up the Hudson River on the big riverboats with Parla, Welthy had it all, or so it seemed. Not beautiful by conventional standards, her photographs of those years show a strong face of increasing attraction, her hair softly upswept, with powerful, luminous eyes. Parla wanted to marry Welthy. Her kisses gave him hope, and more. She was flattered, excited and uncertain. At twenty-six she had the world, and Parla, on a string. But was this what she wanted?

In the early years of the new century, Welthy was paying only slight attention to the wider world, the Wright Brothers having captured her interest with their famous first flight in 1903. Japan had stirred the oriental world with a victory over Russia in 1904, and young Chinese flocked to study in Japan by the tens of thousands, including Chiang Kai-Shek.

In 1905 the United States Congress hardened and extended the Chinese Exclusion Act, provoking the first anti-foreign boycott in China for the brutal treatment of Chinese in America. That same year, in Nanchang, China, a riot forced missionaries to flee the city to Kiukiang. These contradictory signals seemed to Welthy in stark contrast with the benevolent aims of the missionaries, but her knowledge did not go far beyond the newspaper headlines. She was busy working and having too much fun.

Her main interests were still friends, music, study, beaus. Confident and unafraid, life ahead was one large opportunity. It was only a matter of choosing. But could she accept Parla? Something she did not understand was holding her back.

ROBERT SPEER

Her father's example of accepting the spiritual life as natural, her mother's trust that the freedom she permitted Welthy would never be used only for personal pleasure, and her own sense of Christian identity, all came into focus one evening in 1905 at Carnegie Hall. She had gone to buy opera tickets and noticed that those leading figures of the missionary movement, John R. Mott and Robert Speer, were coming to speak there. Parla refused to go with her, but Berr Deyo was ready to join Welthy in hearing them address a packed assembly of the Christian Student Volunteer Movement that Dwight Moody had founded twenty years earlier.

Speer, a staunch Presbyterian, was one of the greatest advocates for foreign missions in church history. To some he was "Weeping Bob" as he spoke of the black awfulness of sin, appealing to the heroic youth to evangelize the world in its generation. "Duty is clear; Christ commands; we obey," said Speer.[2] Many in that hall had come long distances with a will "to be called". They came from small mid-western co-educational colleges in small bands combining school spirit with evangelical enthusiasm — a romantic student movement that provided half the missionaries sent out. They felt privileged and responsible for doing something in the world, fortified with a strong sense of nationalism.

Welthy was several years older, had solid working experience, and was not caught up in that elite camaraderie. She was there on her own, in a chance encounter that would lead to adventure, service and leadership for which she was well prepared. To her, Speer was compellingly earnest as he proclaimed, "The Gospel is either true for all, or it is not true at all."[3]

He saw Christianity as the great unifying force in the world, the deep moral foundation that would transform individuals who would change the evils of ancient societies. "The world knows itself to be one world. Shall we not share the good we know, or only let them have evil? Shall we share only our tangibles and not our hopes and ideals?"[4] he asked. Here was an attitude, an outlook, a desire she recognized as her own.

Speer went on: "Every man has a right to know of Christ. The supreme missionary method is the living of the Gospel. Real love in the missionary heart will overcome the inevitable differences of culture, status, custom and wealth. The human race is one."[5] It was an appeal to the heroic instincts Welthy had in abundance.

"This is what I want to live for," she knew at once, and in that moment of recognition, her long sorrow over Abram's death was relinquished, and she came to the realization that he had not been perfect, but another human being trying to do what he felt was right. The mission field became a distinct possibility.

The majority of missionaries of that day felt that Christianity was superior to all other religions. Speer believed that the good and truth in all religions were purer and fuller in Christianity, an inclusiveness Welthy found very acceptable. He supported reform in other religions, while denouncing some of their evils as he saw them. His goal, however, was to seek converts to Christianity. From the start, the supreme goal for Welthy was to live the Gospel.

That night, she went home and explored her reactions to Speer in her diary. "To be or not to be a f-o-r-e-i-g-n m-i-s-s-i-o-n-a-r-y; to bury myself in some desperately needy country; to be queer but independent; never to taste the abandon of music nor the alluring sweets of applause and success; to grind in the bare room in some unknown part of an unknown country, alone save for the presence of a great ideal that once was brought to us by the Great Idealist of Galilee." (MG, 15.) Welthy wrote of her decision in dramatic terms, still bothered by the old negative missionary image, and indulging in some histrionics of self-denial, in part to enliven the diary she wrote later of her missionary years.

All night long she kept asking herself if she could give up Parla, if she could give up an opera career, if she could "bury" her temptations and live for her larger self by sharing with young women in a distant land some of the ideas and the self-reliance she had been given. Parla had already been conquered and was easier to give up. But the possibility of opera stardom was still remote; it was like giving up the unknown. "To be or not to be an opera singer — that is, provided European masters found in me what American teachers prophesied. And in the end speaking to the multitudes through music, and flowers, applause, curtain calls, newspaper write-ups — perhaps; but before that years of grinding work in a little bare room there across the water, alone save for ambition." (MG, 15.)

Her father's voice in prayer and in song kept reverberating in her mind, and by morning her response to the challenge Speer presented was clear. "I do not know now and did not know then how I made my decision. One morning it was there, unshakable, deep in my heart.

God's will or my own, from that moment on nothing made me waver," Welthy said in her autobiography.

1906

Parla had faded into the background. And so too the "feminized over-civilization"[6] of mainstream, late Victorian America, where women were conditioned to develop taste in clothes and furniture to enhance domestic life, with marriage the ultimate goal. To Welthy, coming from a more progressive background than many of her contemporaries, such conformity to the prescribed standard was inconsistent with the new awareness developing in her.

She had accepted the high values of her parents. Her home was a powerful learning centre from which she sprang into ever-widening circles. And she had seen her mother's confinement to domestic life, understanding more clearly now why she wanted her daughters educated. It was not only Parla Welthy could not accept, but the limited life she saw for herself with him.

WOMEN'S FOREIGN MISSIONARY SOCIETY

If Welthy thought the life of a missionary was full of unlimited opportunity, she had surprises ahead of her as she encountered the Women's Foreign Missionary Society (WFMS) of the Methodist Church. Overcoming her earlier reaction, she spoke first to Reverend Greenfield in Rome, who wisely sent her to see Mrs. J. M. Cornell, of the New York Chapter of the WFMS. Beautiful, charming, well-dressed, of superior intelligence and goodwill, Mrs. Cornell paved the way for Welthy to enter missionary service, on her own terms. Welthy's letter of application was passed on to Mrs. Stephen L. Baldwin, President of the Chapter, with these comments: "Temperament—Nervous; Disposition—Affectionate, sunny; Adaptability—Great, to people and circumstances."[7]

She was accepted by the branch for her "splendid accommodations for tact, adaptability, attractiveness, promise as a leader, very generally beloved," and was recommended to the national body with these remarks: "Of strong Methodist ancestry, sterling Christian character, lovable and easy to get along with. Call definite."[8]

When Parla wrote to the WFMS on hearing the news, they confronted Welthy with his letter. He said it was nonsense for her to go off alone as a missionary, that she was just running away from marrying him. The women wanted to know her feelings and intentions about Parla. "I was disgusted", she said, her determination getting stronger by the minute, and the women were quickly convinced of her commitment and began to describe the training she would undergo for her service.

Alarmed at the prospect of programmed piousness, Welthy told the ladies she had been considering another possibility of taking students of affluent parents to Europe each summer, arranging cultural training for them, and doing some studying of her own on the side. Using her bargaining chip with a subtle touch, she said she had not chosen to be a missionary as an act of desperation. She was seeking a more stimulating, expanding, useful role of service. Her six years of teaching in the formal school system had been excellent experience, but she had felt confined, and even a singing career seemed insufficient reward for the long, lonely effort of training required.

Welthy knew she needed to be working with people, and as she told the women of her struggle to decide, her tact and sincerity won out. They went into a huddle in the corner to review the situation, recognized Welthy's abilities and potential, and agreed to spare her the usual missionary training she dreaded. They would send her out into the world on her own terms, unbound.

They asked if she wanted to go to India; she said yes, having no particular area in mind, but her doctor thought otherwise because of the humidity there and her former respiratory problems. That was the one and only time Welthy was required to listen to a doctor's advice; ever after she either had no physical examination or gave low priority to any medical advice when she travelled or worked in foreign countries, India included.

In 1906, however, she really had no option, nor was she so well acquainted with her body's capabilities. The other available mission openings were all in China and she was selected by Mrs. Baldwin to be principal of the Stephen L. Baldwin Memorial School, built in Nanchang by the New York Branch in memory of the pioneer missionary who had gone to southern China forty years earlier.

In the months while she prepared to depart for China, Welthy got better acquainted with Mrs. Cornell, visiting her home in Seabright, New Jersey, and her New York apartment. Of all the WFMS women, Welthy felt closest to her. She had luxury, but it did not mean everything to her. She was very much of this world, yet devoted to missionary work. She was animated, loved beauty, and there was nothing pious about her. She gave Welthy the courage to believe she could be her happy self, loving all the beautiful things of life, while serving the high purpose she had chosen. "She cemented me to the decision," said Welthy. How shrewd of Reverend Greenfield to have sent Welthy to the one woman in the WFMS who could really understand her.

Parla had not been the only one to object to her decision. Everyone in the family, except her mother, said she was foolhardy. Even Mabel, who knew her so well, was against it. Berr Deyo, too, thought it was a waste of her life. One uncle took all the family to dinner in Chinatown pointing to the inhabitants, whom he considered so inferior. "These are the people Welthy is going to give her life to. She has no business throwing herself away like that," he said, adding that at least she should go as a nun, to be protected.

Welthy was resolute. Nothing would stop her now, and to know that her mother had faith in what she was about to do meant everything. She finished her teaching year and headed home to Rome. Mina was married to Arthur Limouze that summer from the smaller house on West Thomas Street in what was the last of the family gatherings for Welthy.

From Parla she accepted a brilliant red opal ring set between two diamonds. He insisted she keep it on her right hand, and said they would meet in Paris in five years to weigh life in the balance, Welthy sufficiently overcoming her "disgust" at his intervention with the WFMS to keep that door open. Though she always spoke of her clearcut decision not to marry him, a draft of an unpublished novel on her China years shows how truly torn she was between the desire to serve the wide world and the "instinct to mate".

* * *

The young missionary from Agra was crossing the ocean again that summer en route to Boston, because his wife's health had proved to be unequal to the Indian climate. He was reading widely, Confucius, among others, and recording thoughts in his prolific notebooks. One entry stands out: "I cannot get away from the idea that I am to be used of God in some special manner in the world. In dreams by night and by day . . . there seems to be just before me . . . almost within sight . . . a world as yet I know not of." Contemplating Cecil Rhodes' wish to be buried on the top of a mountain to be named 'World View', he wondered "Why not live there?" The following day he quoted from J. R. Miller: "You cannot dream yourself into a character, you must hammer and forge yourself one."[9] He resolved to do so.

* * *

Welthy was given a warm sendoff from Rome by friends, family and church. The local WFMS gave her a guitar and a purse of money, and on October 19, 1906, the eve of her departure, the young people of the Church staged a large farewell reception with a full musical program, presenting her with a set of handsome table linen and a set of silverware. Welthy would enjoy her linens and silverware, but her guitar would win friends.

She sang two hymns at that reception: "I'll go where you want me to go, dear Lord," the battlecry of missionaries. And with her song of farewell, there were few dry eyes as she sang the words she chose especially to seal her commitment:

> *In the secret of His presence*
> *How my soul delights to hide,*
> *He that dwelleth in the secret place of the Most High*
> *Shall abide under the shadow of the Almighty,*
> *His truth shall be thy shield and buckler,*
> *Thou shalt not be afraid for the terror by night,*
> *Nor for the arrow that flieth by day.*
> *He shall call upon me and I will answer Him,*
> *I will be with Him in trouble,*
> *I will deliver Him and honour Him.*
> *With long life I will satisfy Him*
> *And will shew Him my salvation.*[10]

* * *

Welthy was on her way. From her family she was armed with a Methodist blend of action and altruism, the ideals of her father, and the quiet, interior religion of her mother. And she set forth from America at the historic height of the world missionary movement with a native conviction that freedom and responsibility could perfect individuals and the world.

PART TWO

OPENING TO CHINA

THREE

LITTLE SISTER HAN AT BAO-LIN SCHOOL

CHINA, 1906

In the late autumn of 1906 Welthy began her westward journey in Omaha, Nebraska, where she was called upon to address the general executive meeting of the WFMS, a forbidding immersion in the business of missions that made her restless to move on. Carefully arranging for their women to travel in a safe group across the Pacific, the WFMS despatched Welthy by train for Seattle, via San Francisco, with three other missionaries, including Miss Ilien Tang, an American trained Chinese also assigned to Nanchang.

When Welthy's luggage failed to arrive in San Francisco, she merrily waved goodbye to her companions as they went on, for she was eager to explore the city on her own. What she saw in full, devastating detail was the warlike destruction of the great earthquake that spring, an awesome encounter with nature's true power. By the time she retrieved her luggage and reached Seattle, a sobered Welthy found her ship had gone and she had two weeks more to roam this city, reflecting on the high adventure ahead. To be sailing alone across the vast Pacific on the S. S. Tango Maru at twenty-six was the stuff of dreams.

She sailed at night out of Puget Sound, the shore blending with the darkness of the sea, and Mount Ranier's white peak shining brighter and brighter as they moved out. Was it a symbol of the better part of herself, she wondered, rising above the earthly ambition to be an opera singer? She tried to analyze why she had let go of her earlier dream, just as she was now letting go of the shores of her native land. The answer did not come to her clearly, but years later she realized it was the disparity in their religious upbringings that had sent her from Parla. She was reaching for life in a larger dimension than he thought possible for her. As her ship headed west, she turned her face towards the east.

During the four week crossing to Tokyo with eight other passengers, Welthy sat at the skipper's table and made good friends of Willys Peck, a young China-born diplomat, son of the Ambassador in Peking, and of the musical wife of a professor at Tokyo University who loved to accompany Welthy's singing. Each evening they gave concerts to her "aching heart's delight", the west not quite so easy to leave as she imagined.

From Willys she had her first lessons in Chinese language and customs, and as they walked the deck five miles a day and talked about China she realized she knew as much about that country as the average American university graduate—nothing.   Education in America was concerned only with life west of the Suez.   She had thought she was an educated woman, but all she really knew of China came from random accounts of returned missionaries.   There was no time to lose in filling the gap, and she decided to apprentice herself to anyone and everyone who could help.   Her ignorance of the east was a revelation; she knew she would have to study larger maps.

Halfway across the ocean, a young Japanese sailor was thrown down from the crow's nest lookout onto the deck during a tremendous gale. He was killed instantly. The engines stopped dead, and with a simple Buddhist service, his body was offered up to the sea, affecting Welthy deeply. "One moment he was a living soul, another moment he was a disappearing spot on the sea." As they neared Japan, the Captain, whom Welthy had told about her symbolic leave-taking from Mount Ranier as they left America, invited her to the bridge every day to feel the rising welcome of Fujiama, sensing her need for a new sign of life.

TOKYO

In Tokyo she went round the city with Willys, astonished that all the moneylenders were Chinese, apparently highly trusted. Later she discovered why. It was not so much honesty, as the fact that the guild and clan that managed the moneylending was held responsible for each member, including his debts, so that honesty became the best policy for all.   Except for farming, everything in China, the entire commercial system, was a network of those small, cooperative guilds.

She and Willys went by "Lilliputian" train to Kamakura to see in the moonlight the great bronze Buddha, untouched by the fire that had destroyed his shrine, its living power quite overwhelming to Welthy. "He has arrived in the state called Nirvana, where the individual soul is lost in the over soul. The mouth is so tender, the eyes so deep, the head so strong and the all so filled with faith and calm that a little came down to me." (TLC, 18-19.) In the "velvet silence" the Buddha loomed higher than the highest trees. "The white moon lit up its face so that it seemed for the moment a living thing." (MG, 17.)

So strong was that shared experience, that Welthy and Willys were at first speechless, then engrossed in conversation as the train returned to Tokyo. Oblivious to the fact, these two had progressed to the category Welthy described as "little lovers", and found themselves on a return journey to Kamakura, not reaching their waiting ship until three the following morning.

SHANGHAI

In Shanghai Welthy parted from Willys, noting cryptically in her diary: "P. W. has invited me to Peking whenever I must have a dance or a skate or freedom! I cannot quite take it in. That Americans in China live, move, and have their being as they do in America! I had expected to be really — so different!" (MG, 18.) She was absolutely unprepared for the closed little community of the white man in China, so evident immediately on arrival.

Welthy had not thought to cable her arrival to the mission people in Shanghai, who had given up meeting ships in the hope of finding her. Not at all worried about finding her way to them, she had her trunks piled into wheelbarrows, riding off in a rubber-tired rickshaw from the docks, in "all the comforts of a limousine without any of its parking difficulties". The sight of the splendid Sikh traffic officers standing like statues in the intersections, in their scarlet tunics with glistening beards, was Welthy's first magnificent glimpse of India, right there in China. How clever of these British to have one race police another, she mused.

Not trusting herself more than eight hours in Shanghai, she quickly bought her ticket for the next leg of journey. "Having turned my eyes from the fleshpots of America, I would not yield to the lures Shanghai offered." Luggage disposed of, she set off on foot to explore Shanghai in the short time available with a young American major heading for the Philippines, obviously enjoying the male company.

"We two children from the western world went looking for China, but instead found Europe, the city unmistakably western with mediocre western architecture." They wandered miles beyond the western enclaves to a remnant of the old city wall, and underneath it found a fascinating alley that was the China of her imagination. But the major did not share her delight, seeing only the horror and the smells of the congested maze, and predicting that she would not last more than three months "among people like these". In fact, all the way across the Pacific her fellow passengers had been making small bets as to whether or not she would stay.

On that first evening in China she was formally introduced to imperialism while dining at the home of an American professor who raved about the British and ranted against the Chinese. Reflecting the British-Japanese alliance, he was all in favour of the Japanese inroads into China, certain that they could give the Chinese better administration than the Russians. For Welthy he gave a specific warning that she would have no protection from the British or Americans in Nanchang, since the nearest British gunboat was in Kiukiang, and urged her not to proceed. It was all very depressing, but Welthy realized there was much she did not know yet, and would not accept the professor's rigid attitude.

At the end of the day she was relieved to board her Yangtze river steamer, the "spasm" of Shanghai over. "For I have come to China to be a foreign m-i-s-s-i-o-n-a-r-y. I have looked in the glass again and again to see if I *look* different. And I don't seem to yet—to me anyway—but I *am* one and on Chinese soil this minute. . ." (MG, 10.) Though it was all new and wonderful to Welthy, she was in fact following in the footsteps of some hundred and thirty Methodist missionaries who had preceded her to China since 1847, mostly to the large eastern coastal cities. Yet Welthy was heading alone into the interior, alive to the drama underway, at once the subject and object of her own imagination and high purpose.

* * *

The ancient soil she had landed on was troubled and unlike anything she had ever known. Why were the waiters the only Chinese in the hotel where she had lunch, Welthy wondered? She knew that Shanghai was one of five treaty ports opened to foreign trade and residence according to the treaty ending the Opium War in 1842, and that each subsequent treaty had extracted concessions for missionaries as well. The Western traders who poured in saw four hundred million consumers in China and flocked to these port cities. And, too, came "the gentle, numb-to-history missionaries who lived well off Shanghai's body while ministering to its soul".[1]

As peasants had moved in to try to improve their fortunes, Shanghai had multiplied five times to a population of a million during the next fifty years. But it was foreign-controlled. The Sikhs Welthy had admired were armed with blackjacks, and in the French concession the police were Annamese from Vietnam. The city council was dominated by foreigners, a small minority of the population. The Chinese were lost in their own country, Welthy thought, amazed that they tolerated that huge inequality.

The Methodist stronghold, Moore Memorial Church on Tibet Road overlooking the mandatory racecourse, was one of many symbols of the tacit agreement between religion and money to share authority over the Chinese, a combination that slowly fuelled the incubating revolution.

Searching for prestige, influence and new markets, eager to establish their international presence, the Americans had followed in the manner of their European predecessors in China, their missionaries representing a culture as well as a religion. As it happened, the schools and hospitals of a social gospel designed to meet the needs of immigrants to the United States struck a responsive chord in China at the beginning of this century, in part because many American missionaries were themselves children of immigrants, raised in the developing mid-west.

The year 1900 had been a turning point in Chinese history, as Manchu reformers feared Western power and pressed for Chinese control of the nation and recovery of rights ceded to the imperial powers through the previous century. One sign of revolt had been the 1905 boycott of U.S. goods in protest against the exclusion of Chinese immigrants from America. Welthy noted that the Manchus had been on the Dragon throne since 1644, not too long after the Pilgrims had first landed in America.

China's intellectual reformers, the literati, recognized the need for modern education and science to resist further foreign influence, while striving to preserve the monarchy of the Empress Dowager and critical elements of Chinese tradition. But after the humiliating defeat of China during the Boxer Rebellion of 1900, and Japan's subsequent victory over Russia on Chinese territory, the survival of the nation had become the priority. Chinese nationalism was born, to endure a lengthy gestation period—a growth Welthy was to share, for she had arrived in China at a moment of great historic change.

TO KIUKIANG

Welthy's geography lesson began the minute she boarded the British-owned steamer that was taking her five hundred miles up the British-controlled Yangtze River to Kiangsi province. The treacherous Yangtze, driven by snows of Tibetan mountains, longest of China's five thousand rivers, raced over rapids, cut through gigantic gorges, and wound through elaborate bends and a network of lakes, down into the vast eastern lowlands to pour its coffee-coloured waters into the ocean at Shanghai.

The valley Welthy was passing through was the most highly cultivated and densely populated area of China, feeding more than half its four hundred million people, the river absolutely dominating the lives of the great mass of the people. The huge delta area near Shanghai had been completely submerged by massive floods down through the centuries, the latest one twenty years before Welthy followed the Yangtze's course that December when the water was near its lowest level.

The up-river trip took four times as long as the down-river one, with trackers on shore at stages pulling the boat by ropes against grooves hewn in the rock. For two weeks Welthy was astonished. Seeing beyond the immediate evidence of her eyes into the lives of those captives, she began mentally to "sit where they sat"[2], as she so often referred to Ezekiel's symbolic enlightenment, and the word *ku-li*—bitter strength—

took on its true meaning. That very year work was begun to cut through the long river bends, eventually shortening the hazardous journey considerably.

In the Scottish captain of the boat, she was inescapably face to face with imperialism, feeling in him the full force of the contempt for the Chinese so ingrained in many of the British and other foreigners. He told her immediately China was no place for a "mere girl" among "ignorant pigs". Noting that he spoke not a word of their language, Welthy was wryly amused by her chauvinist captain. She was his only non-Chinese passenger and he would have much preferred to return her to Shanghai and send her back home where she belonged.

Thrust together as they were, he accepted her presence and settled in to face the ordeal, shouting to his 'boy': "Two piecie man for dinner," meaning there would be two people for dinner. Welthy feared for her digestion, knowing they would be taking their meals together. As she lay down that night to sleep, just one year since she first had the dream of serving in a foreign land, she was wild with speculation and wonder at being alone in China, facing the unknown.

On the boat, Welthy continued her Chinese studies, seeing how the earlier western respect for Chinese civilization had turned into contempt, so that Westerners now viewed the people as victims, subjects, sources of profit, objects of scorn and pity, and by some as wards. The country had been carved up into pieces by predatory foreigners and its government, isolated in Peking, appeared on the verge of total collapse. Westerners considered the Chinese a supine, helpless people, almost beyond pity—the seething, faceless, subhuman mass—genetically inferior, nerveless creatures who would accept anything. Few Westerners recognized that the Chinese capacity to endure great suffering and hardship in incredibly adverse circumstances indicated strength, rather than lack of feeling and could therefore be disregarded.

As Welthy's boat circled round a thirteen-storey, tile-roofed Buddhist pagoda on an island, she marvelled at Chinese building skills, observing the priests with their shaven heads, drawn to all she surveyed in the land where paper, compass, gunpowder, porcelain and silk first appeared. That backbone of the industrial revolution, the wheel, came from China, its perpetual motion and Buddhist symbolism strongly appealing to Welthy. How could these people be ignorant? Everywhere people were working in fields, or moving about carrying heavy loads.

If she had any fear of the strangeness, it was readily banished from her mind by reading the ninety-first Psalm each morning before she began her study for the day. "He is my refuge and my fortress: My God; in Him will I trust." No matter what the captain said to denigrate the Chinese,

Welthy would find out for herself. Here I am, she thought. "North, east, south, and west I am surrounded by China!" It was comforting, encouraging, a homecoming of sorts.

She read on. The Chinese were said to have an ingrained suspicion of one another, the mutual responsibility and interdependence among men of the clans that managed the boats, carts, sedan chairs, etc. creating this practical skepticism. Maintaining family tradition was top priority, a loyalty that hindered individual initiative and public spirit. No man could be at peace after death without a son to perform ancestral rites for the repose of his spirit, and so early marriages were arranged and concubines installed if no son issued from a marriage. It was a flesh and blood patriarchal autocracy Welthy had entered, with women's movements restricted by bound feet, and children exposed to constant quarreling between the women in the confined home. The misfortune of others was considered the work of a demon, not to be interfered with.

KIUKIANG, DECEMBER 21, 1906

As the boat approached the wharf at Kiukiang (Nine Rivers) on December 21, 1906, Welthy had her first close-up view of interior China. Hundreds of coolies leaped across the water to the boat for the luggage of the passengers. On shore it seemed a swarming sea of ants. "I understand what 'masses' are now—there seemed to be millions of people! And all of them dressed in blue! No wonder the Chinese are called Celestials, for the mass of moving blue made it hard to tell where earth left off and sky began!" (MG, 20.)

Two faces stood out in the crowd—Ilien Tang, a graduate of the Kiukiang school with whom she had set out from Omaha, and Gertrude Howe, an American missionary who had been in China for forty years. "Her blue eyes with the purity of Christ, her fine white hair forming a halo about her head," Welthy was instantly drawn to the woman pioneer. The two women despatched Welthy alone in her sedan chair on the hour-long trip to the mission compound while they tended to her luggage.

For once Welthy knew fear, praying and laughing at herself as the howling coolies carried her past a suicide procession (following a husband who had rescued his unwilling wife from the river), shouting to the people to clear the way, scraping over pigs' backs through the mass, men lifting up the curtain to peer in at her. She spoke no Chinese, the coolies knew not a word of English, and she was cold with fright for the first time. Only nine months ago seven Anglo-Saxons had been massacred in an anti-foreign riot.

"It was much longer than crossing the Pacific to me, though I suppose it didn't take an hour . . . I laughed at myself often, but I prayed more often, and when I arrived I got out of that chair and hugged and kissed every American in sight! It was a terrible breach of etiquette, for some of them, I understand, have lived together for five years and still call each other Miss W . . ., Miss P . . ., etc.!" (MG, 21.) The warmth of her greeting from Gertrude Howe and Ilien Tang, by contrast, won Welthy's permanent gratitude and continuing relief at being billeted with them in the hospital compound rather than with the formal ladies.

Gertrude Howe had gone in 1872 to Kiukiang, the only "occupied" city in Central China then, to use mission terminology. Taking an early stand against foot binding, it had been difficult to get pupils for the mission school because of the fear of permanent spinsterhood parents believed this implied for their daughters, and the general swell of anti-foreign hostility. In 1886, sensing that the WFMS wanted to send her home for taking in foundlings and what they considered her overly sympathetic attitude toward the Chinese, she resigned in protest against their requirement that the girls be taken through the streets to chapel every day, because she understood the Chinese objection to such exposure of their daughters.

The Chinese had respected her greatly and were saddened when she left Kiukiang with the four abandoned girls she had adopted and went further west to Chungking, beyond the reach of the WFMS. Using her patrimony, she sent two of the girls, Ida Kahn and Mary Stone, to train as doctors in Michigan. After a riot in Chungking, the WFMS was moved to ask her to reopen the Kiukiang School, taking only girls from Christian homes. Young Mary Stone had been the first girl of the better classes to grow up in Kiangsi province with unbound feet; she returned to work as a doctor in Kiukiang. By 1902 Ida Kahn was able to begin her medical work in Nanchang because of Gertrude Howe's constant help.

It was a spellbinding story to Welthy, and in the days ahead she grasped the magnitude of this powerful woman. Her father, Isaac Howe, had been a strong abolitionist who had risked his life many times to save slaves from the south, instilling in Gertrude a deep concern for human life that was evident in her beautiful face.[3] She was a saint to Welthy, someone to be followed, whose life Welthy always wanted to write.[4]

"She was an institution built into the lives of the Chinese people. Criticized by the missionaries in almost every idea and action, she listened to God for her instructions. She was right, always, a tower, a little too forward, like me, for those silly women", reflected Welthy on one who had truly served Chinese interests in the fullest Christian spirit, as she longed to do. "I could stand on her shoulders. The struggle was much easier for me because of her."

Christmas day in Kiukiang, and Welthy was too busy to be homesick. She sang at three parties for students and children in the hospital, wearing her Peter Thompson red dress, and was mistaken for a bride. "If they only knew—I'm at least ten thousand miles from being a bride!" Literally buried in bed that night, fully dressed, her fur coat and the floor rug on top, Welthy was too cold for nuptial dreams.

Her personal discomfort was nothing in the light of the anti-foreign aftermath of the Boxer Rebellion, the Uprising of the Righteous Fists, that had taken several years to reach the interior of China. Welthy was now hearing details for the first time. Nine British missionaries had been killed in Nanchang the year before, and a riot had broken out in February when the city was occupied by the military for ten weeks. The Chinese thought they had suffered unpardonable wrong at the hands of foreigners, and focused their attack in Nanchang on the well-established French Catholic and Plymouth Brethren missions, the main foreign presence. The fledgling Methodists had only minor damage because the Governor of the province had sent a boat to rescue them, Gertrude Howe included, and had seen them safely to Kiukiang. Since all boats had been commandeered by the army to take soldiers to Nanchang, the missionaries gathered in Kiukiang were stranded, awaiting permission to return.

Once again, Welthy was forced to wait for her ship, and as she waited for the all-clear to proceed on the last stage of her journey, there was time to listen to all the conflicting tales, the gossip and the urgings of many not to go on to Nanchang. Welthy knew Gertrude Howe fully intended to go back, and simply decided she could not do otherwise, a decision that stood out in her memory in view of the anticipated hostility ahead. Missionaries felt they had a double challenge — to overcome an ingrained, deep hatred of foreigners as well as religious superstition. Han Suyin recalled childhood games drawing pictures of goats, sheep and pigs representing Christians and sticking darts into them. They crucified and drowned rats as foreign devils.[5] Well, Welthy concluded, they'll have a hard time drowning my hundred and fifty-five pounds. She would take her chances.

TO NANCHANG, 1907

With Gertude Howe, Ilien Tang and a deaf waif she had agreed to care for, Welthy set out thirty miles back down the Yangtze to the point where they entered Lake Poyang for the ninety-mile crossing and a further thirty miles on the Kan River to Nanchang. Their boat had "winged arms outstretched to catch the breeze; its face held high to dare the storms and typhoons; it cut the waves and went breast forward. Such a symbol was Gertrude Howe. She cut away traditions; she faced typhoons and weathered them; she feared nothing but cowardice and less-than-the-best," wrote Welthy, rising to the drama of their journey.

But their junk was soon becalmed. "The eight coolies who managed the boat, got out on shore, tied bamboo cables around their bodies as we would harness mules, and literally pulled that boat along inch by inch, hour after hour. As much as I hate mechanical noises, I shall welcome the day when they arrive. For the sight of these men doing the work of canal mules haunts me. And the minor 'labor lilt' which they sang almost broke my heart. If I were a poet, I should write a sonnet to the burden-bearer of China." (MG, 24.)

During the tribulations of the five-day journey the three women became well acquainted and Gertrude Howe told of her long struggle against the stiff attitude of the WFMS. She spoke of poverty, of love, of friendly people who longed to break their ancient chains. Never scorning the Chinese or the prevailing Buddhism, approaching everyone as a friend, Welthy understood why she had won out, and why her plans to build a hospital in Nanchang for Ida Kahn were moving ahead. As for Ilien Tang, she had studied for eight years in the States, including kindergarten training, and though she would be her subordinate, Welthy realized immediately that she could learn a great deal from such a talented Chinese woman.

* * *

"January 1, 1907. New Year's night! A New Year, a New City, a New World, and a new life", Welthy recorded in her diary. Full of hope and wonder, Welthy faced her new responsibilities in a strange, remote part of the world with that sense of adventure and fun she brought to everything, stepping outside of her skin to see herself on stage. Her irrepressible energy and genuine enjoyment of people were immediately evident as the five resident Methodists turned out to greet her. That all this was happening to her filled Welthy with the childlike delight she could never conceal, yet balanced with a shrewd practicality not immediately apparent.

It was not long before the City of the Flourishing South came to know of the tall new stranger heading the School of the Protecting Spirit on the southern side of the city's fifty foot high grey brick wall, near the Virtue Conquering Gate. Well equipped with forts and cannon pits, Nanchang's walls were untouched by a thousand years of wars, empires and revolutions that passed through that strategic mid-corridor of the Kan River valley linking north and south China at the junction of the Fu and Kan Rivers.

It had been the main route of armies, commerce and migration of people for fifteen hundred years prior to the treaty ports, and the area had prospered as one of the most affluent of regions before trading patterns changed. During the Taiping Rebellion of the mid-nineteenth century, Nanchang was the only city spared because the gentry could afford to pay the army to by-pass the city and supply the soldiers with food.[6] Around the wall was a wide lotus-covered moat. Walls, thought Welthy, China is a walled country. Cities walled, women walled by bound feet, foreign policy itself a wall.

Forty-eight yellow-roofed temples could be seen from the wall, with some four thousand businesses flourishing within — shops galore in single storey brick buildings with colourful signs, each street specializing in a product, and as many shops outside the walls. There was not a cow to be seen, for they ate too much to be economical, but pigs, dogs and painted chickens crowded the streets, "every black sow with her cunning black litter claiming full pedestrian rights".

In the centre of the city were several artificial lakes filled with lotus, providing a relief from the narrow alleys, where official families could paddle about in their little boats. Paper made of bamboo, rice or mulberry straw, and ramie cloth with blue and white designs, were famous handicrafts of the area. Porcelain, grass, cloth, tea, indigo and rice moved in and out of the city in a forest of boats sailing in all directions along the connecting waterways. Welthy found herself at the center of a dynamic universe. The gates of the old city beckoned her, and its bright lights, newly installed by the Japanese, were a dazzling contrast to the countryside.

Kiangsi province had a strong tradition of peasant rebellion, the answer to which was over a hundred walled cities in that province alone, where landlords, scholars and officials lived securely. "I feel as if I were living about two hundred years ago," she wrote to her step-brother Henry. "Not a Chinese down here knows anything about geography but thinks China is the world, and they call us foreign devils. A few rich send their sons to the U.S. and U.K. for education, but Peking usually grabs them on return, so we lose them here."[7] Welthy already felt part of her new environment.

The sights and sounds of Nanchang, populated by predominantly Mandarin-speaking Han, soon became part of her daily experience. Of the fourteen foreigners there in 1907, all were missionaries. With its tightly hostile community, penetration of Nanchang had been the most stubborn of all the Methodist goals to realize, the last of seven cities in China with over a million inhabitants to be entered by any mission.

"Here I am four hundred miles from a railroad! There is not a mechanical noise to be heard except the squeak of wheelbarrows and the click-clack of the bamboo clippers of the watchman who beats out the 'watches of the night'. I lie awake to hear them . . . There's the Temple Bell too that sounds every night at eleven . . . a superhuman note that sounds and resounds over the whole wide expanse. It is music that hurts like a Chopin nocturne. It floats on and on, and after it stops I can still hear it singing to me . . . But here the chorus of human agony as well as joyous celebrations and arguments are distinctly heard. What fun it will be when I can understand it all!" (MG, 23.)

It was not fun at all, but harsh reality to know that the loud rumble of moaning souls just outside the school wall that first winter of famine came from thousands of starving peasants, not rioting, but pushing forward in a mass towards kitchens thrown up hastily by the gentry to give out gourds full of hot rice. The walls held fast, the rice held out, the peasants eventually returned to the countryside, and Bao-Lin residents could unlock their gate without terror. This was China. Welthy would never forget it.

BAO-LIN SCHOOL

Baldwin School (Bao-Lin), well situated on a hill near the river just outside the southern gate, had been in existence only four years. The first principal, Miss Kate Ogburn, was home on furlough, leaving Miss Newby alone in charge. A missionary only one year away from Iowa, she in turn left soon after Welthy arrived, due to poor health and the heavy burden. Miss Ogburn and Miss Newby had fled for safety during the recent rioting, returning a month later to find the police in charge of the five-acre campus.

Within an eight-foot wall were a three-storey school building with its three "recitation rooms", a dormitory for a hundred girls, and the teachers' building, or General Board home, as it was known. Flowering shrubs and tall palmetto trees enhanced the atmosphere, but in general Welthy found it indeterminate, like the plain brown dress Miss Newby wore. Worst of all, there was no name at the entranceway, no identity. The budding builder in her was already developing ideas of an environment more conducive to real learning.

The school had four teachers and forty-five girls, mostly upper class, in eight grades. With the arrival of the Honsinger/Tang team, Bao-Lin entered a new era at a moment of significant educational change. The first two decades of the twentieth century marked the awakening of China's women, two hundred million of them, as the major social force underpinning the revolution that was to come.

There was a small feminist movement in China before 1911, but among the urban elite only. Christianity had its greatest appeal in disadvantaged rural areas, where women were the most disadvantaged and thus the most potentially revolutionary force. They were completely dominated by men, who in turn were dominated by feudal politics, clan superstitions, and religious legacies. As they entered the world of modern education, Welthy was entering their history.

In Ilien Tang Welthy had a delightful Chinese companion, one of the three girls Gertrude Howe had prepared for college entrance before the first regular graduating class at the Kiukiang mission school. When shown to her room in the teachers' building Welthy asked where Ilien Tang would stay and found she was to be relegated to a modest building along with the other Chinese teachers. Rejecting such an exclusive attitude straightaway, and determined to learn Chinese customs and language by sharing daily living, Welthy announced to a very perturbed Miss Newby that she would join the Chinese teachers. "She's my tongue and ears," said Welthy of Ilien.

Miss Newby went to consult "the American oracles across the street", as Welthy called "the men". Dr. Bowen, overall head of the Nanchang Methodist mission who ran the hospital in the adjacent five-acre men's compound, wisely assessed Welthy's determination and advised Miss Newby to accept it. Tradition was thus broken by allowing a Chinese to live in a Western ladies' compound house, a real breakthrough in Protestant missions.

Welthy's instinct for survival told her that life alone in the ladies' house with Miss Newby, whom she found static, would be sparse. She knew she needed livelier companionship, and would not accept the institutionalized spinsterhood, with its lack of privacy and freedom, that the ladies' houses represented and that gave the women missionaries their sense of community identity and solidarity in a foreign place. Welthy's sense of her own identity was strong enough without that clubbiness, and she wanted to avoid the special friendships and rivalries that developed between missionary women, at a time when sharing a bed was not an uncommon intimacy. She did not feel she had made a "permanent Catholic commitment to a women's order, but rather a Protestant commitment to follow individual conscience".[8]

ILLITERATE IN CHINESE

Overwhelmed by all she did not know, feeling absolutely illiterate, Welthy was just as determined to overcome her own narrow education. "At home my college degree counted for something, but I can see now that I learned nothing whatever in college." Hardly true, but that openness of mind augured well for the cooperative enterprise she envisaged. Let's get on with it, she told herself. "Tomorrow I begin the ABC's of the hardest language on earth."

With the clearest understanding of her priorities and a real need to know, going to it full force five hours a day, Welthy admitted "it is the first time I have ever known the zest of study. Strange that in college at home we pay our good money and then try to get the least possible that will give us a degree! But here, I *must* know the word in order to use it tomorrow." Her scholarly gentleman teacher Yang, in his heirloom spectacles, three-inch-long fingernails and sleeves that "came down socially to meet them", was a veritable encyclopaedia. "Alas for me," said Welthy, "I am without an index. He expects me to memorize the classics before I understand them, while I am wanting to know 'what time is it?'"

Admittedly defiant and determined to learn everyday Chinese, her opinion of his teaching method matched his disdain of her ignorance. She "ruffled his Confucian complacency" by bringing carrots, onions, and fish from the kitchen, insisting on knowing their Chinese names. Functional literacy was her plea to the scholar. How could she convey to Yang, with his disdain of things physical and his cultivated scholar's stoop, that she needed the language of action? She must act it out for him.

He became interested in her queer ways, laughing inordinately, and began to suggest staying beyond the allotted time. "I quickly saw that to hold his interest in an illiterate Westerner I must help him save his face", and so the scholar and the impatient missionary persevered together with increasing respect for each other. Welthy in her corseted suit swayed back and forth rhythmically with Yang to absorb the cadences of the language, a scene that highly amused children and teachers passing by.

The learner became teacher, and teacher learner, an exchange that was typical of all Welthy's subsequent educational efforts. She delighted in the musical tones of Mandarin, though their subtle variations took time to master and she got soup instead of sugar if she failed to say "tang" in the right tone. Words were magic, she discovered, to be used with respect and great care.

In the end, the scholar learned the dynamics of modern educational methods, and Welthy possessed far more than functional literacy; she gained a window on the history, philosophy and literature of an entire civilization, personally introduced to the rhythmic harmony of heaven and earth. "I'm gradually learning that everything under the sun originated in China if one only traces it back far enough, and I am tracing as fast as I can; I shall soon have the Garden of Eden pointed out."

And now she had her own Chinese name bestowed on her by Yang, proudly proclaiming her new identity on eight-by-four-inch red calling cards in splendid calligraphy with its own rhythmic style: "Han Wei-lo".

"It is a great safety valve to one's pride to write home. In my long letters to the family and to Parla I am an erudite cosmopolitan. But once the letter is written and I look across at that wise, learned, philosophical sphinx, I am limp with stupidity! I would no more dispute him in his field than I would attempt to turn back the waters of the Yangtze." On her daily walks she learned a new proverb each time from a little paperbook she carried along. "Better go than send. Better prevent than cure disease." Wisdom that had seemed Western and modern she now discovered in ancient Chinese maxims. And wisdom was there too in the pictographs, or ideographs of a word in a most intriguing way. Peace, for instance, was represented by the characters for one woman under one roof. Elusive peace, she thought, as she heard tales of life in real households. (MG, 26-33.)

MOTHERS AND DAUGHTERS IN CHINA

Marriage was universal, with fifteen the legal age for girls, to perpetuate the highest blessing in Chinese society—an unbroken male line—and almost all were married by twenty to begin early raising a classical family of five sons and two daughters. Women were inferior, disdained as a source of pollution, the aim of female education being perfect submission to husband and his family, not cultivation and development of the mind.[9] Wives were chosen and marriages arranged by the parents, a measure of progress over earlier times when wives were captured, and later purchased.

For a thousand years the Chinese woman's dependence had been symbolized by her "golden lily" feet, in which foot binding forced the heel under the instep, the smaller toes crumpled under the foot, the large toe bent up and back until the whole foot was no more than three inches long. The muscles of the forelegs atrophied, and in extreme cases the feet rotted off. It was a refined form of cruelty that began at age five, and the undulating walk it produced had great sexual significance, just as did the tightly-laced waists of European ladies. Bound feet became a caste symbol, the poorer classes unable to afford to so immobilize daughters whose labour was needed. By 1902 several edicts had been issued to ban foot-binding, but the custom lingered on, especially in remote areas. Many women chose infanticide for their daughters and suicide by opium or eating soap as the morally accepted way out of an oppressive life. Female suicide, in a society where suicide was a common practice, was more than double that of males.

A young girl had an especially hard time, being fed less than a boy and being likely to be bought or sold as a servant, wife, concubine or prostitute, whatever the traffic would bear. Rape was common, minimum legal rights offering no protection. But with marriage and motherhood a woman could look forward to superseding her mother-in-law, and with age, to commanding far greater respect than in the West. Welthy had read about all these things; now she was hearing first-hand from Ilien Tang of the inner heart of China, of wives stoically enduring the agony of being supplanted by concubines.

Literacy among women in Kiangsi was almost non-existent at the turn of the century. Physically they were strong, their grain diet having five times the food value of meat, and a variety of fruits and vegetables were often available. But undeveloped minds in a land that had revered learning from Confucian times left women as slaves, a means to someone else's end. They could not enter that aristocracy of learning.

MISSIONARIES AND RELIGION

With the Christian gospel, the missionaries sought to make every Chinese life, woman's included, an end in itself. So promising did this look that Bishop James Bashford declared: "If China accepts Christianity in earnest she may surpass the Western world in realizing the new humanity,"[10] an attitude of significant refinement over A. H. Smith's earlier pronouncement that "to capture this race for Christ means the early conquest of the whole world."[11]

The missionaries were confronting a society whose ethics emphasized man's duty to man rather than to God, and a direct, practical concern with this life. There was no escape from facing facts, and the inescapable fact of life was a "pyramid of authority, an immutable hierarchy" of people, rooms, courtyards, with all individual desires subordinated to the virtue and tradition of the family, and the punishments for rebellion severe. Change was the enemy.[12] Right behaviour was essential to social prosperity, the will of the individual subordinated to the group.

The merchant was the strong man, with government remote and in its proper place, in what was a largely self-governing society, with strong democratic tendencies, except for the government's enormous taxing power.

The educational system, with its famed exams, aimed to provide an elite corps of government officials. A land of uneducated masses with little sense of nationalism gave wide scope to growing layers of corrupt officialdom, which were gathering momentum through the years.

Religion was tolerated, but there, too, centuries of creeping bureaucracy had produced China's share of ignorant, vicious priests. Buddhism, Confucianism, Taoism and Islam all had their influence, and many Chinese were attached to more than one faith without any sense of inconsistency, in what was an eclectic, somewhat agnostic view of conflicting teachings. They viewed the different strains of Christianity with equal skepticism, puzzled by the inexplicable contradiction between what Christians said and did, equating Christianity with opium and extraterritoriality.

To a thoroughly Methodist woman such as Welthy, that benevolent tolerance of all religions could have seemed mindless opportunism, lacking in principle. A familiar conversation might be: "To what sublime religion to you belong?" Each would then praise the other's religion, sigh, and say: "Ah well, religions are many, reason is one. We are all brothers."[13] Such synthetic reasoning had great appeal for Welthy, who saw the predominant "three ways" of China as possibilities rather than competing religions, revealing a broader approach to eternal questions.

Many of her fellow missionaries could not abide that Chinese attitude towards religions, driven as they were by the conviction that only through Christ could one be saved. Secure in her own faith, Welthy was anxious to share her understanding of it through education and personal example, yet eager to learn about other faiths and the underlying culture that gave rise to them. She could not put her heart into the numerical race for converts; education was her profession, not religion. It would require wisdom to conduct herself with integrity and respect for the Chinese while advancing mission priorities.

For fifty years the status and rights of the missionaries had been backed by the Chinese Government, and their enclaves had become a haven for many Chinese who feigned conversion, seeing the advantage of foreign backing in any lawsuit, the "rice Christians" willing to live under the aegis of foreign powers in their own homeland. The Roman Catholics used that lever extremely well, exercising powerful authority over their converts, acting as a partner in foreign imperialism. Welthy was haunted by the fact that American missionaries traded on rights and privileges won by European force, and that no foreigner could be brought to justice because of extraterritorial rights.

In choosing from the start to live with Ilien Tang, Welthy had acted instinctively to protect herself from the "mission-centric" outlook, based on psychological and physical separation from the surrounding Chinese society. "The missionaries really did not want to enter the Chinese world any more than they had to. Their whole purpose was to get the Chinese to enter theirs."[14] Welthy was an exception to that pattern; she wanted to meet them midway. Granted that the age of contempt for the Chinese was slowly giving way to the age of benevolence among missionaries, still there were accumulations of practices and procedures to be reversed, and Welthy was ready to take a lead. Why live in China, if not to be among the Chinese?

China's long resistance to western culture was crumbling. The old civil service exams had just been abolished, diminishing the influence of the missionaries' old enemy, the "literati", and a Ministry of Education had been created to forge an amalgam of eastern and western education. With the new century, the old Empress Dowager had finally changed horses, backing the liberal reformers.

In an interior city such as Nanchang, it took time for the missionaries to appreciate that they were the main representatives of the newly favoured western civilization. In the coastal cities, young Chinese were already viewing everything from the West less critically, fascinated by western persons and possessions. It was the start of an unprecedented period of euphoria and physical security for the missionaries and their programmes, their influence for good, or less than good, at a peak. When they returned to Nanchang from Kiukiang in early 1907 the Methodists found themselves in greater favour than they had dared to hope, the door opening slowly to the new interchange of East and West.

Welthy was ready on her side. "It was easier for me to be tolerant of strangers whose customs were wholly different from my own than to exercise the blessed virtue of charity" toward some of the missionaries whose behaviour towards the Chinese she felt was wrong. (TLC, 59.) "You cannot effectively improve a part of any community unless you understand the community, its language, its customs and emotions," wrote Welthy. (TLC, 33.)

With this imperative uppermost Welthy felt most at home with Gertrude Howe and Ida Kahn, and began to refuse invitations from the foreign colony unless Ilien Tang was included. She found her social life sparse, but when she needed to refresh her spirit it was Gertrude Howe, herself too busy for social doings, to whom Welthy turned. It was well worth the two-mile walk to encounter her "sweet fearlessness". Welthy felt strong in the presence of someone who looked her straight in the eye.

Through Ilien she made friends among young Chinese couples, who managed to overcome their initial distaste for the smell of meat Welthy exuded to them, a realization unpleasant enough to cause her to give up meat. No western habit was going to stand in the way of becoming truly acquainted with the Chinese. She decided to adapt herself to what they found acceptable in their country, and laughing at herself along the way, had fun making the adjustment. Thereafter Ilien's invitations from

Chinese always included Han Wei-lo. Welthy was admitted beyond the moongate.

In return, she discovered she would have to tone down her wardrobe and raise the neckline of her dresses so as not to offend their sensitivities. After watching a few westerners who had taken to Chinese gowns yet remained unwilling to allow Chinese to enter their front door or sit at a table with them, she gave up any thought of adopting Chinese dress. She resolved "to remain me while trying to expand that me", the closest she ever came to spelling out a personal philosophy. (TLC, 52.)

In her autobiography she confessed to being fascinated with the intricate houses, elaborate entertainment rituals, and abundant signs of wealth at the relentless feasts of upper class families, describing their perfumes, brocades, pearls, jades, golden bracelets and conversations in breathless detail. In one home she saw the entire sixty room household of one hundred and fifty people (half servants), the concubines, jewels and treasures. What young woman from Rome, New York, would not be intrigued? Besides, if she was to understand her students she must know about the parents and gain their confidence.

Going also among the straw huts of starving squatters and the beggars' lairs, stung by their terrible reality, Welthy was gripped by the paramount importance of women's education as a tool which would allow the Chinese to break out of those extremes of poverty and wealth, a hold that would last a lifetime. "Both ends are lifting the veil and letting me in," she marvelled, yearning to make ends meet somehow.

* * *

Alone at night with the temple bell dinning its mellow notes that seemed to express the agony of the deformed feet she had massaged that evening, Welthy thought of the million souls locked inside the city gates at sundown and the helplessness of the lepers with their disappearing features begging at the city gate. "She prayed as she had never prayed before; maybe her former minister would not call it a prayer; it was a cry in the dark for the stoic suffering of the hushed city, the poised transcendent living the poor achieved; it was her own inadequacy; it was an intense love for her lonely mother; it was Parla's last kiss and her farewell letter to him; it was the realization of the vast ocean that was China and the tiny grain of sand that she was on the shore of its vastness; it was the ache in her heart when Dr. Ida Kahn had shown her how to massage those tiny feet."[15] A great bend must have a great straightening, the proverb pronounced, and that meant one thing to Welthy: the wider education of women. No more emphasis on feet or walls; focus on strength, not weakness, she decided.

Forty-nine undulating vibrations pierced her mind and body as their deep, lingering tones drifted off and she could hear the Buddhist priests and acolytes chanting their mantras in cadences rising and falling. The moon, shining through her open eastern window, offered light and quietness. "God must be hovering over the city, more tenderly even than the moon. His love must be penetrating the city wall, the house walls and the shop walls and the straw huts, even now while the city sleeps. God's love is mine," she said aloud. "I am part of God's love, and I shall simply help him here. The things which are seen are temporal; the things which are not seen are eternal. God help me to see and to expose the Eternal."

* * *

In 1907, Bao-Lin was the only school for girls in a province of twenty-five million. Welthy vowed that she would not only expand Bao-Lin but would inspire other schools to be built, and travel through the interior, preaching her own gospel, talking to the women and to the men about their wives and daughters. Over yang's protestations that it was revolutionary, she had a mammoth sign hung over the main gate announcing in bright red Chinese characters: *Ye Shall Know the Truth and the Truth Shall Make you Free.* Bao-Lin was no longer characterless. Welthy had set her stamp on it, her personal pledge made public. It had not taken her long to "stand up and be what she was". The open gate symbolized her own ever-widening search for the truth that made her feel so at one with her new Chinese friends.

Scholar Yang had warned against Bao-lin declaring liberty as a goal for Chinese woman. "No individual should have too much freedom," he said, quoting a sage, "especially our women. If our women have freedom our whole country will be forever a sheet of loose sand, our traditions will float out to the sea and be lost forever. No, it is the state that should have freedom, but our women must not have it. If they talk thus of freedom our women and our country will be in a state of license. It is wrong. Our women have always had freedom — but freedom behind the walls."[16]

In her autobiography, Welthy summarized her diametrically opposed hopes for the freedom of women: "Such long-suppressed energy, brains and virtue would raise the rate of human progress as a number is raised to the second power, squared, not merely doubled." (TLC, 81.) As for the carpenter who made the new sign, Welthy enrolled his daughter with free tuition.

In Nanchang the highly evangelical China Inland Mission, with the missionaries in their long Chinese gowns and pigtails, was the most important. Protestant missions in general, from Germany, Sweden, Britain,

Canada, the States, grew more rapidly than those of the Catholics due to the predominance of Protestant Britain in foreign trade and the willingness of Protestants to admit non-Christians to their schools.

When Welthy arrived in China, some sixty-seven different Protestant societies were operating, with fifteen hundred men and a thousand unmarried women missionaries. In the coastal cities there were also the YMCA and the YWCA, whose workers generally had higher abilities than the missionaries, and to whom Welthy felt closer. They had already adopted a policy of giving the Chinese control of their operations, which seemed eminently sensible to Welthy.

BISHOP BASHFORD

Bao-Lin School was under the authority of the Nanchang men's mission, within the Central China Conference headed by Bishop James W. Bashford. A former President of Ohio Wesleyan University and the first resident Methodist Bishop in China, he had arrived in 1904, when enthusiasm for supporting Chinese missions was starting to lag in America. He had turned down high posts in the States and abroad to spend his twilight years where he felt he might approach his goal — to relate one's ideals to personal living and helpfulness to others.

He believed the Christian religion should deliver men from paganism and establish a system of education that would produce an enlightened populace, an honest government and a humane system of industry. Taking a long view, laying permanent foundations, he wanted to unite the fragmented Christian efforts that had been disdained by the Chinese for their previous association mainly with the lowest levels of society.

Now that missions' teaching ability was creating new respect, even as it would affect their girls, the rich began to enrol their children and the mission schools had begun catering to this new interest by offering courses in English. Welthy recognized in her Bishop the elements of statesmanship as he urged the Chinese to take more authority and responsibility for the work of the church, and encouraged the gentry to begin looking after their own.[17] Bashford remained in China throughout Welthy's time there, a steady source of strength to her.

The Chinese Government's view of female education as inappropriate had prompted the elite gentry to found their own schools, many of which were closed during the Boxer Rebellion. Some three hundred mission schools were the only alternative for the daughters of reformers and progressive officials. A 1906 proclamation mandated the Government establishment of schools for girls, affording the mission schools an historic opportunity to influence their development. Welthy realized the significance of the moment and lost no time in making contacts and friends amongst the gentry and local government officials, with Ilien Tang her entree beyond the moongate. Until then, girls were taught to stand to one side of and behind their fathers-in-law when speaking, for example, and to obey every command, without question. A girl's voice was to be restrained within her teeth, she must not laugh aloud or make a noise if angry. She should learn women's work, rise early and honour her parents.[18] Her virtue lay in having no knowledge, in living a life of complete obedience and dependence on generations of men.[19]

Welthy was more than ever grateful for the liberating educational foundation her mother had provided, and understood that she was there in China precisely because of that freedom. She must use it wisely. But as for laughing out loud, Welthy was incapable of restraining her own buoyant laugh. From the start, the little Bao-Lin girls were delighted at this tall new authority figure who was so happy she could sing and laugh at anything and make them feel at ease. They crowded round, amazed at her energy and was willing to do any kind of work, no matter what. So young, so smart, her beautiful figure on horseback and a rein in her right hand, remembered student Pearl Chen, Welthy was like "winter's sunshine"to the little ones. Their name for her was "Han Hsiao Ja" (Little Sister Han), amusingly affectionate in view of her towering height and weight. The name may have been Welthy's own invention, but in using it the children adopted her as their own.

Welthy, Ilien Tang and Miss Newby were settled in their small house with an amah and a cook. To take care of the myriad matters she tended to, Welthy decided to build an office with a fireplace for herself between the house and the dormitory, with money a friend from Haverstraw had sent for her personal use, a fateful decision, as time would reveal.

One of the first things she did was to request five hundred dollars from the WFMS for a gymnasium to help the girls fight off consumption through exercise; for herself she bought a small rowboat that she kept on the river nearby. It could carry four passengers, with Welthy rowing. Since the alternate form of rural transportation was a coolie-pushed wheelbarrow on the narrow paths that were the only roads then, Welthy opted for the comfort and control of her own boat. She loved to take Mrs. Chen and Mrs. Won, two matrons of the dormitory, to gatherings of women along the river and listen to their tales of ancient festival legends. Instinct told her to listen for meaning behind these legends, to respect the symbolism that enriched the lives of these "cultured illiterates", whose knowledge came from centuries of oral transmission.

"I am pulled from one excitement to another. Last moon it was hydrophobia, and this second moon brings . . . smallpox." Welthy volunteered to be isolated with the victim to care for her, but fortunately it turned out to be chickenpox. Castor oil was prescribed, Welthy the brave dispenser. "Eighty-eight times did I pour out the hated potion from the gallon can! . . . one of the cunningest Orientals ran upstairs and hid under the farthest bed. I loved her. . . one of the hardest things I've done since arriving is to insist upon her taking the dose after that sportsmanlike attempt to get out of it." (MG, 37, 39.)

It was Welthy, the one who played the piano and sang to the children at night, who could persuade them. They could see she loved them. And love was coming back to her, adding both to her strength and responsibility. She had constantly to adjust her priorities, reducing the nightly brushing of her hair from one hundred to sixty strokes, for instance.

Welthy soaked up China like a sponge. She was observant, imaginative, accepting, and never bored, as Berr and Parla had both predicted she would be. "Here . . . comedy sits daily at my doorstep. . . Tragedy goes stalking over the mud threshold of the squatter's hut as well as the ebony threshold of the palace. Tragedy rides in gilded sedan chairs; it lurks under bejeweled headdress and brocaded garments. Here tragedy and comedy need no stage to depict them. Those other stages that even now . . . attempt it, will . . . forever be for me a puny counterfeit." (MG, 45-46.)

What Welthy did find endlessly long, however, was waiting for the north wind to hasten the sailboat bringing mail from home. More than all the news Welthy loved the imaginative epistles spun out in Mabel's hand from her opinionated cat. In winter, when the Poyang waters were low, only sailboats could get through. After summer's rains small steamers plied with regularity. "I shall listen for the sound of the sailors' song as they let down the sail. I shall love that song forever! It means letters, letters!"

All this she narrated vividly in her diary during the cold nights, fully clothed, bundled in her fur. Sometimes she took her gramophone to the office as she scratched out letters, listening to Caruso sing, transported to the Metropolitan Opera, weeping.

SHANGHAI, SPRING 1907

In six months Welthy was on her way back to Shanghai, not in flight from her missionary life, but with a long shopping list of things the school needed, and to attend the historic China Centenary Mission Conference as Principal of Baldwin School. Gertrude Howe had asked her to go along, and since Welthy could afford to pay her own way, she agreed eagerly. It was a chance to see and hear the best and the brightest of all the denominations, to meet her peers, and take part in the discussions relating to women's education.

She heard her Bishop address the question of the day — should China have a national, independent church or be linked with home churches? Lifting the debate to a higher level than other speakers, Bashford opposed both in favour of a world-wide church with local autonomy. Welthy was impressed, her admiration and respect for him fast on the increase.

In the mission house where she was staying in Shanghai there were several prominent missionaries, including Dr. Arthur Smith and W. A. P. Martin. Welthy sat silently at the dinner table listening to the discourses of these great men. There was much talk about the Hague Peace Conference, forerunner to the League of Nations, and of subsequent disarmament negotiations, then underway in Europe. Finally she had the temerity to ask: "Who will go to represent China?" Silence. She was gently informed that China did not qualify for participation in a peace conference because she had no army or navy.

"Those words burned in my brain and in my memory as though they were buried there. The Chinese have long memories." So did Welthy. How strange, she thought, that China was not permitted among the forty-four nations seeking peace. To her, China was eminently qualified by her very lack of military might to discuss peace among nations, having had her own disarmament conference of warring states as far back as 546 BC.[20]

Once again, the view of China as a second-class nation was driven home to her. Welthy would not stand when "Britannia Rules the Waves" was played at conference sessions. "She may rule them now," muttered Welthy, "but not forever, especially these Chinese waves. They're going to rule their own. I felt I had to say something." (T, 23B.) "And I lived to see the day," she reflected sixty-six years later.

CH'IU CHIN

Outside the conference where they were debating so calmly the spreading of the Kingdom of God, China's leading young woman revolutionary leader of the time, Ch'iu Chin (Gem of Autumn), who dressed like a man, was supervising the making of bombs in a house she had rented in nearby Hongkiu, and editing a fiery women's magazine, *Chung Kuo Nu Bao* (Middle Country Women's Publication.) Ch'iu Chin was a heroic figure in the struggle of Chinese women for education and for emotional and physical freedom. She left her husband to study in Japan, then returned to found the magazine in January 1907, of which only two issues were published before she was executed by beheading in July.

Her revolutionary writings urging modern education for girls and rejecting the traditional female role had most impact at the time on educated
urban women, but by the revolution of 1911, she had become the self-
sacrificing heroine who was the inspiration of the women's armies.[21]

Welthy noted her own interpretation of Ch'iu Chin's writings: "In our
language are two miserable, pitiable, hazardous, dangerous words. They
are Black Darkness, not comprehending reality, not having sight or hearing. If I can waken women from this deep drunkenness of ignorance
and startle them with ten thousand terrors then they themselves will
evolve plans. If you don't act now, even though you sprinkle water, it
can not ferry you to salvation. In the past ten years the wind of custom
has slowly veered . . . Ah, slowly, how slowly the thread of light is piercing the black darkness of women's realm, which has been shut in on all
sides for four times one thousand years."[22] Deeply stirred by these radical outpourings, Welthy's thoughts focused on weaving that slow thread
of light into garments of true power.

The incessant political talk she overheard at sparkling receptions of
Shanghai's foreign elite was of little interest to Welthy, who saw the attitudes and interests they represented as being far more fragmented than
even those of the missionaries and their churches. Only Sun Yat-sen's
call for China to the Chinese made any sense to her. While he was in
hiding in Japan and raising money abroad there had been several
unsuccessful attempts to overthrow the dynasty, and branches of Kwang-
Fu (The Returning Light) were springing up throughout China and
among Chinese students abroad, especially in Japan, Chiang Kai-Shek
among their members. "The greatest mistake my international friends
made was their failure to acknowledge that power in the future lay with
the Chinese themselves. China *was* the Chinese, not the American
businessmen or the missionaries or the British . . . or the Japanese."
(TLC, 68.) It would take her country another sixty-five years to accept
that reality.

CHINA CENTENARY MISSION CONFERENCE

Louella Miner was chairman of the conference committee on women's
education, where the debate touched on the mental abilities of Chinese
girls compared with boys and Americans. Gertrude Howe stated strongly that the girls were fully equal in capacity and their education should
reflect this. Still, many felt that the girls' physical and moral development, especially Bible study, must come first, that intellectual development was the last priority. There was disagreement over industrial
training and work because of the health hazards and temptations of
greed. Should only the indigent students be required to help in school

housework, or should rich and poor alike do these chores? Should girls receiving free education be required to pledge themselves as teachers? Ogburn and Howe were among the objectors to that suggestion.

Early betrothals were also a policy problem for the schools. Howe spoke clearly again, saying that there was no wrong in a girl remaining single if she lived a life of consistent service, but the Conference record stated: "It is well for Christians to keep on the side of conservatism, and to hold before the Chinese the ideal woman, the wife and mother, wisely and lovingly directing the affairs of the home."[23] Still siding with male domination, they cautioned against too much equality with men too soon. "Power without ability and wisdom to use it for home and state means ruin to home and state," they decreed. Not very clear thinking in Welthy's view.

How were young women to develop their abilities if their intellectual education was deferred, particularly in a country that revered learning above all else, to the point that any scrap of paper containing the highly respected printed character that was found lying on the street was carefully plucked up with bamboo tongs and placed in a special urn. And how would Miss Miner's prediction that no influence would be more important to twentieth century China than educated, public-spirited women come true? Welthy was practical enough to want a beginning now, for this life, and for all the girls in her school.

Much discussion centred on the proportion of Christian and non-Christian students to be admitted to mission schools, with wide differences of opinion. Louella Miner raised the level of thinking with her conclusion that "the women of China are turning to us not because we are Christian, and in spite of being foreign, but because we are educators. We have stepped out into the largeness of life."[24] Here was a missionary Welthy could admire. Inspired and enlightened by some, and disappointed in many of her fellow missionaries, Welthy's introduction to China and missions was now complete.

Welthy had also seen the grim effect on young girls arriving in Shanghai from the countryside like merchandise for the whorehouses, each floor specializing in beauties of a certain province. It would take more than Bible study to do the work she had come to do. It was a wiser and more widely committed woman who headed back up the Yangtze to her mission post in far-off Kiangsi. She was re-equipped mentally and physically to tackle her assignment, with bundles of supplies for herself and the school.

NANCHANG

Organizing and managing the school came easily to Welthy, her authority generally accepted. She heartily approved of the Chinese education the girls were being given — history, geography, literature and ethics all from a Chinese point of view. Domestic household arrangements, however, were appalling. "How was I to organize what was not there, never had been there?" said Welthy about garbage disposal and the handling of dead animals, horrified by the absence of the most elementary precautions.

When a social crisis emerged involving schoolgirls and parents, Welthy was challenged far beyond her experience. One girl's parents arrived at the school determined to commit suicide and have Welthy blamed for influencing their daughter to marry a man not of their choice. "Custom — honored, intricate custom, so much of which was wise and good and worthy of respect . . . How firmly should I stand against its ramifications?" she asked herself. "I wanted only to help my girls be the best they could. I could take only one stand."

She staunchly defended the girl's intention to marry her lover, while ensuring that there were men by the riverside to rescue the father after he threw himself in. The mother would not speak to her afterwards, threatening to kill herself with a dagger, but privately she must have appreciated Welthy's fast thinking and acting. Running between parents, daughter and fiance like a mediator, Welthy achieved a compromise. The young man agreed to provide the customary feasts, trousseau, jewelry and whatever else was requested in return for the parents' reluctant blessing. It was a minor diplomatic achievement and a landmark piece of high theatre for Welthy.

A REVOLUTIONARY CRISIS

Another crisis called for rapid soul-searching as the revolutionary activities of student Chang Tren became known to her. Welthy was aware that Chang, Yen-Siem and several of their followers had been reading Liang Chi-chao and Kang Yu-wei, reformers Welthy could admire. What she had not known was the likelihood of revolutionaries right there in Bao-Lin. It came to light when news reached Nanchang of the capture of their leader, Ch'iu Chin, after her cousin and close accomplice, Hsu Hsi-lin from Nanchang, shot and killed the Governor of Anhui, who had begun seizing revolutionaries. Chang Tren and her group identified so strongly with Ch'iu's role in the Kuang Fu movement that she gathered her group in the east corner of the compound for an intense discussion and rededication to Kuang-Fu. That was the first revolutionary meeting at Bao-Lin — or was it, wondered Welthy.

Six days later, on July 15, 1907, Ch'iu Chin herself was beheaded. The students were provoked into agonized mourning for their lost leader and her last eloquent words: "Autumn rain, Autumn wind, Autumn heart grief, slay." To the students it meant that the time of decay and executions had arrived. Student Chiu Min who had been proud of her Autumn name joined the grievers as they gathered later in Chang's dormitory room to chop off their long black braids, the mark of Manchu supremacy that was not of Chinese origin. They sealed their pact secretly, in blood, for what future collaboration Welthy never knew.

Ilien heard and reported to Welthy that Chang had been a distributor of Ch'iu Chin's bombs, received from young male student accomplices at distributing stations in Kiangsi and Hunan, dispersing them throughout the countryside, via the cart of the travelling barber, or any willing patriot, to "heroic souls that dared to come and get them." Welthy understood now why Chang's grandfather or grandmother so often lay at death's door, requiring her to make frequent, mysterious trips to Kiukiang and back to her country village to sit at the bedside and help call back the soul of the delirious, honourable ancient one.

Important looking letters for Chang often arrived at Bao-Lin, letters that aroused Welthy's curiosity when they first crossed her desk. Now she was confronted with the strong possibility of a revolutionary cell in the school. What was she, principal of a mission school, now to do about it? Furthermore, the Governor's niece knew of these activities and was leading her own protest over such revolutionaries being tolerated in their midst.

Welthy called the radicals to her office, and, not prepared to pass judgment on them, calmly asked them if they thought they ought to remain in the school.   She was confronted with her own words over the entrance gate, words of truth and freedom. They wanted access to news of China and the world; she agreed to bring in the newspapers they specified and to hire a Chinese scholar to teach current political affairs. She also cautioned them not to reject everything that had come to them from their forefathers in reaching for new freedom, and allowed them to remain.

They were patriots in their own country, she reminded herself, and who was she to restrain them from what had brought her own rich inheritance of freedom in America?   Having defused the situation with a fine balance, she was relieved that the girls would have more time to grow and develop their own understanding now that their fiery leader's influence was diminished.   At twenty-eight, Welthy was scarcely older than these Chinese teenagers whose lives had been so compressed by accumulated history.   (TLC, 68-76.)

To Chang's classmates Welthy had become their champion. "Partly for my own pleasure and partly to solidify my position with them, I began to take my noon meal with the pupils. They were emboldened by my constitutional insensitivity to teasing and made fun of my Chinese, but did not venture to defy my intuitive knowledge of just how far to let them go. I needed their respect," acknowledged Welthy. In fact, she regularly took lunch with the Chinese staff and dinner with the American missionaries, breaking that routine at the slightest opportunity for stimulating variety.

Sunday evenings she always encouraged her girls of the Singing School, as Bao-Lin came to be known, to sing whatever they wanted, accompanying them on the piano. They were bound together in music, though Chang Tren and a few of the radicals considered it irrelevant to the emancipation of women. Welthy knew the power of music within herself, even fantasizing of a day when there might be mass choral singing as people united for better life, and so she gave them the best brand of harmony she knew.

* * *

In a sudden, ceremonious stroke, Welthy and Bao-Lin received the recognition, both social and political, that she deemed necessary for its expansion. The Governor of Kiangsi descended on the School. Freshly coached by Yang, and well-endowed in the art of role playing, Welthy carried out the elegantly ambiguous, tedious protocol at each turn, even to insisting "somewhat insincerely" that she was unworthy, the school humble, and exchanging a series of low bows. "What a vision of sable! A black satin hat with soft iridescent peacock feathers falling over his back, his amber beads with jade pendants, his large *pu fu* richly embroidered in front and back, his satin boots. How little did I dream I could actually carry on a conversation with this gorgeously bedecked Oriental, who not only filled the chair but spilled out on all sides." It was grand theatre.

When the inspection finally ended, the Governor announced he would send his daughter to the school, and Welthy received an adamant letter in "spidery script" that represented other missionaries' strong disapproval of her actions. An American never bows the knee to any man, she was informed. Welthy, who would not bow to Britannia in China as a matter of principle, replied: "I am in China, deep in its heart, and I believe I should follow its etiquette." It was not worth offending anyone, in her view, when it was a matter of form only, as she saw her relations with the Governor. (TLC, 55-57.)

KULING

When the intense summer heat arrived and most of the girls went home to their families, Welthy welcomed the opportunity to refresh herself at Kuling in the Li Mountains high above Kiukiang, taking Ilien Tang with her. They were carried for eight hours nearly four thousand feet up through bamboo groves, along winding paths to the treeless heights. Welthy, sporting a pith helmet, blue goggles and a huge umbrella for sun protection, required two men to heft her chair.

The beautiful valley atop the Lushan range was scattered with stone bungalows, unhidden by walls. It was an international settlement of a thousand foreigners—missionaries, diplomats, professors and businessmen, mostly British and American, some German and Russian—where the European customs of the port cities were institutionalized to help preserve the national identities in which all faith was placed. The "concession" stretched a quarter of a mile along the bund—Jardine-Matheson, Butterfield & Swire, Standard Oil—all the signs of empire were there. And for a while Welthy played the game of empire.

She fell into an active pattern with people her own age, especially "the Yale boys", as they went on long strenuous hikes, had picnics, played tennis, swam and flexed their Western muscles in the open spaces after the cramped life on the plains. Musical concerts were a tradition and Welthy quickly found herself rehearsing daily the Elijah Chorus which was to be the highlight of the season.

Everyone, including Bishop Bashford, was there and it was a bustling, stimulating change of venue. She could even wear her decollet evening dresses. In letters home to his family, the Bishop's young secretary, Harrison S. Elliott, could not suppress his growing admiration for the bright young star on the mountain.

Jul. 20   At five went for a tramp with Miss Honsinger—a mighty pretty girl—a sunset to remember.

Jul. 22   Moonlight picnic with young people.

Aug. 2   Some of our later recruits are capital people.

Aug. 9   Methodist picnic on tennis court.

Aug. 10   To Miss Honsinger's for dinner with Mr. and Mrs. Hersey (John Hersey's parents) and YM, YWCA people.

Aug. 17   The boys organize picnic to repay girls.

Aug. 19   Dinner at Merrill's and Miss Honsinger's with Bashfords.

Aug. 20   Annual sacred concert in evening. Miss Honsinger had principal solo and is really the best singer on the mountain. She has a fine soprano voice.

Aug. 21   Kupfers, Bashfords, Rosenberg, Miss Honsinger to White Deer Grotto, renowned center of Confucian learning.

Aug. 29   Another concert. China Inland and Plymouth Brethren veto it being humorous, even for encores, as narrow as narrowness. Miss Honsinger was ahead by a good deal of any one else, has the best voice of any person here, and indeed a very fine one for any place. She has a commanding personality — tall, rather heavy, black hair and fine eyes. Mrs. Bashford says about the most strikingly beautiful girl she has ever seen, and she puts her whole soul into her singing so that her solo was remarkably fine.

Aug. 31   Scrapped with coolies for Miss Honsinger as she was getting off for her station.[25]

One mission family lingered to the end of the season every year to hear her singing, as vital to their annual retreat as the good air of the mountain. To young Pearl Comfort Sydenstricker and her Presbyterian missionary parents, Welthy's singing was a breath of fresh air.[26] Summers at Kuling meant hearing Welthy, and the Pearl S. Buck of the future carried that eloquent image of Welthy forever, an admiration that marked their meetings in the decades ahead.

"I have met the Bishop," Welthy wrote, "he doesn't approve of me yet, but he will." She had offered to raise money and take in a family of orphans from the recent famine, and the Bishop had refused to allow it. In ensuing weeks they took the measure of one other, with Welthy's singing opening many doors, and by summer's end she had the Bishop's approval, if not the orphans. Her admiration for Mrs. Bashford soared as Welthy observed an experienced, cultivated woman with real ability taking her place affirmatively beside her husband, one who could readily recognize Welthy's talents and leadership quality, and was generous enough to say so. It was another good alliance. Welthy had covered the ground well in short order, not so much by design as by spontaneous necessity.

She returned to Nanchang to find hundreds of emaciated city children burning up with fever. "Hereafter for me . . . the cross will be a Chinese walled city of seven gates without sanitation, without ice, without sewerage, without a water system, with no vaccination and one hospital — a million people whose sick are for the most part without any medical help." (MG, 53.)

A CHILD ON HER DOORSTEP

She could and would do one thing. On her own birthday that September 18, she took in a three-month old baby who had been rescued from a medieval orphanage and left on Gertrude Howe's doorstep. The schoolgirls named her "Precious Pearl", though her nametag said she was Elizabeth. Child rearing was added to the list of things Welthy must learn quickly. A wet nurse was hired, and Welthy bowed to the amah's traditional notions of caring for the baby except when she was sure she was right.

"Never mind the formalities," said Welthy, when informed that the WFMS would not permit legal adoption. And whatever the Bishop might think, this child had come to her seemingly as a gift, and her love for "Betty" filled Welthy with memories of the glow in her father's eye as he beheld her on the floor years earlier. She had a new family now — Betty, her amah, and Ilien Tang — and the feminine soul of China unfolded to her in generations.

Before long she took a second baby, and soon there were four. "I wish you could see my Chinese girls," she wrote to Henry, "their eyes dance, and they are unusually bright." Delightful as it was to have an intimate domestic life, Welthy soon saw the wisdom of putting Betty in a special section of the dormitory along with the other orphans, under the care of a matron, where she could grow up more naturally.

ILIEN TANG

Welthy had come to depend so much on Ilien that she had a rude shock when she ventured into the city alone on foot one day, wandering through the narrow winding streets with their richly gilded signs "hanging down like stalactites in a cavern", on Silver and Gold Street, Basket Street, Curio Street, spellbound by all until she found her own towering presence the centre of an alarming crowd. She fled into a nearby shop, waiting hours until she could return behind the safety of a sedan chair's curtain. Ilien explained that the crowd was infuriated that she might be masquerading as an official of some kind, as signified by the large feather in her hat. To sacrifice that favorite hat and feather was more difficult than giving up mutton had been. She would have to temper her curiosity with caution from now on.

Ilien was learning from Welthy how to use her own strength in dealing with the students, and in turn Welthy learned from Ilien to control her impatience with slow-moving events and circuitous language. It was a fair exchange, but their "bright attachment of mutual admiration and respect" was not so acceptable to all the students. Some were jealous of Ilien's closeness to Welthy, and more importantly, they could not accept the authority Welthy entrusted to her. They could take orders from a Westerner, but *not* from a Chinese woman.

One girl demonstrated their protest by throwing her rice bowl on the floor and refusing to eat, leading a small mutiny to test Welthy's will. Certain that the answer to their spoiled, assured rebelliousness was not to take the offenders into her office, shed tears and pray with them, as was missionary practice, Welthy told Dr. Bowen and the others who tried to intervene that "I'd rather have ten serious pupils here to learn than fifty who have to be petted into behaving themselves."

She decided to send the rebels home, Gertrude Howe backing her stand in what had become a student strike, eliciting much gossip and speculation about the ruin of the school. Welthy knew Ilien's leadership had to be upheld. "We two are one, and of the two of us, she is the more important. She is the one who provides their model. I can't. I'm from another country," she told her critics.

Mission history was made when Welthy appointed Ilien Tang Assistant Principal in 1908, and in time the girls returned to school, bringing new pupils with them. According to one student, Mildred Sun, Ilien was kind to everyone and generally liked. It was a personal victory for Welthy, allowing her more freedom of movement to be her roving self, but a much greater victory for the mission she represented. (TLC, 48-50.)

Teachers caused their own share of problems. The Chinese teachers were jealous of Ilien's foreign education and her special status with Welthy, evidenced by their close living arrangements, something Welthy had not anticipated in her need for lively companionship and inter-cultural understanding. Single women without families in a strange land, with heavy responsibilities, were prone to emotional breakdown, so her support of Ilien had a good measure of instinctive self-interest in it.

To some, Welthy was setting a good example in her relationship with Ilien and they liked being invited to her quarters for meetings and parties. Others did not think Ilien was intelligent enough to be given such special treatment, partly reflecting their own ingrained acceptance of inferiority, partly envy, and perhaps some misunderstanding of Ilien's lightened work load due to declining health. It was another balancing act for Welthy.

*   *   *

"Prayer is a spiritual exercise, not a means of moral suasion," wrote Welthy, reflecting on the incident and her decision not to plead with prayer. Women's struggle for freedom was not confined to the United States in those years; it was underway on Welthy's frontier right there in Nanchang. It was the fullest freedom she sought for her girls — economic, political, social and spiritual.

Deeply sensitive to her own growth, she later wrote of herself: "Unrelated though the crises that confronted me were, each cut a facet in the rough block of my ignorance until, by year's end, I had begun to learn to learn." Mistakes she must have made to have been so conscious of her own development, but they were more steps along the way than obstacles to her continuing growth.

Fifty years later, reflecting on those times, Welthy wrote:

> *I think the main reason I could take a great deal from any environment was not a childlike willingness to learn, but the fact that I did not incline to doubt myself and my roots, who and what I was. We did not question our souls so interminably in my early days. I accepted myself. I admired my Puritan ancestors, respected my strict, small-town American upbringing, believed in my old-time Methodist religious teaching. My contradictory worldliness, ambition, and love of pretty things seemed natural to me. Modern concern with equality and freedom for women, with education, with the expansion of the religious spirit through all and any sincere worship, did not conflict in me with inherited or older conceptions. I could also love all of China without conflict, the old and the new, the faults and the virtues. Of such was mankind. And if there was so much tragedy in China, it was also true that they faced tragedy with extraordinary endurance and humor. (TLC, 63.)*

No psychiatrist, religionist or philosopher need look further than that lucid analysis for the key to Welthy's personality. The words she used — accept, admire, respect, believe — all strong, positive verbs of value, were her base for clear — cut action. Accepting the large contradictions of life, Welthy mastered the art of coping with the minor ones.

She could respect and flatter the old authority, be it husband, bishop or governor, in order to gain access to those he had dominion over — a timorous wife, the mission field, the women of rural Kiangsi. It was a balancing act that called for enormous confidence and a capacity to translate difficult problems into terms of individual human lives. Welthy had both in abundance, and knowing that real power is internal, all her efforts to create change through education were based on this awareness.

* * *

With the death in 1908 of the "Old Buddha", the Dragon Empress who considered herself an incarnation of the divine Goddess of Mercy, the crumbling of China's external power was accelerated. Welthy got into trouble again for wearing her red dress, a colour forbidden until Tsuhsi's body was buried. For a moment she had forgotten that her Chinese friends expected her to mourn as they did, and so she banished the favorite garment for the required twenty-seven days. Peking seemed so far away and the government there a remote fiction. For all her wide attitude, Welthy's world was very provincial, and government meant the Nanchang officials, individuals hidden behind a mask of bureaucracy and protocol.

Welthy persisted in developing good relations all round and it was not long before the school enrollment had doubled, many of the new pupils from official families. She was pulled in all directions and conducted voluminous correspondence with the WFMS and church people to get scholarships and keep the funds rolling. She dropped in on classrooms, listened, and as she gradually understood the teachers she would ask questions, trying to elicit meaning and interest from the memory work.

By mid-1909 she was teaching ten classes and giving nine music lessons a week, her evenings as full as the days. And she took her turn with Puritan zeal in massaging feet newly liberated from "embroidered bags", in an effort to straighten them for natural walking, a symbolic act that helped burn off pent-up energy. She made sure the matron always bought fish for meals before exams, the brain food her mother had served. As headmistress of all the girls, Welthy's intimacies were limited, and an evenness of attitude grew up in her that kept the usual incidents of mischief to an acceptable minimum.

Monday mornings she held forth on hygiene, comportment and manners, inspiring a certain amount of fear that was generally matched with love. Twice a year, in spring and autumn Welthy organized a boat trip to the countryside for all the students, and there were frequent picnics. The school had become her whole life, and she gave it all her extraordinary energy. Young Wang Fu-tze looked beyond her principal's solemn facade to find her beautiful, and wonderful, seeing in that face the happiness Welthy felt in her heart. "Whether I had come to China guided by Divine Will or more humanly influenced by lively curiosity, impulsive energy, and a longing to stretch my wings, I felt I had come to belong there," Welthy wrote. "I was not inclined to excavate in my unconscious for psychological explanations." (TLC, 62.)

Recognizing Welthy's ability to handle people, Bishop Bashford sent two quarreling missionaries from Kiukiang to Bao-Lin "to be straightened out." Older than Welthy, Faith Hunt and Blanch Search arrived in a state of absolute non-communication with each other. Welthy's mother had dinned it into her that an educated woman could perform any duty, however distasteful or however startling, that needed to be done. Summoning her courage, Welthy told the women she did not care what was separating them, that they were there to be examples of love and could not justify being there unless they acted with love. Reaching deep into her own reservoir of love for the requisite skill, "knocking their heads together," and this time praying with them for her own need as much as theirs, she achieved a reconciliation, appropriately tearful.

ORPHAN BAO-BEI

Occasions for tears were as plentiful as the joyous ones. In 1908 the second orphan, Bao-bei, became ill suddenly in the middle of the night. The matron called Welthy to the dormitory. Assessing the seriousness immediately, Welthy sent someone to fetch her cape, another to bring her half of the key to the city gate. For just such emergencies she had been given one half of a foot-long wooden key shaped like a ping pong bat, sliced down the centre, which was matched with the other half on presentation at the gate. She would not wait for bearers to be fetched for her sedan chair, but sprinted off into the black night with a lantern to get Dr. Kahn, two miles away through the narrow, winding cobble-stone streets on the other side of the city.

Dr. Kahn, all two hundred pounds of her, wisely chose to travel by sedan chair and offered Welthy one, but Welthy had to use her own two anxious feet for the return journey, incapable of sitting still in a crisis. Bao-bei's sickness was quickly diagnosed as diphtheria, and she had to be quarantined with someone caring for her. Welthy felt none of the teachers could be spared, and decided that she herself was the only one not indispensable to keeping the school operating smoothly. For three days and nights the principal stayed alone with the child, singing her favourite lullaby over and over again, until finally Bao-bei died in Welthy's arms.

She gathered up the little body and went outside to dispose of clothing and bedding, remaining outdoors herself for several days, supervising the hair-lipped carpenter in making a special little coffin. She sent to the city for some white satin and cotton and made a tufted lining for it, even making the paste to glue it down.

For the grave, Welthy chose a spot by the river where she often sat at dusk, that spot where the sun fell softly and returned to her homeland. Welthy dressed Bao-bei in her favorite pink dress, put a ribbon in her hair, and placed her to rest, and the staff lowered the small casket into the grave with a sheet, the entire student body passing by one by one to drop a flower on top.

That simple scene at sunset by the riverside was fixed forever in many young minds and hearts, as Welthy closed the service with these words: "We shall plant a cross at the head of her grave, that all who see it in the years to come may know a little child of God fell just here. God loaned her for awhile to us, and she gave us great happiness, and we give Him honor, for now He has taken her to Himself."

* * *

For relief and recreation from the hovering responsibility of the school, Welthy would splash off in her boat, adorned with a pair of English sculls she was not too proud to accept from a friend at the Shanghai Yacht Club. With its brass oar locks glistening in the setting sun as she rowed, Welthy could send herself in imagination to any time and place, freeing herself from all pressures as she rowed through waters of gold.

Watching other boatmen fishing with their tamed cormorants, she commiserated with the birds. "If I could, I would tear off your rings and let you go free. I would let you catch your big fish and float and swim and dive and fly to your birds' heart's content! It must be a terrible thing to be tamed and unnatural. That is what Parla thought I would be, a tamed cormorant . . . if I came to China I could never more fly or take big fish my nature craves. Never fear . . . I am not yet tamed! I'm a wild cormorant still!" (MG, 83-84.)

She could also visit her new friend Barrett Chapman, one of the "Standard Oil boys" she had met in Kuling, whose home was a riverboat because he had no accreditation in the city. It was fun to move beyond Bao-Lin's cloistered walls, to laugh and joke and be complimented by an attractive young man whose blonde hair and blue eyes accented a fine western nose. To Barrett and his cohorts, Welthy was "Maxine", so named after the glamorous actress Maxine Elliott, abundance personified, in sharp contrast to the lofty image of headmistress.

Both sides of the image were valid; Welthy was absolutely at ease in both worlds, each endowing the other. Barrett shared her love of Chinese art, and was a mine of information about new developments in the province and about the latest talk of communications and railroads. Catching his enthusiasm for the new prosperity he envisaged, Welthy could match it with her own passion for mental and spiritual growth. They were both dealing in light — his for the oil lamps of China, and hers for the unfolding of the world through the education of China's women.

For reading material Welthy had the *Literary Digest, London Times Weekly, Staats Zeitung* and Chinese newspapers. Of her salary of fifty dollars a month, twenty went home to her mother and the balance was exchanged for Mexican dollars in Shanghai. Added to that she had some savings from her previous teaching that afforded a few luxuries such as the theatre. But neither glittering costumes nor crude stage devices could compete with the audience, seated at round tables, eating and talking throughout, hot towels sailing over their heads as waiters tossed them about. It was infinitely better than the performance itself.

On Saturday afternoons she took time to explore Nanchang's antique shops with Mrs. Nien as her guide, Chop Stick Row becoming the focus of search for her growing collection of Chinese art curios dating from the Tang dynasty, displayed in her quarters and throughout the school. Chinese dishes, redwood furniture and carpets satisfied her undeniable love of beautiful things.

She acquired formidable skill in the fine art of bargaining, winning the respect of the merchants for her skilful use of humour and proverbs in the transaction. The dynasties came alive to her as she learned the legends depicted on porcelain plates and vases and in paintings. Even her Chinese singing lessons became enjoyable and she could join the girls in singing their music almost as enthusiastically as she led them in hers.

Saturdays meant no freedom for some of the students, however. "We have to keep them here all the time," Welthy reported discreetly, "because there are men members of the family who think the time has come when a girl may be absolutely free from all ties of family and convention. The problems that some of our girls have to face are black." The entire first eighth grade graduating class became Christians, the only ones in their families, and they had a very hard time at home trying to follow Christ's teachings.

With all the enthusiasm of a true reformer, Welthy made her first tentative river trips by junk to tell people about the school and the hospital, bringing some students along as prime exhibits of the new education. Her maiden speech in the countryside had dismal results. For one thing, people never stopped feeling her clothes and asking questions about her queerness. They had never seen a foreigner before and were both astonished and fearful, especially of the eyes so far back and sunken in the face. Welthy had to let them look and touch to ease their fear. And she could not cure their dying children on the spot; she was no saint to them.

On future diplomatic forays into the districts Welthy always took a few carefully selected teachers and senior students, particularly if their parents lived in the area, sending her card ahead to the local magistrate. On one trip she went the last forty miles by wheelbarrow, hovering precariously over the paddy fields as a coolie jogged it along a path made for one pair of feet. The barrow had one large wheel in the centre with pickets and a board seat on each side, and whoever sat opposite Welthy must have leaned hard to their side for balance if they were not equally heavy.

1909

The following year she took a houseboat trip a hundred miles along the Han River, lined by orange groves and palms, stopping at the cities to visit the churches. No women came to the evening services, but in the afternoons she spotted a few in the safety of dark corners, "their faces plastered with paint and powder so their features could not be seen, their hair covered with many brass ornaments, expressions on their faces so blank, so pathetically empty, so in need of His love. They did not understand one thought expressed in good Chinese by the pastor; it may take years to get a spiritual thought through to them. They must be taught by women, *and only women,*" wrote Welthy, determined to see light in their eyes. Her own eyes were growing brighter.

In an article entitled "China's Waiting Women" appealing to the Board to support day schools for girls in every city of the province, Welthy stressed that girls must be taught by women. She depicted women as "superstitious, uncontrolled, untutored, but with a kind of hopeless longing".[27]

Gertrude Howe had strongly supported Welthy's approach while in the States that year, and was a staunch cooperator in the development of the schools. The WFMS saw great growth ahead for Bao-Lin and could congratulate themselves on their foresight in selecting Welthy. Their ability to manage her, however, would become a test of will.

* * *

Halfway round the world young Fred Fisher, still in his Boston parish in 1909, was struggling for the way to reach people. "Thou hast placed me in a hard field," he prayed. "The problem of the downtown church almost overwhelms me. For a year and a third I have labored. I long to preach to crowds of men and women. Our average attendance Sundays is not much more than two hundred. We are in the midst of thousands of people. Give them to me, O Lord, take away the self from my work. Fill my church, and do it soon. Give me a message that will draw them."[28]

* * *

To Welthy the message had already become clear; her method, however, was very different. She stayed in Nanchang that summer to get the industrial department organized, as the heat sapped energy from all living things. The hawthorne trees gave way first, then the mulberry and willow trees. The earth was dry and hard and cracked. Out from the squatters' huts came the inmates like rats leaving a drowning ship. Inside the city wall the streets were lined with bamboo cots with sufferers doomed to die of cholera. Everywhere emaciated men, women and children of all ages crawled out of their germ-infested, windowless houses to die in the open air.

Corpses were continuously being carried away, but the stench of disease and unwashed bodies filled the heavy air. The black pigs and their litters came out to die too, but they were picked up sooner than the humans by the butcher and made ready for sale at the open meat market. As Welthy walked through the streets she saw women covering the eyes of the dying with a cloth or a palm leaf to shield them from the glance of the foreign devil, whose gaze might affect the dying one's entrance into the next reincarnation. She watched flies moving from dead bodies to carts of open melons, the main refreshment.

Her dizzy, wounded mind staggered at the horror surrounding her, the stench overwhelming her. She stopped in the middle of the street and prayed: "Oh God, I will fear no evil, for Thou art with me, Thy rod and Thy staff, they comfort me. And, Oh God, I will not be afraid," she added, "but I will be careful."

She was brought back to her own immediate personal responsibility — all those children who had remained in the school for the summer and who were probably eating melons when she was not looking. For today, she could hurry back and wash the melons with potassium permanganate. For tomorrow, her responsibility was much larger and it would take more faith and energy than she had dared to dream of.

Always ready to take inspiration wherever she could find it, Welthy looked into the face of Jane Addams that hung in her office, and found it not without hope, though she seemed to be carrying the sorrows of the world in her heart. A visiting American tourist woman who happened upon Welthy in such rare repose berated her for not being busy teaching heaven and hell and salvation to the children. "How can I ever make Americans realize that going into a country already heavily freighted with numerous religions one must choose the barest essentials to teach and live by?" Welthy wondered. (MG, 71.) Those clear moments of commitment and vision set her apart from her less creative contemporaries.

1910

"Once I thought East was East and West was West and never the twain would meet, but Ilien Tang and many of her friends have taught me it is false and not what Kipling meant . . . And now I know that there is no border, nor breed, nor birth among young women of any race, though they come from the end of the earth." (MG, 85.) That dramatic diary entry in the autumn of 1910 was Welthy's proclamation of world identity, in all its young purity and innocence. Inscrutability had vanished. She found herself in the potential of each young Chinese woman, and kept repeating: "The veil is being lifted."

That game of real life, arriving at sunset feasts preceded by her flaming red calling card, even imagining that as the only foreigner she had been accepted as one of the set, all was necessary to keep her expanding perceptions in balance amid the realities and contradictions behind those moongates. Even her hat had been reinstated, featherless, as if to acknowledge that she really was different.

However, the real difference about Welthy was in relation to the other missionaries. To begin with, missionary wives lived with many contradictions and often resented the salaries and freedom the single women had, feeling insecure about their own capabilities. Mission boards would not pay wives, who were heavily overburdened, but they did respond to the growing demand for more single missionary women.

In effect, the boards exploited both the married and single women. On one hand the men's boards required foreign service of wives without remuneration, and on the other hand the women's boards reinforced spinsterhood by supporting the services of single women. The salaries were sacrificial, but were just enough to attract school teachers from pioneering, rural mid-west America, who made up the majority of missionaries. Marriage was not on their horizons, and they wanted to make better use of their talents than they could in America, a society largely closed to professional women. Missionary work gave them unusual freedom and security, and was an acceptable alternative to the poor environment they wished to leave behind.

Welthy, however, had not ruled out marriage altogether, nor was her background so rugged. The possibilities and opportunities seemed unlimited to someone with her New York exposure and expansive personality. She had simply evaded one pressing suitor in her pursuit of experience and an opportunity to serve. Her future was an open door, and always would be, but to most of her missionary colleagues, life was prescribed. The ties to family and letters exchanged with them sustained and defined their sense of themselves. Self-fulfilment was less valued than Christian charity, but in Welthy's case, the two goals were in equal proportion or merged into one. Her sense of self-fulfilment lay in finding the best way to express her sense of Christian charity.

Welthy had more in common with the young American women of her day whose Eastern college education and some financial leeway gave them the freedom to choose settlement work. Welthy had moved ahead quickly as a teacher, had good leadership experience and was an unusually articulate speaker, so that she might have made more headway in the States than others who chose the missionary life. Given Welthy's inherent spiritual drive, it was natural that she chose the religious rather than either of the secular options open to her. As Jane Hunter states in her analysis of American women missionaries in turn-of-the-century China, "missionary service was over-determined for Welthy."[29]

While the others were developing their faith in God and His institutions, Welthy was developing faith in the growing power within herself, a power that made her stand out from the rest. With wide contacts at all levels, Welthy did not feel at all inferior to the men of the mission nor did she hide her femininity in the unstylish clothes considered appropriate for spinster missionaries. In the genderless Chinese language she was often called "Ocean Man", but that just added to her feeling of equality. She felt even less inferior to "*those women*" of the WFMS, who used their emerging strength as they began to win seats on the General Board to continue what they had themselves received from the men, and enhance their own stature with an expanding empire of single missionaries who perpetuated the myth of saintly spinsters serving their Lord sacrificially, eternally. It was unhealthy, and Welthy knew it. A high rate of mental disorders among missionaries was the result.

"There were . . . missionaries who despised in their hearts the people they came to 'save'. There were those who thought salvation lay only in the narrow way of the sect to which they belonged . . . others were shabby and unbeautiful because they thought only of the soul and never of the body. Sanctimoniousness put me off, but sanctity was a quality I worshipped in anyone," wrote Welthy. (TLC, 21.) The cool reserve of many missionaries made her appreciate all the more the poor coolies who could laugh and joke even with their heavy life burdens, drawing her closer to the Chinese who could find amusement in everything.

Ill prepared for the crowds, the pigs, the filth of China, many wives retreated into excessive American domesticity in their walled refuges — their Grand Rapids homes as Welthy called them — relying on Montgomery Ward for supplies of food rich in meat and starch as their best defence against the climate, unaware that the amazing Chinese resistance to infection and disease stemmed from much lower meat consumption.

With husbands often away in the interior, those wives with children to protect from Chinese contamination were increasingly isolated within their own small colonial empire, whatever inner desire they had to serve being less and less fulfilled. Childless wives, or those who survived the pain of separation from children sent home to school, were better able to find a satisfying role.

As it happened, there were four missionary wives in Nanchang and none at the larger mission in Kiukiang, nor did they have any orphans there. Welthy therefore had a larger responsibility, but it did not take much effort to draw two of the wives into the work of the school, Mrs. Gage helping in the kindergarten and Mrs. Muir in the industrial workshop. It may not have been their ideal of service, but it went a long way toward developing the school.

*   *   *

At the height of the missionary thrust, the World Missionary Conference summoned Protestants of all denominations to Edinburgh in 1910. Fred Fisher was there to hear Robert Speer's call "to the Western nations that owed all their good to Christianity." They had a heavy debt to do justice and help the non-Christian nations that could not be left undisturbed; they were already disturbed. No Christian could keep the spiritual life and blessing to himself, for God's word was the universal possession of all God's people, and the church itself must be saved from growing luxury and divisions. Denouncing polytheism, idolatry, polygamy, exorcism and other evils in China and India as arising from a false concept of morality, he preached a humanitarian gospel of regeneration and protest against immorality and injustice. The unity of mankind, brotherhood, equality and hope, were the life-affirming, sacred, inviolable truths, calling for a world plan. Evangelization of the world *within our generation* was his battlecry.

Speer feared that the non-Christian nations were likely to imitate the West before working out their own Christian solutions, and warned that universal charity was not the aim of missions, nor were mass movements. Neither were social, educational or political change the main aims, but rather the goal was to plant seeds of an indigenous church—the naturalization of Christianity—that would release the energy to produce vast change. Challenging the Layman's Missionary Movement to rise to the unprecedented moment of opportunity and crisis, Speer urged much greater involvement of people at home.[30]

Listening to the rousing speeches, so many of them focused on China, the magnet of mission fields in the world, Fred was captured by Speer's powerful conviction as Welthy had been four years earlier. Fred reaffirmed his vow to be a planter of seeds, his call to the divine life growing stronger and stronger. Speer had touched both their hearts with his directive that real love in the missionary heart would overcome the inevitable differences of culture, status, custom and wealth. More than anything, his pronouncement that the human race is one was to each of them the single most compelling truth.

* * *

Fully intending to remain in the plains that summer, Welthy was instead despatched early to Kuling when fever hit. She spent the first part of the season there with her orphans and the other foreigners, easily enjoying the European style of life among the elite. But she shared with her less well socially endowed missionary colleagues a strong dislike for the insufferable British condescension to Americans and decided to break out of the stifling atmosphere.

Pei Tai Ho, the northeast seaside resort, though still a foreign preserve, offered change and new interest where she could continue recuperating. Estelle Paddock, National Secretary of the YWCA, the leading organization in women's development in China, was a perfect companion for that interval when Welthy was planning a new high school. Estelle agreed to take Ilien Tang for YWCA leadership training in Shanghai, and helped Welthy with ideas for training indigenous students to make local crafts and ways of selling them. Swimming daily along the pine-covered shoreline, fattening up for the winter, giving concerts many evenings, and later discovering Peking, the time passed all too quickly, but she was more than ready to return to Bao-Lin in the fall.

One of the first girls to enter the high school had been Sally Kiang, a minister's daughter who lived nearby and had come up through the grade school. The following year her mother entered the high school, in a successful bid on Welthy's part to reach adults, stretching established mission practice to include her, as she had done before for Mary Hill.

She encouraged the girls to give a Christmas party for the beggars and derelicts outside the walls, and when the big gates swung open, the tattered creatures shuffled in apprehensively, the girls moving among them serving food they had prepared themselves. A full concert followed, entirely managed by the girls, concluding a memorable evening, and a good lesson in the art of hospitality, part of the loving way Welthy wanted to see her girls grow.

Her own open door and talent for making every occasion a special event was a powerful example. School hospitality was extended to the *tai tai's* (wives of officials) who came regularly on their four inch feet to watch new China playing tennis on their "heaven", or natural feet. They came from all parts of China, since their official husbands were never appointed to their own province, exposing Welthy to the broad universe that was China.

The WFMS reported proudly that Bao-Lin had sent their first exhibition to the Nanking Exposition in 1910, featuring science and mathematics. Welthy herself was teaching botany, and the girls' notebooks formed part of the exhibit. With additional courses in Chinese etiquette, art and literature, plus English essays, Bao-Lin was making its mark as a school of high standing.

The school had also entered into a new contract with parents unable to pay the full fees, agreeing: (1) to baptism or church entrance, (2) no betrothal until after graduation or without the principal's knowledge, (3) the child remained through grade four and would serve the church from one to three years after. For those who could pay, Welthy insisted on raising the tuition rather than using the school to attract 'rice Christians' seeking foreign protection.

The Government had started a new school where tuition was free and students were treated rather like honoured guests. When they called on Bao-Lin to help set up this school, Welthy only too gladly involved some of her senior girls in getting the books and necessary supplies together. What would they learn if she did it herself? Bao-Lin's standards were steadily improving and Welthy was eager to push them higher.

When she asked the WFMS to send a mathematics teacher, Wang Gwei-hsin was sent from the Kiukiang School, relieved to get away from a principal who "liked goody—goody missionaries and played favourites with students." Not at all reluctant to make scathing remarks about some of the missionaries, no one could accuse Gwei-hsin of being goody—goody, and for Ilien Tang she reserved her special scorn. But she taught mathematics well (and much later taught English to Chou En-lai in Tientsin) and had high regard for Welthy. Her unkind tongue, however, was a new factor in keeping harmony in the school. She had been there only two months before disaster occurred.

A NIGHT OF RAGING FIRE

In the cold, black night of December 1, 1910, at 2:00 a.m., Bao-Lin burned to the ground. The fire had started from a smouldering log in the poorly installed fireplace in Welthy's study, where she had been working late paying the November salaries and writing personal letters to scholarship patrons. It spread rapidly with the aid of howling winds to the school, the dormitory and the teachers' home.

Welthy awakened to see the whole compound aglow, rushed to warn Ilien, and tried to cross the corridor to the dormitory, already aflame. She had the wit not to open the door, jumping through a window and down an outside staircase just before it collapsed.

There beneath her window on that "seven coats night" of piercing chill stood the lodgekeeper like a pillar of salt, petrified, still crying out "school is on fire," his initial warning that had aroused her. Welthy had to shake him back to his senses. She had never so much as touched a

Chinese man before but knew he was numb with fright and he must be sent to arouse the American men across the way who could notify city officials. As she began ringing the gong she prayed that the fire drills she had insisted on, and that the Chinese staff thought idiotic, would save the day.

She rushed back to rescue the orphans from the dormitory, rolled them in blankets and put them safely in the arms of young teachers who had responded quickly to the alarm. They crawled along the floor through the smoke, sat low on the stairs and bumped their way down in the dark, Welthy's red gown thrown over their heads.

She made two last rounds to check the dorms, the roof now in flames. Ilien, who took time to dress, was unable to follow Welthy down the smoke-filled stairs and had let herself down with a short awning rope and kicked in a window below, making her escape through the veranda, suffering some burns. One teacher hurt her back badly trying to save her trunk, but the naughty Gwei-hsin was able to pull two children out and drag them downstairs.

Outside, Welthy had all the classes lined up according to drill procedure and took roll-call to be sure everyone was safe. They were. Then she went back for Yang Ma, the orphans' amah, who had gone to get their clothes. Welthy found her, clothes aflame, and pulled her out with the help of one of the Americans, who had just reached the desperate scene.

The other Americans soon arrived. William Johnson, head of the boys' school, told Welthy later that for the next half hour she spoke only in Chinese. In that critical instant, Welthy was Chinese. She moved, she managed, and was congratulated by the Government for saving all the children, who were marched off to the brand new wing of Dr. Bowen's hospital, so new it had no beds or chairs.

The Governor's representative appeared, dressed in satin, along with the Magistrate and the Police Commissioner, and for once Welthy dispensed with protocol and kept moving. They were astonished to see the red-robed figure streaking back and forth, holding her robe up to her knees so she could run, her face black with smoke. For all her courage and resourcefulness, however, she was unable to save any of her precious possessions. Had she loved them too much? She asked the American men to try to save the piano in the chapel, and with ropes and many helping hands they were able to inch out the item she cherished most.

In time Nanchang's fire department arrived. It consisted of some twenty iron carts, each the size of a child's wagon, all empty. A bucket brigade was organized to fill the carts from the river, then a mere hand pump from cart to a little hose produced a pitiful stream against the roaring blaze, "its light shining over the city and surroundings as no other blaze in the city's two thousand years." They were literally playing with fire, but she thought better of her instinct to tell them to stop their hopeless effort. They were doing their best with what they had, they had come a long distance in the middle of cold night, their system would probably be effective against a thatched roofed hut, perhaps the school buildings were out of place. She felt she must stay as a sort of hostess, particularly to ensure that the walls did not collapse on them. Finally she put a stop to their pumping, and sent them to protect the adjacent squatters' huts.

When there was nothing more to be done, Welthy thanked the firemen, observing proper etiquette, taking time now to make three bows in the cutting cold. She sent the lodgekeeper, who had recovered about half his senses by then, to buy tea and sweets for the firemen, and lingered till all had been served. Storing the scene permanently in her heart, she extracted every last ounce of drama. "Only one wall still stands silhouetted against the moonless sky like a sentinel watching over a precious body from which the spirit is gone," she recorded. A few tons of coal and a large wood pile kept the fire burning for days.

As the temple bell announced dawn, she turned her back reluctantly on the smouldering fire that contained all her Chinese musical instruments, her rare porcelains, bronzes, rugs, music, clothes, letters, and all the school's equipment. As she crossed over to join the children and teachers in the men's compound, moving slowly, she knew she was facing the most serious situation of her life. It was a very black moment. By what she felt could only be called the grace of God, she kept herself from falling into despair, remembering that the children were the living part of the school, the part that really mattered. Her step quickened as she approached the compound, where all eyes were upon her, their principal.

The children were gathered together in the assembly hall of the compound, some crying, teeth chattering in the winter cold. Welthy at the piano urged them to sing "One by One", the song of their happy times. As she led them in praying, her calm gradually spread to the children. Gwei-hsin was suffering from nerves, and laughed all through the prayers, afraid Welthy would see, but she just could not stop.

A capable matron urged the cook to prepare breakfast — soft rice congee, with strings of pickled turnip, red pepper and a fried egg on top — and the world began to look a bit better. When one father arrived with a huge basket of mandarin oranges for everyone, Gwei-hsin immediately sat down and ate as many as she could, by her own confession, in frightened reaction to the horrendous night, and even more fearful of drawing Welthy's attention to such bad behaviour on the part of a teacher.

* * *

Though she was never blamed for the fire, the knowledge that the fire started because of her desire for a warm fireplace weighed heavily on Welthy, and was the unspoken motivation for all she set out to do. "I wouldn't fail these children now for anything you or your world has to offer, Parla," she told her diary. "No power on earth can tempt me; I'm theirs for better or for worse. I've got to see them through."

The children had also lost all their possessions in the fire and neither the building nor its contents were insured. Whatever guilt Welthy felt, she rapidly transformed it into action. That ability to push negative thoughts from her mind and concentrate on possibilities was Welthy's prime survival technique, positive thinking personified.

When all the children were settled down, she walked across to the shore of the river and strode up and down in the cold. Suddenly she stood still. This was a crisis — her crisis — and she would have to meet it, alone. Then she walked over to the squatters' huts to apologize for pouring water on them. They greeted her gratefully.

She went on down to the spot by the shore where her friends the cormorant fishermen were cleaning fish for market. Their life goes on as it has for two thousand years, she mused, and now hers had abruptly changed in one harrowing night. Her mind was racing. She had to restrain the urge to jump in her boat and row till she was exhausted. But standing there by the moving waters, always changing, she came to the decision to rebuild the school, to build a school worthy of the city and the province. Statistics took on new life as they raced through her brain. How many eligible school age girls were there?

Scholar Yang appeared at her side, offering assistance, and as they walked along together surveying the wasteland beyond, Welthy's decision grew stronger — the crisis was being transformed into a dream. "Bao-Lin has given the girls of Kiangsi the dessert of the feast," Yang said. "Now they demand the feast proper."

The Dragon Sand, that wasteland they were traversing, belonged mostly to the Temple of Last Prayer, where criminals were permitted their final shriving before their blood was shed, just there, by beheading or crucifixion on the adjacent Executioner's Grounds. Huge camphor trees made a grove of heavy shade surrounding the Temple. Priests were tapping the trees and pouring sap in boiling cauldrons, and all about the air was fresh and healing with the fragrance of camphor. Welthy took that as a good omen. By now she knew herself to be completely fearless, and they proceeded towards the Temple. She bowed to the priests and expressed her hope that the Temple was unharmed; they said they had sounded their gong in the night and prayed for a worthy outcome. With a certainty that surprised her, Welthy told them a greater school would rise.

Scholar Yang impressed her with his diplomacy as he asked them if crucifixions were growing less. They agreed, commenting how inappropriate crucifixions were in the neighborhood of such a fine school. Welthy wondered if the Temple would soon be of no use at all, with so few crucifixions; they continued to agree, for they much preferred to return to their monastery to spend their last years in prayer and meditation. An unwritten, unspoken agreement had been struck. It was enough for Welthy to act on, taking counsel from her proverb for the day: "A journey of a thousand miles begins with one step."

* * *

Her own belief that when a thing should be done, it could be done, put her feet on the road to the cable office. She cabled the WFMS in New York, asking them to stop a friend who planned to come for a year, and Bishop Lewis in Nanking, saying she would take her sabbatical a year early, go home and raise the money to rebuild. She felt a bit sheepish for omitting to say she would leave Ilien in charge, since such appointments were the Bishop's to make, so a second cable added that information, certain he would be reasonable. Both Bishops Lewis and Bashford concurred.

"Well, well," she thought, "I have both Bishops behind me." Even so, they insisted she stop in Nanking en route to sign a promise not to raise money for a college in Nanchang as well as an elementary and a high school, her ambition and impatience by now well known. One missionary in Nanking wrote to her : "Woe be unto you when all men speak well of you."

In Nanchang word of the fire spread rapidly and tales of Welthy's athletic prowess abounded. American children were saying: "Did you hear how Miss Honsinger escaped the fire? She was upstairs, took a piano under one arm and a baby under the other and let herself down by a rope!"

There were countless arrangements to be made for the children. The son of the wealthiest member of the gentry came, full of questions as to the schools aims and activities, and by the time he left, he had volunteered to act as Welthy's secretary, a great catch on her part, and the Governor sent a company of soldiers to protect the ruins from vandals. All this support was enormously encouraging; the school was befriended.

In a borrowed dress and slippers, a man's overcoat, cap and gloves, Welthy observed "I am getting acquainted with myself minus things", though she badly missed her hairpins. Her confidence in always being able to rustle up some clothes from somewhere stems from that frantic experience and enabled her to travel light the rest of her life, the hairpins among her few essentials.

The smallest children were sent off to their homes in borrowed clothes, and those who could not go home were installed in a house Welthy rented. The school would be kept together, with the four wives helping, and Ilien Tang in charge. She was the one person Welthy felt could handle the situation, as the only Chinese in Nanchang who was a university graduate, who had been in the States, knew American ways and could handle communications with the WFMS during the time Welthy was away.

The high school class was packed off to the Kiukiang School along with Gwei-hsin so they would not miss a year. To one of the wives Welthy assigned the task of directing the cleaning and piling of bricks and clearing of debris from the ruins of the school.

Welthy awakened one morning to face a chickenpox outbreak in their cramped quarters; everyone had to be quarantined for three long weeks, unable to see anyone. A few days later Betty became quite ill, smelling so badly that no one wanted to go near her but Welthy, who carried her up and down all night long as any mother would.

At the end of three weeks she was on her way, supercharged for action. She said farewell to the priests, telling them that if the Governor agreed, she would bring money from America, and together they would await a propitious day for their symbolic ending of the dynasty, for it was custom to plow under all the graves in China at the start of every new dynasty. Scholar yang had warned of serious times and danger in buying the wasteland of graves surrounding the temple. Welthy was as ready as any patriot to help end the dynasty.

* * *

No instruction from headquarters was necessary then or ever after. From that time on Welthy became one of the most dynamic, self-generating forces the Methodist Church had ever known. "Beware, America!" she warned, "I'm coming for your money and your goods and maybe your life." The battlesong she was to sing for the rest of her life, with appropriate adaptations at each new decade, had found words. Welthy had made her choice. She was going to rebuild the School, whatever it would take to do it.

FOUR

THIRTY-FOUR THOUSAND BRICKS AND THE TEMPLE BELL

A MERICA, 1911-1912

The destruction of the school and everything Welthy owned was both devastating and liberating at once. As a child of American Protestantism's greatest era, she was filled with confidence that anything could be accomplished if one had the will to summon God's strength. Welthy had the will, the personal skills and a powerful need to erase that black night of fire. Her immediate decision to rebuild the school on a broader and more beautiful scale held firm. By early 1911 she was back in the United States armed with ideas to carry out her plan, leaving her Chinese family behind.

In San Francisco she headed straightaway for the St. Francis Hotel, an odd sight as she scuttled across the thick carpets, nearly tripping in her soft Chinese shoes, western shoes being the one item the Chinese could not produce in her size. In her long man's raincoat Welthy was hardly equal to the hotel's elegance. The lure of its finely appointed bathrooms had such appeal that she gave herself up to a few luxuriating hours before proceeding to Los Angeles, where she had been summoned by the WFMS. She obediently boarded the Night Owl, treating herself to a steak dinner en route to prolong the luxury, but it quickly palled as the sharp contrast with China flooded in.

There is also wealth in China, she thought, in the beautiful expressions of an accumulated culture, never so ostentatious as in America. An incurable sinophile then, even the elaborate Chinese feasts seemed more genteel to her mood. She had gradually lengthened her sleeves and heightened the neck of her dresses to adjust to the Chinese standard. Now the endless variety of competing dress designs in America looked like "non-essential overtones".

The WFMS overwhelmed her with a list of the meetings she was to address, giving a full account of Baldwin and the fire. Unprepared for this demand, Welthy wanted to forget the fire and focus on the future, rebuilding. When she asked if she could sing instead, they insisted on a real accounting. Welthy sang anyhow, to begin with, just a song to break the ice and create a more intimate atmosphere. With her grand voice coming forth out of the long red silk Manchu robe given by a Nanchang lady, the Methodists got more than they bargained for. It was always that way with Welthy.

Mabel and Mina were there for a tearful reunion at Grand Central Station in New York, while her mother waited to embrace her youngest in quiet privacy. They were days of great joy and laughter, endless talking, and whirlwind shopping. Her sisters had decided to dress Welthy properly, since she had almost no clothes, choosing a black velvet dress with long white kid gloves and a smashing picture hat, the kind she used to wear, and a formal dinner dress made of some Chinese crepe she had brought.

Welthy duly presented herself to the WFMS with a wavering heart and was informed they would permit her to have all the money she could raise to rebuild the school, but would not give her any of the personal contributions received from individuals and had no money to pay her expenses. That she had lost all her personal possessions did not concern them at all. They would plan her engagements across the country, speaking three times on Sundays and once or twice on weekdays. It seemed like a sentence handed down by a judge, her wings effectively clipped — reaction to any board or committee meeting where an agenda was strictly followed and instructions given with apparent disregard for her own sense of direction. On second thought, she knew it was a great opportunity and accepted their tight control as necessary to her purpose.

When all was agreed, the nine ladies felt obliged to tell Welthy that her dress and gloves and hat were quite elegant for mission meetings. Welthy turned the scene around by agreeing with them, saying how lucky she was to have such a generous family to reclothe her after she had lost everything in the fire, making her point with a delicate touch. It gained their sympathy, and a few useful tears were shed all round.

She further enhanced her position by telling of her previous day's experience in speaking of "The Composite Chinese Woman" at Marble Collegiate Church to a large meeting of church women of all denominations marking the Golden Jubilee of Missions. One rich woman asked her back to speak in her salon, and the first funds for the school began to flow. Welthy's old ally, Mrs. Cornell (who she noted was the only one of the WFMS women in the New York Social Register) told the committee later that Welthy was irrepressible, broke all the rules, and that she for one loved her for it, not at all threatened by Welthy's style and exuberance. Welthy would win people whatever she wore, Mrs. Cornell predicted, and suggested that the WFMS had better not try to change her but make the best use of her unusual talent. Since the ladies had also received a good report on Welthy from Bishop Lewis, who praised her development of Chinese leadership, they tolerated her seeming flamboyance.

Even so, Welthy was so thin and worn looking that before sending her off on tour, the ladies insisted that she spend two or three months at Clifton Springs Sanitorium to recuperate from an illness Welthy never remembered having. Whether it was compassion or captivity, she stayed only two weeks before deciding that she would sleep much better if she were at work raising money.

RAISING MONEY AND RAISING CONSCIOUSNESS

"People had to take initiative. Those back of us were so slow. I was the only one who knew what to do. You have to do it," insisted Welthy the entrepreneur. In her Chinese silks and satins quickly made up in Shanghai, a white feather hat, and an enormous sable coat hanging to her ankles — the only warm coat in China large enough, normally available only to warlords and such, and a bargain at three hundred dollars — the refitted Welthy was hardly the picture of a missionary returning from the dark interior of China. With a performer's instinct she was certain that her stunning clothes would capture audience attention and draw it from the immediate preoccupation of the day — the horrendous sinking of the 'unsinkable' Titanic on its maiden voyage in April 1912. She wanted to win their hearts and open their purses to the needs in China.

Public relations came naturally to Welthy, whose costume changes fitted whatever role she was playing to whatever audience. Rich people liked style and charm; Welthy could deliver that while speaking seriously about other people's poverty. There was no need for her to look like a miserable wretch herself. "I wanted no pity," she said, "I was doing just what I wanted to do."

On that marathon fund-raising trip across the States in 1911-12, Welthy matched her dramatic skills expertly to the levels of her audiences, bringing her Chinese girls alive for them and expressing the need with such spontaneous enthusiasm that she single-handedly raised thirty thousand dollars. She knew nothing about raising money, thought all platforms were for singing, and found herself a great drawing card as word spread throughout Methodism of her talent and mission.

It was a highly stimulating, if gruelling experience that taught her much more about herself and others, a quantum leap in adult education that established her base for the future. With a keen eye for inflation and the dramatic appeal of a more easily remembered round figure, thirty thousand grew to one hundred thousand in Welthy's retelling of that adventure through the years. Welthy was frankly pleased with herself, and no doubt more than one WFMS lady wished she were still 'recuperating' in the sanitorium rather than doing what came so naturally to her and not to them.

At Chicago the man from the Missionary Training School who was sent to meet her train returned alone, saying no one looking like a missionary was on the train, an incident she relished. Zula Brown, a trainee who was assigned to look after Welthy, remembered well the tall, vigorous looking young woman with snapping brown eyes, so concerned about her plain black dress, toned down for the Training School, because she had a date with a young man. All the trainees rallied round to help her get ready for the evening, polishing her shoes and sending her off with a key to the building in vicarious delight, Welthy happily receiving their attention.

With the image of the fire and escaping children strong in her mind, she was at her best appealing to the best in Americans — their generosity. At the risk of seeming egotistical, she simply could not hide her God-given personality. She decided to put it to work, and made a direct, personal appeal to Dr. Welch of Welch's Grape Juice, dressed in style, unafraid of approaching the top man. His two thousand dollar gift was what she needed to confirm the instinct to follow her own light.

With her customary love for statistics, Welthy noted she had made six hundred and forty-five speeches in those fifteen months in the States, in country village parlours and luxurious city drawing rooms, sleeping in farmhouses and mansions on the way. She met America. "There was but one way to measure the success of my words, I thought each night. How much have I added to the fund today?"

No one could accuse Welthy of specialization or expertise. It was a golden opportunity to find new teachers and she did not confine her energy to fund raising alone. She had the whole school on her mind, which to the WFMS was probably an outrageous overreach of her responsibility. Understanding the psychology of people's need to be helpful, Welthy was drawing them to herself personally so they listened to what she was saying as a human being, not just to a barren idea. Dramatizing the story of the fire to the Student Volunteers, and outlining her rebuilding plans, she strongly reinforced their missionary bent as they hung on her every word. "She had the gift of luring others into whatever project she was engaged in by picturing the need, the opportunity and the romance awaiting them," said Zula, who found herself at Bao-Lin within a year of meeting Welthy, as did Ella Jordan.

Once they arrived, these women came to be regarded by the students as the best teachers at Bao-lin, so that Welthy's selection technique, seemingly random, was based on an astute assessment of intelligence as well as motivation. Welthy looked as much for psychological balance as for intellectual ability. Crossing sectarian boundaries, she also attracted Rosalie Mayer, a young Episcopalian from Waterville, New York, who came to Nanchang at her own expense to teach music. Thus Welthy effectively outreached the WFMS in her staffing, and secured a five hundred dollar salary for Rosalie through a private donation.

Her family was eager to hear everything when she returned to her hometown for several days. Though Welthy was thrilled by the warm reception of her church and family, Rome was no longer home; home was becoming wherever Welthy was, her love and loyalties on an expanding trajectory. Her mother wanted to know all about Betty, of course, but declined Welthy's invitation to come back to China with her. Mabel, the teacher, initially so skeptical of Welthy's adventure in China, became more and more intrigued as Welthy talked on, and ultimately agreed to teach at Kiukiang when her contract in the States ended.

Welthy's talk to the congregations of First Methodist's morning service and Liberty Street Methodist's evening service one Sunday, appropriately tailored, was proudly quoted in the *Rome Daily Sentinel:*

> *Here, little waifs, picked up from the gutters ere the dogs should devour them, have been sheltered and mothered; here, broken-hearted women have found a sympathetic ear and the silver word of comfort; hither, hobbling, crippled girls with tiny feet have come and have gone away normal, healthy, girls leaping and praising God; here, high class ladies of the old order, bound down by fetters of custom and the past, have come to look with longing eyes and bleeding hearts on the girls of the new order in Christ Jesus; here, the ideals of Christian womanhood—ideals of body, mind and soul—have been lifted up and fostered in the lives of the city's daughters; here, a cup of cold water has oft been given in His name to some of the least of these, His children."*

She went on to say that the lakes in the centre of Nanchang became so putrid from the accumulation of female babies' bodies that no one could live near them. In 1909 the government installed baby boxes on the walls of buildings around the lakes with instructions to those who had strangled, or in some other way murdered their infant daughters to "throw babies bodies here". Every morning the bodies were collected and disposed of outside the city walls. She had found one of her own orphans by stumbling over the child in the gutter.

Such disturbingly graphic scenes, described with all the Christian compassion Welthy could muster, communicated instantly a need that reams of more prosaic statements about educational work could not convey. Welthy wanted human response to human indignity. The Christian courage of American women could penetrate the hopeless darkness of blank superstition. And she was mindful of her own very human response to the indignity of that ghastly fire, for she was unwilling to admit publicly how it had started. From a public relations viewpoint, it made no sense to cloud the issue with speculation about the fire.

Speaking throughout New York state on the famed Chautauqua circuit and to service organizations and church groups across the country, she said the new Bao-lin would be a 'central powerhouse' that would send out good teachers and wives throughout the province. Education was the overwhelming need of the day. Driven by this conviction and aware of her own ability to do something about it, none of the several suitors who wooed Welthy on that trip had a chance. She had yet to meet a man whose idealism matched hers.

* * *

It was almost as if she could hear years in advance the words of Fred Fisher: "Modern education is a holy call. No cost is too great, no sacrifice too hard. The first imperative of the ideal world is education that comprehends the training of mind and soul and body." (PS, 186.) Welthy did meet Fred during the course of the Methodist General Conference in Ithaca in 1912, and remembered "looking into the brightest pair of blue eyes you ever saw." And they went on their separate ways about their business.

Fred had begun to hit his stride as a preacher in Boston, and had dealt with every layer of America, from brahmins to the newest immigrants. Important big churches had sought him for summer replacement, but when he was called to be General Secretary of the Laymen's Missionary Movement he accepted the challenge because he thought it a more direct way of helping missions in India. He must have crossed Welthy's path many times that year, as he too travelled throughout the States preparing for their convention in Indianapolis the following year.

With a ready laugh and a natural gift for reaching the hearts of listeners, he too made lifelong friends then and became widely known throughout Methodism. His resourcefulness was a match for Welthy's. When roadblocks appeared he could find alternate approaches, once even mortgaging his Hingham, Massachusetts, home to raise promotional funds when appropriations from the church lagged. The three thousand laymen attending the convention contributed fifty thousand dollars for missions, a distinct success for Fred as a preliminary to the massive Centenary movement which raised one hundred and five million dollars for missions worldwide. But in that signal year, Fred was ahead of Welthy by twenty thousand.

* * *

In Chicago a well-established banker insisted Welthy stay in his fine home where he lived with two spinster sisters, and his limousine sped her wherever she needed to go. She sang and entertained his friends. He fell hard for Welthy's exuberance and her evident enjoyment of high living as they moved about Chicago together. Why couldn't she be a missionary to one family, he pleaded, offering to rebuild the school himself and take Welthy back to see it someday. After refusing his proposals of marriage several times, Cinderella left the ball and retreated to the austerity of the mission training college; the slipper did not fit, her fling was over. She wanted no man hanging his prosperity round her neck.

Another man offered to go back to China to help her for a year if she would marry him at the end of it, throwing a horse into the bargain after teaching her to ride, even soliciting her mother's help in his pursuit. Her mother had been highly amused by a list in a mission report of those "Lost by Death and Marriage", and warned Welthy that the offers would not come forever after Welthy turned him down as too devoted. "No woman wishes only to be worshipped," Welthy said. "I felt with each one of them that I'd be entering into a closed circuit. I wanted an idealist." Most of all, she wanted to rebuild Bao-Lin herself.

Parla was still on the scene, though she was moving too fast to see him often. When they met in Rome, a shrewd mother who knew the measure of her daughter, asked pointedly: "Are you giving him all your kisses?" Sixty-three, action-packed years later Welthy confessed that the very worst thing she ever did in her life was to lead Parla on so far, her strong attraction to him revealed in several different drafts of a novel she attempted to write about that period.

She obviously liked and enjoyed men, and at thirty-three the pressure to marry was at a peak. The hero of her novel was named Boyd Chandler, practically Barrett Chapman, but his characterization was a composite of Barrett and Parla — an industrial engineer with an oil company, virile, his sensuousness somewhat inhibited by a New England background, not given to indulging in the quick easy affairs so many western men had in China, but with some guilt over his intermittent affair with one lovely Eurasian woman.

Welthy depicted herself — called Wally, Prudence and Ruth in the different drafts — as his fiancee just arrived from America, humiliated by his affair which was known to all the foreign community. He wanted to marry her, and she finally agreed on condition that she might carry out her own work plans. When he insisted on a full-time wife, the marriage was put on long-term hold and he went off to work in France, while she remained at work in China. The twin problems were her fear of domination and the strength of her own passion. Welthy listened to her fears and decided she would risk the wait for whatever the future held.

She was determined to be a person who was throwing out ideas to help change the stereotyped view that the Eastern world was hopeless. One man who saw her off at the railroad station for her next speaking assignment infuriated her by saying that it did not matter what she said. All she had to do was stand up there, look at them and let them look at her and the money would flow. His intended compliment backfired resoundingly and made Welthy so mad she could scarcely board the train. She would be heard for her ideas, and she would make them look beyond her appearance. It never occurred to her to dress down, to repress herself.

* * *

Often she talked to children, excelling in communicating to them her own childlike wonder at life. It was a long route to thirty thousand dollars to vie for ten percent of a child's earnings—the payment for weeding a garden being ten cents—yet those challenges from which she reaped the least tangible results were just as important to her as the larger gains. Scores of women came up to Welthy after speeches in later years to say they had been indirectly influenced by her all their lives, by mothers who had heard her speak in those years. "She was the most beautiful thing to look at you ever saw!" remembered Alice Kennedy after Welthy spoke in Syracuse.

Various family members caught different impressions of their swirling relative. Cousin Dee was downright enamoured of Welthy's grand appearance and oriental gleanings. Their relationship entered a new phase when the grand lady invited Welthy to visit in California and began to see in her a new kind of protégée. Welthy of China could be a great asset in her drawing room, with its growing collection of the Chinese art objects that adorned fashionable salons of the day. And Welthy had no objection to meeting the very rich and marvelling at their ways. After mingling with the British and elite at that "finishing school" in Kuling, she could hold her own in any setting.

Sister Mina had married her minister and was settled in Cleveland. Welthy visited and kept moving on at a pace that defined her future life. She loved Mina dearly, but the two sisters were so different in personality and basic interests that their attachment to each other never had a chance to develop far beyond the sibling stage.

Brother Fred, married to Evalina and practising medicine, had suffered a bad fall, the effects of which were to plague him for years. He adored "Babe" more than ever and was bursting with pride over her activities. The magnificent ruby red brocade Mandarin coat lined with white lamb's wool and grey fur piping that Welthy gave to Evalina became an instant family heirloom, carefully preserved in a box for special viewing. To Fred's young family in Syracuse the fabulous coat stood for everything in the world they knew nothing about, in a way creating a vast gap between them and Welthy, whom they rarely saw. To them she was some sort of strange and marvelous creature from another world. Still, Fred urged her to marry before long and be very much part of this world.

There were many firsts for Welthy during that interval in the States. In New York she saw Sarah Bernhardt as Queen Elizabeth in the first feature length motion picture, drama enough to sustain Welthy for some time back in China. To celebrate having her first shower at the YWCA in New York, no doubt in splendid naked imitation of Bernhardt, she fell and sustained the first in a very long line of fractures.

* * *

Politics came alive for Welthy as she heard at every stop the intense discussion about another American who was travelling throughout the land, the intellectual idealist who was inaugurated as the first Democratic President in sixteen years, Woodrow Wilson. She was then, and remained, very pro-Wilson, but took no active part in politics. Still disenfranchised in 1912, women such as Alice Paul were speaking out. The Freudian emancipation had begun to affect middle-class life, with young people of both sexes challenging traditional morals and manners. Welthy saved an article about Christabel Pankhurst who led a suffragist attack on Parliament in London.

Another article, written by an American in Peking, described Chinese women's position as being very good, saying they had keen business heads and were often consulted by their husbands, and that they were happy in isolation with bound feet, serving their husbands and doing embroidery. Welthy could hardly wait to return to the young women of China who sought no such "happiness".

In her talks to businessmen and industrialists she referred to political events in China and the power of the foreign bankers' consortium, showing how annexation of Korea and the expanding power of the Japanese in Manchuria meant betrayal of the American open-door policy. In her draft novel, the heroine learned to be more clever in her speeches, explaining these events in terms of losses to American pocketbooks.

In real life collections were boosted because Welthy left the impression in their minds that by Christianizing China, American business would be expanded. Furthermore, by giving American products for the school there was great advertising value to be had. In retrospect, Welthy was concerned that she may have become a participant in imperialism herself, wondering if her preoccupation with seeking funds may have clouded her broader vision.

Bishop Bashford was also in America that year, urging President Taft to recognize the new Chinese Republic which emerged during Welthy's absence. Taft delayed recognition, waiting to consider the views of other nations, and especially those of American bankers. The recognition came the following year by the Wilson government.

SUN YAT-SEN

At Wesleyan University in Macon, Georgia, one of the famous Soong sisters, Ching Ling (the future Madame Sun Yat-sen) was writing a theme paper on the influence of foreign-educated Chinese in bringing about social reforms and athletics, citing the symbolic cutting of the queue as the greatest event of the century thus far, and insisting that fraternity was the basis of liberty and equality.[1] In her ancient land that esteemed the arts of peace, the pen had always been mightier than the sword, as Welthy already knew.

Ching Ling's future husband had also been trying to raise money in the States in 1911 in support of his revolution against the Manchus, so despised by the Han people for their perceived racial inferiority, so incompetent against the foreign imperialists, and so repressive with their ever-increasing taxes. Sun read in the paper that after sixteen years in hiding he was to be the first President of the provisional Republic, and in London he won the recognition and support denied him by the Americans, raising the British enormously in Welthy's esteem. Delighted with the freedom China was entering under Sun, a Christian, Welthy's idealism knew no bounds.

Her greatest coup resulted from a highly successful appearance at a summer missionary conference at Northfield, Massachusetts. "You were there, tall, lovely, crowned with a coronet braid, singing 'Spirit of God Descend Upon my Heart' with the voice of an angel," wrote Olive Whittier. "I stayed with you all I could, and desired to be exactly like you, even to going over to teach in China. I could not forget that lovely girl."

One woman offered to go to China and develop the school gardens. Another was so impressed as Welthy went on to describe the buildings and grounds she envisaged, encouraging different groups to build or furnish a room or a wing, that she pledged the participation of her architect husband. Never one to let a ball drop, Welthy presented herself post haste before Franklin A. Green, a well-known New York architect from Boston, gave her conception of the campus, and came away with a full set of plans for five buildings. Without specific reference to the WFMS she was going full steam ahead, unwilling to wait for the wheels of bureaucracy to grind out their slow results. She only knew that the school had to be rebuilt quickly, scarcely realizing that she was setting herself up as general contractor, confident that the details would all fall into place.

At Welthy's insistence, Bao-Lin was to be the first mission building adopting the Chinese style of architecture with the rhythmically curving roofs of their culture. Once three hundred iron beds for the dormitory were pledged, Welthy knew the rest would follow. Her strategy was to identify the industries in each city to find those producing items the school needed. The Troy, New York, branch of the WFMS, for example, sponsored the assembly hall, the King's Heralds throughout the country sponsored the kitchen and dining room, Rotary groups offered a windmill and a huge steel stove. "We'll have the first water system in two thousand years, the first bathtub, the first victrola, the first moving picture machine, the first microscope," exclaimed an ambitious Welthy. Using what has become the standard fund-raising technique of matching interests, Bao-Lin was resurrected, and with it more satellite day schools.

* * *

RETURN TO CHINA, AUGUST 1912

If the public was very generous and responsive to Welthy, *those women* disappointed her deeply in a way she could never forget. When she set sail from San Francisco in August 1912, she had been entrusted with a paltry two thousand dollars of the sum she had raised, thoroughly dismayed by their lack of confidence and reluctance to turn over sacred mission funds. Their attitude heightened Welthy's identification both with the Chinese for whom the funds were raised, and with the American service organizations that had been so spontaneously generous. They were more lively, more direct, more anxious to see things done – in fact, more like herself.

If the women were skeptical, stingy and envious, Welthy, as the person in the middle of the transaction, was showing blatant unconcern for the administrative niceties on which organizations depend, often far too heavily. After four years of operating the school largely on her own ingenuity in immediate response to Chinese realities, and sending constant information and stories to the WFMS to help their fund raising, she felt they were dependent on her, rather than the other way around. The mission field was the centre of action where the whole purpose of the WFMS came alive: board tables with abstract discussions of activities on the other side of the world were peripheral. Purpose, not policy was her authority; cooperation, not control the method.

JAPAN, SEPTEMBER 1912

Welthy and Rosalie Mayer sailed on the finest liner on the Pacific, the twenty-seven thousand ton "Manchuria", much upgraded transport from Welthy's earlier crossing. As they passed the international dateline, Monday disappeared, leaving one poor Englishman wondering what to do with his weekly laundry. Rosalie was a delightful companion, her intelligence well matched with humour, who kept busy observing idiosyncracies for newspaper articles she was writing. The "Manchuria" anchored in Nagasaki harbour during a serious typhoon, the government fortifications lining the shore adding to the ominous scene.

On Friday the thirteenth of September, the ladies joined the throngs in Tokyo to watch the three-mile funeral procession of Emperor Meiji. Spinning along in a rickshaw, appropriately veiled, they drew their own crowd of spectators. After eight hours amidst the expectant mass, the great ox-drawn wagon appeared bearing the Emperor, preceded by a guard of honour of ten thousand men. Welthy and Rosalie hushed with the crowd as the court musicians played the lament on reed instruments, the temple bells rang out, and history was theirs for a moment.

An equally vivid impression of Japan remained with Welthy all her life. She saw the steamy mills where hundreds of thousands of rural girls were brought to work on wool from Australia, and she saw the dormitories where they were boxed. "Half of them became prostitutes at the end of a year or died of TB. They could afford to be annihilated. It was a terrible waste of human beauty and love. Cruel things are done," acknowledged Welthy, speaking with deep compassion sixty years later of that chilling memory, adding that Japan had long since abolished such practices.

CHINA, SEPTEMBER 1912

In Shanghai they stayed with William H. Lacy, manager of the Methodist Publishing House, whose home was always a stimulating haven for Welthy. Rosalie's keen eye discerned that the brokers were the busiest of the busy street scene, licensed to go faster than the others in their victorias, one foot hanging out ready to dash to business. Shopping there brought the total of their assorted luggage, mostly building supplies and educational materials, to some sixty pieces as they headed up the Yangtze.

Welthy's houseboy was there at Kiukiang, equipped to prepare their meals on the houseboat journey across the Poyang and to take over as baggage master. As they neared Nanchang, the river was so low that a smaller boat had to be sent for. Unable to wait, Welthy commandeered a nearby sampan as the swiftest sailing for those last ten miles. The foreign bund outside the city wall swarmed with eager welcomers under colourful lanterns. Firecrackers slung by the hundreds on bamboo poles went off in their honour. Welthy was home.

It had been twenty months since the great night of fire, and there had been massive change in China. Since the Government's proclamation in May 1911 to nationalize the railroads, and the decision to contract a huge Four Power loan to finance the construction, rioting had escalated in all areas. The Government thought the railroads would never materialize without foreign money, and so the provincial companies lost their rights to build their own railroads. People were convinced that with railroad rights mortgaged to foreigners, foreign power would only expand in China, and so the question of railroads had become a symbol of nationhood, a unifying influence.

The gentry and merchants were demanding a Chinese owned railroad to develop their natural resources. Taxes to pay interest on Boxer war indemnities and loans from the West had debilitated native industries, giving the advantage to foreign commerce, which was exempt from the ever-rising net of transportation taxes. In early October Wuchang fell to the revolutionaries, a month later Nanking, and by December 25th Sun Yat-sen had ended his exile and was back in China.

THE NEW REPUBLIC OF CHINA

Sun had fulfilled the dream of millions by overthrowing two millennia of dynasties and placing China in the modern world. It was a great moment for Welthy to be returning, with visions of upending dynasties. The confusion and terror of the previous year had forced the school to close, and all women missionaries (except Gertrude Howe) were advised by the Bishop to leave Nanchang. Ilien Tang had taken six children and two teachers to her father's home in Kiukiang, and Dr. Kahn had kept the children who could not get home. Perhaps when they saw the contents of her freight boxes, they might see the fire as a blessing in disguise, Welthy hoped. Only one of the four missionaries' wives had endured the school's upheaval, along with seventeen Chinese assistants.

In fact, Nanchang was not invaded because the gentry paid large sums to the revolutionary leaders to persuade them to refrain from looting and horror. By April the school had been able to reopen in its temporary quarters with one hundred and forty children. The new Republic, established February 12, 1912, was now seven months old, her five-barred flag flying everywhere. Soldiers were practising her song on their bugles. Most importantly for Welthy, an emergency central education conference had been held during the summer, resulting in a new system of education patterned mostly after German schools, announced only a few days before her return. The aim had changed *from*: fostering loyalty to the Emperor, veneration for Confucianism and promotion of public and martial spirit, supplemented with practical learning, *to*: fostering moral education and supplementing it with utilitarian, military and aesthetic education.

Four years' compulsory, co-educational primary school was the foundation of the new system in a country where less than five percent of its population was in schools at all levels. It was an enormous beginning, and it would be years before the planned network of higher primary, middle and vocational schools and colleges would start receiving the new students. It was a totally new situation in a city absolutely preoccupied with a new vision of nation, where not one soul in Nanchang had ever heard of Woodrow Wilson, not even the westerners. America was far behind once again; the present and future were in China.

"Gone are the sable coats, the peacock feathers—gone the amber beads, the embroidered *pu fus*, and all the other gorgeous insignia of rank . . . The queue and the long satin garment are banished . . . The new official will come by pony . . . The Governor banquets us . . . wearing a Prince Albert and well-creased trousers, walking awkwardly in squeaking Western shoes! . . . No one dares to prophesy the future of this country when her womanhood shall be unbound in body and mind and spirit," wrote Welthy. (MG, 115-116.)

* * *

Welthy's absence had been particularly felt on one desperate occasion when a beautiful twelve-year old student was confined to her room and hanged herself, rather than lose face by confessing to stealing some yarn. Everyone thought Welthy would have found a way to save the girl.[2] When Welthy arrived the girl's body was still in its coffin at the school, and since her family refused to remove it, Welthy went immediately to call on the parents, whose initial reaction was to blame Welthy and the school's modern ideas.

It had not been loss of face that caused the girl to take her life, as it turned out, but her parents' insistence that she marry an uneducated boy they had chosen. By some miracle of empathy and diplomacy, Welthy helped them accept her death, and together they planned a service to be held at the school's expense. By the time Welthy left their home, anger and fear had given way, and they accepted Welthy's offer to take in their younger daughter tuition free. On so many critical occasions it was Welthy who found a way to bridge the chasm of opposing views. (TLC, 121-122.)

Zula Brown had arrived with Welthy, and Ella Jordan came soon after, Zula to teach history, geography and English, and Ella to head the

Nanchang Woman's Bible School. Welthy's priority had been for a science teacher, a scarce commodity, and so she welcomed her new teachers for the knowledge they brought, contained her disappointment, and continued the science teaching herself.

SUN YAT-SEN COMES TO NANCHANG

Two memorable events took place in Nanchang that autumn. Dr. Ida Kahn's hospital was formally inaugurated by none other than "the brightest star in China's firmament", President Sun Yat-sen. It had been ten years of struggle since the jolly, plump Ida Kahn first went to Nanchang in response to a plea to help a seriously ill woman. Her sedan chair had been mobbed, stones broke the glass, and she had dashed for safety given only at the sixth door she knocked on. For six years she worked without financial help, until the gentry began to realize what she could do. They gave grain enough that the proceeds from its sale enabled her to buy a five-acre site and build a dispensary.

From that beginning, funds flowed in from America to build a staff home, and later the hospital itself.[3] In park-like grounds it was a beauty spot for the whole city, and its doors were open to all, ecumenical of necessity. The seven hundred Christians of Nanchang had no better spot in which to welcome their new President as he arrived on a white horse, and no better representative of the foreign community than Welthy Honsinger to express their greetings in song.

> *For days before the arrival of the great man one could feel new life astir among the million within the walls. The soldiers of the new army made the nights hideous by their practice of the diatonic scale. Twenty-one guns were fired as the little steamer brought Dr. Sun to the city; a queueless army of eight thousand lined his path, and a queueless, self-respecting populace greeted him as their liberator. Can this small man in common clothing, with his hat in his hand, be the great Sun?. . . . He stood on the veranda of Dr. Kahn's hospital under a red banner and addressed the Christian community as brothers and sisters.*[4]

Stirred to her depths, Welthy rose to sing her song to the multitude in that vast open park, pouring out her hopes and dreams for China's future that was so inseparable from her own. A young student, Hubert Liang, heard the tall, handsome foreigner that day, whose "bell-like quality thrilled and inspired the audience." It was a day he never forgot, nor could Welthy. History was seeping into her bones.

During the feast that followed, Welthy was privileged to sit beside Dr. Sun. When asked by one eager conversationalist if he thought China would soon discard chopsticks in favour of knives and forks, Sun gently noted that in China they had used knives and forks many years ago and had discarded them, for it was in accordance with the law of evolution that the simple and the crude comes before the more difficult and highly civilized. That gracious reply stood out in Welthy's mind as a model rejoinder to the ignorant.

In her draft novel, the heroine went on to seek and win Dr. Sun's help in developing Bao-Lin into a college. Further, he asked her to plan a system of normal schools throughout all of China to train teachers. The visionary in Welthy was working overtime.

* * *

The first priority was to acquire land for an enlarged campus, a near-impossible task in such an ancient civilization. She bought twelve adjacent acres, shrewdly avoiding being taken in by a false deed dipped in hot opium to give it the appearance of an old document, by having Ilien Tang and Scholar yang look it over carefully and consult an expert. Two ponds, twelve huts, one temple and five hundred graves came with the land.

Welthy spread out the linen sheets of building plans before the contractor she had engaged, only to discover their detail was a total mystery to him and the plans would have to be redrawn and explained point by point in the Chinese scale. That done, his attempt to squeeze money out of Welthy resulted in a fierce scolding and his eventual firing. Her dream for the new school was so important that she could not entrust the full responsibility to anyone else. The trust the WFMS withheld from her, she now withheld in turn.

Welthy rode out to the Emperor's Temple on the far side of the city, climbed to its top and measured the roof in detail, cornices, ridge, gargoyles and all. Having assessed the situation carefully, she decided, rightly or wrongly, that she was the only one to do the job and set to it without apprehension, stimulated by a new and different challenge. She needed that school rebuilt quickly, solidly, beautifully. The double energy it demanded of her was an investment in her own well-being. For Zula Brown, who worked into the night with her in rescaling the drawings, it may not have produced such a sense of well-being.

The symbolic start on the new campus was a bridge across the moat by the entranceway, and Welthy was delighted when the City Magistrate decided to reimburse her for this public convenience. She celebrated by taking in another orphan.

As Christmas approached, Welthy and Rosalie were busy making up parcels for all the girls, each done up with their names in Chinese on red paper. For the six orphans now in her charge she had bought little suits in Shanghai. And again that winter the city merchants distributed cooked rice daily to eight thousand hungry.

CHRISTMAS EVE, 1912

Welthy lingered by the embers of the fire, reading Dickens' "Christmas Carol" and St. Luke. "What difference has it made in this old city of the Flourishing South that once a Babe was born in Bethlehem?" she asked herself. "How can it be done, O Man of Galilee, Thou who lived among people so very like these who sleep yonder within the great city wall, where the moon and stars hang even now so bright? Is Nirvana the way to peace, or is it the Via Dolorosa, the more difficult way Thou didst walk on earth?" (MG, 121.)

Christmas Day began and ended with music, the white-robed choir of girls walking single file, each carrying a candle, to the window of every member of the faculty, singing "Hark! the Herald Angels Sing." And there followed Bao-Lin's traditional feeding of her squatter neighbours from outside the wall, the lame, the halt, the blind, the ragged, the filthy, the worst-looking beggars of the city. The girls paid for, cooked and served the food on large, flower-laden tables on the tennis court, and afterwards told them the Christmas story. So spontaneous and free of the self-consciousness of most westerners, the girls excelled at playing roles and improvising, and Welthy loved that quality in them.

One small girl told them in her simple language that they were keeping the baby's birthday because he taught men how to live, that to love God, and to love our neighbours could alone bring the world peace. "A little clutch came to my throat," Welthy confided. "Perhaps after all it has made some difference in the old city that long ago a Babe was born in Bethlehem."

Before having their own Christmas dinner, the girls then went out to call on the sick. Parents gathered for a programme later in the day, when presents were given, each girl pinning her gift on the Christmas tree in envelopes, one by one, and their principal reading them out — promises of food, or medicine, or clothing, or a decision to teach difficult children in remote parts of the city. Not a girl left Bao-Lin without learning that Christmas meant giving, not receiving. And finally, "The Hallelujah Chorus" was sung, and a proud principal could believe that something within the old city was stirring.

It is a fact of history that Nanchang was an important, early centre of all the subsequent stirring that would bring change to China. Its educational institutions produced some of the participants in the first Chinese *soviet* (commune) established in Kiangsi province in the late 1920's. One veteran China hand said that the early Baldwin graduates she met invariably commented on the democratic atmosphere of the school, where students and teachers shared much of their life together, and that the school broke through the feudal traditions intended to bind women by the four authorities — political, clan, religious and masculine. All the mission schools aimed to break feudal traditions, but Bao-Lin was seen to have shortened the distance to the goal.[5]

MABEL HONSINGER ARRIVES, SPRING 1913

That spring Mabel Honsinger arrived in Kiukiang, having paid her own way out, to teach music, art and physical culture, which to a Honsinger girl included plenty of deep breathing. "At six o'clock every morning, strains from Czerny or Mendelssohn, Paderewski or Moskowski rendered by our ambitious little musicians come floating to our ears along with the efforts of China's buglers across the way who are having their own peculiar trials with the scale, and one murmurs half asleep 'China is one huge conservatory of music.' I would gladly see all the arts, especially Music, serving Him who has given them and made them what they be. If this limited study will foster in the girls the love of the beautiful, that they may more clearly see God in His mountains, His lakes and His sunsets, if it will help them to go through this life seeking in nature 'whatsoever things are lovely,' the labor will not have been in vain, for the love of nature is indeed a characteristic of the Christian heart," she wrote for the mission report.[6]

Writing home to the Rome newspaper, Mabel wished she had a "cyntemograph" to show the narrowness of streets, not more than twelve feet wide, houses appearing as one continuous wall, dank alleys never penetrated by sunlight, always damp from water spilling out of buckets being carried from the river all day. Shocked by the blind, the beggars and lepers, she was relieved to report that "when a mother with a crying baby sees us she says: 'Look, a foreign missionary!' The child stops crying and looks in wonder. It is a great pleasure to play the role of an animated bottle of soothing syrup." More reserved than Welthy, less of an idealist, blue-eyed with heavy black lashes, handsome black brows and a sharp, narrow nose, Mabel had the same life-saving ability to see herself objectively and laugh, a shared grace that made them uncommonly good friends.

* * *

When Parla cabled that he was coming to China, Welthy had to face the issue squarely after too many years of indecision. "You live in a fairy world Parla," she told her diary, "and that was where I lived when I knew you, long aeons ago . . . You are only ten thousand miles away, yet it seems millions! Why should you come to this world — the real world? It has no relation to you." Welthy's need to be loved and to be of service was well met in China. "Could I leave those little yellow faces with black beads of eyes and quiet tears running down strained faces? No, Parla, no!"

She had known for some time that she must be free of her attraction to him, and it was clear what she must do. Her choice was made to "bury" herself in China, in the sense of losing or giving, not suffocating or destroying. "The thousand and one rasping mechanical noises of American cities have irritated my soul," she went on, convincing herself. "I have listened for the deep, vibrating resonance of the Bell of the Dragon Light Temple, and every night it came to me over the ten thousand miles and brought peace." (MG, 111.) Her cable to Parla read: "Impossible to see you. Busy and happy. Your coming utterly futile." With that, Welthy finally put Parla out of her life.[7]

In that year Welthy's link with America grew thinner, for her mother died after several months' illness, just as Mabel reached China. Mina, Fred and the Kaemmerlens had been with her at the end in the house that Welthy had found time to remodel and divide into two apartments while in America. Her mother may have had a premonition, when sending Welthy back to China with her blessings, that she would never see her daughter again, but she did not cling to Welthy for care. Her mother had set her free, in every way, and at thirty-four Welthy had a more urgent need than ever to fulfill her mission.

MAY, 1913

The United States had recognized the Chinese Republic, but it was a republic in name only. Sun Yat-sen, considered too radical by many, had resigned within six weeks and Yuan Shih-k'ai was at the helm. "His heart beats for a monarchy, although his lips speak for a republic. He is a dictator. It is hard on the young intellectuals and patriots, and many are already in jail." (MG, 124.) The western powers, mainly the United Kingdom, were backing Yuan with their banking consortium, and few Chinese had any illusions that he was not lining his pockets profusely. Many thought of Sun as deluded by the ideal of universal brotherhood and unable to judge men as they were, not as he hoped they might be. To Welthy, it was very depressing that Yuan had broken China's first effort at democratic government, and with the help of the democracies. All of China was now mortgaged to the western powers.

With Ilien she went several times to the Model Prison to visit a former student, Mai Lau, who had by some clever piece of feminine strategy opened the gates of Nanking for the revolutionary soldiers. Welthy's sympathies were with the younger student element, who saw their dream of a true republic fade away so quickly. She hoped with them for Sun's return and a renewal of his spirit of reform, and she particularly wanted to see Chinese women accept responsibility along with men to achieve this. Mai Lau's time in prison was not wasted. Welthy noted Carlyle's "French Revolution" in Chinese and Matthew's Gospel on her desk, and they were treated to a reading of an article on woman's duty to New China that she was sending to be syndicated in the newspapers. "In prison or in freedom, she removes all obstacles before her and lives fully!"[8] exclaimed Welthy proudly of her student.

She was now Secretary of the first session of the Kiangsi Mission Conference, with Gertrude Howe as President, a formidable team. Their aim was to have a Christian constituency from which to draw future leaders of China. Bao-Lin had passed an important milestone; the entire first high school class of five girls had completed the course and graduated at a notable commencement on an auspiciously clear and cool June day after a heavy storm. Under a huge shed of matting, with flags galore and decorated bunting, over five hundred invited guests gathered. City people were eager to attend the gala, and one school sent its entire population to witness the historic occasion.

All the girls were dressed in spotless white, their glossy braided coronals adorned with fresh white gardenias. The five graduates in pale blue linen gowns "had a queenliness and simple elegance that impressed everyone." Who but their principal, so often described as queenly, with a regal bearing, had coached the girls to their finest performance? Dr. Kahn reported that "our beautiful Miss Honsinger, in beautiful clear-cut Chinese that surprised all, told the girls they had only been prepared for the lessons of life, that their studies were by no means finished."[9] They now had access to a lifetime of learning.

The *China Press* of Shanghai gave front page coverage to the commencement, itemizing the "mixed bag" of events: a piano duet, a dragon fighter, an essay on domestic uses of chemistry, Rubenstein's Melody in F, an essay on a girl's responsibility to her country, calisthenics drill, Godard's "At Dawn" on the piano, an essay on patriotism for women, more piano, an essay on "What Christianity Means to Me", and the triumphant finale of the Hallelujah chorus lead by Miss Honsinger. A mixed bag indeed, splendid entertainment for a festive occasion, and just what Welthy ordered. When asked by a critic why she taught the girls foreign music, Welthy replied that just as she wanted to learn Chinese music, they would want to learn western music. They would never be content only with what they had then. There was enough music for the whole world and they had a right to know it.

Welthy had bought herself a horse for liberating dashes off into the dust, freeing herself briefly from the incessant demands of responsibility. A horse could almost go fast enough, and she would always ride along the shore of the river whenever the school had a boat outing, high up on her horse, as on a platform where her fine posture stood out, a grand image so many remembered, an astonishing sight to their inexperienced eyes.

Cousin Dee had given her twenty-five hundred dollars which she used to build a cottage in Kuling, where she could establish her own brand of hospitality and bring all the orphans and any fellow missionaries or teachers who wanted to enter her open door. A Canadian Presbyterian, Hattie McCurdy, a music-loving friend, came the first year to share the two-bedroom cottage with Welthy and Mabel. Planning and supervising the construction was pure delight for Welthy, a superb organizer who could adapt to whatever the local conditions demanded. Mina had sent out to China a good deal of their mother's furniture, to Welthy's surprise and dismay, for their Victorian look required much Chinese embellishment to fit the surroundings.

All these arrangements were made while Welthy was confined to the Kuling sanitorium by Dr. Vaughn for rest and diet. If her ailment had a name, it was not something Welthy remembered or recorded. What she did recall as the highlight of that summer was the successful sale of crafts from the Bao-Lin's Industrial Department, in which she enlisted the help of all her holidaying friends. Being a friend of Welthy's was fraught with surprise activities.

REBELLION OF 1913

Kiangsi was astir with rebellion that summer of 1913, with Kiukiang in rebel hands for weeks and Nanchang captured in August. Governor Li of Kiangsi, one of the most dangerous rebels, had gone to Bao-Lin and promised Welthy they would be protected if she would lock the gates and keep the school open. It would be considered an act of friendship if she would do this, so the invading armies could see they were standing firm. For once Welthy took shelter behind her femininity, feeling unsure, yet certainly she could not get boats to evacuate her people if she did not cooperate. Bowing to the Governor's superior knowledge of military matters, acting on trust, Bao-Lin stood firm with the rebels, though the Kiukiang schools closed down. Welthy was proud of her decision, considering it an apolitical act of friendship.

Earlier in the year Governor Li had invited the twelve Americans in Nanchang to a feast to mark U.S. recognition of the new Republic. The Tobacco Trust and Singer Sewing Machine people were there, but not

Standard Oil. Barrett Chapman was not allowed into the city. A thirty-piece brass band played "Hail Columbia", and when the Americans were asked to sing their national anthem, the band played "Hail Columbia" again. Finally they did sing "America the Beautiful" (Welthy's all-time favourite song and personal national anthem) and "John Brown's Body." For five hours they summoned all their *kaichiwhah* (guest breath) to sustain the round of complimentary conversation, elaborate feasting and special concerts.

The WFMS report for 1913 noted that "because of political uncertainty, added to the usual drawback to building enterprises in the East, Miss Honsinger has known the pangs of hope deferred," not quite capturing Welthy's frustration over construction delays. In his report for the year, Bishop Bashford commended Miss Honsinger and her staff for their evangelistic tour of the district, yet commented that since Christianity was a personal religion, he expected no mass movement.

Welthy's report said that Gwei-hsin was back in Nanchang and that three of the five high school graduates had joined the staff, another was doing Bible work among women and the fifth was teaching in Shanghai. The thirty-five children in Ilien's kindergarten were collected at their homes each morning by wheelbarrow and brought to the school, which was moving from house to house as expanding needs challenged their temporary shelter. The foreign faculty often had to walk five miles a day from the different homes they were camped in. Despite the hardships, "we have all learned to say with Confucius 'with coarse rice to eat, water to drink, my bended elbow for a pillow, I still have joy in the midst of these things'" the principal assured them and herself.

In Kiukiang, Mabel had entered into a romance with a Scotsman who lacked the approval of the local foreign community because of his brother's misdeeds. Her principal, Miss Merrill, was "just plain jealous" according to the omniscient Gwei-hsin, and an unhappy Mabel eagerly accepted Welthy's invitation to come to Nanchang for Christmas in 1913. She, too, had been treated to an elaborate foreign tiffin given by city officials who borrowed foreigners' cooks, waiters, linen and silver to serve twelve courses.

Wary of boat travel, Mabel wanted to travel overland to Nanchang with another missionary, but the officials considered it unsafe. Reluctant to disappoint Welthy, she made the dreaded voyage by violent river and stormy lake. When the boatman asked the ladies if they had husbands, Mabel reflected, and replied: "Have none, want none." The small boat that took them on the last lap of the journey "looks like an Alexander Douglass shoe box with a whirling egg beater on the back."

Once in Nanchang, Mabel was kept in perpetual motion by Welthy on jaunts into the city to the shops and restaurants. For a time they were living in a tent awaiting completion of the dormitory, Welthy very much on site, and Mabel suffering the primitive conditions along with her. From her sickbed in the completed dormitory, which was home and school to all, she longed for some bracing, fresh American air, deploring the general lack of ozone in China.

With smallpox raging and the stability of China in serious trouble, Mabel warned the family at home that they might have to go to Japan for a year. As she fell back on her sickbed, Welthy finished the letter home for her: "I am so happy that I am perfectly well," adding that Mabel was much better. Other people's illness often produced in Welthy an honest delight and amazement at her own good health and ability to carry on.

Her enormous reservoir of compassion was not inclined to be tapped for an individual sickness, though she would take any and every possible practical step to defeat illness and encourage recovery. For Welthy, half a day was more than adequate time to recover from anything short of a terminal disease. Poor Mabel observed forlornly: "China is one huge graveyard."

And so it seemed to Welthy as well. Her diary for 1914 recorded a "grave April. I have bought a cemetery. Anyone who has a cemetery in her possession in China needs friends." Welthy was warning herself as she prepared to encounter the realities of ancestor worship. She was glad she had spent so many hours pouring tea for the Governor, for he now had signs up all over the city saying that Little Sister Han would pay each one who claimed a grave within three months, otherwise she would remove them — another undertaking of Welthy's in the category of impossible things only a fool would attempt. Few claimants came.

Welthy herself presided over the last rites as the reburying of five hundred bodies proceeded, some of the burials dating back to the 17th century. There was a huge audience, and "a self-appointed committee of the populace came to see if I did it according to custom. Little Sister Han has been walking a chalk line in the method of dealing with the spirits and dragons." She hired two hundred coolies to dismantle the old temple, and had the two stagnant ponds replaced with groves of bamboo, magnolia, oleander and azaleas. "No more malaria is my slogan." At last, Welthy was making things move.

KAN RIVER EXPEDITION

When school dispersed in June, she hired a junk for an expedition up the Kan River to make an informal educational survey of the interior. A gunboat of river police commanded them in harsh voices to halt, hurling out abrupt questions and forcing them to stop. Welthy took command of her ship on the prow, whipping out a small, silk Stars and Stripes flag to signal her identity. Within minutes she was offered the keys to the nearby city and runners were sent ahead to notify officials of her coming. Never a flag-waving American, she was practical enough to appreciate and respect the security of her nationality. President Wilson had said that Americans put human rights above all others, that her flag was not only the flag of America but the flag of humanity. That was Welthy's America, and she could wave her flag freely.[10]

As the first post-revolutionary guest in that city, she was given a wooden key the size of a suitcase to its gate. What she found inside was a city where women had established a tradition of conducting the city business. Their husbands had gone off to fight wars and were killed. The widows had learned to manage affairs, and thereby retained their right to run the city. Apparently the widows had remarried, but on condition that this right remain with them. Here was a city where Welthy could do business, and plans for a Bao-Lin feeder school were drawn up and quickly implemented.

By July the Nanchang temperature was one hundred and twenty degrees and Welthy was more than ready to head for the hills. Unwilling to leave the orphans behind, she set off with sixty-seven pieces of luggage, eighty coolies and seventeen children, joined by another seventeen children Mabel brought from Rulison. It took eighteen men just to carry one piano; the Honsinger girls would not be without their music — the extra dimension to their teaching — and the children came daily for lessons from the nearby cottage Welthy rented and organized for them at her own expense.

AUGUST, 1914

It took six days for news of the shot from Sarajevo to reach Kuling. Welthy was with her English friends at a tea party, singing and playing when word came. Her Scottish escort stopped dead in his tracks. August 10, 1914. "Europe at war! So difficult to talk with German friends in the morning and British in the afternoon. Where will America stand? The strain is almost unbearable."

She swam and took long walks among the pine, cryptomeria and gingko trees — quiet times to reflect on her mother's life, feeling the loss of her dignified assurance. With a group of young people she went on a three-day camping trip and came upon a Buddhist temple surrounded by trees in the midst of the barren mountains. The priests allowed the foreigners to camp in the temple, giving them access to their kitchen, and they talked of many things. "Our Buddha says 'He who is strongest in patience, he is the great man'," said the priests.

DIVINE DISCONTENT

Grateful as she was for their hospitality, Welthy wondered if that was wisdom, "and left them dreaming. In Europe men are dying, the world's mind is on the Marne, but the priest calls his people to prayer, receives their alms and leaves the world just as he received it from his fathers. . . . No, Buddhist priest, I love your temples, and your trees and your calm, but I shall create if I can in the daughters of your people a divine discontent with 'things as they are'." (MG, 140.)

Welthy was building for the future—a solid school campus, a programme of high standards and a plan for continuity. "Miss Honsinger's keen desire is to make Baldwin a source of supply for the teachers needed in District Day Schools, which in the next five years should number two hundred at the least. Her courage and wisdom won out in the climax of troubles in constructing the buildings. Her thrillingly interesting letters were received, printed and circulated throughout the year," reported the WFMS for 1914.

"Two weeks ago I was singing in the mountains. Today I am again a contractor—counted fifty thousand bricks twice." By October the Harrington Home for missionaries opened. In November the large dormitory was ready, and construction of the school proper began. And thereby hangs a tale, recounted by Welthy hundreds of time through the years, each version with a flash of originality to keep the drama of the great event bright in her mind.

WELTHY COMMANDS A FLEET

Rumour had spread that a railroad was to be built from Shanghai to Nanchang, rivetting the attention of political and commercial interests. To Welthy it meant *bricks*, because there were to be stations of machine-made bricks, so much better than the porous bricks she had been using. Off she went to Kiukiang and succeeded, with the help of the Governor and her own intricate persistence, in purchasing three hundred and forty thousand bricks through various middlemen. She then hired forty-nine large junks and had them loaded with bricks, each with its own hieroglyphic bill of lading. "By the time I had filed the thirty-ninth piece of literature I bought a bamboo basket to carry them in." Three hundred white iron beds arrived from the States while she was there, as well as her piano that Mina had sent from home. That called for another ten junks and more skilful unwinding of red tape to get possession of them, duty free.

Setting off for Nanchang with her full flotilla of fifty-nine junks, her houseboy commissioned as commander, no admiral has been prouder of his fleet nor relished the adventure of wind and water more completely than Welthy. On the third day the weather turned extremely ominous, Welthy huddling in terror as they dropped anchor in the raging, ever-rising Yangtse, the roof leaking, the rats scratching. Tennyson's poems, Meyer's Medieval and Modern History, and the Bible were her companions in battle. "Napoleon and Abimelech will from now on be my warm friends, for they shared all my secrets in those eleven days," she confessed.

One clear day they entered the Poyang Lake and were blown up to the Hai San mountain jutting out in mid-lake. Sheltering in one of its coves near a temple, Welthy listened to the priests telling the myths of the mountain, tales she happily added to her ever-expanding reservoir of Chinese lore. They picked their way on in each lull of the storm, Welthy getting well acquainted with the boatman's wife, and eating red rice and bean curd, certain amenities of an admiral being absent.

On the tenth day, Welthy's junk struck the sharp point of the anchor of a neighbouring boat as they were settling down for the night. Water surged in. Welthy crawled out on top as her ship sank in the shallow water — among its cargo, her carefully crated piano. She summoned twenty coolies who took their own time assessing Welthy's statement as to the contents of the crate, their suspicions running high.

Astutely refraining from interrupting their animated, almost threatening discussion, she had her reward and a very muddy piano crate emerged from the water, hoisted by a pulley attached to the top of the mast. Success, but there was still a load of bricks to be recovered from the bottom of the lake, and it was bricks that Welthy had come for. With military determination she planned her strategy for their recovery, a subject not treated in missionary guidebooks.

Wet to the bone and quaking with cold, she was taken by friendly villagers, bursting with curiosity about her foreign presence, to the crude shore home of a boatman. But their courtesy and hot vermicelli were inadequate to warm her in the November cold. Since she could not remove her clothes with so many eyes peeking in at her, all she could do was add a layer of clothes and lie down to sleep. Yes, she was in a predicament. No one in the world knew where she was. She was long overdue back in Nanchang and she could not send a telegram.

There was only one thing to do. She would hire another boat and remain there until a way was found to get the bricks up. Surrounded by the usual self-appointed committee of the populace as she bargained for a boat, their discussion rose and fell until the leader advised her in a calm, philosophical tone that all could be saved. She would just have to wait eleven months until the water was low again. With sad reluctance, bowing to superior wisdom, Welthy abandoned ship and set off on the last lap of her fleet's voyage.

At Nanchang the entire school lined the shore to welcome Han Wei-lo but strong winds prevented the landing, blowing the boat two miles further along. For an admiral, it was an anti-climax to arrive at Bao-Lin by squeaking wheelbarrow at the end of her high adventure. In fact, the arrival of her piano eclipsed her that day; even its sound was weird indeed until she could import a piano tuner from Shanghai.

The velvet tones of the temple bell assured her she was back home, safe and sound on dry land. Looking over the newspapers that night, reading of the war, of splendid British ships going down to the bottom of the sea, Welthy was disturbed that concern for her own safety had dared to loom so large. Perspective restored, she still could not forget about those thirty-four thousand bricks at the bottom of the lake.

Telling of her great nautical adventure thirty years later in her biography of her husband, Welthy took poetic licence and compressed the event considerably by having divers rescue the bricks in a matter of weeks, none of which changed the essential story. It emphasizes her willingness to sacrifice accuracy of detail for dramatic impact, and her unwillingness to admit a military defeat! At the actual time, she wrote: "In spite of my humble words to the men of high degree I feel a victor, for I have waited the eleven months, the waters of the Poyang have subsided, and those thirty-four thousand bricks are mine! They have become historic." (MG, 144-154, 159.) To Gwei-hsin, Welthy's triumph was in winning over the coolies so that they cared for her during that dangerous crisis, attributing it to Welthy's "attractiveness," or ability to see the coolies as individual human beings.

* * *

As for Welthy's household servants, even pressed as they were into extraordinary service, they were devoted to Welthy. She understood and accepted the matter of "squeeze" in household matters that her fellow missionaries considered outright stealing. Where she had looked on it as stealing in the case of construction, it was standard business procedure for servants to get their squeeze when shopping, and she told her cook, Wei-cheng, to shop where he got the best squeeze. As a result, her household ran smoothly. With a healthy appetite and a genuine interest in food, wonderful dishes appeared on her dining table which catered to all comers, and Welthy gained a new recruit for the school in Wei-cheng's daughter (who later declined a college scholarship, trained instead as a nurse in Soochow Hospital and married a doctor).

1915

The 1915 WFMS report announced that "the substance of things hoped for" has appeared, with four buildings open, including Ilien's kindergarten by the front entrance gate. The compound wall now stretched to enclose vegetable gardens to supply the school, under Catherine Baker's care, basketball and tennis courts, swings in a large playground with lots of good hiding places for the little ones, and hundreds of trees lining the walks and winding paths. Camphor, pine, peach, persimmon, bamboo and magnolia trees, all planted by the students, gave beauty and shade. Welthy took an active part in everything she had launched, especially the outdoor exercise teaching. To inaugurate the tennis court, she and Ilien learned the game first. The entire school watched as Barrett Chapman taught them, tittering at the sight of their principal in such a strange pursuit.

Some of the children arrived at the new kindergarten the first day with nose-rings and stiff silver necklaces to hold the spirit within the body and deceive evil spirits. On Sundays, many of their mothers came to a special class when Welthy spoke to them. There was Friday Bible Tea in the missionaries' home, Sunday evening Epworth League services, Zula Brown's Wednesday evening English club, and a YWCA branch. The YMCA had initiated the first efforts in rural reconstruction and urban social work in China, concepts Welthy wanted instilled in her students.

Altogether, Bao-Lin had become home, school and church to a widening age group of Nanchang females, in addition to the one hundred and fifty students. And a fine new brick road from the gate to the city gate steadily attracted more visitors. On the third floor of the dormitory there was a TB ward, and a room set aside for quiet prayer. With running water and a furnace giving warmth there was much to be grateful for. "We shall not be the same Baldwin again," wrote Welthy, "but a vaster, bigger, sweeter, kinder one, fuller of the spirit of service."

Welthy's letters continued to go forth to those Americans who had contributed blankets, plumbing materials, the Delco plant, the pump, clothing, various and sundry school supplies and, of course, the iron beds. Iron beds may not have seemed appropriate for interior China at the beginning of this century, and when criticized by some for making foreigners out of the girls, Welthy asked: "Did you ever try to keep bed bugs out of three hundred wooden beds?" She saw nothing wrong in her girls having the best America could offer.

Welthy urged her teachers to stress hygiene and preventive health since the girls got nothing of this at home. Assisting at the hospital on Sundays reinforced what they were learning. "Encouragement to attempt greater things always comes from the Principal," noted Zula, but

Welthy's encouragement of the WFMS to produce a science teacher had met with no success. Meanwhile, poor Zula, urged on by Welthy, lived in daily terror of blowing up the new building in her chemistry class.[11]

Catherine Baker had arrived to head the Music Department, aiming to produce first-rate hymn players for the Christian Churches. A Normal School opened, headed by May Bel Thompson. Welthy pressed her plan to develop the Industrial Department further, and using her own money sent the sewing teacher, Mrs. Nieh, off to Shanghai for four months of training. Mrs. Gale, wife of Nanchang's ranking missionary and much loved by the children as "grandma", was tremendously helpful in that and the bluebird pattern the School specialized in was ordered by hospitals as far away as Shanghai. Curtains, bedspreads, and many other items went forth from Bao-Lin, thanks to Welthy's strenuous marketing efforts.

Rosalie Mayer had gone home in 1913 about the same time Mabel left Rulison, leaving a large gap in Welthy's life. Barrett Chapman had been transferred to Shanghai, depriving Welthy of another valued friend, but not before she extracted one hundred dollars from him for iron fire escapes for the school. There were no bachelors among the male missionaries, and the mission boards had been sending an increasing number of females. Barrett had been the one man in Nanchang with a strong personal appeal for her, and she missed him sorely. But the new buildings were a source of satisfaction — "strong, plain, substantial" she called them — and proudly invited Dr. Lacy to come from Shanghai to lay the cornerstone of the Administration Building, the last hurdle.

As for work in the district, one of the grammar school graduates had doubled class attendance at the school she had taken charge of at Kien Chang, two weeks by boat up river. In another town a school had opened by the gift of the Chinese teachers of Bao-Lin. In Fuchow, in the Fu River District, Welthy had a building erected for a day school for fifty girls that Ilien Tang launched, encouraged by Welthy and good local support. Welthy was sure it could form the core of a new mission station. On another district outing on the Nan River she reached the isolated city of Ching Te Chen, famous for its pottery and proto-porcelain, dating back to 4500 BC and 0 AD respectively. Ching Te Chen is the birthplace of porcelain. From the kilns of that oasis on the Nan, porcelain was shipped all over the world. Once again Welthy carried precious cargo in her boat back to Bao-Lin.

* * *

In her craving for the empathetic companionship that she did not find amongst her missionary colleagues, Welthy reached out eagerly to make friends whenever she encountered anyone with wide interests. Her strong affection and warmth in receiving one YWCA visitor, who shared her bed out of customary necessity, surprised Welthy when the visitor made advances beyond affection. With Welthy's rejection, "that was the end of that," and the friendship remained intact. The temple bell would be her friend. Much as she loved the children and her busy, responsible life she craved adult companionship.

*   *   *

There were now twenty-two government day schools in Nanchang, all of which Welthy had visited along with Gertrude Howe. Bao-Lin's target was to prepare teachers for these schools, which in future would be doing the main educational work. Welthy was constantly invited to the government schools, and their classes frequently came out to Bao-Lin to see how they did things. Mr. Liu, the Chinese Commissioner of Education, told her that Bao-Lin was the best organized school in the two provinces under his jurisdiction, and with Ilien Tang's kindergarten the school had become a model of teacher training.

By 1915 the first college for women in China, Ginling, was cooperatively established at Nanking by five Protestant missions, and Welthy was an early board member. The Methodists had acquired a site for a future college in Nanchang, a possibility of intense interest to Welthy. She spent many evenings writing to people back home trying to raise scholarships to Ginling for her graduates, but for Betty and one or two of the others she aimed for the very best—Peking University.

PEARL CHEN LIN

Pearl Chen, who taught at Bao-Lin for a year after graduating, had intended to study in the States where she had a scholarship offer, but while waiting in Shanghai for passage to the U.S.A., Welthy persuaded her otherwise. On Welthy's recommendation, a four-year scholarship at Ginling was offered, and Pearl accepted, changing all her plans in a decision she never regretted. Her innumerable poems, published and unpublished in later years, exceed one another in singing her praises of Welthy's wisdom, judgment and kindness, and especially her training in singing and speaking at Bao-Lin. For another graduate, Sally Kiang's sister Frederika, Welthy secured a scholarship to Vassar College in New York State, and felt greatly rewarded when Frederika returned to teach biology at Peking University.

One day back in her high school years Pearl had been bold enough to imitate Welthy during a recess period, when girls were supposed to leave the classroom. "Girls, you cannot stay in this room. You know the rules," Pearl commanded. Then she felt two hands covering her eyes and heard Welthy's voice in Chinese say: "You false Principal. The real

Principal is here." She was terrified of getting a demerit for herself and all her classmates, but Welthy simply laughed with a lovely bright face and left the room, able to enjoy the joke as much as the girls had. "She was so close to us," Pearl said. "She knew our wishes, yet had a way to persuade us to do her wish. If we had any talent, we had a chance to develop and show it. She didn't care about facial beauty, but rather our talent."[12]

WANG GWEI-HSIN

When Gwei-hsin decided she wanted to study in the States around 1916, Welthy felt she was well enough grounded in her Chinese background and actively encouraged this, helping to get a visa and making various arrangements. Decades later, when she attended Welthy's ninety-fifth birthday party in New York and made several extended visits to Connecticut to renew their friendship, Gwei-hsin reminisced about her debt to Welthy. In the beginning she thought missionaries only taught the Bible. At Rulison, her principal had followed a nine-to-four routine on a most impersonal basis. But Gertrude Howe had taught all subjects, and then Welthy came along to follow in the same pattern, giving Gwei-hsin private piano lessons and teaching Latin to four others in her spare time until the doctor ordered her not to do so much. Welthy treated everyone the same, never looked down on the Chinese, and respected Chinese authority. "She knew how to do things. She inspired people to listen. She has greatness in her," said Gwei-hsin, normally more critical. "Chinese can tell if foreigners are capable. One missionary couldn't talk clearly. We knew she didn't think clearly. She was useless," pronounced Gwei-hsin.

Inner control was high on the list of qualities the Chinese respected, and this Welthy had demonstrated repeatedly in handling demanding situations. Gwei-hsin acknowledged that some missionaries did not like Welthy, but considered that mostly jealousy, and stressed how Welthy's appearance and personality made people listen when she sang or spoke. That, combined with her practical common sense, made people like her, and prompted Gwei-hsin later to name her own firstborn Welthy.[13]

Hubert Liang, who attended the boys' mission school, spoke in much the same terms, after learning more about Welthy and Bao-Lin from Miriam Nieh, who later became principal. "Her identity with the Chinese people and their interests . . . a largeness of mind transcending race and nationality . . . a breadth of view taking in the whole of humanity and basic, enduring values, not superficial or transient phenomena . . . far-sightedness that sees man's fate for centuries ahead . . . a spirit that kindles, inspires and challenges the best in those who come in contact with it."[14] Welthy had created something of a legend.

To demonstrate Welthy's powers of persuasion, Gwei-hsin told of an excursion to the Nanking Exposition when Welthy bought crabs for everyone. When her cook became deathly ill, Welthy went to his room to assess the situation. He announced he was going to die, and she would have to care for his family, strong motivation for Welthy to encourage his swift recovery. With her attention, his health returned. On that same excursion Welthy sent some local boys for hot water, and set about washing the very dirty hair of one girl. "You are very kind," the boys said. "Oh, I'm just setting an example," Welthy answered, in her best recorded approximation of a theory of education.

In Shanghai Welthy had a new friend in Dr. Henry Spencer Houghton, first Dean of the Harvard Medical School there, and a closet singer who admired Welthy's musical presence. Through the Lacys or other friends, she met the movers and shakers and was invited to their homes, developing ever wider contacts that could be of use to Bao-Lin and her girls. Many of the scholarships she got for the girls resulted from these soirées, where Welthy's singing continued to draw attention. Houghton was delighted to have Welthy in his home, an opportunity she never missed; once she graciously elicited a dozen sewing machines from the surprised representative of the Singer Company.

Returning to Nanchang was always a relief after such lively sorties, for she had come to identify more fully with inland Chinese — to her the real Chinese — than with the hybrid mix in the port cities. That schizophrenic breed, the Chinese middleman caught between East and West, so evident in Shanghai where western commercial interests dominated, had not penetrated to Nanchang.

Welthy had made friends with the superior nun, a botanist, of a Buddhist temple on the other side of the city. Her head was shaven, with nine round scars burned in when she took a life vow of celibacy and entered the world of the yellow robe. They developed a measured curiosity about each other. She asked if Welthy was a Christian nun. "What am I anyway?" Welthy wondered, "an unmarried woman who had left her friends and her country to help other girls and women find a new *tao* is a tentative description that springs to mind." The nun was well educated and interested in how the missionaries thought; they agreed to interpret customs and philosophy to one another.

Welthy's fascination with the ordinary round of Chinese activities had long since worn thin, the feasts amongst a small exclusive circle, including the Governor's wife, with the unvarying prerequisite pattern of sixteen hors d'oeuvres to begin every feast. "They never tire of discussing the appearance of western women's clothes and manners," Welthy lamented. The "cultural accumulations" had begun to pall. With the nun she could look more deeply at the differing cultures, not in the abstract manner of comparative religion, but on the level of what they thought and said and did as individual human beings. (MG, 155-157.)

* * *

Welthy's impatience with "things as they were" increased the longer she remained in the mission atmosphere. While she shared the experience and cultural background of missionaries in general, her unusual personal power, that inner drive towards a fuller life, pulled her in the direction of many wider interests. In her engrossing study of American women missionaries in China from 1900-1920, written from a 1980 feminist perspective, Jane Hunter described the "illicit authority" the missionaries enjoyed. Purpose, prestige, job security and gratifications were theirs without having to assault established conventions in the way women had to in America.

Nor did they have to struggle against men, since American women and Chinese men were rarely attracted to one another, giving the missionaries a freedom they did not deserve since they had not fought for it. They had a free opportunity to exercise administrative skills, and to develop increasing self-confidence through the kinds of opportunities only available to men in the U.S. It made the Chinese villagers look on them as "she tigers", and defer to them as part of the dominating western power.

The extraordinary physical security the missionaries had within their guarded compounds, with their domestic empires of servants, added further to their ill-gotten gains, in Hunter's view. Their general technique of "intimate evangelism" — soulful eye contact and hand holding to encourage surrender of will, to change lives through individual conversion rather than social change — was in effect acceptance of the status quo. Their "endless love" of China was a form of condescending arrogance to Hunter, depending on Chinese vulnerability and misery. The unmarried missionaries frequently adopted a child, formed special friendships with Chinese co-workers, relying on the economic and emotional power they wielded over the Chinese, and stayed on to die in China, their inability to adjust to life at home motivating many of them.

Concluding that the women missionaries had an enlarged appreciation of their own capacities for action, Hunter considered the "inexplicit restlessness" of personal lives that sent them to China was a reflection of the overall economic attempt of nascent American imperialism to dump surplus goods on China.[15] Welthy's restlessness was an explicit, expressed desire to improve social and economic conditions through education.

It is true that Welthy seized the opportunity to lead and manage what Bao-Lin offered, that it was a great liberating experience, and glimpses of Welthy may be seen in many of Hunter's descriptions. Yet the overall characterization does not apply to personalities like Louella Miner and Welthy. They were exceptions to the general rule, as Hunter acknowledges, who were less tinged with "imperial evangelism" as they laboured against the norm to plant seeds of change within China in the most generous way of all, freely, without imported ideology.

Welthy was only too aware of the shortcomings of the system that gave her these opportunities, and was increasingly concerned about the limitations and contradictions of her role. Her personal style, her impatience, made it impossible to think of trying to reform missions from within, especially at such distance. Women missionaries did not have access to the *Missionary Review* to express their opinions; that was for men only. Women's articles appeared in *Women's Missionary Friend*, whose editorial policy reflected the very attitudes that disturbed Welthy. In gathering information about women missionaries, Hunter had to rely on the only available material, those more personal aspects of mission life contained in letters written home to families.

1915 TO 1917

For the next two years, while she completed the campus, Welthy kept her own counsel and kept thinking about America. She knew she was capable of doing much more if the WFMS would give her the opportunity. It would be a natural progression to develop a women's college now that Bao-Lin was rebuilt, expanded and running smoothly, and she herself was expendable. Her ideas on missions, their strengths and their weaknesses, were clarifying; she felt her armour needed strengthening. China had been going through years of disorder and decline, with alliances being made and broken just as quickly. It had become a dictatorship of generals. The warlords commanded personal armies that pursued their own interests and goals, and were sustained by western power and money. Social disintegration was advancing, national and provincial government posts were changing hands rapidly, and the rulers of the country were at odds with the thinking of the majority of the people. Only the facade of unity remained once the common enemy, the Manchus, were defeated, and the underlying causes of weakness were not faced since even the elite were divided among themselves.

At least half of the government officials were either Christian or Christian-educated, but less than one percent of the population had been won to Christianity. The missions' inability to understand that the Chinese wanted an improved standard of living, calling for economic and political change, lay at the root of their ineffectiveness, though many of the future leaders were educated in their schools. Those few far-sighted missionaries who thought in economic and social terms read the handwriting on the wall and knew that conditions would not always be so favourable. So they made haste while time allowed and took advantage of the support of local officials, as Welthy did.[16]

That alliance between the missionaries and those in power prevented the rise of a strong Chinese economy, either by direct intervention or by competition with nascent industries, catching the missionaries in a contradiction they did not understand.[17] To the Chinese they were part of the ruling class, increasingly alienating the growing left-wing movement. Welthy felt the ambivalence of her role in the agitated political atmosphere, and the Methodist missions themselves had become so populated with women that the Church felt a need to reassert a more masculine image, a shift she also sensed. But Gertrude Howe was where she belonged, a woman over seventy fulfilling her own destiny, staying on to open up new work further along the Kan River.

*   *   *

When Japan made her Twenty-One Demands upon China in 1915, Bishop Bashford immediately wrote to William Jennings Bryan, the Secretary of State in Washington, outlining his reasons why the United States must take a firm stand against the Japanese, and to Woodrow Wilson, who had asked to be kept informed, urging that China's response be delayed until the foreign governments could press their views. He saw the imminent danger of China yielding to Japan and forfeiting territorial sovereignty, and went back to the States to state his case in person. Convinced that friendly relations between China and America were of supreme importance, Bashford cautioned that "if the white races attempt to solve the race problem with selfish motives and through military power, we may witness a race-war in comparison with which the present European struggle will prove only a skirmish."[18] The war meant decreased mission support from Europe and the United Kingdom, and an increased role for the more prosperous Americans, leverage Bashford wanted to maintain in the long term when economic considerations would demand an open door policy with China. No one listened to his voice more intently than Welthy.

In 1916 the Indian poet-philosopher, Rabindranath Tagore, travelled to America after receiving the Nobel Prize for his *Gitanjali* (Song Offerings), words of universal dimension that were to influence Welthy deeply in the near future. He was shocked to find impoliteness and crudeness, and people laughing at his Indian dress. America was like a four-year old child to him, just beginning to ask questions. With the entire population organized for mechanical purposes, their nationalism and material selfishness was abhorrent to him.

* * *

May 1917. "Since the railroad letters now come in a month, still America is too far away. My country at war! Every thought of you, America, has so long been one of luxury, of peace, of sunlight. Here about me it has been continual dusk, with only now and then a ray of hope shining through. But now, America, the clouds of war are over you! I must fly to you! I want to know what you are thinking today! I cannot stay longer than to complete the school — then I shall come and share your fate." Her Chinese friends kept inquiring how the Christians' war was going. There was nothing Christian about it. To her it was deeply troubling and confusing.

June 1917. Welthy's orphans were growing up; still she put lovely ribbons in their hair. Her colleagues said she was spoiling them, for they would only marry carpenters. "If they marry anybody," replied Welthy tipping her hand, "it will be bishops and diplomats." In fact, the gentry had already begun seeking to betroth them to their sons, but Welthy was determined that they should decide their own future in their own way.

Her restlessness crept in again when the buildings were dedicated. "The usual verbal bouquets have been scattered. I replied humbly to the flow of Confucian eloquence and the stifling shower of compliments from high state officials. The test of real work begins . . . with every possibility before us." She was exhausted, overextended and impatient to get on with the next uphill climb.

She remained in Nanchang that summer, the campus quiet except for the perpetual singing of cicadas, and the chewing of white ants invading a valuable pile of pine that was to be made into a platform. There was no siesta for Welthy. Working against time, in the intense heat, she oversaw the workmen pouring on pitch and kerosene against the insects and boiling water to prepare the wood properly, stood guard against theft of materials, and ensured proper mortar mixing and spreading.

It was a lean and mellow time. She had come to know the workmen all by name. Some brought their birds in a cage to cheer them through the day, some their musical instruments to play at mid-day. "If you have two loaves of bread, sell one and buy a lily," the Chinese proverb said. Well, she thought, these illiterate workmen had their lilies with them. Perhaps that was why their brows were smooth, their faces carefree. Long life was surely theirs.

By September she finally managed to purchase the Temple of the Last Prayer. "The air has been blue with proverbs. With the Temple came eleven unburied, lacquered coffins. Ilien Tang and I become our own necromancers and undertake burial by the city wall."

The last of the five buildings, one hundred and seventy feet long, was finished and dedicated by Bishop Lewis, with Frederika Kiang singing the solo, "The Birthday of a King". The furnishings of desks and chairs were made according to Welthy's drawings and pictures taken from a furniture catalogue. It had sixteen classrooms, laboratories for physics, chemistry and biology, an industrial department where sixty girls were earning their tuition, and an extension program at Ban Bu Gai Church where women were taught sewing.

Welthy's various efforts to arrange financing for the students had borne fruit, putting Bao-Lin well ahead of the older mission school in Kiukiang in reaching towards indigenous support. It was a goal Welthy assumed instinctively but was not apparently a priority at Rulison.

The WFMS recognized the heroic effort Welthy had made to rebuild the school. "When one says Nanchang one thinks of beautiful Baldwin Memorial School and Miss Honsinger, for it is to her vision, energy and consecration that this great plant is largely indebted. She has given lavishly and devotedly her whole mind, heart and strength. She comes to the end of the term weary in body but grateful for what the new Baldwin stands for among the millions of Kiangsi's women."

In Welthy's draft novel, the heroine had become aware of her egocentricity, her excessive insistence on self-sacrifice and serving others, all of which was activated by strain. She considered herself essential to fund raising, rebuilding and developing the school to a college. Even the Bishop condemned the egomania her letters revealed. She had become cranky, eccentric, losing interest in music and clothes, seeing herself like the other missionaries, someone who could not do anything else in life. Ilien Tang helped her to understand how she had changed, and the heroine took an honest look at herself, determined to master her weakness. She was also yearning to marry. How much of that reflected the real Welthy is pure guesswork, but it does show that she was taking a long, hard look at herself.

China declared war on Germany in 1917, contrary to Sun Yat-sen's priority of achieving a working government at home. The U.K. began recruiting men from Shantung to work behind the lines in France. "I dread what they will see of the western world at war," wrote Welthy. With the Russian Revolution also occurring in 1917, the world's turmoil had increased significantly.

October 1917. "The Temple of the Last Prayer has become a Temple of Play for the children of our neighbors. In these last few months these neighbors have changed from enemies to friends. I have walked through the narrow alleys of the squatters' huts many and many a time when from one end of the alley to the other I could hear . . . 'The Foreign Devil is coming' . . . mothers who were quick to use the opportunity of my presence to say: 'If thou dost not stop doing that I shall tell the foreign devil to take thee away.' And forthwith the naughty child became the embodiment of meekness. I was the b te noir . . . It has not been easy, for the mothers believed that the spirits of the dead criminals still lingered about the old executioner's grounds, and that belief had to be overcome. We overcame it by tea parties! . . . And now when I walk through the alleys . . . a mother tries with the children, who by this time are all in the alley to greet me, to say "Goo Mawlin". That is the last and surest sign of neighborliness and brotherhood — an attempt to speak two words of my language."

November 1917. "The last dedication is over. The clergyman who led in prayer slowly and reverently removed his glasses, and every man and woman in the audience did likewise. The Chinese do not pray with glasses on!" In the archway of the auditorium, Welthy had written in Chinese: "The Truth Shall Make You Free," and some scholars had worried that "free" might be misunderstood. "When they saw our impressive ceremony by the cornerstone saying "Not To Be Ministered Unto, But To Minister", they thought perhaps the freedom we taught was the freedom China needs."

December 1917. "China is sending men by thousands to war. When foreigners meet, the air is tense. American men are restive here. Little Sister Han too is restive." She was being criticized soundly by the British for giving sanctuary at her Kuling cottage to a German family that could not get away. Welthy, who had taught German previously, had made good friends among the Germans in China easily, and now she was supposed to hate them. She had become unpopular with the foreigners, and in her heart she felt more than ever drawn to the Chinese in her loyalties.

*　*　*

Welthy's five-year term was drawing to a close. She was going home to America and the larger world, having completed the task she set for herself. Her vision of what Bao-Lin could become was a reality. But in that final month she undertook one more task during that winter's serious famine in the north, "the second one since I have become so surely a part of this country. News of it will go to America and they will send money and flour, but they can never picture what a famine really means. We who live here among these people, who walk past the huts and hear the cries of hungry children at night, know that a famine is so many degrees beyond mere hunger. We see the trees stripped of leaves, the animals gone, and the hollow-cheeked people who remain, crawling in the direction from which they hope for food. Then we see them drop by the wayside, dead before the goal is reached." This is what America should be fighting against, she thought.

She was the first woman to be appointed by the Governor to a relief committee, and promptly enlisted his wife as patron for a school fund-raising function to which the elite women came, smoking their water pipes, talking and asking questions throughout the performances. And as Welthy was packing for America, her girls made the decision to go without meat and send the equivalent amount to the relief fund for the duration of the famine.

Believing she had chosen the person with the best overall qualifications, Welthy appointed Ilien Tang acting principal without waiting months for WFMS approval. The displeasure of some missionaries and bishops over that breach in tradition was partly due to their disapproval of Welthy's decision not to return to China. A missionary was supposed to stay on, endlessly. They also depended considerably on Welthy's leadership, feeling she was leaving them in the lurch, a dependency Welthy did not crave. Zula Brown was among those who disapproved, but did not go so far as one newly arrived missionary from Indiana who wrote to the Bishop denouncing Ilien's appointment.

Reading the political signs on the wall, the church had begun to encourage indigenous leadership to be developed as quickly as possible and here was a concrete example of their emerging policy that both Bishops Lewis and Bashford approved. Welthy commented that her accuser could not speak a word of Chinese herself, a large disqualifier. In the end, the WFMS put Zula Brown in charge of the school, according to their 1918 report, overruling Welthy's single-handed attempt to advance Chinese leadership.

Late December 1917. "Great banners of red satin, a gold bracelet from the students, and from the faculty—the Temple Bell! Its mellifluous tones will ever more ring out from the School of the Protecting Spirit. Who is this Little Sister Han they talk about in such high-sounding phrases?" she asked herself. "What little I may have done to help thy daughters, men of China, is a grain of sand in comparison to what they have done for Little Sister Han."

In her doctoral study of Welthy's educational philosophy, Colleen Kelly wrote that Welthy's "most powerful educational contribution lay in being the example of what you teach, and making a conscious commitment to do this." In the vanguard of pioneering female education in China, Welthy was "in the best tradition of the great missionaries, and a forerunner of the Chinese efforts to adapt those aspects of Western learning and technology they deemed useful and appropriate."[19] She had perfected her own personal equation for effective education — the love that she considered necessary to learning.

* * *

In twelve years Welthy had full experience of the five elements of China — her metal, wood, water, fire and earth. She knew intimately China's five colours, five flavours, and five tones. And its five virtues — benevolence, righteousness, propriety, wisdom and sincerity — had woven themselves into her personality. It was time to move on, building on what she had learned, sharing what she had understood, and accepting her freedom.

1 2

1. Welthy Blakesley Sanford Honsinger, Welthy's mother. 2. Abram Walker Honsinger, Welthy's father. 3. Welthy, Mina, Mabel and Fred Honsinger.

3

4   5

4. Bertha Deyo and Welthy in France, 1904.   5. Welthy, left, with her Pi
Beta Phi sisters, Syracuse, 1898.   6. Welthy at 21.

6

7

8

7. Sailing for China aboard
the S.S. Tango Maru, 1906.
8. Ilien Tang and Welthy, c.
1908.   9. Two scholars who
taught Welthy.   10. Main
building of Bao-Lin School
that Welthy built.

9

10

11. Dr. W.S. Lewis, Dr. H.H. Lowry, on left; Gertrude Howe, right, at China Centenary Conference, Shanghai 1907.   12. The staff of Bao-Lin School, c. 1914.

13. The Principal of Bao-Lin, c. 1908.   13

14

14. Welthy at work for the
YWCA, 1918.   15. Anna
Dorinda Blakesley Barnes
Bliss, Welthy's Cousin
Dee.   16. Betty (Ho Chen-
yi).   17. Helen Krayer with
Welthy in Geneva, 1927.

15

16   17

18

19

18. Welthy on top of the world in the Himalayas.
19. Bishop and Mrs. Fisher en route to India sortly after their marriage in 1924.
20. Welthy and Fred with his parents in Indiana.
21. Fred and Welthy in Burma, 1928.   22. Touring a gold mine in South Africa, 1925.

20

21

22

23

23. Welthy about the time of her marriage. 24. Frederick Bohn Fisher.

24

PART THREE

THE GLOBAL FISHERS

FIVE

SHALL WOMEN KEEP SILENT?

The years in China had been "purposeful, exciting, expanding, deepening, humbling, fun, overwhelming, immersing, life-changing and a basis for the future." They were also exhausting. She had given all she possibly could to Bao-Lin and had nothing more to give. "I had raised the money, built all the buildings. I had gotten substantial help from individuals to support teachers and some of the poorest children, and I had started an industrial department to have the poor children earn their way through school. So when I came back I was *free*, you see." There was no need to martyr herself in China, nor cling to her authority and power there.

World action was centered in Europe, drawing Welthy to its source. Because of the war, passports were required for foreign travel for the first time, and Mabel had obtained one hastily for Welthy, shedding one year from her age by guessing at her birth date. Welthy never bothered to correct the error, enjoying the mystery of the missing year until much later when she decided to claim it. At the time, her age had little meaning, as she was being pulled into the maelstrom of the emerging modern world, a world in which the WFMS seemed dwarfed by new attitudes and emotions. But first she would have to encounter her employers. Wondering where she was headed, she had the whole Pacific Ocean as counsel.

If her future work was to be effective, Welthy needed to understand the changed realities of the world, and she yearned for companionship along the way. She had a lot to look for, but China, where she first discovered kinfolk of another race, would always be part of that future. Longing for renewed purpose and fulfilment to match her enhanced sense of freedom, the long ocean voyage was a quiet prelude to new life.

* * *

Just as Welthy was heading home to find the world, another searcher was on the move again, two global stretchings on a parallel path, their travels occurring in the same years as if by omnipotent design. Fred Fisher's orbit drawing ever closer to Welthy's, he spent seven months in 1917-1918 travelling throughout the Orient, including China, as part of his fund — raising effort for the Methodist Centennial campaign. He was reading extensively on oriental religions, history and cultural development. In India his goal was one million dollars for the Indian Mass Movement, a target Fred achieved in promises not fully realized.

It was a turning point in his life, for Gandhi was back from Africa, already proclaimed *Mahatma* — Great Soul. Fred heard him speak at the Indian Congress meeting, where an Englishwoman, the extraordinary Annie Besant, was elected President. Her advocacy of gradual steps towards Home Rule was losing ground to the All-Indian Home Rule League, and she was troubled by Gandhi's non-cooperation methods. Gandhi soon gained full leadership of the Indian Congress, his appeal to the masses personally witnessed by Fred. Travelling on the same train, watching the vast crowds surging to see Gandhi at every station and the strength he gave out to them, Fred realized why Gandhi needed that one day of solitude every week to know his own mind.

* * *

COUSIN DEE'S MANSION, CALIFORNIA, 1917

Whatever ideas were buzzing in Welthy's mind, they were put on hold when she reached California and entered the world of Cousin Dee in her Montecito mansion just south of Santa Barbara. Casa Dorinda was Cousin Dee's dream come true. It was one of the few large buildings constructed during the First World War, eighty-five rooms surrounding a central patio on an estate of forty-eight acres, built over the previous two years. Cousin Dee had been so impressed with the Spanish Colonial buildings at the San Diego-Panama Exposition in 1916 that she commissioned their architect, Carleton Winslow. She wanted the Spanish roots in Southern California to be reflected in a palace equal to the best in the world, to create an atmosphere of elegance and beauty where she could entertain royalty and leaders from around the world and fill her house with people enjoying the finest music and art of the day.

Much of the ground floor was for formal entertaining, with the requisite hand-carved grand staircase leading to a royal suite and other quarters for lesser luminaries. A very demanding, firm, but generous and thoughtful dowager, Cousin Dee supervised every detail of construction. "She was the guiding hand, not always in the velvet glove."[1]

If Welthy's eye had been dazzled by the elaborate homes and feasts beyond the moongates of Nanchang, she was absolutely dazed as she approached this awesome mansion. She was permitted entrance into the grounds, not ejected as many inquisitive travellers were by the grand dame who encountered them on her inspection rounds. Cousin Dee, in a long black skirt, high black laced shoes, white blouse with fichu and an embroidered mandarin jacket, kept a sharp eye out for strange cars entering her gate, and would firmly raise her walking cane and command

"Halt!" Few dared to challenge her, certainly not her forty servants, though they were respectful and loyal.

Welthy's eyes fell first on a romantic bell tower with a commanding view of the estate, then on the ornate ironwork around all the windows and doors, and the great arched entranceways. She was led in along an endless corridor, through massive carved doors depicting the story of Confucius. All around were gold-leafed walls, and above a carved, painted ceiling from Peking. And there in the Chinese Room she was received by a proud and pleased Cousin Dee.

Anna Dorinda Blakesley Barnes Bliss had set the stage carefully, taking immense delight in Welthy's appreciation of each piece of amber and jade, and every art object as they went round the room. Having lost all her own treasures in the fire, Welthy took prolonged, vicarious pleasure in the collection.

In her Chinese silks, Welthy brought a fresh quality to the dream mansion. Though she lacked the formal training of a Swiss finishing school, it was quickly evident to Cousin Dee that Welthy knew her Chinese art and added a lively dimension in interpreting it, talent gleaned from informal absorption of life in China. Firm friendship was inevitable, despite the great differences in age and experience. As fellow construction contractors, the two entrepreneurs had an extraordinary mutual interest and respect for one another. Cousin Dee saw in Welthy a potential protégée, and Welthy had entered a select, advanced finishing school on most favoured terms.

Cousin Dee escorted her through the mansion, first to its heart, the music room with its built-in pipe organ — where a pre-Christian Roman lamp hung from the ceiling — to the panelled Library with its Gothic windows and secret wall compartments, to the Napoleon Room for bachelors — where Prince Leopold of Belgium stayed during his parents' visit the following year — to her private elevator with its gold filigree and mother of pearl ornamentation.

Had Cousin Dee not given her such a warm reception, the missionary would have been quite lost in the mansion. As it was, all thoughts of the outside world escaped Welthy in the overwhelming immediacy of that vast private world of Santa Barbara, where the railroad sidings were filled with private cars of visiting eastern millionaires. Despite the elaborate extravagance, Welthy enjoyed every minute of her visit and the exquisite parties on the Great Lawn under a huge *shamiana* from India, disinclined to pass judgment on others. It would take time for Welthy to recognize the unbridgeable gap between their worlds.

By endowing the children's wing at Cottage Hospital in Santa Barbara and establishing the Blakesley Botanic Garden in Mission Canyon,

Cousin Dee had established herself as a leading figure in the cultural and social life of the community, which she presided over for two decades. And in the east, where she had homes in Washington and New York, she was also influential.

Cousin Dee was a genuine patron of the arts, sponsor, among others, of conductor Ernest Schelling and supporter of Paderewski, the great pianist, in urging President Wilson to press for Polish independence. When Paderewski later came to Casa Dorinda, Cousin Dee paid him five thousand dollars to play for an elite audience of thirty-three people. He returned several times as tribute to his great friend Dorinda, and proclaimed the mansion "the most agreeable private house in which I played in America, the atmosphere of silence like a temple."[2]

Welthy's musical ambitions had long since faded into the background and whatever she might have sung for Cousin Dee would not have been up to her world-class standards. But the two did share a compelling passion for music and appreciation of Chinese art, much in vogue since the days of the clipper ships returning from China laden with treasures. Why couldn't Welthy interpret Chinese art to Americans, wondered Cousin Dee, since she was not planning to return to China as a missionary? Welthy could study in New York to become more qualified in the fine points; doctoral studies at Columbia would be the right thing, she suggested.

What gave Cousin Dee special status in Welthy's eyes, however, was the historic fact of having ridden on the very first train to cross the United States, Uncle Henry Blakeslee's Union Pacific Railroad. In whatever form, the wheel was Welthy's all-time favorite invention—from the Chinese wheelbarrow on up—for the most practical and symbolic reasons. The wheel meant progress, moving towards a goal. That Cousin Dee was a member of the Colonial Dames and Daughters of the American Revolution seemed less significant than her great train ride.

When it came to money, Welthy had a very healthy respect for Cousin Dee's annual income of one and a half million dollars from her Castoria inheritance that enabled her to give an airplane and many ambulances to France, and furnish a Red Cross ship with supplies as her war effort. She was a munificent donor, willing to give her substance, if not herself.

Cousin Dee's daughter Mildred, Welthy's exact contemporary, had inherited an equally large fortune from Demus Barnes. Welthy delighted in telling the story of Mildred's desire to have her mother's pearl necklace, worth a hundred and twenty-five thousand dollars—"a thousand dollars a pearl," Welthy marvelled. Cousin Dee declined to make the gift, explaining that Mildred could very well afford to buy such a necklace herself. Mildred had married her step-brother, Robert Bliss, who was well launched on a diplomatic career, then serving at the Paris Embassy, where Welthy would soon have the opportunity of meeting her cousins.

NEW YORK, 1917

At the end of 1917, Cousin Dee sent Welthy back into the real world with a gift of twenty-five hundred dollars towards her studies, a letter of introduction to the Perkins family in New York, and the promise of meeting again soon when she returned east for her regular six-month stay. Welthy had won her heart and was admitted into the intimacy of her life as a daughter. With no home to go to and her future an open question, she respected the connection.

It took the entire train ride across America for Welthy to consider the ideas Cousin Dee had tossed out and the elegant people she had met. It was a strange side of America she had never glimpsed before, and now she had become a small part of it. By the time she reached New York in May, the culture shock was over and she had almost recovered her senses. Did the WFMS really live in the same world? One thing was certain, they were no longer the source of all wisdom and authority.

Welthy was technically on furlough for one year, the implication being that she would subsequently go out on another mission posting. The Board of Ginling College in Nanking did not want to see Baldwin raised to college level, anxious to have all funds targeted for Ginling. Having served on its board, Welthy admired Ginling, but it was two weeks too far away from Nanchang and she felt strongly that there was a real need for a women's college much closer for the new stream of graduates from Nanchang and Kiukiang high schools. It was a need so obvious to Welthy that she may well have lacked the patience to present it in fine detail, nor was she asked to do so. To her it seemed that the WFMS was questioning her judgment and her commitment, when their prime concern was actually administrative.

In retrospect, Welthy always dramatized that searching interval, saying: "No call came from the WFMS." What she meant was no challenge was offered, and Welthy was incapable of sitting out her furlough, waiting like a tired old rag for opportunity to come along. She was rested and ready for action, but her salary while on furlough was only four hundred and fifty dollars per annum, not enough to live on in New York. The WFMS did ask her to make speeches, but they were clearly wary of her independent strength and did not know what to do with her. In the meantime, the YWCA was very interested in Welthy's experience, and those suggestions of Cousin Dee's were still in the back of her mind.

In her brother's home in Syracuse she found the family in a state of distress and Fred in need of medical treatment. An old hip injury had led him from drug to alcohol dependence, household finances declining accordingly. Welthy gladly offered to pay for his treatment at a clinic his wife Evalina recommended, first asking Cousin Dee's approval for using her money this way, since she had no savings of her own. It was the best she could do in the sad circumstances.

In New York it was fun to be with Mabel again, sharing her apartment. Mina's husband had a ministry in the city, so the three sisters had a semblance of family life. But Welthy needed to be closer to the centre of action and soon took a room at the YWCA Hostel on 38th Street. Then she presented her letter of introduction to the Perkins family, a mother and daughter of impeccable standing with wide international interests and friends. At their dinner parties she made friends among the elite, including Anne Morgan, daughter of the wealthy banking family, who had involved Bessie Perkins in organizing substantial assistance to France during the war, for which she received the Legion of Honor from the French Government.

Bessie, the daughter, became a close friend to Welthy, though a good fifteen years older. Their conversations focused on the war and its effects on people, and at the hostel too the talk was international. Europe was on everyone's mind. Issues involving individual human beings and their needs — the other side of war — drew Welthy closer into the orbit of the YWCA, where Estelle Paddock had paved the way. They asked her to write lectures on China that could be sent around the United States and to consider joining the organization. Welthy did both.

Any thought of studying for a doctorate had dissolved after Welthy submitted her generous outline for a thesis to a professor at Columbia and was told her ideas could encompass three or four dissertations. Welthy always had a tinge of regret at not pursuing academia, but the decision not to ranks as one of her most perceptive choices. It could have been a safe harbour for a middle-aged woman, with the promise of prestige and influence. Welthy laughed at herself for even toying with the possibility. She was totally oriented to people and action, with a mind racing too fast to deal in depth with abstractions and theories. If she really wanted to be called 'Doctor,' she would have to wait for an honorary degree. The first one came soon.

Cousin Dee expanded on her hope to establish her protégée in a fine house in Peking as a cultural hostess, where Welthy could take in a few well-placed, paying guests Cousin Dee would send her way. Leaflets could be distributed to the hotels offering Welthy's services in introducing Americans to Peking's art and culture, and soon Welthy would be at the centre of a distinguished circle, bringing Americans and Chinese together socially for their cultural benefit.

It was a grand fantasy that Welthy enjoyed for a moment, but only a moment. Who but a Chinese could best interpret China, she asked herself? For what purpose that touched the needs of people would she be doing this? Much as she admired Cousin Dee, her proposal was too far off centre for service-minded Welthy.

EUROPE, FEBRUARY 1918

By early 1918 Welthy had found the action she wanted and was heading off to France in her YWCA uniform, one of hundreds of women engaged in war work counselling. "I went to war for them," she announced. Armed with a fifty dollar permanent wave, her first, she wanted to look her best meeting French women. Before setting off she marched up Fifth Avenue in a YWCA-sponsored recruiting parade, and lectured to a huge audience at Ocean Grove, New Jersey about the effects of the war on the women and families of Europe. She followed Schumann Heink—of Metropolitan Opera fame—on the programme that evening, a charged opportunity for Welthy to assess the wisdom of her earlier career decision. Challenged to recover the audience from the famous singer, Welthy won them with the story of a Cockney woman whose husband had gone to war. "Ah, this war's 'eaven, gettin' twenty shillin's a week and no 'usband botherin' about."

Welthy met her war-travelling partner in the crowded YWCA despatching office, as the two waiting women quickly sized each other up as eminently compatible. "Josephine had strong red hair, was smart as a whip with cultivated speech, good looking, breadth of knowledge, humour, a perfect woman, real. She was mentally at home in the world, nothing troubled her, not even the German submarines our shipload of fifty-five thousand soldiers was dodging. We fell for each other," Welthy said.

Except for the red hair, Welthy could have been describing herself, their similarity even extending to prominent relatives from St. Louis. A mother of two children, married to a wealthy man who allowed her freedom, Josephine January was Welthy's perfect peer for months of exhausting tours of France, Germany, Belgium and Luxembourg gathering information, visiting factories, hospitals, refugee camps and touring the fighting fronts.

Billeted by the army along the way, learning the looney lingo of war, talking with nurses struggling against depression as soldiers died, playing piano and singing for the troops, watching the latest Browning machine gun shoot six hundred bullets a minute, rushing from one overwhelming impression to the next, Welthy and Josephine kept each other going. Etain, Luxembourg, on one cold March day, was by far the hardest. "Sick - took 'Pinkie's brandy', got off transport and ran fast and furious over worst road, shell holes, absolute destruction, past our trenches to Commercy to Toul—ate *alone* that night in dining room."

For a few days between tours Paris was both welcome and appalling, as one diary entry tells: "2 musicians, Waldo & . . . played everything, 2 sandwiches—fight. Wreck. 7:30 p.m. at Montparnasse. Taxi! Home! Bed!" The next day she "shampooed, washed, mended and cleaned and sorted papers, bought flowers and fruit, and had three dresses made," a healing day in readiness for the next grim tour. At army headquarters in Chaumont, they dined with thirty generals, seeing the war from the opposite extreme.

On landing in England after crossing the Channel in total darkness, their friendship was sealed forever when the customs officer made them stand back together, in a class by themselves—their names absolutely too odd to be believable—Josephine January and Welthy Honsinger! They saw women smoking for the first time, and heard George Bernard Shaw speak to women war workers in a munitions factory, convincing them with wit and warmth that they were needed. "He was with us in spirit," Welthy said of the sense of solidarity he aroused. "We laughed, we almost wept."

Everywhere there was still talk of Edith Cavell, the English nurse executed in 1915 for helping Allied soldiers escape from German-occupied Belgium. Welthy was so deeply moved by her story that she kept noting: "Patriotism is not enough. I must have no hatred or bitterness toward anyone."[3]

CHINESE STUDENT LABOURERS

In southern France, as at other stops, Welthy encountered some of the two hundred thousand Chinese student labourers manning factories, mines and public utilities, who represented China's contribution to the Allied cause. Among their numbers were Chou En-Lai, Ho Chi Minh and Teng Hsiao-ping, who carried home strong impressions of westerners gleaned amidst the senselessness of war. Many came from Shantung, the holy land of China from the time of Confucius and Mencius, and many from Szechuan, eager to study the French Revolution after the failure of their own.

The British and French treated them more humanely than the American forces, the language barrier a huge problem, but empathetic treatment by YWCA welfare workers helped alleviate the situation among the Chinese, who were mostly illiterate when they arrived in France.

They were learning quickly, thanks to the efforts of Jimmie Yen, an American-trained educator who started the first newspaper for new literates there. He arranged for Welthy to meet the labour brigade at Soisson and see the results of his literacy work for herself.

The Chinese pressed Welthy to speak to them in their own language about a war they could not understand. When she spoke of Bao-Lin and discovered one of the men had often delivered goods there, the effect was electric. They invited her into their huts and their questions poured forth. Why had they been sent halfway round the world to dig trenches and bury the dead? Where in the world were they? They had travelled across Canada in trains with the blinds pulled down so they would not be tempted to jump off.

Welthy was hard pressed to find intelligent answers to their questions, the whole experience leaving her deeply questioning, but she did come away with many promises from them to give their daughters an educational chance when they returned home. And she had one more vivid example of the dangers of illiteracy and inadequate communication.

Welthy often thought of her mother in those heavy days, telling herself how pleased she would be that Welthy had "buried" herself in China, and was reborn into a wider world in which China was playing a part. "Bao-Lin graduates were now building — not walls, but structures of new thought which shall hold the 'open door' policy of China's mind. It was not a burial of life but a resurrection," she insisted. "Somewhere from some other sphere tonight, mother's spirit listens and is not sorry she let me go."

* * *

Easter 1918 in Rome, where she saw more statues of Popes than of Jesus, and "tackled every man I saw for a pass to the Piave front, but we went without one." In a rented Fiat she toured the mountain battlefields to find families living in barracks while rebuilding and planting fields. War, she learned, took on a different aspect with each nationality according to the common wisdom — with the British it is a sport, with the French, martyrdom, and with the Americans, a job. Later, the women workers at a munitions factory at Puteaux told her they were sad the war was over, because for four years they had earned money and for the first time were well fed. And in her diary, she wrote the large question: "If there is to be no change, why are men dying?"

There was time for a gorgeous dinner at the Picadilly Grill Room with Peter, an English doctor she had met on the boat from China. And she had lunch with Peter, a married man, at the St. James Club and at Brown's Hotel where she was staying, and dinners at Hatchet's — wonderful escapes from the reality around them. "Talked to Peter till 12:00. No," was the not so cryptic diary entry for May 20th. The next day he saw her off on the boat train. "He wanted a weekend," said Welthy, willing and able to enjoy a flirtation, but careful of herself in the added freedom of wartime. Later she sent him a Virginia Lucky Stone from Roanoke, the last transaction in their romance.

AMERICA, MAY 1918

After four months Welthy's group returned to the States on a cruiser surrounded by a convoy of a dozen large gunboats, and for once she achieved appropriate naval status when she and Josephine were assigned to the Admiral's quarters, the Admiral being a friend of Josephine.

Welthy immediately embarked on a one-month, non-stop speaking tour; by now she was a highly effective speaker, well able to appeal to the pent-up patriotism of Americans, staying in a different place every night, often in private homes that were not at all restful. "The last time I go to a private house—whiskey fiend, I fear. Talked all the time. Children impudent, house confusion." Or, "heat in hotel awful, can't stay in room." Welthy on the run was oversleeping, missing or near-missing her early morning train departures. She was exhausted, possibly fighting off the pandemic flu that took so many lives that year.

EUROPE, SEPTEMBER 1918

By September she was back in London being taken round by the War Department Munitions Committee to meet factory workers, listening and learning. When she reached France the war had begun to wind down, the Allies' recovery of their positions consummated by the Americans, with the Germans pushed back beyond the Hindenberg Line. Welthy had in fact come to participate in the beginning of peace. By the end of September the final Allied offensive on the western front began and peace initiatives were underway early in October.

AMERICA, NOVEMBER 1918

Recognizing her considerable talent, the YWCA cabled her to return home to help in a massive drive for reconstruction funds, and by Armistice Day, November 11th, she was in Wilmington, Delaware, to lecture, staying at the Dupont Hotel. After Mrs. Pierre Dupont heard her speak, she insisted that Welthy leave the hotel and come home with her. Gathered round the radio with the family, she sat up into the night listening to the great good news of victory coming in from Europe.

Welthy was there among the hushed throng that filled Madison Square Gardens in New York to mark the Armistice. As the Navy Band played, triumphant words came over the amazing radio from all corners of the country, and ten thousand rejoicing voices sang "Nearer my God to Thee." Of that unforgettable day in twentieth century history, Welthy said: "We had reached a day of international thinking—we were truly getting nearer."

In a fast-paced round of speeches on the effects of the war on European families, Welthy was overflowing with a sense of the historic role American women could play in initiating and sponsoring reconstruction work in Europe to rebuild shattered lives. "Radiant with enthusiasm and happiness over life and its opportunities—this is the biggest impression one always retains of Miss Honsinger," reported the YWCA.[4] As light is the other side of darkness, so Welthy saw the immense possibilities for peace growing out of Europe's ravage, and it filled her and her audiences with excitement.

EUROPE, DECEMBER 1918

In December she was back in Europe—in Belgium, Italy, France and England—as the forces were demobilizing and getting ready for "the war of peace, which was to be the greater war for every lonely, thinking woman." Out of their suffering, great wisdom and compassion could flow into a world at peace. Welthy had absorbed some of their wisdom and compassion, and she had spoken with many of the families of the hundred and twelve thousand American soldiers killed in the war. There was little she had not seen or felt of war.

PARIS, JANUARY 1919

In Paris, she was welcomed at the American Embassy by Robert and Mildred Bliss, dining there frequently and mingling with leading figures of the times. When Woodrow Wilson arrived in January 1919—the first American President ever to leave his country—he received a triumphant welcome. A shining, smiling man, he greeted the Allied women workers, and none shook his hand more proudly than Welthy, who never lost her respect for his idealism in striving to end all war through the League of Nations. His warning that unless justice was done to others, it would not be done to America remained fixed in Welthy's mind.

In Paris she dined with C. T. Wang, former head of the YMCA in China and one of the five members of China's delegation to the Peace Conference, who pinned all his hope for China's future on Sun Yat-sen's movement. He expressed confidence that America would never renounce her principles, that her sense of fairness would prevail and she would insist that Germany's rights to Shantung would not be handed over to the Japanese as part of the settlement. When the Treaty of Versailles did recognize Japan's special rights in Shantung, as a counterweight to Bolshevism in Asia, Welthy shared the bitter disappointment of all thinking Chinese, especially the student labourers. Her loyalties were split down the centre, as she felt the Chinese sense of betrayal by the West that sparked their May fourth New Culture Movement in protest.

AMERICA, 1919

Back in the United States Welthy lectured intensively to audiences of fifteen hundred people, eighty-five times in ninety days, as she travelled the Swarthmore Chautauqua Circuit with the Robin Hood troop of players. Her mission was to persuade Americans to face the post-war challenge of sharing their wealth with victims of the war. She was commanding, convincing and absolutely clear, injecting the lighter, personal side with individual human beings the centre of focus. She presented the very positive opportunity for women to act, especially in the emerging atmosphere of freedom.

Other voices were claiming the attention of American women, a chorus Welthy did not join, except peripherally. Women young and old were staging marches, serving prison terms, resisting brutality and ridicule, fighting for their democratic rights. The dominant leader of the suffragette movement was Alice Paul, Founder of the National Woman's Party. Her guiding principle was complete equality under the law. If Wilson wanted to make the world safe for democracy, the place to begin was at home, where half the citizens were excluded from the right to vote. The message was heard, and the Suffrage Amendment was ratified in 1919, with no help from Welthy.

Of the various paths she might have pursued in those years, the women's movement was clearly a progressive, liberalizing option. At forty, however, she had a background of experience and upbringing that gave her a very wide perspective, and except for 'those women', she had not personally experienced any lack of freedom. What she had experienced was the profound poverty, disease and illiteracy in China, and the senseless brutality of war. Besides, direct political action conflicted with her instinctive feeling that focus on the vote was not deep enough, significant though it was. An unformed, implicit idea was stirring in her mind that went beyond the law of any one government. Confrontation was not Welthy's way, nor was structural analysis of the root cause of things. She was an activist on a broader stage.

ILIEN TANG'S DEATH

With her constant travel Welthy had little time to help Ilien Tang, who had come to New York for medical treatment of an inoperable cancer under her breast bone, a fact Welthy had not known when leaving Ilien in charge of the school. However, she enlisted Barrett Chapman to run errands and take Chinese food to Ilien when she was away. The treatment finished, Ilien wanted to return to China, hoping to reach there before the end. Cousin Dee offered to send Welthy back with Ilien, but since Dr. Phoebe Stone was returning to China that summer and could care for Ilien, Welthy decided not to accompany her dying friend. "I didn't feel I ought to go just then. I didn't know what they (the WFMS) were going to do with me." Two wars had brought a new toughness to her compassion — the World War and her own struggle with the WFMS.

Ilien reached her home, and in her last feeble letter nine months later told Welthy not to regret not bringing her home, that she had done everything in her power. The letter was written in stages by different hands, asking Welthy to look after one girl's education, to sell her trinkets and give her pearls to certain people. In her own hand, one last addition to "Welthy, my dear heart. Well, darling, I have scared them two or three times already. How I long darling to have face to face talks with you. How much you have been to me! O, dear, I am too weary to write more. Good bye! darling."[5]

As for Barrett Chapman, he and Welthy were still good friends, and he once asked Welthy if she would ever give up her active work and come along with him; at least that is what she recalled, evidently not considering it a full proposal. She would have married him had he asked her, she later speculated, as suggested by his large presence in the character of her many attempts to fictionalize the China years.

In the meantime, the WFMS knew that Welthy had been offered a position with the YWCA and made a counter offer. She could be their Candidate Secretary, going round to colleges to speak to potential missionary recruits. Welthy was particularly effective at this, her natural, energetic, informed speeches drawing eager students in such large numbers that mothers were wary.

So successful was Welthy that she soon urged the WFMS not to send out all the eager women who responded to her speeches, that much more careful selection was needed to fit qualified people into each position abroad. She wanted a say in the selection process, and told them she would stop speaking unless they agreed to this. They refused, and Welthy was back on furlough, while the WFMS struggled to manage Miss Honsinger's personality. With her unusual experience and confidence, perhaps over-qualifying her, and the other options open to her, she still felt deeply rooted in the Methodist Church, despite the determination to be herself and respect herself. Surely there was a continuing, expand-

ing role for her within the church, but the link was becoming more and
more tenuous with each furlough interval.

Given a freer hand Welthy might well have filled the mission ranks with
highly appropriate women. Her style was personal and informal. "I think
you would be a round peg in a round hole," she wrote to Dorothea
Keaney, a biology teacher at the Carmel Seminary. "Come down and
talk it over!" The Woman's College in Foochow needed someone to
head their Biology Department. Escorted by her mother, Dorothea appeared at Welthy's apartment in New York, merrily greeted by Welthy
despite two cracked ribs from falling in the tub. Both were overwhelmed
by Welthy's enthusiastic, vivid description of the need, and left with
thoughts whirling in excitement. Dorothea took time to decide, grateful for Welthy's patient answers to her questions.

She had been in awe of Welthy for years, listening shyly when Welthy
visited their parsonage home in Syracuse, and her interest in missions
had developed steadily. Now she wanted to be sure the sense of challenge she felt was more than a duty. "Is God really calling me?" she asked
herself, or was it Welthy? To her, Welthy was "strikingly impressive, with
a regal bearing, decisive and charming at the same time, with clear, understandable ableableable explanations and sympathy for a girl's
problems, great tonal qualities of voice and a blithe spirit that
refreshes."[6]

Welthy was a woman who could stop traffic anywhere, and did, by stepping off the curb on a busy downtown street and holding up both arms
while she walked calmly to the other side. Dorothea was wise to be
cautious in her response to such a strong personality, and Welthy had
astutely assessed the motivation, background and training of her candidate, who did go to China in 1920.

METHODIST GENERAL CONFERENCE, IOWA 1920

Welthy attended the Methodist General Conference in Des Moines,
where Mrs. Bashford sought her out to say that her deceased husband,
the Bishop, thought Welthy should be made head of one of the women's
colleges in China. That was heartwarming news, but 'the women' would
not have her.

Together they attended the consecration of new bishops, and Welthy,
resplendent in a long black velvet evening gown with a large corsage of
red roses at her waist found herself sitting on the platform in the august
company of the entire Council of Bishops. When she rose and sang "All
the World is Dying for a Little Bit of Love" to that prestigious assembly,
every bishop in the hall was ready to offer her all the love she needed.

One new bishop, the youngest elected in many years, poked the colleague beside him and muttered: "No woman who looks like that should be singing about dying for love!" Unwittingly, Welthy had been singing directly to the heart of Frederick Bohn Fisher, the new Bishop to India and Burma.

WORLD TOUR 1920-1921

With the knowledge that the WFMS was ignoring Bishop Bashford's recommendation, Welthy had to find a way to overcome her disappointment, to guard against bitterness and channel her interests. If she was going to present the need for missionary work in countries served by Methodists, and get young women to offer their lives, she must know more about those countries. With five thousand dollars willingly offered by Cousin Dee she embarked on a study tour around the world, joining Margaret Slattery, a dynamic evangelist she had met in France who was booked to speak at the World Sunday School Conference in Tokyo, and two other serious-minded women, Alma Adams and Eleanor White.

Crossing the Pacific, Welthy had long talks with fellow passenger Jimmie Yen, now President of the Chinese Christian Student Association of America. China needs to be left alone, he told her, given time to work out her own solution, and it was the religion of Christ, not Christianity, that would help.

Whether she was technically on furlough or was the incoming Candidate Secretary is unclear from the WFMS records. To a woman bent on business and anxious to make her trip count that was a minor detail, and so she had her own calling cards printed as Candidate Secretary. "I had to go as something when I was talking to all those students and teachers. Wasn't that an innocent thing to do?"

* * *

CHINA, AUGUST 1920

It was mid-August, 1920 when the ladies stepped off their Yangtze steamer at Kiukiang, cholera on the rage once more. The technological revolution had begun to touch China, a Ford motor car taking them up to Kuling that summer season. During their three weeks in the mountains, Welthy sold the cottage and her piano, and bought silks and five Changcha rugs for her new apartment. To Welthy, shopping was a peak cultural event, an instant vacation, and for every cent she spent on herself, two or three were always given to others.

On the crowded new train from Kiukiang to Nanchang, it was Welthy who helped the poor policeman create order out of chaos by establishing two distinct lines of traffic within the train aisles in either direction, doing her bit to help in the modernization process.

The entire population of Bao-Lin, some three hundred and fifty people, was there at the railroad station to meet Han Hsiao Ja's train in Nanchang, another celebrated arrival of their returning heroine. Welthy had kept in close touch with the senior girls, ready to assist with scholarships as their graduation neared, her far-flung net still reaching out. The first Chinese principal of Bao-Lin, Miriam Nieh, a teacher Welthy brought from Rulison School, had been appointed earlier in the year; it had taken until 1919 for Chinese to be included on mission boards and committees, and until 1922 for Chinese architecture to be recommended in new buildings. The Honsinger/Tang team had paved the way for others, with scars to prove it.

The travellers were so impressed with the beautifully landscaped twenty-five acres and the sight of hundreds of girls lining up for fall registration that Alma Adams immediately offered to take up a scholarship. For Welthy it was sweet indeed to see the full-grown trees, the grass, her fine buildings and girls flitting in and out among the trees and paths, but there were pangs, too. It was strange to be present on opening day "and I not there at the helm."

On September 18th there was a surprise forty-first birthday tea for Welthy, featuring a dramatic presentation of her life entitled "Never Say Die As Long As I Have Music and Watermelon Seeds", a lighthearted reference to her great social skill in chewing and spitting out the omnipresent seeds.

They made visits to all the girls' schools in the city, the influence of Bao-Lin's help evident everywhere, and she and Margaret Slattery spoke on numerous occasions to church and school. In many informal counselling interviews with students, Welthy discovered that most of them wanted to train in medicine as the best way to be of service.

When Margaret Slattery was to speak to several hundred of the assembled missionaries, with Welthy presiding over the church meeting, they were informed that women must not enter the pulpit but must remain on the same level as the pews, discrimination that triggered Welthy's article "Shall Women Keep Silence in Churches?"[7]

Welthy's Chinese friends invited them back beyond the moongate for a feast, and while she donned her best black dress and black furs, Margaret chose contrasting white, with white furs to match her white hair. What theatre! How difficult to take Welthy seriously when she had so much fun dressing up and enjoying life. The following evening they came down to earth at more prim after-dinner games of spin the platter and drop the handkerchief with the mission staff.

There were fireworks in the yard on their last night, and next day all the orphans, teachers and high school girls crossed to the other shore to say farewell at the new railroad station, singing "Baldwin Will Shine Tonight," their gift of light to Welthy.

Two things struck Welthy particularly in China that year. Everywhere students were reading wall newspapers and discussing the Versailles Peace Treaty, yet another western exploitation to them. The students were themselves "living newspapers", absorbing world news from many sources and becoming highly politicized. Welthy supported their strikes urging the growth of Chinese manufacture, noting one student's fear that their wave of protest might only be a "five minute patriotism".

She heard the term "Bolsheviki coolie" for the first time and understood the choices China faced. Their need for good communication was more urgent than ever to build up a thinking nation. "She came increasingly to realize that the most important aspect of communication was the ability of the ordinary man and woman to read and write in a predominantly literate world," wrote Kelly, "knowledge both preventative and curative, forestalling ingingand removing injustice."[8] In her own mind, peace for Welthy was a matter of working for justice.

Her second impression was of the new life Professor John Dewey, the American educator, had put into some dying educational projects that had relied too heavily on research and endless testing and theorizing. Dewey's learn-by-doing approach struck her as much more appropriate to the practical needs of China with eighty-five percent of adults illiterate. Welthy was becoming increasingly aware of the deepening mutual ignorance between China and her own country.

To the national journal of her old sorority she sent an appeal for American women of culture and sympathy to help in the struggle of Chinese women for new life, giving her own definition of the truly liberated woman: "They need the American woman who is greater than any creed; a woman who puts love before dogma; a woman whose great passion is to serve."[9]

JAPAN, 1920

In Tokyo Welthy continued the pattern of speaking at the YWCA, visiting schools and colleges, meeting as many educators as possible and writing articles to send back home. "All over Japan it seemed to be 'moving day' for schools. City children spend a week in the country each year and vice versa."[10] With ninety-eight percent of the children in primary school for six years, trains and temples were overflowing with children during that massive exchange week as Welthy thrilled to the wheels of motion carrying young Japan in all directions.

She could not resist a shopping expedition in Nikko, pearl headquarters, and was glad that Cousin Dee had not offered her the great
pearl necklace. "I didn't want a hundred and twenty-five thousand dollars hanging round my neck," she insisted, but the influence was there.
Ever after, the necklace adorned Welthy wherever she went. Strung of
real pearls initially, it became less and less authentic through the years
from repeated breakage and loss, until even a variety store version suf-
ficed. She felt naked without that symbol of her choice, even as she herself grew in authenticity.

The travellers journeyed on, taken round Kyoto in the Mayor's car,
giving speeches, singing, visiting schools in Osaka, meeting social service people, touring factories. In Seoul Welthy noted: "Hear and see
Japanese imperialism at work. Torture and arrests." On to Peking by
train via Mukden, Welthy learned about the educational changes stemming from the May Fourth Movement and the anti-Christian organization of students denouncing the imperial alliance of Christianity and
capitalism under American leadership.

Many missionaries still felt that the corrupt, unstable political condition of China was a moral evil correctable only by moral education. "No
increase of technical efficiency will correct this fundamental danger,"
they concluded.[11] Feeling distinctly uneasy over the rapid growth of
government schools, some superior to their own, the missionaries recognized the need for Chinese management of their schools if they were to
win Chinese support. Welthy had understood for some time the missionaries' vulnerability to charges of cultural imperialism, but many
remained blind to the resentment their attitude created until the May
Fourth accusations by the Chinese of moral deficiency of the allies, which
brought the issue to a head. Only then did they allow Chinese
administrators to begin taking over their schools.

As for female education, the collective wisdom of the missionaries was
that it paid to educate girls, as they could earn money and make better
marriages. Welthy was hearing something different. The entire first
graduating class of five at Ginling College had taken a vow not to marry,
Wu Yi-fang, later the first Chinese President of the College, among them.
Their single missionary women teachers had provided the example of
non-domestic women, powerfully influencing the girls away from the oppressive married life in China. But they wanted their freedom to help
build China, not the church. Many had first been politicized at missionary schools, through their resentment of the condescending attitudes of
the teachers, as Welthy well knew from the lesson of Chang Tren.[12] Always with an eye to the future, Welthy talked intensely with teachers
everywhere she went, some her own Bao-Lin graduates, giving her

general impressions in an article entitled "China the Day After Tomorrow".

SUSPENDED IN COLOMBO, 1920

By the time they reached Colombo, the western world had caught up with Welthy, and she was dealt one of the hardest blows of her life, inflicting a wound that never completely healed. A cable from the WFMS was waiting, informing her simply that there was no such position as Candidate Secretary. Welthy was effectively fired.

She imagined that someone at one of the many colleges where she had spoken with potential missionary candidates may have written to the WFMS referring to discussions with Welthy. Welthy sincerely believed that her informal efforts were in the larger interests of the WFMS, where her loyalties lay. She could never understand why an organization with such high aims could act so narrowly, suppressing her talent and ambition to carry out their broad purpose. "Those women crucified me. They never thought about what would happen to me," she said of the deepest hurt ever inflicted upon her. "No doubt I was stronger for it," she conceded years later. If the WFMS wanted to cut her down to size, their dismissal had the opposite effect. It was a distinct turning point; Welthy was not about to vanish into thin air.

INDIA, 1920-1921

In December they reached Bombay, where Welthy's heavy heart was hit even more deeply at the sight of poverty worse than anything she had seen in China as the Punjab Mail took them across the desert to the central cities of northern India. The sight of the Taj Mahal, monument to a Queen who had tended wounded soldiers in the field, unveiled, took on new symbolism as she watched a flock of Muslim women covered from head to foot in black shrouds. "As they turned to take one last look at the white, shimmering monument to a woman, I realized they were seeing it only through two slits of fine white net. This piercing contrast between the unbelievable beauty of the monument and the group of shrouded women who followed the Queen's own culture so disturbed my meditation that I could think of nothing but what the future might hold for these repressed souls," she recalled over and over again.[13] Those veiled eyes became to Welthy the bound feet of India, holding women back from life.

Welthy's distress, personal and public, increased at each stop as they moved about the crowded cities visiting more schools, colleges, and shops. She saw children sleeping on the floor, and many other signs of severe deprivation, a shock equivalent to the discovery of her ignorance on arrival in China fifteen years earlier. Educated and experienced as she was, she had not understood that such blackness could exist.

It was a relief to reach Isabella Thoburn College in Lucknow, the first women's college in the Orient, a bold adventure of the WFMS at a time when American colleges for women were still in the experimental stage. While Margaret spoke to students, Welthy alternated between singing to the girls to ease her heart, talking with the College President, Evangeline Thillayampalam, and grabbing history books off the library shelves to learn how India had lost its strength. At the YWCA she spoke about India's future, but in her heart she found it difficult to see.

WELTHY HONSINGER MEETS BISHOP FISHER

At last they reached the hub of India, Calcutta, city of grand avenues and parks, and home of the most destitute people on earth. The accumulated distress over her own loss and the millions upon millions of diminished Indian lives she had seen as they crossed the country culminated in a powerful response to the one person she encountered who offered believable hope and light ahead for the people of India. There he was before her eyes once again, Bishop Fred Fisher, all dressed up in cap and gown, offering the future to hundreds of pairs of bright brown eyes at the closing exercises of a Methodist school.

Two shining blue eyes then invited Welthy to sing, watched as she made her way to the centre of the platform, and admired the grand posture, the narrow waist, the long, stately legs. The "Boat Song" from Tales of Hoffman came forth from lungs and lips energized by his interest. Welthy and Fred definitely noticed each other, but only that, for Fred was married to his childhood sweetheart from Muncie, Indiana. But a glimpse of Welthy as she came towards his car at the Grand Hotel door lingered in the back of his mind.

Welthy did not go up to Darjeeling with the others, preferring to use the time to see the Methodist work in Calcutta, escorted by the Bishop and other missionaries. She read Fred's book "India's Silent Revolution", the result of his wartime travel there, and felt his sympathy for India's expectation of greater participation in government in recognition of its contribution of men, money and materials for the war when Britain asked for them. She read of illiterate Indian soldiers catapulted from remote villages into modern warfare, and the implications of this exposure when they returned home, as with the Chinese labourers.

In that agrarian society villagers had no alternative income when famine struck because their traditional home industries were dismantled by increasing industrialization. They lost their lands and became lifelong debtors to their landlords and to the moneylenders, who charged seventy-five percent interest on loans for the two main rural diversions — marriages and funerals. And these debts were passed on from generation to generation.

In preparation for India, Fred had studied economics at Harvard to understand working conditions there, such as in the Bengal jute mills, where workers, including children, received the "irreducible minimum wage" under conditions of ruthless competition. A practitioner of the Social Gospel, he sought an economic middle way between the laissez-faire of capitalism and the government control of socialism. His missionary stance was to approach both body and soul as an indivisible whole.

Fred saw fifty million outcastes and a hundred and sixty million illiterate women as the potential silent power base of a revolution against medieval arrogance and brutality. He was not blind to the obstacles, but believed that universal, free, compulsory education, such as the Americans had attempted in the Philippines, and as many European countries and some native states of India were adopting, was the critical factor on the road to freedom for India.

Fred told Welthy about those pioneering Indians who had begun educational reforms, urging the British colonial government to reverse its educational priority from a few at the top of the caste system to the mass at the bottom. His observation that "men have an elemental and instinctive contempt for women which the more primitive societies do not attempt to conceal" amazed her, as they discussed the dismal practice of *purdah*. "Like fishes in the dark cave, who lost their eyes because for many generations they had never used them, these women have lost all ambition for the privileges and responsibilities of normal life. In educating and liberating the women of India, the greatest difficulty will be to break down the prejudices and inhibitions of the women themselves." (SR, 140.)

Fred was talking Welthy's language. As for the missionaries, he urged them to give up their literal insistence on doctrine and the fine distinctions between orthodox and heterodox beliefs. (SR, 92.) The Hindu, on his part, must give up his prejudices about caste, women and Christianity in a generous recognition of all for the elevation of India. Fred cited the leading efforts of K. Natarajan, Editor of the *Indian Social Reformer*, in promoting such cooperation.

Before being elected Bishop, Fred had been Associate General Secretary of the Interchurch World Movement with special responsibility for industrial relations. His mandate was to emphasize the human element in labour relations, and bring employers, employees and the public together in a cooperative adjustment in the post-war period. With the steel strike of 1919, he appointed an independent, national commission of inquiry that pressed the steel companies to reduce the work day from twelve to eight hours. He was also Executive Secretary of the Interchurch War Emergency and Reconstruction Committee.

Fred's liberalism was viciously attacked by the powerful business interests his Commission had offended; they accused him of being a Bolshevist, pro-German, whose name was really Fischer, charges that were later withdrawn. His role had been so strong that the British Criminal Investigation Department (CID) picked up the trail and had him watched in India, only to have the Viceroy himself, Lord Reading, inform the CID they were in error.

Described as a "chubby little man whose convexity of waist line held him at an appreciable distance from the edge of the table, with penetrating blue eyes socketed rather deeply, and pugilistic jowls,"[14] he was hardly the stereotypical romantic figure, except for those eyes. Nor was he the conventional bishop.

He had read widely and deeply, mostly from Greek, Roman and Renaissance philosophy, to learn how to conserve and develop his energy and master techniques for exerting the influential authority expected of him. Consciously seeking guidance, he made his own rules not to allow himself to be offended or discouraged, to keep his ideals dominant, and try to decide how Christ would act in difficult situations.

Earlier that year Fred had written thoughts, from the grandeur of the dominant churches of Paris to the quiet heights of Darjeeling, reflections of the man Welthy saw behind those powerful blue eyes, a man of compelling attraction:

> *I have a spirit of rebellion within me when I see the blasphemy of these forms and ceremonies. When I read the Gospels, with their beautiful story of the simple life of Jesus — how he lived in the villages, visited in the homes, was an iconoclast of past forms and told the people deliberately that they must not trust in them — when I think of his humility and lack of pretense, and then find how the established church has built these shrines of idolatry in His name, I think it is the worst blasphemy ever enacted against God and perpetrated upon mankind.*[15]

and later:

> *Here, climbing the hillside path, is a beautiful burden bearer — a clear-faced woman, with a pack of wood upon her back which would surely break mine. A strap over her head holds the load. Her body is swung forward in graceful and easy proportion. And as she climbs, she sings. And as she sings, she knits. Think of carrying such a burden, with*

*hands free to knit. And think of singing, with back weighed
down and hands employed. This, truly, is the perfect trinity
- to bear one's load with grace ascending, to give one's hands
to useful service, and to let the heart sing withal.*[16]

How could he know he was describing the woman Welthy was becoming? He had heard her sing twice, he knew of her work in China, and now they had spoken directly to one another about the challenge and burden of Christian service abroad. Though he came from Middletown America, as Muncie became known, Welthy knew there was nothing average about the Bishop. In fact, she thought he was the most dynamic and delightful human being she had ever known; she revelled in his company, and recognized his divine discontent as the hallmark of a true reformer.

Fred's sermons and speeches called for democratic reconstruction from the bottom up. He was proud of the democratic structure of the Church in India, for episcopal though it was, it had no central headquarters, its various boards operating from many different cities. In Calcutta, Thoburn Church was fully self-supporting, as was the boys' school, the Industrial Home, and the Seamen's Mission.

There were numerous other Methodist activities in Bengal alone, but Fred was Bishop of Northeast India and Burma, serving a vast population. He was anxious to see change, in education particularly, and had quickly become impatient with bureaucracy "in dim and mysterious recesses of the British Parliament's gloomy halls", an attitude Welthy could understand only too well. He had not only the administrative requirements of the distant Methodist Board in New York to cope with, but the political fact of London's say in all things Indian.

Welthy's experience in China was vitally interesting to him, as he recognized her progressive ideas. He stirred her to study the many religions of India, and as they said farewell after days of intense discussion, he sighed and hoped the WFMS would send her to India.

COLOMBO, PALESTINE, BEIRUT, CAIRO, TRIESTE, 1921

January, 1921. The four travellers shared the general alarm of passengers aboard their ship from Colombo to Port Said when both crew and captain remained drunk. It may well have been Welthy, emboldened by her previous nautical experience, who oversaw the safe transit of the ship through the Suez Canal, twenty hours at a snail's pace. Margaret Slattery wrote "New Paths Through Old Palestine" based on their journey through the Holy Land and dedicated it to Welthy, who confined to her diary her extensive thoughts on every site visited. In Beirut she sang at a British Girls' School, in Cairo she sang in Chinese at the American

University. At Trieste she noted: "We are hated now because of our money", meaning American wealth.

The Simplon Express carried them on to Paris, for a triumphant reunion with their lost luggage at the Hotel Petrograd. In the exuberance of their return to the western world, sharing beds as was the custom for travelling ladies of modest means, Welthy was momentarily in the arms of playful, womanly love, responding freely to an affectionate embrace. But that was not what she really wanted, and, as before, she stopped the affair almost before it began without harming the friendship. At forty-two she retained her faith that she would find her ideal lover and chose not to diminish herself with less.

AMERICA, 1921

Welthy's priority on returning to the United States was to visit her brother in Syracuse. His condition had not improved, and with the marriage strained and Evalina wary of interference, Welthy felt powerless to help.

Syracuse had become a place that kept sending her away, for she had come to say goodbye to her home chapter of the WFMS. She knew it was goodbye, though they did not give a clear reason and she did not ask. Mrs. Wilson was the brave woman who urged Welthy to take her severance pay of four hundred and fifty dollars for the year, placing the check in Welthy's purse, tears on both sides accompanying the transaction.

The official WFMS record shows Welthy having "Retired" in 1918, but that was crossed out to read "Resigned 1921". In the smallest of handwriting the different views of Welthy were recorded: "Great power, crowded hall in Life Enlistment Class — We want W.B.H. but she does not seem to want us. Cannot fathom her attitude — Splendid, great vision and power. We need her — Unusual ability and charm. Do not agree with Bagwell that her attitude to China w'd weaken her influence among college girls. She may prefer to present life service more broadly than WFMS but results good — Need and want her — Organization so closely articulated no room for unsupervised, independent individual however brilliant. Bills enormous, breaks engagements, cancels dates. Salary requirement large." If they were uncertain and confused, it is not difficult to see why Welthy felt her life was on the line.

The Methodist connection was not irreversibly severed, however. The Board remained divided between those women who decided to let her go and those men who respected her strength. "The women didn't want me. They thought I should go back to China. It was none of their business what I had to do," said Welthy at the end of her life, still rankled by their rejection, still certain of her right to freedom. "If they wanted to invite me, it was my privilege to accept."

COUSIN DEE TO THE RESCUE

New York offered the best opportunity to build on her experience, and whatever Welthy was celebrating on return to the YWCA Hostel in the spring of 1921, she fell in the shower again, fracturing her knee — an accident resulting in a visit from Cousin Dee. Welthy's tale of her treatment at the hands of the WFMS prompted Cousin Dee to come to her rescue with twenty-five thousand dollars in bonds. These yielded a six percent income, no strings attached, which Welthy accepted gratefully. But Cousin Dee had further plans. She really wanted to install Welthy in a Park Avenue apartment in the hope of capturing her for high society. She began by sponsoring her for membership in the Cosmopolitan Club and seeing that she was properly introduced. As one of New York's "400" of patrician origins, she had the clout to do it. A prime mover in establishing the Town Hall, which opened that year, she had given sixty-three thousand dollars initially and numerous subsequent gifts towards its development. Built by the League for Political Education, the hall was originally an adult education forum of the suffragist movement, designed for lectures on democratic principles. It had no grand boxes, but the evening lectures were definitely white tie.

In Washington, Mildred and Robert Bliss had just purchased Dumbarton Oaks, the famous Federalist mansion, and were busy with renovations and landscaping. Altogether, Welthy's avenue of entree into elite society and the women's movement was first class. For three years she hovered on its fringes.

More distinguished visitors came to her hostel. Mr. and Mrs. Ellis Phillips, staunch Methodists of considerable wealth, had heard of Welthy's industrial department at Bao-Lin and came to offer Welthy support in building an industrial school for girls in China. Though she had met Mrs. Phillips, Dean of Women at Ohio Wesleyan College, several times when she had spoken there, and had a high regard for her, she could not help thinking that the WFMS had put them up to it to get out of sending her to head a college abroad, thinking that a strong businessman could control Welthy. She did not accept, and declined another offer from the Singer Sewing Machine Company, at a very large salary, to install sewing machines in the schools of China. In both cases, Welthy felt the work was too far from the church and would not draw on her prime talent as an educator.

WELTHY AS METHODIST EDITOR

Beyond the administrative clutch of the church, Welthy was highly regarded. She next found a focus for her energies working as an editor at the Methodist Publishing House on lower Fifth Avenue. "She was the most fascinating thing that ever hit the Methodist book concern. Always bustling, always busy, well dressed, spoke to everybody — just a startling personality. She never came into the place quietly. 'Well, today's a great day,' she would say to the small staff."

For Helen Krayer, her secretary, it was the start of a new adventure in living and service. She became Welthy's right hand and close friend, sharing her dismay at the outworn attitudes of the WFMS ladies. Twenty years younger, Helen was one of those whose mother was initially wary of her daughter's new position, having heard Welthy warning "I'm going to go to your church and I'm going to get your daughter," her familiar battlecry. But Welthy was neither a radical nor a brainwasher, as Helen's mother recognized once she saw Helen begin to flourish under Welthy's guidance and friendship.

Welthy was in effect the editor of *Missionary Education*, a new monthly magazine started in October 1921 for all levels within American churches. She used artistic talent wherever she could find it to enliven the pages, always with an eye to symbolism and strong visual images. Drawing on her contacts in many countries, she elicited a good variety of material, writing on India herself frequently. She was a professional woman, with freedom to use her considerable imagination and abilities. She enjoyed an extremely satisfying working relationship with Dr. Eric North, the general editor of foreign missions, and Hal Luccock, the editorial secretary of foreign missions, a warm-hearted fellow educator noted for his dry humour. "I never had any trouble with those people."

The magazine was well received and grew rapidly. Concentrating her efforts on making East and West acquainted with each other, Welthy succeeded in having its name changed to *World Neighbors*, a phrase that summarizes the insistent theme of her life. A Methodist press release noted that "Welthy Honsinger was again in the country, where her intellect, charm, personality and consecration are accomplishing much for the kingdom."

Aside from editorial help, Helen made all the arrangements for Welthy's many speaking engagements, often travelling with her. Welthy was in much demand at church and service groups, noted for her appreciation of beauty, worth and humour in other civilizations. She expected Helen to know all sorts of things, so Helen put in long evenings at the library filling gaps in her knowledge. For Welthy, it was a happy interval of stimulating work, the opportunity to express her views, lively companionship, travel and prestige, and she often wore her long red necklace to signify her delight.

Helen walked Welthy home after work every day, going far out of her way to enjoy the fun of their light-hearted stroll up Fifth Avenue, scarcely able to believe that such a high-minded woman of service could be so merry. New York was an exciting place to be, with the streets full of the new breed of women who thronged there to seek their futures. There were the flappers, the ambitious careerists and the worldly sophisticates all emerging into the light of the new day. All sorts of new occupations were beginning to open up for women and there was great movement afoot that Welthy and Helen found so stimulating in their daily walk. At forty-one Welthy did not go overboard for the outward expressions of the new freedoms; her skirts remained long, she kept her corset on, and did not take to cigarettes and alcohol.

* * *

At a Methodist meeting in Baltimore in 1922, Bishop Fisher caught sight of Welthy once again, her singing magnetically attractive. He remembered the wife of one of his Indian ministers who could talk of nothing but the powerful impression Welthy Honsinger had made on her.

* * *

In a burst of egalitarianism, Cousin Dee gave twenty-five hundred dollars to each of the Honsinger offspring, Fred, Mabel, Mina and Welthy, but it was Welthy who had caught her strongest interest, whose talents she wanted nurtured. Her gifts to Welthy over the years totalled sixty-seven thousand dollars, in one form or another, assets that Welthy carefully conserved as insurance against an unknown future. With a regular job to support herself, Welthy took a small apartment, but for anyone as irrepressibly outgoing as Welthy, living alone was unbearable. Mabel had moved out to Warren, Pennsylvania as Director of a Community Centre, where she taught immigrants about America. And while Cousin Dee's friends and soirées were enjoyable, they were not really Welthy's kind.

She had more in common with Margaret Slattery, the teacher, writer and lecturer with whom she had travelled earlier. They moved into a small apartment together, each coming and going on their various travels and returning to their shared home. Later they took up joint residence in a special apartment in the Allerton House for women at 57th and Lexington, another of Cousin Dee's projects, where she arranged to have two apartments made into one, allowing each some privacy. The arrangement worked well in the beginning, but Margaret, in her sixties, wanted more security than Welthy, whose future was still an open book. The differences in their ages and outlooks were evident to sharp-eyed Wang Gwei-hsin, then studying in the United States, who described Margaret's writings for high school teachers as "just like chewing soft rice", in comparison to Welthy's vigorous style. But Gwei-hsin conceded that she was a very effective speaker with strong appeal to young people, which was what Welthy most admired in Margaret. Welthy's alma mater, Syracuse University, summoned her to receive the first of many honorary degrees, a Master of Arts for her study of Chinese literature, on the recommendation of Professor Kraus, her former teacher. Rosalie Mayer reported that Welthy was so embarrassed by the President's long commendation that she turned to go back to her seat before being hooded, then returned to the dais, rather astonished, amidst warm applause. Such approval from her own Methodist college was awesome and welcome reassurance, but she did not accept an offer to teach about China, well aware of her unsuitability for academic life.

That recognition prompted another gift of money from Cousin Dee to have Welthy's "Twins' Travelogues" published, four small books on Asian children for young people, presenting their customs and habits. In stories full of Christian content, but with an absence of cultural superiority, her twins made imaginary voyages of discovery to America, where everything different seemed wrong at first.

In addition to editing the magazine, she wrote articles for various religious publications — children's stories for *The Classmate* and general articles for newspapers. One story, "From Confucius to Christ", told of a Confucian scholar who looked for eighteen years to find a Christian who followed Christ, and found him when Sun Yat-sen came to Nanchang. But she also wrote of political matters such as the Soviet Union's influence in India, and Bertrand Russell's in Peking. Reacting to the American Government's ban on Asian immigration, she warned of prejudice against foreigners, recalling her own experience of being a foreigner in China. Mothers had cried out to their children as she passed by: "A foreign devil is coming. Narrow your heart." America could not afford to narrow its heart, she cautioned.

WELTHY'S STAND ON WOMEN'S ORDINATION

In the *Christian Advocate* she deplored the decision of her church to bar women's ordination. "Those of us who have carried the truth revealed by Jesus in far countries to the unprivileged women of the world love to tell what is to them the surprising story of Jesus' conversation with the Samaritan woman at the well. When the disciples came 'they marvelled that He was speaking to a woman'. But 'from that city many of the Samaritans believed on Him, because of the word of the *woman who testified*'. From all that we can learn of Jesus, he seems to have had no prejudice of race or color or sex. Can His church afford to take an ideal lower than that of the Master?" she asked.[17]

* * *

Cousin Dee always took Welthy to the stately headquarters of the Bank of New York on Fifth Avenue, a bank where women do their business discreetly in private, carpeted chambers with their own special entrance. Cousin Dee was writing cheques on the order of five hundred thousand dollars to complete the Town Hall building plan, while Welthy's cheques were mere dots in comparison. Conditioned to the handling of Mexican silver dollars in China, Welthy preferred to use the 77th Street branch and hear the rattle of real change in the marketplace.

Nor was Welthy's fancy captured by the handsome lawyer, so delicately presented to Welthy at several lunches by Cousin Dee, despite his interesting years in Italy. The pressure was definitely on for Welthy to channel her energies into a solid, socially acceptable lifestyle, to settle down into marriage, very much part of the increasing backlash against women's new freedoms.

* * *

"True emancipation of women will come only when the necessity for attracting the other sex disappears."[18] Bishop Fisher was back in the United States talking about Gandhi when he made that reference to women's "slavery" in 1922, pointing out how Gandhi treated men and women as equals in his freedom movement.

He was drawing wide attention in America, describing a six-hour talk with the Mahatma, who had since been jailed. Gandhi had criticized foreign missionaries who came to India for their own selfish advantage, and had read aloud passages from St. Matthew to Fred.[19] When Fred asked what he advised the missionaries in India to do, his clear, incisive answer was: "Be better Christians." The stinging words burned deep into Fred's heart.

Fred's wife Edith, his quiet, cultured companion and unsurpassed hostess, had died in India within three days of caring for a typhus-infected baby, and he had returned home with her personal effects. Speaking three times a day during the intensive "I Will Maintain" fund-raising campaign, grief heightened his eloquence. His speeches were widely reported in headlines across the States. Welthy parted with a hundred dollars when she heard his dinner speech at the Commodore Hotel in

New York. She knew nothing of his personal loss at the time, nor that his own health broke down after two months of the gruelling pace.

In his voluminous notebooks he sought consolation, remembering the mighty influence of his modest, rather melancholy father. "Make your own luck," he had told Fred. "The character you build will determine your life. Study, work, dream big things, then *do* them." And always he could feel the loving touch of his mother, "my Josephine's hands on each cheek." The parental roles were reversed in Fred's case, his gentle father steadily urging greatness upon him, as Welthy's mother had done, and his purposeful mother bestowing the liberating love Abram Honsinger gave Welthy.

Already showing signs of discontent with hierarchy and his elevated role, Fred was telling his church that he thought there should be a bishop in every state in the States, and many more abroad. "One way to keep the bishops humble and industrious is to have plenty of them — and a less isolated office would make for less criticism." The theological and organizational preoccupations of the church were becoming too confining in the midst of the vast human needs. He kept asking himself: "What is a Christian?"

And to his head of state, President Coolidge, whom he visited twice in the White House, Fred pressed the right of Indians to become American citizens, citing their racial superiority and the impracticability of isolation in an interdependent age. He urged Coolidge to foster Pacific trade with a large merchant marine and accept broader cooperation with Asia as a national policy, views that received considerable press coverage, and powerfully echoed Welthy's attitude.

On his lonely journey back to India, via China, it was the S. S. Tango Maru of Welthy's first voyage that carried him across the Pacific. When his health broke down soon after reaching India, his arthritis seriously aggravated by the climate, he used the enforced rest to read ever more, becoming intrigued with the modern psychology of the unconscious. His writings reflect a new sense of the poetic, and a rekindled urgency to grow. Of himself he wrote: "He had reached that season of life when the mind of man is composed of depth and simplicity in nearly equal proportions."

Fridays became a day of fasting and spiritual upbuilding for Fred in his determination to overcome sensitivity to criticism. "Which Road Shall We Take?" was written in that interval, advocating a world-wide federation of Methodism, refuting the popular concept that Methodism was exclusively American. In his notebook he spelled out his personal "cravings", or goals for his ideal Christian service abroad:

To be a persuasive and convincing preacher with a right degree of eloquence, incisiveness and cosmopolitan appeal.

To be a worthy author with pen commanding and thought deep but readable, catching the needs of the times and spreading right principles and methods.

To be an acknowledged authority on internationalism, knowing by travel, social contact, study and reflection the various nationalities and races, and helping break down prejudices and misunderstanding.

To be a leader in interdenominational cooperation and unity, and help bring Christendom into true universal communion, fellowship and cooperative effort.

To be a student of and moulder of public opinion in matters of social and economic life, seeking the practice of cooperation and the reduction of competition, applying the principles of Jesus to the total relations of men.

To think deeply on human problems, and the relation of men to God and men to men. By reflection, meditation, prayer, reading and social intercourse to create ideas and develop policies of world-wide significance and power.

To imbibe the very spirit, personality and attitude of Jesus Christ so that no selfishness, nor irritability, nor repulsion shall control me.

To be truly serviceable in every relationship of life.

* * *

WELTHY THE AUTHOR

Nineteen twenty-four was a watershed year for Welthy. She could never come to grips with her ambition to write the romantic novel of her China years. Well able to express thoughts and describe scenes vividly, organization of material evaded her and she required strong editorial assistance. However, with Helen's help she published two books in 1924, both aimed at young audiences.

"Beyond The Moongate" was presented as her China diary, suitably tailored to appeal to a youthful sense of adventure and service. "A String of Chinese Pearls; ten tales of Chinese girls ancient and modern", was a collection of folk tales, rich in vivid scenes of everyday life, reflecting her hopes for Chinese women. Every page dramatized Welthy's hopes for a better life for Chinese girls whose lives were governed according to roles defined by men for men. The exceptions were her heroines – the Chinese Jeanne d'Arc; the Dowager Empress who though vain, selfish and extravagant nevertheless held incredible power she used wisely; the girl patriot who became a living newspaper to her illiterate audiences.

Summers she taught at the student Christian centre at Silver Bay and Mount Hermon College, personally sponsored by Helen Gould, philanthropist daughter of the famous financier Jay Gould. With all her freedom, Welthy never wandered far from the main path that pulled her towards Christian service. She kept to her own style, in small matters as well as large – even in the roaring twenties, her skirts did not rise above the knee.

GANDHI'S AMERICAN FRIENDS

Along with other liberals of the time Welthy felt the moral shock of economic imperialism the war had revealed. More radical liberals, such as Norman Thomas and Roger Baldwin, saw in the massacre at Amritsar, the Treaty of Versailles and the western response to the Russian Revolution a betrayal of the concept of national self-determination. Welthy was among those thoughtful Americans attracted to the personality of Gandhi, whose movement based on the democratic village tradition of India combined their hopes for democracy and for the moral recovery of the West.

In Gandhi they saw the idealism and realism of Christ, and around them a small, vocal following emerged endowing Gandhi with his own American mystique, even though many of his admirers had little awareness of India's diverse reality. John Haynes Holmes, the Unitarian, and Fred Fisher were two of his strongest admirers. "Gandhi is exemplifying Christianity instead of merely preaching it," Fred said. "He is making a joke out of our Western civilization which pretends to worship Jesus while it is backing up all sorts of materialistic claims with bayonets and battleships." Gandhi had pointed out to Fred that the missionaries were primarily concerned with protecting their property in India if any trouble broke out. "That is not the way Jesus taught you to act," Gandhi reminded Fred. Quoting the Bible, he said, "If any man take away thy goods, ask them not again."[20]

In an article in the *New York World* with the heading "How an American Bishop Has Been Learning Christianity from Ghandi" (with the typical misspelling of Gandhi's name), Fred was described as "a decidedly American American who has not lost his perspective, has not allowed India to swallow him up. He is a driving, hustling, hop-to-it type of Westerner who would pass in the crowd as a super-charged live-wire industrial executive rather than a churchman. Fisher listened to Gandhi, who knows that what we call force is weakness. Gandhi originally thought only of using his wealth and influence in humanitarian service, but then he literally obeyed Jesus and stripped himself of every worldly power, urging people to break from the influences of capitalism and return to family and simple life." The article continued with Fred's views: "Early missionaries gave all without protecting themselves. Then came imperialism and trade and the acquisitive society, with the social organization that has confused us. Now a missionary often comes to a native soul whose light is greater than his own."[21]

WELTHY SPEAKS TO THE BISHOP'S HEART

When Welthy was invited to speak to a Methodist gathering early in 1924 she chose to speak about India, the first time in America she had dared to tackle that complex culture. Had she known that in the audience were two of the leading missionaries from India, she might not have been so bold. Evangeline Thillayampalam from Lucknow, and Bishop Fisher, home for the biennial meetings, heard the words that changed Welthy's life. Hearing her express with conviction ideas and attitudes so close to his own, Welthy's eyes watching Fred's as she spoke, he awoke from the isolation of his personal sorrow. Two days later, on St. Patrick's day, he appeared in her office, inviting her to lunch. "I knew right away," she said. "I knew he wasn't going to fool around."

They lunched at the Commodore, their recognition of each other growing. He invited her to dinner and the theatre a few days later. She accepted, and then cancelled. Was she ready to give up the freedom and satisfaction of her work to leap into the unknown? She knew Fred had another woman friend, an Anglo-Indian lady in India. Margaret Slattery begged her not to get involved with Fred, saying she had such important work to do, and was fearful of losing her companion. Welthy knew she must decide what she wanted before seeing Fred again.

Another matter of the heart weighed heavily in Welthy's deliberations; Mabel had been seriously ill for the past two years. Cousin Dee had given Welthy ten thousand dollars to pay the medical expenses for Mabel's hospitalization in Warren, Pennsylvania after her hip, then her lungs, gave out. The diagnosis was uncertain, her pain advancing, and finally in April 1924 she died of breast cancer. Welthy had been looking after her affairs, and with Mina brought her body home to Rome for the final parting. She prepared a memorial booklet including Mabel's favourite thoughts — "Trouble is halved, once you have laughed."; "Love is a paradox. The more you give away the more you have." Welthy ended the tribute to her beloved sister saying: "For us it is a new, deeper chal-

lenge to give this needy world a richer measure of that service which she
gave so lavishly." Out of that dark moment touching her own mortality
so closely came a clear warm burst of sunlight. Welthy knew what she
was going to do.

METHODIST GENERAL CONFERENCE, SPRINGFIELD 1924

No call had come from the busy Bishop. She and Helen Krayer went
up to Springfield, Massachusetts to attend the Methodist General Conference of 1924 where Fred would be receiving an honorary degree and
playing a prominent role. In a crucial, carefully composed note to him,
Welthy wrote: "I am anxious to see you for a few minutes — will you be
good enough to look me up on one of your least hectic days? Please do —
I can't bear it if you don't. Cordially, Welthy Honsinger." She had made
her move.

That was all Fred needed. He managed to steal away from the spotlight of the conference for a few moments alone with her. On the bridge
across the Connecticut River so aptly named Memorial Bridge, on that
gentle upward arch, Welthy and Fred exchanged their first kiss. Taller
and two years older than Fred, all Welthy's yearnings and experiences
found expression in his arms. "A bishop was over-determined for
Welthy," said one observer, wryly.

The next note despatched down the hotel corridor was not preserved, but Welthy's expression of love elicited this response from Fred:

> *My Darling: What a lovely letter you have sent me. From
> my heart I love you, in deepest, holiest devotion. Life is
> new — you have set my heart aflame. How beautiful you are,
> how wonderful. It is like a dream . . . May God make me
> worthier of this amazing happiness! Yours in deep devotion.
> Fred.*

After four hours sleep, he sent these lines to her at 6:30 a.m.:

> *This is life's best morning to me . . . my dreams a lovely
> reality. Only two months to wait, then thirty-two years of
> active service and glorious fellowship together. And then
> even eternity shall not separate us. And, beginning now, the
> overwhelming love. It floods my being this morning. But
> the most glorious fact is that you love me. If you want to
> lift and inspire me just tell me often. Every glimpse of you
> today will be heaven. Your own, Fred.*

Welthy's next note shows the unburdening of her grief over Mabel's
death and the deep commitment she was making:

*Corners that were dark are flooded with light, flashes of fear
are now strong beams of courage. A heavy heart has become
aglow with optimism . . . all that I have desired, you are,
and all that I have responds to you."*

They became engaged in a taxicab during a dash away from the meetings, where excited speculation about the burgeoning romance between
the progressive, controversial Bishop and the stunning former missionary was rippling through the conference. That Welthy was always mag-
nificently dressed in outfits of a single colour from hat to shoes made
her an even more romantic figure.

Fred's parents had been at the opening sessions, sitting in the Bishop's
front seats. When they left, he gave the seats to Welthy, and joined her
when not on the platform himself. All eyes were on them. "I was one of
the most popular people there," said Helen, "for everyone wanted inside information about the lovers." Conference-goers saw Helen with
Welthy every day, but never at dinner in the evenings.

Sharing a room with Welthy, Helen was her confidante. "I never saw
anyone so in love, in a quiet, dignified way."[22] When Welthy returned
to their room each night she would confess that she and Fred had
slipped off together again. One night the lovers were spotted sitting in
the park after dark and ordered on their way by an officious policeman,
a touch of comedy to remember in later years. After that they contented
themselves with car rides in the rolling New England countryside whenever they could steal away, bribing the driver to secrecy.

Welthy to Fred:

*Good morning, darling. The birds, the sunshine, the roses
which I have kissed are all shouting 'He loves me', and instead of feeling at all like a vampire myself, I feel thoroughly bewitched. I am glad it is you who have to make the
speeches today. Obstacles that loomed so large grow
smaller as I look into your steady eyes, so full of devotion
and humility and courage. God keep us humble and worthy of this great love and through it, may we bring love to
the ends of the earth. Here's 'me' — your Welthy.*

And two days later:

*You are my man of God and I am proud to say that you are
mine. I shall be sitting up in the balcony with my eyes and
my mind and my heart all upon you, praying God to keep
you alert and poised and yet spontaneous. This is your day
. . . You will preside differently from all the others — thank*

*God — and I shall rejoice in whatever you do. Your adoring
Welthy.*

Years later one minister's wife remembered sitting up in the gallery
watching the good looking, attractively dressed woman in the front seats,
and many of the delegates stopping to talk to her. Even from that distance she was drawn to Welthy's gracious manner which reflected her
inner strength, and her seatmates were surprised she had not known
the woman was none other than the Welthy Honsinger whom she had
heard about for years. Throughout the conference she heard no
criticism of Welthy, but Bishop Fisher did not fare so well.

One evening in the parsonage of a Springfield church, several conference leaders were discussing Fisher, saying he was young, unorthodox, moving too swiftly to Indianize the church, and sharply
criticizing him for suspected Bolshevik leanings and lack of concern for
British proprieties in India. The woman's husband, George Vogel, then
said: "Fisher is far ahead of us in thought and action. His methods and
procedures will be the norm on the mission fields of the future."[23] Mrs.
Vogel was proud, in retrospect, that her husband's judgment was proven
correct.

It was official at last. In May 1924, the engagement was announced at
a reception honouring the new bishops' wives, and Welthy on her
engagement. A round of receptions for Welthy followed, then the formal announcement at the final conference luncheon — the delegates had
given their unqualified approval of the romance. Welthy's new status
with the WFMS was a bit of divine irony, and she would be serving in a
much larger capacity than they could have imagined. Fred asked Bishop
McDowell of Washington to marry them in July, then moved it up to June,
one month away. "I should think the earlier anybody married Welthy
Honsinger the better," McDowell replied. "It is an act of special mercy
and grace to you that somebody else has not run away with her long
before this."

Earlier, Bishop McDowell's wife had told Fred that she had wanted to
see Welthy as President of Isabella Thoburn College in Lucknow; now
Fred delighted in informing her that Welthy was going to India in another
capacity. Welthy's last word on the matter of not being allowed to head
a college was that she would have run IT College differently, raising funds
so it could reach out over the country and join in cooperative efforts
with every other women's college in India for maximum impact.

Welthy certainly had a fine new feather in her hat, but Helen had one
of the heaviest ordeals of her life to face when she got back to New York
ahead of Welthy. Margaret Slattery literally went wild on hearing the
news of Welthy's engagement. Used to special treatment, she sum-

moned Helen and paced up and down the floor pressing her for details. Welthy had sent her a telegram saying their engagement was the will of God, a phrase that sent Margaret through the ceiling in rage. Her deep disappointment and outright jealousy over losing Welthy provoked a nervous collapse. A startled Helen bore the brunt of her extraordinary reaction with patience and skill, discreetly arranging for her to recover at a sanatorium near Buffalo and escorting her there. When Helen got back to Springfield to tell Welthy and Fred what had happened, they were profoundly grateful for her handling of the delicate situation. Welthy could safely return to the Allerton.

Fred telegraphed from Springfield: "Darling it's awfully lonely here. Everybody misses you and asks about you. They call it a miracle of the conference. You are their popular queen and my goddess of love. Fred." *World Neighbors* carried an announcement of the engagement, referring to Welthy's appreciation of beauty, worth and humour in other civilizations, a quality of understanding she would need to draw on heavily in the new life ahead.

After a quiet dinner alone with Fred at the Commodore in New York, gazing at her yellow sapphire engagement ring, Welthy wrote to Fred:

> *It has as many facets as we have attractions for each other*
> *and each one shines more radiantly than the one I saw a*
> *moment ago - just as every new discovery of you - my many-*
> *sided man of God — delights and sets me aglow.*

She told him that Mrs. Cornell thought she and Fred together would be a great asset to the church, and that if he really thought it necessary, she would attend a luncheon with him, otherwise she had work to do. Describing a gown she had bought, she wrote:

> *I want you to like them all — it's such fun to have you care.*
> *I love you more every minute — you wizard. I feel as though*
> *I had always belonged to you. I adore you.*

Then she was off to Syracuse and Saratoga Springs to see relatives and give them the news as she bade them farewell. There was less than a month to make her plans. Cousin Dee had generously decided to give the wedding at the Cosmopolitan Club, and Welthy was quite prepared to let Cousin Dee manage her wedding, if not her life. Welthy had an entirely new future to plan for.

When she returned to New York, Fred was away, and the letters kept flying between them. Welthy:

> *My lover, do your ears burn! You've been talked about,*
> *raved about, dreamed about and loved every since I left you.*
> *I live over the hours again and again - they are my rosary*

truly. I think of nothing else but you . . . I admit my complete capitulation.

Going on to discuss details of their wedding announcement, she made no attempt to conceal her impatience with protocol:

If you don't approve speak by telegram or forever afterward hold your peace! My but it's fussy marrying a Bishop!

She expressed some sympathy for him in informing his sisters, living in his Hingham, Massachusetts home, of his coming remarriage, and suggested that being women they just might be curious to see her:

Of course they are hurt, but they are dead wrong, just as Margaret is.

And then the words that reveal the unspoken anguish of Welthy's life since leaving China:

I haven't touched a piano or sung a note since the war, but think I could even begin to sing again now.

* * *

She had another reason to sing. "Beyond the Moongate" was being very well received, her lively narrative and happy conversational style combining to make a dramatic impact. Newspaper articles about Welthy and Fred now referred to her as an authoress. "We make good copy, don't we?" she wrote to him, pointing out that she, too, had been speaking on Gandhi.

MARRIAGE IN NEW YORK

They were married on June 18th, 1924 by Bishop McDowell. Dr. Thillayampalam from India, whom Fred had sponsored at Columbia University, and Frederika Kiang, for whom Welthy had arranged a scholarship at Vassar, were their attendants, with Percy Jewett Burrell as best man. In a white suit Welthy took her vows before a hundred friends at the Cosmopolitan Club, a setting so unusual for a bishop's wedding that no one, not even Cousin Dee, had arranged for photographs. Rosalie Mayer loved it because there were no sobbing parents and thought Welthy and Fred were "perfect peaches."

When the ceremony was over, Welthy gave her flowers to Helen. Cousin Dee's busy eye observed this, and she snatched the flowers out of Helen's hands, saying they should be in the family. This, in spite of the fact that it was Helen who had made so many of Welthy's arrangements, who rode in the car with her, and who knew how deeply in love Welthy was. "But you didn't cross Cousin Dee," Helen said later. "She was a very imperious old guy."

Helen rode back to the Allerton with Welthy and Fred in the Carey limousine, and helped Welthy finish packing her bags, while Fred went to the Commodore for his things. They drove off to Lake Mohonk Mountain House in upstate New York, looking for all the world like just another middle-aged couple.

It was exactly one hundred years after Abram Honsinger was born. He would approve, Welthy knew. She was happy thinking in terms of centuries, for with Fred's love the touch of eternity had come to her. Welthy was on top of the world.

SIX

FELLOWSHIP, YES, FOLLOWSHIP, NO

LAKE MOHONK, 1924

When the newlyweds reached the Lake Mohonk Mountain House resort that June evening, they were just in time for dinner in the great timbered dining room. Exhausted from the emotion of the wedding ceremony and the preceding days' rush, they ate together in rare, reverent silence, as they looked upon each other fully for the first time as husband and wife. Then, inveterate talkers that they were, they began to relish the events of the day in spiraling detail.

Once settled in their room, Welthy began to prepare herself for her first night of love. "I'd give anything to see you in the bath," Fred suggested. Well, here goes, Welthy thought to herself, grateful for a moment's privacy in extricating herself from a medieval corset before her lover appeared. Fred knew how to love Welthy; he revelled in her pure and powerful body, her perfect skin. And Welthy had been moving towards Fred all her life. Nothing held them back.

By morning they could not bear to part and they started then what remained the cornerstone of their married life, breakfast in bed together, an honoured time of intimate talk that underpinned the day. "They were the best times," said Welthy. Two vibrant personalities had come together, heroes in each other's eyes and arms, discovery enhanced on Welthy's side by the faith that she would find it, and for Fred it was the never dreamed of gift of new life.

Hal Luccock, Welthy's colleague at the magazine, sensed the formidable combination the two would make. He wrote to Fred: "I do know there will be a service whose reach can never be measured that you and Welthy will give in these days ahead, and I well know that is the deepest thing in your hearts."[1]

It was not only their shared high purpose and love that bound Welthy and Fred. They were both wide and hungry readers, each had authored half a dozen books, and both were commanding speakers. Nurtured by strong-willed, caring parents, they were both steeped in Methodism, and had both reached maturity under the influence of Robert Speer, John R. Mott and Harry Emerson Fosdick, the leading liberal churchman of the day in New York. At the point where religion, philosophy and psychology combine, William James was their guiding light.

Fred had first been interested in going to the Philippines, where Welthy had begun her serious study of other educational systems and cultures after leaving China, just prior to Fred's 1918 visit there. He told her that he had been the only non-adult in the Bible class at the High Street Church in Muncie, where the discussions usually turned to deep personal problems; Welthy told of her own early exposure to the adult world at Abram's class meetings. When Fred told Welthy of his profound experience in childhood, so similar to her own father's conversion as a young man, their feeling of belonging to each other soared.

It was a day or two before Welthy realized she had married more than Fred Fisher. Early in life he had begun to keep notes and quotes from his favourite authors, scratchings in a bold hand that he called "a moving record of a good man's constant effort to walk with God." They popped out at the slightest opportunity. He had been born the year Emerson died, and carried a little volume of Emerson in his pocket. To his delight, Welthy had her own favourite Emersonian epigram: "The secret of education lies in respecting the pupil."

Unaffected by the stigma attached to marrying a shorter man, Fred was the tallest man in the world to Welthy, willing to let the sensitive side of his nature show. He could stop to look at a glowworm and ask: "Are you reflected light of God?"

The lovers could not escape the real world for long, even on their honeymoon. The Bishop had not brought his secretary along and certain matters had to be attended to. The novel experience of acting as Fred's secretary was one Welthy quietly resolved to circumnavigate in future, but for the moment she tended to the necessary arrangements for their imminent journey to the Orient.

They went on to Pilgrimthorpe, Fred's home in Hingham, Massachusetts, founded in 1638 by pilgrims, where his two sisters lived in a state of determined skepticism over his new wife long before they met her. Pictures of Edith seemed to face Welthy at every turn in the house and despite her best efforts she was never able to win their hearts; they remained loyal to Edith's memory. His brother Harry, however, was genuinely pleased to see the happiness Fred had found with Welthy.

Disappointed in his sisters' cool reception to Welthy, Fred took his bride off to Cohasset on Cape Cod for a few days, and Welthy was thrilled to burst out of her clothes, literally, after the tension at Pilgrimthorpe, joining Fred skinny-dipping in the warm ocean at dusk. They frolicked on the shore like youngsters, with a fervour that always brought a blush to Welthy's cheeks whenever she recalled those carefree hours.

TO THE ORIENT

Orient-bound, their long train ride west in mid-summer was broken with stops in Chicago and Banff, and a lively southern detour to California, for Cousin Dee had rushed back to Santa Barbara after the wedding to prepare for their command performance at Casa Dorinda. Fred took in the grandeur with quiet disbelief, thoroughly enjoying the company of Robert Bliss, Cousin Dee's distinguished lawyer husband, a man of no great wealth himself.[2]

As for Cousin Dee, Fred remarked: "Why, she should be ruling a state!" She did not conceal her jealousy that Welthy preferred to join the men for conversation after a grand dinner, rather than remain with her hostess and the other women. Welthy had already declared her independence by marrying Fred, and she was prepared to ignore the protocol of etiquette to hear her man talk even if it meant risking Cousin Dee's displeasure.

SHANGHAI, AUGUST 1924

The Fishers sailed from Vancouver, reaching Shanghai in late August, just two months after the wedding, setting the fast pace they would continue to follow. Fred's secretary, Walter Miller, travelled with them, but Helen Krayer had been unable to accompany them because of her father's illness. The luxury of boat travel was the time it allowed to absorb the distance between the culture left behind and the one ahead.

Fred had developed the habit of planned study of great writers while at sea, putting down his own thoughts in large black notebooks. Welthy, too, spent the mornings reading. Afternoons they took rigorous turns around the deck, and at dinnertime discussed a topic agreed upon at breakfast. They were so in love they laughed a lot, and alone in their cabin, their ultimate compatibility had reached "a happy plateau" by the time they arrived at Shanghai. Filled with gratitude for their happiness, they re-entered the Orient with boundless energy and a strong desire to do their best in the work ahead.

Fred was as eager as Welthy to set foot on Chinese soil. She had insisted on stopping in China en route to India, to introduce him to her world as she entered his, and he had been easy to convince. For two months she had been telling him all she knew about religions in China, especially the mystic Taoism she respected, and could scarcely wait to get him beyond the treaty ports, on up the mighty Yangtze where the real beauty of China lay.

There had been significant changes since Welthy's last visit and Fred's two previous ones. Intellectuals had established the Communist Party, Mao Tse-tung among the founding members. After the western powers had refused to give up their special privileges in China or help in reconstruction and training despite Sun Yat-sen's pleading, the Soviet

Union had seen its opportunity to befriend the vast, emerging, bordering nation.

Sun understood from the failure of the 1911 revolt to gain national unity and equality for China that in his semi-feudal, semi-colonial land it would take the involvement of the rural masses to achieve his dream for China. The U.S.S.R. was the only nation ready to help in the massive rural work needed, and the famed Borodin had arrived in Canton to help Sun reorganize the Kuomintang and its military academy along Soviet lines, training Chiang Kai-shek as Sun's successor.

Chinese youth had taken great interest in the Russian Revolution when the Soviets began to assist China, especially when they renounced their extra-territorial rights. The long-simmering Chinese revolution was taking a decided turn to the left, though Welthy had confidence that Chinese common sense and ability to compromise would keep them from going too far left. Sun went up to Peking that year in an unsuccessful attempt to seek a compromise with the northern rulers that would strengthen China in foreign eyes and command respect. His dream of abolishing the unjust treaties and winning equal status among nations was only partly realized before his death from cancer early the following year. To Welthy, and to many Chinese, he remained the father of national unity in China.

HANKOW, PEKING

In Hankow and Peking, Welthy and Fred observed the Mass Education Movement underway, and went round the old Russian concession, its beautiful buildings now being used by the Chinese. Russia's Legation had been raised to an Embassy, and only Russia had an Ambassador in Peking. Welthy saw these as highly important moves towards China on Russia's part, deploring the lack of vision her own country displayed in declining to help with the development of China. To her, rural reconstruction was eminently compatible with the Christian way and should have been embraced by America, as some enlightened missionaries interested in cooperatives and agricultural work were recommending. "Five thousand missionaries working unselfishly for the people, great Mission universities, hospitals scattered throughout the country, the greatest medical college of the world (Peking Union Medical College built with Rockefeller money), even these could not capture the imagination of China as did these friendly acts of one nation to another. They felt instinctively that here was one nation willing to treat them as an equal," she wrote later from India.[3]

Christian organizations had begun to feel great pressure to rid themselves of foreign missionaries and dependency on foreign support. The

1922 China Education Committee Report had urged the use of Chinese architecture in schools, Chinese financing and management. Prior to 1920, no major Christian school had a Chinese head, though Louella Miner had proposed it five years earlier and Welthy had attempted to install one. Despite an illiteracy rate of eighty-five percent among Chinese adults, the former patronizing manner of missionaries was slowly giving way to one of cooperation, of working with the Chinese as equals, as Welthy had done on her own authority years earlier.

BAO-LIN

As Welthy and Fred proceeded across Lake Poyang she regaled him with the most expansive version yet of her 1912 shipwreck, her dramatic gestures nearly leading to another disaster at sea. They reached Da Shen Men gate of Nanchang to the popping of thousands of firecrackers, and there was Gertrude Howe's wise old face prominent among the throngs welcoming Han Wei-lo and her groom. Now Fred understood the strength Welthy had found in that face and the courage it had given her.

In a stylish white dress, flashing a large, white feathered fan in the noon heat, Welthy lived up to the expectations of the school children as they peeked behind the fan to say hello, a game she played with gusto. Her seven orphans appeared in the red hats and scarves she had brought them, to show their appreciation. For Betty (Chen-yi), her beloved first 'adoptee', Welthy reserved her special affection, proudly introducing the beautiful young woman to Fred, who was captivated by her charm. She had graduated from Bao-Lin and was teaching there, a model of Welthy's dream for all Chinese women.

One of the original students, Sally Kiang, was the principal of the school briefly, resigning after her marriage. She was followed by Miriam Nieh, whom Welthy greatly admired. Of Bao-Lin's fifty-two high school graduates, ten had completed college, twelve were still in college, twenty-four were teachers, ten were social workers, ten were married, and one had become a doctor.

As Fred and Welthy gathered with the staff, Welthy could hear one of the teachers, Miss Baker, who was not fond of her, remark: "Why, it's the first time I've heard her be quiet and let others speak!" Welthy conceded some truth to the remark, and remained fascinated by everything Fred said, and others' reaction to him. The Chinese he spoke with were curious about India, especially literacy—was it necessary, and did Indians think so? Fred was the first visitor from India to the area, prompting curious scholars and gentry to come out from behind walls to meet him.

Bao-Lin staged a gala luncheon to honour the Fishers, a celebration always accorded Welthy but rarely other missionaries on return visits, according to Gwei-hsin, mainly because Welthy had kept in touch personally and followed through on plans for each girl. Fred got a low rating when Gwei-hsin overheard him suggest that Welthy should have designed simpler buildings such as they did in India, erroneously concluding that he thought the large, attractive campus too good for the Chinese. Welthy showed him her school with eager pride, and always remembered Fred's reaction, and her deflation and disappointment as he explained why he thought simpler buildings might have been more appropriate. Here their different views of the material world conflicted for the first time. Or was it ill-disguised jealousy at Welthy's accomplishment?

Fred's normally profuse notetaking fell off during the early months of their marriage. A few brief, telling entries appear from Nanchang. Quoting Shelley, he wrote: "Nothing in the world is single; all things, by a law divine, mingle and merge in one another's being;" and O'Shaughnessy: "One man with a song at pleasure may go forth and conquer a crown, and two with a song's new measure can trample an empire down." On a less imperial, more practical theme, he recorded: "The man who takes his work to bed with him sleeps with a thief." Fred was learning how to stay married to his irrepressible wife, and not be robbed.

During those days in Nanchang the only serious episode of discord occurred between the honeymooners, Welthy taking to a separate cot for one night. Whatever she had done, Fred merely said: "I wish you hadn't done that," and Welthy's remorse was sufficient to erase the incident from their minds, overtly at least. She would never reveal what happened, and since they did not quarrel openly or confide their troubles to others, the matter remains a mystery.

They went by junk with Welthy's old cook, half blind by then, on the long river journey to King Teh-chen, the famous porcelain city that so intrigued Welthy. An extra coolie was needed to carry their wooden Carnation Milk box full of one thousand Mexican silver dollars, the standard currency used by foreigners. When Welthy bought seventeen huge pieces of porcelain, Fred saw for the second time another aspect of his wife, one he did not fully understand. To him, her pieces were possessions, and as such should be kept to a minimum; to Welthy they were beautiful expressions of a highly developed culture she loved and wanted to share with all who came to her home, as part of our collective human heritage. Despite that discrepancy of attitudes they began to learn to respect each other's need and laugh whenever the gap got in their way.

JAPAN, MANILA, SINGAPORE, CEYLON

In Japan they saw bookshops everywhere, and were impressed with the new achievements in literacy. In Manila, Singapore and Ceylon, the Bishop and his wife were on display to curious Methodists. On the final stretch of their journey, Fred gave Welthy an object lesson to the effect that nothing is unbearable unless one allows it to be. As their train from south India plodded all day and night through the heat, the screeching of flat wheels dinning into her ears incessantly, irritatingly, he said, "Just get into the rhythm of that squeak. Make it a song." (FBF, 114.) A Honsinger could only agree.

INDIA

The India they returned to still greeted Americans appreciatively for their role in World War I, a role based on idealism, not reward. But the British were criticized for supposedly forcing missionaries to spread propaganda for England or leave, for draining India's resources to supply twenty percent of England's national income, and for slaughtering unarmed and unresisting Hindus wholesale.

Of India's population of three hundred and twenty million, some sixty million individuals belonged to the "depressed classes", outcastes with nothing to lose who were the prime target of missionaries. Christianity had little appeal to the more secure caste Hindus.

Welthy studied in depth the complex society she was entering, and Fred warned her that the many British women she would encounter rarely took interest in things Indian. They usually stuck to their own clubs, which denied admission to Indian women, they played tennis, golf, bridge, rode horses, went on hunting parties and to hill stations, and displayed a galling superiority towards the 'natives'.[4] To American Methodists weaned on a policy of equal rights adopted in the States in 1908, it was irresponsible.

Welthy had seen that insularity among the British in China; now she faced culture shock head on in the imperial capital of their prize colony. But she also knew that it was the British who had introduced modern education to India through government-run schools and colleges, supplemented by extensive missionary education, although it was geared to producing officials to administer the subcontinent, as China's classic education system had also been. The British-developed network of railroads was their other major contribution to India. Ironically, both bequests helped to foster the nationalism then on the rise under Gandhi's leadership.

The old image of an India of splendour and wealth, bejewelled potentates, marble palaces, tigers, elephants, snakes, gold and silk, had left most westerners with an unreal picture. They thought only of the pageantry and exotica, the Indian remaining a faceless member of a lesser breed. Descriptions of India's mystical religion and philosophy heightened that remoteness, augmented as they were by exaggerated reports from phony Indian swamis touring America preying on the gullible. It all left a negative impression on westerners that was much stronger than the realistic regard held by a few for Indian culture.[5] Great changes were underway in India after centuries of political domination from outside and inertia within. Emerson had been the first important American thinker to pay attention to eastern wisdom. But it was Gandhi who made the West begin to take serious notice of India when he emerged on the political horizon, attention that began with ridicule and grew into respect. Fred, and by association, Welthy, were part of those beginnings.

The American Methodists' knowledge of India dated back to their first mission in the old Muslim capital of Oudh (later renamed Lucknow) just prior to the 1857 Mutiny which brought them much suffering. Thoburn had begun mass movements of whole villages into Christianity, his strategy being to move from conversion of individuals out of a wicked environment to the conversion of the environment itself.[6] He was as staunch an ally of the WFMS in India as Stephen L. Baldwin had been in China, recognizing early the importance of women's development.

Welthy's later work in India stemmed from her bond with Thoburn, not only because of his powerful influence on Fred, but as much because of the inspiring example of his sister, Isabella, whom he persuaded to come to India. She was the pioneer woman missionary of the WFMS, the first one to venture out into the wider world, and her work led to the establishment of the Lal Bagh Girls' School in 1870 and Isabella Thoburn (IT) College in 1887, both in Lucknow.[7] To Welthy, she was another Gertrude Howe, and when IT College invited Welthy to serve on its Board of Governors, she accepted readily. As the Bishop's wife she was a good catch, but that particular bishop's wife brought an added dimension to the task. Lucknow had become the focus of her hope for India.

CALCUTTA, 1924 TO 1930

In Calcutta, Fred presided over a well-developed network of Methodist institutions — the self-supporting Thoburn Church and Calcutta Boys' School; a nearly self-supporting Calcutta Girls' High School; and the Queen's Hill Girl's School in Darjeeling, which catered to Anglo-Indian and foreign students. There were also an Industrial Home, the Seamen's Mission in Kidderpore, the Lee Memorial Mission for girls, various day schools, the Mission house and business office, and the Collins Institute for five hundred Bengali boys. All the staff of these institutions came under Fred's administration, his area of responsibility extending far beyond Calcutta, throughout northeast India and all of Burma. Welthy knew if she was going to see her husband, she must be ready to travel on exhausting journeys throughout his conference, composing her own special survival song for each mode of transportation they encountered.

The Fishers were a formidable team, and Welthy was very much the Bishop's wife. She gave British garden parties, but included Indians, studied Indian culture, gave speeches, and made solid friendships with accomplished Indian women. Calcutta in the 1920's was the centre of a cosmopolitan commercial, political and cultural life, a sharp contrast with the poverty all around.

Their home was a six-room apartment in the Methodist headquarters at 3 Middleton Street, near Chowringhee, Calcutta's main street. Part of the space was an office for Fred and his secretary, and the large, high-ceilinged drawing rooms, with concrete floors painted red, served as a public reception area for their steady flow of guests and visitors. Their day began at 5:30 a.m. with *chota hazri* served in their giant six-foot bed under a mosquito net, while a servant boy in the hallway pulled the cord of their *punkah* back and forth endlessly to keep the hot air circulating. At Fred's insistence, they read silently until breakfast arrived at 7:00, when a bursting Welthy could commence verbal communication using their new pet names for each other, Han and Bohn. By her own choice, living his life on his terms, she came to understand how the silence enhanced what they had to say to each other.

Mornings they each tended to their business, Welthy looking to household matters and menus, afternoons they both tapped out reams on their portable typewriters, back under the mosquito net, and it was a rare evening when they were not receiving guests or colleagues. Their door was always open. At the end of each day they wandered across the *maidan* to *lowa kana* (literally, eat the air) before crawling back in under the stifling net, occasionally thinking with longing of ice cream sodas. However, they knew very well how privileged they were to be situated so comfortably amongst the elite of Calcutta, as part of an established Methodist show of prestige to educated Indians and the ruling British community, their episcopal trappings designed to compete for attention. Nevertheless, their next-door neighbour, the Maharajah of Burdwan, outdid them by a good measure, and the Viceroy's sumptuous palace was close by.

Theirs was a household run by a hierarchy of servants, familiar to Welthy from her years of managing servants in China. But here the distinctions of caste added complexity. Welthy could not singlehandedly abolish caste overnight, nor could the household function without the servants if she and Fred were to do their work. She read all she could on the ancient structure of caste, why and how it had evolved, and made her decision to live with the reality for the present. "It is the custom of the country to subdivide the work into many tasks," she wrote, "both because of caste restrictions and in order to employ as many helpers as possible." With no refrigerator, the cook had to shop daily, going from shop to shop during the morning hours, while the sweeper cleaned the bathrooms, the *dhobi* did laundry, and the bearer oversaw the household and served the meals.

Welthy's training in Cousin Dee's parlour had prepared her well for her new role and she quickly became a distinguished, if reluctant, social hostess. What she and Fred really wanted was the company of Indians who were thinking and planning a future of equal rights for all. Guided by Fred, she set herself a course of study of the social reform efforts in India, to discover for herself what progress had already been achieved and what the barriers were.

WELTHY'S INDIAN EDUCATION BEGINS

Welthy came face to face with the immensity of Indian history and culture, feeling once again the humbling effect of confronting an ancient wisdom gathered over four thousand years. She felt like the young woman arriving in China, profoundly aware of her ignorance. High purpose alone would never be enough to sustain a cooperative effort with Indians in lifting up the lowest of their people. She would have to understand how they thought and why.

Five basic reform movements stood out: the Brahmo Somaj, a rationalistic group of educated, middle class Bengalis, founded by Raja Ram Mohim Roy; the Arya Somaj, a group also influenced by western thought as it modified their own Vedic wisdom; the Rama Krishna Mission, a service organization based on mystical guidance; Rabindranath Tagore's movement of aesthetic, cultural renewal aiming at harmony of eastern and western thought and action; and Gandhi's spiritually-based national movement of nonviolence.[8]

Tagore's ideas had particular appeal for her, especially since his *Visvabharati* had been inaugurated at Santiniketan not far from Calcutta that year, and his efforts to blend the best of East and West were being much talked about in Calcutta. His passion for freedom spoke strongly to her; he, too, had been in China in 1924, pleading eloquently for the human soul to be rescued from the dungeon of the machine. "Proclaim the spirit of man and prove that it lies not in machine-guns and cleverness, but in a simple faith," he implored.[9] While Welthy studied, Fred was asking himself hard questions about his faith. He knew that socialism aimed to save the individual by regenerating society, the great experiment begun in Russia, while Christianity aimed to save society by regenerating the individual.

It would take a vast spiritual movement in India to reach her people, a movement outside of organized Christian forces and within Hinduism, Buddhism and Mohammedanism, a movement such as Gandhi's, which drew idealism from Christ's very principles. It would not do to continue 'de-nationalizing' Indians with a foreign brand of religion, making of them a different sort of caste, full of pride and imitation of western ways. Christ was a living ideal at work in the world leading social movements. Fred knew that the Christian advance could never be measured by the number of baptisms per year.

While foreign missions were being attacked by many observers, travellers, writers and thinkers both within and without the church, Fred became more and more convinced that missions would do well to heed Gandhi's recipe for the naturalization of Christianity in India: live more like Christ and study other religions to gain a more sympathetic approach towards them. To Fred this meant that missionaries must be free from racial or national prejudice, from religious conceit, from a limited belief in Christ, and especially from administrative control. In short, they must be let loose to fulfil their inherent responsibility. Would his church be willing to place such faith in its workers?

Fred wanted Indians placed at the head of the Methodist schools and colleges; he wanted to develop Indian-based support for these institutions. With large cuts in his episcopal budget in those years, the very survival of the work meant finding new resources overnight, and new ways of operating. He organized a conference with the theme "Building the Indian Church", with women chairing several of the sessions.

He ran into administrative hot water with his board in New York by compensating for some of the immediate drastic effects of the budget cut out of his own pocket, then trying to raise funds to reimburse the cost, in a reversal of the usual process. Reprimanded, he decided to concentrate his energies on his spiritual ministry, the reason he came to India. The burden of administrative and financial matters bore too heavily on him under a system controlled from New York. He was also advised by his friend Sudhakanta Roychoudhury, Tagore's assistant, not to let his political feelings about realities in India interfere with his spiritual mission, advice he respected.

Welthy accompanied him as much as possible on his strenuous travels. In Lucknow she attended her first meeting of IT College, where she noted in her diary that the treasurer was "as rattle-brained as she looks amidst a three hundred and sixty lak debt." Everywhere the talk was about "the cut" in the budget of each Methodist institution. She accepted invitations to speak at every stop, including the Moslem men's university at Aligargh, toured factories and settlement work with Fred, and kept reading history. After meetings that lasted all evening, they delighted in midnight meals alone together in the soft Indian moonlight.

She was particularly eager to meet Sam Higgenbottom, the pioneer agricultural missionary in India, and to walk through some of his reclaimed farmland. He sought Fred's help in achieving union of the Methodists and Presbyterians, and increasing Indian representation in the very practical work of the Allahabad Agricultural Institute,[10] winning Welthy's vote of confidence. "Fascinating personality, and I fear his unattractive wife is jealous of it," Welthy noted wickedly, a reminder of the hazards of marriage to an outstanding man.

Fred's anxieties over a bishop's role in India did not all stem from spiritual questions. His doctor told Welthy clearly that she should get Fred out of the humid climate of Bengal's lowlands, that his repeated attacks of arthritis were likely to affect his heart and his joints could permanently stiffen.[11] Diet and exercise were inadequate to combat his overactive thyroid gland, the trigger of both his ambitious energy and his illness. That disease-prone personality must at times have presented Welthy with daily challenges to harmonious living. Fred's shack in the cool, dry air of Darjeeling offered a temporary haven in which to reflect on his future, but more particularly to prepare themselves for the major journey of their lives. It began with a pilgrimage of their own into the heights of the universe.

THE HIMALAYAS, 1925

In the loveliest of her books, "The Top of the World", Welthy told of that Himalayan adventure, of how they zig-zagged up through the mountains on horseback, his, 'The Intelligent One', hers, as it happened, 'The Foolish One', accompanied by a corps of bearers. At the peak of their upward procession, "we were mysteriously in the hands of a force greater and more elemental and more terrible than we had realized. Four days we have sat in the forceful hands of mystical elemental nature," as they ran out for each glimpse of a brilliant blue sky before the clouds closed in again. Making their way down the narrow paths alongside a huge abyss, avalanche damage everywhere witnessing to the destructive force of the elements, Welthy was sure "the pioneers of the covered wagon had no harder day. Even Douglas Fairbanks would have had a thrill".

The *Rome Daily Sentinel* proudly reported Welthy's "sonata" from the mountaintop in a lengthy editorial on an "exceptional traveller wholly in love with the world wherever she finds it. A very versatile wife for a bishop is this daughter of Rome," the article concluded. Welthy was equally proud of the recognition, noting: "How father and mother would have thrilled and how Mabel would have loved it. I am happy to have the name of Honsinger remembered, and I want to do more and more to make it known and loved in my own native town." *The Nashville Banner* found the book "clear as crystal and fragrant as the winds," while *The Christian Advocate* referred to her "racy language and winsome directness." The photographs by Welthy won appreciation from *The Boston Evening Transcript*: "With their bodily eyes very few . . . will see this vision splendid. But books like this bring them . . . within the range of that inward vision which knows neither disappointment nor disillusion."

As Welthy and Fred left the "heights of God and went down toward the valley of mankind," for days there was no sign of life, their companions the horizon of five mountains. "Not a tree trunk could be seen, not a tree stood alone, but all seemed to need the companionship of the others in this lovely silent forest, and so the limbs reached out and touched each other, vines intertwined them and the soft green moss covered them all so they became as one family. For tenderness, for sympathy, for life, we preferred the valley of men," she declared.

During their descent through a riot of rhododendron trees with giant magenta, pink, carmine and white blossoms in full bloom, Welthy's incompatability with 'The Foolish One' literally brought her down to earth. She was thrown over his head, breaking an ankle, and had to wait hours for a carpenter to make a special chair, of her own design, in which fourteen coolies carried her down the rest of the way to Ghoom. It was one of her more fateful fractures, preventing her from taking part in an opportunity just ahead.

Welthy often indulged in comic relief in the privacy of her diary after tiring days with some of the missionaries they encountered in the valley of humans. One wife "looks exactly like Mother Goose and talks like her, very prim and purses her lips, a monologist. She would be perfect going up in the air on a broom," she suggested.

CALCUTTA, 1925

On their return to Calcutta, a foot below sea level, Fred became so ill that Welthy took him back up to his one-room shack in the hills, stopping in Darjeeling for provisions. Again her reaction to fellow travellers at the Mount Everest Hotel found expression in her diary: "The type of people at the hotel are bleached blondes, plucked eyebrows, salved lips, skirts to knées—parasites—and the men are monocled sisters." She read detective stories to distract herself from self-righteousness and anxiety over Fred's condition. These arthritic flareups recurred frequently, adding stress to an already stressful life, and testing the strength of a young marriage.

Fred made one trip to Lucknow without Welthy that first year, travelling by Ford, elephant and foot to visit remote villages, writing to her during a lengthy train stop where a bridge had been washed out. With no dining car or restaurant, he made do with oranges, peanuts and cold coffee whitened with toothpaste, while remembering the great days of their first year and dreaming of their future. He wrote to her:

> *Sometimes the heat and toil make us weary, but you make me glad and joyful. Yes, people do think we are too enthusiastic, but let them. We'll keep the thrill, eh? Just think that Welthy Honsinger really married me! And loves me and wants to live with me. Let critics 'crit'—we'll just go on working, loving, serving, playing. We've got to play more. Eh? Let's do it.*[12]

His next letter announced:

> *I love you Welthy . . . and I shall love you until Heaven and beyond. My Welthy, my ideal woman, author, graceful personality, speaker and lover. Here's my whole heart and life at your feet.*[13]

Welthy's impatience with the protocol of episcopal life was a problem that was always present. Fred's role demanded constant acceptance of difficult duties by both of them. It was not a role Fred could relinquish quickly, but they had already begun discussing his resignation as early as 1925. On one occasion, Welthy lay down on the floor of their bedroom to think for herself about it, independent thinking that was impossible in the bed they shared. Fred came into the room and joined her on the floor, and they agreed he would resign in 1926 or 1928, whichever seemed wiser. He weighed his decision carefully. His notes during this period were full of information and thoughts on bishops, including all aspects of their tenure, retirement, age, duties, goals, and his analysis of the length of service of every Methodist bishop in history.[14]

TAGORE, GANDHI, ANDREWS AND FISHER AT SANTINIKETAN

Fred's mind was pulled away from his own problem by a weekend visit to Santiniketan to meet again with Tagore, known as *Gurudev* spending many hours in private discussion with him and C.F. Andrews, the British priest who gave up his Anglican ordination to serve India as a simple

Christian. For two rich hours, they were joined by Gandhi, for Andrews was affectionately known as 'The Hyphen' who could bridge the thinking of Tagore and Gandhi, the two wise men who had influenced him most deeply and with whom he was closest. As Tagore put it, The Hyphen stood for brotherly love as opposed to the hymen of conjugal love.[15]

Fred had known Andrews since they both arrived in India in 1904 and from their mutual interest in industrial relations. He was just back from South Africa where he had frequently gone to advance the rights of Indians. Gandhi and Fred had been in correspondence regarding South Africa, and the discussion of the quartet turned to that continuing thorn in India's pride.

At sunset the four set off for a cross-country walk, Gandhi in homespun with a crude walking stick twice his height, Andrews in a thin Bengali shirt with tails flying in the breeze, Tagore in a flowing gown, and Fred with the walking stick Lord Reading, the Viceroy, had given him. "I believe Gandhi could beat us all," said Fred. "That little giant's ninety pounds has every muscle counted and at work. He likes to talk while he walks, in the rhythm of it, but the poet likes to stride on alone, so I walked with Gandhi." (TLC, 203.)

When Fred told Gandhi he had accepted an invitation to visit Australia soon, Gandhi urged him to cross to the other side of the sea to study the Indian situation in Africa, where Gandhi had begun his struggle against racial injustice. Gandhi saw Fred as an impartial observer, neither British nor Indian, with a breadth of vision which would allow him to assess the situation accurately. It was not a request Fred could refuse.

Though she had been invited to Santiniketan, Welthy missed that mighty assembly because of her broken ankle, a loss she always regretted. However she got a full verbatim account when Fred returned, brimming over with a fresh sense of challenge and stimulation. She agreed immediately to the African journey, and to their Australian homework was added another continental history to be absorbed.

TO AUSTRALIA, JUNE 1925

Welthy scolded herself for not having done more preparatory work in Darjeeling. "I must learn to work faster, that is evident." From Scott's "History of Australia" she noted that "the wrongdoings of the white man had extinguished homo Tasmanians completely by 1860. The rapid development of Australia was possible because aboriginals were not warlike, had no arts or animals, no pottery, no cultivation of soil, or homes." Armed also with books on chess and Antarctic exploration, and a fine meal at the Metropole in Colombo, they sailed with ten others on the S.S. Devanah in mid-June, 1925.

"We sit at the Chief Officer's table and Fred sings the Hallelujah Chorus each meal, because his seat is next to the end of the table which is empty, as well as the seat opposite him, so he doesn't *have* to talk, the sinner." She knew they were thought snobbish for not playing mahjongg and bridge with the others, but their minds were on the people and problems they would be meeting and speeches they would be making.

FREEMANTLE, PERTH, ADELAIDE, MELBOURNE

C.F. Andrews had paved the way for Fred with the Australian Foreign Ministry and Commonwealth officials, writing that "Bishop Fisher has brought humanity into our racial problems as few living personalities have done."

In Canberra Fred joined the notables in meeting the Admiral of the U.S. Fleet, some fifty-five ships with forty thousand sailors then in Australia's harbours. Not supportive of the military, the Labour Government did not welcome the fleet as such, Welthy noted, but did entertain the officers. During non-stop meetings, receptions and speech-making, Welthy speaking almost as much as Fred, she bristled with disgust at each mention of the "white Australia" policy of the British. "British dinners are at best an awkward affair. They think we are longing to be paid the compliment that we are like them." The British no doubt found Welthy and Fred naive in their enthusiasm and belief in change.

Welthy was writing a series of articles for *The Classmate* entitled "Under The Southern Cross", beginning with a lively geography lesson about upside down stars, with the Lady in the Moon looking down instead of up. The beauty of the Southern Cross constellation was the crown of her journey. She reported that Henry Ford's autobiography was the most popular book in Australia. But Welthy and Fred's favourite memory of Australia, she wrote, was "the warm hearts and open minds of your students." They climbed Mount Lofty with students, discussed racial problems with them, listened, laughed, learned.

Fred studied industrial and social policies of Australia, and talked about India, Gandhi and imperialism, getting very good press coverage. One paper reported that a visit intended as a health holiday had turned into one of international significance, presenting Fred's view that the destiny of the world now rested on the shoulders of the English-speaking nations in some ways, that their power should be regarded as stewardship, so that they served, not dominated others. The two criteria for judging a nation, according to Fred, were how it treated women and how it treated the lowest strata of society. As for organized Christianity, "the non-Christian people of the East did not understand a Methodist Jesus, or an Anglican Christ, or a Roman Catholic or a Presbyterian one, but a Christ who came to save the world and suffered for it."[16] Fred also spoke in favour of dominion status for India rather than complete independence, and about General Feng in China.

Australians used to bishops in gaiters and apron were uncertain how to treat a Methodist bishop who dressed like everyone else. His visit was seen as a peaceful promotion of understanding at a time when the American fleet was demonstrating naval power. "And we liked Mrs. Fisher just as much," one report said, "and saw in her the best type of 'college woman', a type that America alone produces. Being also a wise woman she allowed the spotlight to rest mainly on her husband, though now and then there were flashes of independent thought that made us feel that even a bishop is molded by his wife."[17]

The Australian Methodists found Fred "strong and friendly, with a widely roaming mind that ever knew the direction it was taking, a man of broad culture and of a daring mind, disciplined by experience to practical use. Yet with it all there was a gentle humility which softened even the most challenging and critical thing he said, and made us feel that he came to learn." Welthy felt she could not have described her husband better.

In Tasmania they visited the huge sheep ranches run by well-educated men living the gracious life in large homes. What Welthy liked least of all in Australia were the old penal colonies of Botany Bay and Port Arthur, where English criminals had been sent in former times for even the most minor crimes, her outrage leading her to read all she could find about that cruel period. "We think in giving up penal colonies we have given up all cruelty and have become more human and Christian," she wrote, "forgetting the child labour and race injustices which are stirring up as much hatred as ever burned in the breast of innocent men who spent a lifetime in the tortures of penal settlements."

Welthy was eager to see the aborigines of Dravidian stock that Darwin had studied in 1836, and found them at a desert outpost called "Fisher" where they came to beg coins and clothes from passengers. She felt great pity for the slowly dying group, and disappointment in their culture, much less developed than that of the Maori of New Zealand. She noted that Darwin had discovered, but not explained their hopelessness.

In her articles for young people she wrote about Australian birds, telling their legends. She traced the development of sheep breeds in Australia, described life on a ranch, the growing of alfalfa, and told how native-born Australians still spoke wistfully of "home", meaning England,

and her delight when meeting a real Australian who thought of the country's future in Australian not British terms.

At a Melbourne reception for the American Admiral, Welthy presented "a striking figure in black brocaded material trimmed with white fur and cropped with the same. She wore a large black velvet hat with a long feather at the side." Such social page interest pleased Welthy; she wanted women to find her attractive in the hope that what she had to say might also appeal, though she was not always sure of herself in Fred's territory. "I made fifteen minutes worth of feeble remarks and decided *never again.*"

At a farewell lunch Fred proposed a World Conference of Methodism to mark the two hundred years since Wesley's first conference, and Welthy's farewell was a stirring speech on women's uplift to six hundred of the Women's League of Churches, proposing a world federation of Christian women and suggesting Australia as the first meeting place.[18]

They had seen Australia from coast to coast, met its politicians and private citizens, toured factories and spoken at countless gatherings — the equivalent of a modern political campaign in miles travelled, people met and ideas shared. Welthy was overwhelmed by the appreciation the church women showed her. "I felt humbled," she said, "but I loved it."

TO AFRICA, AUGUST 1925

August 19th, 1925, the Fishers set sail aboard the S. S. Ulysses from Adelaide with forty-three other passengers on the journey to Africa of six thousand, two hundred and seventy-nine miles, Welthy logging every detail. They decided to take specific subjects for dinner table talk and stick to them, Fred trying to teach concentration of the expansive mind to Welthy. Twenty-two hundred calories per day was their limit, plus a walk of three miles around the deck and exercise in their cabin. Welthy loved the company of the "floating kings of sea air", a family of albatrosses with eight-foot wingspans gliding alongside the Ulysses as she read Darwin's "Voyage of the Beagle".

At their table for two, arranged with difficulty by Welthy, they revelled in each other's company after the rigorous round in Australia, and turned their minds to Fred's mission in Africa — to assess the situation of Indians there. Welthy completed ten articles for her series, and they both managed to escape from their fellow passengers for the main part. "Fred's policy," she noted "is *never* to speak to the British first, and after their first attempt at friendliness to be very reserved."

That was probably the only time either of them seriously attempted to repress their spontaneous American friendliness, their pride too often wounded by British coolness, as they tried to be more British than the

British. By the time they reached Durban two weeks later Fred was scarcely able to walk from exposure to the humidity, though he had written a torrent of administrative letters and Sunday school lessons.

DURBAN, PRETORIA, RHODESIA, ZANZIBAR, NATAL, PHOENIX

Fred had been well briefed by Charlie Andrews in planning his survey of the Indian situation, then at a critical point pending a decision on the anti-Asiatic Bill. In Durban, Pretoria, Rhodesia, Zanzibar, Natal, and at the Tolstoy Colony founded by Gandhi at Phoenix, where his son Manilal lived, Fred consulted mayors, city councillors, legislators, professors, clergymen, YWCA and YMCA workers, students, merchants, Indian groups and writers.

Welthy looked for the legends and folk tales that gave meaning to African lives, the myths of identity, and when Fred questioned whether he truly had a message for an assembled group of six hundred black Christian villagers, Welthy reassured him. "You never talk down to them," she advised. "They may not get the full significance of your words, but they never mistake your spirit. They look you in the eye, and by the time you have finished the benediction, they have grasped something of your message." (FBF, 183.)

Indians were allowed in hotels only as servants. They had to sit in the rear of trains and trams, and were banned from English-speaking churches. The indentured labourers had originally come across the sea on contracts they could not read, signed by thumbprint, and were forever at the mercy of the bosses. "The so-called Christian government is the worst offender," wrote Fred, confirming Andrews' information about an attitude that was driving Christian Indians out of church.

In Johannesburg, Welthy was deeply impressed by hearing native Africans filing into church, singing as they entered, "their tremendous bass voices the great organ pipe that held them all to the key." Even the ushers sang. Everyone sang during the collection, and in that self-organizing group requiring no leader, she saw a vision of the possible.

Gandhi had written about his soul-shattering experience of being thrown off African trains for his colour, humiliation that changed the course of history, as the nervous young lawyer was transformed, almost overnight, into a man of action. He took up the cause of the poorest of the indentured Indians, lured to Africa with promises of land and liberty, and of the traders that had followed them. Now the British wanted to deport them and deny their families admission, for they were becoming educated and starting to compete economically with the white man.

CAPETOWN

While Fred visited the Prime Minister, Welthy went down into the gold mines, where conditions were so despicable her diary sizzles with reaction to what she found:

> *. . . hateful compounds of Cecil Rhodes and his kind, whose gold-lusty brains devised them to prevent gold theft, where thousands of miners were forced to live forty to a room, herded away from their families, working for the lowest wages and two meals a day . . . a situation contributing to the deterioration of the race, not their uplift. The Bishop and all the other missionaries sailed into me with a eulogy of praise for the charitable mine owners (the Chamber of Mines who own the town, white and native, soul and body). It devitalizes, degrades, tears down all that the missionaries build up. Yet these very missionaries fawn before the owners as if they were altruists and the missionaries the receivers of charity. They are singing songs with the blacks on Sunday, teaching them a little Bible on Thursday, and every day thundering forth eulogies of the mine owners. Seven thousand feet below the surface of the city, the soul of the black man is dying, and family life – the only thing that will make a race – is being ruthlessly destroyed.*[19]

Welthy could not get away from Capetown fast enough. She set about writing a series of articles on the African trip in the form of "Letters to Aunt Dorinda", letters that began with gaiety but could not conceal her increasing sense of shock. They explored her developing awareness of economic and political realities. Welthy's compassion crystallized then and there, as Gandhi's resolve had:

> *As I stood on the rim of the great diamond hole, Aunt Dorinda, and looked out on the fields covered with drying clay that would soon yield up the sparkling gems you love so well, I kept saying: 'It's blacker than the Black Hole of Calcutta.' The diamond and gold fields of South Africa are a nightmare to me. I see the glittering gold; I see buckets of diamonds refracting all the colours of the rainbow in each tiny facet; I see the happiness of every girl's face around the world as she looks down at the solitaire on her left hand, but behind it all I see the black man of Africa who has been cast into a hole to produce these glittering beauties. He has long since learned how to hold up the production of diamonds to keep up the price. Isn't it strange that the*

scarce thing has become the most priceless and greatest to be desired? Why can't the rare virtues and graces be made so desirable?

No 'native' may own land or his house. He is a renter and will remain so all his life . . . he is a child, surrounded by circumstances which will keep him a child and make it impossible for him ever to grow up.

Impressed by Africa's vastness, and considering the over-crowded miners' compounds, she wrote: "Two hundred thousand people seem like a few stars in the sky of a dark night. Africa's people have been so few and their lands so limitless that there has been no need for intensive cultivation. When one plot of land wore out, the tribes would migrate to fresh territory; they have left no abiding civilization behind them. How much of our civilization do you suppose our tribal forbears owe to the necessity of living within narrow limits and of living *with* their neighbours?"

VICTORIA FALLS

Welthy recovered her spirit at Victoria Falls. "I sailed up the Zambesi in a tiny steamboat, but Livingstone was obliged to sail in a tree trunk with a place carved out large enough for him to sit in. He dodged ugly crocodiles and uglier black fever. He dodged misunderstanding and distrust more deadly than wild animals. The very opportunity of looking at these Falls was paid by his life. His sacrifice and daring beyond belief is a constant challenge to me. Every tree seems to speak of him. I was amazed to find that it was not his mad desire to find the sources of the Nile that kept him so long in Africa. It was this wicked slave trade . . . his first business in Parliament in England was to strike a fatal blow at this trade in human beings."

She added: "There is an alluring idealism about America that no other country seems to satisfy. Away up here in the very heart of Africa, my own native land calls me. I love her." Her need echoed her homesickness for America after long years in China.

UMTALI

At Umtali, in Rhodesia, Welthy noted that the missionaries did not speak the native language and some would not permit a black man in their house for fear the British would not respect them. But even worse, one of her own countrymen had expressed the same conviction of white superiority and opposition to Asian immigration to America, and to missionary efforts in the Orient in general.

As they sailed for India in mid-October, Welthy wrote: "We leave with no regrets this whole continent of Africa where Christians join wholeheartedly in dealing out the greatest injustices to non-Christians that we have ever seen. Even our Bishop says that American Negroes are no good as missionaries, that '*all they have in common is colour!'* The greatest blow I have received in Africa is the unchristian Christianity. My faith in it as organized is all gone. It is a sombre, dull, hard, cruel, selfish and militaristic religion, and so far from the lovely Christ as darkness is from the mid-day sun."

RETURN TO INDIA, 1925

Welthy's pessimism is explained by her recorded statistic of having travelled seventy-two thousand miles with Fred in the first fifteen months of their marriage. Beside that note is her own record of twenty-one years as the average length of service for Methodist bishops; Fred had only five to his credit. There were miles and miles to go, for Welthy and Fred together, and Welthy alone, to recover her optimism.

Before tackling his report, Fred tended to his administrative problems in correspondence to New York, the endlessly vexing personnel matters, finding replacements for two deceased heads of institutions, urging the selection of individuals with a modern social vision, pleading for a deaconess with a calm disposition, and explaining the vast difficulty of operating with people away on long furloughs. It was a colossal amount of administrative detail which would have been better handled by a different mind and personality than Fred's, but as long as he remained a bishop the burden was his.

CALCUTTA, NOVEMBER 1925

On their return to India Fred was busy moving about in connection with his African trip, consulting with Charlie Andrews immediately and in early November presented his report[20] to Lord Reading at Simla. "Three million Caucasians have taken possession of fifty million blacks, determined to maintain white supremacy," Fred wrote. He described in detail the situation of the hundred and sixty-thousand Indians restricted in every important aspect of living, while the anti-Asiatic bill was before Parliament. He pointed out that such a direct attack on Indians would prove an indirect attack to whites in the rest of the world by making martyrs of Indians.

The Calcutta Guardian commented that "the diffidence which hinders many non-British missionaries in Europe and America from taking a lively interest in a conflict which is confined to Britishers and Indians, even though Christian principles be at stake, did not deter the Bishop from openly avowing concern . . . and set an example which should be followed by all Christians, irrespective of nationality." The writer urged adoption of Fred's report.[21]

WELTHY BEFRIENDS INDIAN WOMEN LEADERS

Welthy was speaking on Australia, singing at Thoburn Church, and receiving Chinese visitors. She found her own way into the emerging Indian women's movement, which was part of the larger national struggle together with men to fight their imperial oppressor.[22] She had a strong new friend in Sarala Devi, Tagore's niece, a vigorously anti-British Brahmo Samaj editor who invited Welthy to join her *Mahamandal.* Sarala Devi in turn came to Thoburn to speak on prohibition, deploring the British custom of drinking alcohol in a country with a traditional religious belief against drink. At the formative meeting of the All India Women's Conference (AIWC) in 1926, Welthy heard Devi claim the future for Indian women, too long intellectually underfed and in a state of senselessness.

The fact that less than seven percent of India's women were literate was not known then. A few women's increasing political awareness made them natural leaders of women's organizations, and one by one the issues of serious oppression of Indian women came to light, with child marriage the central issue that had eluded reform efforts.

Welthy kept listening, studying and making friends. Among the women she befriended were Urmila Devi, one of Gandhi's close retinue, whose brother later became the first Indian Viceroy; Kamaladevi Chattopadhya, founder of the Congress Socialist Party and key organizer of the AIWC; and Sarojini Chattopadhya Naidu, the poet/politician whose weak heart was large enough to embrace all the issues of oppression as she moved beyond caste and home to be the first Indian woman in active politics. These women were powerful influences in Welthy's life that came and went all too quickly as she was pulled back into her role as the bishop's wife.[23]

* * *

As wife and lover she missed Fred terribly during their first long separation of eight days. Finally his train pulled in to Howrah Station and "never in all my life did Bon look so radiant, so noble, so magnificent. I fell in love with him all over again. I felt twenty years younger. We spent the morning (in bed) talking, talking, talking." She and Fred went hunting for picture frames so he could have all her photos with him on his next visit to the Viceroy, wanting her moral support, and then Welthy was alone again. "The wind at night is cool, and my lover is nowhere to be found!" she lamented in the lonely house, dramatizing the moment for herself.

Applying the axiom of David Starr Jordan, she caught up with Fred at Jubbalpore. "Wisdom is knowing what to do next. Skill is knowing how to do it. Virtue is *doing* it." Doing it could well be Welthy's motto.

Fred spoke on "Modern Racial Adjustments" at a reception in Jubbulpore, showing how the missionaries tried to please the British rather than the Indians, to the great distress of the British present, though Welthy thought he had been quite mild — even including a few American sins. Two days later Fred was informed by a representative of the British Commissioner that he was persona non grata in the district for speaking heresy within the British empire. In her next talk, Welthy presented her equally strong views under the title 'Rediscovery of Jesus', her indirect, non-confrontational approach striking a more acceptable balance, softening Fred's stance.

One of the Fishers' regular visitors in Calcutta was Sudhakanta Roychoudhury, former librarian at Santiniketan, who wanted to remain a Hindu yet follow Christ's way, and asked Fred's help. In one of his more unorthodox arrangements Fred consecrated and supported him for experimental social service work with Tagore. Sudhakanta spent many hours with the Fishers, expressing concern that Fred would be too political and not hold to the spiritual side of Indians, a fear Welthy did not share, though she respected Sudhakanta's caution.

CAWNPORE, DECEMBER 1925

In early December, 1925 they were in Cawnpore to observe the All India Congress under a huge colourfully painted *pandal*, the bishop unable to make a sharp delineation between religion and politics, as Gandhi himself could not do. When the Mahatma arrived, the mass of people rose in utter silence until he was seated. The most impressive speakers were those freedom fighters with credentials of several years in prison, and of them all, Sarojini Naidu, the newly elected President of the Congress, had the greatest command — another of Welthy's genuine heroines with whom she became great friends over the years. Welthy also saw that the rest of the women attending the Congress were kept in a special *purdah* section, partitioned behind a tarpaulin, separated from everyone else.

She also met Madelaine Slade (known in India as Mira Behn), the English admiral's daughter who had recently arrived amidst much publicity. To Welthy's skeptical eye, she looked thin and unadjusted, wandering about like a lost soul in white homespun. It took Welthy several years to overcome her reflex reaction against the British, to transcend the slights she and Fred had felt personally and nationally, and come to know and admire Mira Behn.

FIRST MEETING WITH GANDHI

Despite the throngs clamouring to see Gandhi, he sent Urmila Devi to bring Welthy to his tent, her growing reputation having preceded her. Gandhi, who had considered retiring to the hills to meditate and study for the rest of his life, could not turn his back on the active struggle around the large moral issues of the day. He had decided to concentrate his efforts on *Swaraj* from within, preparing his people to be free, and had established the All-India Spinners' Association to restore decent economic life to the villages through decentralized industries. It was a concept much ridiculed by elite, educated Indians, in part because Gandhi spoke of it in the common language of the people, not the scientific language of the educated.

Though it was a Monday, Gandhi's day of silence, Urmila Devi assured Welthy that Gandhi wanted to see her. As she entered, he rose from the floor, took Welthy's hand in both of his, and "gave me a smile of welcome that lasted through the years." He sat on a white covered pad in an otherwise bare room, except for his spinning wheel, a pile of books and papers. He pencilled a note and handed it to her with a mischievous twinkle in his eye that put her at ease. "You may speak but I may not," it read.

"So I sat down on the other white covered pad which completed the room's furnishings. I spoke a sentence or two about South Africa and Manilal, then was silent. The atmosphere of this room was too richly meditative for speech. I was there perhaps for an hour. Now and then Gandhi would spin, now and then open a book and read, now and then would close his eyes. From that moment I never thought of the Mahatma as little. Frail as he was through much fasting, you felt his towering power when his eyes looked straight through you and looked for truth. Yonder in the huge *pandal* the session of the Congress was proceeding but the greatest power behind it and permeating through it sat here, now spinning, now praying — in silence. After a while I rose, took his hand again, he breathed into my spirit another warm smile, and I returned to the *pandal*."[24]

CALCUTTA

On return to Calcutta, Welthy wrote in her diary: "I believe that we have got to renounce something or do something to make a change in our own living in order to make the Indians believe we are in earnest.

Perhaps it is to give up our beautiful house," the perquisite of their position. Or should they give up the position altogether?

Welthy had also met Tagore earlier in the year in his Calcutta home, and later heard him speak eloquently at a world council of religions on his ideal of tolerance of all cultures and religions in preparation for future world cooperation. Fred had taken a step toward that cooperation in appointing a missionary to interpret Christianity at Santiniketan. Tagore had read to Fred his "Broken Prayer to Jesus", which speaks of the "expectation of the great pain of thy coming into my life." Deeply moved, Fred said Tagore had caught Christ's real meaning—the suffering, sacrifice and pain—better than most westerners, only to be reminded by Tagore that Christ was an Oriental, a brown man. "We understand him in India, perhaps better after all?" Tagore suggested.[25]

* * *

Welthy recorded a luncheon discussion with one of their women missionaries. "She didn't like to hear Fred say he was looking for a 'mad man' (to fill the Thoburn pulpit). She thinks the more normal we are the better—but *what* is better? Greatness flies out the window when conformity takes possession of the house."

In the central struggle of their lives, which was greater—to adjust and accept the realities of episcopal life as it was, or to follow their inner light where it led them? The issue was further confused on Christmas day, 1925, when a cable arrived calling them home by March for several months of routine work, rudely interrupting their ongoing search for direction.

New Year's Day, 1926. Welthy was alone dismantling their Calcutta house—the vases, bronzes, brasses, lanterns and hangings, the living art of India and China. "What we want is to resign and really live. We have worked practically twenty-five years at the task of carrying the Christian message. We dream of freedom to live and serve and work as the spirit dictates and not as the Bishops' plan dictates."

The two American missionaries who had just arrived looked alike to Welthy, with no personalities of their own, no understanding of the strength within them. It was not a very hopeful sign for the future of missions. By contrast, her husband loomed large. "It is interesting to me to see a group quicken up under Bon's leadership. He makes them tremble with his prophecy, his warning, his surgeon's work by use of his moral knife. He makes them roar with his humanness and his humour, and makes them weep with his tenderness, and speechless in worship at his reverence. He is a darling as strong as a Gibraltar and as tender as an orchid."

Welthy was feeling so cramped as a bishop's wife in that hectic environment, and in the adjustment to marriage itself, that she was ill frequently that winter as they waited to leave. She tried to occupy herself by
reviewing books on Indian women, editing Fred's sermons, and speaking at every opportunity, but it was not enough. They had one last
sojourn at Darjeeling, honeymoon fashion, reluctant to leave for their
arranged tour through his territory.

Welthy deplored the bishop's burden more at each stop — cause or effect of her recurring illness — creating a strain between them that was
only faintly suggested in her diary. "We talked and talked out some of
our problems, for I had been perplexed for two days." They had reached
a critical point both in their marriage and in their sense of service. That
January, while they were in Benares, Welthy had a miscarriage. Whether
or not she was aware of her pregnancy, and what effect the strenuous
travel had can only be guessed at. But the loss of a life that had begun
must have troubled her in subtle ways, even though she came to consider it a blessing, given their mobile life. In such private matters Welthy
had only Fred as confidante.

Their crisis was temporarily resolved with a decision to spend the next
year and a half in the United States raising money for the Indian projects
they were committed to, and establishing their Hingham home for the
future. The target date for his resignation was moved ahead to 1928,
when they would withdraw to "meditation and creation". They did not
know then that Gandhi's influence was so strong, his example so palpable, that withdrawal would be impossible. They were in the States
from March to December, 1926, but then returned to India. They
remained in India and Europe for the whole of 1927, and returned to
America from March to September of 1928.

On the first long voyage to America in February, 1926, Welthy consoled
herself for their various troubles by reading Tagore. At the Suez she
noted "the ignorant soldiers keeping the status quo of the British empire at Aden." She reread Gandhi's letter to Fred just before their departure:

> *I have no doubt that whatever the present result of the South
> African struggle, the seed sown by you and now being
> watered by Mr. Andrews will bear ample fruit in its own
> time. I cannot be dislodged from my faith in the ultimate
> triumph of truth. Mrs. Fisher asked me for a message. What
> I see happening in America is distressful, either an exag-
> gerated view of the movement or a belittling of it. Both are
> alike distortions. I regard the movement to be one of per-
> manent interest and fraught with very important conse-*

quences. It therefore needs a diligent study, not a mere su-
perficial newspaper glance. May your visit to America then
result in a more accurate estimate of the movement in
India.[26]

Gandhi's measured advice, solicited by Welthy, was a clear signal to
Fred. "Fred will never be able to get away with an incognito resignation," Welthy realized, "it must be the whole hog or none."

As they landed at Halifax, she watched the Russian and Polish immigrants disembark for their new life on western Canadian farms, set-
tlers brought by the Canadian Pacific Railroad. Red Cross and church
people were there assisting the immigrants with helping hands into their
future. Movement of people and ideas, she thought, that's what is important.

AMERICA, MARCH 1926

Fred's personal dilemma took a back seat to his dismay over the thirty-five percent cut in appropriations for missions abroad. He spoke passionately about his shock at the American attitude that the time had come
to relinquish responsibility for the work abroad, that they could let it
drop after seventy years' development in India. Yes, he wanted Indians
to take responsibility, but he definitely did not think the mission work
was done by any means. Missionaries were needed more than ever to
overcome the influence of imperialism and exploitation, to prove that
the white race has millions of people with passions other than selfishness and greed. "The multitude cannot hear without the living voices,
not expressed in old words and old forms, but through living service,"
he pleaded.[27]

He carried out his personal fund-raising commitment, speaking in
terms of flesh and blood, not theories. From the Detroit Metropolitan
alone he got a pledge of one and a half million dollars. In Battle Creek,
Michigan one woman came up to get a close look at the kind of man
Welthy Honsinger would marry. "My how they love you out here," he
wrote to her. Throughout that summer he averaged fifteen hundred to
two thousand dollars per donor in "subscriptions" to support specific
needs in India, often the transit expenses of missionaries. He had particular success with businessmen, whose language he spoke well.

At Fred's urging, his church approved a year's leave of absence for Dr.
E. J. Helms of Boston, founder-director of the Goodwill Industries, to
visit the Far East, especially India. The church took care to underline
that no expenses should be incurred unless specifically approved. Ralph
Diffendorfer, the treasurer, intended to keep a close rein on Fred's imaginative enterprises. In Omaha Fred was taken to task in a newspaper

editorial for criticizing the war theme of "The Star Spangled Banner", pointing out that he would quickly go to war to defend his right to worship according to his own conscience. A strong editorial, representing the conservative majority of the day, in *The Chicago Daily Tribune* railed against Fred's "ignorant wilfulness" in espousing liberal views.

During this time, Welthy visited family and friends, made speeches and renewed contacts. Her brother's health was in steady decline, his children almost all grown up. The second of his five, Mike, had gone off to college, headed for a naval career that would bring him to the rank of Rear Admiral; he became a staunch supporter of his Aunt Welthy's work in later life. Helen, the third child, was beginning college, with help from Welthy. Mina's boys were also treated to a glimpse of their fabulous Aunt, who came and went so quickly throughout their lives.

For Fred, it was a relief at the end of the day to write to Welthy as they both moved about the country:

> *Darlingest; Your two lovely pictures are before me and I have kissed the hair, the eyes, and cheeks and lips — and the bare shoulders too! Nothing in all the world stirs me as you do. Something inside of me leaps and sings and yearns when I think of you. It is wonderful that I found you. My love for you grows deeper, and I am more and more convinced that some great, unprecedented destiny awaits us. We must prepare for it.*

Welthy never stopped preparing herself for the future. She was reading, reading, and thinking. From Upton Sinclair she drew her creed: "Get something really important to do in the world, something bigger and more permanent than your individual self, and then lose yourself in it." Ever practical, she absorbed Moore's "Family Medicine and Hygiene for India", noting the treatment for tapeworms, and the foods high in carbohydrates, since Fred had a chronic need to diet, with certain foods forbidden.

They sketched out broad travel plans. Pilgrimthorpe, with its inviting circular drive off a winding country lane, a three-storey wooden house surrounded by thirteen acres and a low stone fence, offered many possibilities. Fred estimated it would take ten thousand dollars a year to run it in full swing, including service and a secretary; with their joint capital of ninety-two thousand dollars, the annual interest was only forty-five hundred dollars, not enough to carry out their dream.

After making careful calculations, Welthy began that summer on renovations costing sixteen thousand dollars to accommodate Fred's parents comfortably, itemizing each expense meticulously. Fred's delight in planning the gardens was confirmed by Bacon, Voltaire and

Aristotle, his horticultural advisers. Kant and Schopenhauer he consulted on the meaning of success, wealth and wisdom, as his passion for enriching life through Pilgrimthorpe grew into an ideal of living fully through house, garden, people and ideas. He followed Voltaire's pattern of study and research during the days, while guests entertained themselves, and social and cultural activities during the evenings with their guests. The Fishers were rarely alone, nor did they want to be, except for necessary work.

At last their plan was underway, and Welthy was moving in her old sure, swinging manner, the details of construction always stimulating. She would meet Fred at the Seymour Hotel in New York whenever his travels allowed. He told her of one Methodist banquet attended by white bishops only, making him more certain than ever that missionary expansion could no longer be confined to geography; the new adjustment must be in the individual social character of the messenger and those who send him. He was ruffling many established feathers.

Harry Emerson Fosdick, newly installed as pastor at Riverside Church, the large interdenominational centre built by John D. Rockefeller in New York, inspired them spiritually, and his pastoral counselling drawing on modern concepts of psychiatry made great practical sense. Fosdick's church was filled to overflowing every Sunday, his sermons broadcast nationwide, the kind of response Fred had yearned for in his younger days in Boston.

Fred had a three-hour discussion on a train to Michigan with Bishop Nicholson regarding his future, and was advised to make his change now. Nicholson warned, however, that an unattached authorship/lectureship might be considered an evasion of high responsibility, whereas a university chair would not. Since many thought Fred had been elected bishop expressly for India, a home area assignment would not do. On the other hand, Fred could adjust and accept the criticism that usually went along with the work, and there had been criticism of the Fisher expenses. It took four more burdensome years of criss-crossing the globe for Fred to come to his decision, for they were not ready to cut the tie that bound them to the inspiration of their growing years. In late 1926 they set sail for India, closing the doors of Pilgrimthorpe wistfully behind them.

INDIA, 1927

At Brown's Hotel in London Fred gave Welthy a beautifully inscribed notebook as his Christmas gift, signifying a fresh start on their episcopal service and encouraging her jottings. They drew inspiration from a visit to the graveyard of St. Andrews Church in Hingham, England, where the tombstones of his ancestors Frederick Fisher and James Fisher put them in touch with the centuries, easing their immediate impatience with bureaucracy.

They were the only Americans in first class on the P & O boat from Marseilles. They cut down to a seventeen hundred calorie a day diet, while Fred began a colossal notebook on philosophy. Welthy read Dreiser's "An American Tragedy", observing: "A religion that failed at every point — we too must go through all the thinking, the fear, the worry of a weak mind."

January 6, 1927. "Lay at anchor all last night in Bitter Lakes, the mist so heavy that the Pilot refused to take us through the Canal. Fred read until 2:00 a.m. and before we went to bed we had decided to resign and take a Professorship in Harvard or Boston Divinity Schools. How often we long for Pilgrimthorpe — in its fullness, to sleep, to eat, to live, to work and grow there."

Still unable to resist her private reflex reaction to the British, she noted: "The cliques are getting more and more pronounced and our Englishman duller and duller. He eats caviar and cold meat pies, and Camembert cheese and drinks, drinks, drinks."

The long delays in getting through the Suez were increasingly difficult to endure. They gave up coffee, and Welthy occupied herself by discussing the day's run with the engineer, and reading Benjamin Kidd's "The Science of Power", revelling in the prescient chapters on women with glimpses of a feminist future.

At Bombay and Calcutta they were greeted with garlands by the assembled Methodists, but Fred quickly learned of all the gossip surrounding decreased mission support and his own controversial fund-raising efforts. He was deeply troubled by it. Welthy had a frank talk with their physician, who said Fred's aggressiveness in pushing things through made enemies, but that he himself approved of Fred's policies.

It was left to Welthy to smooth the way through the thistles, a skill she possessed in good measure through a talent for focusing on the positive things she saw, such as the simplified, practical village living of Fred Williams, "an unconscious and great educator." Williams was a young missionary selected by Fred to head the Ushagram Educational Colony in Asansol, Bengal, which Welthy never failed to visit when she was near. He pioneered educational reforms to encourage initiative and character development and that year succeeded in joining boys and girls in a coeducational high school.

There was little time to dwell on the criticism and gossip, however, with an extensive southern tour absorbing their immediate attention. On their return to Calcutta, the problems resurfaced when S. K. Mondol, an assistant district superintendent appointed by Fred and one of his special *protégés*, came in full of bitter complaints, convinced all missionaries were against him. It was a blow to sense the hatred he felt, and what Welthy considered a narrow-minded attitude on the part of some mission people.

In Lucknow, Welthy spoke at the IT College on "The Most Interesting Subject in the World—You," and attended a Board of Governors meeting, wryly noting: "It was interesting to see them stretch out three hours' business to a day's work." 'Interesting' was a word Welthy used whenever she was disappointed but did not wish to hurt anyone.

FRED'S DELIRIUM

It helped ease her frustration to roam the market on Hazratganj. She was tempted to buy fifteen hundred rupees worth of Indian rugs, and wrote to Fred, confessing. He wired back: "Congratulations on your acquisitive taste—am proud to be counted one of your possessions." Taking that as permission, Welthy bought the rugs, but Fred insisted she return them. Their views on owning objects still differed. But Welthy, dazzled by the upholstery and carpets of Bokhara and Farrukabad, still had her heart set on creating an Indian room.

The constant travel, the diet of humble, gracious offerings of villagers, the growing heat, and the humidity caused Fred's most serious illness in India. With his arthritis aggravated by a high fever and a pulse of one hundred and thirty-two, absolutely delirious, Fred couldn't stop worrying about the outcastes. He kept repeating: "But what have we done for them? What have we done for them? They never had a chance." Those words haunted Welthy all the rest of her life.

With round-the-clock nursing he recovered, and they ascended into the hills of Darjeeling to recuperate. On their third anniversary they each took one of the Sunday sermons at the Mount Hermon Boys' School started by Fred, Welthy speaking on 'The Smothered Christ' and drawing a fairly good evening audience, while Fred filled the morning service. She delighted in his power, never thinking of herself as a competitor in preaching, and he was proud of her increasing strength in the pulpit. They walked to their hotel happily and dined outside by moonlight—"a radiant anniversary".

Early in 1927 they traversed India once again on the Punjab Mail, sailing from Bombay. They were seated at the Captain's table. "At his left, Lady M., a tiny, tight-corseted woman covered with diamonds and self-possession. Her skin is purple, and this, contrasted to her long, leaf-like diamond earrings, gives a quaintness. Probably her husband made soap or perfume enough to be knighted. Opposite us a Britisher who hates India in the well-bred British fashion and who makes the same cut-and-dried remarks that one has heard since Armistice Day. 'Yours is the Land of the *Free*! Ha, Ha! Your land of the free ends with the Statue of Liberty, and if you will allow me to say it, the most despotic country on God's Earth.' I do not know just why a Britisher should call it God's Earth, when they rule with absolute sway over one third of it."[28] Welthy confined her opinions to the privacy of her diary, however.

That constant presence of the British on a wild monsoon passage, with three sleepless nights of high seas, made Welthy and Fred delighted to reach shore. They celebrated their escape from the ship with a 'breakfast' of filet of sole, cafe au lait and salad at the Marina Palace Hotel overlooking the Suez Canal and the mouth of the Mediterranean at Port Said.

THE HOLY LAND

They were happy to sit up all night on the train to Jerusalem, recalling for themselves the legends and history of the Holy Land. Welthy wrote of their visit:

> We cut across Jerusalem etiquette—no one goes out after dark—the streets are black. We engaged a carriage with difficulty and left Jaffa Gate, past Damascus Gate and out to the Mount of Olives. A haze rested over the hills, but we saw the glittering silver sea—the Dead Sea—made living and brilliant by the white moonlight. Alighted in front of the place of the Ascension, went down under some olive trees, and Sahib spread out his coat, and there we sat, looking down upon the city. The city's life of indifference is even now as it was then. And in that city the Christianity of those who call themselves Christians and worship everything about him—his tomb, his manger, his footprint, his mother, his cross—everything except his message, and so again he is crucified in his own house.

SWITZERLAND

Their destination that summer was Switzerland, Fred as a delegate to the World Conference on Faith and Order, a refreshing opportunity to mingle with their peers. While Fred attended sessions, Welthy went to Heinrich Zimmer's lectures and sat in on meetings of the World Population Conference, admiring the efficiency of the scientific approach. "They say as much in three days as the Faith and Order Conference did in three weeks, but no pulpit attitude or propaganda." Helen Krayer came to spend a month with the Fishers in Switzerland and help Welthy with her writing. "She made you happy you were going through hell to get what she wanted," Helen remembered. "There was compensation for it though — friendship. I don't think she used that power to anyone's detriment. Almost always they benefitted by learning something, or a new contact."[29] Helen continued to be the Fishers' good friend and helper through those years, meeting their boats, escorting them wherever possible, driving up to Hingham to check on Fred's parents at Pilgrimthorpe, and joining them on vacations. She remained the most loyal and durable of all Welthy's friends.

RETURN TO INDIA, 1927

On the return voyage to India Welthy found an American businessman to take to task in her diary, though her sharp observations were as much warnings to herself: "Homesick for hotel, food, climate, he is. Are we building such a country and such a standard that none of us will be happy outside of it? He doesn't seem to be homesick for people."

Modern communications had taken a leap forward in the mid-twenties with the short wave radio bringing news instantaneously from all corners of the world. News deeply distressing to Welthy had reached them in Switzerland of the Communist-led armed uprising in China that began in Nanchang, a revolutionary hotbed, ignited by Chou En-lai. It was hastily conceived and ended ignominiously four days after the revolutionaries occupied the city, when the southern soldiers of the Kuomintang routed them.

But it was a turning point in Chinese history, Nanchang the pivot, marking the beginning of the Red Army which left small bands of guerrillas roaming in southern Kiangsi as it retreated. The retaliation of the southern soldiers was horrendous; soldiers looted Nanchang, chopped off heads, and cut out hearts. It was government policy that foreign interests were to be protected, so the local Chinese crowded into the Bao-Lin School compound while northern and southern soldiers fought fiercely around the wall, leaving it heavily pockmarked and broken in spots. In the end, the southerners occupied the school.

Welthy was deeply relieved that Betty was safely away from Nanchang, having begun her studies at Yenching University in Peking that year. She had borrowed her tuition fee from a fund Welthy had established at Bao-Lin for such purposes, and Welthy sent a monthly check for her personal expenses. Happy as she was about Betty, Welthy's mind was on China, the school, the staff and students, wondering about and not knowing for some time their fate.

Chiang Kai-shek's southern soldiers carried out their worst massacre in Shanghai, purging all Communists from the Kuomintang and killing factory workers and young boys. The scene was repeated in Nanking.

To a young New Zealander who first arrived in China that year by tramp steamer, that vicious killing and the subsequent famine of 1927 were the never-to-be-forgotten shock that jolted him into a lifetime of struggle against injustice. His name was Rewi Alley, and he too had encountered the Chinese student labourers in France during the War and caught an impression of their strength. From that devastating year of 1927 onward, Alley committed himself to the uplift of China's masses,[30] a commitment that was to have a profound influence on Welthy.

To all living Chinese, 1927 stands out sharply in their history as the beginning of the modern era, whatever their affiliations, for that was when Mao Tse-tung and Chu Teh led their small band of soldiers from the eastern coast westward to the mountains on the Kiangsi-Hunan border to establish the *Kiangsi Soviet*, the first peasant-dominated government. From then on Mao's base was the rural peasantry, the vast majority of Chinese. There would be no turning back.

In hindsight, World War I was seen in China as a failure of Christian movements to preach and practise Christian love, a reaction that did not surprise Welthy. Drawing on Fred's powers of observation and analysis, she was honing her skills in direct, clear communication of complex ideas:

> *There must be exhibited by our race and our western nations an absence of race superiority. China asks for two things in this uprising. First, to be treated as an equal in all dealings with foreign powers, and second, the opportunity to put her own house in order, unmolested.*[31]

Though she was back in India, China was always in her thoughts, and she saw then the same pattern of neglect of the rural masses emerging in India, on a different, slower scale, where the movement against foreign control and ownership was gaining ground. "Down with Christian Schools" was the slogan she often saw on walls, which attacked Christians as instruments of capitalism. Meanwhile the fundamentalists and modernists of a hundred and fifty different Protestant denominations continued to fight among themselves in an unchristian manner, unaware of the real message they were communicating.

CALCUTTA 1927

In Calcutta they resumed the heavy round of duties throughout their territory. Welthy studied and wrote with renewed energy, rededicating herself to Fred's mission, trying to develop her own role. "It was always his imagination that ranged far afield, over the universe and into the starry heavens. Then I, like Martha followed along, carrying out his ideas. He kept me so busy that I rarely had a chance to do much imagining on my own account." She made notes on remembering, learning, speaking, organizing her ideas for speeches and noting where they were used. In her notes on greatness is included "endure persecution," the inevitable reaction strong leaders arouse in some people. She was merging herself completely into Fred's position and his view of the needs.

At Jubbalpore she opened the Central Provinces Conference speaking on "The Potentialities of Women in the World," and at Lucknow her pageant "The Day After Tomorrow"[32] was first presented at IT College. It starred six nations—Industrialism, Patriotism, Justice, Socialism, Militarism and Education—and Religion's three children—Love, Peace and Goodwill.

And Welthy learned new tricks of adapting to Indian travel, managing to alight from long, dusty train journeys looking refreshed and sparkling. Words used by the missionaries to describe her then were "graciousness, elegance, vigour and resourcefulness." Her white handkerchief was freshly laundered and pressed dry by plastering it on the train's mirror, a thrifty habit that she practised in the most modern of hotels for the rest of her life.

She invited the American women of Calcutta to tea, and when they left the American Women's Club had been formed, Welthy's Indian room the catalyst in their ostensible purpose to study Indian art. In a long, long walk on the *maidan*, Welthy and Fred decided they had written their last begging letter for money. They had not, of course, for the need was still there. And they decided once again to resign, Fred even writing a letter he never mailed to accept a lectureship at Garrett Theological Seminary in Illinois. The agony of their indecision went on and on, as they waited for a clear sign.

November 15, 1927. Welthy noted that some three hundred people were killed in Hindu-Moslem riots, which was no more than in car accidents on State Street in Chicago. She quoted Gandhi: "No doubt they (Moslems) are too free with the knife and the pistol, but Islam was born in an environment where the sword was and still remains the supreme law. Moslems have an ordeal to pass through. Let us not harbour a spirit of retaliation."

In Lucknow, where Welthy went more than any other place in India, she heard reports of one Christian whose house had been burned to the ground; another's had been trampled by the *zemindar's* elephants. However the main talk was still of the big cut in appropriations, part of a general decline in missions since their peak of expansion a few years earlier.

Katherine Mayo's "Mother India," which many Indians thought had been instigated by Delhi's white bureaucracy, and which Gandhi called "a drain inspector's report", attributed all India's ills to uncontrolled sexuality, which added impetus to the growing trend away from missions. With her harsh denouncement of missionaries for remaining part of a conspiracy of silence, and her thorough rejection of self-government for Indians, Mayo further muddied the unclear waters of American thinking on India. Welthy, knowing what a sensation it was causing and what a slap at Gandhi it was for daring to think of equality, applauded his decision to send Sarojini Naidu to the United States to counteract the book's blunt attack. The only thing clear to Welthy about that crisis of missions was just how fully it reflected on a large scale their own personal crisis.

One critic of the times wrote: "Americans who began to go to India . . . taking with them all their strongly fixed cultural and religious convictions, and bent on persuading Indians to accept these convictions in place of their own . . . this body of views is almost unanimously negative in spirit . . . but a few counterparts of a different sort emerge. There were notable persons, Robert Hume, Jabez Sunderland, Bishop Frederick Fisher, Eli Stanley Jones, who sought common grounds with Indians on the basis of a more sympathetic grasp of Indian feelings and problems. For a committed religionist to yield the principle of the exclusiveness, or at least the superiority of his particular truth is to yield a great deal and to gain in return much painful confusion."[33]

January 2, 1928. Welthy was dismantling the comforts of their Calcutta home once again as they prepared for return to the United States to an unsettled future. En route to Bombay for their ship, Fred gave his Episcopal address at the Baroda Central Conference, his outline marked with Welthy's note not to put women's work separate from the men's. "Fred said power is seldom conferred; it is grasped!" Welthy recorded, impressed by the insight. Mondol thought the speech prophetic, and Welthy thought that he and Chitambar were the best representatives India would have at the Kansas General Conference to which they were all headed.

The Fishers took time to visit the art gallery of the Gaekwar of Baroda, an enlightened ruler who had established compulsory education and built schools and a university in his state, and who hung portraits of Christ and various madonnas in his collection. Welthy's last strong observation before leaving India: "The (Indian) Christians, except in Calcutta, are dupes and slaves of the white man, docile to both *zemindar* and Imperialism."

February 5, 1928. It was a welcome relief to sail on an Italian ship, her officers "nicely non-pompous compared to the P & O, the drinking one tenth and the sports spontaneous. And for once Rex George was not prayed for. Bohn at his best, and I basking in the tropical seas and in the love of the finest bit of masculinity in the universe." It was Fred's tenth and her sixth passage through the Red Sea. Later she added: "This boat is going home, she must look her best, and every Italian workman since we beheld Etna in the clouds this morning has worked like a woman bewitched."

AMERICA 1928

Fred's father and brother were there when they arrived at Boston's Commonwealth Pier, along with the press, for Fred had aroused considerable interest in his article 'To Be or Not To Be a Bishop,' published in *Zion's Herald* that February. It was the most startling discussion of the episcopacy ever published in a Methodist magazine. He told of four years' agonizing over the question, for as far back as the 1924 Springfield Conference he had a resignation letter in his pocket, the prospect of a life-term as bishop crushing at his young age. He confessed to irritability, to losing his temper four times and apologizing three. He feared the powers of the office affected a man's humility, and recommended that power of appointments be taken from the bishops and given to the cabinet, and that the district superintendents be elected, not appointed. No bishop should reside more than eight years in any one place, and he should be supported by the area he served rather than the general treasury. Urging increased spiritual responsibility by greater contact with the Christian community, he pleaded with his Church: "Don't let the machinery of the Church crush our idealism."

In general, his article was taken as constructive and it increased Fred's popularity. But there was criticism of the concept of others doing the administrative work as establishing an unhealthy, comfortable dependence. Some thought he should go ahead and resign, but need not take the whole church with him. Some thought the whole article superficial. Others said he had hit the bull's eye, sensing the feeling of the average preacher. Aware of the growing revolt among ministers against the great power handed to bishops by their autocratic founder, John Wesley, Fred proposed that all bishops place themselves before the General Conference for a vote of confidence.

Above all else, Fred wanted to spend time with his frail mother who was recovering at Pilgrimthorpe from a debilitating illness. When Welthy and Fred arrived they found the house greatly improved, cleaned and polished inside with a grand family dinner awaiting them. And Fred's disapproving sisters were no longer there. Welthy and Mother Fisher became fast friends, two strong women who appreciated each other's abilities, as Fred had known they would. "We went to bed the two happiest people in the world," Welthy wrote, "in our own room, the loveliest room in the world." But it was only a few days before duty called them to the Kansas General Conference.

GENERAL CONFERENCE, KANSAS CITY, 1928

They settled into a housekeeping suite at the Aladdin Hotel in Kansas City for the month-long conference. While Fred attended and chaired sessions, Welthy studied the League of Nations, the World Court, and the Roman Catholic Church, but she was there to hear Fred's keynote speech which drew a great response. "It is hard to think of Fred Fisher as just a bishop," said one account. "He is more than a bishop and every utterance sounds a prophetic note . . . One could not help but feel that he is a voice that will grow more prophetic with the years and all of Christendom will yet listen intently to that voice."[34] Welthy noted that Bishop Welch and his wife were also upset by a system that moved them about like chessmen, and that E. Stanley Jones, whom Fred had initially encouraged to go to India, was elected a bishop that year but declined. Like Fred, Jones felt called to interpretive preaching rather than executive work, and wanted to minister to Indians personally. He presented Christ, not creeds, customs and rites, and he could find Christ beyond the boundaries of the Christian church. In the same vein, Welthy said of Fred: "No Methodist wall nor even Christian wall could hold Fred. To cooperate with Indians who were groping for a better way of life and who were following the Christ pattern was, to his mind, laying foundations for the larger Christendom" of which Tagore and Gandhi spoke. (FBF, 121.)

* * *

A happy family occasion pulled Welthy and Fred to Syracuse. Her brother's daughter Helen was married in Welthy's lace dress to Gordon Halstead, with Fred officiating. They had just graduated from Syracuse, "two of the loveliest idealists, Helen so poised at twenty, and Gordon at twenty-three with lofty, glorious thoughts," Welthy wrote. Gordon had a teaching post waiting for him in Cairo, and Fred, thinking that such a fine young couple would freshen the Methodist scene in India, invited them first to Pilgrimthorpe for a few days and then to India on their honeymoon. Though Helen scarcely knew her Aunt Welthy and Uncle Bohn, they could not decline such an appealing offer.

Welthy had appeared at her brother's home briefly from time to time when she was in the United States, and had bailed out the family financially on a few occasions. Though she had helped Helen at college, Helen was unhappy at Welthy's pressure to study general arts rather than the home economics of her choice. Through the years, the resentment

Helen felt over her difficult home life, as the most vulnerable of the five Honsinger children, and the one who felt most keenly the unhappy relationship of her parents, came to focus on Welthy, whom she saw as the one person who could have done something to improve things.[35]

As a child, Welthy loomed larger than life for Helen. If she could be so wonderful to other people's children, foreign at that, why had she not paid more attention to her brother's family in their dire need? The expectation was of Welthy, not other relatives, because Welthy was seen to be the most bounteous and had the connection with the affluent Cousin Dee.

*   *   *

Fred was on the road again, writing to her from every corner of the United States, reflecting on four years together with his "Wonderful Welthy". He had only two regrets, first for being "such a cad in discontent about our job," laying part of the blame on the hard climate and sickness. Determined to overcome this, he wrote: "Think what an honour my Church has given me, and how noble and beautiful a wife God brought to me. I will rise above it – you help me." His second regret was his "selfish pride and a temper that made a few friends critical." He vowed to win them back, to do his duty, and to save and hope for the future at Pilgrimthorpe. "My heart and mind and soul are *with you* today, my glorious love, with your beautiful, unrivaled body, your high unmatched mind, your radiant purest soul. Love me, Dear Welthy, always, as I love you. Your own devoted and happy Bon."

He told her the resignation question was still up in the air, some thinking he should stay in the States for a year or so, expressing genuine concern for his health; and the women expressed eagerness to have Welthy in their midst. Fred's problem had become the church's problem; they did not know what to do with their controversial "baby bishop". He was already giving speeches on America's place in the world today, and many thought his voice should now be heard in the United States.

Certain that Fred was an original, creative thinker, Welthy resolved to make him write down his ideas as they came to him. In his ambition for noble living, he embraced and distilled the greatest thoughts, ever a student of others, perpetually learning how to think and plan, and to speak extemporaneously with a flow of words not exceeding the flow of thought.

September 24, 1928. "Our last evening at home. One is wrapped round in love and feels the divine present so surely. Mother and Father (Fisher) are the Archangels of that heaven."

MIRA CHAUDHURI   25

MIRA CHAUDHURI   26

25. Rabindranath Tagore still writing at 78, Santiniketan, 1939. 26. Mira Behn (Madelaine Slade) and Welthy at the Kyber Pass 1939. 27. Welthy as Nellie Bly; photograph on her lecture promotion flyer in the early '40's. 28. Gandhi and his wife Kasturba listening to Tagore reading (taken from photo in Welthy's Literacy House house).

27

28

TED KELL

29. Welthy the journalist c. 1950.

30   ARIEL   31

ARIEL   32   Courtesy LITERACY HOUSE   33

30. Welthy, Dr. Kittrel and Dr. Frank Laubach, Allahabad, 1954.
31. Sushila, the strong woman of Chillahwan village, learning to read at
sixty-five. 32. A young man using the Literacy House materials practising
writing. 33. Literacy House staff welcoming Welthy back after a fund-
raising trip, Dr. T.A. Koshy at left, A.R. Siddiqi right.

S. SWENSON 34

CARE 35

S. SWENSON 36

34. The House of Prayer for All People at the centre of the Literacy House campus.
35. With India's philosopher Vice-President, Dr. S. Radhakrishnan at inauguration of House of Prayer, 1958. 36. A variety of traffic passes the gate of Literacy House on busy Kanpur Road. 37. A Literacy House mobile library set up at a weekly market.

ARIEL 37

Courtesy LITERACY HOUSE

38

38. Members of the first Literacy House writers' workshop, 1955; Comfort Shaw, 2nd row on right; R.C. Ariel, 3rd row, 2nd from left. 39. One of the first literacy training classes at Allahabad, 1954. 40. Women's literacy classes are usually held in the home of the strong woman of the village.

Courtesy LITERACY HOUSE   39   S. SWENSON   40

43

41. Sucheta Kripalani, Chief Minister of Uttar Pradesh, and Dr. Radhakamal Mukherjee, Vice-Chancellor of Lucknow University, escorting Welthy to Founder's Day ceremonies at Literacy House, 1964.
42. Indira Gandhi, Minister of Information & Broadcasting, with Welthy at inauguration of a Literacy House training programme in Assam, 1956.
43. Welthy greeting the Dalai Lama at training programme for Tibetan refugees, Mussorie, 1959. 44. Prime Minister Jawaharlal Nehru talking with Welthy at Literacy House book fair, 1958.

45   46

45. Dr. T.A. Koshy and Welthy greeting Hadley Perrin from Canada, 1960. 46. Dr. Koshy and Welthy arriving at 9th National Seminar of the Indian Adult Education Association. 47. Welthy was the only woman with 36 men participating in the Government of India's National Study Group on Adult Literacy and Adult Education, New Delhi, 1964.

48. Literacy House puppets attract the entire village, 49. Dr. C.D. Deshmukh, Sri K. Desai, Durgabai Deshmukh and Welthy arriving at inauguration of a writer's workshop, 1968. 50. Eleanor Roosevelt and Welthy at Wayne State University, Detroit, 1962. 51. Visiting a village in Uttar Pradesh; Mrs. Sheila Trivedi of Family Life Centre on right. 52. Ambassador and Mrs. J.K. Galbraith looking at publications with Dr. Mukherjee.

ARIEL   48

LIBERTY STUDIO, HYDERABAD   49

50

S. SWENSON   51

USIS, INDIA   52

RETURN TO INDIA, SEPTEMBER 1928

Facing towards India once more, their ship lying still in the extreme heat of the Red Sea, she felt differently. Her diary entry unleashed long pent-up emotion, showing the strain of their unresolved issues after four years of marriage, his anxieties dominating their relationship:

> *I lay half the night thinking about myself and my relation to Bohn — something seems to have cracked. He seems only to tolerate me, and I seem to have no buoyant response to him, whatsoever. I have repressed myself, step by step, until I feel like a sponge squeezed dry. Lifeless and utterly monotonous. Bohn remarks about my stumbling over everything, but it is because I don't care what happens to me, since I am nothing but a lifeless sponge, that seems to have attached itself to Bohn — and I don't know why I did it. Of course I shall have to do something to redeem myself. I don't know what. If we had a child, there would be a focus, but now, I'm just an appendage, and not a necessary one at that. I'm merely packing bags, fitting up rooms, rushing for conferences, then trains, and boats, and simply in a confused manner trekking thru life.*

Welthy's surprising lapse into depression may come as no surprise to a modern feminist but was partly caused by "a great congestion in head — sinus and quinsy and mastoid — can't rest or be free." It was strange territory to find herself in, and as always, with no one but her diary for counsel.

Within a few days she was free of her pain and dark mood, and enjoying the company of Motilal Nehru's daughter, Vijayalakshmi, and her husband Mr. Pandit, who were fellow passengers. And she developed a more optimistic view of her husband's role: "Bohn's mission is not to the masses or to the blue jackets, but to thinking youth and thinking middle age and whose who would give their lives to an ideal."

Helen and Gordon were there with the others to meet them at Bombay and they travelled together to Lucknow, where the Fishers were received so warmly that Welthy thought perhaps they ought to live there. They were invited to every centre and home, for everyone was anxious to hear news of the conference and happy in general to have their Bishop and his admired wife back in India.

Fred and Welthy had arranged to pay for Helen and Gordon's travel to India and for a special salary and living expenses for them to stay in Lucknow as missionaries, an offer they accepted but later regretted. They were shocked at the way the missionaries lived, in a style close to that of the British Raj, quite out of keeping with the simple values professed. They seriously questioned the basic motivation of both Welthy and Fred, who did not feel they could discuss with the inexperienced young couple their own ambivalent indecision about their inherited mission role and the lifestyle it imposed on them.

December 14, 1928. "The King is ill. Bohn asks two minutes silence for him." Fred had made his adjustment to British rule, for the moment.

WELTHY CREATES A DEFINITE ROLE

Welthy had chosen a niche for herself within Fred's domain and now had a clear work schedule and responsibilities, along with Fred's other top lieutenants, the Foleys and Wolrath. She would edit and publish their new magazine *The Calcutarean*, assist in writing Sunday school lesson interpretations, give special attention to the development of women's and children's work through the area, make the residence a spiritual, social and intellectual salon, and plan for the best possible presentation of their missionary message in America in 1930.

Fred had understood her need for a role, and Welthy was ready to give it her best effort. She was one of that growing group of wives of foreign service missionaries and diplomats, of whom much was expected and to whom little, if anything, was given, other than the nod of respectability. Welthy was asked by New York to write lectures for American churches on Indian culture, which she happily agreed to do, and was also writing a book on young India. Still unsettled, however, she acknowledged that "all through my life I have longed for my father's counsel and love."

Fred was having a recurring struggle with the local WFMS, "a very conservative, grasping, greedy group," according to Welthy, which thought the bishop had no jurisdiction over them, could not make appointments without their approval, direct funds, or unite men's and women's work. Oh those women, Welthy thought, they haven't changed, they're still the same. She considered it a great step forward when the men and women of the conference planned their first united programme the following year.

They marked their wedding anniversary in 1928 by reading together Carlyle's "The Great Empire of Silence", then talked till three in the morning. Trying to follow Fred's system of planning, Welthy made a gallant effort to set down her goals: "My remote aim is to be a great and brilliant wife of a great and brilliant man, to be a charming hostess who attracts men and women of note, and to write a great novel. My immediate aim, to make our home attractive, artistic and comfortable and to write the lecture for the Board." Was Welthy building her own empire of silence?

BURMA, NOVEMBER 1928

Within a few days she was aboard the S. S. Angore as it pitched its way through the monsoon en route to Burma. They decided to spend ten weeks in the summer heat studying the country, because they were dissatisfied with their superficial knowledge of that part of Fred's territory, which was still under British control. Welthy was an eager student, observant of detail, interested in the people, their history and their aspirations, profusely recording all she learned as they travelled throughout the land of pagodas. Her critical eye saw that the missionaries were uninterested in Buddhism and seemed not to think of the Burmese as human beings with recognizable feelings. The colour and gaiety of Rangoon delighted her, while the "dreary Methodist Church barn singing dreary Anglo-Saxon tunes" was painful. Music was meant to lift, not deaden.

Welthy went alone to Mandalay Hill when Fred was too ill to move about, meeting the hermit U Khant who had the idea of capturing the hill in the name of his religion. The missionaries would throw her out of the church altogether for doing that, she speculated. "What autocrats they are—I am almost afraid of them." Almost. The very thought of the missionaries sent her in the opposite direction to Mogok's ruby mine, there to buy the brilliant red cut stones she would have set into a red gold ring, its sparkle giving her lively companionship through the years.

Fred spoke to groups of prominent Burmese who had hitherto looked on Christian gatherings as offensive. He convinced them that Christian and Buddhist men have a common ideal and must work together, that victory is not won by trying to destroy other religions. "Christ does not antagonize. He magnetizes, He heals, He draws out, He calls forth, He rebuilds." Practising what he preached, Fred had a thrilling experience as the first Christian to speak in the main Pagoda at Thongwa, with Welthy and several Burmese women present—the first females permitted entry. (FBF, 157.)

At the Buddhist monastery in Pagan, Fred spent long hours with the head Abbot, U Wilatha, and his monks, in reverent discussion. As they departed, the Abbot brought out a precious small Buddha heavy with gold leaf, made from the wood of the Bo tree from Buddh Gaya in India, and brought there in 1091 A.D. when the Temple was built. It was his gift to Fred, a rare and beautiful object in every way that became Fred's talisman and symbol of tolerance.

Their visit to Burma was extraordinary in many ways. At every stop, the CID kept very busy conspicuously checking on their activities while Welthy and Fred accepted Burmese, Indian and Chinese hospitality in private homes. The CID presence kept some of the missionaries from associating with the Fishers. To W. W. Bell, one of their own Methodists, however, "they were a handsome, exciting couple and one had the feeling to do everything to make them at ease."[36] Whatever controversy surrounded Fred in those years, the missionaries generally admired Welthy's ability and retained a vivid impression of a well-dressed, gracious and resourceful lady bedecked with fine beads.

FRED FISHER AND THE BUDDHISTS

Burma's mathematician-philosopher, U Ba Sein, presented Fred with his 'Mathematics of Buddhism' and invited him to a debate, an invitation Fred suggested take the form of each presenting the best of their respective religions since he was disinclined to debate religion. Welthy quickly read U Ba Sein's esoteric work along with Fred as they planned his discussion, and she was the only woman in the hall as some eighty scholars listened to U Ba Sein turning again and again to Planck's Constant Pi to prove the validity of the Buddhist circle of life. Fred seized his opportunity, using the Quantum Theory as the most significant element in Planck's discovery, citing the law of the radiation of energy and the law of coordination and response in nature, and showing how those physical laws support Christian belief in divine energy emanating from God. Fred challenged Buddha's claim not to have seen or found any God, in what he considered the climax of his missionary career. Welthy was absolutely awed, as she described:

> *Fred Fisher, the student of B.P. Bowne at Boston, posited in the very heart of the circle the Divine Living Christ. The little electric bulb lighted the faces of the two protagonists until long after midnight. A gentle breeze from the river broke the sultry stillness. The dignified elders would willingly have continued the discussion until dawn. I felt as though I had been a silent listener to Paul on Mars Hill when he said: 'Ye men of Athens, I perceive that in all things ye are too superstitious. For as I passed by, and beheld your devotions, I found an altar with this inscription — THE UNKNOWN GOD. Whom therefore ye ignorantly worship, him declare I unto you. (FBF, 162.)*

CIVIL DISOBEDIENCE IN INDIA

When Sir John Simon came to India in 1928 to head a parliamentary inquiry on Indian conditions and recommend reforms, no Indian members were appointed, and the commission was boycotted everywhere it went. Gandhi launched his civil disobedience campaign against a huge tax increase, resulting in dispossession and jailing of thousands, and mass sympathy for the victims. The government was moved to repeal the tax increase, release the prisoners and restore their possessions, a success which led some nationalists to call for immediate violence to achieve full independence. Motilal Nehru recommended acceptance of dominion status as India's minimum national demand (as Fred had), but his son Jawaharlal broke with him and pressed for full independence. This was the background against which the Indian National Congress held its meeting in Calcutta in December 1928, where Gandhi achieved a compromise between the two factions in the form of a one-year delay. If dominion status was not granted within a year, the Congress agreed to adopt tactics of non-cooperation and non-payment of taxes. The Fishers followed in fullest detail the proceedings of the Congress, where some twenty thousand squatted on the ground under the vast *pandal*.

1929

Fred began 1929 with a tough ultimatum to the women of the WFMS to join cooperatively in the overall work or go home. "They knuckled down," Welthy noted with satisfaction. And she herself swung into a brief interval of "wifing it", taking up housekeeping in earnest, and hunting down furniture at rock-bottom prices. "Bohn returned and raved about the house. It really is beautiful, and to make it so I have talked Chinese and Cockney, and have bargained in Hindi and Esperanto. The living room is blue, the study red, the guest room green, our room mauve, the reception room and dining room a blending of green and brown. It was wonderful to have him just as enthusiastic as I am. I can scarcely believe it," wrote a rejuvenated Welthy. And from Rangoon she received the black and gold lacquer dishes she loved. "We love the house to distraction," she wrote, delighted with their shared pleasure in the nest they both wanted.

The euphoria was not to last, however, for Welthy had an odd recurring fever and abdominal pain, which she did not consider important enough to identify. Fred's arthritis was steadily worsening and at times he was unable to write or walk, yet he was determined not to resign for health reasons. In one personal letter Welthy said Fred had not had one day of freedom in eight months. He found a very helpful Indian private secretary, a Hindu, which troubled some Christians who were concerned that the secretary would be privy to confidential personnel matters.

Often travelling without his busy wife, Fred missed Welthy increasingly. He was still struggling with his tendency to rush in and lead too strongly where ideas and attitudes were different. "You and I think so beautifully together," he wrote. "Even our differences of opinion are inspiring to me because I have such profound respect for your judgment and experience. I will not weaken my ideas, but improve my manners, eh?"

To a colleague in Indiana he wrote: "We are caught over here in a wave of strict European Imperialism where one's free speech is denied him because he is an Alien. To a red-blooded man this is unbearable."[37] He was focusing on the end of his eight-year appointment, when he might honourably seek a transfer, perhaps to his own Hoosier State of Indiana.

Setting out on the next trip with Fred, Welthy wrote: "I often look at our numerous pieces of luggage as we travel through the villages of India and wish we might go as simply as the Indian evangelist goes. I wish we might live as simply as Gandhi. We have eliminated and eliminated until we feel we have narrowed things down to the stringent measure of necessity. Still the book bag, the typewriter, the tiffin basket, the stove kit, the two rolls of bedding, the suitcases piled high sometimes seem like unsurmountable barriers between us and the village Christian."[38] When they both became ill from accepting the varied refreshments offered on those extended tours through towns and villages, they took long walks and worked together on the lectures Fred was preparing on racism.

They heard Mondol preach so profoundly that one American said he could now believe Fred about Indian leadership. Working together on a book on building the Indian church, Fred and Welthy were invigorated by the hill air and their commitment to the heart of the missionary purpose, as Fred encouraged indigenous interpretation of Christianity in Indian languages, such as Sudhakanta's translation of the Sermon on the Mount into Bengali.

GANDHI'S ADVICE TO FRED

Fred's earnest query to Gandhi as to what Americans could do in India brought clear, practical advice:

> *Don't send doles of charity, but send experts who are not exploiters in the disguise of philanthropists but true philanthropists who will give knowledge for the sake of giving it, and who will study the conditions of India's cattle and show us the way of improving our cattle breed and the supply of milk from the existing cattle.*[39]

Aware that the use of his personality was his own greatest asset, Gandhi sought intelligent help from other individual personalities of deep moral commitment. Personalities—the universe existing within activated individuals leading the way—were at the core of the bond Gandhi and Tagore shared, and that moved Fred to begin writing a book on the meaning of personality.

WELTHY IDENTIFIES WOMEN'S ROLE

Welthy was still aspiring to write a great novel about a woman, this time in the form of "The Red Nun", another of those never completed ideas. And in one of her last talks in India, to Calcutta's Cosmopolitan Club, she spoke passionately from her own experience, with clear warning:

Women have had much to do with causing the continuation of war by allowing sentimental talk about men going to war on their behalf.

Always prodding women to wake up and be full personalities, to bring the quality of the home out into the real world, she continued:

The spirit that has enabled woman to throw herself into and, if necessary, sacrifice herself to the interests of the family, is needed in the wider corporate life of the community and nation. Education is of little value to women unless it enables them to make a vital difference to the life of the country. We live in a man made world — with laws and organisations, made primarily for the convenience and happiness of men. If women enter public life merely as competitors with men for positions in the established order of things, their contribution will be of little value. They must create a new emphasis and new position in society for themselves.[40]

She was her own best example as her thinking moved from the personal to the more political.

Welthy's article "Missions True and False" urged a parallel decolonizing of the minds of missionaries, stressing cooperation rather than control, a shift from the inward looking of mission compounds to a wide outreach. She said the church's preoccupation with mission property and organization seriously diluted its main purpose. In India she was highly respected by an ever increasing circle of friends, colleagues and leading personalities. Welthy and Fred were both moving into a wider realm.

1930

In India the majority of American missionaries still adopted or adapted to the prevailing British view of Indians, and the few dissidents who chose to identify with Indian interests never lost the maverick label. Bishop Fisher was still expressing a minority view in 1930 when he wrote: "Gandhi is living and acting the thing we dream of."[41] Almost all news of India filtered to America through British sources.

As Fred's eight-year term drew near the close, two issues assumed overriding importance, providing the final push for the Fishers to make their long-running decision to endure or not to endure. The first concerned the Fisher Fund which Fred had established to help Indian and Burmese projects without having to wait for sanction from New York.[42] They were so preoccupied with building up the Indian church, sensing a new vitality to their efforts and response on all fronts to the process of naturalizing, rather than nationalizing the church, that he could not sit quietly waiting for the slow hand of bureaucracy to move. Leaping ahead without waiting for approval from New York, as Welthy had done in China, his risk was strongly challenged and then criticized. Eight years later, the church did agree to his stand and acknowledged the value of the assistance the fund provided, but in the interval there was misunderstanding and pain for Fred and Welthy in the matter.

Nevertheless, Ralph Diffendorfer considered Fred one of the greatest minds and hearts of the church, realizing that "it is his point of view and in the direction of his program that we are to look for a revival of a missionary movement in America as it is interpreted to our people. The old missionary appeal is gone forever. The missionary enterprise has to be re-thought and re-interpreted and re-shaped in many of its policies. No one is working at this in our Church more than Bishop Fisher."[43] In the transition from pitying the poor to creating a self-sustaining church, Fred was in the forefront, "dragging an unwilling church behind him." Some were listening.

The second issue, also administrative in nature, revolved around S. K. Mondol's engagement to an American missionary. Mondol, who had made a strong impression in the United States, was an obvious leader and fine speaker whom the Fishers admired greatly (and who later became a bishop). However his indiscretion in relations with an American woman missionary made it impossible for Fred to keep him as a district superintendent, the question of a pregnancy at issue. Fred took pains to consult New York, and when the day came to decide the case, Welthy tucked a note into Fred's pocket as he left for the meeting. "Be a Jean Val Jean bishop," she suggested, meaning be forgiving, for she thought Fred had overreacted. He did soften somewhat, giving the woman the choice of resigning or returning to the United States, but Mondol's reassignment was interpreted as a direct racial slur against his marriage. To Fred the issue was the example of a Christian leader engaging in questionable conduct.

There were repercussions throughout the church as the result of the pamphlet Mondol's friends had printed in which Fred was viciously attacked for discrimination.[44] Fred conceded it was "my heaviest blow in recent years, my deepest episcopal sorrow." As the storm brewed around them, Welthy and Fred kept their own counsel throughout, painfully aware that some would see the Mondol issue as their whole reason for discontent.

Fred was now convinced that by removing an irritating and confusing issue, that is, himself, the Indian church could begin to stand on its own. "I could not afford to drift, nor to fight," he wrote. "I took a sweet leap out into the unofficial ministry where I hope to find joy in liberty. I wish to teach rather than to judge, to live in a home rather than in hotels, and to minister at an altar rather than to preside in conferences over delegates. I want to drink again the fresh waters of American freedom. I crave freedom from bitter criticism against mere official acts. If it must come, I'd like it for ideas and not for machinery. Mrs. Fisher and I have spent so long in the Orient trying to remake the past, that we'd like to try now to grow with the expanding western present."[45] A decision was imminent.

To Welthy, he wrote in pencil from a wobbling train:

> *I do want to make some contribution to the world. You must help me be somebody. I find no objection to our going. Do you? I think we are loved and respected except in certain sections and everybody is that way more or less. We express ourselves too freely and fight for too many causes to be universally popular. And what's the use of living without expression and loyalty to some ideal and conviction? I see Wesley said: 'I never fret; I repine at nothing; I am discontented with nothing.' You help me be that way. Eh? Just think of having you for a wife. Malcolm Pitt says he wants to find a little image of you for himself. I said if there were others like her I'd be a polygamist. My heart loves you, my whole life thrills at the thought of you. Saturday will be a day of glory because I shall see thee face to face.*

Pitt, a missionary teacher at Jubbulpore Theological Seminary, admired Welthy as one capable of making fast friendships with all kinds of people. "With Welthy you don't need a lot of time," he sighed, adding that Fred had the right ideas but was a bit of a bulldozer in pushing them. He knew Mondol well, having roomed with him once, and considered him downright jealous of Fred. Pitt totally disapproved of the Mondol signs — *GO HOME FISHER* — posted on all telegraph poles.[46]

Fred tried hard to get the Indians to agree on an Indian bishop to succeed him, and left as his last message this convocation address given at Serampore College in February, 1930:

> *For hundreds of years, India has described the visible world as an illusion, denying the reality of existence. The world is not illusion. We tread upon solid earth. For generations,*

India has played hide and seek with reality. Reality is harsh, but wholesome and disciplinary. What India needs is not individuals practising renunciation for their own souls' sake, but men and women who will undergo regenerative sacrifice for others. True education prepares for effective evaluation of human situations and needs, as well as gives direction to the impulse to serve mankind in remaking unfavourable conditions.

* * *

AMERICA, 1930

As Welthy and Fred boarded their steamer for Europe and home, Fred was physically and psychically spent and could barely hobble, arthritis had so immobilized him. His immediate destination was a surprise assignment to the North Indiana Conference of the church, while the Methodists debated the best method of handling his unprecedented resignation from the episcopacy. He was too great a force to lose, and within months his special talents were assigned to an area where he could well fulfil them, as pastor of the University Church in Ann Arbor, Michigan.

Welthy had participated in the decision, prodded by their good friend Bishop McDowell who suggested that she encourage Fred to spread his wings and follow the dictates of his own heart, despite whatever criticism resulted from his liberal appeal to students. She used her connection with Dean Kraus, who had shifted from Syracuse to Ann Arbor, to hasten matters along, well aware of the slow grinding wheels.

There were more university students in America then than in all the rest of the world combined and Fred was stirred by the prospect of so many young minds to touch. The world was in a shattered state after World War I, and American optimism was deeply shaken by the economic catastrophe of the depression. It was time to be at home, taking a stand against isolationism, trying to bring the world into the minds of America's future leaders who would determine the new forms of international service. Ten thousand students at Ann Arbor, a hundred of them Asian, a lively university faculty and a community congregation were to Fred a direct, personal challenge equalling his call to India a quarter of a century earlier.

* * *

As Welthy prepared for her new life in America she reflected on the attitudes and experiences of their six years in India. Fred's passionate, intelligent, personal love was hers, in a giving and taking that had propelled them through painful decisions to greater heights. She had gained more experience of imperialism and the American need to prove itself in the world. She had experienced subservience as a wife, searching for a larger role, and she had understood to the core the far greater, absolute injustice of racial wrongs, and the ignorance and poverty they prolonged for large groups of people. She had seen more of the world, had come to know many of its leading personalities, and was filled with a need to share the insights she was privileged to have gained.

India followed the Fishers to America. Most reactions to Fred's departure were sympathetic, but N. H. Mukerji and J. R. Chitambar were despondent, feeling Fred had let them down in their hour of greatest need, fearing reactionary forces would set in, even reminding him that Christ suffered at the hands of his own people but endured with love. Fred knew he was not indispensable, however, and recorded his deep satisfaction at Chitambar's election that year as bishop to succeed him, the first Indian so elected in the Methodist Church: "There may come a time ten or twelve years from now when tremendously constructive things can be done in India. All over the world we are in for a decade of reaction against all forms of liberalism in state, church and society. I cannot afford to give up my liberalism, but I can afford to give up any position or possession. There is a sweet consciousness of having chosen the better part."[47]

* * *

When Welthy and Fred reached Hingham that summer Fred wanted the two beds in the room they had used so briefly to be put together with one headboard, age and his frequent infirmity taking little toll on their intimate life and early morning talk sessions. "Perhaps never before have I felt such a sense of maturity and satisfaction," he wrote. "Welthy is on the new terrace in the morning sun and wind. Father walks out to the garden. Mother's frail step is heard climbing the stairs to her room. Biographies of LaFayette, Pasteur and Jesus are before me. So different! Yet all breathing the revolutionary and constructive essence of something new." What was past for Fred—his old fear that while preaching against imperialism he was himself leading an imperialistic life—was gone. And what was present was the feeling of family, deeply missed during extended travel and service abroad.

ANN ARBOR, MICHIGAN, 1930

In the fall of 1930 they began their new life in Ann Arbor. Each morning and evening they walked over to see the day's progress in repairs and alterations to the home they would soon occupy. Welthy knocked down one wall of the large study so she and Fred could converse as they read and thought. Exploring other minds was their intoxication; one book led to another, one glimmer to its opposite, as the two of them absorbed more and more of mankind's inheritance in the printed word. It was a warm, expansive period in their lives, enriched by the presence of Fred's parents whom they brought to live with them.

Both Welthy and Fred had books published in 1930, a happy *entree* into their student constituency. Hers, entitled "Freedom; A Story of Young India", tells of a Bengali family from the aspect of each family member confronting the new social awareness of the 1920's, in vivid scenes attractively illustrated by Tagore's students. Writing to youth about youth, Welthy put herself on the side of their idealism and hope in a presentation of Christian spirit.

Fred's book, "Personology", was a compelling expression of the need for new personalities, changed through practical idealism to face the future, conscious of God and responsible to man:

> *We belong to God by nature, and nothing short of identity with him will satisfy the inherent hunger and thirst of our souls . . . Know thyself is an old maxim; know thy world is a new necessity . . . Religion is a universal instinct so deep as to be as dependable as the law of gravitation . . . Science and religion both live and advance by faith which leads to experienced reality.*

He called it scientific mysticism, encompassing the parallel forward thrusts of science and spirituality toward unity:

> *All the evolutionary force that drove plant and animal life onward to newer forms and higher perfection will inherently operate as an internal, insatiable social law to drive mankind forward toward the higher social idealism . . . Its full realization will depend upon socialized personalities . . . No religion has all the truths. No nation has all the patriots. No race has all the virtues. And none can do without the other. If there is any truth anywhere, it is the fact of the unity of the human race and the interdependence of mankind.*

There was no doubt or drift in Fred's mind now. The call was strong and clear, his ideas echoing through the large sanctuary of his new church. His reputation had preceded him and soon enormous crowds filled even the basement to overflowing to hear his messages on the loudspeaker. Not only students but their parents and a mixed crowd of all ages stood on State Street to hear his regular broadcasts throughout Michigan, with crystal radio sets coming in one ear and the loudspeaker in the other.

1931

Within a year of returning to America he hit his full stride. "Dr Fisher is good to look at," reported *The Michigan Christian Advocate.* "He is the picture of health, ambassador of a robust faith, attractive to youth because he is so virile." He was heartened that the church in India recognized his and Welthy's leadership in indigenous development, but in the States he felt discredited in official church circles. "I feel its chill," he confessed. Nevertheless he was using his powers to the full. "You and I don't really belong to this crowd of meticulous administrators," he wrote to Welthy. "We can't seem to stay put on party loyalties. We break the harness."

Welthy was as active as Fred, asking the Business and Professional Women "Can We Retain the Feminine Qualities in Business and Professional Life?" Her answer, we must. To the YWCA she spoke on India, and at the Congregational Church her topic was "Prophets of New India", focusing on Ram Mohan Roy, Keshub Chunder Sen, and Tagore's father Devendranath.

The Fisher's home, with its Indian and Chinese lore, attracted large numbers of students, welcoming them to share a very warm, informal hospitality. Often the students would cook and serve the meal, Welthy practising her favourite educational technique of allowing people to do things for her, neither doing it for them nor insisting on being independent. In India she had often found that difficult, since many Indians expect others to serve them. And always she wore beads, beads, beads, the one thing her young nieces and nephews who came to visit remembered vividly.

While her brother was recuperating from an ailment Welthy went to Syracuse to see how she might help. His wife Evalina was still rather overwhelmed by Welthy's powerful presence and remained proudly independent. Welthy loved her brother deeply despite his years of personal difficulty and for all her power, felt powerless to do anything.

In her own home, Fred gladly yielded all financial responsibility to Welthy. He was rather stunned at her prowess in handling their savings, mostly her money from Cousin Dee. "Whew!" he wrote. "What speed in investments. *Gosh* but you move when you get going!"

PLANETARY PATRIOTISM

Fred's speeches were calling for "planetary patriotism", insisting that complete adaptation to our present circumstances, as known here and now, is death. "Prayer is born of human discontent," he wrote, "for we will not accept planetary limitations as final," let alone national limitations. Welthy was teaching a class in comparative religion and met often with teachers and superintendents of Michigan schools to encourage wider exposure to eastern life and thought.

When she went to Hingham to make it ready for their next visit, Fred felt her absence more keenly than ever:

> *Love is such a strange, intoxicationg thing. Intangible, yet all absorbing. Mystical, but the deepest reality. Your mobility, personality, walk, eyes, look, lift of head — all thrill me. Body and mind and soul you are high, exquisite, desirable. The strength of you, the independent capacity, swing, sweep, glory. I love it all.*

Welthy installed a pair of stone elephants to guard the entrance to Hingham, and in the foyer she placed a stunningly handsome Kashmiri carved walnut screen draped with a gilded sari. Beside that was a beautiful Korean chest. Even Fred could not resist the desire to adorn Welthy, and he gave her a beautiful brooch, which she thought too expensive and returned. So he kept writing to her instead, identifying himself as her Best Old Noodle:

> *Sole mate and soul mate, never stalemate. Deep, radiant, attractive, full, vital, living, glorious, I love you. My goddess building her own shrine there among the trees — and welcoming me to her secret place.*

That summer of 1931 he remained in Ann Arbor throughout the university session, taking only a brief rest with Welthy at Martha's Vineyard. There was no time for their usual holiday reading, starting with a binge of detective stories; he took only one book, the Bible, and read it from beginning to end, culling sermon topics for the year and developing a system for handling ideas and themes. "God is universal energy," he wrote, and therefore he could not accept the pessimism of Hinduism that holds that God is unknowable, beyond the universe. With the certainty of the scientist pursuing a theory, he proclaimed that God is here and now present within all. Welthy was not living with a coward, for any man who made such public proclamations was inviting sharp rebuke from reactionary minds. As Fred was growing into his full stature, the students loved it. So did Welthy.

* * *

Nanchang caught the world's attention once more, in 1931, when Chiang Kai-shek, recently converted to Christianity, moved into the city to deal with the Red Army. Missionaries were experiencing their greatest tribulations amid looting and burning as the Communists and Nationalists struggled for control. Even more ominous was Japan's invasion of Manchuria.

One Japanese, the famed social reformer, writer and pacifist, Toyokiko Kagawa, was in the United States witnessing to the fact that all Japanese were not cut in the same aggressive mould. His voice caught the Fishers' attention and held it for years, a warming voice in that time of deepening depression, when Americans began to realize they were in a long-term crisis that went beyond the economy, a crisis that made it increasingly difficult for the Fishers to think of making their utopian withdrawal to Pilgrimthorpe.

GANDHI'S SALT MARCH

In those depression years movies had become the popular escape from ever worsening bad news. And from India via teleprinter, replacing the slow dots and dashes of telegraph codes, came fuller news of the main international story, as *Time* magazine placed Gandhi on its cover as Man of the Year, winning out over the Chairman of the Chase Manhattan Bank, Bobby Jones the golfer, Sinclair Lewis, Ramsay McDonald, Stalin and Hitler. The issue Gandhi had chosen that spring as a declaration of independence was the British Government's monopoly on salt, a necessity of life, God's gift; his famous Salt March took on a high symbolism which attracted America's first serious attention to his movement, indeed the world's.

Vincent Sheean captured the mood well: "There is no Hottentot or Eskimo who could not understand the Salt March. I go to the ocean of God, he said, and I make salt with my hands, and the foreign government will arrest me and put me in prison for it, but this is my truth and I will die for it. The imagination of the entire world was seized and almost obsessed for a time."[48] In America, Fred's voice was strong among a growing number of liberals backing Gandhi's steps towards independence.

While Gandhi was in jail his autobiography was published, edited by C. F. Andrews, and reviewed by Fred. Tagore had made his second visit to America, speaking in Carnegie Hall, but as before he was unhappy about the visit, as he wrote to Fred: "Leaving this country not with much success but some wisdom of resignation. The obstacles are great and I do not know how to overcome them."[49] He enlisted Fred's help in having his poem "The Babe" published, something Fred never did pursue, and it was left to Welthy to include it in her biography of Fred. (FBF, 136.) Despite his own poetic outbursts, Fred's passion was more for the practical ideals Gandhi personified—his struggle in the harsh world of reality—than for artistic exploration.

India was becoming of continuing interest to America, especially to men who joined the League Against Imperialism—John Haynes Holmes,

J. T. Sunderland, Roger Baldwin, John Gunther and Fred Fisher. A series of talks between Gandhi and Lord Irwin, the Viceroy, earlier in the year, had provoked Churchill's famous diatribe against "the nauseating and humiliating spectacle of this one-time Inner Temple lawyer, now seditious fakir, striding half-naked up the steps of the Viceroy's palace there to negotiate and to parley on equal terms with the representative of the King-Emperor."[50] That arrogance of Christian England accentuated the bitter experience Welthy and Fred understood very well, adding another nail to the coffin of empire.

Gandhi had agreed during the talks to call off his civil disobedience. The prisoners were released and salt was made freely available on the coasts of India. Furthermore, Gandhi was to attend the next Round Table Conference in London, an agreement symbolizing equality for the first time. But it would take another seventeen years for India to progress from this symbolic gesture to the full equality of independence. When Gandhi went to London his agreement with Irwin was nullified when his Congress colleagues insisted on complete independence, resulting in much factionalism amongst the Indian delegates and the ultimate failure of the conference. Gandhi spent three months in London trying to explain India, his food and dress getting more press attention in the United States than his ideas.

GANDHI RESPONDS TO FRED FISHER

Eager to have Gandhi visit America, Fred sounded out statesmen and college presidents, whose encouragement led him to spend a hundred and twenty dollars to urge Gandhi by telephone to make the trip. But Holmes and Baldwin were against it, believing Gandhi's cause to be woefully garbled in America, with cartoonists too ready to ridicule him, and no organized group to receive him and make proper arrangements.

Gandhi was suprised at Fred's urging, mindful of Tagore's American experiences and the mixed atmosphere of hero worship and ridicule, and declined. But he did respond to his American friends in a radio broadcast, speaking of the limitations of machinery as a means of achieving happiness, warning that production would reach a saturation point. Mass production was only possible because weaker nations were exploited. Only when production is localized can wealth be more equitably distributed, he said, and that was the need for India.[51]

In response to Fred's request for a message, he wrote:

> *My message to American Christians on World Peace and Disarmament is that Peace and Disarmament are not a matter of Reciprocity. When real Peace and Disarmament come, they will be initiated by a strong Nation like America*

—irrespective of the consent and cooperation of other nations. An individual or a nation must have faith in oneself and in the protective power of God to find peace in the midst of strife, and to shed all arms by reason of feeling the loving power of God and his protective shield, and I hold such peace to be impossible so long as strong nations do not consider it to be sinful to exploit weak nations.[52]

When Gandhi returned to India at the end of the year, he was once again imprisoned. On release, in September 1933, he wrote again to Fred saying:

I really have no message to give through the lips. I am delivering a message through my action and if the action that is going on in India can unmistakably demonstrate to the world the success of non-violence on a wide scale, I would regard it as a completed message, but just now whilst everybody around is saying that non-violence has failed (which so far as I know it has not) what is the use of my coming to America and preach the message of non-violence. Though I know its efficacy I could not demonstrate it, and apart from that message I have no other to give. Have I made my spiritual difficulty clear to you? If I have, I would like you to plead for me that it is much better that I keep away from America for the time being. If and when the call really comes I shall not be held back by anything.[53]

ANN ARBOR, 1931 TO 1933

The Fishers received many notable visitors in their Ann Arbor home — Vallabhai Patel, K. Natarajan, and the peripatetic Charlie Andrews, who would arrive possessionless and depart with a bag of clean clothes that he would then dispense to the first needy people he encountered.

After the Sunday morning service Fred would discuss the sermon with those who stayed behind, and to those who still lingered on he extended an invitation to lunch. John and Minnie Kopsi, the Finnish couple who kept the Fisher household running, would quickly expand a table set for six to one for two or three times that number, Fred resplendent at the head of the table in the handsome red velvet jacket Welthy had given him. Luncheons during the week would include forty or more people, always with students and foreign visitors.

Welthy was far too busy to involve herself domestically except for planning large parties, her forte. For the Kopsis it was a heavy duty, having to respond so often to unplanned guests, but they did not feel badly used and remained with the Fishers throughout their time in Ann Arbor, Welthy's charm keeping them happy, if exhausted.

Thursday afternoon was the special time when all students were welcome on an open house basis. "Before the leaping flames in our fireplace young India met young Brazil. It made me feel at home to find smiling Chinese faces always with us," Welthy said.

The Fisher household expanded by four when Helen and Gordon Halstead took up residence with one child and another on the way. Following very much in Fred's footsteps, though he questioned his motives, Gordon had written a manifesto in India calling on Christians to support Gandhi and Indian independence. It was a very strong appeal to all who professed to love truth, justice and goodness, to support India's right to express and develop to its highest capacity. The result was a British edict that he leave India, or else the grant to Lucknow Christian College where Gordon taught would stop. He left. Unable to find a job in the United States during the depression, the Halsteads lived for two years in the Fishers' extended family household while Gordon took a Master's degree, still harbouring disapproval of the Fisher expansiveness.[54]

Welthy won her greatest approval from and had the happiest relationship with Fred's mother. In that elastic household of four generations, Welthy became the daughter she never had. Mother Fisher developed a salon following of her own among the students sitting round her on the floor; she glowed in their interest in the civil war stories she told of negroes being hidden on the third floor of their Maryland home, while colonels were downstairs on the first floor. She also felt the reverence for their openness that appealed so much to Welthy and Fred.

When the last guests had gone after dinner, Welthy and Fred would walk out through the snow-silent avenues, often stopping at the soda fountain of the corner drugstore to watch ice cream sodas disappearing down thirsty throats, remembering their wistful hunger in India for a taste of that all-American symbol.

* * *

From China in 1932 came the formal request of T. S. Lauh (Ernest) for Betty's hand in marriage, after lengthy consultations with an English friend on the proper procedure. Reluctant to conform to such protocol, Ernest felt he had done his duty after mailing the letter, and the marriage took place well before Welthy's hearty approval was received. Ernest was much more concerned with his own family's approval, because his father was skeptical of Betty's name, Ho Chen-yi, literally "where female virtues", a name of questionable standing to old gentry, for whom all was in a name.

But Betty won the family over quickly, her beauty and grace compensating for the unusual name, and Ernest's father willingly paid off her debt to Bao-Lin.[55] Shortly afterwards Ernest came to New York to work in a Wall Street bank, and duly presented himself to the Fishers, who found his wit, wisdom, and thorough knowledge of Chinese art refreshing; they could see why Betty had chosen him over the man to whom she was previously engaged.

* * *

Fred's book "That Strange Little Brown Man Gandhi" (the publisher's title), published also in 1932, brought the kind of mixed reviews Fred usually attracted. One said it breathed Anglophobia. Some intellectuals thought it lacked substantial elaboration of Gandhi's thought. Another said it was the first time a white man had successfully made the transition from his point of view to that of the Indian. J. B. Kripalani thought Fred's absolute regard for truth must have been a sore trial to the average missionary and the imperialists, and marvelled later that such a book was written so early, when Gandhi's personality, thought and activities suffered from false propaganda financed by an imperial government.[56] One American wrote: "Let the little heathen stay where he belongs, rather than bring him to the U.S.," reinforcing Gandhi's own assessment of American opinion. It was not a book that could be ignored, and the best indication of its potency was that it was promptly banned in India by the British Viceroy's edict, a ban that included quoting, discussing and translation.

One chapter stood apart from the rest, considered the storm centre of the book in many circles — the chapter "Re-Thinking Missions," written by Welthy as an elaboration on her earlier article on missions. Insisting that it was a travesty of religious liberty that missionaries to India must prove loyalty to the British Government to get a visa, she wrote:

> *We who offered ourselves spontaneously when we were young thought we were radical, thought we had declared our religious independence, thought we were bound to no particular flag when its demands conflicted with the flag of this higher allegiance. Today's youth says we've made Christianity subservient to nationalism. If Indians can't keep up buildings or run schools after all these years, there's something wrong with the buildings and institutions we've built — everything is foreign and Anglicized. Missions have fallen victim to the spirit of conquest rather than change from within. Missions have served their apprenticeship.*
> *(SBM, 120)*

While Roosevelt and Hitler dominated world news, Fred and Welthy spent the summers of 1932 and 1933 in Europe. Fred attended international meetings and lectured at universities, always fighting the increasing pain of arthritis. Once he was hospitalized by a shocking, acute attack. In Paris Welthy looked at clothes and perfume and jewelry—and bought books, their book bill always exceeding their food bill. Among other things, she read the important new novels and summarized them for Fred.

1934 TO 1938

"No house should decide our future," Fred told Welthy, as they continued to find such enjoyment in their infrequent stays at Pilgrimthorpe. Life pulled each of them in many directions. Fred often wished Welthy would not make so many speeches, insisting on his way occasionally, and she would break engagements reluctantly and be there with his slippers and velvet jacket when he came bursting through the front door calling "Hello, Hello, Hello!" to her. When Welthy's investments became a crisis of conscience for him, even though he did not know what or how much she owned, he begged her to dispose of them. Owning a house was acceptable, but not stocks and bonds. Welthy sold the securities and wisely invested the money in houses; her faith in God did not extend to a lifetime of financial provision.

Fred wrote long, lingering letters to her from the sanitorium in Indiana where he went for frequent extended treatment:

> *I have caught a chiseled embodiment of divine dreaming and have crushed it into sweet armfuls of loving, living and response. I have put more life into her life, more love into her original abundance—and she has so yielded her substance of cultural beauty to me as to renew my soul a thousand-fold and touch me with a new sense of beauty, adventure and realization. I am a new man now—not the one I was when I saw her afar off—I have been measuring myself against her ideal standard and have stretched my soul to new permanent heights.*

Fred was well aware, however, of his morbid moods and driving enmities towards people and events. He turned to Welthy:

> *When they begin to manifest themselves you must take us out into expressive activities—even theater, or trips or games or parties . . . don't let me drive you or wound you or break your will. Take control. Forgive all that has ever wounded or limited you. Catch me up in your own lovely*

strength. Hold me to my best — beside you. Hold me to your ideals, teach me your swinging stride.

Welthy tried again to write, this time basing her work on Christ's words at the Last Supper: "This is my body, broken for you". Those words held her in voluminous pages of notes for a historical novel that never materialized, but they served a purpose in absorbing Fred's reflected pain and in developing thoughts she would draw on long into the future. Fred's searching struggle to grow, and his willingness to share it, made her respect him all the more. Impatient as she may have been, she did not see it as weakness.

On the whole, the Ann Arbor years were very satisfying for Welthy, with the world moving in and out of their home and her mind stimulated by myriad personal contacts. But Fred's old yearnings, his need to make time count, his attacks of illness, surfaced too often. He was urging the world mission board to cooperate with, not control, their missions abroad, to transfer church-owned property to local owners, to unite the boards of the men's and women's work, even to unite the boards of all the Protestant missions.

By mid-1934 his tension reached a peak. He had received many requests to lecture at foreign universities. His love of world travel made exclusive attachment at Ann Arbor seem confining; he wanted to learn more about the personalities and ideas of that critical period when Hitler's power was growing, the Japanese were moving deeper into China, and India's independence seemed on permanent hold.

He was offered a professorship of philosophy at Boston University but even that could not hold him. With the idea that he and Welthy would visit the Orient for six months and then be free to go on speaking tours, he sent a letter of resignation to the church, but they refused to accept it, appointing a special board to persuade him to stay, hoping to build up a Methodist centre around him. *The Ann Arbor Times* reported that "the Church had come to be a movement rather than a mere formal organization. Among members are scores of persons not organically part of Methodist denomination nor the Christian church. Emphasis is on the spiritual side, not creed or dogma. The Sermon on the Mount was the highest social standard for human living."

The Detroit Free Press listed five factors in Fred's resignation — ill health, the missionary call, or recall, internal policy dissension, criticism of liberal sermons, and financial difficulties. Fred was still trying to pay off the Fisher Fund, that chronic problem, by having three thousand dollars deducted annually from his ten thousand dollar a year salary.

His letter to Welthy written on a train in Canada in June 1934 shows his struggle to choose the right path, the difficulties in their way, and his profound sense of interdependence with her, which formed part of her own confidence:

> *I do not know what is just beyond the horizon . . . I feel a stirring within me — what it forbodes. I do not quite grasp. For that reason I keep you in confused doubt. And I am sorry for this. But soon, the bright sun will dispel every cloud. Our Resource is within us — we draw it from the everlasting energy of life. Those were lovely but costly words you said ten years ago . . . People have fooled us, and I have not always been worldly wise, but there is no scar on my soul. Silver cups of ours have dissolved in the acid of experience, but God's grace is now precipitating the silver for another richer, rarer one . . . I love you, with a mystic yearning, unquenchable, and not always expressible. Myself is inadequate for the thoughts and dreams that grapple my being. That is why I stumble now and then. I gaze at the far-off and stumble over the near. And you too are like that — really! Our souls belong together — the open road is our home. Tomorrow beckons, and casts her shadow on today. What doth she offer us? Glorious joy, salted with a little pain; beauty, wrinkled with a little disappointment; Eternity, limited with a little time; love, pricked with just enough thorns to require kisses of comfort and healing. And forsaking all others I keep me only unto thee so long as we both shall live, and that means always.*

DETROIT, 1934

Fred decided to answer the strongest call that came to him, that of keeping faith with his church. He responded to Bishop Edgar Blake's plea that he accept the pulpit of Central Methodist Church in Detroit, a city dying on its feet in the gathering years of economic catastrophe. Blake urged Fred to save that oldest Protestant church in Michigan which was about to be sold to pay off mortgages of other churches. It would take a giant to revive it, Blake said, appealing to Fred's sense of nobility. Detroit would have its giant, and Welthy would play her strongest role yet, though she was not eager to leave Ann Arbor.

"The conscience of a city", as Central Methodist has been called, stands prominently at its heart on East Adams Street at Woodward, facing Grand Circus Park. Fred saw the city as the most powerful industrial centre in the world, next to Moscow, as he prepared himself psychologically and intellectually to enter an environment different from anything he or Welthy had known. As his associate he chose E. Shurley Johnson, who had served with him in Calcutta, who with his wife Jet, came to live with the Fishers initially, an arrangement Jet disliked because the Fishers owned the house. Determined to establish strong personal friendships by having a home where large numbers of people could be welcomed and stay as guests, Welthy chose to buy her own home rather than occupy the traditional manse. Two returned missionaries from China, Oscar and Adelia Starrett, who led the Chinese church within Central Methodist along with Reverend C.C. Hung, added to the international flavour.

Welthy and Fred set about their homework, discovering Detroit as if it were a foreign city, making friends among its people in all ethnic groups and occupations, visiting different centres every Friday night. It was Welthy who made their strategic plan for getting acquainted, and for learning from the citizens how the church could best strengthen them. Her systematic, astute, and open-minded method of assault on new territory was later set down in her "Handbook for Ministers' Wives", an engagingly direct and highly practical book. To meet the wealthier inhabitants they even bought "golf sticks", but neither of them needed eighteen holes' worth of time to feel the pulse of a person and the clubs joined the collection of ornaments in their study. Rich people who had moved to the suburbs came back to Central in large numbers anyway, attracted to the power, charm and intelligence they recognized in the Fishers.

Two letters Fred received were typical of the controversy his sermons and talks inevitably aroused. One lawyer wrote: "You are giving me the feeling that I want once again to come to church, feeling I have not had in years, due primarily to the fact that we were asked to love a social system that was built on a profit motive rather than on social justice, and no pastor had the courage to point his finger at the high places."[57]

Another lawyer differed: "Suppose you preach Jesus the Christ with say one tenth the energy that you put into this *BUNK* and *JUNK* that you are now passing out. You might yet earn your salary, provided you get right with God and preach His Word and His Redemption. If not . . . get out of the pulpit . . . and take up the pick and shovel."[58] To the second, Fred replied: "Accept my thanks for your dandy letter. It is straight from the shot gun and I like the sting of the lead. Let's get acquainted. I think we'd like each other."

What the man objected to so strongly was Fred's series of lectures on Hitler and Germany, which displayed a social activist stance that some considered unrelated to religion, the perennial problem liberals face in remaining within a church. Fred was speaking not so much of religion but of the spiritual unity underpinning all religions, and within all people, so they could not be separated by man-made systems of religion, politics and economics. Many understood; many did not. Many appreciated his ecumenical joining with St. Paul's Episcopal Cathedral to celebrate Holy Communion; many did not.

One prominent woman described Fred's preaching style as "a sparkling river rushing down the steep mountain side — the words cascade one over the other so swift and vital — and suddenly you say softly (it always startles me) 'Shall we pray?', and then the swift stream has found peace in a still pool at the foot of the mountain."[59] No one responded more than Welthy, always his student.

Fred wanted the basement bar in their house converted to a chapel for private weddings and communion, entrusting Welthy with his plan for altar representations from Muslim, Hindu, Confucian and Buddhist faiths, with the cross of Christ towering over all. There was a Syrian dossal and altar cloth, a Buddhist tabernacle, Hindu candlesticks, and Confucian vases and murals on the walls. It was one of the few Methodist places of worship with an altar symbolizing the international message of Christ, and there in the basement Welthy played the organ for many intimate wedding ceremonies.

1935

Symbols, that so easily lose their meaning or fall victim to misinterpretation through time, had taken on great importance for Welthy and Fred. When the city of Detroit decided to widen Woodward Avenue and cut twenty-four feet off the church to do so, Fred seized the opportunity of moving the church spire out of the way of motorized progress and remodelling the building. Traditionally the chancel of a Methodist church was a raised platform with a lectern as pulpit; Fred transformed the old meeting place into a sanctuary, recessing the chancel, and adding an elevated pulpit, high altar, carved oak choir stalls, cathedral pillars and Gothic arches.

The main altar frame was thirty feet high, with a large gold-leafed cross and altar cloths signalling the four seasons of the church year. The three hundred and twenty panels of the ceiling were painted with Christian symbols through the ages. In defending the use of symbolism, Fred said he considered it the most beautiful approach to reality, which is eternal, and therefore the beautiful sanctuary was a symbol of the eternity of God.[60] Many agreed, and the church has remained as Fred designed it.

Dorothy Probst, a landscape architect, was one of the congregation who helped in Fred's plan, working closely with Di Lorenzo on the art, ensuring that Fred's concept, of symbolizing the common man and his contribution to the church through the years, be represented, rather than an exclusive array of saints. Fred would often bring Dorothy home for dinner after the Sunday service, where she was initially awed by Welthy and the strange oriental adornments that seemed remote and rather sinister. She felt ashamed of her ignorance, as others in the congregation had felt uneasy at first with their powerful new minister and his equally strong wife.

Welthy's enthusiasm sometimes made her seem just plain bossy, as when she tried to persuade the Ladies Aid Society to do things they did not want to do. Welthy assumed that everyone shared her commitment to service. She knew perfectly well that many did not, but risked their criticism to win those who could be led.

When funds were needed for any purpose, such as enlarging and gowning the three choirs, Welthy turned on her sales ability. As Dorothy watched her being so solicitous of Fred at home, making him comfortable after the Sunday ordeal, being joking and easy, she saw the other side of the Fishers and developed an enduring friendship with them. As leaders, Welthy and Fred knew they had to act with a certain dignity, but that was matched with equal time in warm, informal friendship with their congregation.

When they first moved to Detroit they decided it might be time to try separate beds, Fred's frequent attacks often forcing him to rest, but they quickly traded these in for a double bed again. They treated themselves to afternoon 'naps' whenever possible: "I would have to take off all my clothes," pearls, buttons, the sturdy corset, everything, Welthy complained years later in mock dismay. Their partnership included Welthy's research for Fred whenever he needed an important book analyzed quickly. Then she would take a room at the Statler Hotel to do the concentrated job, no 'naps' interrupting.

* * *

She joined the Board of the YWCA, wrote on Harold Gray's experimental agricultural cooperative after visiting his five hundred acre farm in southeast Michigan, conducted the confirmation class, made the church bazaars occasions for beauty as well as business, developed the choirs, campaigned for Judge Homer Ferguson to regain his seat on the bench, urged young audiences to "use less and do more", and by every imaginable means pulled the women of the church into greater cooperative efforts. "It will take all the grace of God, the help of your husband, and prayer beyond belief," she wrote, "to find the right niche in the church for those older, untrained, yet willing and ardent Christian workers." (HB, 38.) Jet Johnson was one who simply did not want to be kept so busy. She loved Welthy but resented her efforts to manage the women. Welthy understood, and they remained lifetime friends.

Speaking in her spontaneous, conversational style to an audience of four hundred and fifty at a World Day of Prayer service, Welthy's patrician forehead, melodious voice and red scarf tossed over the shoulder of her tailored black dress were noted along with her suggestion it was time we learned from the Orient, and discovered how to take from it rather than just trying to give to it. The same evening she addressed two hundred young people on "Yourself and your World," in the kind of crowded day that had become typical. It was also typical of the press to be fascinated with her appearance.

In time the Fishers moved to a house in the fashionable Grosse Pointe area some miles from the church, where Welthy could have some life with Fred away from constant invasion by the congregation. Many of the women made themselves available to cater to Fred's every need, often driving him to meetings. Welthy took the risk of not doing those same things herself. Fellowship, yes, she thought, followship, no.

Visitors to the newly bought Tudor style house never failed to be surprised by the oriental wonders within. Their Buddhist tanka from Nepal, prints from south India, marble plates from Agra, lovely rugs and carved teakwood furniture, suggested a lifestyle in sharp contradiction to the poverty of India. Welthy would spend many long years later atoning for those years of mainstream living, but through that home they were able to attract the interest of many distinguished Detroiters, to prod them for cracks in their reactionary thinking, to pull them towards their world neighbours.

Through club memberships Welthy made friends of many prominent Detroit women, none of them Methodists but many of whom came to hear Fred preach and remained close through the years. Through her continuing study of music, she met Mrs. Edith Tilton, a believer in the cosmic force of music, and promoter of the Detroit Orchestra and music study in the schools. She sought out the Fishers, and invited them to a children's concert where they shared a box with one of the orchestra's main benefactors, Henry Ford. His story had gone round the world as Welthy had discovered in Australia, yet she found him a simple, genuine man, as many great people are. Simplicity to Welthy consisted of personal warmth, the ability to make one feel welcome and able to ask any question easily, and the openness to accept a stranger freely, not allowing divisions. With Ford she felt immediate rapport; she was pleased at his keen interest in Gandhi and eagerness to hear all she could tell him in subsequent visits to his Greenfield Village.

ANGELA MORGAN

Welthy's intelligent empathy for others and the world was attracting a following of her own. Angela Morgan, a frequent visitor in the Fishers' home, she with "the blaze of eternity in her veins",[61] noted for her poems dedicating the Tomb of the Unknown Soldier in Washington and the memorial to Will Rogers, expressed that attraction in her ode to Welthy:

> *I love the regal texture of your mind,*
> *A fabric starred with charity and grace,*
> *A tapestry no purchaser may find*
> *Though long he tarry in the market place.*

> *No broideries upon your dreaming walls*
> *Bestow the beauty that your presence brings;*
> *Like cloth-of-gold within a prince's halls,*
> *Your spirit traffics with eternal things.*

> *I sing the royal pattern of your soul,*
> *Imperishably dyed with lovely deeds;*
> *No life so broken but you make it whole,*
> *You know the answer to our human needs.*

> *The rich Bokhara, sumptuously hung,*
> *Is not so warm with knowledge nor so kind;*
> *Your understanding is a mantle flung*
> *To shield the traveler against the wind.*

> *My debt to you may never cancelled be -*
> *Such values have on earth no counterpart -*
> *That you are friend is like a crown to me;*
> *I love the regal splendor of your heart!* [62]

* * *

Welthy mourned the loss of Father and then Mother Fisher during the Detroit years, and wrote a memorial article about the gentle lady, unafraid of change, who had accepted her into the family.

When Cousin Dee died in 1935 several years after a stroke, her daughter Mildred Bliss wired Welthy to come to the funeral and stay at the Colony Club in New York. Their lives had drawn apart over the years and Welthy thought her going would seem to be making a claim on the estate. Deciding that her place was with Fred, whose need for her presence was so strong, she did not go, a decision she later regretted. Mildred was naturally distressed, promptly returning all Welthy's photographs from her mother's mansion, and it was years before Welthy was able to recover that relationship.

The fate of Cousin Dee's opulent estate at Santa Barbara mirrored the history of the times; first it was a Navy rest and recreation centre during World War II, next a school for girls, then it lay empty until Hollywood discovered its suitability for film locations, and it is now a luxury retirement community with two hundred and fifty apartments spread out over the grounds.[63] Dorinda Blakesely Barnes Bliss' death marked the end of an era for which Welthy had no nostalgia.

Outwardly, Welthy and Fred were still being pulled in different directions. He struggled with his disease, retreating to the sanitorium occasionally, seeing an osteopath, while Welthy spoke at the Women's League on "Woman as the Psychic Center of the World." Her need to keep actively following her own light conflicted with the demands of church and domestic life, and she found some solace in a helpful thought of Harriet Beecher Stowe: "When you get into a tight place and everything goes against you, till it seems as though you could not hold on a minute longer, never give up then, for that is just the place and time that the tide will turn." Welthy's diary went blank after that cryptic entry, but the tide did turn, this time in the form of airships that carried Welthy and Fred in opposite directions for the first time.

MEXICO CITY, JUNE 1935

> *Why did I come? Whether it is wise to have left Bohn I do not know. I am missing life with him desperately, but I'm learning Spanish by leaps and bounds and it gives me great hope. I think this experience will make me wake up intellectually, which is something to accomplish for I was certainly down.*

Registered at summer school, Welthy met other students, shared quarters and moved about Mexico on weekends, happily observing and recording legends and folklore in a two-month burst of recreation and refreshment.

Fred went to Europe that summer for a World Faith and Order Conference in Denmark, wives not invited, and then onward through Scandinavia and ultimately to the Soviet Union, armed with letters of introduction from Roger Baldwin. He had agreed to Welthy's Mexican adventure, somewhat reluctantly, and wrote constantly during their separation:

> *That tall, Spanish looking Queen down in Mexico this summer; her dark straight hair, those dark penetrating eyes, her aristocratic profile, the perfectly formed and arched lips and eyebrows, the distinctive nose, the George Eliot chin, the Ethel Barrymore stride — Oh, how I love that divinely human*

ensemble. God will touch it with his spirit of creative genius to draw forth its depth and height of artistic expression. Let those long fingers play over the keys as though they brought forth music. I love you for everything you have been, are now, and for what you will yet become. Be the old big and glorious dramatic Welthy, and tell me some thriller when we snuggle up against each other again.

A few days later:

And what love my whole being has for that big brunette down in Mexico. I can just draw in my breath and feel the thrill of her soul. The streams have separated around some hills for a time but flow consciously on toward the great meeting place beyond. And how I shall enfold her then. Dear old Welthy, I love you beyond all else in earth and sky and sea. May the great God of love care for you, and give you all the glory your soul can absorb. Go to it strong and big and free.

From Finland:

Glorious Old Darling, I had not realized the initial letters spelt God . . . an ideal, normal, non-complexed human personality must be the best image of what we call God. And all the legends tell us the marvellous influences of Goddesses. I find I miss you more than anything in all my world of experience . . . Decisions cannot be made without you. I just drift along . . . without that clear sense of direction which surrounds me when you and I are together. I love you, all the day suns and midnight suns and Baltic winds sing it to my soul. I hear them now like a lovely chorus — I love Welthy and she loves me.

His next letter discussed plans for the Detroit Church, vowing to be less demanding, not to have a one-track mind:

As soon as the conference is over I am going to take a straight streak to your arms and never again be separated like this. Nobody else has a Welthy Honsinger, and I can't afford to miss it. Won't you speak Spanish? I'll be so glad to see you and feel you that you may talk in ANY tongue whether I understand it or not. You and I must learn to LEAD that church, including trustees, official board members and Detroit citizens. After this you are going to be with me, even though other people are interesting to you. Not monopolized possession, but permanent presence is my motto henceforth.

The crack in their grand alliance was mended once again. The Mexican sojourn dissipated all the negative energy which had been building up, including Welthy's disgust at being told by the Mexican Consulate that she must carry a letter saying she was travelling with her husband's approval and bearing his signature. The outward sign of her independent rejuvenation was a car, which she bought and learned to drive up and down the streets of Manhattan while waiting to surprise Fred on his arrival with her fait accompli.

She returned to Detroit in high spirits, speaking on Albert Schweitzer, on India, on Peace, and on Mexico to the many groups that invited her — churches, professional clubs, even the American Institute of Banking, where Welthy's respect for money fostered a friendly flirtation with those august gentlemen.

Fred's speeches after he returned were overflowing with his Soviet experience, drawing larger crowds than ever, both admirers and detractors. Reconstruction in the Soviet Union was on the vastest and speediest scale in all human history; some of it he liked and some he hated. He gave up the idea of going to Siberia, feeling it was too great a risk just to get canned information. One traveller to Russia in those years, Malcolm Muggeridge, did penetrate the monolith and saw the deliberate starvation in Siberia, and returned to England knowing he must never pretend that he had not seen it. The net effect of the visit was to strengthen Fred's religious spirit and determination to fight injustice.

Fred had met Romain Rolland in the home of Maksim Gorky, who had recently returned to the U.S.S.R. from exile. Their long conversation ranged from Gandhi's non-violence to illiteracy. Rolland thought Fred had made Gandhi too practical in his book, that the only way to view him was as a saintly idealist, which has been the prevailing view of Gandhi in India itself. As for literacy in the U.S.S.R., a society emerging from centuries of illiteracy, Fred found the Soviets eager for reading material; the train porters, for example, preferred newspapers to currency for tips. And for Welthy, he could not resist buying a painted wood carving of Catherine the Great, Madame La Ressource (Madame Quick Wit) that he saw in the house of a Russian archbishop. It marked the secret entrance to her French lover's apartment that had been a family treasure for four hundred years.

1936

Welthy served as Chairman of the International Relations group of the Detroit Branch of the American Association of University Women, and was active in the Detroit Women's City Club, where Gertrude Stein once spoke. She rode alone in the elevator with "Gertrude the Silent", observing her sparse, masculine plainness, and the pockets in her skirt. She told Welthy that her whole effort in literature was to show the dual nature of everything, that people are not different ages inside but have a contemporary feeling of everything existing at one time. These were things Welthy had long known about herself, but she never warmed to the Stein manner of presentation.

A much more appealing author was Pearl S. Buck, whom she had known in Kuling as a young girl, and who had changed American thinking about China forever with her Nobel prize-winning book "The Good Earth", which depicted a family's grim trials with famine and hopelessness. For the first time for many readers, the Chinese came alive as individual human beings enduring and surviving with dignity and wisdom, people Americans could understand. When the book was made into a film, Welthy was there in the balcony beside Pearl Buck at the historic premiere showing in New York in 1937.

As Fred tackled more complex, difficult topics for his sermons, working in his study undisturbed until late morning, Welthy kept callers away and handled many pastoral matters herself. At the end of each week he completed his sermon notes in large pencilled script, kneeling in front of the prayer desk in his library, with a crucifix over it, his discipline for keeping his ideals dominant while he was editing. His sermon "If I Were Dictator" received full front page coverage in *The Detroit News*: "Money should be a medium of exchange yielding equal profit to both parties, not a commodity in itself. He would bar unearned income, and called for a new political party based on the Sermon on the Mount, as necessary to purify capitalism. Governments of the world could establish a universal currency and take over all functions of money, credit and banking."

The personalities Fred brought together for symposia at Central Methodist, men such as John Haynes Holmes, Rabbi Stephen S. Wise and Reverend Charles Clayton Morrison, stirred reaction and fear among anti-communists. This did not bother Fred, whose awareness of the powerful changes in Europe led him to predict accurately that the world would have first to fight fascism before communism. America's decline in purpose and prosperity saddened him, pervaded his sermons, and dominated his poems, such as this one expressing the duality Stein personified, and that to Fred was the ever-changing pull of God, inching us forward by trial and error into harmony:

> *Something in my heart longs for peace,*
> *When war is in the air.*
> *And somewhat yearns for war*
> *When peace is there.*

1937

Welthy felt the passing of time with the death of her sister Mina at age fifty-nine, and asked herself what more she should be doing with the precious gift of her own life. "When one door closes, another opens," she would say, and in fact her beloved Betty did walk in through the door on arrival in America in 1937, as Japan's full-scale invasion of China got underway. All of Asia was aroused by Japan's arrogance, and it was India that offered help to China in the form of a medical mission and supplies in response to a request endorsed by Sun Yat-sen's widow, Soong Ching Ling, who greeted the five Indian doctors at Canton Wharf. Rewi Alley accompanied them on the very dangerous passage north to the Red Army in Yenan. Alley had become the lynchpin of the civilian cooperation behind the lines to oppose the Japanese, as China literally picked up her tools and marched west across the land to escape the invaders.

Welthy had kept her Chinese contacts through the years, receiving in her home people such as Wu Yi-fang, President of Ginling College. Betty and Ernest had escaped the invader to arrive safely in the land of the free. But not not all Americans had read Pearl Buck. There was a powerful prejudice against orientals and only the poorest accommodation was available to them. Welthy appeared on their doorstep unexpectedly soon after their arrival in New York, and proceeded to help them get more comfortably settled. They had left their daughter Miriam behind in Shanghai with Ernest's family when embarking on their uncertain future as aliens in an economically depressed time, and while Ernest took up his work as representative of the largest raw silk filature manufacturer in China, Betty studied child psychology at Columbia. Being present at the planning and building of their new life in a new land gave Welthy great pleasure and a fresh sense of family.

* * *

During the latter part of the thirties, foreign missions encountered more financial cutbacks, prompting Welthy and Fred to raise five thousand dollars for the Fisher Fund to support Indian projects facing abandonment. The money came from the sale of their oriental art treasures, in all, some three hundred and niney-eight items, including Tibetan dragon lamps, inlaid Damascus furniture, Mohammedan daggers, the painting of Catherine the Great, Chinese camel hair hangings, and a Coromandel screen. It was not the first time Welthy had been parted from her treasured possessions, and she would start all over again many times in the future to collect, and then to sell or give away, everything she owned. She never lost her attraction to objects of beauty and originality, but she did learn to love them and leave them.

New Years Eve, 1937. Welthy was alone in the library, Fred was away on business when she wrote these heavily laden lines:

> *Sometimes I feel we live together more*
> > *When we are far apart.*
> *Our lives are strangely set*
> *Within the public gaze . . .*
>
> *So sure are they that you are here to give,*
> *To share your soul, your mind, your wisdom*
> > *All with them,*
> *That even they can not believe that*
> *We have words, we too would say —*
> > *Just we alone . . .*
>
> *Each book upon the many shelves speaks*
> *More than any author dreams.*
> *It speaks of you —your comment here —*
> > *Your humour there—your look beyond*
> > *What even Plato dreamed or*
> > *Epictetus analyzed.*
> *Sometimes I think we live together more*
> > *When we are far apart.*

And Fred was turning more to poetry to express the passionate yearning "that only the dawn, the spring, the song can satisfy," recognizing the signals from his biological timepiece, knowing "for native home my soul aspires." As the nations of the world lurched towards war, he wrote this lament:

> *They knew not what their souls required,*
> *But thought all service could be hired.*
> *They combed the world to find the hands,*
> *To make the things their purse demands.*
> *Their hot-house sons grew into youth,*
> *Their daughters, spoiled, became uncouth.*
> *They bought the mines, and sold the ore,*
> *At profits never known before.*
> *The blinded miners, whipped and cowed,*
> *To every insult meekly bowed.*
>
> *These sins were piled in one great heap,*
> *And set on fire with flames that sweep*
> *From heart to heart. Fire licked the sky,*
> *Consumed the rich, piled ashes high.*

Self-ruined daughters, hot-house sons,
Remain, the broken, helpless ones.

Fred's book "The Man That Changed The World" was published in 1937, witness to "a universal, insistent yearning, unwilling to accept limitations, only the pursuit of possibility." Fred wrote that Jesus, springing from a land that was literally a highway between north and south, east and west, embodied the truth of all religions and nations with his inclusive message. Christ was a peripatetic teacher, whose school was wherever he sat down and talked to his followers. Christianity is a moving faith, from the Middle East to Europe and America, and back to the east again in new forms, as Tagore and Gandhi have enriched their Hindu mysticism through Christian philosophy. Only a changing religion can last. A great church requires light and air to breath and live. Truth cannot be suffocated. If he had the power, Fred would not snuff out any religion, for they are all parts of the universal truth.

The underlying theme of the book, which Fred dedicated to Tagore, represents the last thoughts of his ever-questing spirit for:

> . . . *the social incarnation of God in society itself, where personality transcends property, and cooperative peace supplants the pagan technique of war. . . We have called ourselves children of God. It is time we were reaching our majority as citizens of God's democracy . . . catching the essential rhythm of the inward and outward aspirations of our personalities, balancing belief with action.*

* * *

January 1938. Fred wrote to Welthy from Chicago that "a solemn sense of the meaning of our love has settled down upon me," as he planned to weave it into a series of Sunday night sermons, without anyone but Welthy suspecting. When she went to Savannah, Georgia, to fill a speaking engagement he was unable to keep, he urged her onward:

> *Let your whole personality speak. Let your best clothes, and beauty parlour modernness decorate the mental charm of the inner soul of my Welthy Honsinger. You are a great mind, inspired by a living soul, housed in a beautiful body. Let it all speak to them — as it speaks to me across these miles today. Never have I loved you so deeply. Vows of deeper and more radiant devotion fill my heart.*

Drawing on her China experience, Welthy warned that meeting of the General Missionary Council: "I dare not take a white-faced or European interpretation of Christ," adding that she had lost faith in the rigidness of legislation, but never in humans with their capacity to change. She suggested: "We are going to have a peace table of women someday. Japan will be the hostess and China the business manager." And on her return journey north she sat down at a western peace table in Washington, representing the American Association of University Women at a conference on the "Cause and Cure of War".

Early in 1938 Welthy and Fred motored south in their Ford to Florida Southern College in Lakeland, where he gave a series of lectures, and both received honorary degrees, Welthy's for her books on China. In Virginia a large truck bumped them from behind at a railroad crossing, shoving Fred forward over the steering wheel. The blow forced him to cancel his lectures there as he complained of soreness over his heart. The doctor who examined him could find no damage and so they drove on to be back in Detroit in time for Palm Sunday.

As he worked on his Easter sermon, "Learning to Live Forever," Fred thought of his own mortality. One of the very attractive, well-groomed widows who catered to Fred collected him by car, as she had frequently done before, to drive him to an engagement, while Welthy went to call on sick members of the church. In the car, Fred suddenly collapsed. The woman took him to a nearby chiropractor's office and called for help. Joseph Shaffer, his physician, came immediately to find the chiropractor manipulating Fred, and rushed him to the Ford Hospital. He was conscious but in deep shock, his pulse varying in different parts of his body, numbness shifting.

By the time Welthy was informed and reached the hospital the doctors told her the soreness he had been feeling in his chest was a torn tendon connecting the aorta to the heart, and its final rupture was now killing Fred. Pain beat down on him like bolts of lightning, reverberating through Welthy, a pain she would have to learn to banish from her heart, daily, for the rest of her life. Even had Fred's condition been diagnosed earlier, there was no remedial surgery possible then.

"Good Friday, at dawn, his spirit took wings . . . the light of the rising sun was lifting the darkness into what was for him an Eternal dawn. Songs of birds broke the awful stillness and made a symphonic overture to accompany His universal spirit so ready for the Great Adventure." So wrote Welthy in the memorial pamphlet she put together a few months later in a gallant effort to lift herself out of despair. In their last hours together Fred said to her over and over: "Remember, I love you more than anything else in the world."

* * *

It was Helen Krayer Schwartz, now married to a New York business-man, who came immediately to Welthy — Helen, the person who had seen their love beginning, maturing, and enduring. She slept in the same room with her, and all the time Welthy talked and read, talked about Fred and their dream of freedom, talked to keep herself going, talked about his Easter memorial she would plan.

It was the only Easter funeral Detroit had ever known. Welthy helped Fred's loyal secretary, Grace Macpherson, execute every detail and send telegrams to friends everywhere. Welthy had no tears; she only wanted to be by herself to plan the lying in state before the high altar, where the casket rested after the Easter service until the funeral, viewed by six thousand mourners.

Welthy walked into the sanctuary alone, and the combined choirs, her creation, sang the Hallelujah Chorus in celebration of Fred's life among them. In her grief, Welthy was stung that only the Michigan Bishop was present, Easter duties keeping the others preoccupied. In his eulogy Bishop Blake said: "Dr. Fisher had an ear for things others could not hear, and an eye for things others could not see. He was able to rightly interpret things in the light of the Eternal, where he was completely at home."

A portion of Fred's ashes was placed in the altar of Central Church, the bruised and discouraged church that had been saved by Fred and Welthy. They had increased its membership from eight hundred to over twenty-five hundred, and established a permanent bond with the community, assuring its future. It was a brilliant era in the life of Central Methodist Church, marked by a small bronze plaque where his ashes remain, with these words of Tagore chosen by Welthy:

And when you had taken your leave,
I found God's footprints on my floor.

PART FOUR

RECOVERING THE WORLD

EXQUISITE LONELINESS

1⁹³⁸

At fifty-nine, Welthy was a widow. Her grief would somehow have to absorb four hundred thousand miles of living with Fred. Inundated with condolence messages from around the world that "burned deep into my waiting soul," there were enough practical details to fill the immediate days ahead, with well-meaning friends and relatives making too many suggestions and recommendations for her future. To friends everywhere, including Gandhi, who had responded to her telegram and the announcement of Fred's death on the national radio, Welthy sent a printed memorial pamphlet, "Good Friday to Easter", written as her first act of recovery.

Tributes to Fred invariably included Welthy, as in *The Christian Advocate*: "These two were deeply one; they could speak from the same platform, accept the same degree in equal honor from the same college, write with like clearness to power on the same great themes, and give themselves to the church's work with the same ardor and effectiveness." One letter said Fred had done more than any other man to debunk Methodism of some of its useless weaknesses, wondering if Welthy would now be John the Baptist, pointing the way to better things in the church.

Ralph Templin, a fellow clergyman, wrote that "no charge can be sustained against Fisher except that he was almost out of sight in advance of his day, and somewhat lacking in the patience necessary for tactful statesmanship. Fred Fisher was the worst missionary of all, in the best sense of the word. He had become the arch-fiend of missionary heterodoxy. Christianity cannot permanently remain tolerant of imperialistic control. It is inevitable that the mission will some day wonder that it was ever at variance with his thought. But if he was a poor missionary, he was a poorer bishop. Glorious man who was willing to admit it. In the pulpit, Fisher was without peer in America." Referring to Wesley's failure as a missionary, and the failure of Jesus and Paul in the eyes of contemporaries, Templin said: "These 'failures' to cope with the requisites of the Church's legalistic and outworn slavishness drove them back into a reliance upon the inner spirit."

One young Indian, Tarini Sinha, a graduate student who had come from Chicago to pay tribute by sitting all night by Fred's bier in the Church, wanted to live with Welthy and work with her on Fred's biography. A Detroit bachelor businessman offered to move in and take care of her affairs, business and otherwise. "I couldn't fill my house with men," said Welthy. Gordon Halstead urged her to take in her brother's two youngest children and see them through college.

In the months that followed Welthy was offered several university positions teaching oriental culture, and her own Syracuse University invited her to be Dean of Women. But none of these roles of collaborator, lover, aunt or academic could call forth the deep strength that was in Welthy, that she knew she must use.

Welthy weighed her options swiftly, and decided she had no choice but to follow the underlying course of her life, the course that had brought her to Fred, and would now pull her onward if she could find the path to pursue. She stayed in Detroit long enough to participate in the selection of Henry Hitt Crane to succeed Fred at Central—a superb choice—and decided it would be wrong to remain in Detroit with a new leader coming into the church.

For a short while she lived at Pilgrimthorpe, restless when friends and relatives came to keep her company. Betty came quickly, anxious to play the daughter's role to one who had been a loving mother to her. The white land otter coat Betty gave her then was one of the few treasures she would never part with.

From her wartime comrade Josephine January, now a widow returning from months abroad to her Washington, D.C. home: "Oh my Welthy beloved . . . all the years of faith and discipline and unselfish living are your staff and strength now." Those words from the depth of shared feeling, sustained and inspired Welthy more than all the other well intended logical advice. She mined her letters for the all the nourishment they could give her, feeding off every glimmer of understanding.

LAKELAND, FLORIDA, SUMMER 1938

First she carried out Fred's plan to establish a garden of meditation at Florida Southern College, already sketched out by Dorothy Probst. Welthy's assumption that Dorothy would go with her to Lakeland that summer of 1938 came as a complete surprise to her, since she was unaccustomed to such swiftness and the necessary improvisation it meant. But she packed her bags pluckily to accompany Welthy.

They had two simple rooms in a dormitory, sharing a bath with ants who loved mangoes and guavas as much as Welthy did. Welthy just brushed off the ants and stood over the bathtub eating the ripe fruit. Armed with citronella, the women searched the local nurseries for plants to surround the Hindu temple Fred had brought back from India in pieces.

They arranged for it to be erected, its spire dominating a reflecting pool. On one side was the Hindu symbol of eternal life, and inside, an altar with cross and candlesticks replacing the usual Hindu idol. Surmounting the small tower was the cross — the arms of man in the world, supported by rising spiritual awareness, centred on compassion radiating from the point of intersection. Though she was fully conscious of her need to carry out Fred's plan, the symbol would be with her for fourteen long, lonely years before she would understand its full truth and express it in her actions.

She was cheerful and talkative when busy that summer, after she succeeded in mollifying the reluctant students who had no desire to help 'damned Yankee women'. Appearing each day in a man's shirt and man's felt hat under a farmer's broad-brimmed straw hat, Welthy demonstrated her willingness to work. She joked with the boys while overseeing their labours, and managed to harness their energy to her will, greasing the wheels with liberal applications of Coca Cola and Dr. Pepper. For Dorothy, twenty years younger, it was a long, hot, tiring, sunburnt, bitten summer she would never forget, as she tried to keep pace with Welthy's driving energy. But it was offset with laughter and fun during quiet weekends at the Gulf of Mexico when a lifetime friendship was built.

Welthy gave many of Fred's books to the college to start an Asian collection that bore fruit years later when the college launched its Asian programme; and the garden became the most popular place on the campus, a place where students chose to be married. She considered building an Indian house as her permanent residence in Lakeland, one of innumerable possibilities, but nothing was clear. In diaries and poems she was living through the emptiness:

Magnificent Sorrow
is mine.
Love strains my ear to catch
the conversation of that sphere
where he now talks and walks
and serves unencumbered.
Grief leads me staggering to the
unplumbed deep
of awful silence,
Where silence echoes silence.
Faith forces me to find his God,
Ever growing
Ever expanding
Ever suffering.

*His going companions me
with magnificent sorrow.*

By the end of August 1938 she returned north with some of her old
momentum back. Fred's silver Damascus cross, symbol of her summer's
work, hung round her neck as she appeared on the platform at the
Michigan State Fair, principal speaker on the women's programme. On
the eve of the Munich crisis, Welthy reminded her huge audience that
in the last war it was women's part to make the war endurable and
provide amusement for their men. "We'll never do it again," she
promised. *The Detroit News* carried her message prominently.

She moved on to Chautauqua, New York, to speak as a well-known
author in their evening programme. It was a natural home for Welthy
in every sense. Originally housed in tents, it was now a town in itself,
with narrow shaded roads, Victorian houses on tiny lots adorned with
flowers, hotels, recreation facilities, a huge amphitheatre, music in the
air, and everywhere the American flag flying proudly. It sprang from a
time when people believed in the perfectability of man. At its peak, some
thirty million came to breath its fresh and hopeful airs. In late September 1938 Welthy was ordained a Deacon of the Methodist Church in a
unique service. In a costume of her own design—a purple crepe cassock bordered with red, over it a white silk surplice with flowing sleeves
and a purple fringed stole, Fred's cross and a purple velvet biretta—
Welthy took her vow and was licensed to preach, baptize and marry.

Reports of the ceremony said she hoped to receive elders' orders
within a year, which carry the full authority of the ministry and would
be a precedent in the church for a woman. But Welthy thought again
about that distinction. "If you become an elder, and anyone had anything against you, they could put you anywhere, somewhere up in
Michigan. They could have traded me. I felt I had some other things to
do." Position and security were not her priority.

She preached her first sermon in the High Street Methodist Church in
Muncie where Fred found his spiritual life, and where they asked for a
portion of his ashes to remain. Except for Harry and Florence Fisher,
the other members of Fred's family did not keep in touch with her and
she always felt they disapproved of her, never certain just why, though
she was well aware that many thought her too strong for a woman.
Another portion of the ashes was kept for the Himalayas, where Fred felt
closest to God.

FINANCIAL WORRIES

There were distressing business matters to settle before she could
make a significant move. She named Helen Krayer's husband, Arthur

Schwartz, and the Methodist treasurer, as co-executors of Fred's estate to deal with the insurance company's intent to pay Fred's life insurance based on natural cause of death, rather than a larger amount for accidental death. Welthy's eyes were on India and possibility of building a chapel of Indian design at Jubbulpore Theological College in Fred's memory. But the Church pushed its claim to the outstanding Fisher Fund money. It acknowledged that Fred's motive was to help needy projects of the church, but said it was still a personal debt, since both Welthy and Fred had signed a letter saying they would pay it, certain they could raise money after the fact.

Welthy had received no family inheritance, and had no income except that from the carefully managed money Cousin Dee had given earlier. With no pension as a bishop's widow, as a result of Fred's resignation, she suggested to the Methodists that they put the outstanding sixteen thousand dollars in trust, with the income coming to her. Nothing would satisfy the treasurer however except cash in hand, and efforts were made to have Welthy raise money for two debts on churches in India which were to be memorials to Fred and his first wife. "We will probably get more with molasses than with vinegar . . . if we can interest Mrs. Fisher in providing funds for needed projects in India that is better than any threats of legal procedure or antagonistic attitude," wrote one official. Another recognized that Welthy would be in the public eye and in a position to raise a good deal of money for India if they cultivated her, but suggested discretion lest Welthy think they were working her too hard.[1] It was a strange strategy, but Welthy was sympathetic and cooperative to the appeal.

The whole issue left her with a wound equivalent to that from her own dismissal years earlier from the WFMS. In both cases the situation resulted from the Fisher lack of concern with cold, administrative detail. Method took precedence over motive for the church, a fact Welthy could never understand. She felt the pressure of the church for its pound of flesh. How did they value the unpaid services she had rendered as Fred's wife for fourteen years, she wondered? The Church's Committee on Policy and Program felt that its case was not strong enough to take legal action against Welthy. It is easy to see why Welthy had no desire to be an elder.

WORLD TOUR, DECEMBER 1938

December 17, 1938. "Eight months ago the choirs were singing the Hallelujah Chorus. Today I stand on the deck of the Excambion with its sixty-six passengers and its heavy cargo. I have taken passage to India," wrote Welthy to her wide circle of friends. She would re-enter the world to recover her spirit. For one whole year she would look into the faces of India and China, meet everyone she could, find out what they did and why, learn all her shattered mind could absorb, try to grow, try desperately not to look back. She began with her fellow passengers, observing their manners and conversation, and felt at one with them, briefly, when heavy rolling seas deposited passengers and furniture unceremoniously in a heap on the floor, only to discover in that intimacy that she alone among them had not read "Gone With The Wind". By 5:00 a.m. that omission was corrected, and she began on "All This and Heaven Too" to enhance her social skills. A woman travelling alone needed friends.

In Cairo an astrologer predicted she would live to ninety-three or four, an improbable Christmas gift for one struggling to get through the immediate present. It was a new year when Welthy set foot in Bombay, a city transformed in eight years with modern apartments and houses springing up, signs of life everywhere. Welthy was home again.

BOMBAY, 1939

Her good friend S. Natarajan, took Welthy in hand immediately, sending his daughter to meet her ship at Ballard Pier and escort her to the missionary settlement for university women where she had arranged to stay. That evening they took her to hear Kagawa speak against war at a World Faith meeting, and the next day Natarajan gave a party for Welthy in his home in the Bandra suburb of Bombay to meet prominent people in all spheres. They had all read Fred's last speech, published in Natarajan's journal, and showed a genuine desire to make her Indian visit successful in any way they could. It was the first time she had felt stimulated since Fred's death, and with wise counsel from Natarajan plotted her time in India.

She was struck immediately by the contrast between the narrow outlook of missionaries at the settlement residence and the wide, cooperative attitude of the Natarajans and their expansive friends. "I can plainly see that we have left the little missionary circle, and when I think how many years we stayed in it, I marvel." She met Bombay's elite at the home of the Vice-Chancellor of the university, formed a friendship with Hansa Mehta, the leading political woman in Bombay whose *swadeshi* home of Indian handicrafts was wonderfully appealing, was entertained in homes of distinguished people on Malabar Hill, met social workers and heard about their adult literacy classes for six hundred women.

Travelling about the city in an open one-horse Victoria, Welthy spoke at the Alexandria School for Parsee girls under Sophia Wadia's sponsorship, found little to enjoy at the Willingdon Sports Club except the beautiful Indian women, and met a Muslim congress worker just released from prison who told of training non-violent women workers. She went twice to observe Ivy Child's work with young girls and speak to them, noting that "Indian girls are so intelligent, and so friendly, but they need to be approached with an open heart."

Her days were full. Welthy was on the move again and recording everything for a series of articles published by the Methodists. She returned to her settlement quarters only to sleep and for prayers, feeling Fred's absence terribly in that atmosphere where she was "alone in the high-ceilinged rooms. Privacy is all here again, but without him. I do not know what to do." Split by the pull between her new associations, and her old loyalty to missions, she decided to immerse herself in the mission atmosphere next, keeping an open mind.

Stopping at Poona en route to Jubbulpore, she was tickled that the Indian sent to meet her train wired back that she had not "reached," since he saw no one old enough to be a bishop's widow. Despite her resolve to be open, she felt the missionaries there made no effort to know or become interested in Indians on a personal basis. "I wonder where the mission thing will lead," she mused.

The six months Welthy spent in India saw her pulled more and more away from the point of view of the missionary, towards a broad appreciation of all of India and of all Indians, from the highest to the lowest, as she moved about the sub-continent renewing friendships and establishing strong new ones, creating an invisible network which would form the base of her later work. Excerpts from her diary show wild swings of mood during that first year of raw vulnerability.

January 23, 1939. On seeing a decaying widower: "May God help me not to live in the past. I am sure Bohn is living in the future as he always did here."

January 25, 1939. At the end of her first day with the missionaries at Jubbulpore: "It was hard and maybe I didn't do well in coming. Oh these institutions where the missionary has been everything. It makes me feel cold. Perhaps when I have slept over it I may feel differently." The lack of beauty was deplorable.

January 27, 1939. All my life now, I shall have to be studying something—it is my solace—not cigarettes as the Mohammedan woman on the train. At least it will keep the grey matter in my brain moving. Bohn would probably say 'sit down and think.' And perhaps I shall some day learn how. But as yet, I know only how to study."

January 29, 1939. After hearing Frank Laubach, the American literacy pioneer in the Philippines and elsewhere: "He's a real find, a sweetly mystical sermon. He revels in his work. Laubach uses love and help and they occasionally have a conversion." Welthy saw his 'each one teach one' system in operation in a veranda night school at the college, a school that had begun with ten students and now had eighty.

January 30, 1939. "Nobody mentions my Beloved here. I am going to believe they reverence him, feel I do not want to talk about him." In fact, her silence stemmed from the lingering impression that Fred had been asked by the British to leave India, and that he had ceased to believe in missions. How could they understand his belief that missions were needed more than ever, but on a different basis?

"Oh how I long to talk it all over with Bohn. I realize how I fed upon his mind and how little I have of my own. I wish I could live with Indians. This campus is dried up, not awfully deep. How the Methodists hate Gandhi. It leaves an unpleasant taste in my mouth. I cannot stand it very long. There is no feeling for India in this house. They are against the Congress."

February 2, 1939. "I do not know how I am going to live and not talk to anyone. I am almost afraid to stay here because I'm afraid I will talk. I feel I am compromising myself in staying with the missionaries. The WFMS has not made one move. I had decided to try to love them in spite of everything, but it is not going to be allowed I reckon."

MEETING WITH GANDHI

February 6, 1939. Welthy made a one-day excursion from Nagpur to Sevagram Ashram with Indian friends to see Gandhi. Ten years her senior, he had retired from politics several years earlier to develop village industries and education, focused particularly on the *harijans*, children of God, as he named them. He was still sought out for political advice and at that moment was undergoing a fast for political purposes. A doctor came in to take his blood pressure during the brief time she was with him in that "heavenly quiet of a place," but it was long enough for Gandhi to offer her a place if she wished to join the Ashram.

He suggested that she first talk with Nehru, and with the two best exponents of *ahimsa*, B. R. Prasad in Patna and Rajagopalachari in Madras, to find out for herself what was in their minds, since he was uncertain whether Welthy's interests were more political or educational. He also recommended that she see the Christians in Travancore, who had joined with Hindus in the freedom struggle, and several other areas of India, especially Santiniketan, where Tagore's constructive education and revival of Indian culture had greatly influenced the basic education movement. "Then come and pool experiences and after hearing your reactions I will put you right if I find you have any wrong impressions," he wrote a few days later.[2]

February 10, 1939. On receiving a letter offering her the New York Town Hall for a lecture series, Welthy decided to accept and try to carry on expounding Fred's interpretations of religion and politics. On the chapel she wanted to build at Jubbulpore, Bessie Perkins "wonders why I try to make a monument for Fred when he needs nothing in brick and stone."

February 12, 1939. Still at Jubbulpore, hoping for some breakthrough in her plan to build a chapel, studying Hindi, taking evening meditations for the students, attending faculty meetings with no Indians present, Welthy felt the confinement more and more, always looking for a friend to ease the lonely hours. With a new white sari to enable her to sit on the ground decently, she planned to join the seven hundred thousand who would attend the upcoming Congress meeting, the real reason for her long stay in the area. With no one at Jubbulpore interested in her chapel idea, she wondered if she was losing her mind.

February 14, 1939. Friends in America cabled greetings on Bohn's birthday. "I had hoped by putting up a chapel along Indian lines to persuade silently to Indianize this campus."

Welthy's solitude amid the crowd was delightfully broken with the arrival of Frances Shepard, a young college teacher from New England with experience conducting European tours. In a moment of discouragement Frances had written to a friend that she was ready to take off and go round the world, and received by return post the recommendation that she contact Mrs. Welthy Honsinger Fisher, who was planning such a trip. The name was well known in her family; her father was a Methodist minister, and her mother had joined the other young ministers' wives in trying to get a good seat in the balcony at conferences to see what colour Welthy was wearing each day — her all lavender, all blue, or all red costume. Frances went immediately to Hingham to meet Welthy, and on the spot they agreed to join forces in India, as soon as Frances could get away. Welthy offered to pay her one hundred dollars a month for secretarial assistance.

Adventure was back in the air with Frances' arrival in 1939. Here was someone to travel around with, and help with correspondence and the articles Welthy was sending home to the Methodists and *The Syracuse Herald*. Movement was the best antidote for Welthy, and few young Americans have been exposed to so much of India, inside and out, as Frances was that spring.

INDIAN NATIONAL CONGRESS, TRIPURI, 1939

Riding in tongas they went out to the tent city at Tripuri, a rural atmosphere chosen to expose city people to realities, where the fifty-second session of the Indian National Congress meeting was underway. Welthy circulated widely, from Sarojini Naidu and Jawaharlal Nehru to village level workers, in her comprehensive study of a changing India, represented in miniature under the big tent.

Sometimes she stayed overnight on a rope bed in a mud hut, insisting for health reasons that Frances return to the college, and glad for freedom to roam around on her own. It was an unruly session, with Nehru shouted down frequently by Bengalis and questioning his own ability to lead in the face of overwhelming differences between Hindus and Moslems.

It was the basic education exhibition that really caught Welthy's interest with a vast array of hand-made products from all the regions of India, showing Gandhi's idea of learning by doing. It seemed the constructive way to improve Indian life, by recognizing individual humans in a concrete way. She was particularly drawn to the posters announcing the new Wardha system of education with a richly carved tower of a Hindu temple, the dome and minarets of a mosque, and equal with the two a church spire mounted with a cross. She could not resist writing to Gandhi about the Hindu temple in Florida, and the two engaged in an animated exchange of biblical quotes.

Gandhi was leading a fundamental effort to overcome the illiteracy of ninety percent of India's population. British education had not touched the villages where most Indians lived, and only five percent were in primary schools in cities, where European materials in the English language were used to produce an elite corps of loyal clerks, alienated from their own culture. Though some private educational experiments had been undertaken, mass primary education had been ignored. This was now Gandhi's main concern in response to the immediate need of villagers.

Nehru's sister, Vijaya Lakshmi Pandit, invited Welthy to her hut for a talk over tea, as did Sarojini Naidu. Both were busy women preoccupied with the pressures of Congress, yet they took time to extend the unique brand of hospitality and friendship in which Indians excel, keen to hear the views of an outsider they respected. Sarojini was both commanding and serene at once. A short, dumpy woman, she had the presence of a queen, able to rally Indian women to the nationalist movement. Humour was her ally, and underneath her power was a poet's spirit, drawing Welthy irresistibly to her.

* * *

In Calcutta Welthy went first to the old banyan tree in the Botanical Gardens, its massive network of protective aerial roots encompassing an area large enough to shelter a small army. Its outspread arms, separate but joined to the core, the whole growing in both height and width, gave her a much-needed sense of involvement in a living movement, just as Sarojini and Gandhi had claimed her as one of their own and made her feel she belonged in India.

Sudhakanta and Charlie Andrews each called on her at the YWCA to reinforce Tagore's invitation to Santiniketan, where Fred had often thought of starting a Christian centre in his retirement, and where they now urged her to build a cottage for herself, an idea that she considered for some time. But before entering Tagore's world, she carried out her symbolic mission in the mountains above Darjeeling.

HIMALAYAS, 1939

Some Indians had wanted Fred's ashes at a large Hindu institution, and it may have been more appropriate to put them in a Christian chapel, "but I decided to bring them to these great heights where he found God so near, these great piles of mountains and strength, and these tender orchids that grow so luxuriantly on them represented his strong intellect and his tender soul and the universality of his spirit."

She set off with Frances and the principal of Mount Hermon School at 3:30 a.m. for Tiger Hill eighty-four hundred feet above sea level, and "just as the sun was coming up over Everest and Kanchenjunga, which he loved above all others, the great crests were soon aglow — first pink, then mauve, then brilliant white. 'I am an offspring of the sky, Child of the Sun, For native home my soul aspires' — well darling, you sang that song in your notebook a year ago," she reminded herself. Reading out her prayer to the mountains, Welthy could see the purple color of his robe even in the ashes as she gave him back to his Cosmic God.

> *Here on these Himalayan Heights, O Beloved,*
> *Where here you taught me to know the Eternal —*
> *His Majesty, His Humanity, His Universality,*
> *Here, facing Everest and Kinchanjung,*
> *I give you back to Him.*
> *These parts of you that laughed,*
> *These parts of you that loved,*
> *These parts of you that suffered.*
> *I, too, will follow you,*
> *Greeting you here or there on even grander heights*
> *Where you and the Eternal dwell.*

TAGORE, SANTINIKETAN

February 27, 1939. Tagore at seventy-nine was the most impressive human being in physical appearance Welthy had ever met. "Something in his long garment reminds me of a clergyman's cassock; something of a Chinese gentleman's long robe; and something scents of the old Gupta era when Indian art flourished and there still lingered a strong Persian and Greek influence. In his person and poetry he embodies a lingering essence of India's mystical past, a little of her complex present, and much of her vital future."

Despite the tranquil beauty of *Santiniketan* and Tagore's serene countenance, Welthy was still subject to disturbingly swift mood swings. "I talk too much with these people. I know that I talked too much when Bohn was talking. He used to say that I would not let him finish a sentence. I want to fly to you over the border into the other world and hear you talk of the things of God forever. What I might have learned from you."

Sitting on the veranda of the Guest House under the shade of a neem tree, with mango groves, sal trees, chattim and a few palms just beyond, and the song of birds everywhere, Welthy studied the plan and progress of Tagore's creation, reading again his poems that spoke so intimately to her, as if he had known her need long before.

And in that silence she listened to Tagore's graceful words, written and spoken, visiting him frequently in his exquisitely simple mud hut to learn of that freedom of the mind he sought to cultivate. In his book "Personality" she found the very ideas Fred had expressed in seeing identity with God as the true personality:

> *Religion is the true centre of gravity of our life, the truth of our complete being. It can never be imparted in lessons or measured by outward standards.*

His school was the outgrowth of his life, not a mere carrying out of doctrines, and its ideals changed with maturity, starting from an act of benevolence struggling to achieve results, and growing into his own development of spontaneous creation. What he wanted above all was a university where everyone should learn cosmopolitan tolerance of all cultures and religions in preparation for world cooperation. His teaching spoke directly to her:

> *Truth cannot be communicated to those on whom you look down. You must be able to see the divine light that shines within them, for it is your own lack of vision that makes all seem dark.*

Tagore had learned that trying to overcome problems by tightening organizational screws gave meagre results, that the answer was to be found within oneself. Having suffered as a youth from "the tight-fitting encasement of school, like the shoes of a mandarin woman, which pinched and bruised" his nature, he rejected discipline and uniformity as limiting human development in early schooling. The object of education was "to know man and make yourself known to man." If his intellectual and physical education were developed at the expense of spiritual growth, man had only fragmented knowledge, was ever left in a state of contradiction. His spiritual nature was as compelling as the physical law of gravity, a belief Fred had expressed in the same terms.

What Welthy found particularly perceptive in Tagore was his clear recognition of women's strength, and of the feminine aspect undeveloped in most men. His words of 1917 aroused her with the prediction that men would have to give way to women, who have broader development, just as the dinosaurs had to give way to humans with their more compact development:

> Masculine creations of intellectual civilization are towers of Babel — defying their foundations, toppling over and over again. Woman, like a tree, sends out branches, but deeper bonds are held firm in soil - broad, deep and stable. Not mere growth, but harmony of growth. Not always relying on outside stimulation. Woman must come into the bruised and mained world of the individual; she must claim each one of them as her own, the useless and the insignificant. The individuals must find their true value, raise their heads once again in the sun, and renew their faith in God's love through her love. Woman's responsibility has become greater than ever before; her field of work has far transcended the domestic sphere of life.[3]

When Welthy visited the adult night classes in the villages surrounding the experimental rural development work at Santiniketan she was surprised at the lack of conviction among Tagore's educators that all Indians should be able to read their own language, believing that other things came before literacy. The concept of universal literacy throughout a future democratic India, and the wisdom of establishing a basic literacy requirement for voting privileges was an issue of varying opinion, one that was never completely resolved in Nehru's mind.

In 1939, Welthy had no doubt in her own mind that everyone had a right to his or her own cultural and spiritual heritage in his or her own language, regardless of political considerations. As with the missionaries, she did not argue the point but listened and observed, reserving the argument for her diary. She knew that Gandhi had changed his mind about a simple adult franchise after observing the working of Congress, and now favoured a literacy test for two reasons; first because the right to vote was a privilege and should carry some qualification, and secondly, that the much desired literacy would come quickly if the government was sincere and solicitous about upgrading the disqualified illiterates. It was a view based on idealistic assumptions.

Despite her reservations, Welthy felt that a fundamental shift was taking place in India under Tagore's guidance, with his focus on villages, inclusion of women and revival of the best of Indian culture. As his teachers and students extended their work to the villages, they purposely put themselves in the position of learners, studying indigenous crafts, folk art and music, rediscovering their own heritage.

*   *   *

March 6, 1939. "Now as I go about India I find I do not see it with my spirit. I seem more like a body without a soul. I walk in dreams, striving to make myself interested in all the throbbing new life of India."

Introducing Frances to the historic sites of Benares and Agra also helped Welthy to see things anew. Welthy disliked the Hindu temples but admired the devotion of the worshippers, a devotion she found generally lacking among Christians. In contrast, she found the high level Indian Civil Service officials serving under the British extremely noncommittal, remote from their own people, and chillingly professional.

April 7, 1939, Good Friday. "For one year now I have looked into every crevice of the world where he has been. He is not there, not here, and not in India. I have been like a body wandering to and fro about the earth, without a soul." In the pre-dawn shadows, Welthy consoled herself by writing:

> *The white moon lingers high in the morning sky,*
> *Fragrance of night flowers still pervade the air.*
> *An expectant hush blankets all sleeping creatures,*
> *Men in huts and palaces, in streets and fields,*
> *Await in slumber the call of the dawn.*
> *Birds are silent, the wind withholds its motion.*
> *The moon hesitates to give way,*
> *Knowing full well that when she fades*
> *The burning sun will announce this Tragic Day of Sorrow.*
> *Oh mystery unsolved, I search for him in the fading*
> *   moonlight,*
> *Only to find myself at the dawn of Eternity.*
> *Make my road swift to the Eternal.*

As they had done every day since their arrival in Delhi, Welthy and Frances attended Gandhi's prayers at G. D. Birla's house at dusk, all seated on the floor for the singing, chanting and quiet meditation. She observed how few attended the prayers, Nehru never, Sarojini always. Gandhi had asked Welthy specifically to bring some foreign friends that

Good Friday evening to sing his favourite Christian hymn, "Lead Kindly Light," with words he would have the Christians hear, words meant for Welthy:

> *Lead, kindly light, amid th'encircling gloom,*
> *Lead Thou me on.*
> *The night is dark, and I am far from home,*
> *Lead Thou me on.*
> *Keep Thou my feet. I do not ask to see*
> *The distant scene; one step enough for me.*

From that high moment of Gandhi teaching his Christian friends, Welthy went in his son Devadas' car with an English woman, Agatha Harrison, to see Charlie Andrews in the hospital, and then with Sarojini's daughter Padma Naidu, to see Gandhi off at the Old Delhi railroad station in the crowded third class, while one of India's wealthy princes travelled by special car in solitary splendour — a striking image of contrasts.

On Easter Sunday, 1939, Welthy went to early communion alone at the Methodist Church and then to the morning service at the Anglican Church, where the Viceroy read the lesson against the background of those white, barren walls she found so unrevealing. From there she went with Sarojini to a discussion on South Africa at the Arya Samaj Hall. "I tried in two churches, and then in this meeting of ethical protest, but none of them seemed to lift me spiritually. Well, there is one yonder, and one here so much of the time with me, that I feel the exaltation of it. But with the triumph I should act. And where? And how? These are yet unanswered."

Andrews wanted her to settle at Santiniketan, and Agatha Harrison suggested she might run a centre in Delhi part of the year where people of all religions and races could meet. As she travelled by train in a compartment full of women in purdah, saddened by the thought of their darkened lives, Welthy looked back briefly at what she had found in India so far in that critical year. What she had gained from Tagore and Charlie Andrews would have to sustain her for life, for both men died shortly after.

Mahadev Desai, Gandhi's secretary, came to urge that the story of Fred's life in India be written, and gave her a letter to Sir Reginald Maxwell, the Home Member, who could get Fred's book "That Strange Little Brown Man Gandhi" removed from the banned list. Andrews had also pressed her to try to get 'brown' out of the title. Welthy prepared to do battle by donning her blue and white polka-dot dress, one she reserved for special occasions for its supposed appeal to men, according to Frances.[4] It did not work. Her first "official imperialist experience" was negative, Maxwell remaining adamant against removing the ban, "so I take it that their gesture toward releasing India is only a gesture."

G. D. Birla, the prominent industrialist who gave his home over to Gandhi whenever the *Mahatma* was in Delhi, often drove Welthy back to her YWCA hostel after the prayer meetings, offering her flowers from his garden for her room, and demonstrating to her by his support of Gandhi that wealth and power do not automatically corrupt.

Nehru's wife and Raj Kumari Amrit Kaur, one of the women closest to Gandhi, befriended Welthy, recognizing the level of her interest. Welthy attended several meetings of the National Council of Women, and was invited to address them. She was well informed of the religious and social traditions that kept most Indian women living in dark shadows — echoes of Chinese women's lot at the turn of the century — and committed to an educational solution, she was drawn to these active women. Sarojini had been the first to break out of caste and home into active political life, and because of Gandhi's strategic inclusion of women in his movement, others had come forward in increasing numbers to initiate voluntary organizations in an unprecedented wave of national effort.

BASIC EDUCATION

At Gandhi's urging Welthy went to see Dr. Zakir Husain, head of the Muslim college in Aligargh, and a distinguished educator who would later serve on Welthy's board, become President of India, and present her with the first Nehru Literacy Award. On that April day in 1939, he told Welthy in a soft voice which masked his strength that educational workers could not be political, that his group did not take government grants but depended on the support of the public. Big contributions were dangerous because when they stopped, the work stopped, but his educational programme had built-in self-support from the production of crafts.

That concept of the scientific teaching of crafts to enable students to produce and make education self-supporting was the basic educational thrust endorsed by Congress as the mandate of the All India National Education Board established at Sevegram that month. Basic crafts, not literacy, would serve as the basis of education of the whole personality. For an impoverished nation it was the only approach to universal education that seemed possible. Husain told Welthy not to interest any millionaire in the matter; they needed to work out their own educational salvation for the multitudes, by the multitudes.

She analyzed and compared the three approaches of Tagore, Gandhi and Husain, each with a slightly different emphasis, but all aiming at the education of the rural majority. Tagore insisted on including the joy of life, convinced that natural enthusiasm gave an enduring motivation to learn. Gandhi, himself from the commercial class, put the emphasis on the political and practical, which Welthy saw as a possible detriment, though she could not argue with his aim of self-government and self-sufficiency as a protection against tyranny within and without. "The end of all knowledge must be the building up of character," said Gandhi. Much as she believed in work experience and incidental earning as partial support, she felt the emphasis should be placed on learning, not earning, and that the temperaments and talents of people should be understood first, with some practical adult psychology applied.[5] On balance, she thought Gandhi's concept of learning from the ground up, not from centralized education trickling down, had the ultimate common sense of a democrat. In response to the new movement towards basic education, the Indian Adult Education Association was founded that year, another in the wave of voluntary organizations adding strength to India's drive towards freedom.

For letters to Helen Schwartz Welthy reserved her light banter and personal feelings, including a desire to feel thin and a resolve to give up soup, white bread and desserts. "I am covered with bites of sand fleas," she wrote. "They do not announce themselves like the gentleman mosquito, so all I can do is to flit the bed and myself, but even flit is just a perfume for them. They are unteachable."

She reported that everyone loved the white hat Helen had helped her buy that resembled a northern Indian *Mawari* hat and won a joke from Gandhi every time she wore it. That interval in Delhi, seeing Gandhi daily, was the happiest Welthy had been since arriving in India. "I am not straining or striving any more. I am just experiencing what comes and trying to sense the value of it. Something will work out."

April 11, 1939. The ladies went by intermediate class train to Lahore, travelling in a compartment with twelve Muslim women who threw off their *boorkas* as soon as the train departed. Welthy met Begum Shah Nawaz, Parliamentary Secretary for the Punjab, and attended an Assembly session, the wedding reception of the Begum's daughter in the Shalimar Gardens, and a huge luncheon of the All India Women's Conference, observing the power of those women even though cloaked in *purdah*.

Distinguished Indians called on her, thanks to introductions sent ahead by friends. Nehru's uncle, Brijlal Nehru, introduced her to many more. She visited the Golden Temple and studied the origins of Sikhism intently, noting that the services consisted of music, reading and meditation, no "lecturing."

April 15, 1939. "I should have stayed with him the last night and known what was in his mind. I carry his name — a sacred trust — I must try to carry his message — but how — and where?" she asked herself over and over again, fearful that in sleeping a few hours in an adjacent room she had somehow betrayed the trust after Fred died on that Maundy Thursday, a day of such symbolic meaning in the church.

At Peshawar she and Frances were taken in graciously by an Indian family with whom Mira Behn was staying while planning to establish a demonstration spinning centre for productive education in a village near the Khyber Pass. She intended to try friendship and love in action as an antidote to the failed military solution to problems in the area. A refugee from the "frightful affectation" of life in London, she sought to alleviate the physical and spiritual hunger of the village, finding there the sweet simplicity and sharing in the midst of stark poverty that was absolutely revolutionary to the way of thinking and living she had known.

Though Mira Behn had shaved her head in what Welthy considered slavish devotion to Gandhi's cause, now as she watched the expert, wise way of helping a low caste group with a problem in spinning, she saw the English woman as a new kind of nun. Unarmed and unafraid, Mira Behn had government approval for her plan.

THE FRONTIER GANDHI

They drove out with the comptroller of finance for the Northwest Frontier through the austere, grey hills past miles and miles of camels and armed soldiers to meet the Prime Minister of the province, Khan Abdul Ghaffir Khan, "the frontier Gandhi." A giant of a man, he insisted that the tribes could be won with cooperation and economic help, with wells, not guns, and described his efforts to establish popular education for the *Pathans* in the face of opposition by the British and the *Mullahs*.

She made sharp notes on a talk given in Lahore by J. C. Kumarappa on village economics: "develop labour intensive industries — support local market — emphasize duties rather than rights — western centralized production rotten to the core — don't want standardization but human beauty — advance of man is in direct proportion to the extent he can go unarmed."

After a few hours spent at the Gymkhana Club among the elite, Welthy escaped to the only movie in town, "Son of Frankenstein", a strange import indeed, and quite inadequate to meet her need for distraction from the rush of people and ideas.

KASHMIR, 1939

"My beloved is still in my mind. He looms all important. And probably woman has been like that down through the centuries; nothing seems to change it, not education, not travel, not independence, not so-called freedom. Love has no freedom — it has chains forged by itself and woven with joy. Death does not break the chain, nor would I have it so. He lives with me here in this little houseboat — he would love the colour, the Bokhara rug — the red davenport — flower vases everywhere — and on the roof a large awning covers a space where we can sleep in warm weather. I am awake at three minutes before five every morning — the time he went away."

Welthy and Frances had taken up temporary residence on the Astora, Houseboat No. 243 in Srinagar, Kashmir, complete with bearer, cook, water carrier and sweeper for nine rupees a day. During the Muslim *Id* festival they were towed out to the middle of the Dal Lake to accommodate the influx of Muslims, one of the many events Welthy described in vivid detail in her articles. Beneath the surface gaiety she found the houseboat a ramshackle place, spending the day fending off hawkers and traders who tried to earn a year's living from two months of summer visitors.

April 29, 1939. "Yesterday Hitler gave his epoch-making speech and we have no radio and will have to wait for the Delhi papers."

The daily round of tea-time entertainment back and forth with visitors in nearby boats, of walking and riding treks, and of listening to people quarrel about trivialities, quickly began to pall. Welthy certainly did not want to camp or trek or live with women who kept fussing over who would do what with whom, and who never studied what they were seeing. They filled her with a need to move on. Even Frances, delightful companion that she was, cramped Welthy's style. "I tell you she wore me out with her fantastic energy and tremendous spirit," Frances said, marvelling at Welthy but hoping to enjoy their escape from the heat in a more relaxed manner. But Welthy never did anything in halves; when she relaxed, it was complete and over so soon that others had hardly begun.

May 17, 1939. "These mission people think I'm a radical so I must watch my step."

May 18, 1939. "I must be soft — shall keep going — must have health if I am to accomplish anything and wiriness that will carry me through hard things."

May 19, 1939. "I shall have to practise much to get the present day swing of style. Alexander Woolcott is terse and colourful, Pearl Buck is colourful and piquant, while Dorothy Thompson is piercing and direct.

If I'm going to write I'll have to write every day and cast out thousands of words."

She and Frances shifted from the houseboat to a tent where Welthy tried to begin writing Fred's biography, but anxiety over her future invaded her thoughts constantly and all she could manage were letters, and notes for articles. It was only mildly satisfying work. Her whole future was up in the air. Should she work in India, in China or in the United States? Should she spend half the year teaching in Florida, where Dr. Spivey had invited her to Florida Southern College? There was no pull of family strong enough to draw her. "Oh mountains, help me to stretch up as do the trees on all these hills. I need to be bigger and to put my mind on helping the rest of humanity. Instead of riding ponies, walking over the hills and baking beans I should be writing. Why does anyone come here where there is no place to work, no light to read by and no books? Eating is the main pastime."

* * *

In early June Welthy descended from the mountains into the plains once more. Seeing the missionaries in Jubbulpore again she could not help commenting on the "pious and prudish spinsters. I wonder if the mission school has done it?" She went back to *Santiniketan* and worked on plans for the chapel which she had asked her Bengali philosopher friends to draw. She saw the plot of land where Sudhakantha and Charlie wanted her to build a house, but neither plan materialized.

She knew she disappointed Andrews in not placing her future work under Tagore's umbrella, and her own disappointment was huge when the chapel design was rejected by the Anglo-Indians at Jubbulpore who wanted everything Western. They kept the five thousand dollars she gave for the chapel, proceeds from the life insurance battle she finally won, but the war intervened to prevent any construction. Much later, with years of accrued interest added to her gift, they eventually compromised by building what Welthy called an auditorium, but what was in fact a larger, multipurpose hall along the lines of her Indian architect's plan. Welthy could never bring herself to go back there. "I couldn't bear it — I knew Fred Fisher would love the chapel," but the Methodist board would not consider that money as partial payment on the Fund debt.[6]

In her distraught state, Welthy was no doubt a trial to church officials, but she retained warm relations with O. L. Davis, principal of Leonard Theological College, who wrote that he hoped "we can really take Indian culture more seriously now — that's where we want you to help us when you come back. Let me know when you really plan to come." Much as she would have liked to settle the nagging debt problem, her future was uncertain and she needed the income from that money to live.

"Pearl Buck says she has to earn money. So do I," Welthy noted. June 14, 1939. "What a heavy heart — tears are ready to burst forth at any moment. I've done a good many foolish things — should have left Kashmir earlier." Wavering and insecure, widowhood kept Welthy captive.

June 18, 1939. The fifteenth anniversary of her wedding. "He was the horizon of my life and his being there has made all the difference in the plane beyond. I feel he wants me to hurry up and do all the necessary things here and come where he is. Did I do all I could to make him happy? Fifteen years ago we were finding each other. Where did we go astray. I should have kept him thinned down and insisted on giving up such heavy tasks — but I knew we were led by a spirit greater than we were or are."

Welthy's swing through India concluded at Bombay, where a message from Gandhi to see him at Birla House on Malabar Hill awaited her. They met in a huge marble-floored room, Gandhi seated on a white mat in one corner and providing chairs for Welthy and Frances. He teased Welthy about his silent Mondays, saying Fred had been responsible for them, by having first come to see him on a Monday, so full of ideas and talking so much and so fast that Gandhi could not get a word in edgewise. "The rest did me so much good that I have ever since kept Monday as a day of silence," he jested, a gentle caution to his loquacious American friend. (TLC, 146.)

Welthy told him that she could not join his ashram, that she was unclear about her future and would for now try to interpret in America what she had seen and understood in India. She did not tell him that she found the ascetic, puritanical atmosphere created by his followers repressive to someone of independent thought, or that she found Tagore's celebration of life a more natural environment. In Gandhi himself, however, she found much to spur her own thinking. He urged her to be a judge and a critic, to tell the story unsparingly, and inquired when they would meet again. "I said two years, but who knows?"

* * *

As they sailed for Colombo aboard the S. S. Corfu, Welthy sorted out her reactions to all that had happened in six months. Gandhi's amazing ability to win the rich and powerful to his cause, along with the masses, convinced her that real progress depended on such an alliance and that only one committed to leading others could achieve it. His basic education programme was more substantial than all the political talk she had heard, and everywhere she had seen the need for it. Frank Moraes' article "When India Becomes Literate", describing the campaigns launched in seven provinces within the past year, gave her hope, though he noted that mass literacy would inevitably result in a pronounced swing to the left, and would require the kind of biblical faith which moves mountains. "India has become village conscious," she wrote in her article "Inside India," which focused on literacy. In some provinces where Congress (the nationalist political party) was in power, she reported, every literate person was required to teach an illiterate or pay a fine, showing a determination to tackle the problem that had been absent from the India she knew before.

Welthy tried to start a book on women of Asia, but that too eluded her, as she continued producing short but significant articles such as "International Etiquette," urging an open mind on American travellers:

> *It is easily possible to go around the world with blinders on*
> *. . . of prejudice and race superiority, completely insulated*
> *by American or European standards, comforts, language,*
> *ideas. It is easy to come back home with your bags and*
> *trunks plastered with the gay tags of all the hotels in far*
> *away ports - and remain un-inoculated with humanity. We*
> *insist on our way . . . and make such an excellent case for*
> *ourselves that we have had much of the world magnetized*
> *into thinking we possessed the God-given pattern of life, and*
> *that the struggle of all other civilizations toward a fuller life*
> *will be rewarded in direct proportion as they adopt our*
> *ways, our customs, our language and our parliaments.*
>
> *. . . If you can hear his point of view with poised, intelligent*
> *interest, if you can treat him without prejudice, and like him*
> *for himself while disagreeing with some of his ideas, you will*
> *have made possible the foundation of the only real interna-*
> *tional cooperation there can be in the world.*
>
> *. . . The passport into international society is courtesy — an*
> *essence of mind and spirit that sends forth its fragrance in*
> *every word and act. Within this one body of ours we carry*
> *about all the culture we possess, and our only contact with*
> *the world is through this one body.*
>
> *. . . If all your travel has been done by inclusive tours, you*
> *have missed that exquisite yearning, that sweet loneliness*
> *which comes from being an utter stranger in a new and*
> *foreign country. What a golden opportunity to hear the point*
> *of view so different from your own.*

For over a year Welthy had felt herself to be that utter stranger. The message was for herself as much as anyone.

CHINA, SUMMER 1939

July 22, 1939, Chungking. Welthy had left Frances behind in Hong Kong for her dangerous flight to the wartime capital of China. She had tried to enter China through the new Burma highway, but monsoon floods prevented that. Every day in Hong Kong she called the Chinese National Aviation office waiting for an answer about a flight; there was much questioning and secrecy. Finally the okay signal came, and Welthy departed at three o'clock in the morning in heavy rain with eight other passengers, paying exorbitant customs duty on the hospital supplies she was carrying in from Anglican Bishop R. O. Hall in Hong Kong.

They landed at dawn on an island sandbar in the Yangtze with the plane curtains drawn closed, the shining Douglas aircraft a target for Japanese bombers. They disembarked into a rowboat which took them to a waterplane for the twelve miles to that city of hills and stone steps, where the bombing of May 4th had cut the population in half. Twenty-seven Japanese planes had bombed Chungking during the night. Wounded soldiers and civilians still lay everywhere in the streets. It was a desperate scene.

Her first call after checking into the hostel where foreign journalists were staying was at the American Legation, where her old friend from the memorable trainride to Kamakura, Willys Peck, was Charge d'Affaires. She was invited there frequently, meeting a barrage of people, gathering information, and assessing attitudes.

All day there was the noise of the populace chiselling dug-outs in the rocks, and at night, the bombing. They went to sleep dressed and ready for the *Gin Bao* cry that sent Welthy, Tillman Durdin, Edgar Snow and the other correspondents dashing each night into the dugout shelter in the compound of H. H. Kung, the Finance Minister. "Three squadrons expected tonight . . . Chinese quiet in face of danger . . . swift and efficient handling of fires, dead, injured and refugees. China will not be terrorized. What philosopher ever designed a balance for weighing the fine essence of courage?"

Each night Welthy helped with the wounded, observing that "in war work we took people for what they were, for their capacity, their spirit, and their humanity, and forgot about dividing walls." All her energy, physical, spiritual, and emotional was fully absorbed by the horrendous need all around her. Thoughts of Fred no longer dominated; Welthy was back in her own territory among people for whom she had a great affinity.

In the long hours spent waiting for the 'all clear' Welthy kept to her studying, noting that Chungking had been settled in 2200 BC and that their particular dugout was the mausoleum of a former aristocratic family. "Who knows what little bodies have rested in the tomb-cave which has now become our shelter from enemy air-raids?"

REWI ALLEY AND GUNG HO

She quickly ascertained who were the key people and projects to be seen, beginning with Rewi Alley, lynchpin of the *Gung Ho* cooperative movement, whose prime aims then were to hold an unwilling Kuomintang to the war of resistance against the Japanese and attract international support. Beginning the year before, in 1938, they had established some three thousand small production units employing a hundred thousand people making blankets for the army, repairing equipment, and producing innumerable items for the war effort. Over ninety percent of China's prewar industry had been destroyed or immobilized, and when the Japanese invaded, in a mammoth upheaval, thirty million refugees from eastern China had trekked a thousand miles west, their possessions on their backs or in wheelbarrows.

Alley, a New Zealander, was an adviser to the government "who draws his dividends from the thrill of rehabilitating human life, a missionary whose churches are the workshops of China,"[7] wrote Edgar Snow of that vast movement which would form the technical base of postwar China. Conventional economists scoffed, certain the Chinese could never cooperate with each other, but Alley knew the Japanese could not bomb every village, that the cooperative spirit was not foreign to people who had traditionally worked together in guild and clan. Convinced it could be extended, Alley prevailed and was able to persuade General Chiang Kai-shek and his wife of the need for decentralized industrial cooperatives near the source of supply, fitting the goals of both wartime and peacetime, and transforming refugees into producing and useful citizens.

Alley had envisioned a native products guerilla industry of small factories spread across six provinces supporting an army of two hundred and fifty thousand. Mme. Sun Yat-sen, sister of Mme. Chiang, was so certain that *Gung Ho* represented the best possible way of putting her husband's beliefs into practice that she established her own organization in Hong Kong to win western support. Despite his humble high school education in that land of educational aristocracy, Alley was the first foreigner to be entrusted with responsibility for organizing an economic movement in China. His years spent as factory inspector in Shanghai and organizing famine relief were the real test of his ability. "Who can say that in the end Rewi Alley's achievement may not prove of more lasting benefit to mankind than the current battles of empire . . .

may not in fact be the most constructive result of the battle for Asia itself?" Snow speculated.

In Rewi Alley, nearly twenty years her junior, Welthy recognized a strength of spirit in action that filled a large part of her emptiness, engaging her restless energy. Rewi spoke her practical language; he told how they salvaged aluminum from the Japanese bombs to make spinning wheels, how they converted tung oil into gasoline. Ten percent of the profits from the cooperatives went into a fund for clinics, schools and nurses in every village. He showed her a large rural production unit being planned by young Chinese engineers assisted by Purdue and MIT graduates. The imagination, resourcefulness, cooperation, opportunity for learning and sheer scope of the project roused a vital response in Welthy and impressed her far more than anything else she saw during three months in China. Two months earlier, Alley had been near death with typhoid and malaria, his recovery taking place on the move from bombed hospital to warehouse. He was just back on his feet when Welthy encountered him.[8]

MADAME CHIANG KAI-SHEK

She met Mme. Chiang, who also impressed her initially, as she visited the hospitals, orphanages and new cooperatives of her New Life Movement. Travelling to Sun Chi with James Endicott, the Canadian missionary, in a small tug full of soldiers, "we hung on by our fingernails for a day and a half on the Yangtse," as the river's current competed with cries of *Gin Bao* to keep them alert. The town's temples had been transformed, come alive as orphanages, to Welthy's happy relief. At one Temple of Hell she thought: "What could these gruesome plaster representations of an imaginative hell offer to children wise in suffering beyond their years? *San Ming Chu Yi* (Three Principles of the People, the national anthem) rang through the temples and down the raging Yangtse," a striking sound that in time would become shrill to Welthy's ears.

"With her feminine sensitivity," wrote Welthy, "Mme. Chiang has discovered beauty in the West China farmer's hat and saw in it a realistic, democratic symbol. Few women had worn hats before. Swathed in a scarf of silk tied under her chin, she startled her war workers by declaring she was ready for both sun and rain. Every *warphan* loved his hat more than any other earthly possession. Wearing a coolie hat, she has made women's work fashionable. What a woman for such an hour in China! The Chiangs are people of destiny. They have complete understanding together," Welthy reported, awed by Madame's electric words and fearlessness.

What she could not know then, although she discovered it later, was that a display orphanage could be set up for visiting foreigners one day, and dismantled the next.[9] It was not easy for foreigners to discern the fine differences between the many organizations working against all odds in those critical years.

Welthy talked to everyone she could, and saw as much ongoing work as possible to learn of the extensive rural reform efforts that had been underway for a decade, with special attention to education and literacy.[10] With no political axe to grind, she kept an open mind and listened closely. She talked with Jimmy Yen, she saw the cholera, dysentery, typhus and smallpox everywhere and the tremendous need for medical help. World War II broke out while she was in Chungking, adding greatly to the confusion and speculation about continued western assistance.

MADAME CHOU EN-LAI

She also talked with Teng Ying-ch'ao, Chou En-lai's wife. Welthy plied her with questions about the Communist approach with villagers of the Northwest, asking how such a change had been effected so quickly. Mme. Chou told her they taught the villagers about modern Japanese ways and what they must learn to combat them. In three months the majority had learned to read. Welthy took careful note of their strategy of beginning reform with the written word. That made such sense in a society that had evolved out of an aristocracy of learning. With villagers thus equipped for communication and study, sanitation, nutrition and cooperative production had followed readily.

Mme. Chou talked on about their work, then suddenly stopped and looked Welthy straight in the eye.

"We want just what you want," she said.

"But what is it I want?" asked Welthy.

"You want the Kingdom of God," Mme. Chou replied softly, and after a short silence added, "but you are so slow."[11]

Welthy remembered that Madame had herself been taught by a British missionary in Peking and had benefited from the slow-moving Kingdom, but she knew all too painfully how cumbersome the missionary movement of western civilization had been.

Speaking of her impressions wherever she went and observing reactions, Welthy met many Chinese who were not Communists in 1939 but who were also skeptical of the Chiangs and felt the Kuomintang would sell China to the enemy. Gwei-hsin was among those who thought their New Life Movement of social regeneration was inadequate to meet the crisis; the virtues of orderliness, cleanliness, simplicity, frugality, promptness, exactness and honesty were not enough. In her usual frank manner, she told Welthy to stop singing the praises of Mme. Chiang.

There were also many who thought the Kuomintang was an exclusive mutual aid club engaged only in tactics and organizing, while the Communists were fighting for land reform and China for the Chinese, with commitment to a long-term struggle. Among all the literature from many sources that she collected, Welthy read Mao Tse-tung's "The New Stage," in which he predicted a long war, cautioned against too much outside aid, and cited as their main task raising the people's self-respect and confidence in developing their own strength.

The stronger medicine of *Gung Ho's* strategy was winning increasing regard from a very practical-minded people. As Welthy realized this in the months and years ahead, her attitude toward the Nationalists became increasingly negative, her allegiance finally falling completely within Mme. Sun Yat-sen's camp. She discovered the strained relations between Mme. Chiang and Mme. Sun when the former sharply refused to give her a letter of introduction to her sister in Hong Kong.

MADAME SUN YAT-SEN

Welthy found her own way to Mme. Sun Yat-sen (Soong Ching Ling) in Hong Kong, where her China Defence League was trying to avoid Kuomintang interference in seeking support from the West for the war effort and the cooperatives. The League had broken with the tradition of appealing for support as charity or as conscience-money; instead it presented the Chinese and their cause as being in the vanguard of the world fight against fascism, joining with allies as equals. Israel Epstein, who wrote much of their English publicity, told Welthy they were determined to overcome the Kuomintang's monopoly on contacts with foreigners, and sent her off armed with material about all the activities they assisted. The West was supposedly anti-fascist, fighting Hitler, yet its support went largely to Chiang, considered a dictator by many Chinese. Even though the majority of refugees needing help were in the areas liberated by the Red Army, the United Nations was giving almost all of its support to the Kuomintang.[12]

Whose priorities came first, Welthy wondered — those of the people needing help, or those of the politicians so far removed from the harsh reality? The politicians seemed to spend all their time wrestling over ideology. Mme. Sun was not then or ever a member of the Communist Party; she took her direction from her husband's three principles laid down long ago: first, to unify the nation and get rid of foreign influence; second, to establish a people's democracy based on literacy and voting rights for the masses; third, to develop the people's livelihood through land reform and socialization of industry so that no one had to beg.

In Mme. Sun, Welthy found a powerful example of a widow extending her husband's visionary work, using her own personality and name, Soong Ching Ling, in work that brought hope, training and help to individual human beings struggling to save their country. They became warm friends after Welthy told of singing at her husband's reception in Nanchang back in 1913. Though their paths crossed infrequently through the years, it was a friendship based on mutual regard for courage and leadership that endured for more than forty years until both died within a few months of each other.

* * *

Nanchang had been occupied by the Japanese for a year after heavy bombing which destroyed Dr. Kahn's hospital and the Ladies' House at Bao-Lin. The school had taken to the hills, carrying on by tenuous means, but Welthy was able to pick up the threads in her contacts with alumni she met in Shanghai, many of whom were teachers. The Women's Corps in Kiangsi, seventy thousand strong, had been organized by well-educated women who travelled to rural districts to step up efforts in education, hygiene, land reclamation, production and war service. It was a pattern of leadership that can most likely be traced to the training and model that Bao-Lin provided to an expanding educational network in the province.

When told that Chinese families feared to send their young daughters to West China for college education, Welthy undertook to arrange scholarships at different American colleges for ten young women, seeing to the paperwork immediately on return. Only five were able to get away from Shanghai before Pearl Harbour froze all movement. For one girl, Phoebe Hsia, the daughter of Miriam Nieh, Welthy enlisted Arthur Schwartz as co-sponsor and together they managed to delay the departure of her ship from Shanghai while cables flew back and forth clearing her visa.[13]

In Peking Welthy's contacts were more with Chinese than missionaries, and when she was invited by John Leighton Stuart, President of Yenching University, to tell the students what she had seen and heard in Chungking, she happily obliged.

Frances rejoined her as they travelled by British ship from Shanghai to Tientsin, then blockaded by the Japanese. Blacked out all the way, they were required to produce stool specimens in order to land. Whenever new regulations were posted they laughed and speculated: "Well, which war is this test for?" From there they took the Trans Siberian railroad under, over, and through the Great Wall up into Mukden and down through Korea, all under the watchful eye of the Japanese.

*   *   *

As her 1939 travels through the Orient drew to an end, Welthy had touched the essence of current thought and action in India and in China, and had established personal connections with their leaders. In both countries education was significantly in the forefront. Gandhi's basic education programme was getting underway in India, and a high priority being given to education in China by both the communists, in starting with functional literacy, and the nationalists, with their emphasis on morality-based civic education in China. These were encouraging signs.

Women were asserting strong leadership in both countries, far more so than in the West, and Welthy saw no role for herself in either India or China, believing that development should come from within a country. What she could do was tell America about the women of Asia, portraying them through her personal experiences of their courage and commitment. She could carry on the effort to bring Asia alive in American minds, minds that had scarcely been scratched by the deep historical reality of the East.

There was symbolic meaning also for Welthy in the fact of Nehru's arrival on the sandbar in the Yangtse on the incoming plane as she departed from Chungking, Asian brother from the south come to assure the Chinese Government of India's sympathy and support.

Once again, Welthy had the long voyage across the Pacific to help find her way back to life without Fred. It no longer seemed impossible. She walked the deck around and around, not with the old swinging stride but surely and steadily, marshalling her thoughts for the new life she was entering in a suddenly changed world at war.

1939 TO 1946

Over the next seven years Welthy became one of the foremost American women speakers, in perpetual motion by train to all parts of the States where she was booked by her three agents in New York, Chicago and Hollywood. She was Welthy Honsinger Fisher, proudly using her full name, earning between two hundred and three hundred and fifty dollars per lecture, enough to pay her expenses and more. She had sold all but the Hingham house after Fred died, and would have disposed of it if the Halsteads had not pressed her to keep it in the family. Now she sold some of the surrounding land, which eventually became a small housing development on Fisher Road when she later sold the house itself.

New York was her base, the place where fast-moving people met, and where Betty's young family was growing. She used the Hingham house some summers and rented apartments in different sections of Boston or Manhattan for variety when not travelling abroad. Long summer walks and evenings at Fiedler's Boston Pops with friends kept her American sense of fun intact. Helen Schwartz tried to supervise her shopping to keep her costumes suitably dignified because "if Welthy wasn't watched, she'd drape herself with a gay shawl or add a flower or feather to her hat." Welthy happily tolerated such concern and expressed her exuberance anyhow.

Her companion for many information-gathering journeys to South America and the Middle East during the war years and after was Bessie Perkins, financially secure and free since her mother's death. They were stimulating years full of people and places and ideas and study, but restlessness and anxiety were never far beneath the surface. She kept moving so that she would not get trapped in one mindset, knowing she could not rely on the American press alone to keep her informed about what was happening in other countries. Drifting around the world from place to place like a ship without a compass, constantly sending and receiving signals as she searched and probed among an endless parade of people, she tried hard to fix on a destination. And at the end of a long trip she would often dine alone in the Oyster Bar of Grand Central Station in New York, adjacent to the Commodore Hotel, scene of former romantic times.

SOUTH AMERICA

Welthy and Bea travelled in style on their many South American trips, staying at the fine hotels Bea could afford and carrying introductions to leading political and social figures through Bea's Pan American League connection. Welthy was soon appointed a representative at large by the League. The Chinese Consulate in New York put her in touch with their ambassadors and a well-arranged programme was mapped out in advance for each winter trip.

Prepared by a month of studying Spanish in Middlebury, Vermont, Welthy proceeded to absorb the history, economic, social and artistic background of each place as her entree to the individuals she met, aware of the distance from that day at Rome Free Academy, when she won a prize for drawing the map of South America correctly. How strange that the 'other America' was the last continent she should visit, and stranger, that the ship's library had not one book that would make poor neighbours into good neighbours.

November 27, 1941. Passing through the Panama Canal, Welthy marvelled at every detail, taking pride in its American engineers: "Gives one a lift of the chin."

November 28, 1941. In Colombia, seeing barefoot boys, and envying them their freedom from uncomfortable tourist shoes: "I wonder how much nearer the heart of the eternal we are than the barefoot. . ."

December 1, 1941. Flying in a small plane in Ecuador, Welthy thrilled at the adventure and the American pilot's skill: "A fine American look about them a finer crop of humans than any civilization has ever produced." Welthy lacked no pride in her country; in fact her hopes for its moral leadership in the world were in direct proportion to that pride.

December 15, 1941. On a blacked-out ship en route to Peru a week after Pearl Harbour: "To be sure Japan was treacherous, but will we make the world more moral by using all our forces for war? That is the question which makes it all seem wrong."

December 19, 1941. Lima, as they set up temporary housekeeping in a spacious apartment: "I somehow died too on April 15, 1939. I somehow can't get going again. . ." The war news overshadowed their busy round of meetings, teas and dinners with diplomats, politicians, editors and educators.

December 25, 1941. Welthy awakened hearing Bohn's voice in the singing of birds. They continued work at the Red Cross and she had radium treatments on her nose for a reason not identified in her diary. January 22, 1942, Arequipa. Reflecting on the war: "each of us wants the same — food and shelter, home and love, work and play, freedom and peace."

Mme. Prado, wife of the President of Peru, gave a luncheon for Welthy and Bessie to meet leading women. "She is a member of the modern school of First Ladies," wrote Welthy, "who conceives of her position to be not only one of presiding at palace functions but of leading her country's women one stride forward, ready to play an intelligent part in the post-war chaos."

However, Welthy noted that Peruvian women were not politically minded, were not even interested in their own franchise but were moving toward reform by the side door of social service. She speculated privately that when baffled in their social programme they might sense the need for political power sooner than they thought. Speaking at the School of Social Service, Welthy suggested that it was time to do away with charity and put the rewards for labour on a self-respecting basis. The Indian, forming sixty-five percent of the population, was the forgotten man of Peru, Welthy noted, while the old families spent much time in Europe, tossing off a few charity cheques here and there as conscience money.

PROFESSIONAL LECTURER

Welthy gave good value in her talks in America. The Women's Canadian Club of Toronto and many others invited her back for repeat performances, for which she earned between two hundred and three hundred and fifty dollars. "A magnetic platform personality," said one review. "A charming speaker who has *lived* in the fullest sense of the word on four continents and knows intimately the great, the near-great, the humble, the poor as well as the wealthy," as anyone who has ever travelled with Welthy can testify. "One of the five best-informed and most brilliant speakers of America," said another. "Tall, aristocratic and crisp. Builds immediate confidence in her knowledge without creating the impression she is excluding all other authorities," reported *The Bostonian*.

From town hall to tea party, for every kind of organization across the country, often featured in the Talk of the Month Clubs in those pre-television years, Welthy earned her living, speaking to Americans about her growing convictions on the approach to a peaceful world. A paid talk was usually matched with an unpaid appearance at a local Methodist Church.

Fall, 1939. At the Maxwell School for International Affairs, Syracuse University, Welthy said the British Government was making a serious mistake in refusing dominion status to India, that India could never be Russianized because of its spiritual heritage. Theirs was a religion that appeared to have no beginning, which gave it a quality of majesty and truth. She felt her own government was making a mistake in refusing to recognize the potentialities of the Pacific, recommended it abandon the "cash and carry" approach to munitions (referring to selling scrap metal to the Japanese for bombs), and said that helping China now would enhance future relations in the area. She thought the Chinese could accept Russian Communism but that they would adapt it to their own ideals as they did everything else. Insisting that the world could not be saved from the top down but only by the people themselves, Welthy warned that war was steeping them in hatred so they could not work together.[14]

Johnston, New York. "We are being watched and weighed in the balance by the millions in China to whom we have pledged support . . . Under pressure, Colonel Edward House struck the race equality clause out of the Treaty of Versailles, to Wilson's dismay, and Japan set out then and there to further her plans for a race war . . . China cannot understand our inconsistency . . . our oil and scrap iron is killing them . . .

China will not become an aggressor unless we make it so by unfair business practices."

March 1944, Los Angeles:

> *We cannot go on with vast populations with low economic level. We missionaries have not understood this any better than anyone else. It does little good to take one young person from a village and make him a Ph.D. if you leave the village as it was before. The religions can only meet the problem if they are simplified so that all people of good will can subscribe to them, and this has not been done. It has been tried by Tolstoy and others but their followers are not many.*[15]

January 1945, Palm Springs. In talking of world neighbours, Welthy pointed out that all the prophets and leaders who found God had the concept of a world family, of human unity.

1945, Los Angeles:

> *We with thin, lightly pigmented skin are in the minority in this world. We had better face the race issue. China's eyes are slanted toward us . . . Survival in the world of tomorrow will be a matter of casting our lot with our allies in China and India . . . we must face the ethical issue of race now, by an attitude of mind, to get away from the absolutism of our ancestors and face a realistic future.*[16]

February 1946, Peoria, Illinois:

> *We have talked in terms of the masses, but we have never divided them into grandfathers and grandmothers, mothers and fathers and children to study their problems. Race is a myth.*

1946, Boston. Talking to students at Harvard University, Welthy urged them to keep their hearts warm for others who are cold:

> *The battle of democracy is not fought on the battle field, but on rice fields . . . The educated must accept the responsibility to cooperate, even compromise . . . The goal — international trust and cooperation — is to make life free and give opportunity to all people everywhere . . . We can't give up . . . Each generation brings us nearer.*

Welthy was happiest when the theological students came to Hingham for her weekend 'seminars,' when they sat around on the floor of the large paneled library, lined to the ceiling with books, where she and Fred had worked together. Welthy had steeped herself in Fred's notebooks, writing short summaries in the front of each, not knowing how best to use them, and wanting others to know of their existence.[17] With the students Welthy talked about how to build sermons and what they really wanted to say, sharing everything she had absorbed from Fred.

Often tense from worries about her uncertain future and the strain of travel, Welthy visited an osteopath in Chicago and learned a technique of relaxing muscles and nerves that became an automatic habit. She took a moment, too, for nutrition study, settling on a moderate diet, supplemented with brewer's yeast and vitamin B-1 for invigoration. Cooking was fun, if not indulged in too much.

When she was with Betty and Ernest in New York there was always a Chinese feast, perhaps one reason their children's feelings for Welthy were reserved, since their young appetites were more geared to the peanut butter syndrome of America. Just as the role of aunt was not enough to keep Welthy fulfilled and occupied, neither was that of grandmother to Betty's children, for she was there one day and gone the next. Granddaughter Lennie, who once visited Welthy in Hingham and helped her move to a New York apartment, remembered only her "stubbornness", or single-mindedness in getting the job done.

Another of Welthy's favourite stopping places was Saratoga Springs, New York, where the Cyrus Ellmore home was a warm refuge. Welthy claimed that in those gypsy years she would drive alone from Winter Park, Florida, to Saratoga Springs in a single day on old Route One, along the coast — one of her classic compressions of detail. Cyrus's wife Adele Kaemmerlen, daughter of her step-sister, Lizzie Kaemmerlen, offered a family haven Welthy cherished, briefly. She would stay four or five days, give a few speeches, take the baths at the Springs where Cyrus was head engineer, make more friends, and enjoy a social life not restricted to church people. Anxious to see Welthy remarry, the Ellmores had a widower in attendance for her one year, a doctor from Utica with whom she had mutual friends, but "he was too serious." Welthy kept moving on. "I prowl around," she said.

She often went to York, Maine, where Bessie was restoring her heirloom house, and they would go antique hunting. Bessie wanted to give Welthy the boathouse on her property and suggested ways of expanding it into a studio, but Welthy respected her independence more. Frequently her Chinese scholarship students would be with her and she would rent a small adjacent cottage in that popular watering spot where New York's elite summered and she made important contacts.

CHINESE INDUSTRIAL COOPERATIVES

She was readily drawn into the INDUSCO committee in New York in support of the Chinese cooperative movement. Eleanor Roosevelt was Honorary Chairman, Pearl Buck was Chairman, and Bishop Hall the International Chairman of that movement which gave many Americans gave hope that China would hold to an anti-fascist, democratic path.

The prime task for INDUSCO was to keep Rewi Alley's efforts going after he and his workers were isolated behind enemy lines in the Chungtiao mountains, and to prevent the reactionary Kuomintang elements in the United States and China from taking control of the work.

Helen Foster Snow was the power behind INDUSCO, having participated in its initiation. She urged Ida Pruitt to give up her position as head of the Social Service Department of Peking Union Medical Hospital to develop foreign support for INDUSCO, as Secretary of the Committee. "These 'self-governing workshops' which we thought we had invented anew," wrote Mrs. Snow,[18] "were inherent in the whole Protestant Reformation in England, as a line of socialist group enterprise coming all the way down from Wycliffe to the Puritans in New England and the Methodist class meetings. The century of Protestant missionary efforts in China did blossom like a century plant in INDUSCO, as an anti-feudal revolution at the grass-roots, in the villages. INDUSCO at last put the Protestants on the right track in China."

Mrs. Snow wanted Welthy to join because she knew her to be someone who could think straight, see to the essence of any issue, and take responsibility efficiently.[19] Besides, she knew Welthy had survived her oriental missionary years with grace and had not become a disagreeable, intolerable queen, ordering people about.

In siding with such progressive revolutionaries, Welthy was taking a big risk, but she believed in China as a democracy of local self-government, the reality on which INDUSCO had built. Forty years later, her friend Soong Ching Ling wrote in her strong, bold hand in recognition of Welthy's unstinting support of an immediate need in China: "China is indeed moving along in the right direction, and you will be proud that you helped us in our work."[20]

In one three-month sweep down to Florida and back Welthy gave forty-three speeches in seventeen cities in aid of INDUSCO and the China Defence League. Some ten thousand people heard her at the various clubs, schools, colleges, churches and private homes where meetings were held, and many more heard her radio broadcasts. With her sweeping knowledge of Chinese history from ancient to modern times, and her stories of experiences with living personalities, Welthy was a powerful fund-raiser:

Ancient China built walls; modern China builds roads. Walls were a part and parcel of Chinese philosophy, the etiquette and psychology of old Chinese character. Walls slowed up the approach to personalities, to homes, to officials, to transactions in the market place. Walls made an altar of etiquette and made possible the quality of character that could 'think twice and say nothing' . . . Today China's walls are razed and the bricks and stones made into roads. Her foreign policy is expressed by the Burma Road, seven hundred and twenty-five miles of highway from Lashio to K'un-ming, Chungking's life artery and one of Marco Polo's routes. It was built by thousands of Chinese men, women and children — an epic. Each day Chinese come out of their caves to mend the damage of the previous night's bombing. It is their declaration of independence.[21]

Of Rewi Alley, she said: "He knew that soup kitchens for this mass of humanity was too poor a substitute for reconstructive work. It wasn't good enough for the brains and the industry of China."[22]

As Hong Kong fell to the Japanese, Soong Ching Ling returned to Chungking to lead the work there, using her apartment for meetings, as did Welthy in New York when asked. Welthy did not resign her membership in those committees as some did when their names appeared on the Attorney General's List of Subversive Organizations, but continued staunchly to support them.

At the end of the Japanese war in China, Welthy publicly endorsed Soong Ching Ling's appeal to the American people to prevent the expansion of the civil war in China by halting their government's military assistance to the Kuomintang.[23] She was also a member of the Committee for a Democratic Far Eastern Policy, but played a less active role in that essentially political pressure group during those years of intense debate about America's role in the post-war world.

CONTINUING LINK TO GANDHI

For all her interest in China in those years, Welthy did not lose contact with India. Gandhi's secretary, Mahadev Desai, kept in touch, asking for American news clippings and wondering in 1940 what America's attitude would be towards the war. "She will have to play the game," he wrote, "and if she throws her weight on the side of the Allies . . . we expect her to do so on the express condition that India is given the right to frame her own constitution."[24] A few weeks after Pearl Harbour, Gandhi wrote to Welthy: "To send you season's greetings is a mockery when hatred reigns supreme and God of Love and Truth is disowned."[25]

Welthy joined the India League of America, headed by J.J. Singh and Roger Baldwin, founder of the American Civil Liberties Union, to support Gandhi's movement and try to get quota rights and citizenship for resident Indians in the United States. She continued to talk about India in her lectures and to maintain her contacts there through extensive correspondence.

After two world wars, it was humanity itself, not any one nation or political approach, that was her central concern. She could hear Tagore's voice signalling that patriotism can become a magnification of self on a stupendous scale, a form of devil worship dethroning God. Independence was not an end in itself; we should be striving to be free from the limits of political life if we are to become whole.

And when Gandhi was released in 1944 after twenty-six months in jail his voice reached her in the form of a thin penny postcard that miraculously found its tattered way through several forwarding addresses. "I miss your great and good husband," wrote Gandhi in his own hand. "A double burden rests on your shoulders."[26]

* * *

Uppermost in Welthy's mind was her commitment to write a biography of Fred, which took five years and substantial assistance from his secretary, Grace MacPherson, to complete. When it was finally done she felt the freedom of having surrendered her personal hold on Fred's legacy. In the process of writing the book, she had absorbed every last thread of Fred's thinking, and her own mind had recovered its balance.

"Frederick Bohn Fisher; World Citizen," was published in 1944 with an introduction by Bishop McConnell, and this tribute from Gandhi: "I had the privilege of coming in close contact with Bishop Fisher. He seemed to me to be one among the few Christians who walked in the fear of the Lord and therefore feared no man."

The book was well received as no mere wifely sentimentality. Welthy kept the focus on Fred's thoughts, ideals, actions and achievements, largely remaining in the background herself, realizing she had barely scratched the surface. At the end, for future searchers she included some of the meditations from Fred's vast notebooks which she had pored over, especially those on the concept of social service as religious practice. One reviewer said: "In every realm which calls for acting upon Christian principle — ecclesiastic, political, social, racial — he was of the type we can not do without."[27]

Friends urged her to pursue her long-standing desire to write, knowing she needed an outlet for her tremendous energy, and she did try, again and again. The archives abound with draft articles on grief's slow wisdom, washing your mind, the feminine quality, voluminous notes on the seven last words of Christ, on human rights, on the internationally-minded woman, on Einstein's concept of interdependence, an outline for a novel about voluntary exile based on her China years, and very sharp observations from extensive historical readings.

Her mind chased itself in diaries, notebooks and disorganized scraps of paper brimming over with ideas, sketches and facts all mixed in with names, addresses and appointments. Welthy was obviously not consciously preserving her thoughts for posterity or she would have practised better housekeeping, her approach to filing random at best. Whatever book she was reading served as a file folder and her notes were hopelessly irretrievable. One batch of clippings on India was pinned together with a large sewing needle. Notes were simply a memory device, but the act of studious note-taking, of thoughtful time with pen to paper, was a life-giving exercise at any time of night or day. Extracting meaning from whatever people, places or ideas she experienced, Welthy steadied herself.

Not addicted to perfection, she never aimed at highly polished form in speaking or writing, nor at absolute consistency. The uphill slant of her penmanship, the frequent dashes, the lack of punctuation show an open reaching to convey a single idea. One consistent theme, however, for all her speeches about the lives and customs of people on all continents was the belief that peace depends on human beings understanding other human beings.

Welthy was teaching herself, thinking and feeling with all her faculties in those reflective years of partial withdrawal from the main course of her life. Her body was also speaking, for though she claimed not to have noticed it much, she was going through the menopause (many pause, as she called it) and guessed that it occurred belatedly at sixty-four when frequent nosebleeds interrupted her speeches. The likelihood is that it affected her more than she realized as her powers of concentration consistently evaded her.

She tried to write an educational book on the achievements of negroes in the United States, another on India for high schools, and a novel on India's freedom struggle. Her frustration at being unable to complete any of these projects as she moved all over America is captured capriciously in a quotation she noted: "I think there should be two of me, A living soul and a Ph.D."

A clue to the missing ingredient she sought jumps out of these notes: "We Anglo-Saxons are drab compared with the Orient. We need colour, rhythm and humour in our religion, the Christian rhythm of working together."

In voluminous notes on womanhood of the world, Welthy urged women to be internationally-minded, not to mistake differences for inferiorities. Everything she did and said was shaping her own future:

> *It will be in our attitudes to other races, toward food, and toward those with different political and economic theories from our own that we will rise or fall as Christians in this new era. The Kingdom of God is still within us where it has always been and always will be. The expression of it comes out in our attitudes. Can we agree to differ and resolve to cooperate?*

FOREMOST METHODIST WOMAN SPEAKER

Billed as the foremost Methodist woman speaker, Welthy returned regularly to the pulpit of Central Methodist Church in Detroit. Her topic in 1945 was "My Patriotic Creed; The World is my Home." One member of the congregation, Gladys Coon, recalled a Good Friday sermon of Welthy's: "I have never been a very religious person. My worship has always been in music. But from the moment you said 'shall we pray' until the last word you uttered I felt a surging of deepest emotion. You took me to the depths and brought me to the mountains. It seemed that you actually knew — it came from your heart and not from a book or another's experience."

Welthy maintained her connections with the Methodist Church, attending their General Conferences regularly, and in 1942 she paid into its treasury the outstanding sixteen thousand dollars owing from the Fisher Fund. Many years later while visiting friends who had invited a seer to meet their academic friends and hold a seance, Welthy heard him say the name "Diffendorfer" (the Methodist treasurer) and then: "tell the Board I want to give a salary to Welthy Fisher to make up for her loss." Nineteen years after Fred's death, Welthy began to receive his pension from the church, a rather hollow victory but welcome funds nevertheless.

She toyed with the idea of buying a house in the Georgetown section of Washington, D.C., where she often went to enjoy Josephine January's company and together they would call on Eleanor Roosevelt. Mary Dreier, the protector of women's rights in factories, was a good friend, as were many other movers and shakers in the capitol. Having declined to run in Michigan on the Republican ticket for Congress, Welthy nevertheless took a close look at her government, interviewing the few women senators. Mildred and Robert Bliss were back. Their mansion, bequeathed to Harvard, was being used as their centre for Byzantine Studies and was the scene of the 1944 Dumbarton Oaks conference that led to the establishment of the United Nations. Mildred was very much the grande dame of Washington society, in her genuine pearl choker, and happy to befriend Welthy in her widowhood.

Roosevelt's sudden death in 1945 literally threw Welthy off-stride as she heard the news while walking to a function and had to stop to regain her composure. As a leader of the free world, F.D.R. was as great a hero as a nation ever gets in Welthy's eyes. But she could not forget how much of the world was not free, those parts of the world she knew so well and loved, still beckoning. The Allies had achieved military victory over Germany and Japan, but at the cost of the atomic bombing of Hiroshima. For the entire world it was a new era of cynicism and disillusionment. Victory was not where it seemed to be, and for Welthy the world was a deeply troubled darkness in which she struggled daily for an outer action to match the inner harmony she was beginning to achieve.

CHINA, 1947

With the war over it was possible to travel to the Orient again. Bessie, older and cut in a different mould, would not proceed beyond the Middle East, for all her internationalism. Though she was always in the middle of people and seldom without friends around, Welthy had come to terms with the fact that she was alone, that no association of family or friends could hold her. Sailing once more across the Pacific towards the Middle Kingdom, freedom was the exquisite companion of her loneliness.

Shanghai, spring 1947. When Welthy arrived at the MacTeiyre School for girls (now Middle School Number Three), the principal, Hsueh Cheng, a college-mate of Ernest's, lodged her in the house with the American missionaries, quite unprepared to discover what an unhappy mix that was. Welthy's dislike for the Chiang Government had intensified, and she wanted to learn about non-Kuomintang China, to the distinct discomfort of the resident missionaries. And her ideas on education, which stressed the value of Chinese culture and stated that foreign was not always best, struck a better response in Hsueh Cheng than in the missionaries. On her next stop in Shanghai, Welthy stayed in the dormitory with the students and Chinese teachers, to everyone's satisfaction.[28]

The old school network worked well for Welthy. One of her former Bao-Lin students, Mildred Sun, principal of another Shanghai school, sought Welthy's help in going to America and in return looked after any and every kind of arrangement for her extensive travel in China.[29] Nanchang was first priority, not seen for twenty-three years since her honeymoon visit.

BAO-LIN REVISITED

Welthy arrived at Bao-Lin in time to speak at the school's first commencement after nine years of Japanese occupation. The city wall was gone, its path now the main boulevard of Nanchang with Bao-lin centrally located. From Principal Lan-ching Chou-Chang, a former student married to the head of the rural welfare service, she heard the harrowing story of the school's survival under heroic leadership.

Inspired by Welthy's example of carrying on after the fire, and her foresight in building larger, stronger buildings for the future, Lan-ching had gone to Bao-Lin from the Kiangsi Women's Life Improvement Association. The Japanese Army was moving toward Kiangsi, and she did not want to see the school closed after all the former principals had struggled so hard. She urged all the students and faculty to participate in the Women's Movement to help drive out the bandits, and when the Japanese arrived she moved the school to Yuntsen, with support from the Bureau of Education and the alumnae. Then they shifted to Shia Chuen, an interior village where food provisioning was very difficult.

With the overseas connection to the Methodists difficult to maintain, decreasing funds, few teachers, and sick children, it was an almost impossible situation. They occupied ancestral halls and very damp Buddhist temples made of mud brick, earning their keep by helping farmers and workers. In 1940 they moved to Yutu but were forced to hide out in the countryside. There were eight more moves before they were able to return, victoriously following the 59th Army of China into Nanchang after the Japanese left.[30] The long march of Bao-Lin led by its gallant Principal Lan-Ching had saved the school.

With only the classroom building still in reasonable condition, she repaired and rebuilt Bao-Lin with Methodist help and started with a hundred and eighty students, soon doubling the enrolment so that students had to sleep on the floor. This was the situation Welthy found that summer. "I realized that I myself should work first and set a pattern for my co-workers and students," said Lan-Ching, recalling the overwhelming effort everyone put forth.

For Welthy that epic tale was her full reward for the faith she had placed in her students. When she rose to receive their magnificent embroidered silk scroll with its brilliant, prophetic inscription, Welthy knew she was a happy woman. "To Han Wei Lo Hsiao Chang," it said above a burst of chrysanthemums and a cock crowing; "In the autumn of your life you still announce the dawn." Their voices, speaking to her as one in that exquisite offering, eased her loneliness and lifted her towards the future. It was one of the signs she needed, recognized and cherished.

* * *

There was a flood of Americans looking at China in 1947 and writing books and articles on "whither China?", with great differences in the information being reported on the nature of the Communists. Among the Chinese masses there was a growing awareness that there was not time for Chiang's economic modernization programmes to trickle down from the rich, urban elite to the hard-pressed rural peasantry. Because no acceptable alternative was offered, whole cities surrendered to the advancing Communists without fighting.

Most Americans found it difficult to understand the revolutionary forces that had been developing for over a century enabling the Communists to win the people. In trying to blow out that flame, in their panic, the American provision of lethal weapons to Chiang created more anti-Americanism in China than any Communist propaganda could.[31] Missionaries were receiving particularly harsh treatment as a result, the Christian church having become a symbol of immobility, of dealing only with symptoms. The unconscious arrogance of the missions' generous help was itself corrupting.[32] This was no surprise to Welthy, who had seen the seeds of self-destruction years earlier in administration by remote control.

CHINA WELFARE FUND

She had been commissioned by INDUSCO to take a close look at the work being done by Soong Ching Ling and Rewi Alley, to better understand the present needs. After the Japanese war, Soong Ching Ling's China Defence League had become the China Welfare Fund (CWF) with children's centres in Shanghai reaching out into the communities, orphanages, schools and cooperatives, raising almost all the operating expenses within China. The CWF was determined to counter the thinking that unless help to China was foreign-controlled, it was like throwing money down a rat hole.

Activities were locally managed, a far more effective approach in the liberated areas where self-help and mutual assistance were the theme. The Quakers were their closest cooperators in standing against foreign agencies that were extensions of their government's foreign policy to save China from communism.[33] For Welthy, who did not put political considerations first, that commitment to maintaining the dignity of the Chinese people — proving they were not helpless wretches — and that there were reliable organizations deserving support, won her continued allegiance to the work of the CWF.

TO KANSU WITH REWI ALLEY

The Sandan Bailie School was established in the Kansu desert of the northwest by Joseph Bailie, the Protestant missionary who pioneered in developing Chinese orphan boys into engineers. Between the Japanese and the Kuomintang, the network of industrial cooperatives, which had received some four million dollars help from private Americans, had been reduced to that single centre. Several billion dollars of U.S. government aid to the Kuomintang had helped deal the blow. Administered by Rewi Alley since its beginning, Sandan Bailie had a history of successive evacuations similar to Bao-Lin's, a tale Welthy had heard blow by blow as Rewi escorted her on the difficult travel by dirt track, winding tortuously over hills and mountains, jumping furtively on and off trucks.

Passengers were forbidden on commercial or military trucks, but "as love laughs at locksmiths" travellers found a way by alighting at checkpoints and climbing aboard later. "You came at a time when going over that road, especially Ding Chiang Miao, was dangerous," Rewi wrote to Welthy many years later.[34] "A whole truckload of people were killed there, just after you crossed back, by the bandits supported by the Ma general. Your coming gave strength in ways that perhaps you did not realise, especially in Lanchow where there was a plot afoot to get rid of us. Your backing of us was a very present help. With your flair for explaining things and your breezy confidence, you had a way of sweeping away problems and contradictions."

August 17, 1947: "I'm rocking in the cradle of Chinese civilization in the narrow corridor of ancient Kansu," wrote Welthy, from the compound of the temple of Fa Ta Ss where Ashoka's hair was buried, where the desert dust blew through the door, conveniences were non-existent and she slept on a mud slab. Here Mongols, Turks, Tibetans, Chinese, Persians and Afghans met on the Old Silk Road that carried great camel caravans across the Eurasian continent. "This is a mud world. I have talked with men and women of every class . . . and they admit regretfully that so long as America continues her military aid the war will go on . . . They say sadly that America is building up a great mountain of hate that will take generations to live down. China is over eighty percent agrarian and until we have helped the eighty percent we have not helped China."

But to see a symbol of hope in a school of four hundred students, operating in the ravaged, half-deserted city, was worth the treacherous journey by truck and foot. After ten years of struggle, Rewi and his workers needed every bit of encouragement they could get, as his lines from *"Gung Ho"* reveal:

Co-operative days, co-operative nights,
Co-operative lice, co-operative fights. . .
Beginnings of the idea that there must be training . . .
Can we, will we ever learn how to decentralise,
Put maximum responsibility on the maximum number,
Stop bureaucracy that stifles initiative,
Lead from behind, let the mind
Have scope, give it depth, emotional outlet . . .
How to learn that pretty clothes
Do not make pretty minds, that mind and hand
Must work together, that in Kung Ho
All one's longings may be expressed,
Creating, analysing . . .
How can we get people who will stay and struggle?

Fertilisers, farm tools, glass, and porcelain
For the millions - textiles we all must have;
So why these bankrupt villages, villages with peasants
Crouching defeated on k'angs, diseased, hopeless,
Hearts full of surly hate, no way to wait for release . . .
Fools, knaves, fat little bottoms on swivel chairs,
Fat little faces slyly watching for profit,
Yet all so immaculate, so charming, and so remote
From anything as clean as a machine or
A peasant's mind . . .
And there are those who creep in
Where there was understanding, leave chaos;
Yet again are those, whose feet are steadily set,
Who cannot be diverted until they get
Past first beginnings.[35]

In Rewi Alley's passion for the eighty percent, the heart and mind of a democrat spoke clearly to Welthy. In the tough reality of his survival against the harsh ravages of man and nature, amoebic dysentery in constant competition with his faith, the courage of a strong spirit commanded Welthy's attention. Watching Rewi getting a cooperative education from the two Chinese boys he had adopted, Welthy found a man of action, practising what he preached. They were days of intense communication and understanding. In Rewi's blue eyes Welthy saw the horizon, while his strong legs seemed as rooted to the earth as the limbs of the great banyan. Tagore's words had came visibly alive in Rewi's highly practical efforts to reach for minds so they might be free, with heads held high.

The American factory-size wool spinning machine whose passage Welthy had helped through the complexity of Hong Kong customs had arrived in small pieces and been assembled. Corriedale sheep from New Zealand were improving the quality of wool, and a once important industry had been revived. Welthy ordered all the rugs she could afford, selling them in the United States to help the school, whose sale of products met nearly half their operating costs.[36] It was the kind of self-supporting basic education Zakir Husain had spoken of as the only sure path for India.

In fact, Nehru tried several times in the succeeding years to bring Rewi to India to launch a cooperative training programme, a project Rewi would not undertake because of the lack of a supporting infrastructure.[37] In China he had built on the existing cooperation in clan and guild, and he saw no comparable possibility in a land of such diverse cultures and peoples as India. But Welthy was looking and listening hard, a synthesis of her own creative and analytic faculties emerging.

"Welthy had the knack of finding the important thing," Rewi remembered. "One had the impression of a person with immense drive and ability, yet withal sensitive to the situation in which she found herself. She did a good job for us at Sandan, spreading better understanding about us, and despite many snags and difficult personalities — part of the situation of that period — was not fooled, and held to her belief in us. It was not so simple for a woman her age to travel hinterland and never let difficulties frazzle her. She had to divide the sincere from the insincere and decide on whom to support."[38] Rewi summed up his dilemma and that of all reformers perfectly, little knowing that in his succinct manner he was describing Welthy's future when he said: "We are a thousand years too early for the officials and a thousand years too late for the people."[39]

INDIA, 1947

Welthy continued her search. In the brutal turmoil of a newly independent India ablaze with religious rioting, Welthy found "the important thing" upon which to fasten her gaze. He was a deeply saddened man, his worst fears realized, his life teaching seeming a horrible mockery, his main mission of non-violence an apparent failure, but it was still from Gandhi that Welthy sought strength to comprehend the shattered fabric of an India torn asunder by the massive gap between the vision of the few and the reality of the masses.

She talked at length with those valiant Indian women who had been so close to Gandhi through the years and were now in positions of high government authority. Sarojini Naidu of the mellifluous voice Welthy loved was Governor of the United Provinces (now Uttar Pradesh), compensating for feeling like a bird in a gilded cage by turning the *Raj Bhavan* into a showplace of Indian colour and crafts. There was nothing austere or sombre about her, and for Welthy she was a superb example of a woman following her own light, never pretending to follow Gandhi's lifestyle.[40] Vijayalakshmi Pandit, Ambassador to Moscow, and Raj Kumari Amrit Kaur, the only woman in Nehru's cabinet as Minister of Health, and many other friends Welthy had known over the years, were all striking signs of India's freedom reflected in her women. Welthy could share their pride in power and feel the awesome responsibility each one faced.

And Indian women were eager to hear her, Mrs. Fred B. Fisher, Speaker of World Women's Party,[41] as the notice advertised her address to the National Council of Women and the YWCA in Delhi on "Some Aspects of the Women's Movement in Various Countries."

Through them and many others she met during several weeks in India, she gained a direct sense of the new era India had begun, the vision and struggle of former years now the present reality, demanding of the same individuals strength of a different kind in the wielding of political power. In the instant of their swearing in to government, the freedom fighters had become the force to be reckoned with, and because of that very power Welthy looked beyond it for wisdom. It was Gandhi, and not the aggregation of earnest politicians, who saw clearly into the future and the dangers ahead if the rural root of that democracy was not recognized and given priority. To Welthy he had the authority of utter conviction.

For many evenings she had gone to Gandhi's prayer meetings at dusk in the walled garden of Birla House in Delhi, now attended by large numbers. Gandhi would come out of the east room, his arms on the shoulders of two grand-nieces, and walk slowly down under the long arbour to the portico at the foot of the garden. He would step up and then seat himself on the white dais. Hanging above him was an openwork brass lantern and before him an inconspicuous loud speaker. As soon as he was seated the prayers began, chanted by those nearest him, from the "Mahabharata" and finally ending with "Sita Ram, Sita Ram", when many would join in rhythmic clapping. Then Gandhi would talk on the issues of the day in a low, gentle voice, scarcely audible, analysing the moral implications. To the uninitiated, his tremendous simplicity seemed like a sequence of remarks lacking cohesion. To Welthy, he spoke the truth.

The year 1947 had moved swiftly with Lord Mountbatten's priority a transfer of power to Indian hands. When all parties realized that the Muslim League would agree to nothing short of partitioning the sub-continent, the British and other Indian leaders agreed and Gandhi acquiesced reluctantly, against his better judgment. His advice to Nehru to make the Congress an organization for services to the people, dedicated to building an agricultural commonwealth to revive the villages where three-quarters of the people lived, was rejected in favour of the scientific path of industrialization, centralization and urbanization. He was further distressed by Nehru's acceptance of the British administrative system, an old model he distrusted.

Welthy appreciated Nehru's desire to release the vast stores of suppressed energy in his people, to arouse them from "generations of shameful subservience and timid submission to an arrogant alien authority."[42] Like Nehru after the death of his wife, her own profound discovery of the new reality of India was emerging from her study of the immense cultural diversity.

The year-long outbreak of violence in different sections of India reached a climax on August 15th with the ceremonial transfer of power from British to Indian hands, a ceremony Gandhi boycotted. He had spent the previous months in the riot-torn areas, walking from village to village, preaching forgiveness, brotherhood and purity of heart, trying to assuage the desires of Hindus and Muslims for revenge against each other. India, land of extreme contrasts, rejoiced at her liberation from nearly two hundred years of colonial rule as the Union Jack was lowered and the Indian tricolour raised at the majestic Red Fort in Old Delhi. But it was equally a day of mourning over so many lives lost and the uprooting of eight million Hindus and Sikhs from Pakistan.

Fine words were said that day, but those which were engraved on Welthy's heart, words that became her own song and call to action, were Tagore's poetic offer of freedom to his people, written decades earlier and read out to the huge assembly and radio audience in all corners of the new nation. Welthy felt them as deeply as any Indian patriot:

> *Where the mind is without fear and*
> *the head is held high;*
> > *Where knowledge is free;*
> > *Where the world has not been broken*
> *up into fragments by narrow domestic*
> *walls;*
> > *Where words come out from*
> *the depth of truth;*
> > *Where tireless striving stretches*
> *its arms towards perfection;*

Where the clear stream of reason has
not lost its way into the dreary desert
sand of dead habit;
Where the mind is led forward by
thee into ever-widening thought and
action -
Into that heaven of freedom, my
Father, let my country awake.[43]

LAST MEETING WITH GANDHI

Welthy saw Gandhi for the last time on her final evening in Delhi, December 15, 1947, six weeks before his martyrdom by assassination. "I followed him back into Birla House by appointment. He insisted that I leave my shoes on, noting that 'this is a foreign carpet, isn't it, so follow your custom.' His sandals came off and he sat down on the low dais as I sat on the floor. 'Until and unless reform reaches the villages of India,' he said, 'there is no reform'." Remembering the double burden he had placed on her shoulders after Fred's death, Welthy asked for more specific guidance from him, which came simply in the form of a plea to come back to serve India's villages. "India is the villages," he assured her. The cities are a mere drop in the ocean of villages. "You love us and understand us," he said gently, "go to the villages and help them." That was all. It was for Welthy to find the way.

"We talked about the refugees I had seen that day and he said he must give the next portion of his life to those people who are not to blame for their present condition. I mentioned the fast he was contemplating to bring Hindus and Muslims nearer together, and the last words he said will go ringing through my life: 'Do not be concerned about me, my life is in the hands of my great counsellor'."

GANDHI'S ASSASSINATION

On January 30, 1948 humanity's attention was fixed on a single moment in an Indian garden with the stunning news of Gandhi's assassination by an ultra-nationalist Hindu for holding India back from a war against the Moslems. That irrational act of violence ensured that Gandhi's voice would be heard through the ages.

For Indians there was a tremendous sense of revulsion against threatening war. "What the assassin achieved was peace, not war," declared Vincent Sheean, witness to that pivotal event. Once again, Welthy was present at a poignant time in stark history that seemed to powerfully reflect her own exquisite loneliness and questioning.

"India gives a moment, between the setting of the sun and darkness," wrote Valerie Fitzgerald in words that capture elegantly Welthy's suspended state, "when man is forced to recognize his own mortality. Creation then stills to a breathless hush before the dark finality of night; all eyes look inward, the most fervent heart grows chill and old memories of sad happenings beat at the mind like bats. . .It is a moment that nurses negation, that fosters awareness of omnipresent tragedy, unmasking each man's knowledge of inevitable failure. It is seldom that one escapes the insidious languors of this moment. . .Then as though a blindfold were pulled from the eyes or a heavy hand lifted from the brow, the world struggles back to the familiar and, quietly still, one turns with relief to the necessity for effort."[45]

For a woman as impatient as Welthy for action, to have taken five more years to come to her critical decision to serve the villages of India shows how carefully she weighed her intelligence and compassion to be absolutely certain of herself and the specific path she would follow. The effect of the killing would take its time to work its way through her to the point of resolve and affirmation. Even with Gandhi's signal so direct and personal, it was not possible to believe in 1948 that she could be of any help in India.

* * *

In both China and India Welthy had heard the same message from their messiahs — a call to the middle-classes to stop over-intellectualizing their nations' needs and identify with the impoverished masses. She understood the ancient values of self-governing community life Gandhi wanted renewed. His practical programme was aimed at nothing less than restoring the authority of God in everyday life, building up the nation from the base of its five hundred thousand villages through the cooperative efforts of self-governing individuals.

While she did not meet Mao Tse-tung in China, she came away confident that China's base for its future had already been built, with education a strong plank already in place. Welthy understood that there was no longer any need for foreign women and missionaries to attempt to lead the way in China after women's freedom became part of the overall revolution.[46]

Of India's intentions on education for her rural majority she was less certain, despite a plan for every literate person to teach two people a year or pay a fine of two rupees. Education and literacy were very much discussed, but it was too soon to know what priority they would have. Still, the pull of Gandhi was strong, intensified by his personal appeal. History itself had 'given a moment'.

PAKISTAN

Wanting to find out what plans the new Pakistan had for education, Welthy travelled there in 1947 under the prevailing conditions of war and martial law in the company of Mrs. Ellis Phillips, a visit recalled with some amusement by Arthur H. Peacock, the International YMCA War Services Supervisor and Church World Service representative who was assigned to escort the ladies. He received a call from the airport that two American women were stranded there with all public communications and transport broken down. Peacock collected them in a truck which was visited by a bullet passing through the tarpaulin sides right over their heads.

He delivered them to the Palace Hotel, where they had an appointment that evening with Begum Jinnah, sister of the new President, to discuss women's education. "I nearly dropped my teeth when I went to pick them up," said Peacock, "beautifully dressed in full evening clothes, long white gloves, mink capes, the works." He loaded them into the truck and drove them to the heavily guarded palace.

Next morning they were again perfectly dressed. This time they passed through cordons of military, giving the password of the day at each check right up to General Rahman's front door, for a breakfast appointment with the Minister of War, who was also Minister of Education. After an hour's discussion, the General begged off to tend to his other portfolio, and their anxious escort saw the ladies safely back to the airport. "Mission accomplished," sighed Peacock, relieved to wave goodbye to the intrepid pair, still travelling in the grand manner in those years of ocean travel and steamer trunks.[47]

JAPAN AND KOREA

Welthy wore her fine clothes to her appointments with other dignitaries on that Asian journey as a sign of respect for their offices. In Japan she interviewed Prime Minister Katayama and one of Japan's many women parliamentarians, and she was an overnight guest in the home of Kagawa, the poet. She learned about the work of the Christian churches in Japan from the United Church Moderator, and observed the Christian Women's Service Centre assisting vast numbers of refugees from Siberia, Manchuria and Korea. In Tokyo she enjoyed being assigned military rank at the Correspondents' Club. In Korea she went straight to President Syngman Rhee, with the instincts of a veteran journalist, to inquire about education and women's role in his government.

MANILA, SINGAPORE, HONG KONG

In Manila, Singapore and Hong Kong she kept up her efforts on behalf of INDUSCO. Speaking to the American Association of University Women in Manila, she urged her audience to realize that the focus of history had shifted from the Atlantic to the Pacific, where the oldest cultures and largest populations were, and where the new order for the world would be decided. In so urging the women, Welthy was speaking first and foremost to herself, and in fact she had entirely by-passed the Atlantic and Europe at both ends of her trip.

AMERICA, 1948 TO 1952

On her return to America in 1948, Welthy was immediately pulled into a rigorous round of speechmaking, with fresh insights and vast information to give out from her various platforms: as Chairman of the World Day of Prayer (WDP), as chaplain of the National Woman's Party, as a supporter of INDUSCO, as a member of the Committee for a Democratic Far Eastern Policy, of the Committee for Peaceful Alternatives, and of the United Nations Speakers Bureau.

The UN had become "the town meeting of the world," stimulating beyond measure to those whose idealism could conceive of world thinking and decision-making in the absence of conventional power. Liberals were given a boost when Eleanor Roosevelt became the Chairman of the Human Rights Commission after the Declaration of Human Rights was finally adopted by the UN in 1948, the result of years of Roger Baldwin's efforts in the American Civil Liberties Union. Baldwin and Welthy had a similarity of attitude, though he preferred to lead from backstage while she chose front and centre.

Nearing seventy, her energy level was still extraordinary as she moved about the country, seeing it anew, presenting ideas and observing the response. She was not making her ultimate decision in a vacuum, but in trains and planes and crowded halls and homes, in the very midst of America, in the manner of the national politician she would not be. She was called back to her university for another honour in 1948 — the George Arents Medal for distinguished service in international cultural relations. Citing her quick, omnivorous mind and the infectiously warm personality that made her an influential leader in the cause of world peace, the presentation speaker told Welthy that "the real secret of your wealth is that you have constantly added to it by giving it away." On this occasion, her gift to her audience included a good fashion show as she accepted her award wearing her pearl necklace and a wide brimmed hat overflowing with flowers, attached to her head at a jaunty angle.

WELTHY'S VISION CLARIFYING

Her speeches, articles and interviews show the gathering urgency to respond to the still, small voice of Gandhi.[48] Feelings released in the compassion of personal grief were now transformed by relentless study into ideas and thoughts of her own. And the melancholy tone of previous years was gone. No longer did Welthy lean on her diary for communion; it been replaced completely by sharply focused research notes. There was a new toughness in her talk — plain, straight talk Americans could understand:

I don't think China will accept anything wholesale in the way of ideologies or governments, but will adapt those that fit her civilization. Most Chinese are praying for a coalition government. China will hold her place in the world. As China goes, so will go all Asia. We must think of China in terms of centuries.[49]

The writer referred to Welthy as "one of those wide awake, world conscious people who stir the imagination and waken you to wonder what you've been doing all your life." By her own expressed purpose, Welthy was hitting the mark.

At the New York Rotary Club:

We must study large maps — the history, religion and economics of peoples. Our best help to Asia is through the non-political agencies of the United Nations, sending teachers, doctors, agriculturalists and technicians, but Asians must be free to attain their own goals by their own methods and parties.

Again at the Rotary Club of New York, the reviewer seemed surprised to hear a woman with the ease and grace of an accomplished speaker as she told how Gandhi dared to put religion into politics — a taboo subject in the land of separation of church and state — but that Gandhi's religion was large enough to include all brands of faith and political persuasion. "I came to feel that I was part of his circle, and I think this was the secret of his power, that he could draw millions of people into that circle with him," she said, seeing an inclusiveness akin to Christ's. "That smile of his gripped me and I felt the sensation of friendship."[50]

An interviewer for *The Scranton Tribune* had difficulty pinpointing the peripatetic Welthy. "Born in Rome, home in Massachusetts, car licensed in Connecticut, votes in Michigan, lives in New York City, when not travelling," the article read, going on to report Welthy's very specific views on America's blindness in China. Beginning with the clipper ship trade in 1784 and fortunes made in tea, china and silk, at China's expense the United States "played" with the decadent Manchus in the Taiping Rebellion, their victory setting China back fifty years in uplifting the peasants and underdogs. In 1911 the States guessed wrong again in supporting Yuan Shik-kai instead of Sun Yat-sen, the 'simple man in a rumpled suit'. American bankers kept upholding puppet warlords, and completely disregarded China in the 1919 Peace Conference. It was old history, but the Chinese have long memories, she warned.

In Des Moines, Iowa, recommending that the United States adopt a hands-off policy towards China, she said:

> *If China splits into two camps, as it may, we should help both sides. Why punish the Chinese peasants who haven't had a square deal in fifty years? I believe in China's middle-of-the road thinking and natural stability to moderate Communism so it will best serve Chinese village life.*

Regretting that the Communist leaders were firm Marxists, she pointed out that Chiang had started out with the Communists, and that Japan and Russia were the two greatest influences on him. "If you read the uncensored edition of "China's Destiny" by Chiang, you will know he has no love for western countries."[51]

Welthy's views were strong enough that she risked official disapproval in the United States in lobbying for more liberal immigration laws as a member of the Planning Committee of the National Committee to Repeal the McCarran Act (anti-subversive). The Committee urged President Truman to reverse the alarming tendency to abrogate civil rights in what they considered unjust discrimination against Asian immigrants.[52]

In that era when American economic interests dominated world order and the powerful influence of the China lobby in Washington prevailed, that liberal effort was defeated on national security grounds for fear that the country would be flooded with orientals. The issue was intensely debated during the early fifties, and the closed door atmosphere created by that defeat was to Welthy a denial of the very heart of America, the symbol of all she stood for.

WOMEN MUST ADVANCE FREEDOM

In a 1948 speech entitled "An American Woman Looks at Her World," Welthy struck out on all fronts of her growing realization that real peace in the future would depend on the women of the world standing up to say and do what they knew to be true. Excerpts from that speech all point in the direction that Welthy was leading herself, thinking on her feet in her struggle with the vast political gap she saw:

> *In this day the question is asked, not only by those of us who live in these lush 48 states — and we stemmed from a per-*

secuted, non-conformist group who paid a heavy sacrifice for freedom of worship and education and government — but by over 60 countries of the world; and because we say we have "true democracy" the world is watching what we do. Professor Harold Lasswell's committee of scholars met a hundred times over twenty months surveying everybody from Plato to Harry Truman, and came to the conclusion that democracy can be measured by two signs and two conditions. The signs: Shared power and shared respect. The conditions: Economic balance and enlightenment.

Because I am a woman I must look at the world from the eyes of femininity — not that I wish to divide the world by dividing the two sexes, or to say that one is superior to the other. It was femininity that the old German philosopher, Schopenhauer, who did not like us very well, said was the quality of enabling a person to put the individual in the background and the larger unit in the foreground. Benjamin Kidd, in "The Science of Power," says that whatever group leads in this quality will lead in the next era and will dominate the world. If you will allow me to say it reverently, I believe the great quality in Our Lord was his quality of femininity, for which he went to the cross.

Down through the ages, east and west, the family has been the unit for which women have lived and died. But now the family has been extended to community, community extended to nation, and the walls of nations widened to include the world.

The quality of femininity is still in demand if we are to save the world. Women do not have a monopoly on this quality. To preserve it, some nation or group in that nation must be willing to lay aside its sovereignty.

American women are the most coddled, best housed, best fed and longest lived in the world, with a life expectancy of 68 years. We are tough, we can endure, we have the opportunity for the best education. Why is it we have not changed our nation? Why is it we are not completing the democracy which our fathers founded and which Lincoln moved forward such a long distance? I believe it is because when we got the franchise in 1920 we thought of it as a finished achievement. We thought we had only to rejoice. Instead, the franchise should have been recognized as a tool, which

*we did not use. We made bricabrac of it, admired it and
put it on the shelf. Now we struggle because we cannot influence Congress, because we are not in Congress.*

In 1949, shortly before the final outcome of the civil war in China,
Welthy agreed to represent the Communist position in a nationally
broadcast debate on whether the Kuomintang or the Communists would
win and bring improved life to the people. A group from the Henry
Street Settlement acted as the jury. She was introduced as a board member of the Committee for a Democratic Far Eastern Policy (which had appeared on Senator McCarthy's list of subversive organizations), in an
attempt to prejudice the jury against her. Welthy straightened up in her
wheelchair, her current fracture forgotten, and interrupted the
moderator: "Sir, I think we are here to discuss the question of China.
Let us proceed to the point." They did, and the verdict came down on
Welthy's side.[53]

It would be incorrect to deduce that Welthy was a Communist. She was
never active politically in the Communist or any other party, but she did
believe that in China the Communists were the one group looking to the
real needs of the majority of Chinese. She also believed her own country
was wrong to rely on military strength to fight Communism, but should
fight to remove its causes — poverty, hunger and disease — beginning
with disarmament to release funds for social reconstruction. With the
establishment of the Communist Government in China in 1949, Welthy's
direct involvement with China was interrupted for a quarter of a century. The cooperatives had done their job and had been long since
phased out. While the cooperative philosophy had been democratic
socialist instead of capitalist, many considered its decline symbolic of the
failure of the whole western effort. Helen Snow, Welthy and many others
believed that the cooperatives did achieve their goal of pushing back the
Japanese invaders and creating a working base for China's future.

COMMITTEE FOR PEACEFUL ALTERNATIVES

Regarding her participation in the Committee for Peaceful Alternatives
in the forties, Welthy saw it not as a women's issue but as one of overriding significance for all human beings. Urgent work by thoughtful
women with the men in power was needed to break through the
materialistic mentality of those who put their faith in war to solve
problems. She spoke on behalf of the committee whenever and
wherever asked. As Joint Chairman with Dr. Mark Dawber, the Director
of Home Missions of the National Christian Council, she was among
those prominent individuals on the Attorney General's list of suspected
subversives when the committee was infiltrated by Communists. That

Welthy—with her deeply-rooted belief in the inherent divinity of the individual human personality—could be labelled a Communist, reflects sadly on the tenor of the times. She kept her own counsel in the matter, inwardly deploring that ominous aberration of the McCarthy/McCarran period. It was not a proud moment for the American idealist Welthy was, and added weight to her impending decision.

ALBERT EINSTEIN

When Welthy looked into the eyes of her exact chronological peer in his study at Princeton University in 1950, she found in Albert Einstein the kind of resigned sorrow she had seen on her last visit with Gandhi. She told Einstein that fifteen years earlier she had worn his two percent peace button, in the days when he still believed that if two percent of the population objected to war it could be stopped because the prisons simply could not hold that many. Seeing that now as a negative approach, he spoke sadly of the spiritual distance increasing between races and nations as their physical nearness increased. "Man is his own greatest mystery," said the great scientist, who had found common ground with the poet Tagore.

When Welthy reminded Einstein that the Mayor of Hiroshima had said that if all statesman visited his devastated city peace would follow, Einstein considered that too simple. He knew that people would not do the simple thing. "They are making peace more difficult with every international conference," he said.[54]

After the visit, during which Welthy had asked Einstein to sign a peace petition, he wrote these solemn words to her:

> *The voice of a few private individuals will not have the slightest effect. People have been convinced that America is threatened by Russia and China. Things are so advanced that salvation cannot be reached anymore by normal political procedure. I now feel the same way as I did among the Germans in 1914 before they started the first world war.*[55]

He was dedicating the rest of his life to making atomic fission useful to man, but Welthy felt his deep despair at mankind's persistent inability to comprehend "what is truly valuable in our bustle of life is not the nation . . . but the creative and impressionable individuality, the personality . . . he who produces the noble and sublime."[56] In Einstein, the physicist, Welthy heard echoes of Tagore, the poet, and Fred Fisher, the pastor.

Einstein was feeling his age and was soon to die, carrying the burden of our century's dis-ease with him. Welthy could understand his gloom but could not accept it for herself, and she left that critical encounter with an almost unbearable urge to find the paths to peace, believing it humanly possible to do so.

The peace movement had attracted powerful adversaries in the confused post-war years as America struggled to replace a fragmented Europe as the strongest voice in the world. Missionaries and church leaders had been particularly vocal on both sides. Welthy's stance, however, was clear. She saw hatred and hunger as the two cancers eating at the world. And she believed with all the strength of her heart and mind that freedom comes to those who act out of their individual conscience to demonstrate universal love, and not out of the barrel of a gun or a government policy.

* * *

Earlier she had worked with Pearl Buck's East-West Centre promoting greater cultural awareness, often speaking as Pearl's representative. Pearl urged a much closer association on Welthy, but "Gandhi's words rankled in my soul," said Welthy.

Sorrow touched Welthy again with the death in 1949 of her beloved Betty, whose inner and outer beauty had kept her heart warm with its light. Stricken with cancer of the esophagus, she died a painful, lingering death at forty-two, with Welthy frequently at her Memorial Hospital bedside reading the twenty-third psalm. With her own good musical training received at Bao-Lin, Betty had seen that her five children were trained at the Juilliard school—Welthy's indirect legacy to her 'grandchildren'. The funeral service at Riverside Church, where Betty had taught Sunday School and sang, gave Welthy what she needed to go on, with a full farewell from the magnificent choir, their finest tribute to yet another life that would no longer accompany her on the long journey.

WORLD DAY OF PRAYER

Yet even through those sad days, "living with Welthy for a year and a half was like a bit of the kingdom of heaven," said Miriam Evans of 1951 and 1952. "Peace, order, joy, deep friendship, giving one a sense of power and gratitude for life. Many friends from all over the world came and went—there was an undercurrent of delight in it all."[57] Evans was the Executive Director of the World Day of Prayer (WDP) while Welthy served as National Chairman, and it made good sense for the two to share not only their work but expenses and meal preparation. Whoever got back to the apartment first did the cooking, and fast as Welthy was, she was usually the last one home at the end of an out-of-town speaking tour. Her domestic elusiveness was awesome.

After living in several different apartments around New York, alone or with whomever happened into her life, Welthy had finally sold her Hingham home and purchased a cooperative apartment in one of Manhattan's more cosmopolitan sections, that block of West Sixty-Seventh Street between Central Park West and Columbus Avenue known as Music Street. From the Hotel des Artistes at the corner and from each handsome building on both sides, violins, pianos, and soprano, bass, baritone and tenor voices could be heard at all hours. It was an atmosphere that attracted many famous writers and actors in whom Welthy delighted, at ease with the spiritual quality of great performers. Fifty West Sixty-seventh Street suited her perfectly, gave her a new sense of security, and remained her headquarters for two decades.

Another colleague at the WDP, Myrta Ross, was grateful for an invitation to lunch in Welthy's apartment to meet Gandhi's son Manilal, editor of *Indian Opinion*, who came from South Africa to observe a UN debate, during the time when Mme. Pandit was Indian Ambassador. He ate half as much of the vegetarian meal Welthy served him as the others, chewed twice as long, and said he felt his energy doubled thereby.[58]

Evans and her husband Emory returned the honour by inviting Welthy to their apartment for breakfast to meet another traveller from Africa, Albert Schweitzer, whose work they wished to help. Welthy was expected to talk to him about Gandhi, but she did not want to confront him about not developing indigenous leadership as Gandhi had done. She thought Schweitzer should have gone beyond importing Europeans to the continent, and begun training Africans. But out of considerable respect for his achievements, she felt there was nothing to be gained by saying that, and so declined a rare invitation to meet the famous humanitarian.

Welthy had her own work to do, giving a great deal of time and money to the WDP, which was the international, interdenominational and interracial effort of the United Council of Church Women (UCCW) to focus on one day a year when women of the world united in prayer. With interest in the WDP declining after the war, Welthy had been challenged to recover and expand the programme. She was extremely effective in further developing the WDP. It became a national world observance with an annual offering of a quarter of a million dollars, divided equally between home and foreign missions, with women in ninety nations participating, thirty-one more than were in the United Nations Welthy noted with pride.

She had distinguished assistance in the WDP from the black woman who was her secretary there, Uvee Mdodana Arbouin, and who went on to lead her own Christian Retreat for black women at which Welthy spoke for many years whenever possible. Welthy drew Mrs. Benjamin Mayes, wife of the Atlanta educator, into a leading role in the WDP, frequently staying in their home on her fast travels.

"Many a day she wore me out," said Myrta Ross. "I tried to keep pace with her ideas for programme and outreach, with the quick back and forth she sparked in committee members, to record for minutes and action, but I was no equal to her velocity. When the day was done she seemed alert and sparkling, the rest of us fagged and wilting. I think God must have exploded a spiritual as well as a physical atom within her."

Welthy had served happily under Mrs. Georgiana Sibley during her term as President of the UCCW, and was then appointed Chairman of the World Day of Prayer by Ruth Worrell, the Executive Director, in 1948. When a new Executive Director from the south arrived, Welthy was dropped unceremoniously along with many board members. Accustomed by now to the ways of organizations, Welthy left it at that, refraining from the speculation and gossip surrounding such upheavals, and aware that she was too energetic for all tastes.

Miriam Evans remembered once when Welthy was asked the secret of her long, active life, how she smiled and seemed about to divulge a deep secret: "Every morning I take a great stretch like a big cat and thank God for a new day," said Welthy, not taking herself too seriously.

But when she had to answer for the universal meaning of life, Welthy was ready for the challenge as she told the UCCW in her 1949 Call to Prayer:

> We are the message — in a thousand different tongues our prayers will rise and from a thousand differing temples, but the Lord of Life hears all. His spirit hovers above those who pray under the shade of His trees; it warms the hearts of those who worship in cold, barren rooms; it moves up and down the aisles of high cathedrals; and the Presence will be real in thatch-roofed chapels and bring a glow to mud-walled huts. God will precede His worshippers into hospitals and factories and radio stations.

Her greatest fear was an unbalanced world that ignored spiritual progress, and Welthy's call grew clearer as she urged new thinking:

> Women praying, mothers of the human race tilling the soil to the rhythm of their God. Saints, known and unknown, praying for the tomorrows through their sons and daughters. Brooding world-wide prayer heard only by their children and their God. Praying women — the force of the future.

*We would not stand still . . . and yet our faith is shaken over
and over again . . . by the violation of old laws and customs
. . . by things that tear down and disintegrate our human
society. We know our fathers have been mistaken in many
ways. New science, new learning reveal to us that those
things that were once settled have to be changed and must
be seen afresh. Yet we know that our fathers' love and loyalty must center in our thought of their ideals and achievements. In the old days of absolute power when armies and
navies held nations in sway . . . things seemed very quiet
and peaceful . . . there were not so many revolutions or
violent changes. Yet that era was not so good for men as
this very turbulent age in which we live. Whole nations are
having release today. We pray, our Father, that we may see
things as a whole.*

Along with her prayers she had plenty of good, common sense advice
that she presented in her "Handbook for Ministers' Wives" in 1950,
blending general words of wisdom with concrete details on the management of life in a goldfish bowl. She had become well-known for conducting institutes for ministers' wives across the country, sponsored by
various denominations, which she considered to be one of her best efforts in drawing out women's strength. Such institutes had never been
organized before, and she brought Rachel Vixman, the authority on parliamentary procedure, to teach them the correct way of conducting meetings. Oddly, it was not the church, but her old faithful, the YWCA, who
underwrote publication of the book. In an uncanny mix of lofty ideals
and practical common sense, there was no romantic mystique about
domesticity:

*You must decide your role. Don't let others do it for you.
    Church members dearly love to make the minister's
    wife the chief chaser of details. Don't do it.*

*Where is leadership required? Think in broad terms. The
    church should make an imprint on the community.*

*Practice intelligent neglect of housework. For quick
    relaxation during a busy day, lie on your back on the
    floor, hands above your head, close your eyes and let
    go.*

*Good posture reduces fatigue. Flex your abdominal
    muscles.*

*The parsonage has a definite contribution to make in
    bringing national and community leaders together*

> *with people who have travelled afar. That is the*
> *drama of life in a parsonage.*
>
> *Never close your door to church groups in the home.*
>
> *Overall, the wife's role is subordinate to her husband,*
> *who is an eternal source of delight and despair.*
>
> *Woman is the psychic center, whether in sorrow or in joy.*
> *She must always and forever put first the good of a*
> *unit larger than herself.*
>
> *You will soon learn to take adulation and criticism in*
> *equal measure.*
>
> *You may think budget limitations are the problem but it's*
> *more likely to be your attitude. No basic problems will*
> *be solved by increased budget.*

As a shortcut, Welthy borrowed a chapter from the Household Finance Corporation booklet on managing household time in order to become "motion-minded." She listed the broad range of resources and methods available within a community for understanding how it works, giving the wives substantial tools to help them grasp their role. The book was well received and has continued to be used.

* * *

During one of her summer visits in Maine, Welthy had decided to repay her social debts with a Chinese dinner, helping Ying Hsueh and Bei Tsung-li, her student companions, in the kitchen. She ran out to gather flowers, slipped on a stone in the deep grass and lay there with a broken knee, hollering to passers-by from strong lungs well developed through the years. Welthy excelled at being rescued, but it was an excruciating introduction to Dr. Henry Field, the anthropologist, one of Bessie's guests, who came to her aid and remained a warm and helpful friend. The break was set rather inexpertly at a local hospital, leaving Welthy with a deformed left knee that knocked against her right knee with every step she took for the next forty years, in effect leaving her crippled. "They must have had plenty of time that day," her orthopaedic doctor in New York remarked later on seeing the long incision.

Welthy was forced off her feet for a few months, but it did not keep her from speaking commitments. "I'm sure it's the first time you've ever had a speaker appear feet first," she muttered as her wheelchair was rolled out onto one platform, turning her disadvantage into a plus. She had her audience laughing with boisterous applause, ready to accept her and willing to be held spellbound by her presentation.

There was one last study tour with Bessie Perkins in the Middle East in 1949 and 1950, with Welthy still in her wheelchair for the ocean voyage and climbing about on crutches thereafter, all the while overcoming constant difficulties of travelling with a broken knee, her purse and briefcase in one hand, and typewriter in the other. The trip was described in a series of "Dear Welthy" letters; Helen Krayer Schwartz' daughter Anne Welthy was the fourth child among Welthy's friends and relatives to bear her name.

Damascus, December 23, 1949: "In bed with diarrhoea, sore mouth, cold, thinking of Ernest's devastation at Christmas, and reflecting on refugees. There have always been these problems caused by War, and until we make war the archfiend and settle the disputes by law of the world government—which must come—we shall not get out of any difficulty." At every refugee camp, the call was the same: "Have you work for me? We have nothing to do."

In Iran Welthy noted: "The fundamental need is adult education, social and technical, to instruct the peasant in improved agriculture, sanitation, housing and cooperative living."

In Cairo: "Moslems in different countries differ so widely in their reactions and traditions, it does not seem reasonable to suppose they will hang together on world-wide issues. Powerful nationalism seems to be more powerful than the oneness of religion."

At Marseilles, she wrote after seeing the statue of Jeanne d'Arc "standing out in front of the Church of St. Pierre and St. Paulin, one of the busiest and noisiest squares of the city. Raucous traffic and rushing people pass by, even as she was disregarded as a young girl of sixteen and heard God speak to her. I thought of you four Welthys, and of myself, and wondered whether we would dare to stand for the truth we believed in though they would burn us at the stake. She let them shun her, laugh at her, imprison her, and burn her body, but they could not destroy her soul, and she waited hundreds of years before they called her a saint. So I thought, standing on two crutches, letting people pass by me and gazing at that young pure white face. It lifted me to a high moment of inspiration."

Speaking about her trip back in Syracuse and Rome in 1950, wearing a red silk print tunic over a long black evening skirt, "the tall, stately Roman" told of changes in the eight Middle East countries since World War I in regard to literacy, education, religion, women, social work and government priorities. She found Israel the only enlightened country, the others still with economies unbalanced between rich and poor, with no middle class.

* * *

New York in the early 1950's was a stimulating metropolis; the United Nations attracted interesting people from all continents, many of whom she met at innumerable meetings and social gatherings. With her personal flair for style and exuberant personality she could hold her own in any social setting.

For all that she was learning, however, it was always India that was on her mind, and Gandhi's plea to her. As Pearl Buck said: "He was right, he knew he was right, we all knew he was right, the man who killed him knew he was right. There is no weapon, no bomb, so powerful as the force of a great good spirit . . . In that personal example was Gandhi's secret. He did what he told others to do."[59] Nehru had said that the light had gone out of their lives with Gandhi's death, but to Welthy he stood brightly for the one thing the Christian Church had always advocated—overcoming evil with good—while Christians kept waging wars in search of peace.

With Eisenhower's defeat of Adlai Stevenson in the 1952 Presidential election, the cold war was officially institutionalized and globalized. Welthy needed to choose her side carefully. At one point she had considered buying a house and settling in the Georgetown area of Washington to be close to the political scene, but her concern for democracy as she understood it was leading her far beyond a government that claimed to trust in God yet had such difficulty hearing the voice of truth.

In the post-war prosperity and attitudes of America Welthy could not pretend she did not know about conditions in Asia. Everything she had learned from her family, her church and her experience told her that truth and freedom depended on individual awareness and response. She had been in a position to look closely at the churches and could find no role for herself in their busyness, as she concluded:

> *When I watch the leaders of our Christian movements leaping from one conference to another, I wonder whether they do not feel as Savonarola did about the saints of his day, that they were "too busy talking to God that they could not hearken unto him." Lasting movements must spring from aloneness. We can create solitariness anywhere. We have only to feel the need of it. We can find the center of calm in the midst of whirl.*

Preoccupied with the democracy of her inheritance, she thought most about education, the liberating factor at the root of democracy, not as something to be handed down from universities, but caught from those who live it. In South America she had learned that it was not enough just to give radio teaching; the personality and example of a teacher in the flesh, genuinely interacting with students, is what sparks the mind and motivates the beginning of real learning.

In upstate New York she had been highly impressed by a residential centre in which unemployed youths learned by doing, basic education taught with trades, as Gandhi wanted for India. In China she had seen the literacy materials that soldiers mastered in two months in addition to learning their trade.

She had long talks with Dr. John L. Peters, founder of World Neighbors, and with Dr. Frank Laubach, President of World Literacy, both of whom came to her apartment for intense discussions of the needs in different parts of the world and ways of meeting them. Laubach's work, largely focused on India, was particularly interesting to her, and in fact he urged her to come out there with his group. A highly effective, commanding speaker, Laubach drew support from the National Council of Churches as well.

Ideas were racing in her head now, and ringing in her ears she could hear the eternal wisdom she had so often given out to others: *if you want to change the world, start with yourself.* And so after fourteen years in the wilderness of indecision, she began on cold winter nights to take Rudolph Flesch's course in readable writing at New York University. The class rewrote articles and editorials from *The New York Times* and *The Herald Tribune*, condensing flowery sentences and pedantic paragraphs into simple English. The adjective was the enemy of the noun, she discovered. A frustrated writer all her life, Welthy was finally studying the art of writing. Why? She wanted to know the new streamlined methods, was her answer to curious friends.

* * *

She had kept up her many contacts with India, belonged to the India League of America, and was described by Kamaladevi Chattopadhya, Congress member and leading women's activist, as the best informed woman on India she had met in America. A decade earlier, Fred, in his last delirium, had kept insisting: "We must do something for the outcastes. We have raised money to preach to them and they are no better off than before. We must do something to help them lift themselves out of their despair." Faith, choice, action—words demanding individual response—her response, kept beating at her brain.

In her loneliness after the loss of so many she had loved and admired, Welthy had dipped into genealogy, tracing her ancestors, and had looked for the future in the faces of her nieces and nephews. But her surest, steadiest companions of those fourteen years of search had been the words and thoughts of great men and women through the ages. If they had been a crutch, they were no longer. If she could walk on a wounded knee the rest of her life, she could conquer her wounded heart. Welthy was ready, prepared by seven decades of profound experience.

All the powerful influences of her life—Abram, Christ, her quiet mother, Gertrude Howe, Fred Fisher, Tagore, Gandhi, Rewi Alley, Soong Ching Ling, Einstein and her own seventy years of world experience — were pulling her towards action. Raised and educated in the patriarchal mindset, Welthy had looked largely to men for strong ideas. Yet the one quality her male mentors had in common was that they dared to explore their full nature, unafraid of the feminine within. To Welthy their discovery of wholeness within themselves made their lives magnificent, their thoughts for all of humanity significant and worthy of deep study.

She had reached out for all the understanding of mind and heart the world offered; it was hers now to give back in full measure, in one concrete, symbolic act of universal love. How could she do otherwise? Wasn't she the woman who had said, "the world has always been one — we have not recognized it"?[60] With her life, she was about to do so.

PART FIVE

INDIA — FREEDOM REGAINED

EIGHT

BUILDING LITERACY HOUSE: 'MATAJI'

INDIA, 1952
There was a marked sense of purpose in the seventy-three year old woman who made her first trans-Atlantic flight in the autumn of 1952, speeded on her way to her chosen destination. As India had won its freedom, Welthy too was in bold pursuit of her own path, a powerful woman recognizing her opportunity to act.

Her need to be of service, to love and be loved, was not being met by travels and speeches. It was not enough to work on committees for world causes, to pray and talk about peace and sharing. Love demands action. To find her own equivalent discipline in response to the destruction of war and the ideology causing war Welthy had made her choice to become the person she urged others to be. She was listening to her own words:

> *We do so much group thinking, group discussions, group findings, we are in danger of losing the reality and responsibility of individuals. It was a lone figure that hung on the cross that day, and the call of it is to you and me as individuals.*[1]

In Gandhi's plea that she return to help the villages of India she could hear Christ. India, the grand workshop of spiritual experiment, the laboratory of the soul, had a chance to recover its real freedom once more, from every kind of oppression, material and spiritual. Welthy was drawn towards that search by a vintage blend of knowledge and experience imbued with compassion, endowing her with a rare credibility among the other westerners pouring into India. Deeply read in the world's history, already present during the fall of one civilization and the rise of another in China, with understanding of India's historical place in the world—history written by men—Welthy was much more than an American abroad. She was global in thought and deed. And she was a woman with a vision.

Few Indians or Americans were adequately prepared by all that had gone before to meet each other on the equal basis India had been dreaming of for so long. Americans with their trickle-down economic theories were overly eager for results and under-informed about conditions; Indians accustomed to life's disparities were touchy and sensitive, and both were caught in a fluctuating pattern of superiority and inferiority feelings, of over-acceptance and over-rejection, of deep resentments and frustrated striving.[2]

In the early 1950's, during a small luncheon discussion of famine in South India, Welthy had asked Sir Benegal Narsing Rau, India's leading jurist and representative on the UN Security Council, what Americans should do to help. Should they jog their government or the UN to increase aid? "Mrs. Fisher," he said, "I would hope that from now on, aid everywhere could come less and less from governments and more and more from people to people."[3]

Welthy's simple plan was to go back and look again into those beautiful brown eyes of the villagers, the ones whose future determined the future of India, at the heart of freedom as Gandhi had understood, and find a way to include them in the twentieth century, on their terms. There was wisdom in souls living near to God and nature that could emerge as a great force in India's social and economic survival.

*   *   *

She had rearranged her personal affairs with Ernest's advice and appointed the Bank of New York to manage her investments of one hundred thousand dollars, yielding five thousand annually, to cover her modest living and travel expenses. Having learned how to travel light, paring down to essentials mentally and physically, she was ready to make an instant home wherever she was, the old dream of a personal paradise on earth no longer even a fantasy.

From 1952 on, Welthy seemed to grow younger, defying the law of gravity in eyes and jawline, if not in the rest of her body. It was a buoyant, rejuvenated woman who landed in Bombay that September, filled with energy and determination, her mood equal to the stirrings throughout independent India, five years into its quest for new life.

With the British no longer dominant, Welthy too was free of their infuriatingly superior manner, and could begin to appreciate their real contribution to India and understand the affection they still inspired in many Indian hearts. Without question the British had brought the beginnings of education, justice and hope for the masses to India, and they had tried to teach obedience to a higher law than personal ambition or caste advantage, in a society whose main religion accepted inequality and misfortune as coming from the gods.

Through the new constitution outlawed the concept of untouchability, the ancient caste system was still the main social determinant in India. Countless reformers had not succeeded in erasing it. Western democracy, the alien parliamentary system India had accepted, when its whole history was set in an autocratic mould, confounded efforts needed on so many fronts to develop a free and prosperous society.

Of nearly four hundred million people, eighty percent were illiterate, eking out a harsh existence in remote mud villages. For Welthy, this ignorance was the primary problem, standing in the way of any real change in poverty, primitive conditions, and the caste system that helped to maintain these bars. It had been the same in China, with the rural masses predominantly uneducated until Mao Tse-tung had equated education with irrigation in his priorities. But India was a democratic society and could not impose literacy upon her people. Somehow the people themselves would have to understand the need for learning even before they could understand the modern world, a reversal of the traditional ways of thinking.

The Indian Constitution aimed at universal, compulsory primary education, but only a third of the children who did have access to a village school continued through the fifth class, usually because they were needed to work in the fields. For those who had no schooling, or who dropped out, an educational safety net was needed to catch the youth who would soon be forming families of their own, who comprised India's immediate future, and in whom all her dreams of democratic nationhood lay. The system of education inherited from the British was based on western culture and language, and ignored India's traditional system, which was steeped in religious ideals and service.

Educators had become increasingly aware of this inadequacy, but had so far been unable to persuade the government of the priority need to change the approach. The uneven results of past experiments, and the stifling of initiative by centralized administration, left education, particularly of adults, in the background.

The scientific centres that Nehru called the new temples of India based on massive hydro-electric energy for rapid industrialization would bypass the villager, whose urgent needs were far simpler. Gandhi's reputation had been diminished as a result of the killings at partition; some thought his way too slow, and many of his followers abandoned his ideas once rewarded with high office. But Welthy could not so easily turn off that voice. His democratic instinct to build upward from the people rather than impose programmes from the top was the correct analysis, she felt certain. Even then there were signs that the service and sacrifice that initially characterized the Congress were turning into power and prestige seeking that Gandhi had feared as a result of the westernization of government and industry.

Nehru had identified India's chief problem as the political and economic structure based on a semi-feudal land system, imposed by the British and incompatible with democracy.[4] Yet in his own study of human history and search for direction during years of imprisonment he had concluded: "that a divorce from the soil, from the good earth, is bad for the individual and the race. The earth and the sun are the sources of life."[5]

Welthy had studied everything she could about India and came to her own conclusion that a direct assault on India's illiteracy in the villages was the key to unlocking the potential of millions of individual human beings. Each had his or her own rhythm to bring to India's song in the world's chorus, each had an inherent skill to be developed into a productive livelihood. Was literacy not the critical element that could bring the spark of democracy alive?

Through the years there had been intensive efforts to promote literacy in different parts of India, begun by dedicated people fighting long uphill battles. But their campaigns usually lapsed into despair at the complexity and cost of the task, even after some promising results. Without careful motivation and suitable follow-up reading material, those isolated campaigns had never met their targets. The exceptional, steady work of Satyen Maitra's Bengal Social Service League in Calcutta and the efforts of Kulsum Sayani among *purdah* women in the *chawls* of Bombay were well known to Welthy and highly regarded for leading the way.

There were few politicians who did not wax eloquent over literacy, each surpassing the other in defining the goal, so that it became more ambitious than the goals of the most prosperous democracies. Impossible expectations that the illiterate would become the citizens of the future overnight, fully developed in all their faculties, led to increasing confusion. While publicly espousing literacy, Indian leaders from Nehru on down, privately had deep, understandable reservations about the potential dangers of extending a little learning too quickly, of social progress endangering the delicate balance on which their political achievement rested. They feared that a majority of new rural readers would be left more credulous than critical, paying undue reverence to the written word, open to exploitation.

Literacy was a perfect tool for authoritarian regimes to train their flocks to conform, and India was taking care not to harm the process of democratization. Welthy understood that caution, but was prepared to give the process a prod with her crooked walking stick. She had a healthy awareness that any regime, benevolent or otherwise, had the power to exploit its people. Literacy was a risk, but as with women's education in China, the first steps must be taken. If the villagers could keep themselves free to learn, err, adapt and invent, a solid grounding could be created.

DR. FRANK LAUBACH

Among the Americans in the early 1950's who were eager to buttress India's democracy with various nation-wide programmes of communication was Dr. Frank Laubach, the Congregationalist missionary who had pioneered his phonetic "lightning" literacy method among the Moros, a Moslem tribe on Mindanao in the Philippines. Laubach had worked in many parts of the world, and for years had been actively developing literacy teaching materials and training workers in India in his "Each One Teach One" method.

He had won a contract with the Government of India, under the Point Four assistance programme of the U.S. Government, to produce a full set of his materials in twelve of the Indian languages. He and his wife Effa, along with Philip Gray and his wife, had worked strenuously to develop what they considered to be the finest primer, charts and follow-up readers ever made, the result of countless revisions and testing in the villages to find one thousand of the most commonly used words as the base.

Laubach was thinking big, and felt that his team was truly on the eve of conquering illiteracy in India, with the key to success the availability of reading material for millions of new readers and large-scale training of writers. This is where Welthy entered the scene. She had enormous respect for Frank Laubach, a dynamic Christian capable of inspiring large numbers of people, and ambitious to see results from his long years of work. But she was wary of the political implications of Laubach's strong Christian stance in India's new secular democracy, as was his own son, Robert, who has carried on the Laubach literacy work.[6]

JOHN PETERS AND TOM KEEHN

Welthy reflected on the approach of her friend John Peters, who had withdrawn from Laubach's organization to focus on an integrated approach to development, combining agriculture, health and industry with literacy training. Welthy had met Peters shortly before coming to India at a conference on international development in Washington, organized by Thomas B. Keehn on behalf of Nelson Rockefeller, and later the three met in her apartment for further talk. In describing his own organization, World Neighbors, and its concentration on long-term development, Peters gave Welthy added incentive to trust her own thinking, and from Tom Keehn she found friendly encouragement.

Though she was five years older than Frank Laubach, Welthy was attuned to the thinking of these younger men as she rapidly assessed the different approaches to development. Neither Laubach nor his colleagues could realize that the elderly woman they had attached to their team for a few months' work in India in 1952 was seeing things with a third eye. Welthy had her own idea, and it definitely did not include seeking converts to Christianity.

Laubach's records show that Welthy went to India at his request and travelled to different cities with the Laubachs, Grays and Richard Cortright as part of their team, gaining extensive exposure to all aspects of the work. Though she had paid her own fare to India, she received a token salary for those months, paid by World Literacy and Christian Literature (WLCL).[7] Once again Welthy found herself in an awkward situation with untidy administrative arrangements that would lead to misunderstanding. In her own mind, she had made no commitment to Laubach.

In keeping with the times, WLCL soon dropped the 'CL' from is name to become World Literacy, Incorporated, and deleted "promotion of religion" from its objectives, evangelism's first step in a long adjustment towards a new, secular gospel.[8] The specific reason was to be eligible to receive Point Four funds from the government, especially for India. The strategy worked, and Laubach soon had a six-month contract to carry out his work and advise the Government of India on the intended adult literacy component of the Community Development Programme.

Welthy fitted right into Laubach's plans and was assigned to the development of literature for village women. He also hoped she would assist Margaret Lee Runbeck in starting a journalism course at IT College in Lucknow. The need for literature for new literates was already firmly in Welthy's mind after three weeks' discussion with her hosts in Bombay, the Natarajans, in an atmosphere where all the past, present and future of India surrounded her.

She was back in touch with her old network of Indian friends, meeting officials, attending seminars and listening with a deliberately open mind to what everyone was saying and not saying. If she was learning the ABC's of literacy work from the Laubach team, particularly Dick Cortright, she also injected a new element into their approach. "The first demonstration of group dynamics was presented by Mrs. Fisher with chief education workers . . . as a practical demonstration of active democracy and a technique for beginning literacy," the team reported to New York.

And despite the name change in his organization, Laubach was still trying to capture Christians from Communism, the prime concern of many Americans then in India. "Teaching illiterates and evangelizing while we taught," said Laubach, "was a wonderful way to win them to Christ. They are touched with gratitude for our help and want our religion because it does so much for them."[9]

Welthy could not accept that approach forty years earlier, nor could she now. "We cannot give these villagers the story of Jesus as the first thing they read. First and foremost, we must live the story." Knowing that all religions have a way of deteriorating if people are unable to go back to the source, she felt the villagers had a right to read their own scriptures, to find their own way out of the past.

ALLAHABAD, FALL 1952

As in China, a single telegram put Welthy's feet on the track she would finally follow. It was a message from Allahabad, 'City of God,' centre of India's spiritual and practical power, home of its political leaders, destination of millions of pilgrims who come to bathe in holy waters where the Ganges and Jumna Rivers meet the invisible waters of the Saraswati, where Gandhi's immersion ceremony was held, and where Indira Gandhi had lived the lonely years of her youth. Coming from Arthur Mosher, Principal of the Allahabad Agricultural Institute (AAI), the telegram requested Welthy and Cortright to help plan special courses in literacy literature as part of the Laubach contract plan.

Carrying her bedroll on the night train to Allahabad that December, Welthy answered the call. The AAI had the practical approach she believed necessary and would provide the right environment. Sam Higgenbottom, whom she and Fred admired so much in the twenties, had long since retired from the institute that had evolved out of his own experience — of overriding the fears of his mission board that it was not a legitimate mission activity, of applying his own incredible confidence in fund raising to begin soil reclamation, of winning Gandhi's approval for it as the ideal missionary activity, of seeing the AAI through each financial crisis by the sheer force of his own personality, however dictatorial, and of achieving wide regard for it as the pioneering agricultural mission.[10] "To a people famishing and idle," Gandhi had said, "the only acceptable form in which God can dare appear is work and promise of food as wages."

THE JUPAN PROJECT

Welthy was in Allahabad by chance at a most opportune moment. On Gandhi's birthday that year the Government of India had launched an expanded phase of the Community Development Programme begun at Independence, and the new JUPAN project (acronym for *Jumnapar Punarnirman* — across the Jumna River reconstruction) at AAI was part of that massive effort, aided by U.S. Point Four funds. The idea was to test in four hundred villages four different approaches to village development — literacy, agriculture, home and family, and perceived needs — and to assess what category of workers achieved the best results.

If Laubach had not gone back to the United States to receive the Man of the Year Award from the Salvation Army, Welthy would not have been asked to substitute for him in the literacy planning session. She felt he was spreading himself too thin with frequent absences from work in the field, an occupational hazard for early global pioneers living in two different worlds.

From the start Welthy had a glimmer of something no one else could see. Within a few weeks all other thoughts of her future flew out the window. Beginning as a very small cog in a large wheel inching slowly forward, she worked from a small desk in the office of the administrator of JUPAN, Dr. T. A. Koshy, one of the Institute's earliest and most illustrious graduates, who had done his doctoral study in plant pathology at Ohio State University.

"No one dreamed we were starting an institution, I least of all," said Welthy, who had been asked to come for three months. And no one dreamed that within a few years Ted Koshy would have the courage to follow Welthy's star, shifting his career path, recognizing literacy as the critical element in development, and jeopardizing his personal future in agreeing to head up Welthy's institution with its very uncertain future. There were three rugged, confusing and exhilarating years ahead before the crystal cleared.

LITERACY HOUSE

ALLAHABAD, 1953

February 13, 1953. Literacy House (LH) began on Welthy's veranda, with the forty men and three women who had been selected from eight hundred applicants for training as *gaon sathis* to teach reading, writing and agricultural extension work. She had arrived to an empty bungalow that was allotted to the Laubach group for one year as residence-cum-training centre, with no preparations for either.

The institute had already assigned Betty Mooney, a Baptist missionary on their Extension Faculty, to the non-existent centre, and Welthy knew that Dick Cortright and Margaret Lee Runbeck were soon to arrive. Dr. Laubach was also due to return for the first training session, which would never have materialized if Welthy had not taken things into her own hands. With four or five different sponsors, no one had pulled the strings together or knew who would pay for what until Welthy simply jumped into the breach and the experiment began.

Courtesy LITERACY HOUSE 53

SEVA MANDIR, UDAIPUR 54   ARIEL 55

53. Literacy House staff. First row: P.N. Shivpuri, K.C. Gupta, Welthy, Mushtaq Ahmed, Comfort Shaw, A.R. Siddiqi, R.C. Ariel. 54. Mrs. K.N. Srivastava and women of Seva Mandir welcoming Welthy in Udaipur. 55. Puppeteer Naitani helps the announcer puppet greet Welthy, 1973.

56

56. Welthy's family. Front: Freddie Hynes, Toots J. Kimball, Welthy, Helen Halstead, Julie Lauh. Back: T.S. Lauh, Gordon and Wm. Halstead, Pei Fong Loh, Mike Honsinger. 57. President Zakir Husain, Dr. M. S. Mehta and J.C. Mathur, at Nehru Literacy Award, 1969. 58. Dr. James Draper and Welthy, 1970

GOVERNMENT OF INDIA   57   58

S. SWENSON 59   Courtesy WORLD EDUCATION, INC. 60

DIRCK HALSTEAD 61

59. Welthy with the Pradhan of Bijnaur and P.N. Shivpuri at inauguration of Young Farmers' Institute campus, 1968. 60. Education Minister V.K.R.V. Rao, Dr. H. Hunsaker, T.B. Keehn and Welthy at workshop sponsored by World Education, New Delhi, 1970. 61. Welthy with village women near Indore, 1970. 62. Caught off guard in 1973, Welthy's face reveals the pain and fatigue of her years.

S. SWENSON

62

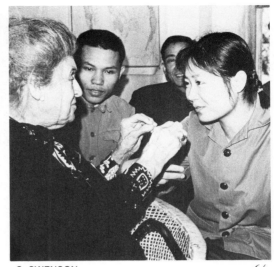

S. SWENSON 63

63. Touring a Chinese commune with cadres, 1973.
64. Talking with trainees at
the Kwantung Teachers
Training College, 1973.
65. With the staff of
Kwantung Teachers Training
College.

S. SWENSON 64

GOVERNMENT OF CHINA   66

S. SWENSON   67

S. SWENSON   68

C. O'KEEFE   69

66. Soong Ching Ling receiving Welthy in the palace of the last emperor, Peking, 1978. 67. Welthy reading a World Education newsletter, Southbury, Connecticut, 1978. 68. Talitha Gerlach, Rewi Alley and Welthy enjoying their reunion in Rewi's Peking apartment, 1978. 69. Arriving at her 100th birthday, New York, with Sally Swenson.

70. Receiving an honorary degree from Chancellor Hidyatullah, Delhi University, 1980. 71. Greeting Prime Minister Indira Gandhi, 1980. 72. Mrs. Gandhi looks on as flowers were presented by Ministry of Education. 73. Newly literate village women talking with Welthy at Founder's Day celebration, 1980.

THE STATESMAN, NEW DELHI   70

GOVERNMENT OF INDIA   71

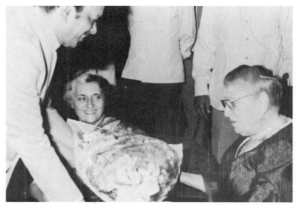

GOVERNMENT OF INDIA   72

S. SWENSON   73

74. In the Gatineau hills near Ottawa after her 100th birthday, with Sally and their cats. 75. The last summer, the last photograph.

MARIJKE GEERTSEMA   74

S. SWENSON   75

On the first day the shops of Allahabad were turned inside out as she scoured around like a new bride for tables, chairs, beds and touches of Indian beauty to create an instant home for the assortment of people with whom she would share Bungalow Number Two, day and night. Fired by her own "unerring instinct",[11] each purchase adding to the unformed idea emerging, Welthy went full steam ahead, applying her own money and method to the situation, as she had always done. Betty Mooney provided any needed encouragement, eager to begin her part in the training.

Welthy loved to tell the story of that day of decision when she moved managed so much, and of the cook she hired on the spot who was so British-trained that echoes of Empire appeared on her table in starchy puddings she could not abide. During the first weeks alone in the bungalow, Welthy and the cook appraised one another thoroughly in a fair exchange of information and ideas leading to a happy modus vivendi, with the cook a valuable ally in Welthy's living and learning centre.

To sustain them in the face of the harsh reality of the villages, Welthy asked the first group of trainees if they would like to begin each day's training with Gandhi's prayers. They chose instead to have her give a meditation theme and promised to organize a schedule of prayers from different faiths. "It is a new day in India," she began, "and we shall try to catch from other religions whatever enriches our own, while we learn to work together." In those two simple resources, a warm home and a prayerful start to each day's work, Welthy placed the human imprint on Literacy House that would be its distinguishing feature.

She felt terribly alone even while making scores of new friends who were to be her colleagues in the great adventure. She had no peers. No one around her had the experience, creativity, energy and spiritual resources on which she was drawing—the 'exquisite loneliness' which characterized most of her later life, demanding that she reach beyond her external surroundings for survival. No one knew all that was in her heart and mind as the programme developed. From each training session they learned the next step, and each night in the villages the trainees found out if they had learned anything at all about teaching adults.

Working closely with the team at each stage to build flexibility into the training, she won Ted Koshy's approval of her trial and error approach. There was hardly time to scratch the surface before the two-month extension to Laubach's grant expired at the end of March 1953 when Laubach moved on to Assam, with no plan for continuing, except in Welthy's mind.

As Margaret Lee Runbeck's three-month contract ended she too wanted to stay on and see the centre become permanent. Soon to die of cancer, at that point she was a writer full of life and imagination whose daily lectures Welthy attended studiously and whose short days with Literacy House were seminal. In a report to New York Margaret wrote:

Last night I watched our trainees teaching in two villages. A brilliant starlit night, and the whole landscape dotted with lanterns and candles around which sat little rings of villagers reading loudly. The air was full of their happy chanting. Animals, always close at hand in India, listened and watched. It was an unforgettable picture, for every element in it was a return to the primitive and good things of the world, simplicity, love of wanting to know, and brotherly sharing. I wish everyone on earth could have seen it. A wave of love for the goodness of mankind would have rolled over the world.

Welthy's imagination carried the image further as she watched a young man squatting in a mud corner, tentatively taking a small book from the tin-trunk library, holding it reverently and peering intently at the characters on the page, unable to decipher them. The printed word! Mysterious, elusive, unattainable — symbol of other people's power — the Brahmin, the politician who came once a year into the village and the government officials in the Block (administrative unit). The word was theirs. Everything about the world beyond his village seemed hidden in that printed word just in front of him. But it could not speak to him. For such a young man, hovering on the brink of awareness, the will toward knowledge was keen and Welthy knew he would learn quickly. For others less eager, the literacy team would be sorely challenged to arouse that desire.

Betty Mooney was worried about the centre, fearing the work would be too heavy for Welthy. Alfred Moore, Secretary of World Literacy in New York, had hopes of sending a man to take over the project. "It is a cause of thankfulness here," he wrote to Welthy at the end of March, "that you have been in India with Frank. You have a kind of enthusiasm and drive that keeps its feet on the ground that is most valuable where Frank's dreams are concerned. You wrote you needed twelve thousand dollars for the training centre. Frank wrote the need was for thirty three thousand. What's the difference? A building?"[12]

The difference was that Laubach's mission was to the whole world. He had other countries on his mind as well as India and thought in large numbers as he moved around the globe. For Welthy, who had been global all her life, the challenge was to translate global thinking into a specific local project on the ground. Thinking small, she held to Gandhi's view. Laubach and Welthy were both larger than the organizations backing and trying to control them. Both were pioneers, having to find their way in the face of stifling bureaucracy. Both admired each other's skills and motivation, different aspects of the same coin.

Welthy was now, ironically, in the position of being herself administrator of an institution! Almost an institution, that is, for it still lacked form and space, but its shape was becoming more visible daily. Emerging out of chaos in fits and starts, the beginnings were intensive, extensive, exhilarating, demanding and exhausting for everyone involved.

* * *

While Welthy pressed boldly on, literacy and education for adults were still as controversial as they had been for a hundred years. Many thought that time, and universal education of children, would take care of any problems. Planners in Delhi were confronted with challenges on all fronts. "It is doubtful if without her this most vital but often forgotten aspect of the Indian citizen's capability for sustaining democracy and development would ever have received the attention it deserves," said C. D. Deshmukh, "amidst the welter of problems this ancient land was called upon to face after achieving independence."[13]

Groups of experts debated and planned in Delhi, foreign advisers studied the problems, new bureaucrats deliberated on what action others should take, and still others tried to cope with the overload of information about the massive needs competing for attention. Welthy acted on her own understanding:

> *We could not afford to dwell on the overwhelming total need; we had to concentrate on the immediate need that we could see and feel around us in the four hundred villages where we began to try and test all our plans and programmes. I realized that argument would not suffice. It was a cheap form of conversation. I would not be able to change their minds. I would do something as a pilot experiment.*

Whatever doubts she may have entertained, she found the answers from the villagers themselves, whose inherent wisdom she respected and to whom she communicated hope. "If you take a cynical view of the world, you feel very old and spiritually dead," she said. "If you take a hopeful view you feel young and enthusiastic." Long before literacy experts elucidated the theory that learning was a two-way process between teacher and learner Welthy was out in the field practising what she had always known. Because she did not state this in painstaking detail, professional educators could not then understand what she had grasped.

Her reaction to the prevailing view was the agile mental shorthand she offered in explanation: "I disobeyed the pundits—we can't wait for children to grow up."

* * *

Welthy commuted in and out of the newly international Delhi gathering ideas and supplies and trainees for her fledgling institution, and dashed down to Mysore to look at the first UNESCO pilot literacy experiment underway. She threw out her encircling arm to everyone who passed by that bungalow, inviting them in with outrageous indiscrimination, from poet to politician. For anyone keen on specifics, Welthy was impossible, but in keeping her door wide open she knew exactly what she was doing at the centre of that creation. In her mind that wide outreach was very specific focus:

> *It was the welding of the cultural with the practical and the integration of both in the Indian character that helped me understand the tremendous job we had undertaken. In both facets there was inspiration . . . as electricity must be generated by both negative and positive forces. It was on the real and the unreal as they knew it to be that I knew I must build. Adapting myself, but maintaining and instilling workable truths common to all.* [14]

Operating on all fronts, Welthy reached to New York to bring Rudolph Flesch—a leading proponent of phonetic teaching—for a writers' workshop, and lost no time in obtaining Ford Foundation and Government of India sponsorship. She convinced Durgabai Deshmukh to send a trainee from her newly created Central Social Welfare Board that assisted and coordinated the work of twelve thousand existing voluntary agencies. Welthy was tapping into the partnership of two of India's strongest leaders, for Durgabai's husband, C. D. Deshmukh, was Nehru's Finance Minister.

Continuing her diplomatic offensive, Welthy invited the entire faculty of AAI, with families, to a tea party, searching for contacts and exposing her staff and trainees to the larger group. Welthy's parties were not the exclusive gatherings most AAI missionaries held; she had an irrepressible urge to be inclusive, often leading to near panic for anyone trying to provide the refreshments. Welthy would dash into the city to buy boxes of Annapurna sweets and then leave the rest to fall into place.

Many Indians with varying backgrounds of experience stayed to join her growing band of workers, captured by the enthusiasm in the air. Before long the buzzing bungalow came to be known as the literacy house, and the name stuck. It was just right, and Welthy was pleased at the spontaneous recognition of her eclectic band of workers.

COMFORT SHAW

Comfort Shaw, a social worker with literacy experience at a Christian rural education extension centre, was drawn by Welthy's obvious leadership ability and her awareness of the underlying religious differences which affected all endeavour in India. When he came to AAI for extension training, Welthy asked him to speak to her trainees on cooperatives, a process by which she identified him as the man she wanted to organize the work of Literacy House. For Shaw the challenge was worth the risk of leaving his secure position, and he lent a strong right arm to her practical brand of idealism. Though both lacked administrative flair, Shaw's commitment enabled him to work well with her in a partnership that held things together through the critical building years.

RASHID SIDDIQI

Rashid Siddiqi, a Muslim trained in dairy development, had boundless energy and skill in organizing men for the evening classes in villages where he did extension training, after taking the Literacy House training. When Shaw offered him a job at Literacy House it was not difficult for Siddiqi to decide between his intense attraction to Welthy and an offer to work in Saudi Arabia. Despite the greater insecurity, he never regretted his decision to join. "It was just a passion to work. The sense of achievement, happiness, contributing, sharing, learning, growing, respect and love and attachment to a group I'd never had before," he recalled.[15] "Those who couldn't adjust to Mrs. Fisher's hurried decision-making left. Before an idea comes out of her lips, because it has been in her mind, she expected the whole thing should be executed. That very nature gave birth to Literacy House. It was real life. All the senses of human being were devoted to one point, the challenge. When she can put in sixteen hours a day, why can't we?"

That sense of belonging that Welthy created gave a unique quality to the work that no one could replace, at once both the strength and weakness of Literacy House as an institution.

ARIEL AND KARNWAL

Clancy Ariel was assistant librarian at AAI when Welthy asked him to help grade books for the new mobile, tin-trunk libraries she designed for the villages, and he soon joined the staff, developing into a key training officer and photographer. Writer S.P. Karnwal was another of those first staff members found by Welthy who grew with Literacy House through the years, rooted in the affective principle and dedicated to Welthy's vision.

And so the work gathered momentum. Welthy insisted that methods and materials be carefully tested in the villages, and that every trainee do practice teaching in villages at night, the only time villagers could attend. They demonstrated improved cooking arrangements so the smoke would be carried away by chimneys, sparing eyes and lungs, and how to build platforms around wells to avoid contamination. They explained how the moneylender caught people by words and documents they did not understand, and they kept asking villagers what they wanted to know. The answers were, first, agriculture and religion, and then, surprisingly, the stars and stories of the movies.

From the Government of India, British Government institutes and *Santiniketan* Welthy got lists of words most frequently used, and by constant testing in the villages the staff compiled a working base of two thousand words. Each group of trainees was involved in improving the teaching syllabus as the courses developed in writing, teacher training, audio-visual materials, and the libraries. Knowing that the overall teaching challenge was one of attitude, Welthy denied a certificate to one trainee from a rich Delhi family because he would not carry out his village practice teaching.

EDUCATIONAL PUPPETRY

As one of her more enduring supporters put it, Welthy was not one to tip-toe around an idea,[16] and when the possibility of using puppets struck her, it was swiftly translated into a trial project, growing out of the traditional puppet troupes that had moved from village to village giving colourful entertainment. Why not let the puppets educate while they entertained? Their enchanting personalities were the only ones free of caste . . . perhaps they could say things villagers would listen to. Later known as educational puppetry, the concept began with Welthy and became a cornerstone of the LH approach.[17]

SIT WHERE THEY SIT

With a 'still small voice' inviting her trainees to speak softly to the villagers, Welthy hoped to awaken them to the possibilities of change, as she cautioned them to respect genetic memory:

They are five thousand years old and tough as a tetanus germ. You must know what they think and why.

Their own scripture, the Upanishad, means "to sit near," for the teacher to communicate the wisdom living in him, his spiritual spark making the wisdom believable, allowing the student to receive it. Sit where they sit, Ezekiel implored, and Welthy emphasized empathy again and again, as the critical factor in teaching, infinitely more important than all the techniques.

The will toward knowledge had first to be aroused by a caring teacher. Motivation to pursue literacy comes from some fundamental, mysterious act of the mind in discovering itself. The brand of literacy Welthy was promoting was neither the old missionary evangelism, nor the newer evangelizing of literacy in the socialist vein. In a land with powerful oral traditions of wisdom handed down by professional storytellers round whom an entire village gathered to hear the great epics, the literacy to be evolved would take its own distinctive character from within the soul of India.

Fully conscious of the immensity of the task, it was an act of extraordinary faith to be planning for a century, while others still thought in terms of quick campaigns. But Welthy brought a profound sense of urgency to the work, and in the charged atmosphere of energy and purpose she created, it was easy to fall short of her high expectations. Her saving grace was her readiness to forgive anybody anything as long as they were out in the villages, listening and learning, experimenting with new ways to motivate interest. Welthy knew she did not have the answers, but she was determined that her staff would find approaches, and test, adjust and adapt them. Theory was a luxury that would have to follow their practical efforts. This was new territory.

Welthy used the materials developed by Dr. Laubach because they were good and were the only well developed set available, but she knew that a far greater, indigenous effort on a continuing basis had to be established for the future—broader, deeper, stronger—and Literacy House would serve that purpose as the first permanent institution committed to that role.

Whatever the subsequent failings of Literacy House, there was no fickleness in its founder. It was Welthy's persistent, strategic focus on the thirteen-to-thirty age group in rural areas and her use of Indian personnel as much as possible that characterized the work.

Like an anxious mother trying to house and protect her brood, Welthy had to relieve the uncertainty about the future of Literacy House. "Almost from the beginning she started talking about their need for more space for classrooms, staff housing and offices," Mosher said,[18] recalling his skepticism about a woman of seventy plus who sounded like Laubach, a man not known for sticking tenaciously with projects he launched. When Mosher suggested that Welthy integrate her project into the overall programme of AAI, she declined, knowing Mosher was resigning immediately and convinced that the project needed freedom to continue experimenting. The JUPAN experiment had been too short and it would take years before its inconclusive results were available.[19] Her attempt to buy adjacent land was blocked by AAI, leaving her to mutter: "My personality should have been darkened in some way or put in a box for a while." In April she asked Alfred Moore for five thousand dollars to continue for ten months until they had to leave the bungalow, believing she and Betty Mooney could operate on such a thrifty budget, simply not prepared to give up. "I start out on a path and I suppose I have gone toward the sun all the time," said Welthy.

It was in every sense a new dawn for her. She stopped signing her name "Mrs. Frederick B. Fisher," no longer leaning on Fred's reputation, and became Welthy Honsinger Fisher again. Thereafter, no obstacle could deflect Welthy, though she was sorely tried and tested at every turn as she put literacy on the new map of India.

Welthy knew that literacy in itself would not bring the changes that would improve village life, that it was as full of the human contradictions as life itself, and in the extreme can even alienate a person from society. But at best, the ability to read could bring an individual a unique access to his or her culture and beyond, an approach to equality, an avenue away from entrenched habits of servile thought. It began with a teacher revealing in his attitude a quality of understanding that made learning desirable. Without it, the mere mechanical literacy needed in a technological society was farther down the ladder of learning, but important even so. There was no longer time for the cultured illiteracy of simpler civilizations.

1954

Juggling the meagre funds at her disposal, tossing in whatever she had in hand of her own, she rented a house adjacent to the AAI for one year and supervised the instant construction of a miniature tent city for the growing, makeshift centre, with a teahouse in the garden for gatherings. Welthy always had time for fun, for relieving the stress and strain with instant vacations in the midst of hectic activity, a rhythmic weaving of work and play. "Our mood was golden," she said of the compressed, challenging turmoil in which their creativity and camaraderie thrived. Bukhnu, the *mali* who was a landmark at AAI and looked as if he had grown from the soil, came along one day and thereafter made the place bloom with beauty and colour. Wherever Welthy went, Bukhnu was never far behind.

The mammoth *Kumbh Mela* held every twelve years was the focal event of 1954 in Allahabad, providing a superb opportunity for Literacy House to show its wares in two special tents to the millions of pilgrims in the vast eight-hundred acre site. *Sadhus* and *sanyasins* by the thousands converged at the confluence of the sacred waters for purification in that first *Mela* since independence.

When a stampede suddenly occurred killing over three hundred people, Welthy, who spoke no Hindi other than a few basic expressions, was standing in their midst. With commanding resourcefulness she did not panic but somehow communicated clearly her intent, asking four men nearby to lift her up above the crowd. The instantaneous response to the impending crisis saved herself and the four men.

September 18, 1954. Recuperating from an accident, Welthy marked another birthday in New Delhi's Willingdon Nursing Home. Returning to Allahabad after a conference in Patna with S.C. Dutta, Secretary General of the Indian Adult Education Association (IAEA), her car swerved to avoid a peasant, rolled over three times and landed upright with two stunned passengers.

The usual committee of numerous villagers surrounded them, their chatter like the tower of Babel to Welthy and Dutta, both unable to move and their driver vomiting blood. In time Welthy persuaded two men to take them thirteen rugged miles to a small village hospital where the extreme lack of facilities was compensated for by great attention while they awaited the Keehns to rescue and despatch them on the mail train to Delhi.

In her report of that long day Welthy omitted to say what the injuries were that required a month to mend. But when Shanti and Humayan Kabir (the Minister of Education) visited her sickbed they found a highly animated Welthy talking and laughing at full tilt despite four broken bones and a head that would not turn to the left. Giving a wonderful performance in telling of her plans, Welthy captivated the Minister.[20] As the toll on her anatomy mounted, there was no longer much speculation about her staying power and ability to transcend obstacles.

She spent the time in hospital writing to women in Greenwich, Connecticut, about the jeep with a special chassis she had purchased in Bombay, their gift transformed into a bookmobile. To another group she told of the welcoming garland of Literacy House publications placed round her neck by the senior staff on her arrival at Delhi's Palam Airport earlier that year.

1955

Literacy House moved again to a former Maharajah's compound at One Bund Road across from Allahabad University, a most agreeable interlude with lively companionship of students and professors. But at four in the morning Welthy was frequently up and on her way to Lucknow with Shaw and Siddiqi, racing to get on the road before the endless chain of bullock carts carrying goods to market slowed their passage. Having discussed the various possible sites with innumerable key figures, Welthy had decided that the permanent location for Literacy House should be near the capital of the largest state in the nation.

The lure of Lucknow was magnetic for its publishing and printing facilities, with an equally strong pull as a Christian stronghold, leading her back to the locale of Isabella Thoburn. She wanted her experiment to be visible, especially to the Christians. In the pre-dawn, her mind racing to the rattle of her little Austin, she asked herself over and over again if she was sure she could help these people when she was not one of them, and if it was right to try.

DECIDING ON A PERMANENT SITE

Governor Munshi of Uttar Pradesh had seen their work in the hills the previous summer and urged her to locate permanently in Lucknow, suggesting a location beyond Sarojini Nagar where he and his wife had built a centre in memory of Sarojini Naidu, his predecessor. But they would not have a distinct entrance off the main Kanpur Road, and would again be linked to another institution, however noble. Welthy wanted Literacy House to stand out and be known.

Other sites had been suggested to Welthy. Six acres near the Muslim Jamia Millia college were recommended by Kabir and Douglas Ensminger, head of the Ford Foundation who had taken strong interest in the work. Indirect government support would also be available through the college. Four acres near the Christian Ingraham Institute were approved by the Bishop if Welthy wanted them. There was a possible site near the AAI, one at Nilokeri, and another possibility of *bhoodan* land that Vinoba Bhave might make available. But she knew that literacy had been too long an ad hoc effort tacked onto other programmes, and the Social Education projects of the government did not have a secure place within the Community Development Programme, as evidenced by a mere three percent share of funds in the First Five Year Plan.

Going against the advice of Albert Mayer, the Planning Adviser to the U.P. Government, to buy a site ten miles from the city and rely on the promise of the Minister of Supplies, C.B. Gupta, to extend electricity to them, Welthy chose a smaller site just beyond the city limits, right at the last electric pole. "I take issue with him (Mayer) with a good deal of caution," she admitted, but a politician's promise would never equal electricity in hand, and she was certain that a modern institution representing the light of learning required electricity, which ranked next to the wheel on Welthy's list of great inventions.

With that critical decision behind her, the minute parcels of land which together made up the site she wanted were skillfully negotiated by Siddiqi and purchased one by one from her new neighbour, Mr. Gurnani, who had a home and factory directly opposite. Painstakingly, on repeated visits, they assembled ten acres of completely barren, alkaline land. "We have decided we cannot afford a brick wall so will have pillars with fine strands of barbed wire and a thorny hedge to keep the hungry cows from our precious saplings," she reported. Welthy was back in the business of building.

Her attention turned to Lucknow, the heart of Hindustan in ancient and medieval times, melting pot of race and cultures, eastern outpost of six hundred years of Muslim supremacy in India, and site of the first Methodist mission. With a single institution she aimed to focus on literacy as a permanent part of the overall educational effort, by strengthening existing Indian organizations, non-government and government, training leaders and developing mobile staff services and materials, using maximum Indian personnel, and providing post-literate publications.

While she was concentrating on specifics, Wallace Speers, the President of World Literacy, and Moore were engaged in extensive communications with Humayun Kabir and William Haggerty, the American adviser to the ministry, concerning an ambitious network of centres covering the fourteen languages of India based on the Laubach method and materials. Laubach was pressing hard for this, his impatience scarcely concealed, fearing that the moment would be lost. "There is a widespread philosophy of social education in India which regards literacy as of minor importance or even dangerous," he reported.

Welthy had read Ensminger's advice to Speers that no outside organization or funds would be effective unless Indians organized and gave leadership to their own literacy programme, and she wanted to be the catalyst to bring that about. By being free of other institutional connections she had a chance to try it in her own way. Some would misunderstand, she knew, but she had done her homework thoroughly, thought deeply and had approval in writing from the Planning Commission to start her experiment in Lucknow.

Welthy's visit to Vinoba Bhave provided a touch of inspiration, for she knew Gandhi thought Vinoba had understood his philosophy best. In asking for gifts of land to use in the service of the poor, Vinoba walked from village to village, into areas where Communists were cutting off landlords' heads, venturing into their midst in a manner that was Christ-like to Welthy. He stayed among them and they stopped the slaughter and withdrew. Without such inspiration Welthy knew she could never face the task she had set herself. What could she do on a piece of bar-ren land to reach barren minds untouched by the gift of knowledge?

WORLD LITERACY SPONSORS PLAN

In the spring of 1954, Comfort Shaw had been appointed administra-tor, and Welthy had returned to New York to seek support for the plans Bill Haggerty had given so much help with. There, she was invited to a World Literacy meeting, attended by Laubach, where the trustees ac-cepted her idea of literacy as a "functional tool of life" and of a fixed programme in one place, allaying their anxiety over what they con-sidered the unfocused, fragmented Laubach projects. They approved her operating budget of thirty-three thousand dollars for one year, as well as a ten thousand dollar gift she recommended for the building fund of the IAEA.

World Literacy was clearly relieved to have a definite centre in one country with a non-religious programme, though they still had ideas of establishing ingingingingother centres in India. Welthy took the money, grateful for one year's reprieve. The fact that it came from different sour-ces within the Laubach network of organizations would pose some reporting problems for her, a reflection of the continuing confusion of organizations in New York. World Literacy's decision to spend fifty per-cent of that year's budget on administration in New York did little to lessen the confusion and only added to what Welthy found to be exces-sive administration by remote control.

In India, Welthy was struggling with changing, unskilled secretaries, pushing herself to the limit, often tapping out informal reports to World Literacy late at night. The new staff in the New York office seemed un-aware that Mrs. Fisher was not an employee to be tightly supervised and controlled. She had over five hundred trainees to attend to and some twenty books for new literates to be written and published, as well as finding staff for an insecure institution.

INDIA LITERACY BOARD

At the end of the year Welthy requested two weeks vacation from 'her employers' to travel by boat instead of air when she returned to New York that year with documents for their approval. These were the found-ing papers of the India Literacy Board (ILB) that Dutta and Ensminger had helped her plan as the entity to own and manage Literacy House. This time she would make sure that the deeds were where they belonged, remembering the Chinese Communists' disdain on discovering that the missions were owned by Americans who did not think their Chinese Christians could be entrusted with buildings.

But Welthy was moving too far too fast for World Literacy, who envisioned the ILB more as a holding company acting with their consent and approval. They wanted more control than Welthy thought wise, especially over the funds Literacy House realized from sale of publications, fees, bank interest, and so on, fearing that a switch of allegiance by Welthy to some other organization would put them out of Literacy House and literacy work in India. Literacy House was their foot in the door and they intended to keep ownership and control of it. Welthy's critical decision to acquiesce for the moment got her plans moving, but with consequences that were to cramp progress in the years ahead.

She took her greatest encouragement from the response of growing numbers of visitors from official and unofficial India who valued the development of graded reading material, the setting of standards and the model of training. The Joint Development Commissioner from West Bengal observed that "an adult literacy centre imperceptibly transforms itself into a social education centre, where the object of study is the individual in relation to society, his role, his rights, responsibilities, privileges and duties."

In P. D. Tandon, an editor and freelance journalist who had been imprisoned with Nehru and was close to the family, Welthy found a delightful companion for early morning walks in Alfred Park. P. D. became an ardent supporter, frequently bringing visitors to Literacy House, introducing Welthy to many helpful people, and observing and reporting later on some Americans who saw Welthy as an obstacle and were less than helpful. Such people turned up regularly and were inevitably more concerned with administrative control than the experimental development of a new programme.

By now Welthy had established many watering stops in Delhi, homes where she could arrive unannounced and stay for a few days of bustling activity. She loved the warm family atmosphere in the Keehn's home with their growing youngsters, the sympathetic, helpful attitude of Marge and Bill Haggerty, and the open friendliness of Colonel Gouman's apartment in Connaught Circus, or Evelyn Hersey's, or the Ensminger's. A lively presence popping in and out of their lives, Welthy never stayed in one place long enough for her underlying weariness and strain to show.

There was something extremely attractive about her spirited energy and her conviction that it was possible to tackle illiteracy that made others want to help in various ways. Seeing illiteracy as a deep cultural condition cutting across all disciplines and classes, Welthy never turned down any offer of help from any source. Working the elite salons of New Delhi in her shimmering silks provided just the blend of pleasure and purpose she thrived on.

People in Delhi listened to what she was saying as she moved in and out of meetings and receptions. Ambassadors became her friends and collaborators, half a dozen American envoys taking up their posts during Welthy's pioneering tenure – Allen, Bowles, Bunker, Galbraith, Keating and Moynihan. One admitted that "I and all the American Ambassadors who have preceded me in this sensitive post would agree that whatever success we have enjoyed has not equalled the lasting benefits of Dr. Fisher's Literacy House in Lucknow."[21] But her reluctance to articulate a theory that educators could comprehend only increased the urgency to make her experiment visible.

MARGE AND BILL HAGGERTY

Welthy talked night after night with the Haggertys about the possibilities for Literacy House and they encouraged her to work on her own. Bill drafted the first budget for her and suggested ways of institutionalizing her ideas. Aware of Welthy's strong foothold in India and her wide knowledge, they had confidence she could do this big job, recognizing a power of communicating with people that they had never encountered before.[22]

With Marge Haggerty and Tom Keehn she went off to Kashmir for a brief impromptu houseboat holiday in 1954, an interlude that established an enduring link with both families. The two delighted to find Welthy such a plucky traveller as she kept their heads cool with a wet cloth from an earthen pot of water on the drive north.

As with all the people who were part of the creation of Literacy House, each one felt they were a major influence and none knew the extent of the vast network she was tapping, nor the different pressures on her. It was Welthy who secured a barracks at Landaur from the commandant of Dehra Dun to hold the first summer course in the hills for fifty trainees. She made the contacts and arrangements for Literacy House staff to hold training sessions in neighbouring states and as far away as Assam at the invitation of the Ministry of Education there. Welthy rarely said no when asked, nor did one easily say no to Welthy when she was doing herself what she asked of others.

LITERACY IN SECULAR LANGUAGE

In New York, Frank Laubach's relations with World Literacy were going from bad to worse, as WL's interest focused mainly on Welthy's growing centre and the non-religious emphasis WL insisted upon. "When the religious motive is cut off my power with audiences ceases and my own enthusiasm dies," Laubach told WL. "I crave and need the support of praying people. This cutting from the churches is for me a personal tragedy. I do not know how to talk in any language but that of religion."

Welthy's deepest motivation was akin to Laubach's, and certainly he strongly urged support of her centre, but she had learned that Christian love can speak a secular language. The literacy organization of the Protestant churches discussed issuing a statement that World Literacy was not a Christian organization, but Laubach's wisdom prevailed and the statement was voted down. Nevertheless, by association with WL, Welthy was labelled as being less than Christian in some minds for a number of years.[23]

April 7, 1955. At the end of another training course, Welthy succumbed to illness again, briefly. "Lying in bed for an entire day is hard work, even tho I'm too exhausted to work." After three days in bed the doctor insisted she continue resting, but by 3:30 a.m. the following day she was back on the road to Lucknow, "running toward the sun" in another round of negotiations.

NEW YORK, 1955 - WORLD LITERACY APPROVAL AND PROBLEMS

In the summer of 1955 under Welthy's guidance the bickering WL Board considered her building plans, the possibility of appointing Tom Keehn as Executive Director, and an ambitious TV pilot proposal Gordon Halstead's brother hoped to start in India. Only the building plans were accepted, with Laubach's strong support, but in noting the board's enthusiasm for that one project he warned that they must not allow Welthy to dry up their other dreams for India or the world.[24]

Reading the writing on their bare wall, Welthy got busy raising money. "Went for dinner with friends and got five thousand for the water supply." One of those friends was Mary Dreier, the social reformer, who shared Welthy's outlook, created fund-raising opportunities at her cottage in Southwest Harbour, Maine, gave a thousand dollars for several years, as well as warm hospitality, a good pen, a warm shawl and extra money for a solid bed for Welthy.

Being a friend of Welthy's was hazardous to say the least, for she had no compunction about accepting whatever personal gifts were offered as she moved about with one suitcase, or asking for money for the work. Was there any other way to get it? Restless at the slow-moving pace of the office, she kept her distance, steadily increasing the building fund through her speeches and contacts.

Richard McFadyen, the Vice-President and Treasurer of World Literacy, took a hard look at the then all-male organization and suggested to the trustees in late 1955 that the work abroad was fine, but that their "turbulent lethargy" at home was not solvable by changing officers and personnel. New York office costs needed drastic reduction, Laubach's global ambitions could not be supported with tired old fund-raising methods, all trustees and officers should resign except three required for legal purposes, and Mrs. Fisher should be invited to ask people interested in her programme to become trustees and officers. For once, Welthy and Frank Laubach were on opposite sides of the bureaucratic fence.

In calling for such a thorough housecleaning McFadyen shocked the board into recognition of their own serious administrative confusion. But they considered his plan inappropriate, looking instead for ways to maintain the Laubach connection and possibly transfer Literacy House to some other organization. Whatever security Welthy may have felt, it now hung in the balance.

Throughout all these difficult deliberations, though it would appear to have been a power struggle between Laubach and Welthy, there was never any discord between them. Rather, the people surrounding Laubach felt jeopardized by organizational shifts and changes affecting the three organizations he had launched and the overlapping policy and fund raising problems. Some harboured resentment against Welthy, believing she had been given her start by Laubach and owed allegiance to his method. Laubach was a wise and wonderful man in many ways, able to see in Welthy a fellow pioneer well advanced on her journey, and did not share their narrow view.

Dr. Paul Means and his wife found themselves caught in an awkward situation resulting from that overlapping when they were sent to India for two years in 1955 and 1956 by Laubach as "co-operators," expected to promote the Laubach materials and method throughout India, but based at Literacy House with no clear role. Well qualified, Means felt under-used and highly frustrated in a subordinate position to Welthy and Shaw, whose goals differed considerably. Welthy informed Means he could not make visits to other parts of India and set up training sessions under Literacy House auspices without an invitation in writing to do so. That was only one of the many tangles she had to cut through with a certain toughness.

Harold Miner, who headed CARE, was one of the key members of the WL Board who sensed that Laubach was no longer welcome in India, a situation Tom Keehn later found himself in was when he was head of the organization. Because her motivation was above suspicion, Welthy remained persona grata in India throughout the years, even among those who questioned her informal methods and large ambitions.

October, 1955. "The pains in my head are still with me – they streak down into my spine until I feel shattered as I did immediately after the accident. But I work on because I do not know what else to do, and always believe in the therapy of work. Isn't it a miracle that I live? And move? And have some little sense left? I thank God every day and would like to make one more contribution to life."

It was a miracle that she was living on, for during a two week stop with Helen and Arthur Schwartz in the United States she had been hospitalized with pneumonia and diabetes, ready to let them treat the former, but dismissing the latter diagnosis as nonsense.

Work and the stray cat she had adopted were the best medicine, the cat accompanying Welthy on her dashes to Delhi, happily resting on her head in lieu of a hat, its independent spirit a source of constant delight and amusement. Now that the staff and trainees were separately housed, dinners alone were the hardest part of Welthy's long day. She asked innumerable friends to come out to India, longing for companionship and help, plenty of help. A few came and were gone all too soon, for it was not easy to help Welthy, to keep up to her incredible pace and meet her enormous expectations.

"I'm so tired of always having to flirt with FAO, UN, Ministry of Education, Extension and Training, UP Everything and Central Social Welfare. I'm exhausted and have no one to plan with." Her house and office were one, the bedroom like the rest room at Grand Central Station, as she dealt with everyone at once.

Frank Laubach was in transit and about to reach India. Both Welthy in Allahabad and Dr. Means in Hyderabad had advised him not to come to Literacy House. Instead, Welthy met him in Delhi, having been warned by Dr. Ensminger that the names Laubach and even World Literacy were so strongly tied to pro-Christian anti-Communism that Literacy House could suffer by association.

One friend discussed her concern over Welthy's health with Helen Halstead, who came out to help for a short period, and they wondered if anyone could actually relieve her. She was such a rugged individualist. "This is a uniquely personal organization . . . what has been accomplished is no less than a miracle performed by Welthy. She has had the fortitude and endurance to do what ten average individuals would find it difficult to produce. The worry over receiving funds regularly has been a great concern with the number of men on the job. Welthy's greatest service is in her contacts all over India. She needs assistance here."[25]

Allahabad, December 31, 1955. At the close of an anxious year, Welthy noted that Dr. Ensminger had written to Laubach that Communism was not the issue. "If we are going to help the illiterate we must do it for their sakes," she wrote in a firm hand, "not for the sake of killing Communism. India believes in co-existence." So did Welthy. If 1955 had been a heavy year, it was only prologue to Welthy's finest but most frenzied time.

1956

January 3, 1956. Welthy was in Delhi typing into the early morning to complete a proposal for the Ministry of Community Development. After delivering it to S. K. Dey the next morning, she immersed herself briefly in the cool darkness of a silk shop, basking in the flowing rich colours, bantering and bartering with the owner who sat cross-legged on a platform covered with white sheeting, the smell of incense pervading everything. Her urgent need for an enema bag and a zipper took second priority to the need for diversion from her all-consuming mission. The game of buying silk and having a beautiful dress made to her design was Welthy's choice indulgence, and it mattered not that her feet were firmly housed in a pair of old-fashioned white oxfords and her brown hair was topped with a quaint little white lace half hat, the disparate parts of a many-sided individual.

January 12, 1956. Welthy was in bed with fever, fasting and taking sulfa drugs and penicillin. For an Indian visitor arriving unannounced she got up, put on her dressing gown and the omnipresent strand of pearls to receive him, then took to her bed for four days.

January 18, 1956. A young American sent by World Literacy to oversee building plans for Literacy House tried to take charge and change everything, offering Shaw ten thousand rupees to back him against Welthy.[26] Shaw refused the bribe. Welthy's diary reflected the tension. "Dear God—You are Love, and Love is the strongest force in the world. Make me big enough, and my prayer sincere." A staff blow-up engineered by the overseer was resolved, grace prevailing as he and Siddiqi shook hands at Welthy's instigation.

JAWAHARLAL NEHRU AND INDIRA

February, 1956. Nehru and daughter Indira were in Allahabad at the family residence, and Welthy was invited to tea, thanks to P. D. Tandon. Later Nehru and Indira visited the Literacy House booth at the *Khadi* (homespun) Fair, pausing there longest and showing careful interest in their prize-winning books for new readers on citizenship and democracy. Nehru told Welthy that his servants read them and so had he.

In those few minutes Welthy gave the Prime Minister a broad picture of Literacy House, and from his daughter, then Minister of Information and Broadcasting, got her agreement to speak to the current group of social education officers in training. Welthy knew that in prison Indira had taught illiterates and hoped to strike a sensitive chord by involving her directly.

March 8, 1956. Welthy was in Assam, studying local history, geography, and Hindu classics, and playing her role along with Clancy Ariel and Siddiqi in training forty social education officers for the government. Indira Gandhi, also in Assam on government business, lingered among the trainees after speaking to them.

March 11, 1956. Revisiting Thoburn Church, Calcutta, where there were too many empty seats, Welthy's thoughts were painful, and reinforced her need to act: "I wonder what we have done, something no doubt, but with what depth that may carry over to the generations I don't know. Thoburn seems a church of tablets."

April 28, 1956. Welthy was in Lucknow selecting temporary houses. Cabling World Literacy for funds to commence building, she asked for forty-five thousand now, and fifty-five thousand in six months.

INDIA LITERACY BOARD

Welthy reported to New York that the India Literacy Board had held its first meeting, Welthy having personally engaged the interest and willingness of each member to serve on the board. She followed up with personal letters to each one, seeking their views and trying to involve that distinguished group of Indians in different aspects of the programme. P. E. Dustoor, Zakir Husain, Hansa Mehta, and G.D. Birla were among the first members. Tom Keehn was on the list originally, but Ensminger advised Welthy to keep the board all-Indian, as that was the only kind his foundation would support. It was acceptable for Welthy to be on the board, however.

Welthy pleaded with New York for a mature American educator to take her place, to work with the Indians for at least two years, and offered to remain as a permanent consultant — a refrain she sang repeatedly. The replies she got from New York all asked for increasingly detailed financial reporting and building plans.

To a seventy-seven year old woman engaged in every phase of creating an institution half way around the world, working against extreme odds of climate and lack of amenities, to be chastised like a child for irregular reporting was unfathomable. Repeatedly she asked if WL would guarantee the total of one hundred thousand for the buildings, with no response. The truth was World Literacy was in deficit, with high-priced staff in New York consuming eighty percent of the dwindling income.

Bill Haggerty, was back in New Paltz, New York, heading the State College, and Iva Gorton Sprague joined the board, giving Welthy hope of action on fund raising. Between Bill, Marge and Iva there was a concerted effort that did produce some money. But nothing equals the conviction and commitment of those working in the field to raise money. So instead of relieving Welthy's burden, World Literacy added to it by prodding her for increasingly detailed information for fund raising purposes.

LAURIE BAKER DESIGNS THE CAMPUS

It was time to translate the dream into buildings. She asked Humayun Kabir for building plans, but what his people sent without seeing the site was a pattern of sharp Western right angles.   It was a psychiatrist at Lucknow's prestigious Nurmanzil Institute who sensed the kind of campus Welthy envisaged and pointed her towards Laurie Baker, an English Quaker architect.

Baker had been an anaesthetist with a Quaker ambulance unit in China during the war and stayed on to work three years with lepers. Stopping in India on return, he met Gandhi and was moved to take a missionary assignment in Uttar Pradesh amongst lepers, but quickly balked at having to submit plans for leper missions to New York officials so they could decide what India needed. Dressing for dinner was still in vogue among his missionary colleagues and Baker soon pulled away from them, adapting himself to Indian conditions and customs.

Travelling by bicycle, he decided to stay on and began designing village schools, libraries and auditoriums, using locally available materials rather than relying on reinforced concrete.   Renowned as India's modern wizard of circles and curves, the human dimension he gave to buildings attracted government interest but was often rejected by vested interests in engineering and architecture. "The length of a wall enclosing a given area is shorter when the shape is circular," he pointed out. "I have found the answer to many planning problems by using the circle and the curve instead of the square and straight lines, and how much more fun the building becomes."

Attracted by the rhythm of his slow, graceful curves, Welthy knew right away that Baker was her man. To Pitoragargh she would go, since he would not come down from the hills where he had built a hospital for his Indian doctor wife. He would accept no payment, so Welthy went armed with drawing supplies and food as alternative payment, setting off with Siddiqi on a journey whose difficult passage became a symbolic challenge to pull her on.

On the third day they braved a hazardous footpassage across a rushing river where the bridge was washed out, the thin planks sagging and bouncing beneath them as they clung to the slippery rope railing. They had to leave the car behind and proceed on foot. Siddiqi was terrified that it would all be too much for her.

When Welthy could walk no farther, Siddiqi dissuaded her from unrolling her bedding on the ground for the night, bargained with a passing peasant, and hefted her atop a small pony, straddling bags of grain. The odd procession made its way through the darkening night to a point where bus and *dandy* took them the last miles. For the next three days Welthy spilled out her ideas to Baker and his pencil moved swiftly, surely across his sketchpad.

Dormitories, library, classrooms, offices, houses, indoor and outdoor auditoriums wrapped themselves invitingly around curves on avenues radiating from a central prayer house in a park-like setting. Simplicity was there in understated beauty. Welthy got what she wanted, and Siddiqi was ecstatic to see the pleasure on her face as they made their way down into the plains, imagining the new campus. (TLC, 262-5)

May 18, 1956. At last, the cable came from New York approving fifty thousand dollars. "I asked for forty-five; they gave me fifty to have some control. They didn't have very much," muttered Welthy. They insisted on the extra five thousand as her salary. Welthy however interpreted this as an attempt to gain leverage over her. Haggerty, who had been ready to give up everything to go and help Welthy, but was restrained by Marge, had insisted on the salary. The other key player in pushing the approval through had been none other than Laubach, who chastised New York for interfering in the contract bidding process, thus causing the loss of many months of work during the rainy season and unnecessarily vexing one who was working her head off to make this a success.

Welthy also contributed to the approval by finally getting so annoyed that she wrote a rare letter of complaint that gave the detail they had been pressing her for. "Be patient with us, Welthy," wrote the President, "and know that we are behind you one hundred percent." Action was needed, not more patience. When she heard the New York office had appointed a building sub-committee to speed things up, she knew the result would be just the opposite. It was.

May 28, 1956. Welthy went to the Planning Commission regarding a proposal for writing workshops, before taking to her sickbed once more. "Doctor — twenty rupees." Tom Keehn wrote again to the Haggertys about his deep concern over Welthy's health, her extreme fatigue, and her inability to bounce back as quickly as before, and urged them to send someone to relieve her of the hated administrative burden.

June, 1956. The move from Allahabad to the temporary buildings in the Krishna Nagar suburb of Lucknow began. The temperature was a hundred and nine degrees Fahrenheit, there was no bathroom in the Krishna Nagar house, and the open drains were a real health hazard.

June 18, 1956. Remembering 1924: "something happened — my life was enlarged . . . the love that began its completion that day is with me still."

July 9, 1956. "In bed — fever — two days."

July 20, 1956. Welthy wrote to New York: "I have been on the point during this last month of sending you my complete resignation, but God won't let me. I've set my hand to the plough and cannot turn back, but I simply cannot understand how you think I can do it all. I have no one with whom I can really consult. This Government will help me if nobody else sees my difficulty. We *must* begin these buildings in September. We have greater difficulty here because all the graduates are unable to adapt themselves to work. There are very few mature educators who believe in social education and who are administrators."

Nehru himself spoke of the split personality afflicting so many Indians, between a narrowness of outlook stemming from caste restrictions, and a broad, tolerant wisdom inherited from their ancestors.[27] That essential conflict in many of the people Welthy worked with daily demanded the utmost in tolerance, a quality Welthy had to nurture regularly.

July 21, 1956. Iva Sprague wrote that they planned to send Gordon Halstead to her for a few months as an answer to her prayer. Welthy cabled back: "Halstead no answer to prayer. Need mature educator and administrator." He was not sent.

UNESCO invited Welthy to a regional conference, as other countries had done, but she could not leave Literacy House when trainees were beginning to come from other countries. The ball she had started rolling was gathering momentum fast.

August 9, 1956. The New York building committee cabled a request for tenders, plans and itemized costs. In an apparent about-face, Laubach questioned whether buildings should have priority, uncertain whether building a campus was a sound plan. He urged other projects be undertaken, and expressed concern over high administrative costs in New York.

LITERACY HOUSE PUBLICATIONS SELLING

The Government of India ordered two thousand Hindi books from Literacy House for Indians in the Fiji Islands, and altogether sales of primers, books and charts reached a hundred thousand for the year. Even under the very unsettled conditions in which they operated, nearly seven hundred people received training from LH in 1956, three quarters of them women, in courses tailor-made for each group. They were District Board teachers, Extension teachers, Health visitors, Home Economic teachers, U.P. Leather Cooperative workers, District Women Welfare organizers, District Cooperative Education officers, and U.P. Community Education officers. Others came from the Tata Institute of Social Sciences, Bombay, and the J.K. Institute of Social Sciences at Lucknow University.

As they experimented with other teaching methods and primers, it was obvious that training was needed at different levels for those who would be planning and administering for the actual village teacher, and that improving and expanding the teaching materials was a continuous process requiring special training, including development and use of audio-visual materials to motivate and reinforce literacy. The initiative to conceive, plan, organize and conduct each aspect of training came from Welthy, drawing on all those wide contacts she had been cultivating with such political skill, that talent she would not turn to politics itself.

August 11, 1956. "Exciting day—all seventeen tenders delivered by a parade of contractors paying three hundred and fifty rupees to bid. At 4:00 p.m. they all crowded into my house for the opening of the bids. There was everything but a camel outside in my yard. There were pedal rickshaws gaily decorated with tin and coloured glass. There were noisy motorcycles. There were one or two sporty American cars. There was a horse tonga. There were many Austins and Hillmans and there was also the humble bicycle. The Town Planner said he had never known so many tenders for one job."

August 15, 1956. Independence Day in India. Welthy began her early morning hour of Hindi study, then welcomed a new batch of trainees and the rain, copying Nehru in her speech: *Aj, Gandhike Din Hai.* (Today is Gandhi's day.) In the evening she invited all the village workers for dinner and entertainment.

August 19, 1956. "Going to Delhi for (1) a puppeteer, (2) answer from the Ministry, (3) a secretary, (4) cement and steel." She also did a quick study in the art of proposal preparation with friends at the American Embassy.

August 30, 1956. "The heat roars on. I think often I can't endure it. I shall not stir out of this country until the buildings are finished. Would like to get a place in Maine and will have five thousand dollars to put down on it by spring when bonds are due." That was another *Shangrila* that Welthy dreamed of sharing with the Haggertys, a dream never to be pursued.

September 11, 1956. "Ground breaking ceremony. Hindus always begin on Tuesday." Welthy dug the first clod of soil for the administration building in the rain, in India the sign of God's blessing.

October 10, 1956. Welthy asked the trainees finishing a course what they learned. "The real education I got here was the education of my heart. Ideas lying dead with me came to life."

October 18, 1956. Welthy, Ariel and Siddiqi were in Bombay giving a course. Welthy spoke at the Tata Institute and made several high-level contacts seeking Indian support.

October 25, 1956. "Exhausted, stomach pains, doctor. How uneventful days in bed can be, the doctor says one month." She stayed two days.

November 7, 1956. "I have no 'go ahead' on any director or any help. I am at the end of my strength but the men in New York do not seem to realize it. I know I have their sympathy, but that doesn't give me consultation and help."

TOM KEEHN APPEALS TO WORLD LITERACY

World Literacy was close to insolvency, with no money to continue the buildings, and no money for salaries. One trustee, William A. Meteer, expressed concern that contributions were not reaching Welthy in India, where she used one thousand dollars of her own to pay a contractor. Tom Keehn wrote three times to Haggerty, who had saved the organization from going under by agreeing to be President. He urged Welthy be guaranteed a three-year operating budget, that the balance of building funds be promised, and that Welthy be given authorization to seek other support in India and employ an Indian Director. Literacy House is Indian, he told Haggerty, and cannot be run from New York.

Keehn's appeal worked, and Haggerty closed the Madison Avenue office and fired the staff, while he and Marge undertook a holding operation with one person in more modest quarters. Still, while it was evident that no one but Welthy could or would be able to raise the money needed, the Keehns clearly thought Welthy was not up to the physical effort, and urged that she be used only for long-range planning and the top level contacts she was so good at. From the long strain Welthy had become impatient, irritable and domineering.

WASHINGTON SCRUTINIZES WELTHY

Welthy had not realized that part of her budget was to come from the United States' AID coffer until she was later summoned to Washington to face hostile interrogation by two members of Senator Joseph

McCarthy's committee, the committee whose purpose was to hunt down suspected Communists. They demanded to know why she was so interested in India, what she had been doing in China with INDUSCO, and what was her connection with Mme. Sun Yat-sen. Welthy was astonished to hear from her own government that she was a suspected Communist.

When cornered or confronted so aggressively, Welthy neither turned the other cheek nor answered in kind, but transcended the issue by explaining it in simple human terms no one could fail to understand. If their children were ill, she asked her inquisitors, wouldn't they want them to have modern medical help? INDUSCO had provided much needed medical books and supplies with money she had raised, and their cooperatives had saved China from the Japanese invaders. Were they not eager to have their children learn as much about the world as possible? India's children were prevented from doing that without the skill of literacy. By the time Welthy left, the two were convinced of her commitment to helping human beings, not political ideology, and her name was crossed off the incriminating list.

LITERACY HOUSE UNDER FIRE

Literacy House had endured the anti-Communist fire, only to suffer repeated attacks from the other extreme of the political spectrum for being a suspected CIA enterprise in a nation understandably wary of the foreigners who kept visiting Literacy House. The CIA, worried about Nehru's socialism, gave top priority to India, helping his right wing opponents and cultivating the bureaucracy through widely scattered operatives. In response, the Indian Central Bureau of Investigation (CBI) looked skeptically at foreigners' activities, making Welthy the subject of a surreptitious search. "I asked them point blank if they weren't CBI," she said, "not as bluntly as that. I softened it with a soft voice and smiles and appreciation . . . you know how it can be done . . . just the way you treat a policeman at home when you're caught speeding." They left her alone after that.

When Beatrice Pitney Lamb came to see Literacy House gathering information to revise her textbook on India, Welthy played her public relations role to the hilt to the skeptical Mrs. Lamb, a shrewd observer who wanted hard information. She had been asked by the League of Women Voters to seek precise answers to several questions relating to Welthy's request for further publications support. Welthy was full of enthusiasm and the importance of what she was doing, but Mrs. Lamb instinctively barricaded herself against what she considered to be immodest exaggeration. In fact, Welthy seemed to her to be downright evasive when cornered about specifics, insisting on putting a human face on the enterprise when hard facts were wanted.[28]

In spite of that, Mrs. Lamb was drawn by the special quality that made Welthy look twenty years younger. When Welthy asked her to serve on the New York Board she agreed, still prodding Welthy unmercifully for detail, and amazed that Welthy could forgive her highly critical appraisal. As Siddiqi put it: "Her faith in the Lord, the programme and herself . . . that got her going and got us going. It is that faith in other people which has won affection, cooperation, achievement for her. Had it not been for that, her misbehaviour, misconduct would have bothered." Because she forgave first, Welthy was easy to forgive.

1957

February 14, 1957. Haggerty cabled that he was now President of World Literacy, a fine Valentine's day present for Welthy, for Bill was an educator who understood her thinking. His first priority after the reorganization that eliminated Laubach completely was to change the organization's name to World Education, Incorporated (WE), and state its purpose in broader educational terms that included literacy. The organization was going through a traumatic transition bridged by Harold Miner's leadership and Iva Sprague's loyalty to Welthy. From relying heavily on government funds, they were now challenged to raise money independently.

Haggerty had heavy responsibilities of his own and took this on reluctantly, but he and Marge wanted to continue their support, for they had encouraged Welthy in her daring effort from the beginning, and knew she was tired, frustrated and discouraged, yet would not give up. "Her quiet prayers in the morning, the first thing . . . made her way of life and purpose possible," said Marge. "I felt she was secure inwardly and would not crumble. By the time we got her letters she would have found a new resource or another avenue and was already pursuing a solution of one kind or another."[29]

"I think I can scarcely bear the joy of it," Welthy wrote back, " to know that I may write you all that comes up, and that you will understand. Do you remember that when the bell-ringer at Philadelphia was told to ring the bell for liberty, that war was over and the Colonies had won, he started to ring it and fell over dead — he died of joy. I do not intend to die, but my heart is lighter than it has been for some time. I have known that something was radically wrong and asked Dick to tell me the truth . . . that I could take the truth rather than live from hand to mouth this way. It seemed so squeamish and inconsequential to have Burnet count our cement bags here and to pay that big salary to him there."

DURGABAI DESHMUKH

April 13, 1957. "Today I had the opportunity I've been wanting to get for four years. I spoke to Durgabai's entire Central Social Welfare Board, and also to the directors for each state. I made them all become illiterates in Hindi while Siddiqi gave them a demonstration. I know enough psychology to make it all short and sweet. Lady Rama Rao, Indira Gandhi, and all the elite were there and it was a great opportunity."

May, 1957. Welthy moved to the new campus, staying alone in the administration building except for the night watchman in that hottest month. Giving a headstart to the plans, she was the resident contractor, her attention on concrete and wires, windows and pipes, roofs and tiling, as she spent endless hours bent over blueprints measuring and translating quarter inches into feet. Climate and cash were the limiting agents as ventilation, septic tanks and a well were planned.

Shaw had advised against a residential campus as being too like a mission compound, but that did not deter her. He did succeed in convincing Baker not to use thatched roofs on the houses. Welthy's dream of building a fountainhead community from which education could flow was taking shape before her eyes. She wanted to support and strengthen the lives of staff members, so that families could see their fathers taking responsibility for a larger community, and the community in turn reinforcing the family. Her own awareness that everyone's effort was needed to make the community run gave workers a sense of their importance, and none needed to feel useless or alienated.

Welthy never reported how she broke her wrist, but it probably happened when she was poking around the site. It was a nuisance similar to the nosebleeds she suffered, to be expected occasionally and endured for a moment.

AMERICA, JUNE 1957

June 30, 1957. "The money lenders and letter writers of India have made a powerful enemy," said the *New York Times*. "She is here to gather more ammunition against them . . . who have preyed on the illiterates for centuries." Harold Miner was still questioning the wisdom and morality of raising money in New York where fund-raising costs were so high. He wondered if they should advise Welthy to seek some or all of her support elsewhere so she could get on with the job, believing she had the stamina and enthusiasm to do it, but instead WE named her their Representative in India.

She was somewhat more than that, leading off an American fund-raising tour with ten thousand dollars of her own money. On an overnight stop in her New York apartment she noted the "wonderful satisfaction in being able to walk into your own home and get your own breakfast, having only run around the corner for a few supplies."

WORLD LITERACY OF CANADA

In Canada she spoke at a 'Camps Farthest Out' meeting, where Laubach had already interested people in the work of Literacy House, and a supporting organization, World Literacy of Canada (WLC) was forming, led by Hadley Perrin and J.H. Corrigan. Welthy's tall, commanding presence in their midst, softened by her easy intimacy, drew in a growing circle of friendly supporters who carefully developed an organization to respond to needs they were learning about. Hadley Perrin's subsequent visit to India determined that LH was not taking a political stance and resulted in regular support of specific projects for over a decade. Ethel Dean and Ethel Eede were the mainstays of the organization in its early years and kept the connection with Welthy open and warm.

EUROPE, FALL 1957

Travelling alone, Welthy stopped in London, Paris, Vienna and Rome for a fast-paced round of opera and meetings on education. "There is a temptation to go out in the avenues of the rich city—rich in foods, rich in music, opera, theatre, but alone it's not fun. So I walked to the Rivoli and past the old Hotel de Cambon and looked in. The air is mild." In Vienna, "the traffic moves so fast that it is a matter of the quick or the dead . . . so I move fast."

At UNESCO in Paris she discovered they knew far more about Literacy House than the New York trustees did. In Rome, addressing an international conference on illiteracy, Welthy said she did not believe literacy could be achieved by campaigns. The need was for basic education on a permanent basis, a simply stated idea later translated into a theory adopted by UNESCO. Travelling by ship through the Suez, she read Edith Hamilton's "The Greek Way", summarizing: "Egypt thinks of death, she says, and builds tombs. The Greeks think of Life and build Theatres. It's fun."

SCHOOL OF WRITING PROPOSAL ACCEPTED FOR LITERACY HOUSE

Lucknow, Christmas Dinner, 1957. Welthy was back in the house she had built on the new campus with her own money, surrounded by the entire staff and their families, thirty-four in all. She was "Mother Fisher" or *Mataji* to them, and knew each child by name. She had spent the day studying writing, her mind very much on plans she and Dr. Radhakamal Mukherjee, a prolific author and Vice-Chancellor of Lucknow University, had made for the proposed School of Writing.

After the Government of India had turned down that proposal, Welthy had approached the Ford Foundation. "We have to live on faith and hope and keep on working, never stopping and never giving up hope and never changing our beliefs if we know a thing is right. This conviction that we needed a permanent school of writing was deep." And she had made a personal commitment to provide accessible reading matter to women who needed it most.

On that day her faith was rewarded when a special letter arrived from Ensminger with a check for sixty-nine thousand dollars and approval to proceed with the School of Writing—an exalted moment for the extended family of Literacy House gathered around Welthy's table in the dry bleakness of an Indian winter.

1958

Literacy House needed a director urgently to deal with the many matters resulting from a growing campus and expanding programme. The demand for detailed reporting from New York and now Toronto were beyond what Welthy and Shaw could manage. Everyone was alarmed when Welthy began having profuse nosebleeds, especially with the added drama she brought to everything. They insisted she take to her bed and sent for the only western-trained doctor in Lucknow, a Swiss psychiatrist, who thought it was a blood pressure problem. No one was more alarmed than Welthy to find a psychiatrist at her bedside, and she leapt to her feet again. But the problem persisted and she was persuaded to seek help in Delhi.

S.C. Dutta made a gallant effort to help out during Welthy's absences. Even when she lay in Holy Family Hospital early in 1958, Welthy was constantly dispatching letters and messages here and there, searching for the right director and various specialists for Literacy House.

Of the half dozen Indians Welthy had interviewed, her first choice as director remained Dr. Koshy. After a stint in Delhi as Adviser on Social Education, Koshy was back at AAI as Vice-Principal and Head of Extension when Welthy pressed him to join her. Financial security and a job for his professional wife, Sucy, were important concerns, so Welthy promised to help Sucy find a suitable position and sent off more letters on that front. With the Ford grant in hand she could guarantee Koshy's salary for the three years of its duration, and personally guaranteed two more years, offering him a five-year contract.

March 28, Holy Family Hospital, New Delhi. "This now-over-a-month-in-bed-business has greatly cramped my style. I weigh a hundred and thirty eight (down twenty pounds). The doctor will take me to a radiologist and X-ray my innards. Ridiculous, isn't it? Tom is golden."

The Keehns had taken Welthy under their wing. They moved a precious air-conditioner from their own bedroom to the one Welthy used when in residence with them, and made a noble effort to help Welthy manage things from her hospital bed. Tom sent someone from his organization to help prepare a fund-raising brochure on Literacy House and advise Welthy on many administrative matters. WE was pushing for an Indian Director of Literacy House, which Welthy also wanted, but she felt it would take the combined efforts of an experienced American educator along with an Indian to bridge the two years needed to develop the campus and find Indian sources of support.

Confined in bed with no visitors allowed (although the Keehns were often there), the diagnosis was: high blood pressure, fluid on the lungs, inflamed gallbladder and swollen liver. The doctor's orders were to rest, rest, rest, and plan to go home. Welthy got up and went to see a doctor at the American Embassy clinic who told her to return to the hospital immediately, which she did, for the moment. She took her castor oil and salt-free diet, noting: "I will have to take digitalis the rest of my life." But the little white pills were forgotten as soon as she felt better, and she left the hospital paying only half her bill; the Sisters were so moved by her mission they insisted on paying the other half. Welthy was well on the road to recovery with that endorsement.

Back in Lucknow she made friends with a lively white-haired woman at a fruit market on Hazratganj, a prominent doctor who had tended the freedom fighters and was fearless enough to take on Welthy as a patient. Her diagnosis of the bleeding made more sense—a small spot on the septum from the dry air, not at all serious—and her cure for any ailment Welthy had thereafter was a 'good old chat' sitting on the edge of her bed, their hilarious laughter sealing a delicious conspiracy that confounded the experts.[30] Dr. Sarah Itty's unique skill and Ted Koshy's acceptance of the directorship were all the medicine Welthy needed.

She had survived repeated assaults on body, mind and spirit, with no sign of giving up. She had overcome not only her own exhaustion but that of her band of workers and board members, whose spirits needed continual refreshment for each new advance in the assault on illiteracy that she was consolidating. The campus was half built—dormitories for seventy, fourteen small staff residences, cafeteria, school of writing accommodating twenty-four, pumphouse and tubewell, tank and sewage, electricity, administration building and open air theatre. Every detail had been carried out under her watchful eye, every inch of ground trod over and over again by the lady with the crooked cane. Colourful murals of teachers and students on the curved entrance wall invited passersby to come in through the wide gateway where the campus was visible, its park-like gardens, shade trees and stretches of inviting green grass a striking scene in that dry land. The flag of India dominated the circular entrance drive where everyone gathered spontaneously each morning to greet one another and catch the first warm rays of the sun in winter months, and again in the late afternoon as they dispersed from work. There was a rhythm and richness to those early years as the developing campus environment worked its magic.

The programme was taking shape, meeting an obvious need within India and beyond. FAO had sent thirty people from throughout Asia, escorted by an Indian Government official, to see their work in action, and support from Canada gave added security. Best of all, her missing cat had returned. The Shaws had a yard full of hens, the Ariels had three white geese "with more humour than most people I know." Though Welthy had no cook and was eating on the run, having turned over her own house to the Shaws, she could take a deep breath of satisfaction. But she knew how much remained to be done. Early in 1958 she took steps to marshall the New York Board, addressing an open letter to all trustees about future plans of that organization, questioning, as their representative,tivetive its fundamental objectives and relation to other groups.

If her frustration from dealing with boards had been high, it was only the tip of the iceberg, for she was entering a new phase of management drama where her own administrative anarchy would create innumerable problems for herself and everyone around her. As before, few on the WE board could see beyond the administrative need to confine and control, to impose order, when a certain planned disorder was necessary. The India Literacy Board had already been undermined by World Education's insistence on budgetary control, effectively emasculating them by withholding financial and administrative reponsibility. The ILB was left to deal with programme development and lesser administrative matters. Despite Welthy's earnest intent to create an Indian institution owned, managed and directed by Indians, WE insisted that LH was "their project". Until that critical issue was resolved Welthy knew the problems would only increase.

In 1958, at seventy-nine, Welthy was trying to hold together three organizations — Literacy House, the ILB, and WE — functioning at all levels vertically and horizontally. Her unconventional theory of management, if she had one, was to lead with one's personality, pulling from out front and pushing from behind, which she did with extraordinary executive skill. Seeing the best in people and accepting them as they were, Welthy did not practise rational personnel procedure in choosing her co-workers. In fishing for their potential best she was trying to communicate the essence of teaching, a concept that was often lost on the administrative mind.

Uncomplicated, honest, Welthy said: "Of course you want to be at the head of whatever you're doing, it's more fun." An impossible woman, so impossible in fact that when Bea Lamb once considered writing a biography of Welthy she quickly abandoned the idea, pronouncing Welthy 'unbiographable,' her innate sense of freedom making it impossible to pin her down. Welthy simply did not feel the need to explain herself, which made it extremely difficult for board members, whether in New York or in India, to get the detailed information they sought. They were miles behind Welthy in experience and understanding and kept insisting on pulling her back to a level where they felt comfortable. Yet the whole held together by some miracle of wit and will that was Welthy's genius.

BACK TO FUND RAISING

Welthy felt she had earned a measure of trust, and that board members should concentrate on raising money. With notable exceptions such as Iva Sprague, few did. So it was Welthy who combed the United States and Canada year after year with the highly effective personal style she had discovered so long ago. A quick study, she had extraordinary physical stamina as she made her broad sweeps of the service clubs, churches, sororities. With an ever increasing, carefully cultivated network of personal friends and power-brokers she broke down a narrow-minded distaste for things Indian.

While New York office costs were sharply cut, the trustees confined themselves to advising on fund-raising approaches, every one of which involved Welthy doing the actual work. For it was Welthy who was committed to the point of credibility, Welthy who sought no administrative definition or reimbursement for her role, Welthy who worked night and day, relentlessly. If she sounds too much, she was.

Many left the board in frustration over their inability to control her; but some grasped her goal and remained staunchly loyal. To a few she was a prima donna, to others a tower of strength, an inspiration, and most importantly an achiever. Welthy did not arouse luke-warm feelings; it was was either hot or cold. Even Arthur Schwartz, who loved her dearly, found her difficult to work with, but said it was impossible to argue with the fact of Literacy House.

Oddly, it was Bill Haggerty, so attuned to Welthy's purpose, who pressed for stronger control from New York, despite gentle urging from Tom Keehn to give Welthy the benefit of the doubt, when he insisted that any funds Welthy received in India from Laubach supporters be returned to New York. Only through World Education were funds to go to India. To Welthy who needed money to pay the bills, it sounded like the outmoded refrain that only through Christianity could one reach heaven!

She wrote to Miriam Evans to say how odd it was that although the Christian colleges in India had only a third or less of their students Christians, money kept flowing to them from America, yet her work was cut off just because it was not controlled by Christians. When her frustration level became too high, she simply shifted gear, turning her mind to the broader perspective of the programme and the individual human beings involved.

There were those who dealt in hard, concrete facts measurable on a short yardstick who thought Welthy often overstated her case. A questioner prodded her gently one day:

"Aren't you sometimes rather dramatic in your presentations?"

She looked up with amazement and shot back:

"Why else was I born?"

HOUSE OF PRAYER FOR ALL PEOPLE

For all her critics, the greatest strength came from Laurie Baker, who spent two months on the campus overseeing the growth of the curved structures he had shaped to her idea. He and Welthy played like gypsy children, tossing meals together in whatever building they camped in as construction proceeded, their light-hearted banter reflecting their pleasure in the simplicity and beauty appearing before their eyes as the House of Prayer for All People emerged at the centre of the campus. The "little rascal" understood her purpose with absolute clarity, and translated it into sun-dried brick and glass.

Set in a circular park, approachable by gentle paths leading up to doors on the north, south, east and west of the small chapel, its large windows inviting the campus beyond, and the finger of its thatched roof pointing to the Godhead, the House of Prayer spoke simply of the larger Christ Gandhi had understood so well. Inside, the only symbol was a small jet of water symbolizing eternal life welling up from its heart, and falling into a simple concrete pool of the living water that nourishes all in a hungry land. In translating Fred Fisher's words into that simple hut radiating outwards to undergird all the work, Welthy made them her own:

> *No religion has all the truths . . . No nation has all the patriots. . . No race has all the virtues. And none can do without the other. If there is any truth anywhere it is the*

*fact of the unity of the human race and the interdependence
of mankind.*

Spiritual imperialism was as unacceptable as economic and political dominance. Freedom from spiritual immaturity was essential for modern workers to accept that different people require different methods to deepen their consciousness, that none are inferior or superior. In nurturing her own natural tolerance, Welthy had drawn heavily from Buddha's teaching of compassionate oneness with all life.

India was hungry in many ways in those early years of independence, not the least of them spiritual after centuries of increasingly alienating divisions and sub-divisions of caste. During the Muslim and British regimes, no higher authority of religion or state could overcome the ever-narrowing social customs. Now with unity at the political level and a Constitution aimed at equality and liberty, there was a legislative possibility of freedom for all. But laws alone would not make people love one another, Welthy knew. Spirits so long repressed would have to be reached with the message of a new day. The truth embedded deep in each heart, as in the closed bud of a lotus, could not be contained in any single expression of two thousand years ago, or by what was understood by any one of the ancient prophets or *rishis*. The seeking of truth is a living, moving process available to all.

And so the House of Prayer was lovingly surrounded by a small moat of water, filled with lotus, the national flower of India, symbol of regeneration and creative energy. In China too the lotus was a symbol, rising spotless and pure from muddy waters. In such a shrine a day of dedicated work could begin, the circle symbolizing inclusiveness to each one present.

EASTER 1958

The central significance of the prayer house was proclaimed by Dr. S. Radhakrishnan, eminent philosopher, Vice-President and later President of India, whom Welthy had invited to inaugurate it on Easter Day:

> *Here in this House, cooperation is a matter of principle. Men
> and women, abhorrent of bigotry and committed to serve
> the new world, will meet together. The quest for a univer-
> sal faith will retain a continuing solicitude for its diverse
> manifestations. But we shall recognize that at the root of
> all faiths is God who is neither Hindu or Moslem, neither
> Christian or Jewish. Faith feels the light of day even when
> the dawn is dark. In all humility I dedicate this House of
> Prayer for All Peoples to the worship of the one God that He*

*may free our spirits, enlarge our vision and increase our
capacity for love.*

Dr. Radhakrishnan had written eloquently on the need to clear away
the dead wood of ancient faith, acknowledging that "growth is slow
when roots are diseased. But those who light a little candle in the darkness will help to make the whole sky aflame."[31] Welthy had understood
his meaning, as she had understood Christ and Gandhi, and she had
acted to light that little candle. As if in further description of Welthy, Radhakrishnan had earlier written that "family and country, nation and the
world cannot satisfy the soul . . . the last part of life's road has to be
walked in single file".[32]

It was that aspect of her journey that Welthy's Indian board recognized
and respected, and her American board did not. Nor was her House of
Prayer acceptable to most Methodist missionaries and other Christians
in India, who now considered her unorthodox because she would not
proclaim an exclusive Christian path to God. It is said that to shed light
one must endure burning, and as some Christian trainees boycotted the
simple morning prayers, Welthy underwent her share of pain from their
rejection.

To Indians who felt the creative flame of greatness languishing after
Gandhi's death, Welthy's offering was a welcome warm glow in their
midst, and it went a long way to overcoming any distrust still in the air
that Literacy House was a missionary institution with a particular cause
to promote. That Shaw, Koshy and Ariel all happened to be Christians
had aroused some skepticism, but in that expanding staff seated on the
layered floor around the water fountain each morning were Hindus and
Muslims in larger numbers meditating and chanting the prayers of their
faiths.

That Easter Day was the turning point, when everything LH had to offer
was made splendidly visible to everyone who came to the grand opening of the full campus. The Governor inspected the dormitories and staff
homes, puppets played their role as arresting communicators, an impressive array of publications for new literates was displayed, including a new
weekly magazine of light reading. With tea and sweets for all, it was a
new kind of garden party, and for Welthy, it was all the theatre she ever
wanted.

* * *

"Industrialization means you must have workers who are intelligent
cooperators with management," said Welthy, whose grasp of the practical was as incisive as her spiritual awareness. That perception was translated into night schools for young adults in cities as well as villages, and

the important visitors she invited became significant allies in the work. Zakir Husain had visited, given a nod of approval to puppetry for education because of its wide acceptance among the people, and agreed to join the ILB. Violet Alva, distinguished member of the upper house of India's Parliament wrote after her visit: "Your Literacy House was an eye-opener to many of us." Welthy's technique with visitors of all kinds was to have them talk to whatever group of trainees or villagers could be mustered, the immediacy of involvement forging a human link that diluted academic objectivity.

John Spencer from England and Louise Leonard Wright from the United States were both intrigued by the fact that there was no light in the villages; Literacy House teachers had to take their own light with them, externally and internally. They arrived by half-ton truck with Coleman lanterns, primers, slates, chalk, blackboard, and charts, all in kits provided by CARE at twenty-five dollars each. And libraries were moving out to villages in tin trunks of fifty books on the back of bicycles, or going to weekly village bazaars by truck.

Puppet plays were being written in the School of Writing teaching facts about hygiene, agriculture, rodents, home-making, reducing dowries, and life insurance. A cast of miniature characters moved out to villages by night, drawing every inhabitant round the mobile puppet stage. A jolly, jumbo puppet, the announcer, popped out from a special curtain within a curtain to warm up the audience with the quicksilver improvisation at which Indians excel. Nobody loved those elemental village nightscenes better than Welthy, as the old and new worlds met. The tin-trunk libraries of Welthy's early imagination had grown into a network of library services, from mobile libraries in small vans at market stalls to the *kitabwala* plying his bicycle to remote villages. Comfort Shaw had trained Harkesh Singh to manage the libraries while he worked on extending the concept into a network serving all of U.P., in what was the first organized effort in India to provide rural library services.[33]

On the campus, the pace quickened. Dr. Koshy had won government support for a building to conduct the Panchayati Raj Training Programme, a comprehensive plan for elected village leaders from all parts of the state. He had taken charge well, and Sucy was a valuable presence in the increasing public relations work necessary to make the endeavour known and understood.

The IAEA held its Ninth National Seminar there, with prominent officials gathered. Welthy made sure no one got away without exposure to the full range of Literacy House activities. Sudhakanta Roychoudhury came from *Santiniketan* to see the work and reported to his Vice-Chancellor on the amiable behaviour of Welthy's workers, their remarkable progress in bringing Muslim women out from their homes to learn, and in overcoming the traditional contempt for women teachers.

MUSHTAQ AHMED AND P.N. SHIVPURI JOIN STAFF

Zakir Husain had sent Mushtaq Ahmed from his institute to meet Welthy, with the result that Ahmed declined a lucrative UNESCO offer and agreed to head the School of Writing. Dr. Radhakamal Mukherjee sent another young man, P.N. Shivpuri, the social education adviser to Nepal, who was also willing to join the training department at the low salary of two hundred rupees a month. Soon after, Nepal sent a group for teacher training. And so the basic building blocks of Literacy House were put in place.

TRAINING FOR TIBETAN REFUGEES

Rinchen Dolma Taring, the former Princess Mary of Tibet, whom Welthy had entertained in Calcutta in the twenties (TLC, 187), was again in her home. The first Tibetan girl to be educated in English, married to a prince of Sikkim, Mrs. Taring had been asked by the Dalai Lama to organize a school at Mussoorie for the Tibetan refugees fleeing to India. Along with four other Tibetans she had come to Literacy House for training and to compile a textbook.[34]

While Koshy worked out the details for the Tibetans' training, Welthy secured financing through the Junior Chambers of Commerce in the United States and Canada that bridged the initial administrative hiatus. She found an artist to illustrate the Tibetan primer and pulled all the other bits together to get the actual teaching underway when it was urgently needed. Meanwhile CARE, the Lowell Thomas Committee and India's Central Relief Committee sorted out various tasks for their eventual responsibility for the Tibetan training. The New York office predictably quibbled about Welthy's direct dealings with the Junior Chambers.

Informal education required informal methods and Welthy was prepared to risk minor administrative wrath for the sake of action. And she was there in Mussoorie for the opening of the school, presenting a white silk prayer scarf to the Dalai Lama, and chatting in Chinese with his mother. "After two nights on the train to Mussoorie, I felt I have given something more to the Tibetans than I had planned," she chided herself. As S.N. Misra, the accountant at Literacy House put it, she couldn't say no, and was blessed with the willing cooperation of Ted Koshy, whose wife, however, frequently wished to see more of the man who worked such long hours with Welthy.

THE FEMININE QUALITY

Welthy's theme in many speeches was women and their unrecognized power. She knew herself to be strong. She personally knew many of India's powerfully capable women in high office who had played pivotal roles in the freedom movement because of Gandhi's strategic recognition of their strength, and she understood the meaning of *ahimsa* — the infinite love in the sacrifice and suffering of women that personified non-violence. "When you educate a woman you educate the whole family and the next generation," Welthy told the assemblage under the colourful *shamiana* on Founder's Day. "It's going to take religious motivation that reaches over empathetically into the minds and hearts of the villagers," she said, echoing Gandhi.

In her notes she kept Tagore's thoughts in the foreground, of the unknown peacemakers armed only with love and understanding. "He knew as few have known that peace will stem from freedom and justice; freedom of woman, justice to the races of man." She wrote of the unconscious liaison between generations, the dynamic centre women occupied. Women's education, concentrating on quality of manner and attitude, and springing from respect for different personalities within the family, was a necessary step in enhancing the prospect of peace in the world:

> *The feminine quality of putting ourself, our group, our racial unit, our nation in the background in the interest of others in a spirit of humility and cooperation was inherent in all the great souls — Buddha, Jesus, Gandhi. Peace is not an entity. It is a by-product of cooperation, whether in the family, in the community, in the nation or in the world of nations. Cooperation in the family requires the feminine quality to be dominant. Peace in the world of nations requires the dominance of this same feminine quality.*

A decade before modern feminist analysis began to emerge, Welthy, essentially alone, found the perspective she needed to motivate the work after ten years' struggle in the villages, where darkness was easily overwhelming. One of her many unpublished, untitled, unpolished poems, written on July 9, 1964, ground its way into her identity:

> *We are the women of the world*
> *Our voices still are muted.*
> *Age after age*
> *we were the submerged world.*
> *We too, went through the earthquake, wind and fire,*
> *with voices hushed in awe.*

Times there were in ages past
They bound our feet to keep us
in their grip.
In other years, even till to-day
with draperies black, and faces covered,
We walk in fear, and see our works of art
through tiny squares of net before our eyes.
We were unlettered.
Unlettered still we walk.

We bore the race
And gave our offspring all we had
Of life and spirit.
Their fathers often left for wars or study
So we, too, reared the race
with our scant understanding
of God, His sun, His moon and stars.
We were afraid.
God's minions spoke to us
In thunder, quake and lightning.

And now the world is new,
or so they say.
But yet we mothers of the race
Still walk with superstitious fears
because we know no better.
We are unlettered.

We are unlettered.
We are the women of the world.

PRESIDENT OF WORLD EDUCATION

In New York, the clarity and consensus Welthy had sought produced unexpected results in a period of continued wrangling among the board. Iva Sprague feared that Haggerty sought a global programme, with Literacy House funded within India and Welthy being called home to advise from New York, her age on the agenda for the first time. Iva summoned other trustees to Welthy's defence. "Welthy was just in the midst of her great ideas," said Mrs Sprague, "and there was no way she should have retired then." Welthy knew it was too soon to push Literacy House out of the nest, that there was much more that needed to be done to consolidate the programme and secure its financial future. She had no intention of walking away from it yet. As a result of the conflict, Haggerty dropped out, leaving WE in better financial shape than he found it.

Because the board had come to realize Literacy House was her project, not theirs, that she was the only one they believed could carry the ball and not let it drop, Welthy was elected President of World Education. She certainly did not need or want another hat, but she accepted the added responsibility as the only way to see her mission through to completion. "She is due tremendous credit for what she had accomplished," the board acknowledged, "and she is determined to see it through." Welthy was the spearhead, without question, and they finally recognized that she was beyond organization. Without her leadership WE would have dried up. "Welthy was sometimes impatient," Harold Miner said, "but it's a good thing she was a visionary or it would never have got anywhere."[35]

Miner also dropped out to assume larger responsibility at CARE, believing World Education was secure in Welthy's hands with Dick McFadyen, Iva Sprague and Arthur Schwartz giving firm support. He was right, and Welthy drew several women to the board, such as Bea Lamb and Louise Leonard Wright, who had first-hand knowledge of Literacy House from visits to India. Laubach's staunch devotee, Mrs. Esther Kramer, also rejoined the reconstituted Board.

To personally guarantee the salary of a new executive director of WE, Welthy sold more of her stocks, a sacrifice that was not rewarded when the young man found the incoming cash from Welthy's fund raising too tempting. Arthur Schwartz had to deal with the situation and fire the fellow. Thereafter, for a long time, the WE office was held together by one woman, Doris Ward, who made a valiant effort to help Welthy carry out her fund-raising responsibilities and keep the board informed. And though the added burden was heavy, Welthy had full freedom to move at her own pace. "As I pay my own travel, I can leave on short notice."

Speaking at the convocation of Syracuse University Journalism School, Welthy turned her new title to fund-raising advantage, as one press report quoted her: "Being elected President was just a way of telling me, 'Welthy, come home and raise the money you need for your work.' She's out for two hundred fifty thousand dollars."

1959

For a short period Welthy had an engaging assistant and fund raiser in Leela Singh, and got to her appointments on the right day at the right time. Leela was twenty, well educated in a privileged atmosphere in Tanganyika and Kashmir, and held as much attraction for Welthy as the eighty year old woman did for the young beauty. "Her enthusiasm, her zest for life was so genuine and contagious, she fascinated, that is mainly why I joined her," said Leela. Though they worked hard, they had fun together shopping on Fifth Avenue, for Leela's fashion flair was equal to Welthy's. "She often had the whole department at Peck & Peck waltzing around her and usually left with some donations," recalled Leela. "She never missed an opportunity," to the point that Leela was frequently embarrassed by Welthy's flagrant begging for Literacy House.[36]

Leela would often walk into Welthy's bedroom in the New York apartment to find her doubled up with laughter at a pop show on television, saying she must see what the new generation was up to.   But she was less accepting of Welthy's thrifty insistence on bus travel in mid-winter, and of her refusal to take a taxi even though Leela was barefoot in open sandals. After a deadly silent return to the apartment Welthy would busily make hot cocoa to warm Leela, hoping to have taught a lesson to her extravagant young friend.   But Leela was young and lovely and in demand, squired by such men as the editor of *Fortune* and Gandhi's grandson, when she could get away from Welthy.   There was so much to be responsible for, as when Welthy was hospitalized for one of the major ailments she refused to acknowledge and was injected with a diagnostic dye in her veins for suspected kidney disease. A violent allergic reaction to the dye prompted doctors to notify next of kin as Welthy swelled grotesquely to twice her size. Within a few days, she walked out of the hospital with contributions to her work from several staff members, the irrepressible urge still operative.

Leela was too good to last. She left to pursue her own career and family, aware that she had had two of the richest years of her life with Welthy. Remaining in close touch, she and her young family were usually there to greet and help Welthy with whatever she needed during her brief stops in Hong Kong.

THE PRESS KEEPS AN EYE ON WELTHY

Welthy on the run was sharpening her message to raise enough money for the next development in India. Her speeches received press attention everywhere: "She is proof of her own statement—'we are the toughest women in the world'—'this is not a changing world—it has changed.' 'America is my country; the world is my home; humanity is my family.' 'The world is too dangerous for anything but truth and too small for anything but brotherhood.'"[37]

Constantly being asked by Americans when Nehru was going to come off the non-alignment fence, Welthy told them he had never been on the fence. "He's a complete democrat—he's for India. Give Nehru sympathy and cooperation, and don't always ask if he votes with us in the UN. Trust him a little. Let him run his own country."

Life magazine did a brief piece on Welthy in her eightieth year. And Eleanor Roosevelt supported her fund-raising efforts in her "My Day" column.[38]

"When she talks," said the *Tucson Citizen*, "one feels the thrill, the strength, the magnetism of a great spirit who has in turn been touched by other great spirits."

There was a surprise eightieth birthday party for the "first lady of literacy" with children of the United Nations International School, and greetings from many notables. The *New York Post* described Welthy at eighty as handsome, vigorous, with a classically Grecian nose, and a manner which was a harmonious blend of intelligence, experience, humour and purpose, who seemed twenty years younger.

Welthy touched the frontier generosity of Americans by evoking their desire to help their neighbours, wherever they lived, and thus made them feel good about themselves. "She is clearing a wilderness," said a San Francisco journalist, observing that Welthy had taken a leaf from her ancestors' notebook as she laboured in the wilderness of illiteracy. In San Francisco, her earlier travelling companion Frances Shepard escorted her on an exhausting round of appointments, finding it difficult to gallop at Welthy's pace. In Phoenix, Arizona, Welthy met Dr. Emily Brown, a journalist turned professor of Far East studies, who was ready and willing to do a stint at Literacy House if Welthy could swing a Fullbright Scholarship for her, one of many such arrangements Welthy made.

A young Indian writer, Som Benegal, marked that birthday with this tribute: "In all these years while the world kept growing older, you kept growing younger; while the world wavered between reason and unreason, calm and fear, wisdom and folly, you remained steadfast in your courage and high purpose, in your compassion and cheer, the brightest candle in the darkness, the warmest glow in the light." Welthy loved him for it, and squeezed something a little more practical out of him in the form of a professional brochure on Literacy House and several helpful articles.

Welthy sat in on a UNESCO conference in Montreal, and went next to Bogota, Colombia, to look at the radio-phonic schools of Monsignor José J. Salcedo, which provided a mix of arithmetic, literacy, hygiene, agriculture and religion over the airwaves. It was impressive, but she could not believe that the warm and lively presence of a teacher with empathy was not the critical factor in learning—the affective principle alive.[39]

Welthy was talking about two kinds of illiteracy—the actual inability to read and write, and the cultural lack of knowledge of one's self, one's place in history, one's heritage and that of other countries. Both were undesirable, and too many people in the United States were victims of the second kind. It was no longer possible to be a cultural isolationist. Overcoming the affluent world's ignorance of the realities of life for their fellow humans in India was as important to her as educating the Indian villagers, two sides of the same coin, worth equal time. In so speaking, Welthy was pioneering 'development education.'

Her own organization remained the hardest of all to educate, having so little apparent understanding of the Indian environment in which she operated and such a strong need to control detail from afar. "I want to know what money and what trustees are at work, how and where. I want to know how we stand financially," she implored them in turn, but instead they kept demanding reports from her, their President. Welthy pushed the WE board to raise money from American companies with business interests in India, and in India she and Koshy sought funds to complete construction from large concerns such as Birla and Bata, with meagre results.

1960

Koshy had taken firm hold in India, and Welthy might well have relegated herself to the role of consultant, as some people urged. Instead, she marched to Washington three times that fall, prodding the U.S. Government for PL 480 funds[40] to underwrite the publications of the School of Writing and to explore the more global ambitions that always intrigued the board in New York, though she was wary of the latter.

She could never forget that in China the Christians had had trouble conveying their message simply because it was not a reflection of their own individual courage and dedication, but rather of the religious, political and economic entrenchment of an elite. Welthy had seen the missionary system break down there, and was determined to convey a simple message in India, through her own actions and through the House of Prayer for All People at the core of the campus, symbolizing unity.

To Mary Dreier she expressed her dismay at "our inexpressive President and stolid Secretary of State" as "we go on putting sixty percent of our income into armaments and cry to the world that we want peace." She confessed to having gone through a dark, deep depression the previous summer; it was too hot to work in India and the wrong time of year for fund raising in America. "Oh, Mary dear—sometimes I wish I were far away—but that is cowardly—we must all face everything that confronts humanity."[41]

While her American zeal for education, community service and social justice was still fundamantally intact, Welthy was no longer part of the fragmented church society with its quarrels over dogma and domination. The real struggle was between the privileged and under-privileged in the quest for peace.

Welthy found expression for her whole being when she planted Literacy House in the heart of Uttar Pradesh. "I couldn't help myself," she said. If she had a physical home on earth, it was there in the House of Prayer with thought and feeling radiating out to all corners of the busy campus.

Her impatience to get on with things was not the grim imperative of a life nearing its end, but rather an energetic, joyful response to life's beckoning possibilities. That was the source of the magnetic sparkle, the essence of the person so many wanted to help. She had found the appropriate action for her energy, and in *Sakshartaniketan*, the Abode of Light, shining with life energy, Welthy was a happy woman.

THE LONGEST STRIDE

THE SIXTIES

As Fred Fisher had admired her long stride in the prime of her life, many were now moved to join with Welthy. For some her steps were too swift and too large and they tried to rein her in. For others she was entering the ranks of immortality. She had been sustained largely by the strength of her own conviction and a small band of loyal supporters, but all that changed when almost overnight she became known as the Literacy Lady.

AUTOBIOGRAPHY PUBLISHED

In 1960, World Education had decided that its best fund-raising tool would be a biography of Welthy. When completed the book proved to be both a help and hindrance to her mission. It was highly readable and did attract many to support the work, but it excluded many more because of its emphasis on her missionary past in China. And for the first time, Welthy's age was used as a promotional factor, though she had still not reclaimed the missing year.

To Lael Wertenbaker, the war-time journalist and author who was asked to write the book, it was quickly apparent from the taped reminiscences Welthy did on the run in fragmented sessions, that "it was Welthy's book,"[1] and it would sell better if done in the first person. What was to have been a biography, therefore, became Welthy's autobiography, "To Light a Candle", the title drawn from the oriental proverb: "It is better to light one candle than to curse the darkness." The publisher's preferred title, "Born Welthy", was rejected by Welthy, who imagined such headlines as "Rich American Widow Seeks Funds," which actually did find print in spite of her caution.

During the year she worked on the book, Lael was frankly skeptical, not liking Welthy much in the fund-raising persona she assumed in the western world. "She tried to make me love her," said Lael, who was at a distinct disadvantage in not getting to India as intended, thus missing Welthy in action in the field. However, other New Yorkers who were involved in the book—Mavis McIntosh, Susan Gleaves, Jacqueline Kornfeld and Nancy Wilson Ross—kept up Lael's morale while the book emerged from the chaos of Welthy's 'papers.' The last tapes were done crossing the Atlantic on the S. S. France, Welthy recuperating from a compound fracture of her right wrist, and desperately wishing for someone to transcribe the tapes.

Lael's efforts were aided by Welthy's recognition of her own outdated Victorian style and ready agreement to any changes suggested. "She was quick to see a point and select the things she thought were useful," said Lael, pleased to find Welthy so pragmatic and objective, never fussing about details if the larger idea was presented her way and the fund-raising purpose kept dominant. Welthy was rather awed to be collaborating with a best-selling author whose classic work, "Death of a Man", had opened on Broadway that season as "A Gift of Time" starring Henry Fonda.

1962 TO 1965

With the publication of the book and a strenuous promotional tour aided by Martha Keehn, Welthy was launched into a new era as a public personality. She took to television with style and ease, an old professional who could graciously turn the tables on the most cynical interviewer. In all the excitement of the tour, Welthy found time to break her hip while rushing in the dark across her apartment to answer Iva Sprague's long distance call.

Mrs. Sprague called Doris Ward, who in turn called an ambulance and a neighbour in Welthy's building before speeding to the scene herself. Doris went mornings to the hospital to work on the fall fund-raising plans while Welthy recuperated, a painful way to escape the dreaded board meetings with their endless debates. Within two weeks she was up and hopping about on crutches with only minor disruption to the promotional tour.

Crutches or cane were not shameful signs of disability to Welthy, but great props to be used when the script demanded, as on the first of several appearances on the Today show. "A Grand Woman Returns Home" announced the lead editorial as Rome Free Academy chose Welthy as Alumna of the Year.[2] Thrusting forward precariously on her crutches, Welthy pressed her theme that we are what we think. She praised those Indian women who had already cast off the burdens of slavery and drudgery to seek an education, and challenged the young school girls, who would never have such burdens, to seek greater opportunity through education and take up their responsibilities in a widening world.

Inevitably the press found Welthy herself more interesting than the work. She accepted that human response because her mission was such an intrinsic part of herself that she had no false modesty. Her book received mixed reviews, sold fourteen thousand copies in eight printings in the United States, and made many new friends for the cause in several countries. Welthy assigned all the royalties to World Education. Had the publisher followed Lael's recommendation to promote the book at each stop on Welthy's fund-raising tour, many more copies would have been sold.

With a British edition and translations into several Asian languages, Welthy became something of an international figure. But its singular aim of attracting support, the heavy accent on her positive successes, and the omission of any reference to Frank Laubach and other significant people along the way was noted, as was the absence of disappointments, obstacles and failures. Though Lael knew Welthy's weaknesses, she chose not to reveal them, nor did Welthy have any inclination towards public introspection, confession or dwelling upon things long since put out of her mind.

The *Atlanta Journal* caught Welthy well in that busy year, describing her still brown hair, and saying she looked more like sixty than eighty. "In a pretty red dress, with a fierceness to the jut of her nose and chin and a calmness, deep and spiritual, in her eyes, she seemed in energy and certainty much the youngest person in the little crowd in an Emory dining room. . . There was the spirited idealism . . . a gentle, goading imperative to her words, with not a little corny cajoling . . . there was a broad spiritual view, typified by her respect for all religious experience . . . and there was humor, worldliness, scorn for the phony, insights about India, China and Africa, femininity and, overriding, a strong sense of the practical. An assured, tough old lady," the article concluded, adding that though she rambled from one anecdote to another she never lost her central theme or her audience.[3]

In Honolulu she was described as magnetic, aristocratic, vibrant, ageless, with enthusiasm and vision. Her talk was quoted: "I believe that people should be educated, but educated to make a choice. Freedom comes with a higher intellectual standard that includes an understanding of the religion and philosophy of others. Literacy is the first rung of education. I'm merely making the ladder available. My work has just begun."[4]

She drew heavily on quotations from her reading and from the battered file of idealistic thoughts she stuffed into any nearest drawer with apparent unconcern for future retrieval. Welthy had a spontaneous eloquence in weaving other's ideas into her own thoughts. These lines of Christopher Fry's, from "Sleep of Prisoners" were typical of quotations she presented:

Thank God our time is now when wrong
Comes up to face us everywhere,
Never to leave us till we take
The longest stride of soul man ever took.

Honours and awards accrued to Welthy in increasing numbers beginning with the first Watumull Award presented in New Delhi in 1962 by
the widow of G.J. Watumull to highlight the significant development
work of eleven individuals; Welthy was the only non-Indian. Mrs. Ellen
Watumull became one of the strongest of the many strong women who
backed Welthy, arranging frequent opportunities for her to appear on
the family owned radio and television stations in Honolulu. She considered Welthy and Margaret Sanger the two was most important women
of her time.[5]

Touching down at San Francisco, Welthy stopped off at Mare Island
where nephew Mike was commander of the shipyard, able to provide a
captive audience of workers for his admired aunt.

In Detroit she received a citation from the Merrill-Palmer Institute of
Human Development and Family Life, not only for her current work in
India but as a way of acknowledging the value and meaning of the great
religions of the world she had brought to the faculty and students in
three decades. She was there at Wayne State University when Eleanor
Roosevelt received an honorary degree, and was seated next to the
former First Lady at dinner. A photograph of the two taken that evening
at one of the last of Mrs. Roosevelt's public appearances before her
death.

When Welthy finally checked in with her dentist after years of disregard, he said her teeth were in the worst shape of anybody's he had
ever seen still walking. More image conscious in the new television era,
and always laughter prone, she decided on a fine set of platinum-back-
ed uppers to preserve her teeth and jaw line. It was a good investment
of time and money.

FIRST UNESCO CONFERENCE ON LITERACY

Speaking with renewed dental confidence, Welthy aroused a clear
response at the first UNESCO World Conference on Literacy and Society
in Rome, Italy, in 1962, when she observed shrewdly that one notable
lack at the meeting was the presence of a single illiterate, the object of
their deliberations. "The illiterate of the world number fifty to sixty out
of every one hundred, whose invisible presence dominated every session. But how could an illiterate find his way there and how could he
move in such an intellectual society?"[6]

Welthy never stopped trying to place the individual illiterate human being on centre stage, in place of others' theoretical assumptions. The Government of India sent no one to join the forty-six nations assembled in Rome, so Welthy and Mushtaq Ahmed had been invited to represent India, with Mushtaq presiding over the sessions on technique and methods, and Welthy, still on crutches, participating in those on motivation and objectives. As an indication of Welthy's reputation, she was told by a literacy worker at the Conference that Indira Gandhi had called her the outstanding person in India on literacy.[7]

* * *

The teachers' sorority, Delta Kappa Gamma, and the non-university sorority, Beta Sigma Phi, both invited Welthy to be an Honorary International Member, invitations she gratefully accepted for the opportunity they gave her to reach more people. And wherever she went thereafter there were groups of the two sororities offering a forum and welcome assistance, for she was travelling alone without help.

In Tucson, when challenged for political comment, she said with directness: "I don't believe in these anti-Communist groups . . . it is better to form a candlelight club than curse the darkness of Communism. By cursing it you make it more important." Convinced that Russia and China had no ideological bond, only a political one, she felt certain that China would change Communism just as she had changed Buddhism centuries earlier.

Accepting hospitality and help from her hosts in each city made strong bonds and kept travel costs low. In Detroit, Betty Brown Pinkstaff took Welthy under her wing on her dashes through Michigan, her home becoming an instant office and public relations centre."A fifteen minute nap always resulted in a deluge of new thoughts to be put on paper,"[8] Betty said, exhausted at the mere remembrance of trying to be all things to Welthy. Betty was impressed by her stately, elegant appearance, her delighted laugh and quick humour, and her ability to gloss over unimportant things. That the old missionary was flexible enough to join them in a cigarette and martini before dinner made her dedication to literacy all the more compelling.

Welthy would have loved Betty to help her in India, but as with a long list of people Welthy tried to pry loose from domestic responsibilities, she did not succeed in finding that "mature woman" she longed for as companion/assistant. Helen Halstead spent six months with her one year, and Litta Roberson, a retired public health worker from Ohio, went twice as a Vista volunteer, providing a sympathetic sounding board for Welthy's difficulties with the WE Board and doing some solid work on a trachoma campaign in the villages.

Nari Bajaj, a handsome, extremely capable young man, assisted Welthy for two years as travelling, living and working companion. Nari swept many of Welthy's admirers off their feet with his physical and mental agility and Indian cooking. But he felt Welthy needed a woman with her, and had begun to think that she was not accomplishing anything,[9] an understandable opinion from the perspective of his youth. He won the admiration of Welthy's Lake Placid friends, Lucile Kyle and Louise Carson, who kept offering Welthy the self-contained cottage on their estate as her home base, one of several efforts friends made to help Welthy settle into comfortable retirement. In declining the offer Welthy risked offending her supporting friends, but much as she appreciated their help and companionship, she valued her independence more. When Nari wanted to move on to become an econometrician, Welthy helped him get a visa to immigrate to the United States, grateful for the help he had given. Alone again, she kept moving.

* * *

The presence of the Fisher/Ahmed team at the Rome Conference opened up new opportunities for Literacy House and led to plans for trainees to come from Turkey, Iraq, Nepal and Sierra Leone. A woman from Iraq went back to head the fundamental education centre in Basra. And the two American women representing the League of Women Voters at the conference, Anna Lord Strauss and Lucille Koshland, looking for a project to support, found Literacy House the best bet.[10] "Know Your Constitution, Vote and Be a Partner of Government", and "We the Government" were the kind of civic publications they were pleased to sponsor for LH. The latter won first prize from the Ministry of Education in India, was translated into many Indian languages and widely used throughout the country. The Government of India, which had not yet set up its intended training centre for Tibetan refugees, asked Literacy House to train another batch of Tibetans during the interim. Literacy House was obviously not engaged in subversive activities, but contributed to the national purpose in training citizens in democratic skills.

In India, Welthy's book brought people of many nationalities to her doorstep. She exercised immeasurable goodwill in introducing many visitors, especially American, to the various Indian officials and women leaders she knew. Rama Mehta, writer and wife of a senior Indian diplomat, expressed what many felt: "Rarely does one come across a person who challenges one's course of life or in whose presence one is forced to think anew the purport and quality of one's own life. . . Dr. Fisher is alive in every sense of the word. There is nothing about her work to suggest a superior mission or message. She is where she is because there is a job to be done and she finds it deeply satisfying. Her work has the sanction of all religions . . . she has no desire to win converts."[11]

In her talks, Welthy emphasized the sense of a new world era she felt so strongly:

> We can build all the dams, hydroelectric plants and factories we want, but if we don't care about educational progress we will fail, because the future is in the people. . . Today is the greatest period to be alive, not because of missiles rising to the moon, but because the minds of man are rising to their full stature.

For all the recognition that was coming Welthy's way, it was sharply balanced by the growing irritation of the WE board members with her extravagant personality. It was "those women" who again caused the most grief. Three of them had ambitions to build up WE as a professional organization with an expanded programme and headquarters, and to relegate Welthy to a peripheral role. The men on the board either backed Welthy or left; the women stayed to do battle. To Welthy the democrat, strength at headquarters meant weakness in the field. Bea Lamb, one of the three, confessed to having been practically in love with Welthy for a while, writing newsletters and raising money for WE, which was Welthy's main desire from trustees. She described Welthy as "the irresistible force before which all seemingly immovable objects have had to move."

But now, the women were no longer inclined to move. Welthy had met her match in the trio, of which the other two were Mrs. Elinor Wolf and Louise Leonard Wright. Their concern was for financial accountability for the money raised; Welthy's concern was the real, practical difficulties of pioneering a programme in the hardship and corruption of India.

Americans had been badly disappointed by their aid experience in the forties. They gave large sums to the Chinese nationalists only to have a good portion of it used to support the powerful China Lobby and keep the aging, ailing Soong family in elegant exile for years. The notable exception was Welthy's friend Soong Ching Ling, whose loyalties lay more with the people of China than her clan.[12] In the sixties, the U.S. Government was ultra cautious in giving aid resulting in tight bureaucratic control of private organizations receiving public funds.

The efforts of the three women had been preceded by Gordon Halstead's proposal to raise fifty thousand dollars seed money for WE to hire a professional fund-raiser. He offered to do the job, but disagreed with Welthy on salary.[13] As a complete volunteer paying her own way, Welthy never believed a full-time fund raiser was required; her priority was for an educator with knowledge of India and administration. Having already given sixteen thousand dollars for Literacy House, Welthy told Gordon she did not dare give the seed money. With no health insurance and no children to care for her, she felt she must retain enough capital to provide for her eventual old age, whenever that would arrive.

It was the first of several unsuccessful bids Gordon made to take charge of WE. He intended to be of help to Welthy, but instead aroused an aging sensitivity in her which left Gordon embittered and increasingly critical of the effectiveness of Literacy House.

MCFADYEN ENDORSES WELTHY

Despite her plea for someone to relieve her of responsibility at WE, Welthy saw no one on the horizon in whom she had sufficient confidence. In June 1963 Welthy was made Honourary President in response to her repeated requests, and Mrs. Wolf was elected President. McFadyen, the Treasurer, resigned over the others' too eager acceptance of Welthy's offer of resignation, saying: "I am quite sure it was an offer and not a conviction. Now we are an organization top heavy with well meaning amateur directors. . . The only salvation I see for WE is strong leadership largely centred in one person and renewed fund-raising activities based on personal contact and personal conviction."

Speaking against hiring a professional fund raiser, he went on: "Except for Welthy, no one seems to be working at approaches to new large givers, and we ill-advisedly turned Welthy out of the office of President, apparently in contemplation of handing the operation of the organization over to a professional whose concern with WE would be as an income producer. I wonder if we will not impair our ability to attract Government contracts and project funds from the more astute foundations if it is known our affairs are in the hands of a professional fund raiser, working without a backup staff of volunteers."[14] His concern reflected Welthy's views exactly.

Responding to her distaste for management, Harold Miner and Arthur Schwartz helped Welthy look into three possible homes for WE within related organizations — CARE, World Neighbors, and Beta Sigma Phi. But Welthy's high-powered board would not relinquish its hold, and negotiations never got off the ground.

SENATOR KEATING SUPPORTS WELTHY

With a two hundred thousand dollar grant from the U.S. State Department for Literacy House publications and audio-visual materials, and Senator Keating's recommendation of the work two years earlier,[15] WE had new status and responsibility in administering those PL 480 funds.

In a letter to President Kennedy, Keating had written: "If all our foreign aid projects were as carefully directed to the needs of the people, as devoutly and sincerely carried out, and as successful in their results as the work of Dr. Fisher, the world would have nothing to fear from Communist dictators."

KENNETH GALBRAITH VALUES WORK

Welthy also had the support of John Kenneth Galbraith, to whom she had written before his ambassadorial post to India was confirmed, because he had urged priority foreign aid for literacy. That initiative resulted in the Galbraiths spending three hours at Literacy House with a large entourage during their first visit to Lucknow in 1962. Calling Literacy House "one of the most intelligent enterprises of our time," Galbraith's interest was electrifying, and plans began immediately thereafter to seek increased PL 480 funds for the greatly expanded operation some WE board members envisaged. The three women were actively involved in reaching for that new goal and Welthy was pleased, though that first grant had been the real breakthrough in recognition.

The WE Board was rightly concerned about the financial irresponsibility of successive executive directors charged with supervising the aid money, who would go on expensive inspection trips to India and yet fail to achieve the desired control. When in New York for meetings, Welthy would not follow carefully prepared agendas, but gave full accounts of the good impression her work was making in India. According to Bea Lamb, she had created a false front.

But Welthy was first and foremost a promoter, a species not noted for modesty, and she was last a complainer. In fact, several trustees who did visit Literacy House were astonished, commenting that Welthy had never taken time to do it justice. Had she been able to convey to the board members, patiently and at their rate of understanding, the range of achievements and the overwhelming odds against which LH worked in India, she might have won greater sympathy from them.

LOUISE LEONARD WRIGHT

"It took all they could chew," said Louise Wright, to cope with Welthy's relentless championing of the vital importance of literacy. While she did alienate some with her impatience, there was no substantial criticism of her by former board members, most of whom admired her tenaciousness, and continued friendly relations with her after leaving. "If she'd gone into the business world she would probably have made large fortunes," speculated Mrs. Wright. "Her techniques were good, almost unique amongst so-called do-gooders — daring, imagination, dramatic, takes liberties, always attractive."

Louise ranks at the top of the list of those who saw more deeply into Welthy's work and personality after several visits to India, recognizing the spiritual energy that sustained her and inspired others. "I don't think she's ever said 'what's the use?' to herself," reflected Louise. "I think she's affected a great many lives of people who've encountered her personally. It's an admiration which leads a person to be productive, helps generate creative energy. She assumes everyone can do what she can do. That's bound to be flattering, and it brings out latent energy."[16]

Louise drew on that energy to become a very effective leader of WE in the years ahead, skillfully reconciling opposing views with her understanding of Welthy's strength. Widow of Quincy Wright, the international lawyer, educator and author, Louise personified the best of American world intentions in the middle of this century, bringing the kind of experience and perspective WE needed and Wlthy respected.

Within a month of her ouster in 1963, Welthy was reinstated as President in her eighty-fifth year, at the urging of Iva Sprague and Dick Mc-Fadyen. Compassion, common sense, or a mix of both, had prevailed, and in Marshall Clark the Board found a good steadying influence.

Welthy was speeded on her Air India way at the end of a long session in the United States by her new-found friends and generous supporters Louise Carson and Lucile Kyle, friends of India and Indira Gandhi. Louise and Lucile took proprietary care of Welthy for several years, always insisting that their gifts be sent directly to Literacy House and maintaining a strong, personal link with the work.

RICHMOND MAYO-SMITH

Half way around the world, the leadership of Literacy House was in a state of flux because Dr. Koshy's five year contract as director was about to expire. Welthy had chosen as the WE representative an American science teacher, Richmond Mayo-Smith, who was spending a sabbatical year in India helping to revise the science curriculum and writing textbooks. His impeccable credentials, social worker wife, presence on the spot, and willingness to accept the seven thousand dollar salary she offered all appealed to Welthy. No large travel, moving and storage expenses would be involved, and he was prepared to use his own money to cover additional expenses, just as Welthy did.

With fierce determination, she overrode the WE Board's preferred choice of an expensive Ph.D. whom they had selected with no reference to her. The representative's role was a difficult one, not clearly defined, and the best of personalities would have faced difficulties. In the circumstances, Mayo-Smith handled the situation well, and was considered by the Literacy House staff to have been by far the best, the most empathetic of all the Americans who came after him. The problem was living right on the campus, being so close to day-to-day affairs, and responsible for funds, yet with no clear administrative authority.

It was almost inevitable that he and Dr. Koshy would clash, given the nature of WE's relation to the ILB. There was one issue of Koshy's judgment unrelated to Literacy House, which Mayo-Smith did not discuss with Welthy, causing them to "fall out for a time," she said, and enabling Mayo-Smith to take advantage of the situation to push Koshy out of Literacy House. In retrospect, Mayo-Smith was not too proud of his role in that situation, particularly since Koshy went on to be an effective leader of literacy programmes in the Government of India. At the time he found Koshy's playing off of the four power centres of Literacy House against each other—Director, Founder, Representative and Chairman—too sly for his sense of rectitude.[17]

Welthy was less naive about the modus operandi in India, more tolerant of Indian survival skills. Keeping her eye on the broad goal, she wanted no fight because there was a large AID grant to be won requiring a united effort.

On one point Mayo-Smith and Koshy agreed, and that was on Welthy's realistic understanding of the relationship of literacy to rural life long before others caught the idea. "She had an uncanny way of knowing what people need,"[18] said Koshy, recalling how she would go and sit and listen to the villagers. No one before had thought of expanding into family life and economic activities, leading to the integrated approach of a total programme. That and her ability to keep literacy before the public as no one else had done has made literacy a respectable field of endeavour. "It was a major public relations contribution in a positive way. She had the nerve to carry it off," said Mayo-Smith, who urged WE to build a financial cushion to carry LH through lean periods.

Mayo-Smith wanted Mushtaq Ahmed as director. He got him, but not for long. With the increasing attention paid to Literacy House, Ahmed's work in developing the primer *"Naya Savera"*,[19] and the follow-up teaching and reading materials, made him a sought-after expert. He had done this work in full consultation with Welthy, who encouraged production of materials that would help villagers form new habits, heal their attitudes towards work and develop a cooperative spirit. The result was his acceptance of a two-year assignment to Nigeria as UNESCO's Adviser on Literacy to the government. It was an immediate loss for Literacy House, but one that turned to gain in the long run because Ahmed never forgot what he learned with Welthy and eventually returned to serve on the ILB.

* * *

New Delhi had become a world crossroads from which Welthy's network of contacts spread in all directions. She literally commuted between Delhi and Lucknow on the two-propeller Fokker Friendship plane that plied the route with great irregularity. In fact, she was by then a global commuter, moving from continent to continent each year. Lucknow, however, was definitely not on the tourist map, though Welthy was once seen buttonholing the Minister of Tourism in a Delhi elevator trying to change that. In Lucknow she had to settle for an audience of those travellers who dropped down en route to Benares or Calcutta and could be exposed for whatever time they could spare.

The tenth anniversary of Literacy House was the kind of *tamasha* Welthy loved, drawing in a large crowd under the big tent, the campus astir with activity and exhibitions. Presiding as Chief Guest was Sucheta Kripalani, Minister for Labour, Community Development and Panchayat Raj in the U.P. Government, freedom fighter and wife of Acharaya Kripalani, who would soon become the Chief Minister of U.P.'s one hundred million people and a solid ally of Literacy House. Growing out of a strong bond with Welthy, her support was one of many strong steps into the future Welthy built at every turn.

But Welthy did know that her strength needed curbing if LH was to make its own way. "Once again the heavy personality struggle not to see everyone who comes," she confided to her diary. "The great need for me here is protection, someone to meet the comers to find out what they want and try to keep me out of it until absolutely necessary."

With a passion for variety and change that sustained her, Welthy gave equal time to the humblest gatherings, as when she went to Bengal to address a village meeting. Lacking secretarial support, she may well have arrived in Calcutta on the wrong day, for no one was there to meet and escort her. So she summoned her good friend Satyen Maitra, venerable founder of the Bengal Social Service League and indefatigable literacy worker, and they set off by car through extreme heat over the often roadless way. "Anyone else would have called it off," said Maitra, but they found the meeting of village people, without the customary V.I.P. to dignify Welthy's arrival. That Welthy stayed three hours talking with the villagers and returned fresh and cheerful impressed Maitra as unusual sensitivity for a foreigner.

AFRICA, 1964

"I am going down into Africa to see some governmental people during the month of May because it is cool there, below the equator," Welthy wrote, but it was more in the nature of a break away from the bickering of boards. The Keehns were in Lusaka with AID. She was accompanied on that hastily planned and executed trip by L.C. Jain, a leading promotor of Indian cooperatives and friend of the Keehns, who delighted in Welthy's abundant laughter and marvelled at her fast pace and faultless dress throughout. Welthy subsequently invited him to serve on the India Literacy Board.

She discussed the perennial problems of WE with the Keehns, who were still actively interested and advising Welthy. Making a stab at following up the African interest of the WE Board, Welthy had an interview with Prime Minister Kenneth Kaunde. Evenings Welthy was included in the parties of the international set, cunningly observing the antics of her compatriots at ease. "Marguerite Higgins, the journalist, was there in all her glory. . . danced with everybody. . . every new-fangled dance that moved her ample buttocks in wide rhythm."

Nehru's death was announced on the car radio while she was in Africa. The shock hit her so deeply that she had the car pull over and stop by the side of the road while she absorbed the news. Welthy could love what Nehru represented to the people of India and the long dedication of his life to serve them, even though she was well aware of his general skepticism about literacy. He had come to resent American support of her work and the praise it received, regarding it as foreign competition.

Citing the example of Communist Kerala, he had told Lisa Sergio, Welthy's writer/lecturer friend, that he was against adult education because they read but did not know enough to understand what was wrong with different ideas.[20] But when she was asked later to speak about Nehru on the African radio, Welthy talked of the larger man's dream for India, who saw beyond the political realm in which he laboured so faithfully.

LITERACY HOUSE WINS LARGE AID GRANT

In that watershed year of 1964, everything seemed to be coming to Welthy in abundant reward for ten years of labour. On June 30th Tyler Wood, Head of U.S. AID in Delhi, called to give her the good news personally that the entire grant requested by Literacy House was approved. 'Those women' in New York had worked hard to secure it, as did Mayo-Smith despite his concern that it was too ambitious to be planning other centres when so much consolidation was needed right at Literacy House. But it was Welthy marching down to Washington, looking the aid givers in the eye, who had carried the day. "If I had been in AID I wouldn't have given such a big grant to an old lady," muttered Arthur Schwartz, shaking his head in amazed recognition that it was Welthy's track record that swung the deal. It was the largest grant ever given to a private agency in India, close to a million dollars over a five-year period (eighty-one lakhs of rupees).

The *Times of India* welcomed the news with an editorial on the vigour of new ideas, saying that "the vision and drive of one person have enabled an idea to grow into a force."[21] Welthy herself observed that ten years ago it would have been unheard of for eight to ten women to meet daily with the village worker for classes in literacy, nutrition and sanitation. The village elders (men) would not have allowed it.

John Peters of World Neighbors wrote to congratulate his old colleague: "When I see you in my mind's eye, I always see you with a feather in your hat, a laugh on your lips, a tossed hand, a flashing eye and words that sparkle with both wit and wisdom. (I must be in love with you.)"[22]

With that degree of financial security for Literacy House Welthy might well have retired and gone home with no small sense of achievement, after years of trying to interest Americans officials in India in her work. Instead she announced she was staying in India for the summer "come hell or high water, and both have come in the form of heat and floods." There was the Panchayati Raj Training Center to be built on new land finally secured from neighbour Gurnani by the enterprising Shivpuri. Laurie Baker was too busy in Kerala to come, so the requirements were sent down to him to make the plan. It came back to Welthy with this note: "I dreamed you and I met in heaven and you were being reprimanded for using your harp as a spring bed!"[23]

Welthy's underlying anxiety was the difficult-to-accept fact that AID insisted on the grant being given to WE, and not directly to the ILB. Both Arthur Schwartz and Welthy had made repeated efforts to have the ILB as grantee, but 'the women' won out and WE became the responsible authority, approving all budgets and work plans of Literacy House. It was a profound error, in light of which Welthy's ability to hold the Literacy House board and staff together is all the more remarkable.

"There are twenty-one women who are trying to direct the use of our funds and the selection of personnel," she wrote to one WE trustee, inflating her two strongest opponents (Lamb and Wolf) outrageously, and deploring the overweening posturing of a board whose only claim to fame was her own work. It seemed deeply wrong and overly ambitious that she should be expected to raise the money at both ends, and that others would control it. Welthy's perennial problem was aggravated in the extreme, the sensitivities of her age adding to her distress, but she would not surrender Literacy House into the board's hands.

WELTHY FISHER COMITÉ IN THE NETHERLANDS

A Rotary scholarship sent a young Dutch woman, Siepie de Jong (later a member of Parliament) to India, where she learned about the work of Literacy House. On return to Holland she was able to interest the Rotary group in literacy to the extent that they wanted to send some money. Wait, said Welthy, recognizing the opportunity; she would come and collect the check personally, which she did on her next journey out.

By the time she left the Netherlands after several days with her new friends and a visit to the Folk High School, an international, residential adult education centre, the seeds of the Welthy Fisher Comité had been sown. Marijke Geertsema, head of the school, was quick to cultivate them further. As a fellow educator, two points Welthy made struck Marijke as significant: that unskilled people were expected by governments to solve the problem of illiteracy, and that the private sector was insufficiently involved, most notably at the big conferences.[24]

MAGSAYSAY AWARD

In mid-August a cable came from the Philippines inviting Welthy to Manila to receive the prestigious Ramon Magsaysay Award on August 31, 1964. Would she come? Welthy was on the next plane to Delhi to assemble a suitable wardrobe for the round of public events scheduled. Seated beside President Marcos at the awards banquet, it was the peak recognition of Welthy's life to be receiving the ten thousand dollar honour, the only non-Asian among five recipients in different categories of what is considered the Asian peace prize.

"I believe that the little man is entitled to a little more food in his stomach, a little more clothing on his back, and a little more roof over his head," said Welthy in her acceptance speech. She was joining the august ranks of individuals such as Vinoba Bhave, the Dalai Lama and Mother Teresa, all of whom she preceded to Manila.

Accepting an honorary degree at Centro Escolar University, Welthy's inclusive feminism sent a strong signal to the assembled elders:

> *There is a new era in this world, gentlemen, and it cannot be carried by you alone. You have had your day and I don't think you have done very well. You need us desperately. We must move together.*

WE downplayed the personal attention being accorded Welthy in press reports that invariably focused on her individuality. The more publicity she received (from which they benefited), the more they turned away from her, especially newer staff and board members who did not know her. A natural skepticism grew around someone so magnified in print; it became easier to regard Welthy as an old woman with a band of loyal admirers.

YOUNG FARMERS' INSTITUTE

Literacy House had stressed the need to teach basic, work-oriented skills in addition to reading and writing long before that doctrine became the by-word of UNESCO as the "functional literacy" of its experimental world programme. Emphasis on feed-back evaluation also predated that of other organizations.[25] Now it was time, Welthy knew, to put that approach to the test on the ground, in the strategic need to produce more food.

By the time her plane returned to Lucknow, she had decided how to use the award money. She would buy some barren land and build the Young Farmers' Institute, where literacy would speak the practical language of agricultural needs and young villagers could come with their wives for residential training on the land.

Her decision was announced at two gleeful parties she threw immediately — one for all the campus children and their twenty-six mothers, with gifts from Manila for everyone, and a birthday party, her own eighty-fifth. It was also a welcome back from Nigeria for Mushtaq Ahmed as everyone gathered under the stars in the open-air theatre, with the puppets presenting a panorama of the life of Literacy House. There was tremendous sense of well-being to have those two far-flung leaders returned to the fold.

BIL AND CORA BAIRD

The puppet troupe created by Naitani and his trainees had undergone advanced education by Bil and Cora Baird, America's leading puppeteers for whom Welthy had arranged a grant. In describing his own branching into educational puppetry, Bil gave credit to Welthy, for in coming to India to teach at her urging, he had learned, doubling the impact of his communication.

Bil and Welthy were on the same wave length, their creative bond enlivening the Literacy House puppeteers with new inventiveness as they travelled throughout U.P. and into other states with their easy brand of learning. They were featured entertainers at the gala farewell outdoor dinner for the Mayo-Smiths, with puppets representing the three Mayo-Smith children.

LITERACY HOUSE ATTRACTS INTERNATIONAL RECOGNITION

As the reputation of Literacy House travelled ever wider, it became more international both in trainees and support. Three UNESCO Fellows were sent from Tanganyika, the Philippines, and Uganda, and there were frequent visits by members of the three supporting organizations in the U.S., Canada and the Netherlands.

Welthy on the wing dashed a note to the UNESCO Regional Representative in Bangkok, hoping she could attract him to take charge of the expansion of Literacy House made possible by the AID grant: "I am dropping down in Bangkok for an hour or so on the 16th, Pan Am Flight 2. We need a statesman in this field." She did not succeed in that instance, but that is how many of the appointments to Literacy House had been made in the past.

Literacy House staff members were reaching beyond their initial perspective as Welthy sought grants for their further training, never as many as the staff might have liked. Shivpuri went to Denmark for nine months and met his wife there; Siddiqi took his master's degree in extension education at Cornell; and Shaw went to Canada. Without enlightened personnel management, however, Literacy House had a very difficult time making the best use of its staff, and several who received outside training left the institution.

A number of the colleagues Welthy attracted to Literacy House gained unique experience that enabled them to step out into the international field, most notably Mushtaq Ahmed and Harbans Bhola, a Sikh with an American Ph.D. whose knowledge and personal charm exceeded his tolerance of the underlying communal problems that plagued Uttar Pradesh and came into sharp focus at Literacy House.

PROBLEMS COME WITH AID MONEY

Representative of many who left, Bhola soon returned to the United States as the base for his international work. There he wrote a scathing criticism of everyone at Literacy House and Welthy Fisher, thinly disguised as fiction,[26] his frustrations brimming over on every page. While he was acting director he said: "We don't deserve all this. It should all be burned to the ground and we should start all over from scratch."[27] It was an understandable response of someone with a young family to consider, whose life was several times threatened by disruptive staff members as the new influx of money and staff began to change the environment of Literacy House.

It was a very emotional reaction to his realization of the problems caused by the unwillingness of staff members to work together, the general lassitude, and New York control over the financial decisions of an Indian project. Nor did he realize that the seeming impossibility of accomplishing anything in this situation was the very reason Welthy was still there, using her personality to keep things going, when all else so often failed.[28] In his disappointment, he chose to distance himself from the work, seeing it essentially as inappropriate and poorly administered.

There was nothing very new in what the experts required by the AID grant had to say during their short stays. Welthy remained on the battlefront, having long ago learned what Bhola was discovering so painfully. Vulnerable in her advancing years, she was easy to blame for any and all wrongs, and some did.

In his carefully articulated response to those who consider it necessary to prove the value of literacy Bhola has since come closer to the "bleeding heart" he considered Welthy to be. "Don't we know, in our bones," he asks, "that illiteracy is oppressive?"[29] By a different route he has arrived at the point where Welthy began, his common sense intersecting with compassion in strong advocacy of massive literacy campaigns in developing nations.

With each year of the AID grant (1964 to 1969), the fundamental organizational flaw compounded existing difficulties. When Mayo-Smith's term expired, the new WE representative tried to dominate ILB meetings and did succeed in instituting a stifling set of bureaucratic regulations at AID's instigation. It effectively eliminated all flexibility, signifying an end to the creative years. The only way to remove an employee was to kill or maim him, and such attempts were made. As well, the psychological warfare of the anonymous letter was frequently used to undermine an individual's resolve.

Shortly after meeting with the WE Board in New York where he was rigorously questioned on Literacy House procedures and expansion plans, Mushtaq Ahmed decided to accept a permanent assignment with UNESCO rather than submit to New York's tight control and implied lack of trust. Welthy was left to hold all the strings together.

The net effect was that Literacy House entered upon an era of rapidly changing directors, representatives and ILB officers. The only real continuity for the remaining core staff was Welthy who continued to follow her own agenda. The AID grant, which was intended to provide the basis for extensive expansion, came close to being the kiss of death. Had Welthy not persevered there is little doubt that Literacy House would have fallen apart.

In the midst of the heaviness Welthy kept dashing off letters in all directions to keep her angle of vision wide. To Tom Keehn she wrote: "How I would like to do something frivolous with somebody. I think I am getting to be a dull boy because I work all the time."

It was plain to a keen observer of Literacy House that Welthy was the one with the ideas and the commitment. The staff all looked to her for decisions rather than to the director because she could empathize. And while she did not directly undermine the director, she did not refrain from throwing out suggestions that were often taken as decisions. "She was clearly the moving force, the tower of strength, the one person with absolute belief in what she was doing, and that gave her the moral force and certitude to ask greatly of others and to receive from them," said one of the steady stream of visitors to whom Welthy gave quality, equal, time. "If it was a personality cult as a basis for an organization, I realized that without such dreamers of great dreams nothing new would ever be created on this earth in human society."[30]

Welthy felt she had to circumvent the rules, regulations and policies others find so necessary because they are essentially uncommitted. She consciously took the risk of receiving heavy criticism for using her personality as a tool. In a purely organizational sense she was a poor manager in her willingness to gather up all kinds of people and try to fit them in, as Gandhi had done. Those whom she could accept, others could not, in that land of unending prejudice, though her American colleagues were frequently less tolerant than the Indians.

* * *

Hospitality was still the cornerstone of Welthy's approach; her door was always open no matter how tired she felt. Each year at Christmas she lit dozens of small candles set in the open spaces of the brick wall which protected her house from the sun. On Christmas Eve she led the Christian families from door to door singing carols, and then invited the gathering group round her fireplace for stories, song and prayer, memorable parties of ready-made tea cooked with milk and spices, which everyone joined in eagerly.

As for those Christians who tended to exclude Welthy, she continued to invite them to her gatherings, and trainees were frequently sent to Literacy House from the National Christian Council. A young Australian missionary took pains to inform Welthy that she was not a Christian because she did not believe that only through Christ could God be found. Welthy listened to his earnest effort to win her to the only way, and was not offended.

One prominent Indian Christian, Dr. Eva Shipstone, remained grateful to Welthy for the tactful way she dissolved the tension of transition when Shipstone was appointed head of IT College. Welthy set the tone by saying at the outset: "Thank God a new era has begun."[31]

Dr. Shipstone also appreciated Welthy's clear, strong minority objection to a rule against having married women on the staff—a rule it took

another decade to change. A large tablet detailing Welthy's long association with the college now adorns one wall, and IT students have taken
up the village work Welthy kept urging upon them in her frequent talks
there.

At the highest level, Welthy urged the Methodists to stop pouring high
salaries into the Indian Church from abroad. "It will be a shell until the
system is changed and the Church digs in its roots into the life of India,"
she wrote, recommending that local pastors be helped to earn their own
living off the land within the community they served. She urged the
bishops to send pastors to Literacy House for training as teachers, convinced that teaching by example was the modern need for preachers.

As for the Indian Bishops who chose to retire in the United States on
comfortable pensions, Welthy's message was in her own active involvement in India. She could never forget the mixed message the Christian
church had left in China and was devoting the final portion of her life
to living the message she wished to communicate in India.

Ultimately the Methodist Church did recognize Welthy as a member of
the serving flock and granted her the widow's pension she had earned.

* * *

Aware that the measure of their work could not be grasped in the
present, Welthy was not seeking triumph today or tomorrow in the quantifiable results experts measure, but in building up a whole nation
through educating its people, especially those who were at the low end
of the cycle of centuries. Some visitors and short-term consultants found
it difficult to see the range of LH activities; others went overboard and
endowed it with impossible expectations. Welthy worked daily to
remain centered, never missing morning prayers.

In her multi-persona as teacher/founder/hostess/planner/fund
raiser, she kept her door open, searching out every new face for signs
of interest and cooperation. A random look at her guest book shows
the variety: "Loving mother—marvellous dinner—expand x 100,000—
I see future India—*Namaste*, I worship God in you—Always rejuvenat-
ing—Great breakfast—Dedication and inspiration are contagious
here—Ideas, ideas, ideas—A revelation".

Literacy, the basic building block of communication, was Welthy's
strategic weapon for peace. While WE regarded her as increasingly unnecessary in India, Welthy was urging the Planning Commission of the
Government of India to include literacy as an integral part in their plans,
offering suggestions and the services of LH. She was also forging a
powerful alliance with the strong women of India—Durgabai Deshmukh
at the Council for Social Welfare, Kamaladevi Chattopadhya of the Indian Cooperative Union, Raksha Saran at the National Council for

Women's Education, and Begum Ali Zaheer at the U.P. Council for the Education of Women.

To the pastor of her beloved Detroit church she wrote in 1966: "I decided we must have a new approach as Christians . . . I am trying to follow the commandments of our Lord . . . to be a neighbour to all my neighbours and to love them equally . . . We try to worship him in spirit and in truth . . . and take gems of thought and inspiration that have come from God himself down through the ages to different individuals who have been god-like men."

In an interview in Copenhagen where she studied Peter Manniche's folk high schools, Welthy tailored her message more succinctly: "I don't think we have a monopoly on a direct contact with God. God is love for everybody." That was the plain, simple fact of life for Welthy.

In Lisa Sergio's collection of the prayers of women from the beginning of time,[32] Welthy offered a meditation beginning with the profound intimacy so many experienced when she spoke in the House of Prayer: "Oh Infinite One, to whom all hearts are exposed . . . " Her own heart sought ever more deeply for that exposure as the battle raged on around her and the years advanced.

She could also adjust her terminology to the changing facts of the world, having discovered that 'literacy' was not nearly as acceptable as 'communication.' Asked by students of Rome Free Academy for a message for inclusion in their time capsule, to be opened in 2067, she wrote: "Some of you may have already spent your vacation on the moon. We are perhaps the first to be awakened to the fact that communication on this earth is essential for every human being on it. The lack of it has kept us all apart in little clans . . . on all the continents and islands. I believe that you will have found a universal language . . . that has become the link language of the world . . . I feel confident that killing each other has ended."

THE FUTURE IS NOW

Welthy's speeches inevitably focused on the future. She based her discussions on her historical perspective, but always insisted that the future begins NOW. That meant attacking the huge communication blank between those empowered with literacy and the illiterate, the haves and the have-nots. "God speaks to all men who have mind and heart open to receive him," she would remind listeners. "Perhaps there are men and women in the lowliest villages who have known him better than the philosophers and the scholars, but with darkness still over half the world, what geniuses are stumbling away in these unlighted paths of the villages?"

To broadcaster Betty Furness she wrote thoughtfully: "I have just been reading Tagóre who said that those of the world who have been suppressing the great majority are only forging their own chains. This I believe, and until we begin to develop whatever capacity there is in the human being, we shall finally find ourselves in chains."

As Malcolm Adiseshiah, President of the IAEA, put it: "She brought the concept of human development to adult education. She saw people as pulsating, hoping, despairing, producers, consumers, fathers, mothers. There is a major lesson to be learned from her work."[33] But thought Literacy House was not the right name for the breadth and depth of Welthy's work.

V. K. R. V. Rao, India's economist Education Minister in the late sixties, pinpointed the writers' workshops at Literacy House as the first example of an action-oriented, policy-modulated research for human welfare. Write, try it out in villages, get reactions, come back, discuss, change — all new ideas needing careful integration into the Indian psyche.[34]

From yet another vantage point, A. N. Roy, the contractor who worked so closely with Welthy in the building of Literacy House, observed that many careerists had let her down, that her one weakness was believing in people. He marvelled that she had not lost faith. The love and trust she placed in people, even though many disappointed her, was a fundamental contradiction, showing both weakness and strength, acceptance and endurance.

Tom Keehn, back in New York and serving as treasurer of WE, urged Welthy to focus her attention on WE: "What do we want to do at Literacy House; in India; elsewhere?" he wrote, and asked her to invite Indira Gandhi to a WE meeting in New York. Welthy declined, thinking it unwise to ask a world leader to a meeting of a few people.

As she drew more people from all sides into her orbit, the ranks of her critics grew in proportion, but Emerson had warned her to finish each day and be done with it. "I did the best I could with the brains I had at the time," she would say, and get on with her thinking, studying, probing.

She was at her creative best talking with young writers wherever she encountered them on the campus, leaning forward on her cane, a brilliant scarf tossed over the shoulder of her great red suit, her spontaneous animation an inspiring delight to the eager scribes, and a worrisome impediment to the administration's timetabling. A photograph of Welthy talking with young writers on her final visit to India in 1980 shows the dynamics of that interaction.

Staff and trainees wanted close connection with Welthy, referring to her as *Mataji*. The rational in Welthy recognized this as cloying dependency; the spiritual in her could not turn away. And so she gave them the love they wanted, remembering the disciples who had loved Christ because he loved them first, and asked the writers to turn their active minds to their village brother's interests, offering them provocative, practical suggestions.

Again and again Welthy was rewarded with manuscripts that found their way into her house before anyone else saw them, love offerings of awakened, aroused individuals, just what she sought. The manuscripts were quickly placed in the proper organizational slot for editing, testing, rewriting and publishing, with no interference from Welthy, yet something special had happened.

Welthy understood the needs of writers. All except herself, that is, for she remained unable to produce a book on her own, though she tried once more at an American publisher's urging[35] to write on village India, focusing on the controversial issues of caste and cows. Welthy struggled through many chapters but she obviously could not do it; she could translate her thought and emotions into action, but could not set them aside to look at. She had become one with her ideas, inseparable, in simple authority.

JANUARY 1966

It was a heavy month of camping out in temporary quarters while leaks in the damp house were repaired. Welthy's leg was hurting and her patience oozing away. Never had she been so physically uncomfortable from the plumbing and electricity problems or felt such stress from the far greater strain of constant visitors and meetings. A visit to Mati village for the opening of the new diesel pump restored her perspective, since it allowed her to see the evident impact of Literacy House in the new junior high school.

But then, in Delhi for an ILB meeting, "all day boresome committee of intelligent people. They used up one hour discussing what were 'workers'—industrial, agricultural? Aren't we all workers, I asked. The semantic argument continued."

There was a thrill when Indira Gandhi was sworn in as Prime Minister, and Republic Day was a first in India that year, seen by the elite, and their servants, on the few television sets then available, the communication gap both widening and lessening at once. Welthy's mind was on the village women who would slowly begin to understand what had happened in their homeland, that a woman headed the largest democracy in the world.

The month ended with Welthy pecking away at her typewriter during regular power outages. "I am now prepared with plenty of candles. It can be done, as it was in Abe Lincoln's day, and my grandfather's and my own father's, who would have been a hundred and forty-four years old today—a span of change—in external matters—but the mind of man? I wonder." On January 30th, Martyr's Day, thinking of Gandhi, she wrote: "I must learn to rise above my physical discomfort and rise in Love. I feel tired and lonely and I pray for President Johnson—a lonely man—with the world's biggest burden. WAR."

February 1, 1966. "You can't sit down and rigidly plan a thing before you know the people. Will we ever get going?" By day she was trying to persuade the Xerox Corporation to buy a forest and back the printing of a weekly rural newspaper, and she threw out suggestions to the New President of WLC, Jack Corrigan, and to a visiting Canadian adult educator, Dr. James Draper, to join with Comfort Shaw in forming another Literacy House. While Eva Shaw rubbed her swollen knees, Welthy poured forth ideas for such a new centre and for a self-supporting, literate Indian church with income-producing land, ideas that settled firmly into Comfort's mind and stayed there in the years ahead.

In response to WE's concern over slow progress and the deteriorating relations between LH, AID and the ILB, the WE Representative had come to the conclusion that "the expectations we Americans have probably should be scaled down considerably," as he suggested accepting the Indian pace and quality of achievement on their own steam.[36] A positive result of that state of tension was a new constitution for the ILB, by which they could enter into agreements with WE on an equal basis and amend their own constitution.

In the mid-April heat Welthy gave a farewell ice cream party for all the children, and a telling meditation in the House of Prayer using Olive Schreiner's thought: "They will climb on my stairs—they will laugh at them, polish them, but climb on them." She needed to believe that her work was a base for the future after such an agonizing six months in India. She headed for America with persistent fever, dizziness and nosebleeds. Amateurs were always ready to diagnose hardening of the arteries and predict that Mrs. Fisher could not live much longer.

* * *

She went wherever she was called in the United States—to receive a large check from Beta Sigma Phi bringing their total support close to a hundred thousand dollars; to accept the Recognition Award from the Women's National Farm and Garden Club; and to receive a number of other honours at gatherings of all kinds, none too small to prevent Welthy from giving her maximum effort in return.

Before the WE Board approved a plan, Welthy was raising private funds for the Young Farmers' Institute, leading with her own ten thousand dollar award money. So conditioned as a speaker herself, Welthy never slowed down to get a consensus from her board, and for all her understanding could not or would not accept what motivates people to serve on such boards. "She's a loner," said Arthur Schwartz, "and so often they're the people who get things done in this world. I love her but found her impossible to work for." And Bea Lamb could not tolerate Welthy's disregard of WE policy in concentrating on one centre and not establishing new centres.

She took belated satisfaction in being the only wife or widow to be included in the new Methodist encyclopedia, the old boys recognizing her after all. After lunching in Washington with Ambassador and Mrs. B. K. Nehru, her diary jumped with exclamation marks as she recorded that one Indian lady said that of course she knew of Welthy, but did not expect to find her so elegant. Travelling with one suitcase as she did, it was more an elegance of manner and spirit than of costume. With inexpensive clothes, Welthy knew how to use red, black and white to dramatic effect.

Increasingly aware of her deepening fatigue, she yearned almost frantically for a mature, unencumbered person to relieve her and keep her from missing engagements on the fly. Welthy was shocked into full realization of her need when she fell asleep in the Beirut airport en route back to India for a TV documentary film about her work,[37] and missed the boarding call. It is some indication of her magnetism that Air India returned from its takeoff position to reclaim her.

Fever and nausea persisting, she went through the grueling filming under hot lights, making a score of new friends among the crew with her personal hospitality. With the phone not working, as was frequently the case, she saw everyone who arrived at her door unannounced, whatever the time, and for whatever reason. Everyone knew Welthy could not say no, and they came to bask in her sunshine.

In six weeks she was back in North America for a WLC conference in Ottawa and, among other events, a banquet in Rome where two former classmates, Susan and Marjorie Comstock, sang the 1896 class song: "Ninety-six forever, we're very very clever, will each member be ninety-six forever?"

Despite her need for help, Welthy's survival instinct kept her evading people in India and the United States who tried to manage or discipline her for administrative purposes. It often seemed that as her public recognition increased, fewer could hear what she was saying as the media pressed for instant understanding and entertainment. She longed for someone close to have fun with along the way, to break from endless focus on work.

SALLY SWENSON

December 12, 1966. Shortly after midnight Welthy was indulging her taste for colourful creativity in a handicraft shop in Teheran Airport during a stopover en route back to India. Highly animated when she spotted me, also in transit, she told me to hurry on to Delhi and wait for her plane which would arrive shortly after mine.

Welthy never expected that after fourteen years of growth with Fred, fourteen years of painful searching, and fourteen years of lonely creation of Literacy House, she would find companionship for her last fourteen years with a Canadian woman more than half a century her junior. I did not know very much about who she was when I waited for her in Delhi, nor was I the mature creature she sought. But I did know who I was not, and that Welthy Honsinger Fisher held some powerful clues for me.

Welthy had written astutely in her diary a few weeks earlier: "Sally Swenson came down last weekend and came twice to 50 W 67th St., but she doesn't know her own mind — she is enamoured of me — but the cause must come first and not me. Now she has sent me a letter telling me she would like to come for a month — to help me! But what can she do in one month! Nothing for me — but a great deal for WLC and if she will look at it that way I think it will be wonderful — so, we shall see."

I was still reeling from five years' exposure to the wider world as a secretary in the Canadian foreign service,[38] followed by five years as a professional librarian developing an industrial research library in a scientific environment, and I knew I had some growing to do in another direction after a brief marriage. Four years earlier I had visited Literacy House by chance during an eye-opening trip to India. The encounter with poverty changed my perception of everything. I scarcely knew what kept gnawing at my mind, but I did remember meeting the 'old lady who was doing good,' as someone referred to Welthy.

At thirty-five, my unfocused restlessness pulled more in the direction of Welthy's world-minded service than the ecstatic, often self-destructive protests of the young, radical left. Unaware of the incipient women's movement, I did share a deep dissatisfaction with the affluent, mindless society in those protest years and sought clues outside my limited life. Perhaps if I sent some money to India I might feel better, I thought, and Welthy Fisher would surely use it well.

I wrote to her, and as she did with thousands of other such letters, she quickly replied and wrote also to WLC, telling them to catch me. When I sent a check slightly larger than their average contribution, they lost no time in following Welthy's suggestion, and soon I was producing a promotional booklet for them — step one in my education. Step two was some deeply thoughtful guidance by the quiet man of WLC, Will Mowle.

Step three was organizing their 1966 conference in Ottawa, to which Welthy came. When I presented myself on the tarmac to receive the jet-speeded octogenarian I might have been squashed by her abrupt: "Who are you?" as she arrived tired and alone, dropping down out of the mid-night sky direct from India. But she had asked the right question.

In the two days that followed I knew that something extraordinary was happening to me, and that it had everything to do with the exhausted eighty-seven year old woman who had collapsed into bed after midnight, and then presented herself full of vibrant energy on the platform at Carleton University early the next morning. The previous speaker had pontificated long beyond his allotted time, and as Welthy swung onto centre stage with her cane I heard her sing softly a sublimely naughty "I could have danced all night."

After an awesomely laudatory introduction, Welthy set an informal, working tone to the conference with her first words: "She sounds kind of queer, doesn't she?" She was just the saintly sinner that someone with the initials SS could recognize. And when she got to the heart of the matter, the reality of her work, she made her point spontaneously, without the laborious logic that limits understanding, freely offering a glimpse of something more complete. There was beauty in her spirit dancing out from clear, sparkling eyes, in her laughter richly short of mischievous, and in the strong embrace of her cascading voice.

One trustee of WLC, Grace Hampson, a mature high school teacher from Pembroke, Ontario, recalled vividly her first meeting with Welthy at that conference: "She flashed to me an experience of the greatest thing I had ever met — love on a world-wide scale — and won my loyalty. . . I never knew anyone who radiated such love — it was so obvious.[39]

Welthy had to be taken whole; it was not possible to divide her up into parts, though some people doggedly kept trying to do so. She was a moving force and one had to be quick to leap into the stream with her. The time was right, and I was ready.

It was literally a leap into the unknown. I had gone to New York on the weekend she described in her diary to pursue the idea of being her secretary. People were milling in and out of her apartment, soup and sandwiches could be made if anyone wanted to help themselves, but I was not getting any idea of what I wanted to know. Suddenly Welthy turned to me and said: "Well, are you ready to come with me and live my life?" That was all. During the next few weeks while I went through the mental motions of rational decision-making, I knew perfectly well what the answer was.

Still, I set off from Ottawa on what was intended as a three-week journey combining business with vacation, leaving open the option to return to my neatly ordered life. At the end of three weeks I cabled family, friends and my employer that I was staying on with Welthy.

Like so many others before me, I was captivated by Welthy, with her sense of purpose, her vigour and eloquence, her warmth and charm — and her intense need, at eighty-seven, for someone to help smooth her road if she was to continue her work.

She was unforgettably assisted in capturing me by a Lucknow woman, Dr. Alankaram, who had given her services in the Literacy House eye camps removing cataracts. As she lay dying of cancer on a *charpoy* in the midday warmth of her garden that winter, she turned her luminous brown eyes on mine and told me with finality and clarity that I must stay and help Mrs. Fisher. The softly penetrating voice and eyes dissolved any lingering questions about my decision.

Litta Roberson had come back to India with Welthy in 1966 because she could not bear to see her go off alone, unassisted, and had no idea that she would be sharing the second bedroom in Welthy's small bungalow with me. Fortunately, she was as adaptable as Welthy to details of personal comfort. We were awakened about 4:00 a.m. each morning by Welthy on the rampage, turning out all the drawers of her chests and trunks full of sheets, blankets, tablecloths and napkins, and then leaving them in a pile on the floor in an unmistakable expression of her discontent with the static situation at Literacy House.

All programme work had stopped, and the effort was entirely focused on research and planning. AID in Delhi had told her how disappointed they were, and the ILB sought clarity from her about the intention of the grant. The ILB wanted a large integrated programme in the block; AID wanted new centres opened throughout India. The representative was caught in between, and it was Welthy who carried the burden of sorting out the impossible standoff.

She desperately needed help, of any kind, of every kind. I knew there were some things I could do to help her, even though there was plenty I did not know. Litta was as relieved as I was when my decision to stay was made, and I simply sat down in a dark, dank corner in the dining room and began typing. I never worked so hard in my life. It was not a job, but a response to a dynamic force swirling all around me night and day.

I could just afford to pay my own travel and expenses, plus minimal room and board in Welthy's house — an arrangement that pleased us both. Instinct told me to preserve some independence from Welthy's moments of imperial impatience, which were frequent that first year as we adjusted to each other. My volunteer status struck the balance.

1967

Welthy was not used to having someone hovering so closely and naturally sought her accustomed freedom. At the end of January 1967, she executed a delicious escape from me in Delhi and presented herself uninvited at the American Ambassador's Republic Day garden party. But it caused no problem because she had carte blanche with her compatriots, especially with their excellencies Chet and Steb Bowles, to whom Welthy was a reigning American in India, a reference point. The Ambassador was amazed that Welthy had been able to do so much with so little[40] and delighted in hosting the premier of "To Light a Candle," a USIS film, in New Delhi. When diplomatic duties pressed her too hard, Steb often came to Literacy House to restore her perspective in the reality of Welthy's back porch.

The day after my first overnight break away from Welthy in six weeks, I returned to our room at the old Imperial Hotel to discover that she had had an accident and was in the hospital. No one could tell me more than that. A thousand reprimands ran through my head as I dashed to Safdarjung Hospital, where again no one could give me any information. There was no record of her presence. I raced up and down the labyrinthine corridors of that complex of buildings, frantically poking my head in here and there, until finally I saw the sleeve of a red woollen jacket through a door.

Inside sat the director and the representative, ashen-faced. They told how Welthy had left a meeting at the IAEA to go to the washroom and as she was coming back down the darkened staircase had fallen near the bottom, where the railing ended, landing on her elbow on the hard terrazzo floor.

"With her remarkable presence of mind and composure, retrieved in hardly more than two or three minutes," reported the representative later to WE, Welthy advised her stunned male colleagues to find Dr. Doraiswamy, the top orthopedic specialist. During the two hours she lay on the floor awaiting his arrival, she was in complete command of herself, calm, cool and collected as a queen holding court, as she continued with the business of the meeting. She knew she had broken her elbow badly, and probably something else; it was a painfully familiar feeling.

Soon the rest of the red wool suit was wheeled out on a stretcher and the crumbled old girl was left in a curtained corridor — since she was only an out-patient — to come out of the general anaesthesia after surgery to piece together her severely shattered elbow. When she regained consciousness she asked for me, her teeth, her rings and her pearls. She was released immediately, and her generous bulk was transferred to a tiny stretcher in an ambulance, and we set off into the Delhi darkness . . . to go where?

Delhi was overcrowded with tourists, all the hotels and our friends' homes were bursting at the seams, and we would never be able to get to our second floor room at the Imperial in their mini-elevator with Welthy on a stretcher. She was in great agony, and her greyness terrified me; I thought she might die.

I learned then to do what I had to do so many times thereafter—to insist on the impossible—and a very distinguished Indian gentleman graciously gave up his spacious ground floor room to us. When Welthy arrived on her stretcher, still looking ghostly, she saw that the entranceway to the room was too narrow to pass through. "Move that cupboard in the hall," she advised, "and then we can get in."

Somehow we got her onto the bed, and then the door finally closed on the retinue that had gathered, leaving us alone. As I lay on my cot that night and for weeks afterwards, listening for each breath, thinking she could expire at any moment, I discovered what Welthy Fisher was made of. She was not about to die, even though the pain was compounded by a touch of pneumonia and a pelvic fracture that went undiagnosed too long. She was kept off her feet and confined to that room for six weeks. I gave up expecting her to die, and learned something about my own strength in addition to necessary hands-on nursing care. I had hired a nurse the first day but quickly realized I could handle Welthy myself and spare both of us the incessant talking in our one-room hospital, cum office, cum reception area.

Dr. Doraiswamy carried greetings back and forth between Welthy and another of his patients, the Prime Minister, whose nose had been broken by a stone thrown from an angry mob. Indira sent exquisitely fragrant flowers and it was not long before some of the most beautiful souls of India passed through the room at all hours as Welthy lay so ill, people who had worked closely with Gandhi, and others who had come long distances to be at her bedside.

I remember particularly the Aryanayakams, longtime workers at Gandhi's ashram, but not all were so considerate for it is Indian custom to cluster round the sick bed in perpetual vigil, often having come long distances. I did not realize that everyone who came thought Welthy belonged to them, and I never learned to handle their intrusions well. My western sense of privacy and concern that she have quiet for her recovery may have offended some Indians. I was also exhausted, partly because I had no retreat for myself except the bathroom. My own needs were of no concern to most visitors; it was Welthy and only Welthy who mattered.

More important was the fact that Welthy and I had endured a crisis together in the most intimate circumstances. We were close in a way we had not been before as I took care of all her personal and nursing needs. When the time came for Welthy to strut her stuff, I wheeled her down the wide, carpeted main corridor of the Imperial to one of the reception rooms where we had arranged an important ILB meeting. All the men were seated, awaiting the arrival of Welthy, whom they had elected as Chairman.

As we reached the door, she and I knew at the same instant that she was going to get up and take her first steps walking into that room, creating her own stage. Proudly, to a round of hushed applause, she gave a magnificent performance, and they loved her for it. In that magic moment she and I discovered how to walk together naturally, so that no one noticed I was supporting her. We were a good team.

One of the many letters Welthy wrote during her recovery in the hotel was addressed to President Lyndon B. Johnson regarding the mixed signals America was sending, as the Christians had done half a century earlier in China:

> *We cannot help both the poverty program in the world, or in one part of the world, and bomb villages of innocent people in another. I am unequal to the eloquence required to present the anguish and despair in my mind and in the minds of many here over the role of our powerful nation in Vietnam.*"

My initiation into Welthy's world was complete. Ever after it was easier to stay than to go, no matter how heavily I allowed the burden of total attendance to weigh on me.

1967 TO 1971

Welthy included me in every part of her life, despite those Indians and Americans who regarded me as an insignificant servant, to be ignored. She had a subtle way of bringing me forward to them as if to say no one is excluded here. Some got the message readily; others never bothered to understand her meaning. I began to see through her eyes, to realize the wide gap in personalities between those who were sensitive to others, open and cooperative, and those whose egos and underlying fear kept them in a narrow, aggressive stance.

That difference became very apparent in the thousands of people we encountered, cutting across a wide spectrum of occupation, status and culture as we moved around the world, spending half the year in India and the rest fund raising and contacting groups in several countries. Welthy put it very simply once: "The world is divided into those who care and those who don't." She had put her finger on the root cause of illiteracy—it was not money or method that was going to make the difference in the long uphill struggle of the illiterate.

THE AFFECTIVE PRINCIPLE

While the experts produced endless reports concluding that lack of motivation was the major obstacle in literacy programmes, Welthy kept demonstrating the "affective principle"[41] in her speeches, in meetings with staff and with villagers, and with the Prime Minister. It was not through theory but through personal action that she communicated her intent, so simply that it seemed like an old lady's softness to some, but Welthy's compassion was solidly based on a deep awareness of human psychology. Even the puppets caught it with their winning ways of wooing a village audience, making learning come alive. She proved this time and again in winning the less caring individuals, sometimes only briefly, by touching the person behind the hard mask where their own need was raw. When they could no longer bear it, the mask went on again and they took shelter in their accustomed role. All her life Welthy had been working with people who were running from themselves. Knowing how large were the steps in the journey forward, she displayed extraordinary patience with the difficult ones who lagged along the way unsure of themselves.

The treatment was genuine friendliness mixed with subtle or not-so-subtle prodding, depending on the situation. While setting her own priority for the next months in India—making the ILB the grantee instead of WE, getting support for Comfort Shaw to build a centre, holding extra-curricular study groups with the staff, and getting plans made for the Young Farmers' Institute on new land finally acquired—she turned and asked me: "Now what are you going to teach in India this year?" Considering myself rather busy at it was, in my lingering nine-to-five mentality, I still relished what I thought was free time and had never thought of doing more.

Having taught me some culinary basics in the tiny kitchen of her New York apartment, where she wielded a mighty knife with efficiency and determination, always finding a new, thrifty way of mixing, cooking and serving leftovers in the shortest possible time, Welthy was ambitious to pull me further along. She thought I could do anything. Watching her give her all cleaning, scrubbing, polishing, organizing in the kitchen, yet making it an adventure full of mystery and zest, I saw a marvelous example of rechannelling energy. Those 'instant vacations' enabled her to return to the main work immediately, her life and work one and the same, no separation of time or space required.

In my first three years with Welthy we travelled to every major city in the United States on strenuous fund-raising tours. Staying in peoples' homes and being constantly entertained in each place was exhausting, as were the speeches, radio, TV and newspaper interviews at each stop. When I wilted, Welthy braced up to greet everyone who thronged to meet her, unable to say no, but grateful when I finally rescued her. While I tried to keep the media focusing attention on the work, they invariably were drawn more deeply to her personality, their cynicism temporarily suspended, to the point that A.M. Rosenthal, of the *New York Times* wrote that "she is one of the few people . . . who impart confidence and strength by believing and proving that life and love do have meaning."[42] That and similar expressions were the clearest sign that Welthy was doing something important in the world in her relentless strategy of creative friendship to build bridges of communication between people.

In the beginning I stayed because Welthy was fascinating and I could not believe she was real. I waited with small-minded readiness to find her fatal flaw. She had flaws to be sure, minor ones enhanced by age and easy to recognize, but they were insignificant in the light of her consistent commitment to serve her chosen cause. She had a greater affinity for someone with my raw instinct than with the careful postulations of specialists and academics who often seemed self-serving.

Living round the clock and round the year with her, I knew that Welthy put as much internal energy into the effort as the external magnetism the public saw. She crumbled with pain and weariness into highly disciplined prayer and meditation, drawing on inner resources for balance, seeking strength to sing her song one more time. She needed me, and I obviously had a need to be needed, basic psychology she understood well.

There was the accumulating mental stress of leading a reluctant international movement towards literacy. There were not just organizations to entice into action, but each one of their varied individual personalities wanting direct nourishment from Welthy. And there was my own increasing dependence on her spiritual strength, which she recognized and used to guide or goad me into more concrete activity in areas where I had some talent that met her purpose, though she never told me precisely what to do or how to do it.

WORLD LITERACY OF CANADA

Specifically, I found myself making the building and programme plans for the new campus library, working with Comfort Shaw on his plans for the new Eastern Uttar Pradesh Adult Education Centre in the poorest area of the state, with the redoubtable Durgabai Deshmukh on plans for the Literacy House South building in Hyderabad, with Shivpuri on the dormitory at the YFI, and with Sheila Trivedi to develop Welthy's ideas for the Family Life Centre. All these efforts were designed to give teeth to her concept of functional literacy.

In each case I was reluctant, believing the initiative should come from an Indian. When there was such need, Welthy thought it extravagant to worry about one's nationality, and prodded me to action. I was then the representative of WLC, and with the strong assistance of Bryan Wannop of the Canadian International Development Agency (CIDA) and George Jackson of Canadian University Students Overseas (CUSO), WLC readily agreed to support each of these new projects. The Canadian government doubled, and later tripled any funds raised by WLC through the national Miles for Millions marches, and WLC became well established as a responsible non-governmental organization in international development work, increasing their annual budget tenfold during those years.[43]

Through me Welthy had been pulling some Canadian strings, and won the personal support and respect of Lester B. Pearson, a statesman with intuitive capacity who relished her company during informal summertime gatherings in Canada and lent his support to WLC. James George, the Canadian High Commissioner in India then, took a personal interest that helped make things move in a way his predecessors had not.

With innumerable individuals Welthy repeated the performance, reaching into every kind of microcosm represented by friends, relatives, colleagues and total strangers, enlisting their various strengths in outreach. That brainstorming was genius at work, and most of us through whom she achieved each step are strangely quieted after such a strong flooding through our beings. Depending on our individual states of development, we have gone on, marked time, or slipped backwards since her death, but none of us will ever be the same. A seed was planted that has a life of its own.

FOLLOWSHIP, NO, LEADERSHIP, YES

Was there some law of nature that said leaders must face their largest opposition from within their own inner circle, from those who profess the principle of cooperative association? The more I saw of the organizations Welthy led, and realized my own erratic response to her challenge, the more I understood how terribly alone she really was, without peers. She was surrounded by people who could catch her vision in isolated flashes, but who were unprepared by learning or experience to weave it into a strong fabric of their own. But Welthy had no desire for blind followers; she wanted leaders. And if she seemed impatient, her very enduring presence was a profound act of patience as she waited for us to grow.

The few exceptions were people such as Laurie Baker, and a handful of Indians who had the advantage of ancient wisdom at their disposal, and each in his or her own way did establish the centres the AID grant had envisaged. But the ILB knew better than to be bound bureaucratically to a network of organizations for which it had responsibility but no authority. What actually transpired was a spontaneous, natural outgrowth resulting from the many off-campus workshops, training sessions, and translations of teaching and reading materials into the many languages of Indian cultures, sponsored by Literacy House in different parts of India.

It is difficult to believe that Welthy could move and manage so much, that she could lift herself out of the chains of her battered body and the stress of difficult travel to rally for each opportunity to promote literacy. In Nepal, for instance, where U.S. Ambassador Carol Laise brought Welthy together with the Nepal Women's Organization and Sushila Thapa, a leading parliamentarian, Welthy made a vivid presentation of the meaning of their ninety-five percent illiteracy. In Benares at the Gandhian Institute, Welthy was the self-appointed chairman of a meeting that laid the groundwork for Literacy House cooperation in building literacy into the ongoing social service work of the Sarva Seva Sangh.

In Madras she marched into the office of the manager for tractors and farm equipment at Massey Ferguson with a proposal for assistance, and went on to Kerala to find Laurie Baker, who sat right down with Shivpuri to make the YFI second stage plans. Welthy was a facilitator extraordinaire as she brought people and ideas together, and created the opportunity and incentive for them to work them out.

LITERACY HOUSE EXAMPLE FOLLOWED

In addition to Literacy House South started by Durgabai, Dr. Mohan Sinha Mehta, whom Welthy and S.C. Dutta attracted to the ILB, established Seva Mandir in Udaipur and his dedicated leadership brought continuing support within India and from WLC and the Dutch Comité. In Madya Pradesh, Krishna Aggarwal's work was inspired by Welthy's example, and shows a similar durability of purpose and support. Comfort Shaw's centre in Deoria, designed to be self-supporting, has won consistent government support for extension under Madan Singh's leadership.

As head of the Directorate of Adult Education, Government of India, Dr. Koshy was thoroughly imbued with the Literacy House approach and materials in developing the beginnings of the national literacy effort.

The WE representative reported to WE that "no institution in India I can learn of has the resources of all kinds that exist here at Literacy House. One of these resources is very definitely Welthy's own intuition regarding programme needs. What is required is someone to translate her ideas into sound pedagogical and administrative terms. There is little wrong with her basic ideas. Things fall apart in the implementation, with which she should not have to concern herself at all.[44]

Welthy had proclaimed food and family life the other points of the trinity she called the Three F's of functional literacy. J. C. Mathur, then the Joint Secretary of Agriculture and a prolific Hindi author, followed Welthy's lead by providing the needed educational and administrative framework in developing the Farmers' Functional Literacy Programme on a national scale, attracting large support from UNESCO and the interest of all developing countries. The most consistently active member of her board, Mathur gave impetus to India's first large-scale experiment in literacy, forerunner to the present National Adult Education Programme.[45]

The representative reported that Welthy had borne the brunt of the ILB meeting in which they insisted upon the director's resignation. "The more I see of this incredible woman and her indomitable spirit, the more impressed I am."[46]

WORLD EDUCATION'S TIES TO AID

Welthy had done what she set out to do, and what she was instructed to do by WE, but because the structure was informal and WE lacked control, few of her compatriots could see what she had achieved. They wrote and talked about it in public promotions, but they missed the essence as they turned increasingly to the U.S. Government, the only agency with sufficient funds to provide for New York administrative overhead and high-priced experts to move into strategically selected countries. Welthy had repeatedly urged more modest salaries for the people WE sent out in their new global push, with family planning the new banner of its flagship.

I heard one of WE's experts say that he saw no reason why he should lower his standard of living, as he spent far more time in the watering holes of Delhi than at Literacy House or in the villages. Such people caused much curiosity in the Indian Government and among some Indian educators, who waited with relish, and the occasional boost of anonymous letters, for them to fall into their own trap. With the pressure for zero foreign aid building up and accompanying suspicions of CIA involvement, few of the "experts" remained for any length of time.

As WE's annual meeting rolled around in 1969, Welthy had her first real case of hypochondria and was very easily persuaded to stay home in bed, resting her aching legs. That was the meeting that decided to seek AID family planning funds and change the very nature of WE's work, with literacy no longer the focus.

In pursuit of the largest pocket of U.S. Government money then available for aid to non-government organizations — population control — WE forfeited Welthy's imprint. With that shift in both programme and funding policy, WE turned away from the people-to-people approach she nurtured and relinquished the spiritual imperative which she identified at the root of motivation for teacher, learner and supporter. From its pioneer beginnings WE was moving into the new era of corporate global development.

NEVER TOO OLD TO CARE

Welthy saw all this happening and did not lose faith in any of us who disappointed her. "I dare not become too old to care," she would say to any who could listen, but all her boards in four countries felt they had no further real need of her, that they knew what to do and how. She loomed too large for them, overshadowing their own ambitions, and when she had the floor she waltzed too merrily, talked too long. Times were changing, the pioneering days were ending, and if Welthy felt the chill from her organizations she did not let it affect her relationships nor keep her from moving about the world at her own expense.

Commenting on her distaste for committee meetings, I once suggested that she might be a bit undemocratic. "Yes," she admitted, "but I'm democratic in my dealings with people."

It was good to be warmly welcomed back at Lal Bagh Methodist Church in Lucknow each time we returned, and by workers and students who appreciated her practical Christianity. When she felt the need for change from organizational anxieties, she escaped into a teacher training session, taking pleasure in reminding the young men and women of Emerson's dictum: "What you are speaks so loud I can't hear what you say." The words were always made memorable by a dramatic dance of hands, arms and feet that added a good laugh to the learning. How she loved those trainees, and how they knew it!

TICKETLESS TRAVELLERS

There was one hilarious occasion when Welthy joined the ranks of thieves and criminals. We had been in West Bengal visiting Tagore's *Santiniketan* and the Mount Hermon School Fred had begun in Darjeeling, both places where Welthy got and gave inspiration, and were heading back to Lucknow on a Sunday to receive the President of Florida Southern College early the next morning. Alas, our seats on the plane were not confirmed and it took off full of school children with long-standing reservations to go home for the holidays, leaving us virtually stranded.

We sped to the next small town, Siliguri, in a taxi that was not supposed to exist, to catch a westbound train on the verge of departure. We had no rupees left, only travellers checks and American dollars, with no way of changing them in the still, dry, hot Sunday town. So we simply boarded the empty, spacious air-conditioned salon car, the only available space, establishing squatters' rights in the splendid comfort of its two long settees.

All the railroad officials of Bengal seemed to appear out of the air, pressing in to our coach to repeat and repeat again that there was no rule they could follow to permit us to travel. "Only rupees, memsahib. Please get off the train." Time and again I explained our predicament, pleading for compassion, pointing out that in that International Tourist Year the Indian Railways might accept our travellers checks. I assured them we would wire ahead for Literacy House to meet the train with our fares. Meanwhile all the passengers from the other cars got down and gathered outside our window to assist in the debate about the foreign ladies, peering with interest through the curtain as they learned about Welthy's work in my expanding plea.

I kept trying to get her to look ill and aged, to lie back on the couch, but she could not play that role and leapt into the discussion with vigour. The officials insisted: "There is no way; we must follow the rules." We kept saying: "You must find a way." They disappeared, returning after a tense interval to say we could stay. East and West had met, reluctantly, and the train departed an hour late.

The young Bengali worker who manned the air-conditioning from a cubicle in our car became friendly after that and spoke to us often, between times of writing a letter to his mother, on the twenty-eight hour journey. The next morning as we neared Lucknow he presented the letter to Welthy, a simple, painstakingly penned, magnificent testimony of his gratitude for her work, along with fifty precious rupees. It was one of the many unforgettable faces of India, of an individual who could see the world in a grain of sand, one of the many lives touched by Welthy in ways beyond measurement.

Word of the "Two Ticketless Travellers who boarded the train forcibly" had preceded us, and we were greeted instantly on arrival by two suspicious railroad officials, who were themselves intercepted by Ariel with the rupees that prevented our arrest.

INDIAN RESENTMENT BUILDS

For all her strength, Welthy was subject to bouts of distress at efforts to relieve her of burdensome detail, but she managed to have enough say so that there was confusion as to who was doing what, when and with what funds. A major need was to encourage the ILB to assume full responsibility for Literacy House, make the hard decisions and select strong leadership.

Welthy asked her good friend Mathur for his opinion on the dilemma. He reported that the representative was dictating to the ILB in a peremptory, offensive manner, doling out monthly rations of money. The ILB wanted direct consultation with AID rather than through the representative tativetativeof WE. Mathur felt the ILB's absence of a link with the Government of India in that impossible triangle was a basic problem that could lead to misunderstanding, since the outreaching purpose of the grant was not consistent with the government's cautious stance on literacy.[47]

Feeling some urgency about the problem, I tried to act as a filter between Welthy and the board, but she quite naturally resented my involvement, leading to an interval when her suspicion and anxiety over my motives was discouraging. It was not difficult to see it all as impossible, and I contemplated running away.

Such brooding was inevitably short-lived, interrupted by the next batch of visitors, such as the Philadelphia String Quartet, whom we had heard at one of its Indian concerts. "Come on out to Literacy House," Welthy urged the musicians, "we'll have some fun," and they did, starting with a lively lunch in Welthy's cottage, followed by a tour of the campus and capped with a puppet show in a village. By the end of the day the Quartet had decided to give a benefit concert in Seattle, not so much as a charitable act but to express their involvement with something powerful the players had sensed in a fleeting moment of oneness with the villagers. No one was safely beyond Welthy's reach.

RETURN TO LAKELAND, FLORIDA

In the months we spent fund raising in Holland, Canada and the States between 1967 and 1970, the scene varied from gold-plated splendour in a private Palm Beach palace to simple gatherings in church basements. One superb memory of Welthy stands out, in all her glory at Florida Southern College to celebrate the thirtieth anniversary of the temple and garden of meditation she built there, and launch its new Indian exchange programme.

The students put on a stirring performance of Tagore's "The Sacrifice" around the reflection pool by moonlight and torchlight with the audience seated on the gentle grassy slopes enveloping it. In her pale green silk sari gown, the wind and moonlight enhancing her sparkle, Welthy was at her radiant best. Standing on a little platform in front of the pool, the gleaming temple in the background, she spoke from the depths of her heart, her strength renewed in response to life and beauty around her. Frailty dissolving, no one saw her crooked cane that evening.

From the sublime to the mundane, overnight, we arrived at the Bank of New York on Fifth Avenue for a private luncheon to celebrate Welthy's fiftieth anniversary as a customer. It is a bank with a difference, where the rattle of small change is not heard, and ladies enter through their private door on a side-street to freshen up in a beautifully appointed rest room before conducting their business with the woman manager of that discreet salon. Shades of Cousin Dee who had introduced Welthy there.

In Detroit to speak at Central Methodist Church, we were guests again of the Pinkstaffs, entertained at a lively luncheon. Afterwards I urged Welthy to rest for her next engagement, but it was not long before we all ran in to investigate a noise. There she was, prancing about trying on everyone's hat in the guest bedroom, banished but unbowed.

In our travels we always stopped in Rome, N.Y., and in Syracuse, whenever possible, going by car, staying in motels, and grabbing a quick rest and a snack before an event. Welthy adjusted her prayers to our timetable: "Thank God for Sally and the soup." As for soup, there was only one kind, tomato.

* * *

The pattern of colonial, imperial control was cracking all around the world, nowhere more strongly than in America, whose stunned majority found difficulty accepting the problems as their own. Seething emotions after years of the Vietnam War, John F. Kennedy's assassination, then Martin Luther King, Jr. and Bobby Kennedy, culminated in soul-scarred youth unable to heal themselves with their anguished songs. Eternal dimensions thrust to the forefront, demanding recognition. America's innocent sense of virtue could never be the same, a change Welthy welcomed, recognizing the pain of real growth.

The United States was troubled, pressure building up throughout the sixties and erupting on city streets everywhere, until one year near the end of the decade we came back and there was a noticeable difference. We had been so much in India, mentally and physically, that the change seemed sudden. Young blacks in colourful clothes and Afro haircuts were highly visible in their newfound pride and confidence. They had decided to be what they were, Americans, and claim full citizenship.

Welthy had quietly kept her ties to blacks through the years, always going out of her way to speak at Mrs. Arbouin's Negro Christian Women's Annual Retreat, not an affluent source of funds but as important as any other group which gave her an opportunity to reach out to people. They presented Welthy with several hundred dollars for Literacy House, sacrificial support by many individual Americans that may never have been fully understood in India. On the rare occasions when someone faulted Welthy for not taking up the cause of blacks in America, Welthy tried to explain that out of her own experience she was better qualified to put her energy to work in India.

The new Indian Ambassador in Washington, Nawab Ali Jung, came to lunch and told Welthy he had first heard of her from Zakir Husain when they spoke of foreign aid to India. Now President of India, Husain said that Mrs. Fisher's Literacy House was the best example of the kind of help India needed and the kind that really works. It was a rewarding testimonial, considering his warning to her years earlier that education should be self-supporting. Even with the power of the government trying to meet it, Husain now recognized that India's educational need was in a class by itself in complexity and size.

Welthy needed and loved those salutes to her long efforts. And her heart was greatly relieved when Mike Honsinger announced in 1968, after visiting Literacy House and finding it much more than he had appreciated, that WE would be his main retirement interest. With assistance from Doris Ward, he injected new life into a dwindling board and succeeded in keeping the organization from crumbling during several difficult years. For that he won Welthy's eternal gratitude.

TOM KEEHN AT WORLD EDUCATION

Tom Keehn's arrival as full time executive director that same year was a turning point for WE. She personally guaranteed his salary for two years, the condition on which he agreed to take the position. With a large family to support, his great concern was that Welthy's impatience would not allow him enough time to build up the organization from its weakened position. Welthy's concern had never been to build up WE, and she kept her energy focused on LH in search of financial security for the staff and their families.

My diary reflects the increasing solidarity between Welthy and me. "She just loves to get her hands on a sinner like me and try to work wonders. I think she is bored by people who aren't struggling. We have achieved a kind of unity that seems indestructible, despite my resentful moods and her impossible expectations. We have a lot of fun and the days rush by, but I must learn to share her more and not try to reserve her affection for me. She believes in being accessible to anyone at any time, and I must help her do that and not always try to spare her energy. For such a strong, determined old gal she is amazingly pliable on some things and this is where I must not act in my own self interest."

I did learn that even though she might agree on some particular action, it could well be the opposite of what she really wanted. Things worked best when I allowed enough time to be certain of her wishes. Small matters of trains, planes, boats, food, hotels, etc. she left to me entirely, as well as the managing of her checking account. By some miracle she was always ready sitting on her suitcase in the front hall long before I could get out the door, and could guess almost to the cent the balance in her bank account, though inflation had changed all the figures. Years of careful living on limited funds had given her a keen sense of value that telescoped into our domestic expenses.

In Anchorage Welthy spoke from the pulpit of the Methodist Church at both morning services and took on the Presbyterians in the evening. She repeated the performance in Los Angeles, and in Honolulu spoke to students at the East-West Centre at a memorial celebration of Gandhi's birthday. Giving the students just what they wanted, she made Gandhi come alive with warmth and humour. I had never seen her so sharp and smooth, though there was absolutely no fund-raising potential on that occasion.

Finally Hong Kong, arriving late in the afternoon when the sun spreads its magic touch on the panorama of sea and mountains and skyscrapers centering around that eternally fascinating harbour that Welthy saw with fresh eyes each time. She could scarcely wait to disembark — I teased her that it said 'Don't walk on the wings WELTHY,' such was her eagerness to be out of the plane first, to dash around the shops and reabsorb the scene. I had a genuine appreciation of Chinese food from my time in Indochina and could enthusiastically share meals with her former Chinese students in their homes or in the multi-layered restaurants of Nathan Road which was the ultimate qualification for companionship on the move.

INDIA, 1969

Those moments of delight were brief. Once back in Lucknow in 1969 we found the new director in a mood to simply close down Literacy House when he finally looked into the books and realized how dependent it was on AID. I had been trying with little result to encourage the ILB to plan an income budget targeted at different sources of income. But in the absence of real financial authority they had continued to operate with an expense budget only, believing that AID or Mrs. Fisher would provide.

The five year term of the grant was ending, with considerable money still unspent. An expanded campus and staff with an outreaching programme was about to have no support unless something was done quickly, and in default of others I jumped into the breach to do the only thing immediately possible to save the institution. At the time I was a trustee of WE and felt responsible to act. I later resigned.[48] No one at Literacy House had any taste or talent for reporting in detail to AID. There was no record of real progress under the grant, and so I went painstakingly around each department insisting that they produce the quantitative information required to build a composite picture of progress, the only foundation on which a request for extending the period of the grant could be based. I was relieved when Martha Keehn arrived and put all the material together in an impressive report which convinced AID to authorize a two-year extension to use the unexpended funds.[49]

At the meeting in Delhi where AID officials agreed to recommend the extension, I urged John P. Lewis, head of AID in India, that the extension be granted directly to Literacy House and not World Education. That was already his inclination, and Literacy House won the extension, entering a new era in its institutional life.

When Mrs. Martin Luther King, Jr. came to India in 1969 to receive a posthumous award for her husband, Welthy wanted to meet her, to feel in the flesh the link of democratic idealism between India and America. After a moving speech, Coretta King's secretary tried to whisk her away but several prominent Indian women insisted that Welthy was a woman she must meet. For a few all-encompassing moments the two women made profound contact. It was a good sign to me to keep the door open, not to impose my pedestrian sense of time on opportunities for those spontaneous moments that meant more in the long run than all the policy and paperwork of organizations.

Speaking on Founder's Day at Literacy House that year, Jayaprakash Narayan, Gandhian follower of Vinoba Bhave and reluctant politician, said in the plainest language that the illiterate democracy had given birth to corrupt electioneering, and the villagers remained slaves to arbitrary power thrust upon them. Rural literacy was of paramount importance, he warned from Welthy's platform. And in a lighter vein, drawing a good laugh from the crowd under the *shamiana*, he said that Welthy must have owed immensely to India in her previous birth to have come out so late in life to found Literacy House. Despite the high visibility of prominent educators and high-level state and central politicians that day, Welthy was seen to be "the most attractive and dominant personality on the dais."[50]

NEHRU LITERACY AWARD

Rashtrapati Bhavan, New Delhi, March 10, 1969. In that elegant Presidential palace, Welthy rose to her full stature, the deep mauve of her georgette sari gown matching the glitter of the occasion with its regal trim of red, silver and gold, taking her rightful place on centre stage as Zakir Husain presented the first Nehru Literacy Award. The award was given on behalf of the Indian Adult Education Association which had polled its members working in the field for their recommendations, with an overwhelming vote for Welthy. In accepting the award Welthy told the assembled dignitaries:

> *India has a deep and enduring message to share with the rest of the world which desperately needs it... There remains the tremendous communication gap, that division of humanity between the educated and the uneducated. Until India's rural people can unite in extending this message, it will never be heard clearly.*

Referring to the symbolic scattering of Nehru's ashes over the villages of India, Welthy said that she took the honour as a new directive to focus her efforts on the villagers, to engage more fully in the discovery of India hidden in uneducated village souls.

Dr. Mohan Sinha Mehta, then President of IAEA and a member of the ILB, urged Welthy to put her ideas on paper for the future development of Literacy House, which he hoped to see grow into a truly national institution. Welthy did not respond, convinced as she was that Literacy House had no future unless the ILB took the responsibility for shaping it, and that they, not she, should elaborate the specific policy and plans.

The publicity of the award sparked fresh interest in literacy and in Welthy, one of the national newspapers running a cartoon on the editorial page showing Prime Indira Gandhi chairing a cabinet meeting of large, old men — asleep around the table — and quoting Welthy: "The average Indian woman lives in a world of no change!" And in the Indian civil service exams that year one of the general awareness questions related to Welthy and the break-away she led from the former narrow, limited meaning of literacy.

As if to will her vision for Literacy House vicariously into enduring form, Welthy did respond to the request of the Vice-Chancellor of *Santiniketan*, Dr. K. Bhattacharya, to give critical direction for their future work. Welthy urged revitalizing the creative workers, saddened as she was by their output: "I felt that the enthusiasm was in the past, not in the present day needs of industry. They were not finding out what things they could create with their trained fingers that would appeal to buyers." Dr. Bhattacharya found her criticism acceptable." What of Mrs. Fisher strikes me most," he wrote,[51] "is her straight manner of approach. . . all the essential features put so tellingly without indulging in any vague platitudes. . . with the good points that she found still lingering. . . and the pardonable and unpardonable defects that had crept in and developed to appreciable dimensions. She has very effectively shown how the whole educational policy of *Gurudev* grew out of his philosophy of life, and how, because of this she insisted so much on creativity, beauty, life that is both physically and spiritually healthy, genuine universalism, and humanism, village work, adult literacy and all-round integration."

If she could reinterpret Tagore to his own people, how long would it take, Welthy wondered, for Literacy House to grasp the full purpose of its founder. She believed she had made her statement of intent with her very life, yet they looked for theories and specific guidelines from her. When would they overcome their indirect approach and authorize themselves to touch the imperfect reality of bruised and dusty individual villagers with essential love? Giving that love had become as necessary to her as life itself. It was life. "Who will write the anthem of freedom for the illiterate?" was her haunting question.

MALCOLM ADISESHIAH

Dr. Malcolm Adiseshiah, who served as Minister of Education and Deputy Director General of UNESCO, articulated his country's approach to literacy clearly: "Hitherto we have been used to looking at illiteracy as a social evil. . . we have not yet realized it could be an important factor obstructing the development of the nation in so many respects. In a country like ours where the problem is colossal and resources limited, adult literacy programme should be primarily for those who are in the teenage and working age group. Production of books on an immense scale would have to be taken up. We need competent writers in different languages and bulk production of books at cheap rates."

The politician in Adiseshiah was speaking after the fact of Welthy's prophetic act of placing her strategic pilot project on the harsh Indian soil. "In our country," Adiseshiah went on to say, "except for a few isolated, far-sighted individuals and a few voluntary organizations. . . there has not been much enthusiasm and whole-hearted support for this movement from Governmental sources."[52]

It was more than fifteen years since Welthy had begun her efforts. Would her work really make any impression on the overwhelming facts of Indian poverty? She dared not speculate. Whatever life remained for her could only be used to reinforce her conviction of the possibility. My own thought was increasingly towards finding ways to help Welthy wean Literacy House from her, financially and emotionally, and also admittedly to lessen the strain. I felt I was unofficial liaison between the ILB and WE. I was beginning to understand the situation and the needs, tempted to act where I really should not — by administrative criteria at least — and feeling pulled in all directions, not the least by Welthy, ever impatient for action. The situation looked more and more complex; something had to give. Welthy was not about to. I hoped it wouldn't be me, and escaped to have an electrocardiogram, to Welthy's astonishment. My heart was fine; the problem was elsewhere.

We kept moving — London, Paris, Amsterdam, New York, Ottawa, California, Hong Kong, New Delhi, Lucknow — servicing an unformed, implicit, quasi-international association for literacy, adding fuel to the idea with each global sweep. For Welthy there was only one approach — press on, press on. For me, fifty years short on experience and many more in understanding, there was a need to stop and think, assess, consolidate, find my own approach — the slow, cautious way of my conditioning. Her need for help was palpable and her push so certain that I never doubted her basic committed wisdom. My incipient stretching could continue gestating as we worked within her chosen battleground. I remained in perpetual attendance. And there was the undeniable fun and fascination of our fast pace.

PEARL BUCK REVISITED

In April 1970, en route to speak at a college in Pennsylvania, Welthy suddenly pointed to a road sign marked 'Perkasie.' "Let's stop and find Pearl Buck," she said. "I spent a weekend with her here twenty years ago and haven't seen her since." We found the old stone house in the countryside as though pre-arranged, presented Welthy's card and within minutes were warmly welcomed by Pearl, a white-haired vision in a beautiful floor-length Chinese silk gown of emerald green, which she had obviously donned in haste expressly for Welthy. I was star-struck while Welthy greeted her good friend and the two settled into intensely animated conversation.

Pearl said it had taken her four years to translate "All Men are Brothers" into Chinese, the classic text used by the Communists as a handbook for guerilla warfare. Mao always carried a copy in his knapsack. "Whatever his ideology," she said, "Mao is a great man. China went Communist because the ruling class did nothing for the people. I never thought I'd see the Asian revolution in my lifetime. The war brought it on. I thought colonialism would last at least another hundred years."

We learned later that the Chinese refused Pearl admission to China when it reopened to foreigners because of that very lack in her vision, charging that her books exploited Chinese poverty.

SUCHETA KRIPALANI

We had more female intensity in the person of Sucheta Kripalani, former Chief Minister of Uttar Pradesh, visiting with us in Welthy's New York apartment for a week. She told of her severe disappointment in Indira Gandhi as Prime Minister for her lack of vision, willingness to listen to the Communists and depending on advice from a small, ambitious clique. Welthy understood that Sucheta's view was predicated on a strong pro-American, pro-Taiwan stance of an earlier era; she also understood the vast realities Indira faced as leader of all India.

At the time, Sucheta's husband, *Acharya* Kripalani, was being mentioned as successor to Zakir Husain, the deceased President of India, but Sucheta was certain Indira would not want him because he had a strong wife and spoke his mind sharply. She was right about that.

NINETIETH BIRTHDAY

There was another swing through the United States to mark Welthy's ninetieth birthday in fund-raising style. Central Methodist Church in Detroit established the Welthy Fisher Career Enablement Fund to help students complete their education.

In Rome Welthy was quoted: "Let's believe that we can become world neighbours. We're going to make better landings in this world, because it can be done."

At Mount Ida College, where she had been a trustee for some years, they saw "a tall, vibrant woman speaking with such confidence and hope, a woman of courage and goodwill, charm, compassion and wit. Her strong face with lines of hard work, study, sympathy and many summers. Her eyes twinkle with the sense of humor that only the really wise can know. She is dressed in ageless chic."

Of the many who wrote congratulating Welthy on yet another chronological milestone, distinguished men consistently referred to her energy, enthusiasm, youthfulness and capacity for friendship. Women responded in a deeper vein, as Nancy Wilson Ross wrote: "Your warmth, loving-kindness, unselfishness and buoyant sense of 'sharing' keep me — and my likes — from ever feeling inadequate or even stiffly deferential in your presence. You seem to possess the singular power to arouse a sense of being at least potentially equal to your challenge."

And from three who knew her well from collaborating on her autobiography: Lael Wertenbaker classed Welthy with Pablo Casals and Pablo Picasso, the only two other human beings she knew who had been as totally alive for as long, with the same quality of creative dedication. "You have lived to see many of the fruits of your labors harvested," wrote Lael, "and you have settled without despair for those fruits which were destroyed." Mavis McIntosh, her agent, saw Welthy as "a real revolutionary, not just helping people but giving them the tools to set themselves free." And Susan Gleaves said that ever since she first walked into Welthy's apartment life had been more. "To work with you is unlike working with anyone else. We laugh more, for one thing. And feel more deeply. You bounce so beautifully, getting higher all the time. (I half expected you would be waiting for the astronauts on the moon.) And we bob along behind you enjoying the altitude."

In India, land of the verbally effusive, Jayaprakash Narayan's birthday tribute to Welthy cut eloquently to the core as he called her "the other Nightingale."

* * *

Love and honours had come to Welthy in abundance but it was never enough to make her sit down and reflect on a job well done. She turned the momentary reward into restorative fuel to live out the rest of her days in the only way she knew how, fully out on the world stage.

A few days after her ninetieth birthday, we packed up Welthy's New York apartment, which she had sold for thirty-seven thousand dollars to generate needed income, disposed of most of her possessions and shipped the rest to India. We had come from the first joint meeting of the WE and WLC boards where they dipped their oars gingerly into the concept of international association with the ILB and cooperators in Holland, the U.K. and Jamaica, a concept implicit in everything Welthy did.

Papers on purpose, policy and procedure were emerging far too slowly. As Welthy had done in 1920, she simply took the ball and ran, daring to believe there would be a team to catch it. She was more than ready to risk a broader plan, to carve more crude steps into the future, using whatever means were left to her in her tenth decade. Let the critics crit. She knew that the imprisoned illiterate was more than ready.

In November 1969 we set out for India once more, stopping in Europe to win people to the expanding idea. One magical day floating through Europe on the Rheingold Express Welthy was nearly overwhelmed by a profound clotting nosebleed that I knew was a sure sign of exhaustion. She rested for a day. Back on the train the following day she almost choked to death when a piece of meat caught in her windpipe; I was observed by wary Europeans clouting an elderly woman mercilessly on her back, a technique I had mastered through varied experience with Welthy on the run. We were surviving together.

As Welthy returned to India in late 1969 there was yet another American Ambassador new to the scene, but not to Welthy. In Kenneth Keating she found a good match. Those two up-state New Yorkers sparked each other in rambunctious, informal banter that eased their way. He was her fifth American Ambassador to India and she knew by now what made them tick, how to enlist their cooperative support. Her reputation had preceded them to India,[53] each new face presenting her with a challenge to leap over protocol to the practical possibilities of working together. The new idea of an international association for literacy, based in New Delhi, would need just that kind of collaboration.

TEN

ENDURING VISION

There was method in her movement. For survival Welthy had to satisfy her unquenchable need for new friends and new ideas wherever she went in the world, reaching out to that point of human connection where life is enhanced. Certain that the best was yet to be, she created her own reason for living in promoting a broader coalition for literacy as a fundamental human right and anticipating the adoption of this stance by UNESCO.

Her confidence and hope were plain to see, her face strong and warm, open and wise. When Welthy was in a room, you knew it. There was a glamour to her goodness. The movement of people towards her was as natural as the sea rushing to meet the shore. That others drifted away was just as natural as waves receding into the vastness of the ocean. One could feel the erotic impulse of her presence, spiritual and sensual at once.[1] We wanted what she had. It was as if she knew the way home.

Publicly Welthy became one year older, almost flaunting a deliciously outrageous sureness of self as she claimed the missing year. Living as if each day were the morning of her life, she seemed indestructible, but as the daily domestic struggle grew heavier, we both knew she was not.

From the time I first went with Welthy the conventional wisdom of friends told me to look to my own future, that Welthy could die at any time. From my family I heard the less-than-subtle message that Welthy was too bold, too confident, too talkative, and that my supporting service to her in a distant part of the world was demeaning work of questionable result. What did I have to show for it?

Living and working in an unstructured, cooperative, floating commune of two, Welthy and I were not following the established ways of society. That we both had some financial resources made it possible.[2] That neither of us could be pushed or pulled off course affirmed our joint pursuit.

Our lives were so intertwined that by osmosis some of her essence attached to me. I felt her ultimate loneliness acutely and became committed to Welthy and her work, an indivisible, authentic whole. In some ways she had become as dependent on me for physical and emotional security as I was on her for intellectual and spiritual strength.

Whether it was a mother/daughter, daughter/mother, sisterly, guru/student, boss/secretary, dowager/companion, invalid/nurse relationship is irrelevant. What was real was the enhancing energy we gave to each other freely, moving ourselves to action under very difficult circumstances, living within the elastic boundaries Welthy wisely allowed. We both knew that whatever we continued to do together would evolve freely on its own, no strings attached.

INDIA, FALL 1969

One of the most difficult tasks Welthy ever faced was letting go of Literacy House. I felt strongly the need to ease her way in this, to take up the enormous slack. We had found a large house in New Delhi for the Literacy Information Centre. Beginning tentatively by gathering and disseminating information on literacy work underway in the world seemed an obvious place to start, since no one else was doing it and I had the necessary skills. The house, mainly financed by Welthy and me personally, was large enough to serve as residence, accommodation for some staff and visitors, office and meeting place.

Welthy was interested and anxious to help develop the international work, but always it was Literacy House pulling her, that place on the ground where the truth would find its way or not. She needed to be there. On the very day our ox-drawn liftvan of belongings was finally cleared through Indian customs and made its way along the Ring Road to Maharani Bagh on the outskirts of Delhi, Welthy and I caught the night train to Lucknow after accomplishing the move into our new quarters. How she loved creating an instant home, rushing about as excited as a young bride putting everything in place.

Immediately on arrival at Literacy House she pressed me to arrange transport to the Young Farmers Institute. Well aware of the Literacy House staff's tendency to please her with preparedness, Welthy wanted to see the state of affairs at the farm with her own eyes, unannounced. We set off for the Bijnaur campus by jeep with the *Gurkha* driver, turning off the *pukka* road onto the *kuchha* road for the last few miles. Suddenly we came upon an accident; our overseer had got word of *Mataji's* movements and was speeding ahead by motorcycle when he caught a village woman's sari in the wheel, dragging her along the ground some distance. He was bleeding profusely from the head and nose, and she lay on the ground moaning.

Villagers streamed to the scene from all directions. We looked at each other swiftly—the injured, the villagers, the driver, ourselves. We wanted to take both injured to the hospital in Lucknow in our jeep. The gathering crowd grew excited; they would not let us move the two victims. Our driver could not interpret for us. The crowd closed in, brandishing their barbaric-looking curved harvesting knives at the wheels of the jeep. It was an explosive impasse, demanding immediate action. I knew we had to get away from there fast, and indicated so to Welthy. In quick, unspoken agreement she jumped down from the jeep — a difficult manoeuvre for her — we turned our backs on the mob, and started the long walk back to the highway, arm-in-arm, along the kuchha road.

That instinct was sound, for by the time we had made our way a mile down the highway the jeep came along carrying both injured parties, with arms and legs of accompanying villagers dangling from the windows. Once our foreign presence had been removed, the crisis had been readily resolved. The woman had only minor injuries but had been feigning to elicit cash from us. The overseer paid for his precipitous good intentions with ten days' hospitalization for a broken nose and teeth.

Welthy and I then hitched a ride back to Literacy House in an ingenious, three-wheeled scooter trucklet, and were gently scolded by the director for our recklessness. He did admit, however, that the overseer would probably have been killed if we had not come along, but then the whole incident would never have happened if we had not been travelling unescorted. The lesson to us was never to travel without an interpreter, never try to be a good samaritan, get the police quickly and remember that the villagers have little to lose. Should Welthy have known better? Literacy House was built on Welthy's calculated risks in which she put herself on the line.

* * *

As a loving mother is forever a part of her children's lives, whether they like or permit it, Welthy needed her connection with Literacy House. To think that she could remove herself or sit idly by waiting for things to happen was an impossible expectation. She was still the one with the bold, imaginative ideas and the personal commitment to match them. In accepting her continuing, often demanding presence, we were all learning a lesson in loving.

Welthy could have paid much more attention to her bodily needs, to the frighteningly profuse nosebleeds, and settled for an easier life in Delhi. But she forgot them the moment they finally stopped. In her diary she kept scratching the words: "And I have miles to go before I sleep." She marked one of those miles in celebrating the hundredth anniversary of IT College, rejoicing in the eagerness of young Indian women who thronged to meet her after the unveiling of the commemorative stone bearing her name.

INDIA LITERACY BOARD

The ILB was happy enough to leave it to Welthy to terminate the employment of the director of Literacy House she had pressed them to hire so the position would not be vacant while she was in America. There followed a barrage of anonymous letters, slanderous insinuations and polarizing of the staff against Welthy and me, all very devious and destructive to Literacy House. The pressure on Welthy surrounding that particular incident was typical of the price she paid for continued involvement. The ILB did not intend to assume real responsibility until she was permanently gone from the scene. They too had a love/hate relationship with her, very much wanting her personal warmth and presence, and the money and stature she brought, yet anticipating the time when they could settle into policies and rules to fit their more bureaucratic way of operating. The British had taught them well how to wait.

As long as Welthy remained there continued to be bursts of creativity; once she was gone, Literacy House would consolidate and solidify. She knew in her bones she had to strive for as much of her vision as her beloved, adolescent institution could bear, confident of ultimate maturity. That perpetual dilemma was the result of Welthy's symbolic leadership in two different cultures, unified within herself, but still only a glimmer of possibility in those around her, no matter how nobly the words of "brotherhood" were spoken. Sisterhood was still in its infancy.

When Professor Girijapati Mukharji, retired director of the Indian Institute of Management, agreed to head the ILB, Welthy felt for the first time their sense of real administrative responsibility. At her urging,[3] he planned ways to generate revenue within India, particularly through the expanded sale of Literacy House publications and farm products. The Welthy Fisher Literacy House Endowment Fund was also begun to receive private contributions.

When Mukharji in turn sought out his mentor, Sri Bhagwan Sahay, artist and retired civil servant of distinction,[4] to chair the ILB, he left it to Welthy to make the actual catch, her eloquent, aging presence dissolving Sahay's understandable reluctance to take on an extra burden in retirement. Recalling that first encounter with Welthy,[5] Sahay said that she was a woman who made her own destiny, that she could well have been head of a state. After seeing and hearing her in person, how could one not work with her?

The ILB that Welthy had loved into being was largely an old boys' network of retired Indian civil servants, trained by the British to authority by remote control, and themselves emerging slowly from the cultural contradictions of their experience. Initially, Welthy had needed a substantial board to receive funds, and found several Indian women who played strong roles on the ILB. But as their terms expired, the men took hold when Welthy was present less often. To them it was more convenient to have fewer, less powerful women. Besides, they still had Welthy, present or absent, and she was plenty of woman to deal with.

In those difficult transition years there was a definite uneasiness as to whether Literacy House had any future at all. Welthy was restless, often difficult. So was I, but I knew I could not leave her. Welthy knew exactly what she was doing, her eye always on the larger vision. I was groping from day to day trying to help. Everything moved slowly, demanding great patience to wait for creative openings, an essential skill to learn where survival itself was priority for the majority.

Our western notions of pace and progress were irrelevant, as were some of the American "experts" who came for brief periods to advise. There was a mystery to that moment when an Indian might actually accept one into his/her realm of possibility, and unless and until that happened, an Indian 'yes' was more likely to mean maybe, or maybe not, or even definitely not. The shaking of a head in assent or dissent is in itself quite misleading, having opposite meanings between East and West. Often an Indian would agree to something simply because that was what we wanted to hear, our transparency inviting polite acquiescence. The truth is that few Indians could understand why we were all running about India trying to rush them into changes, and those who had secure positions were the last to want change of any kind.

LITERACY HOUSE SOUTH, HYDERABAD

Durgabai and C.D. Deshmukh summoned Welthy to lay the cornerstone of their Literacy House South in Hyderabad, which had come to fruition as a result of cooperation between the Deshmukhs, World Literacy of Canada, the Canadian High Commission in New Delhi and the Canadian International Development Agency. The dedication stone pays tribute to that support, much of which came through Miles for Millions Marches in Canada.

C.D. Deshmukh paid tribute to Welthy in acknowledging their motivation for establishing the centre on the Andhra Mahila Sabha campus. "The concept of functional literacy first empirically and instinctively sensed by Dr. Mrs. Welthy Fisher," he wrote,[6] "has since been clarified, refined and worked out in the field in a number of countries, to which India was added as the result of Dr. Smt. Durgabai's efforts in UNESCO."

It had been the cooperation since the mid-fifties of two powerful women, Durgabai and Welthy, that ten years later resulted in UNESCO's experimental world-wide literacy programme taking root in their largest functional literacy project in India, with wider implications in many other countries. Durgabai had seen the beginnings in Welthy's living experiment, and had the power and presence to persuade the world's

Education Ministers at the UNESCO meeting in Iran in 1965 on the future direction of their cooperation in India. This fact has been obscured and is possibly unknown by the documentors of literacy development. Under Durgabhai's strong guidance, Literacy House South became the regional centre for functional literacy in South India.

LITERACY INTERNATIONAL

Welthy and I spent most of our time in New Delhi at the new centre, trying to nudge our American, Canadian, Dutch, British, Jamaican and Indian colleagues into closer cooperation. We knew they found it difficult to appreciate our informal methods, that they wanted to be certain of their control over the development of Literacy International (LITINT). J.C. Mathur, the most insightful of Welthy's Indian colleagues in adult education, wondered why we were bent on establishing LITINT. When we met Indira Gandhi to inform her about LITINT and seek general approval of locating an international organization in New Delhi, she sniffed through the plans and indicated that international cooperation was less helpful than regional efforts in such matters.

Our timing seemed wrong, with deep distrust between India and America, intense nationalism and pressure for zero foreign aid. We knew that there would never be a perfect time, and that words alone would not convey intent and meaning. Action might. When the Government of India sent their security people to scrutinize our accounts and activities, the CIA menace looming large in their thinking, they found nothing but two foreign women renting a large house and running a small information centre with minimal financial support from a few voluntary organizations abroad.

To our western colleagues, our ad hoc methods were perplexing to say the least, but they did serve to get some good information work begun at little cost. Their old need to dominate and control from the other side of the world kept them unsure of us, a lack of confidence I felt more keenly than Welthy. She had experienced it so many times before.

We continued to probe the possible, but Welthy had little interest in the necessary organizational work to become international, and with her increasing restlessness and need for movement, I had neither time nor the requisite skills to move beyond the information work.

My preoccupation with that work left Welthy with too much time to fill, time to worry about Literacy House, leaving herself prone for another fall. I can still hear her shriek as I turned and saw her fall to the terrazzo floor of the Maharani Bagh house, scoring another pelvic crack. For a few seconds she sobbed in a dramatic outburst of self-pity: "No one knows that goes on inside of me every day . . . God should take me now . . . why do I live on?" The pain of fracture was all too familiar.

Her recovery from the shock was far swifter than mine. She instructed me to go downstairs and bring one of the dining chairs on wheels to serve as her means of transport — she was not planning to be immobilized, but was confined to bed to mend, expressing her general distaste for inactivity: "Why you're nothing but a little dictator!" A benevolent one, I suggest.[7]

By the time Welthy was able to travel we had accomplished enough work at LITINT to present a proposal to UNESCO in Paris seeking consultant status. UNESCO officials urged us to establish the LITINT headquarters in Iran, where they already had the International Institute for Adult Literacy Methods, and we went on to Teheran to discover that they too felt the need for a literacy information clearinghouse.

BRITISH COMMITTEE ON LITERACY

Welthy was invited to speak to the high-powered British Committee on Literacy at their formative meeting in the House of Commons in London. Organized by Professors John Spencer and John Bowers, and co-chaired by Conservative M.P. Sir Bernard Braine and Labour Education Minister Shirley Williams, they aimed to press for existing funds to be channelled to literacy. Welthy followed up directly with Shirley Williams: "If we women of the world take a deep interest in this entire matter of literacy, we shall begin to have a world of people in all communities and races who can communicate with each other." Language and linkage, link language, were words often on Welthy's lips.

NETHERLANDS COMMITTEE

In the Netherlands, Queen Juliana took a highly intelligent interest in the work of the Welthy Fisher Comité, speculating about the future of Literacy House after Welthy. The scene: four women at tea in a palace, Juliana and her lady-in-waiting, and Welthy with me, not so serene. Juliana, among the more liberated of the crowned, poured the tea, sign of the more progressive approach to international cooperation our Dutch friends practised. The tea party served to cement the ongoing support of NOVIB (The Dutch aid agency) for the Comité's projects so carefully developed under the leadership of Rob de Coole, the president, with the constant attention of Marijke Geertsema and Maria Schroeder Van-gogh. The Comité concerned itself with the broadest social and political consequences of literacy and the process of assisting it, endorsing literacy for freedom of the mind.

JAMAICAN ASSOCIATION FOR LITERACY

In Kingston Welthy met members of a newly forming group called JAMAL, Jamaica's first consolidated voluntary effort to promote literacy in a highly charged political atmosphere. Her visit reinforced their own sense of the purpose, lending visible support and inspiration as well as organizational connection.

THE LITERACY FACTOR DEFINED

In London again, Welthy addressed a LITINT meeting of people from eight countries organized by John Spencer, offering her vision of literacy as a function of human growth for all. "I believe in a basic ability to learn how to learn," she said, while urging acceptance of change all around us, including changing teaching methods, shifting from formal ways to unstructured, continuous learning and integrated rural development, with literacy a part of the whole. Rejecting popular theories promoting productivity or political revolution as priority for development, Welthy insisted on literacy as the cornerstone of learning.

She recognized the twin needs to re-educate the attitudes of elite opinion makers while ensuring that literacy efforts were focused on achieving the greatest human good. She called development non-violent revolution:

> *The techniques of functional literacy must be applied to a broad range of activities, not only work-oriented situations. There is a growing appreciation of the human and social elements in addition to the economic factors which have predominated in the past.*

> *Our approach to literacy must recognize its potential energy for transforming the total culture of the one who gains the insights it affords.*

> *We must find ways to insert the literacy factor into a wide array of development activities that are planned on a true partnership basis.*

> *We are asking you to be the architects of a continuous learning alliance that could elevate man's function on this earth by creating a living link between literate and non-literate man.*

Welthy marked her ninety-first birthday by travelling from Lucknow over a severely flood-breached road through a massive sea of swirling mudwater to reach Kanpur, where she was invited to address the Rotary

Club. The next night she repeated her request for cooperation to the Lucknow Rotary Club.

Her diary notes under "Agenda for Tomorrow" indicate the tenor of her talks:

> *We must act in the service of our beliefs, and believe that the challenge for the remainder of this century is to make a livable society in every sense of the word — that reveres life and honours the individual and places human values at the top of agenda.*

> *It is not illiteracy itself but what illiteracy breeds that denies all rights — hunger, disease, hopelessness.*

Those were broad, sweeping years moving about a world in which literacy was just beginning to come of age as a respected goal and a vital part of development. In Welthy's ninety-second year she slept in ninety-two different beds! I picked her up off many a hotel room floor when she had fallen in haste or fatigue while my back was turned. And when we collapsed into our bulkhead seats at takeoff for each flight, I put my neophyte hand over Welthy's gnarled, knowing hand reposing on the armrest, in silent acknowledgement of our continuing voyage. By the time we were airborn she would be asleep, leaving me to fly the plane alone.

HUMANITARIAN AWARD, LAS VEGAS, 1971

From Lucknow to Las Vegas in one swoop is a journey of light-years. At Caesar's Palace, on April 30, 1971, Welthy was chosen by Variety Clubs International over U Thant and Danny Kaye to receive their Humanitarian Award. Swishing into the grand ballroom as the band struck up "There's No Business Like Show Business," Welthy gave her grand theatrical performance at last. Regal, proud, and thrilled, she pulled a distracted ballroom of after-dinner party-goers celebrating the end of a week-long convention to their senses and their feet in standing ovation with her vision of the new dawn:

> *Your desire to give children all over the world an equal chance to be happier and more productive through programmes of health, education and recreation is my desire . . . whatever their creed or circumstance or geography. My children are the adolescent boys and girls of vast rural India . . . deprived from primary school . . . dropouts . . . pulled back by non-literate parents to the fields to help eke out a livelihood from the weary soil.*

*But they are children only in one sense . . . for these young
men and women are confronted with adult responsibilities
so early in life . . . and yet have only a child's knowledge of
the skills and attitudes necessary to develop their own lives
and that of their nation. But they are wise in the ways of
the spirit that sustains us all. They have an abundance of
innocent trust that nourishes my soul, so that I cannot hold
back.*

*We performers — teachers, entertainers, and any who would
share with others — must first learn deep lessons ourselves .
. . this generation as no generation before has a sense of the
oneness of the human family, in our various predicaments.*

*They reject the barriers that separate man from man, those
artificial barriers of race, of creed, of education and wealth.
Can we catch our breath a moment in this technological
rush through eternity? Can we think deeply enough together
about where we are really heading?*

*Can we accept some of the ancient wisdom of the past, and
blend it to meet our modern needs? Our young people say
we must, they are pulling us into the future. The spirit of innocent truth demands that we share all we have — not just
our wealth — but our very selves.*

*Educators today are beginning to think of learning as a life-
long process for all . . . whether one is a dynamic executive
in a skyscraper or a farmer toiling in the field. I pray and
believe that we are facing the dawn of a new day, when the
minds and hearts and souls of men everywhere will be free
to be their best, when non-literate man will no longer be
separated from his brothers.*[9]

Having focused all her anxiety on the future of Literacy House, Welthy
had seemingly overlooked the fact that she was homeless. Leaving Las
Vegas behind as we headed east, I drove five hundred miles a day, egged
on by Welthy's hilarious greetings to the infinite variety of cactus trees
saluting her progress across the American desert and the occasional
reach of her cane toward the accelerator. I was driving more than fast
enough, but Welthy's clock was racing. She was living on the edge of
tomorrow as we pressed on to uncertainty.

Though we had not discussed it, I think Welthy had always known that
she would return some day to the ground of her ancestors. In Rome,
New York she took me to the family burial plot under the huge pine trees

she planted years earlier to honour and protect her family. For the first time I saw a distant look on her beloved, weary face. Abram, so long gone, drew her into his realm. . . and Mabel, her adored sister and mirthful companion echoed his pull. Welthy often said that the good times she and I had together reminded her so much of Mabel, and my name often came from her lips as 'Sabel.' She fashioned many other word compressions as her time crunched on, our laughter punctuated with invisible tears.

SOUTHBURY, CONNECTICUT, FALL 1971

We continued east until we reached Blakesely territory in Connecticut. I had not realized how much Welthy identified with her Blakesley ancestors. She began signing her name Welthy BLAKESLEY Honsinger Fisher, turning more towards her mother's spirited energy for strength to keep active as long as life lasted. In one day, almost coincidentally, Welthy bought a condominium home in the adult community of Heritage Village in the gracious, rolling hills of Southbury. In nearby Waterbury and in cemeteries surrounding were Blakesely descendants of the original colonists that I kept discovering.

Welthy was going home, her own way. She realized happily that her sister Mina's son, Charles Limouze and his wife Grace lived nearby, and before long nephew Mike, the retired Rear Admiral, and his wife Norma moved to Heritage Village partly to be closer to Welthy. Ernest Lauh and his new wife Julie were still in New York City, close enough to exchange visits frequently for animated Chinese feasts. Helen and Gordon Halstead were farther away in Vermont but able to visit often enough for Welthy's sense of kinship to flourish.

Two cats completed the circle of domesticity we created. Furniture we bought almost as an afterthought one day as we sped by Syracuse on return from my cottage in Canada during a long weekend. "Stop! There's a Sears store down there—it's open," Welthy pointed from the superhighway. "Let's buy what we need here. We can take it with us and we won't lose time over the weekend." We ran through the store, Welthy's crooked cane selecting this sofa, that bed, until we had enough sale items to fill a U-Haul, which I rented, hooked up and learned to navigate on the New York Thruway. If I'd had more time to think, I might not have done it. On arrival in Southbury late that afternoon I found two workmen willing to carry the heavier items up to the new house, and we settled in that night. Welthy was ecstatic—another instant home.

It was not long before the world was tugging at her—friends, family, speaking engagements and World Education. We went all over New England, seeing everything anew. America rediscovered. A drive of one block through any town impressed Welthy with enough provocative detail to weave into many subsequent speeches. She wanted me to see the little graveyard of her Honsinger ancestors in Alburg, Vermont. We lingered in Hingham, Massachusetts, where Welthy and Fred had dreamed their future together, their house now a retreat residence of the Glastonbury Benedictine Abbey across the road. The surrounding property had been subdivided, with Fisher Road circling around, home to many more.

TEHERAN, DECEMBER 1971

Our Connecticut respite had not lasted long before Welthy wanted to be out in the world doing what she did best, meeting and moving people to action. We got as far as Iran, when the world said stop. I had been seriously concerned about the wisdom of returning to India that year, wondering if Welthy should not try staying away for longer periods. Now we had an answer.

It was midnight. We had checked out of our hotel, arrived at the Teheran airport to catch our flight to India. Chaos reigned. The entire fleet of Pakistan Airlines sat out there on the tarmac. Nothing was moving, crowds were milling restlessly, almost menacingly, no one knew what was going on. Finally, the announcement came over the loudspeaker that Pakistan had bombed India, war was on, nobody was going anywhere that night.

We stayed ten days in Teheran waiting to see if we could or should proceed to India, and eventually doubled back to the United States, spending Christmas with my family in Florida. During a phonecall to friends in Washington, someone asked Welthy what she thought about her house burning. Her first thought was of the House of Prayer in India, not the still-unaccustomed home in Southbury. It had indeed burst into flames from a fire next door, neighbours pulling out all our belongings in the middle of the coldest, blackest night. By the time we returned the roof had been replaced and everything restored to order, but the incident gave us pause, and we settled into a new reverence for the life that lovely house afforded. With Welthy's Buddhist tapestries, bright Indian embroideries and Chinese artifacts, the flavours of the world created a warm atmosphere.

WORLD EDUCATION

Now that she was living in close proximity to the World Education office and board members, Welthy was summoned frequently to their meetings. She had never been entirely comfortable with the name of the organization she headed. "What a big word 'education' is," she muttered, aware more than ever that education is not something we do to others, but a continuing process necessary to all parties in any educational effort. She knew that she herself could no longer refer lightly to her begging bowl, that it offended Indians, and that from here on we would all have to think in terms of sharing an opportunity. Whatever messages World Education was sending out would now have to reach around the world, not just India. Our minds would have to expand into a wider, deeper inclusiveness, as again and again she urged us closer to her old dream of world neighbours.

Many were drawn to serve on the World Education board, some out of a growing sense of guilt or uneasiness about inequities in the world. Everyone had fine titles, nudging them close to toppling Welthy. She poked fun at herself to make her large question to World Education tolerable. "I'm the Chairman . . . it doesn't mean anything . . . so I go and talk to them . . . talk, talk, talk," said Welthy of the lingering years between active work and death itself. "We have a debt to pay, and that is to be our best. You are doing this thing for the love of people, and until we come to this point we're not going to solve the problems in our own country nor in any other country. Our purpose is to help build up the community of living human beings."

In their increasingly complex, expanded operations, Welthy's words sounded simple, naive, outdated, unnecessary, self-evident. They were no longer listening, caught up in their own sophistication and enamoured of their ideology. Welthy tried to spark some brainstorming at a WE meeting that was announced as an informal exchange between the younger staff and the board members, but was chided for not following the agenda. "Wait until the afternoon," she was told. But I did see a spark of light on the face of one young staff member who loved Welthy for trying to cut through the compulsive verbiage, endless foreplay to a living grasp of an idea.

That afternoon Welthy asked: "Now tell me something . . . what did you decide?" No one could answer such a simple, direct question, convinced that she did not understand the complexities. Only her bold action had swept them forward before. To me, Welthy was 'the only man on the Board,' to use a euphemism of the times.

"My hands are off now," Welthy acknowledged to herself. "No one can break through the rigid plan." The rigor of institutionalization was hardening. The board members had no further need of Welthy except as a warm, old friend to be put on a pedestal, where she had never been content to rest since her youth. She pointed to the example of the World Bank in trusting the people of the countries where they gave money, but her misgivings about both WE and the U.S. Government sending so many foreign experts abroad went unheeded. There was so much she knew that they still had not understood, while they reinvented the wheel to suit the times.

She felt that she had failed to communicate the essence. Would those boards of hers in America and India ever learn to truly share the opportunity, to permit love to enter the equation between their nationalities? They were eloquent in saying yes, intellectually. But they were not yet ready to live it. Someday, someday, they will be free, she prayed. It will happen. Nothing else kept her alive but that belief in the possible.

Welthy accepted World Education's movement away from her as necessary growth, and kept her friendship with the individual members who were taking responsibility—Dick Mayo-Smith, Tom Keehn and Mike Honsinger. WE had let the Welthy Fisher Fund, established with thirty thousand dollars' seed money from Welthy and built up to nearly half a million by private gifts and pledges, "slip through the cracks."[10]

Nor did she receive recognition of her twenty years' work in India from her own government, despite recommendations on two occasions for the Freedom Medal. While Kenneth Keating was Ambassador to India he wrote a strong letter to President Nixon proposing the highest honour for Welthy. Several years later the State Department nominated Welthy, at Ambassador Carol Laise Bunker's instigation.[11] India was out of favour and Welthy's individual efforts were not seen by politicians as worthy of such acclaim. For Welthy, the nine years of substantial U.S. AID backing for her work was the most tangible recognition.

INDIA, 1973

Welthy turned from what she perceived to be the brickwall of World Education and sought space for her ever-expanding idea. It was Richard Nixon's America now and she wanted to be in India, as if to personally disclaim association with the menacing presence of the U.S. Seventh Fleet in the Bay of Bengal—a blow as humiliating to India as the Chinese found their western overlords fifty years earlier.

"What kind of opposition can Cambodia put up?" Welthy asked. "She can only offer her people to die a horrible death. God help America and Americans, the Government and the people, to see the ethical and holy brotherly light." Welthy rarely allowed tears to show, but she could not bear what her country under Nixon was doing in bombing Cambodia, communicating to the world that show of force that was against everything Welthy believed in as an American.

From the moment we set foot in India, Welthy's heart was heavy as we sensed the hostility of a historic reversal of friendship. Many Indian minds were liberated from belief in free association between democracies of such disparate military might as India and America. Welthy understood that there had to be a higher loyalty among peoples than nations; her whole life was based on that vision.

The 1973 visit was intended as Welthy's farewell to India, to show her love, faith and confidence in her colleagues there, and publicly indicate that Literacy House was an Indian institution. She had resigned as Chairman of the ILB, and the two-year AID grant extension had been approved to go directly to Literacy House. It eliminated World Education's role in India since they had come to rely so heavily on that one source of funding.

Welthy's return to Literacy House had a particularly festive atmosphere as staff and families gathered by the gate to pull *Mataji* home to them, spilling out all the news of births and marriages, illnesses and deaths in each animated greeting. She belonged to them and they knew it — all except for the newer staff who had not shared the intimacy of the most creative days and could not break through their skeptical reserve. It was for them to give news about the progress of work.

LITERACY HOUSE INFLUENCE EXPANDING

The U.P. Government had just purchased three hundred and twenty-thousand sets of *Naya Savera* teaching materials, UNICEF had given contracts to produce teaching aids developed by Virendra Tripathi on applied nutrition and para-medical training, the National Dairy Development Board gave a three-year grant for a regional dairy cattle breeding centre at the Young Farmers' Institute, the Population Council of India held their regional meeting at Literacy House, the Family Planning Foundation of India granted funds for a workshop to produce teaching materials, and UNESCO's Education Adviser to the Government of India urged Literacy House to use its influence to enlarge the scale of programmes underway before worrying about operational evaluation.[12] Welthy's Three F's were expanding into Four F's — Food, Fuel, Fertilizer and Family Planning — as the concept of truly functional literacy integrated into all aspects of development gathered momentum.

PRIME MINISTER INDIRA GANDHI AT 20th FOUNDER'S DAY

To house the growing concept it was appropriate that the new library building, a project of World Literacy of Canada, was ready for inauguration by the Prime Minister herself when she came to honour Welthy at the 20th Founder's Day. Their different perspectives on literacy illuminate the essential reason for India's gradualist approach to achieving full literacy.

Welthy, the practical idealist speaking of literacy as a transfusion of energy:

Literacy is developing human beings who will themselves change society for the better.

And who but woman can change society more humanly, more effectively and more helpfully for future generations? It is for us, the womanhood of the world, to take our place as creators of the new world society. Woman thus will develop the capacity for faith in herself, because faith in her own particular and vital capacity will change her outlook and in time will change society.[13]

Indira Gandhi, the practical politician, speaking of literacy as a questionable asset:

Perhaps we could have done more for literacy, but I don't know how important it is. What has it done for the west? Are people happier or more alive to problems? On the contrary, I think they have become far more superficial . . . Literacy should come by the way, rather than be the focus of education.[14]

When we called on Indira at her residence in New Delhi, a courtesy she always extended to Welthy, she emphasized the need for institutions like Literacy House to develop income-generating projects for future long-term support, and expressed strong interest in television teaching as the potential breakthrough in achieving literacy in India. Indira pushed hard to achieve India's present satellite communication system to make this possible.

There was a growing awareness that the Indian educational system was dysfunctional.[15] What had been introduced by the British and subsequent generations of missionaries was inappropriate to the needs of an impoverished developing society, where education derived from foreign experience could not create employment and opportunity.[16] The need for a strong voluntary effort was recognized, with excessive reliance on government seen as a real danger to an adult education movement which in effect sought to alter the status quo.[17]

Literacy House was caught in the gap between a rapidly changing approach to education at the international level, and the reality of operating in rural poverty, with no ready-made infrastructure for integrated programmes of functional literacy linked to employment.[18] International experts had unrealistic expectations of the staff, which was less than helpful, and the sheer fact of their expertise precluded understanding of Indian culture with any depth. There was huge need for education on all sides.

In the farewell tribute to Welthy published by Literacy House, "Abhinandan; Homage to a World Citizen", J.C. Mathur's artistic brush touched on the eternal dilemma of dynamic leadership: "We, her fellow-workers, have got so much used to the sugar and pepper in her, that now in February 1973 we begin to wonder how in the absence of the *madhubala* (wine-girl) our carousing group would hold together." Another spoke of the "tons of tenacity" Welthy poured into the candle she lit. Laxmi Menon, former Minister of External Affairs in the Government of India, pronounced Welthy a *karma yogi*, who exudes optimism. Sucheta Kripalani wrote: "Whenever I went to her mentally weary with my burdens (as Chief Minister of India's largest state), I came back strengthened and full of joy."

Welthy's own farewell words were simply stated in the poem she read on that last Founder's Day:

> *To see that greatest of skills . . .*
> *we call it literacy . . .*
> *find its place in each effort*
> *on the field, in the family, in the community,*
> *in industry and the new youth centres,*
> *that the village mind may share its truth*
> *in our planet's renewal.*
>
> *So I'm thinking today of '53,*
> *now that there's not much left of me!*
> *recalling with pride*
> *those things we have done,*
> *aware of those that have been left undone,*
> *and enquiring . . . into the future*
> *. . . which is yours.*

Two comments from Indian men at the top of their professional fields who had worked closely with Welthy convey some sense of Welthy's impact. Mushtaq Ahmed, former director of Literacy House and senior UNESCO international literacy adviser wrote: "She is a born humanitarian. Some members of the staff of Literacy House would approach her with their difficulties. And she would usually promise relief—monetary aid, promotion, change of job—anything to make the applicant happy. We would hold our breath, seeing somebody emerge from her quarters, with a piece of paper in his hand, and marching toward us as the conqueror of the earth. We knew at once trouble was on foot. Once when the rules would not permit us to fulfill her promise I approached Misra, the accounts officer, and said in exasperation: 'Now Mishraji, how can we do this?' I was surprised at the understanding shown by an accounts man when he replied: "Mushtaq Sahib, she is a giver. She doesn't understand rules and regulations. They are made by people like us. And she isn't like us.'"

"Hardly anyone is a hero or heroine to a hard-boiled newspaperman," wrote S.N. Ghosh, for twenty-five years editor of *The Pioneer* which Nehru had founded in Lucknow, and a member of the ILB. "There are, however, exceptions and it is their presence that restores the cynic's faith in human nature and corrects his somewhat jaundiced outlook. Before I met Mrs. Welthy Fisher I had conjured up not a very flattering image of some Lady Bountiful, stinkingly rich, slumming in the East for the greater glory of her home country. I met her for the first time after I had lost my son in an accident and was overwhelmed with grief. Restless, I was roaming the city, when passing by the Literacy House I was attracted by the Chinese Pagoda with its thatched dome. I walked in uninvited and found Mrs. Fisher engaged in a silent prayer with a group of young village girls. Physically and intellectually they were poles apart but I could sense her communicating with the girls, for I too felt the presence of a spirit exuding not only compassion, but enlightenment and understanding.inging The silent prayer over, Mrs. Fisher turned to me with a smile. She has a wonderful smile. I cannot explain how the barrier broke down and she could communicate at my level. Private grief, I understood, had to be sublimated to love, deep and purposive, for a sincere and dedicated work was the most potent anodyne."

Comfort Shaw was the director of Literacy House then, long accustomed to Welthy's ways, and while she was on campus he established visiting hours at tea time. No one had private time with her and there could no longer be suspicion that someone had gained her special favour. Long after Welthy had any real involvement in the workings of the institution her presence was an irritant to the director's authority, a fact Welthy really did not understand because she herself did not deal in power and authority. Authority came from within oneself. She always needed the human contact with the staff, but by 1973 wished to be spared the anguish of each person's problems, and probably just out of sheer weariness she adjusted to the tea parties. Welthy would try to conclude the parties graciously, but unless someone, me, said a firm farewell, no one would leave. You see, there was love, and laughter, a warm informality that provoked creativity, Welthy always drawing out each one's personal thoughts, never talking in the abstract. It was irresistible.

I got tougher and tougher in the struggle to help Welthy let go. But she too made an effort, her own way. Once in the midst of telling a good story to a staff gathering after Comfort had announced she would speak only three minutes, Welthy looked at her watch at the height of her drama and said: "Now I'll stop. I'll finish it another time — he said I had three minutes." In the hilarious laughter that followed, excessive really, *Mataji* had us all by the heartstrings. Were we hopelessly adolescent? I think we were learning the "affective principle."

Siddiqi would have his say on an occasion such as Welthy's farewell visit, Siddiqi the one everyone counted on to master any and all situations with his infectious verbosity. "The future of Literacy House may be a bit uncertain," he said, "but it will never die. This fact will always be the same — Literacy House is ours. The fundamental purpose will continue. Literacy is a means for service to the people, our prayer to God. Literacy is now a factor in our national plan, accepted as necessary. What we started in 1958, other countries are now doing."

To formally bid farewell to Welthy, official functions were given by the City of Lucknow and by Governor Akbar Ali Khan, the latter's enchantment with Welthy distressing to his security guards, when he stole away to Literacy House to present one more gift — a large sandalwood carving of *Saraswati*, goddess of learning. "You have not imprisoned yourself in Christ or Buddha or Mohammed," said the Governor. "You have love and respect for everybody. The affection and respect we have for you will always remain a bond between India and America. I judge the people of the U.S. by the qualities you have shown. I trust the people of the U.S. have love for truth and justice. You go with the good feelings of millions of my people."

A large reception was held in the spacious gardens of the India International Centre in New Delhi, where the President of India, V.V. Giri, Dr. Mohan Sinha Mehta, Dr. V.K.R.V. Rao and C.D. Deshmukh saluted Welthy as a world citizen who had identified a real need in India in targeting her work at young, rural illiterates. "Welthy Fisher has shown us the way," said Giri. "Functional literacy aims at the total development and is in complete accord with my own ideas of solving poverty and unemployment . . . It is people like Mrs. Fisher who build bridges of understanding between different peoples and cultures that will make one world a reality. She is in every sense of the word a citizen of the world."[19]

Welthy responded by saying that for once she would not talk about literacy, and reminisced warmly of her fifty years association with India, revealing a deep connection with beloved leaders who had shaped the nation into being. She gave them what they wanted. History was in the air that afternoon — a moment everyone felt was worthy of prolonging, even if it was Welthy who was doing it! As the President's aide consulted his wristwatch anxiously, my gentle proddings were useless; Welthy's terminal facilities were just not working that day.   The procession of distinguished Indians wishing to salute Welthy continued.   On her last day, Padmaja Naidu (Sarojini's daughter, who had been Governor of West Bengal and a stalwart friend to Nehru), Ted and Sucy Koshy, Acharaya and Sucheta Kripalani, all came to the Ford Foundation guesthouse where we had been invited to stay.

Daniel Moynihan had just arrived as yet another American Ambassador and requested a meeting with Welthy before she got away.   "He has the juice to do a big job," Welthy commented after an animated hour as he spoke of plans to build up relations with India again, especially on the non-government side, where there was a good opportunity to avoid the schizophrenic swings between adult nationhood and immaturity on India's part. Americans were still stinging from being called bad names for the first time in their young history, revealing their own relative immaturity.

In February 1973, at a time of general anti-American sentiment in India, the good news of Welthy's durable work in India, and India's regard for it, was suppressed by the American press.   No American journalist in India could have been unaware of the profuse, public honour India lavished on Welthy's 'farewell' visit,   emphasizing the very qualities professed as the highest aim of democracy. Every national and regional newspaper in India carried a picture front and centre of Welthy and the President, Welthy and the Prime Minister, Welthy and the Governor. I had informed the *New York Times* bureau in Delhi of the various events, so it was no oversight that not one word of this appeared in the American press but deliberate devaluing of an old woman's wise work.

Development was still seen more in material than human terms. Literacy was soft stuff compared with big dams and hydroelectric projects.   There was no hard news in the struggle for literacy, and Americans were left unaware of the deep, underlying connection Welthy had made that was preserving a residue of goodwill in India toward America, a pathway for the future, as a succession of American Ambassadors to India had acknowledged.   Deprived of genuine news by the tough mind-set of journalists and/or their editors, who chose to write Welthy out of history, love itself was being censored.

CHINA, 1973

It was for another ancient society to recognize a good story when they saw one. The People's Republic of China (PRC), having denied our request for visas to visit, decided to reverse that decision. They had read all about Welthy's visit to India and realized she was not just another old lady who might become ill and die in China. We had left Delhi early one morning dejected by their refusal, reaching Hong Kong that afternoon, where the welcoming message from China awaited us. Welthy's eyes shone with pure delight at the prospect.

As we walked across the wooden bridge at Shum Chum, the actual border point between the New Territories of Hong Kong and the PRC, Welthy's mind and heart turned to China. That quarter mile transfer on foot between two worlds was the road Welthy always wanted to walk. Sixty-seven years after her first arrival in China she had another chance at bridging the gap between East and West as one of the first Americans permitted into China in the new era.

It stirred an old woman's soul to be cutting the creative edge once more. The Chinese were clearly interested in Welthy, as evidenced by the calibre of guide assigned by our hosts, the Foreign Friendship Association, who whisked us from the railroad station in Canton to a suite of rooms in a Tudor-style former apartment building.

A week of steady visiting to kindergarten, commune, ceramic factory, middle school, industrial night school and teacher training college gave Welthy's eye a shrewd insight into changes, achieved and yet to be achieved. Initially the Chinese had limited the visit to one week in Canton, but were encouraged by its success to extend it to several more days in Shanghai.

Our little plane actually touched down at Nanchang's small airport in the dark for a quick meal, tantalizing proximity for Welthy to a place so central to her heart. She did learn that Bao-Lin School was now Middle School No. 10. Nanchang itself was off-limits to foreign visitors in that very early stage of opening to the West. It had been a focal point of revolution where unrest still stirred easily, not to be excited by outsiders.

TALITHA GERLACH

At Shanghai Talitha Gerlach rushed forward to greet Welthy. It was Talitha's persistence that helped to obtain our visas. Talitha and Welthy had both set out for their mature work in the Orient in the early 1950's after working together in the forties in New York on various committees in support of China. A YWCA worker in China from 1926-1940, she was asked by Soong Ching Ling (Mme. Sun Yat-sen) to return and help develop children's education at the China Welfare Institute. At eighty-one, she was among a handful of foreigners commanding deep respect from the Chinese.

It was awesome to realize how strong were the threads binding the spirits of Welthy and Talitha to practical, progressive work in two ancient societies. The twenty years' gap in their friendship slipped away instantly as these two veterans pioneering the world put their heads together to compare notes. Womanpower! Time and space, race and religion, all the divisions that plague us, fell away in the clearing they created.

After days of hearing our guides speak of serving the lowly peasants, Welthy made the pointed remark that surely after twenty-two years of revolution they must by now be self-respecting farmers, that to speak of them as peasants did not reflect well on their achievements and may prolong the peasant's awareness of his lowly status. Whenever Welthy raised the point again, our guides deliberately changed the subject, as if they considered her politically naive.

Welthy asked about literacy, and was told it was such a minor matter that no figures were available. Formal schooling had taken care of illiteracy. Welthy suggested there might be a large number of women, especially in rural areas, who remain untouched by education. Yes, they conceded, but they are happy their children are being educated. Welthy chose International Women's Day to make this point. She told our guides that in the U.S. women got the right to vote in 1921; they immediately responded that it was in 1921 when the Communist Party was established in Shanghai. It was also the year when Welthy's world tour provided the basis for choosing her future.

What did Welthy see in the China of 1973, so recently reopened to the West, so preoccupied with their own revolution that they expressed no interest whatsoever in her work in India? Welthy understood change as a process, that China was a society in a state of regeneration after long, multi-layered decay had solidified. To crack that would take a century, but the beginnings were there and she thrilled at the energy of Shanghai, a city of Chinese, for Chinese, and run by Chinese. It was drab and serious by western playboy standards with propaganda terminology not to be taken as gospel. She sensed the pride and purpose in the faces of Chinese women and men on the streets, and when asked for the impression she carried away from China, Welthy said: "They are taking 'love thy neighbour' seriously."[20]

AMERICA, 1974-1976

As long as there were stimulating people, new faces, Welthy had what she needed. Because of my need for rest and refreshment, we spent more time each summer at my cottage in the Gatineau Hills north of Ottawa. She called my country "topside", a touch of imperialism I chose to ignore. I did whatever possible to keep Welthy there for a moment while I caught my breath. People and cats were the best bait. Old and new friends gathered round to meet Welthy, including our former Prime Minister, Lester B. Pearson and his wife. Two special cats found their way permanently into our mobile menage. There were times when I wished Welthy could be like everyone else, relax and take it easy. Instead, she would arrive, exclaim: "My, what a lovely place! Where do we go next?" But the cats' antics, and the ever-changing, beckoning clouds hanging over the sweeping high hills and the clearest limestone lake helped her to live happily in the woods, in her mind, for my sake.

When I built a second cottage with more conveniences, she wanted to share in the cost of one hundred concrete steps that enabled her to climb down and be part of the waterfront life each day. Once when I left her to oversee the new construction, Welthy confronted me with the full force of her determination. She had climbed up the steps and rugged terrain of the gravel road beyond, and there she was tottering on the two-inch side of the two-by-four girders on cinder blocks, picking her way by cane across the abyss below in her open-heeled, orthopedic sandals. How she had pushed, pulled and shoved herself high off the ground with no steps in place remains a mystery. I was so startled and alarmed I simply got mad at her. That night she wrote in her diary: "I don't think I can live with Sally." Old builder that she was, her message was clear: "Look at me—you can't leave me out of anything."

There was a gnawing anxiety that she had not done enough, that as long as life lasted she should be doing more. Writing letters was the best therapy. Her graciously impatient communications kept rushing round the world to prod and praise whomever she thought might act. "All these little things mean something." I was the nearest object, trying to be beyond reach occasionally.

Welthy's eyes had begun to give her serious trouble with cataracts forming slowly. "I'm a pretty dwindling 'Fish'—losing all my scales," she wrote to me. "Waiting to go into the pool with the big whale in Florida, still talking while going down!" That was as close as she came to talking about the inevitable.

Not inclined to reflect morbidly on death, Welthy was ready to accept it whenever and wherever it came. She could never share my panic on airplanes, for instance, comfortable with a feeling of having done her best. She had a sense of a reincarnated future life in another body, a continuing process until ready to join the celestial, but offered no abstractions on the matter.

Whenever I was away from her for short periods to attend to personal matters, she kept scratching out barely legible love notes, well aware that I needed her as much as she needed me. Nevertheless, I recognized the emotional bribery. "The house is so dark. The days are planned and all I need is to acquiesce. I'm getting so weary of having people look after me every minute, so I'll be on the lookout for you always and all the time. Who am I? Yours for as long as Life Lasts. Your old gal Welthy."

UNESCO APPROVES A DEFUNCT LITINT

The efforts we had made to create Literacy International had foundered as a result of bad timing, a basic lack of trust among the cooperators, and the uncertainties of dealing with Welthy and me. Even so, UNESCO thought we had something worthwhile to offer, for we received a communication stating that they would now grant Status "B" Consultancy to LITINT.[21] While our broader purpose was far short of the mark in this endeavour, the literacy information and coordination work we had started among voluntary agencies was meeting an obvious need. UNESCO did not know that LITINT had closed down two years earlier, a bittersweet irony. Had they come through sooner with this public endorsement, we might have been able to hold the group together for useful work. As for LITINT, what we did achieve was to goad existing organizations to become aware of one another's efforts by greatly improved sharing of information. UNESCO itself took the lead in documenting literacy work around the world and the Indian Adult Education Association made more detailed documentation available to its members. At least we had established a pattern.

ONE REALITY

I was fascinated with people's reactions when Welthy spoke, recording in my diary and on tape what was most provocative. Her thoughts were so direct and seemingly simple that the distillation could be missed if one was not listening.

When asked how her spiritual values were surviving the current onslaught of skepticism, Welthy said:

> *I can't believe in any one government any more than I can put all my faith in any one race or one language or one religion. The world is one reality, and I belong to it.*

Listening to world news and America's domestic agonizing over the Watergate scandal, Welthy felt the familiar drag of unwilling change: "Well, we're beginning our knowledge, I suppose."

Talking to Protestant churchwomen in Waterbury, Connecticut:

> *If we go to share anything we have, we must first make friends with the people . . . If we've learned to talk to God I don't think we need objects of worship . . . We were once called the Christian West. Now what are we, where are we standing? Poor countries are becoming poorer and we are*

becoming more destructive and it is more difficult to explain ourselves anywhere in the world.

What are young people going to do, what are we old people going to do? There isn't any such thing as old — just arthritis. We can do things. Speer talked to us about the quality of youth willing to share with others. That was the beginning of my real life. We must have young people, old people, middle-aged people unite.

I see God in the faces of the underprivileged, the unemployed and the underdeveloped — and in the hands of those who work to bring justice their way. Justice is not a law or a political system. Justice is a human being listening to the still small voice, and acting.

Asked if she could have the power to do one thing to improve the world, what would it be, Welthy paused, reflected longer than usual, and gave her most serious reply: "I'd work for a link language, so people could begin to have a chance to communicate with each other." Those were carefully chosen words, the emphasis on "begin".

Welthy was asked who decides what is justice for another. "The main rule is that slavery is wrong. When one enslaves another it's not doing justice to either human being."

"I keep thinking of this great mass of human mentality that in a way hasn't been touched in the villages. India has it, but it will take some time to unwind herself from the colonial regime, when a few were trained as government servants and did so well. We know it is only the beginning. They've somehow got to figure out their own development — for the family, the community, the country. If they don't, they'll be cheated."

When asked what she really wanted to do in this world:

I'd like to convert people to an interest in the basic mass of people, because that's the only resource there is in the world . . . it can't all come from the few that are Ph.D.'s. God holds the world in his hands, but he has to have people helping lift up others . . . because we are God. We're the only gods there are.

* * *

That same wise crone could play from the east to the west coast of America, revelling in freedom on one of her few flights unaccompanied by me. Swinging down the ramp from the plane at Los Angeles airport with a giant bottle of champagne, Welthy had won the in-flight game of guessing most accurately the total age of the eight crew members of the big jet. She was not exactly helpless! Welthy was so modern she was in perpetual jet orbit around the world, yet while speeding along the New York Thruway would remark: "How strange we don't see any horses." A reporter in Hong Kong observing that few at ninety-three were equal to any challenge other than survival, asked Welthy the secret of her success in persuading the rich to support her. "I pay my own expenses," said Welthy, "and then instead of reciting statistics, try to tell people something interesting about the work."

Speaking to the Heritage Village Women's Club: "Why don't we have more women in the Senate and Congress? Are we going to let the world be run by men? You and I are responsible people. Oriental countries have three women prime ministers." She pointed out that Indians always believed there should be masculine and feminine in the godhead, which she illustrated in telling the story of Hanuman organizing the monkey bridge to bring Sita back from Lanka to Ram in India. "Now you hear Indians chanting 'Sita Ram, Sita Ram,' the woman always first. Gandhi looked deeply into the roots of his own culture, religion and philosophy from the perspective of his Oxford education and proclaimed that 'woman shall be as free as man to choose her own path'."

Welthy was often challenged to make comparisons between India and China but never allowed herself to get caught in that trap. The only time she spoke of the two ancient societies in the same breath, she compared the warlords of China with the landlords of India, who both used the people as mechanical creatures.

We talked a lot in the less active years after that big trip, while I began to think of writing this book, and she recovered from a broken hip, broken ribs, etc. She was happy that I wanted to do it, eager to have her life known, proud of the choices she had made. But though she was willing to share much of her intimate life, there was always an inner reserve, a point beyond which I could not reach in excavating her soul.

Free as she had always been, Welthy was disinclined to cover her tracks with self-explanation. She knew what she had done and why. How many times had she said that love is something you don't put down on a piece of paper . . . it's what you give to each other that creates love. And she spoke of being open to friendship, Even those with unattractive aspects she could find the way to be 'link friends'. Why then are people unfriendly towards others? "It's man's desire to have more than his brother," Welthy said. Was that deliberate or common usage of the masculine?

Growing restless with an old woman's wisdom, I asked her point blank one day:

"What do you really know?"

If I can make friends with so many people of different nationalities and races, then I'm sure I can make friends with all the world. If I can do it, we can all do it.

The dream of mankind is to know the rest of mankind. We're curious about other people — to see it as one world. Must it be done by the same belief in the spiritual line, or may it be believed by the love and the truth expressed — by truth I mean integrity — by individuals. Maybe there are others on the other earth, some with great leadership, some with ideas.

It's the mountains and the non-ability to reach each other by thought that has kept different languages developing all over the world. I hate to praise the British Empire, but I think they've done more to make a link language than anyone. I don't like empire.

* * *

At ninety-six Welthy had a cataract removed from one eye, after doctors had repeatedly said it was not worth the risk. She celebrated her excellent recovery at the thanksgiving service in the Woodbury Methodist Church one brilliant morning, rising up spontaneously to give thanks for being able to see the sun shine through the colonial whiteness of the church, feeling its essential connection. "My eyes were interviewed for years," she told them, before Dr. Richard Getnick was ready to risk it with her. If Welthy was looking for signs, she had a clear one that year not to give up on her vision.

Even with eyesight partially restored, Welthy relied on tape recorded books for her main reading each day, a step removed from personal discovery in the darkness of her own illiteracy. But there was no drabness in her appearance, for she followed faithfully Cousin Dee's early advise to brush her hair up and off her face. "It makes a woman look optimistic."

That daily regimen of hairbrushing and rubbing Noxema vigorously, and upwards on her cheeks kept Welthy looking and feeling vital. She cared how she looked and would stand in front of "the glass" striking a pose, throwing a shimmering silk scarf over her shoulder, adjusting her dimestore pearls, and always the earrings. A quick but careful composure; then she was free to forget herself completely. Her hair grey with traces of the original brown in a strong hairline that matched her erect bearing, Welthy was still an eyecatcher moving briskly about in her red sandals with the distinctive cane.

Despite certain physical limitations,[22] her general health remained very good, and doctors were amazed at her steady blood pressure in the low range of normal. She took no medication of any kind until her last year, other than the B vitamins she had always used. Unaware that her instinctive combination of laughter and meditation was emerging as "psychoneuroimmunology," Welthy naturally triggered tranquilizers in her body to handle stress.

One very visibly charitable, rich woman came to show Welthy coloured slides of her extravagant world travel. Welthy did not precisely remember meeting the woman before but welcomed her heartily with wide open arms and conversed animatedly for an hour. At the end of it the woman remained annoyed, aware that Welthy had not recognized her. "Why she treats everyone the same," she said in disgust as she departed.

Of course the ravages of age made her an increasingly disadvantaged woman, and there were some who turned away from her. She became invisible to them. So-called senility may not be a deterioration, but a progression to timelessness and spacelessness, a freeing of the rigid mind by clearing out accumulated mental debris. When I found myself resisting Welthy's fading image occasionally, out of the depth of her character she pulled me back to that point of connection where we acknowledged the interdependence of our strengths and weaknesses. That crystal quality was certainly not the work of a feeble mind. I understood then that those who do not have the tolerance to work with older people, or any disadvantaged people, are probably inappropriate actors in development work, where exasperation with limitations and differences can run high.

When she found the time long in Connecticut between trips and events, she would do something dramatic or playful to prod me away from the desk, appearing suddenly in my doorway outlandishly garbed in indescribable conglomerations of clothes — the actress commanding attention to a live performance — at any time of night or day. Whatever stress I felt with our increasingly confined life it was dissolved in prolonged laughter.

Television became another companion of Welthy's lengthening days. A soap opera kept her mind actively involved with its characters: "Have a care there, dear," she would warn one headstrong temptress, "give another thought before you do that." But there were few programmes of deep interest. "It's time to stop telling stories of pioneers in the west and start to tell of pioneers in the world," she muttered to the cats. And to a TV Cinderella watching the horrid mother and her greedy daughters prancing off to the ball Welthy urged: "Come on Cinderella! Don't just dream. Do something."

Music had always been Welthy's salvation and I carried tapes wherever we went. Her old vigorous hymns still beckoned, but she readily made friends with the best of the pop music of my younger years. If I tried to sedate her impatience with Bach she absorbed the elegance for a few minutes, and then laughed, unwilling to hear the ceaseless repetition of the theme, always ready for a new statement. When the overall repetition of daily life became overwhelming, it was time to move on.

INDIA, 1977

Welthy wanted to be at Literacy House for Founder's Day. Travelling first class was the only way I could conceivably get Welthy, her walker and wheelchair needs met as we made the familiar flight halfway round the world once more. Even so, it was a strenuous trip for both of us, but Welthy didn't want to miss a thing, especially the good food. She had perfected the art of sleeping while eating, or vice versa, a phenomenon that caught the amused attention of observant fellow diners at various high altitudes.

We went first to Literacy House South in Hyderabad, in the March heat, resting briefly at a modest hotel with no water, the shift from privileged living a natural transition for Welthy, and a challenge for me. Durgabai Deshmukh's dream was accomplished and visibly flourishing on the campus with its bustling female student body moving about in colourful *saris*.

Durgabhai had the names of all her cooperators on various cornerstones installed on the Literacy House building, and I felt deep pride in seeing mine among them. Welthy's words to the group Durgabhai had assembled were clear, and carefully recorded, her message not exclusively for India:

> *No nation dares to measure its development only in terms of its resources of oil, minerals, steel and agriculture. First on the list must be the development of that greatest of all resources — the human being.*[23]

In Delhi Welthy held court at the Imperial Hotel, the rambling old colonial relic we preferred for its central location and accessible gardens. Both there and at the India International Centre where we often stayed, we could live more easily and avoid the touristic excesses of the big modern hotels on the outskirts of Delhi.

We encountered Welthy's old friend Mme. Pandit in the lobby, who hastened up to our room to lay out her attack against Indira Gandhi, as if rehearsing her next speech in the national election campaign underway. It was the last stand of a woman ambitious to be President of India, allowing vengeance full play. It was a sobering lesson in the ability of politics to devour the human spirit, as Gandhi had always known.

The parade of callers in that hotel room was exhilarating and exhausting, each one requesting exclusive time with Welthy:

Mary and Jigme Taring came down from their Tibetan centre in Mussoorie with a prayer flag from the Dalai Lama;

Mushtaq Ahmed, now member of the ILB, described his literacy work in Nigeria and Zambia;

Dr. S.N. Saraf brought the latest thinking and experience of India's Planning Commission;

Anil Bordia, Joint Secretary in the Ministry of Education, also on the ILB, said the Government's National Adult Education Programme (NAEP), to be launched in 1978 with the goal of making one hundred million young adults (age 15 to 35) literate in five years, heralded the first significant commitment of funds for literacy and adult education;

Sri Bhagwan Sahay, Chairman of the Board, sought a long personal talk with Welthy, his artistic mind absorbing her whole personality;

Girijapati Mukharji, the Vice-Chairman came for a lengthy paying of respects; and

J.C. Mathur insisted on meeting Welthy in his new home where all the family could see her.

These and many others crowded Welthy's first days in India, evidence of her still high drawing power. For details related to the actual work I was capable enough by then to shuffle papers and find relevant spots on pertinent pages to handle whatever specifics were discussed. If she took an occasional catnap during those intervals — almost talking while sleeping — no one minded too much.

In truth, there were no matters of business for Welthy any more, only the everlasting bond of creation on Welthy's part, and respect on the part of her Indian friends. But it was Welthy who gave an atmosphere in which people could feel genuine warmth, the environment in which growth and change and continuing development occurs. All her Indian callers were exceedingly capable individuals who needed no instruction from her. That they sought for a moment to steep themselves in the ever-widening, ever-deepening aura of love they perceived was all the evidence I needed that Welthy had truly accomplished something in India. These were not blind followers. They were leaders, understanding their need for that sense of profound connection that makes true international cooperation possible.

LITERACY HOUSE, MARCH 1977

Up at 4:30 a.m. for the forty-minute flight to Lucknow, Welthy ready ahead of me, and Welthy the first one off the plane at Amausi airport, its simple, short runway transformed to accommodate the big Arabian jets carrying young Moslems to work in the Middle East. Many *malas* around her neck, smiles, tears, laughter, everyone talking at once. Welthy was home even before reaching the freshly painted entranceway, now including "The Welthy Fisher School" offering grades one to five for children of staff and the surrounding area.

Inside the gate, the announcer puppet officially garlanded Welthy, as she danced to his tune, and the entire staff, with all their families, presented floral offerings, one by one. Welthy knew them all, with a special word for each one. The overwhelming beauty of the campus, bougainvillaea in extravagant bloom, Welthy's house colourfully decorated in welcome, and the general atmosphere of profound joy on so many faces made that festive day a sign to remember. That some of the newer staff remained aloof was sad, but understandable. They didn't believe the myth, had not shared in the glory days of struggling to create LH, and knew only the present difficulties of an ongoing institution.

As the State Resource Centre for U.P. serving other Hindi states as well, LH had become totally self-sufficient within India, its budget needs met one-third by sale of their own teaching and follow-up materials, one-third from the U.P. Government, and one-third from the Government of India. If the degree of independence from foreign support is a measure of success for development projects, then LH has to be counted successful. Welthy's strategy of creating an Indian board, and sticking with them through the thick and thin of WE's controlling machinations, had borne fruit in the independence Mukharji and Sahay had achieved for LH.

At the Bijnaur Farm of the Young Farmers' Institute, Welthy practically spoke to each of the cows and chickens personally, so thrilled to see that campus at last fully operational with green fields expanding beyond its boundaries, all helped by the extension of electricity, tubewells and a *pukka* road to the area. Their produce was sold through the LH staff cooperative, with additional income generated through the dairy cattle development.

Welthy inaugurated a training course for village women, half of them unmarried, yet allowed to live on the campus for five days, reflecting a significant change in village attitude, according to Mrs. Trivedi, head of the Family Life Centre.

At Isabella Thoburn College in the city, Welthy dressed to the hilt for the occasion, almost clowned her way through her speech, poking fun mostly at herself, looking every inch the grand lady but insisting by her behaviour that no church was going to inhibit her freedom to be her own best self. She struck a responsive chord, not quite overstepping the line.

Lucknow itself had a new look that year. Divided main arteries kept the traffic more orderly, uniformly painted fronts of shops and houses in two-tone beige pastels, overhead street lights and a beautiful new garden park with twinkling lanterns along the Gomti River all added to a feeling in the air that things were on the move in India as never before. Swollen, stinging legs and feet could not detract from Welthy's deep happiness in seeing LH truly coming into its own in an atmosphere of positive energy and hope.

25th FOUNDER'S DAY, MARCH 21, 1977

The day began as usual with breakfast on the back veranda in the fresh early morning air. Welthy gave the meditation in the Prayer House and afterwards everyone moved in a body to the adjacent hedged enclosure for the raising of the LH flag she had asked Martha Keehn to have made with its symbol of a *deepa* showing the light of their beginnings. Welthy stepped forward to unfurl the flag before the sun-basked assembly, faces all upturned expectantly. There was a slight hitch when the flag would not unfurl. Ever-ready Siddiqi grabbed a young boy and sent him shinnying up the flagpole from his shoulders to release the flag. A gentle breeze arose to let the rose petals it contained sail out among us as all voices combined to sing almost inaudibly their song of reverent celebration. In that still moment, everything, and nothing was said.

The nation was still in a state of total shock in the aftermath of the shattering defeat of Indira Gandhi and the Congress Party in the general election the previous day. Many were exultant that democracy had fulfilled its long promise to the masses; many felt deep regret at dismantling the mother image of Indira in the Indian national family of such immense diversity. There was a reasonably good turnout of Lucknow citizens for the afternoon *tamasha* under the big *shamiana* but the unprecedented political turmoil pervaded the proceedings and the prospects for literacy advancement.

Dr. S.N. Mehrotra, Director of Education for U.P. and ILB board member, urged me to press for more international cooperation for LH, that it not depend on government links alone. Girijapati Mukharji and D.P. Maheshwari, the Director of LH, expressed concern about the lack of clarity in the concept of non-formal adult education for purposes of organizing and monitoring. S.B. Saran, the Education Secretary for U.P., elaborated on the elusiveness of the concept, referring to the immensity of coping with ten million children entering primary schools each year in U.P. alone. That officials in India's bastion of democracy were groping for an administrative handle on literacy, and had the funds to do so, signalled a real step toward the goal. In the past, it would have been dismissed out of hand, while paying lip-service to the ideal.

In a publication of the Overseas Development Council that year on the failure of aid to address the problems of the very poorest, it urged a more participatory approach to developing self-reliance, and recognized the use of literacy by World Education and Literacy House as a tool to improve daily life a valid goal. Their puppetry increased the likelihood of multiple educational messages sinking in. But the transfer of these methods on a wide scale could not break through the entrenched, tradition-bound system in place. The tragic flaw was over-reliance on Welthy's charismatic leadership and personal ability to attract funds, with the result that her retirement and the end of aid funds meant staff cuts and lower morale, until Indian government resources came to the rescue. "Can the lost momentum and resulting bureaucratization be reversed," was the question.[24]

To have endured through all those years of struggle and chaos, holding together disparate personalities, policies and perspectives from that risky, experimental beginning, was Welthy's monumental achievement. There were still problems of dependency by LH on remote control by outsiders, as the staff often regarded the state and central governments, but LH retained considerable autonomy as a private institution. Twenty-five years after its inception, India had the beginning infrastructure for literacy, imperfect as it will always be.

NEW DELHI, MARCH 1977

Everyone was waiting for the new President of India to be named. We were waiting to see Indira Gandhi, the pre-arranged appointment postponed for one day due to the upheaval. Welthy kept an appointment with *Acharaya* Kripalani, then ninety-two, a widower, lean and argumentative as ever, and deeply bitter in denouncement of the "nightmare" Indira had put India through. He had actively campaigned against her and still clung to his vitriolic verbal assassination. He was one of a two-man selection committee to choose the new President.

Welthy heard him lash out in the privacy of his home, remembering Sucheta's love for the *Acharaya*, the freedom fighter who had been the first President of the Congress Party after independence. Welthy kept her mind on the spirit of Sucheta's cooperation in the early years of LH, acknowledging her gratitude to that part of their joint association, and aware of the seeds of destruction in the political process as practised by scarred warriors.

Indira by contrast showed no bitterness when we saw her the next day at No. 1 Safdarjang Road, the relatively modest residence she had chosen as Prime Minister. Overnight the compound had been transformed from heavy security to minimal protection, heightening our sense of Indira's vulnerability. She looked more petite and less robust, with a yellow cast to her skin and the facial twitching more pronounced. Welthy thanked her for handling the question of the tax status of LH so that it may continue to receive funds as a voluntary organization.[25] Despite her frail and solitary demeanour, Indira seemed genuinely pleased to see Welthy again, marvelling at her strength, and summoning daughter-in-law Sonia to meet Welthy. Having done what she intended to do — demonstrate continuing friendship — Welthy bade farewell once again. As Indira escorted her to our waiting taxi, she made a point of giving a special *namaste* to our young Sikh driver and friend of many years, Gurmail Singh, whom she knew to be a supporter.

One final meeting reflected the new political reality in Delhi. Welthy's good friends Lakshmi and Devaki Jain came with their son and Kamaladevi Chattopadhya. Lakshmi was staunchly pro-Janata Party, his office having been used as their campaign headquarters. He and Devaki felt their labours had been rewarded and democracy vindicated, despite the deep misgivings so many westerners had about Indian politics. Serious and sensitive, the Jains and Welthy had long mutual respect and love.

As they were leaving, in walked Som and Suman Benegal, who had shared an equally long and warm connection with Welthy dating back to the days of Tom and Martha Keehn in the fifties. Som, the artist with irrepressible wit whose eyes still appreciated Welthy's long, slender legs, contemporary knee-length red suit and red sandals, had actively worked for Indira's election, resulting in a total freeze on his long friendship with Lakshmi. In Welthy's presence, they found a way to clasp hands and greet one another again, perhaps only as ships passing in the night, but the glimmer of hope was there.

It was time to leave India again, to move on to whatever was next. Was it intelligent for her to have made that visit in 1977 at ninety-eight years of age? Was it merely sentimental? Should a founder be present and accounted for at her 25th celebration? Was she accomplishing anything by going back there? To me it was profoundly wise and wonderful. An Indian account of the visit gives their view: "Welthy Fisher refuses to be an idol to be worshipped, a memory to be recollected in the peaceful irresponsibility of the non-doer. She embodies the unfailing challenge to flagging spirits among adult educators in India, the beam in her eye bright and infectious as ever."[26] How do we value that which is immeasurable?

AMERICA

Welthy tried to keep busy and interested in the things we could find to do. Friends and family visited, all very enjoyable but no substitute for her own active engagement with life. Hearing Han Suyin speak at Boston University Library, a fellow contributor to their Special Collection of Twentieth Century Personalities, intrigued Welthy. Their animated conversation afterwards excited her, and in the diminutive author's shining eyes China came alive to Welthy in a torrent of ideas.

I remember thinking I should get my camera out and capture that image of Han Suyin in her glittering Chinese silk, squatting in front of Welthy, who leaned precariously forward on her chair, their eyes and hands reaching for each other in first meeting of acknowledged regard. It was a choice of staying in the conversation or reverting to archivist.

In that unpremeditated moment when I chose to stay a subtle shift in our alignment occurred, though nothing was said or consciously raised. As always between Welthy and me, the important understandings were unspoken. My own interests were moving into equal time with hers, and I was clearly interested in China, having already done considerable research on Welthy's early years there. And Welthy was ready to be bewitched into shifting her gaze west towards China across the Pacific once more.

APPROACH TO CHINA, 1978

We left from San Francisco after a reunion there with Pearl Chen Lin, prolific poet of Bao-Lin, and planted ourselves in Hong Kong. Our request for visas through the Chinese Embassy in Washington had been declined, Welthy's age their great concern. Han Suyin introduced us to her old classmate Lee Tsung-ying, editor of *Eastern Horizon*, who shot off our request to Peking immediately from our hotel room after appraising Welthy's vigour. At the other end, Rewi Alley had been pulling for us, with the result that an informal approval was given.

We poised ourselves in Tokyo to await travel documents, an interval not without incident. Welthy's legs had become so weakened that in Hong Kong I had purchased a wheelchair which she used for any but the shortest walk. I developed a severe flu, requiring medical attention, but the Japanese doctor who came to our room preferred to minister unto Welthy, not one to sit quietly by. When the final okay came, I staggered off to get our Chinese visas, leaving Welthy alone with some foreboding.

I returned to find her on the floor in the bathroom where she had fallen. She quickly dispelled my alarm, and I knew from experience to trust her assessment of the damage better than mine. But after six hours of agonizing pain I bundled her off at midnight to the only hospital open to foreigners at that time because of a major accident in the city. The emergency area was closed, but a nurse came down from the wards to give Welthy indocin for pain and she promptly went to sleep on a narrow cot. I was the sole ambulatory inhabitant of the emergency room throughout the night, guarding my patient. Suddenly at 8:00 a.m. the doors burst open with hordes of Japanese in ski clothes, skis over their shoulders, pouring in. The staff had returned after a weekend.

X-ray, aspiration of knee, broken tibia, leg bound stiffly, no bending knee or bearing weight for three weeks. We were due to leave for Peking the next day when Welthy's transit visa for Japan expired. No one was willing to extend it, and only through cajoling the American Ambassador's secretary did His Excellency get into the act to win a one-day extension. That Welthy at ninety-nine was considered too dangerous to bend rules for should be a warning to anyone with a yen to arrange oriental travel tours for centenarians. But the senior staff of our hotel, meticulously dressed in black suits, unafraid, came to the hospital and carried Welthy with utmost delicacy, as though bearing a corpse discreetly through a private entrance and elevator back to our room and laid her gently in bed, beside the most exquisite bouquet of sweet peas.

She fell asleep again instantly, and finally I climbed into my warm, clean bed, deeply fatigued. The moment my head hit the pillow the world turned upside down. Was I having a stroke? I heard the bathroom curtains moving, and saw the building actually swaying; cowering in the entranceway I watched Welthy sleep on through the 6.3 earthquake.

There was one more hurdle to overcome that required my doing an end-run around Tokyo airport security to find a way to do what they said was impossible. Welthy had to be forklifted up to the Chinese plane since she could not walk or bend her knee. I located the one obscure elevator in the airport that would get her to a level where we could approach the plane, then found an unmarked door to the tarmac ramp that would make it possible to get her there.

Throughout all this there was never any question of giving up on getting to China. Welthy kept her mind focused on her destination, simply assuming that I would find a way. Her basic psychology was rewarded in that short, slow forklift up, up, up the outside of the plane that was carrying her back to China. Another landmark in a lifetime of transportation thrills.

PEKING, JANUARY 1978

As soon as we touched down in Peking, four Chinese appeared in the plane, placed Welthy in a wheelchair, picked it up and ran off with her before I had my seat belt undone. There she was waving merrily to me from the ground when I emerged from the plane. She always did enjoy getting places ahead of me![27]

Within her lifetime Welthy had seen China perceived as a worthy missionary cause, a valiant wartime ally, the most implacable of enemies, and now by 1978 a strange new friend. Small wonder she did not put all her faith in governments; she had seen the Chinese as friends all along.

The Great Wall represented the limits of understanding of the time, a need for protection, to keep strangers and strange ideas out. City walls too limited people's vision to what was within or immediately outside the walls. Now the nation-state was the wall setting the psychological limit on most minds, based on the assumption of conflict. But Welthy's whole life was based on breaking through those barriers. In 1978 she was once again where the action was as the world's crude efforts at cracking the walls of nation states was gaining momentum with a steady parade of foreigners peaking into China.

Her host was the Foreign Friendship Association, who provided a Red Flag limousine, a large suite at the Peking Hotel and all expenses, with careful attention to every need and desire. Welthy was persona grata not so much as a former liberal-minded missionary but for the real assistance she provided during the years of resisting the Japanese.[28]

Wang Ping-nan, Chairman of the Friendship Association and seasoned diplomat, gave a small banquet in her honour. Throughout the dinner he and his associates watched Welthy carefully as her arthritic hands wielded chopsticks with knowing agility, as she chatted in Mandarin with alternating jokes and jabs of thought, even with the mind-dulling influence of indocin. The Chinese were not at all inscrutable. They were just plain fascinated, as our interpreters later informed subsequent travellers.[29] Wang was moved to see the photo of close colleague Chou En-lai and his wife that Welthy had taken in Chungking in 1939. No treaties were signed that evening, no secret agreements made, but there was real friendship in the air. Who can measure the full impact of such things?

Talitha Gerlach, eighty-one, appeared at our door immediately. Rewi Alley, eighty, came across to the hotel from his quarters in the old Italian

Legation compound. By then he was the prime foreigner in China, living in the apartment where Anna Louise Strong had held forth, well cared for by the government and his own extended family of adopted Chinese sons and grandchildren. To celebrate the reunion, he asked his cook to produce the best possible dessert for our dinner in that apartment filled with the essence of brainstorming conversations, his books and porcelains so carefully collected through the years. With the arrival of the creation of ice cream, cake and chocolate, an almost spiritual reverence hung over that silent communion table as eyes, lips, tongues devoured the rare treat. Clear minds, happy hearts, and satisfied stomachs — a simple enough occasion to mark the meaning of that moment.

* * *

Welthy was looking for a symbolic sense of the historic change in China. She found it in Tien An Men Square at the recently-opened Memorial to Mao Tse-tung. My robust, eloquent friend wept softly in speechlessness with a recognition that struck deep in her being, evoking images of the turn of the century when China had only the faintest dreams of itself as a unified nation, when misery and fear marked most lives. Along with the grinding inequalities she had seen the raw strength of the people, a bitter strength as *ku li* signifies. Now, three-quarters of a century later, as two men and two women carried her wheelchair up the series of steps approaching the Memorial, she was overwhelmed by an image of her old sedan chair moving upward from her wheelchair.

Proud, strong men and women of the future were lifting her towards the memory of the man who changed the world for all of us, not only for the quarter of humanity that resides within China. Mao, mighty in white marble, commanding eternal attention to his philosophy and teaching; Mao, frail and finite in his casket, reminding us of the contradictions, the ceaseless struggle, the sacrifices.

As thousands of Chinese filed by in awesome silence, Welthy wondered if Mao was going to be idolized and worshipped. No, she decided, there had been too many adjustments and corrections along the way, and too much regard for Chou En-lai's balancing partnership. But Chinese at all levels will never forget who taught them the basics of self-respect and self-reliance on which the entire nation is now building. Not oblivious to problems and pitfalls in present-day China, Welthy chose to focus on the larger signs with their more enduring messages. It was not as if she did not understand obstacles.

SOONG CHING LING

Word came that Soong Ching Ling wanted to see Welthy, though in her declining health she was being very selective about meeting all the foreigners who sought her. She had still never joined the Communist Party, but was the Vice-Chairman of the National People's Congress, fifth in the overall hierarchy of China, and preparing for the fifth Congress meeting soon to take place.

Talitha and Rewi were with us for the twenty-minute drive north to the lakeside estate that was provided as her residence, formerly used as the palace of the last Emperor, Pu Yi. Soong Ching Ling remained seated to greet her guests, presenting small Christmas gifts to each from a basket on the table beside her. After the photographers were dismissed, she stood with the assistance of two aides, and we moved as a body through the stripped-down palace corridors to the room set aside for our 'banquet' of eight. A male secretary of the household, a woman from *China Reconstructs*, Dr. Ma's son, and the lovely ballet dancer Ching Ling had adopted years earlier made up the rest of the group. It was the closest facsimile of family she had, and the atmosphere was relaxed while she poked fun at Rewi with her pet name for him—Alley Baba. Her questions to Welthy had to do with American attitudes towards China and exposure of Chinese culture there.

Ching Ling's aides were not so relaxed, and we left right after dinner. She, supported on both sides, escorted Welthy, supported on one side, the full length of the palace—an interesting procession that went unphotographed. Ching Ling, who was several years younger, insisted on seeing Welthy to the car, keeping a watchful eye on me. I heard her say: "See how she cares for her," and as we exchanged glances I realized she understood better than most the partnership between Welthy and me.[30]

Though she was old and quite large, there was deep warmth shining out from her still beautiful eyes. As Welthy prepared to leave, few words were said, but I sensed the unspoken recognition of abiding alliance between two seasoned comrades, their presence to each other a gift of the ineffable. Fastidious hostess, Soong Ching Ling showed her personal concern for Welthy in several subsequent hand-written letters, seeking assurance that she had safely returned to her Connecticut home and relishing the visit in retrospect.

Welthy's original assessment of Soong Ching Ling as a woman of compassion, integrity and commitment to the uplift of her people remained constant through the years since they had first discussed education and social development. Her courageous struggle through bereavement and the break from the rest of her family, whom she considered greedily ambitious, was of historic proportions, played out in the public eye and thereby doubly difficult. Because of China's taboo on personal biography and focus on individuals, Soong Ching Ling's story is little known, but the view Welthy held of her was also held by some writers.[31]

Watching Welthy and Talitha, Welthy and Rewi, Welthy and Soong Ching Ling, mindful of the immense struggles and sacrifices involved in their chosen tasks, and now to be present at their consummate reunion was to know what we are missing in our attitudes and expectations of the elderly. Where else will we learn courage, values, sharing, wisdom if we don't cast our gaze their way? Welthy in her very advanced years felt herself no alien in China where she was recognized for the quality of her years and allowed her full freedom. As the visit ended there was a feeling of triumph in the air — hers and theirs — at the human victory of endurance through years of struggle.

AMERICA, 1978-1980

There had been tears in the eyes of our interpreter as Welthy was settled into the plane that was taking her from Peking, but she felt no sadness. Her mission was accomplished and she moved on with ease. By the time we reached Los Angeles, however, her whole body let down in answer to the extreme demands on it during the busy week in Peking and the long flights. In fact, we were both in bad shape, free to feel all our aches and pains. Just as well Connecticut was snowbound, all flights cancelled; we had ten days' enforced rest in a California motel.

My own developing flu, sinus infection aggravated by a cold and high altitudes, plus exhaustion, culminating in my only migraine, rendered me immobile. Welthy in the opposite bed had leg pains, a respiratory infection and serious constipation. She was not good at complaining but I knew it was bad. It was almost time to give up the game. We slept for twenty-four hours. Then I got out to a doctor and got medicine that would kill or cure me. A Chinese doctor friend of Ernest Lauh's came to look at Welthy, brought his wife and a feast of Chinese food, and after a miraculously wonderful 'banquet' with them, he announced Welthy should be hospitalized. I wondered, and waited for a sign.

That night, in her increasing agony, Welthy for the one and only time revealed her anxiety. "Do you think I'm going to die?" she asked. I had always been totally honest with her — she was too smart to fool. I thought carefully, assessing the previous medical crises we had endured. Then I climbed into her single bed and held her, saying: "No, I don't think you're going to die." We laughed and laughed, and she slept.

I knew that if Welthy went into a hospital where I had no connection she could get lost in the system. Decisions could be made based on age alone and she might well die there. Legs would have to wait till we got back to Connecticut; respiratory infection was treated by antibiotic and inhalation as an out-patient; and the severe internal blockage was relieved by a dynamite drug combined with a nursing procedure I learned out of sheer necessity. The gamble worked, and within two days Welthy was much improved. She had shown absolute trust in me throughout, as she did with everyone who helped her.

Soon after reaching Connecticut, her doctor came to the house to examine her legs and despatched her to hospital immediately, showing more than usual concern. The multiple clotting of deep-vein phlebitis in her right thigh and calf, as I learned from the nurse, was usually fatal in older women. A coloured dye was pumped into her leg in the diagnostic lab of Waterbury Hospital, showing such an unusual, clear picture of the disease that the technicians were fascinated and injected more

A sharp-eyed private duty nurse kept her eye on Welthy's face, which was rapidly reacting to the dye to which she was allergic. She suddenly gathered her patient and raced back to the ward where the emergency code went out. Welthy's ears and face bloated out of all recognition, no pulse, no blood pressure. The rescue team went to work, Welthy came back to life, and several nurses at Waterbury Hospital will never be the same. On the wall opposite Welthy's bed a large colour photo of our two cats in playful embrace kept everyone amused and connected during the days of blood-thinning treatment.

Back home we began a new regimen to protect her legs from further attack. Welthy endured with grace my little dictatorship of exercising leg muscles, frequent standing, etc., as one more adjustment to the reality of life. In that dark night of anxiety back in the California motel, we both knew her real question was did she want to continue living, and if so, what for.

We both doubled our efforts to keep her going. She massaged her stomach to keep all organs functioning, and exercised her legs in bed. I rubbed her back after her shower more vigorously than ever, and strained hard each day to pull on the strong elastic panty hose prescribed for her circulation. If I ever felt discouraged by the difficulties, the sight of Welthy, walking naked en route to the bathroom with her knees still knocking together from the old injury, was enough to catch me up quickly.

We settled into a quieter existence, more careful of diet, and of finances. Inflation had set in with a vengeance, calling for a new strategy of resource management. Welthy wanted to leave an estate for her work, but the Bank of New York was invading principal rapidly to provide income for her. My own situation was more limited, although I was living free in Welthy's home with a few small expenses paid. In return she was

getting round-the-clock care. I never promised to remain with her till
the end, nor did she ask, directly.

WASHINGTON, D.C., SEPTEMBER 8, 1978

At the White House-sponsored conference on International Literacy
Day, Welthy enlivened a day of dispirited speechifying at the State
Department, still unable to understand why educators insisted on
dehumanizing their endless debate.[32] She was dramatic and playful in
her presentation, sharp and serious in intent as she presaged the possibility of universal lapse into illiteracy:

> *I have often thought the world is divided between those who
> care for the other and those who do not. Illiteracy stems
> from carelessness. We know now that it can afflict us also.
> Let us continue to care, so that everyone will have that great
> chance to grow.*

The Freedom Medal having eluded her once again, she was given a
consolation prize in the form of a citation sent from Vice-President Walter Mondale.[33] Welthy seemed destined to be a prophet without appropriate honour in her own country.

NEW YORK, SEPTEMBER 18, 1978

Welthy's ninety-ninth birthday was celebrated at a glittering event in-
augurating World Education's centennial fund-raising campaign for the
Welthy Fisher Fund, to which she gave the lead gift of eighty-two
thousand dollars. Lillian Gish, Roger Baldwin, Betty Furness and Mme.
Pandit were the leading luminaries among an interesting assortment of
Welthy's friends. The idea was to raise a million dollars in one year, but
from the beginning World Education thought the goal unattainable and
was never fully committed to it. They felt more comfortable with a one
hundred thousand dollar goal. "Why not a million?" asked Welthy.

As a result of that disparity and general stress, I was at odds with the
World Education board and staff for the year leading up to Welthy's one
hundredth, as we tried to plan fund-raising materials and events. I felt
they were trying to erase what Welthy stood for when they refused to
put the House of Prayer for All People on the reverse of the centennial
medallion to be used as a gift to large contributors.

I saw it as the one symbol that represented Welthy's purpose and action most clearly. It showed a spiritual, humanizing underpinning to
her work and an unlimited inclusiveness towards everyone involved. It
was dismissed as smacking of religion by the newest member of the
board, an expert in fund raising. I felt that World Education had missed
the essence of Welthy's life as an educator.

In opting for a global, professional, government-aided programme on a scale requiring large salaries and job security, WE had turned sharply away from the people-to-people path Welthy had built. They had reverted to a previous era of relying on government and experts, where Welthy first came in.[34]

In fact, the woman who was in charge of their centennial fund-raising campaign, gave up on our idiosyncracies and told me bluntly that the world did not need to know about Welthy Fisher. In their new role, WE needed to dilute Welthy's image and she resigned herself to the inevitable cycle of progress far better than I did. She kept her love warm for the individual members and had faith that they would each find their way.

Individual trustees with continuity on the board tried to preserve the integrity of Welthy's approach,[35] but the heady atmosphere of international development and large grant funding had taken hold. The grantors' priorities dominated, and the grantees' corporate identities burgeoned with administrative muscle. In their corporate loyalty in an era of control and consolidation, board members were spared the need to question themselves individually as to broad purpose. It was the old paradox of a leader having to die to followers while they grew through living experience into the realm of new ideas.

The board said if Welthy wants a million, let her raise it, and set up fund-raising events for her in cities across the country where there were still remnants of support from her earlier efforts. Welthy was hoping the board would use the occasion for raising the funds itself, and I was hoping it would seriously look at her life work in the process. But we were both dreaming. It was simply not possible to commit ourselves to the kind of scheduling they envisaged. Unfortunately we were at cross purposes.

Admittedly a disagreeable thorn to WE, I had reason for concern over their financial management. They would admit a serious problem, bring in a new financial officer and still the questions would remain unanswered. I lost confidence in WE, removed myself from the fund committee, and was resigned to getting through the centennial year as best we could, with a grand celebration for Welthy.

Welthy was not actively involved in any of this, but she responded to the stress she sensed in me by falling in her bathroom again. This time it was a compressed fracture of the sacro-ilium, with plenty of pain, and a chance to do some fund-raising in the ambulance en route to hospital. Could this really be happening again? Wonderful doctors and nurses, who got from Welthy as much as they gave; Welthy singing merrily on the return ambulance trip two weeks later, irrepressible, cooperative, and determined to be one hundred. The rest was detail. Her broken bones always mended quickly, her falls due to precipitous movement, not osteoporosis. In no time she was poking down the hall with her walker at a fast clip, mentally a youngster.

We got stronger medicine for her arthritic pain, therapy to strengthen her hip and leg muscles, new moulded shoes, new teeth, and a plan to lose ten pounds to lessen pressure on her weight-bearing joints. You see, Welthy wanted to swing into that big birthday party in grand form. Someone had sent her a card with advice on how to reach one hundred years: "Get to be ninety-nine and then be very careful."

She loved the times when people came to talk about her work, especially the two women who had chosen her as subject of their Ph.D. theses, and gladly gave them whatever time they wanted.[36] And I was able to direct them to sources of information I had already uncovered for this biography.

The highlight of that penultimate year was a beautiful banquet in Welthy's home town, Rome, New York, where three hundred people poured out love to their native daughter in a shining affair organized by Viola Gaylord, a retired teacher with keen international understanding. Lael Wertenbaker was one of the brightest stars that evening, having rediscovered Welthy, and remained close from then on.

At WE's instigation, Lael had been asked by the *New York Times Magazine* to do an article on Welthy, which never got published due to a strike at the paper and skepticism that Welthy was some kind of cult figure. WE's confusion about Welthy carried over into their presentation of her to others. She did not ring true. There was no solid evidence to prove the impact of her work. But the Romans recognized Welthy for who and what she was. It showed in Welthy's unabashed enthusiasm as she spoke of the freedom cultivated in her at the Rome Free Academy on their Liberty Street in the early stages of her learning.

One week before the big birthday a private celebration took place at our home, Bao-Lin style. In all the years of focus on India Welthy had not forgotten her first love and the people who were part of it. Wang Gwei-hsin came from New York, as she often did in those years, with a basket of Chinese food, and Sally Kiang, one of the five in the first graduating class, came with her younger sister. Welthy joined in the food preparation, largely in conversational mode, as the years rolled by and the stories told. At one point I heard Gwei-hsin, more feisty than ever, confess how angry she had been with Welthy when she sent Sally Kiang back to China after one year at Oberlin in the U.S. Sally was staying with Mabel that year, with Welthy paying her tuition. Word got back to Welthy that she was seeing too many boys and was not serious enough about her work. What other tidbits of truth might have emerged from an extended banquet one may only speculate.

The mood was happy, and the three gathered round the organ as Welthy, in her brilliant scarlet robe with broad white collar and cuffs, looking absolutely ecclesiastic, proclaimed the old Bao-Lin school song in robust, rhythmic tones. Never has there been such singing! I was witness once more to a mystic bonding that defies description.

The organ was a recent addition, my idea of a potentially satisfying way for Welthy to use her energy. So I, the non-musician, proceeded to teach Welthy, the songstress and pianist, how to make that complex instrument work. Her fingers wanted to race. Her eyes couldn't make out the notes. I pored over the instructions. The cats paraded on the keys. Finally, some sounds began to come out, and Welthy was making music again. What a thrill! Every afternoon, garbed in her long, black velvet skirt and red stole, she would soar away with America the Beautiful and Onward Christian Soldiers, the two tunes most deeply encoded in her musical memory.

ONE HUNDREDTH BIRTHDAY, SEPTEMBER 18, 1979

Welthy had a fantasy that suddenly everything was hers free from here on, especially flights to anywhere in the world. For that day at least, it was. The centennial edition of her autobiography, "To Light a Candle," published in India with a new prologue and epilogue, arrived that morning, a good portent. And the beautiful centennial medallion was also ready just in time,[37] inscribed with Welthy's 1947 universal insight: "The world has always been one. We have not recognized it."

That evening, one hundred and sixty-five of Welthy's family, friends and loyal supporters gathered on the roof of the St. Regis Hotel in New York City for an evening of total celebration.[38] Lael Wertenbaker and her husband Bramwell Fletcher, the English actor, co-hosted the party, warming up the mood during dinner, awaiting the appearance of Welthy.

As the orchestra struck up Purcell's triumphant march, Welthy arrived at her moment of glory in an elegant, red Indian silk gown of her own design, preceded by ten 'escorts' in black tie. In a body everyone rose to their feet for an extended ovation, shouts of 'Bravo Bravo'. All seemed unwilling to let the magic moment go, as each one exulted in their share of Welthy's dream.

Out came a brilliant birthday cake with one hundred candles ingeniously engineered by Charles Limouze, and the old sung was sung with gusto. Bramwell read out the telegrams: From Indira Gandhi, from Soong Ching Ling and Talitha Gerlach, Han Suyin, Syracuse University, the Governors of New York and Connecticut, and so many others.

Literacy House sent a tape from morning prayers with the worship song
"*Raghupati Raghava Raja Ram*" that had become etched in Welthy's
soul through the years. From the President of the United States came a
brief greeting.[39]

In song and word Welthy's life was unveiled before our eyes,
punctuated with some good old hymn singing that brought a glow to
many hearts. Welthy had requested "America the Beautiful", anthem of
her early dream whose spirit she extended beyond seas and verse.
Welthy knew who she was, and so did we.

Of the speakers, Betty Furness was superbly and respectfully amusing,
Marijke Geertsema thoughtfully informative, Belen Abreu from the Magsaysay Foundation in Manila, humble and sincere, Lisa Sergio at her
prayerful best. Ambassador Carol Laise Bunker said: "You showed us
long before the women's liberation movement that an open heart can
open minds and really liberate us all."

Not surprisingly, several people remarked that the women speakers
outshone the men noticeably, though the men all rose to the occasion:
Bishop Ralph Ward, Jr., Benjamin Mayes and Tom Keehn. When it came
Welthy's time to speak, few could hear her well because the microphone
had gone off and seemed to be saying let Welthy do it on her own. As
they strained to listen, her voice moved out into the room and they
caught her meaning:

> *What a wonderful way to begin a new century!*
> *I wish the same for each of you, my beloved family and*
> *friends.*
> *I look around and wonder, am I in heaven? I see so many*
> *glittering stars and radiant lights in your eyes.*
> *You have given me a new song to sing as I face the future.*
> *(I won't try to sing it just now.)*
> *We need all our courage for the new beginnings awaiting us,*
> *for the heavy tasks to be done in this world, for sharing our*
> *lives and our skills with those who need so much.*
> *I have deep faith in each one of you, whatever your work*
> *may be, in building the new dawn in an ever more caring*
> *world.*
>
> *I thank you a hundred times from the depth of my heart —*
> *your love means everything to me - and I thank our God of*
> *all people for the gift of your friendship and for allowing me*
> *to be so richly blessed. Forgive me please for arriving late*
> *at this great gathering — I hope you weren't worried.*

*Now I want to greet you each one, to hold your hands in
mine,
in a moment we shall never forget.*

In the final tribute, Bramwell said what we all felt as he spoke of
Welthy's inexhaustible vigour, her decisiveness, her refusal to be discouraged, and her great sense of fun. The evening ended with a rousing round of "Of Thee We Sing Welthy" to the Gershwin tune, as Welthy
received each of her well-wishers individually, giving them what they
wanted that she alone possessed — "that certain thing" of the song.

The feeling in the air that magnificent evening was something akin to
what generations of assembled elders might feel in welcoming the arrival of a new child into their community. Welthy belonged to us, and
she gave us light and beauty and hope.

* * *

To celebrate Welthy's indestructibility we went up to my cottage in
Canada, where the October winds knocked down trees, blocking the
road and leaving us isolated in the woods without electricity. And the
snows began. Welthy had the time of her life watching me carry wood
and water, learning the facts of daily life she had known as a young girl.
The mini-crisis did not worry her at all. She had fun watching the fire
dance, but I made a silent memo to get a telephone line brought in so
we would have a phone the next time I took her there.

And I paid closer attention to Welthy's desire to make a final revision
to her will, with instructions on the disposal of her ashes. She wished
part of them to go to the church in Detroit, and part to Literacy House,
and it was agreed Mike and I would carry out her wishes respectively.
Some time later Welthy, the great participator, asked: "Will Mike be with
us when we take my ashes to Detroit?"

Welthy's family of nieces and nephews gave a large reception in the
church in Southbury for their friends who did not come to the New York
party. There was no separation between her private and public life and
her family had no more success than her boards in trying to capture
Welthy. Since I was taking my cue from her, often providing a quick get-
away, I was not exactly beloved. Mike and Norma Honsinger were particularly attentive to "Aunt Welthy", along with Grace and Charles
Limouze. To Ernest and Julie Lauh, Welthy was always "Mother Fisher".

INDIA, MARCH 1980

Welthy had been invited by the Ministry of Education to celebrate her
centennial in India as the government's guest, but the invitation was temporarily suspended when a general election was unexpectedly called.

We waited, poised to move. After Indira Gandhi returned as Prime Minister, the come ahead signal arrived.

The Government of India was offering full travel and expenses to both of us for a one-month visit. I went through the motions of rational decision-making, but knew in my heart we would go. Even Welthy's doctor said: "Go ahead if she wants to and you think you can handle it. You know her body as well as we do and you have various prescriptions you can use as you see fit." For Welthy, if there was a chance to go, to know and to see more, of course she was going. One hundred years of age, Welthy gave no visible signs of concern for her safety, health or the hazards of a long journey. She had been in global orbit so long, that the abnormal thing was to sit at home endlessly awaiting the ultimate call.

Our time was divided between Delhi and Lucknow, seeing as many people as possible each day. It was a tremendous switch from the quiet time in Connecticut. Suddenly we kept appointments by the hour, giving interviews, calling on the President of India, the Governor of Uttar Pradesh, being honoured at receptions by the YWCA, the Indian Adult Education Association, the Gandhi Peace Foundation, the Lucknow Printers' Association, Isabella Thoburn College and the Minister of Education. Welthy was determined to look her best, always selecting the most brilliant, shimmering red silk scarf to toss over her shoulder.

At a colourful function under the big *shamiana*, Bhagwan Sahay came to Literacy House to preside to over the Government of India's release of a thirty-*paise* commemorative postage stamp showing Welthy Fisher and the House of Prayer for All People. And Literacy House released two publications in honour of Welthy's centennial.[40]

At a special convocation at Delhi University an Honorary Doctorate of Letters was bestowed on Welthy whose "life is a translation into action of this spirit . . . of making the struggle with darkness narrower." Welthy's speech was strong and clear, and brief. She insisted on standing, while I propped her up from behind.

The American Ambassador, Robert Goheen, came to call on her, a happy switch after all her years of calling on American Ambassadors in various capitals around the world.

At a reception by the Minister of Education of the Government of India in the grand ballroom of the Ashoka Hotel, Mrs. Gandhi arrived by helicopter after a day's touring dusty villages. Great armfuls of flowers were presented to Welthy and Indira; Indira turned and gave hers to me, in gratitude for bringing Welthy back to India. On the whole Welthy got through the demanding public occasions with her faculties intact.

The following day Indira came to our hotel to call on Welthy, though her new staff had tried to have Welthy come to her. After the inevitable swoop of photographers had left, we three sat down for tea, and I realized that what I had feared all along was actually happening. As I had been juggling her medications on a trial and error basis to meet the dual needs of sleep and pain relief, I had guessed wrong, and Darvon was in command. Welthy was not making much sense; night was day, black was white, but she did seem to know something was wrong and wisely decided to keep quiet. Programmed old fundraiser that she was, however, Welthy gave me a nudge, nodded towards Indira and muttered: "Be sure to get her address." In that moment, Indira and I had a good laugh, established an intimacy of understanding, and went on to chat.

Anil Bordia brought the key staff of the National Adult Education Programme, then two years underway, to brief Welthy on its progress, during the statistical part of which she napped. Adult education was now established as part of the government's minimum needs programme. Motivating illiterates remained the root problem. Voluntary agencies were playing a prominent role, with LH by far the largest supplier of teaching and follow-up materials in many languages, as well as training and retraining planners, administrators and supervisors. The momentum for literacy was at last in place; they said there was no turning back now.

My cousin Corinne Swenson Scott, who had first introduced me to Welthy and was now involved with the NAEP at the field level, told us there were still great difficulties and discrepancies in the Programme. But there was movement such as there had never been before.

As old friends and staff came to greet Welthy, there was love and respect and joy on so many faces as they clasped her hands and sought her blessing. Is there some index to measure that absolute trust? How do you plan for that love quotient in project proposals, that extra dimension that soars beyond theory and textbook, that makes friends and plants seeds, that inspires and sustains those who do not fear it or embrace it for the wrong reasons? I thought about this book and knew it would never be fully written. At best I could suggest that what I had seen was significant. The radio, television and newspapers were all saying so prominently.

Our plane rose from Palam Airport as Welthy's long journey was ending, she turned to me and said: "I left something in India, didn't I?"

THE LAST MONTHS IN AMERICA

We returned to Connecticut where no news had come through of India's regard for Welthy and her journey there. Once again, the American press chose to ignore it. I wondered how many Americans have been so honoured in their lifetime, their faces carried to all corners of India on a postage stamp. Why was her work being devalued, and along with it, India's recognition of it? Is the light too bright to bear?

Welthy was deeply tired, with no more tomorrows on the immediate horizon. Mysterious abdominal pains began to dominate her days and nights. The home stretch was upon us.

We did get back to my cottage for the last summer in time to use the telephone I had finally had installed to call an ambulance when her pain suddenly sharpened, unbearably. After a night in the small local hospital, she was sent to a large hospital in Ottawa where the diagnosis was acute cholecystitis, acute pancreatitis, non-functioning bowel, hemoglobin 50%, dehydrated, congested chest. The head nurse told me later that there were one or two days during that interval when she felt Welthy's death must be imminent. As I sat by the bed, listening for each breath, the process of mourning began.

A very wise and wonderful Dutch Catholic priest, himself recovering from open-heart surgery, came and sat on Welthy's bed, took her hands in his and asked her to pray. Her words poured out so strong and clear, more faithful than I had ever heard her, not for her own life, not for release from suffering, but for the people of the world whose basic needs are still unmet. In that act, her life was renewed, and she gave it back to the young nurse who sat through the critical nights and later wrote of that extraordinary experience.

In late August we got back to Connecticut with difficulty. Since I could no longer handle Welthy alone, she was hospitalized briefly. But soon I took her home with the support of her doctor and visiting nurses. Gradually our privacy gave way to her need for more care, and I was confronted with my need to begin the separation process. Allowing others to look after her, and showing gratitude, Welthy was beautifully cared for, her skin still in exceptional condition.[41]

One quiet autumn afternoon while we sat out in the garden having tea I asked Welthy very simply:

"What's the most important thing you've learned in life?"

> *To love those who gave you life and brought you up and gave*
> *you everything — and to give it back to the world's people.*

On October 20th she wanted a new robe to look her best for all her new medical friends, and I took her to Naugatuck Mall in her wheelchair to buy yet one more red velvet thriller robe. She was happy, but in a sudden glance at her grey countenance I knew how close it was. She could still put on a good performance for visitors.

Bishop Ralph Ward, Jr. came in early December in response to my call. I felt Welthy needed to pray with one of her own Methodists on high. She was there in her wheelchair in the living room in her ecclesiastical red robe when he arrived, the fireplace adding its own welcome. They sat close and talked, he was "surprised at her vigour and ability to discuss things in her usual beautiful and careful manner of speech." After he offered a prayer, Welthy took his hands in hers and "prayed in a most personal, articulate and inspiring way," her spirit soaring so that he was oblivious to the fact that her frail body was immobilized in a wheelchair and she was close to death. "Then she arose," he recalled, "and with you at her side walked quite smartly back into her room."[42]

That afternoon, while listening to majestic music with arms uplifted to the heavens, Welthy became strangely subdued, a grey chill coming over her. It was a mild heart attack. Quietly that night she prayed: "O God, take me home."

She was confined to her room with its blue velvet chair that she and the cats loved, then limited to her hospital bed with its metal railings. Life's movements fell from her one by one. I had imagined that she would slip away painlessly, that she of all people had earned it, but it was not so. The last weeks were increasingly painful, requiring morphine near the end to ease her way.

She was surrounded by loving attention, visits by her nieces and nephews, music, the cats, in her own home with a sunny view over the advancing winter scene. She struggled a while to get out of bed and go downtown again, but her breathing pattern was in the last stages. The nurse said it could not be long. She rallied many times, and the pain increased. "Will God ever forgive me?" she asked.

On December 10th she turned to me and said: "How will I live without you? I love you more than anything on earth," the last words Fred Fisher had spoken to her that Maundy Thursday in 1938.

When Ernest came two days later and sat by her bedside with his fingers caressing her forehead and hair, her eyes were fixed at a distance as she said: "See how beautiful the sunlight is."

On December 15th Helen Krayer Schwartz arrived from Albuquerque in time to speak with her beloved old friend, who was slipping in and out of consciousness.

As an embryonic spirit gestates in the womb, it had taken nine months from the time of Welthy's last, bold worldly connection for her spirit to separate from the body. In the early morning of December 16th, 1980, Welthy smiled once more and slipped away peacefully. For thirty-seven thousand days she had borne her gift lightly through the noise of the world's marketplace and did not lose her way.

EPILOGUE

For ten decades Welthy's reach was sufficiently beyond grasp to keep her fully engaged with the world and its people, consciously trying to narrow the gap between real and ideal.

As an educator, she learned to ask the right questions of herself as well as of others. She understood that the answers were in the unfolding process of living. Welthy considered example the most credible form of education, and universal values the most reliable asset in life.

Living and speaking with the authority of her own conviction gave her a very personal style of leadership that leaves no legacy of theory or policy. She wanted to be judged by her actions. The power she sought was her own deepest sense of connection with people everywhere in past, present and future generations, and the strength to share that awareness.

In the messages that arrived from various parts of the world and in the three memorial services after her death, the spontaneous tributes from a wide range of individuals offer clues to the impact of Welthy's century of action.

At the small service in the Methodist Church in Woodbury, Connecticut, two days after Welthy's death, these words from Bishop Ralph Ward, Jr.:

> *Christ was the one who gave her the vision of the world that brought her into contact with the other great religions. Not just the Christian faith or one branch of it had the answer. Her deep love of life for all persons was the supreme characteristic of her life.*

Rev. Thomas B. Keehn of World Education:

> *There is a litany of life — eternal life — which leaps forward in certain words — caring, for absolutely everyone; loving, critic and friend; laughing, full and joyful; divine impatience, moving forward to new tomorrows; being at home, wherever her feet took her and her body rested. We feel we are an intimate part of the endless links she forged which literally circled the world.*

Central Methodist Church in Detroit offered their memorial tribute the following April, the full choir and orchestra performing Faure's Requiem, with the spotlight on the freshly installed plaque in the altar marking Welthy's ashes beside Fred's. Welthy could not have planned a more appropriate homecoming. A single rosebud was illuminated beside the inscribed words Welthy took as her motto: "It is better to light one candle than to curse the darkness."

Comfort Shaw of Literacy House wrote from India:

> *Mrs. Fisher and we worked not as an employer or employee, not as a giver or recipient or with any consciousness of being superior or inferior. We worked as common persons, for the common people that lived mostly in villages. What lovely days were those when we thought of nothing else but of work.*

Rewi Alley from Peking:

> *Welthy was one of the great American women of her day, direct and forceful, with an ability to pick out the thing to back and give it her strength.*

Bhagwan Sahay of the India Literacy Board:

> *She had a unique sense of oneness with all kinds of people which rendered communication between them and her very simple, very direct, very natural. She set out to assist large masses of people to conquer the darkness of ignorance through lighting the candle of education. On the way, her own personality became a supreme symbol of enlightenment.*

From her Indian physician, Dr. Sarah Itty:

> *It was as though she had some kind of a dynamo inside her to supplement her willpower.*

From Prime Minister Indira Gandhi:

> *Beautiful, efficient, enthusiastic and energetic, she lived life to the hilt . . . and put hundreds of thousands of young women on their feet.*

From the Indian Government's National Adult Education Programme Newsletter:

> *Mrs. Fisher's integrated approach to functional education still remains the guiding principle in expanding nonformal education in developing countries.*

From puppeteer Bil Baird:

> *This tower of strength will be around us for some time. Her purpose and direction gave us confidence.*

From her skeptical biographer Lael Wertenbaker:

> *If anyone ever understood the nature of friendship without regard to cultural, ideological or color barriers, Welthy did.*

* * *

Welthy's physician had found no disease to cause her death, though an undetected cancer may have been the source of the pain she suffered at the end. "She just fizzled out," he said, commenting on her remarkable skin and a mental attitude so positive that it must have contributed to her longevity.[1]

A year later, I carried out Welthy's wish to take the remaining portion of her ashes to Literacy House. The entire campus had assembled inside the gate for that last arrival, as the black velvet sack containing the small brass urn of her ashes was handed over to Shivpuri, the acting director. The urn was then carried to Welthy's campus house and placed on the large round copper table amidst Bukhnu's flowers. Many came by to scatter a few more petals, silently acknowledging the great transition.

The next morning Dr. Koshy led a procession bearing the ashes to their final resting place in a niche in the wall of the House of Prayer for All People. During a simple service representing the religions of India, everyone passed by to place their petals around the urn before the wall was sealed in with a marble plaque commemorating Welthy's life.[2]

Immediately following the service the group processed to the library building to inaugurate the permanent exhibition of Welthy's life prepared by Ariel and the opening of a three-day National Study Group on Adult and Non-Formal Education, where to my surprise I was requested to make some opening remarks. I fell back on Olive Schreiner's words as paraphrased by Welthy,[3] to remind them of her faith in the unfolding process, that all the answers would not be found in those conference rooms:

> *There are stairs of literacy that must be built. It has been my striving to build some of these stairs here and there. The stairs are crude and difficult . . . but others will come after me and they will climb — and on my stairs. And soon a world half in the darkness of illiteracy will begin to climb, to make better stairs and finally reach the top step in individual freedom and development.*

* * *

Welthy's experiment on the plains of India had taken root. By an act of faith she had made that spot on the desert of Uttar Pradesh blossom into life. Now, thirty-five years after her beginnings on that verandah in Allahabad, there are signs that Welthy did indeed leave something in India.

Three leading government figures, aware of my mission, received me immediately upon arrival in Delhi, each indicating in separate ways their recognition of Welthy's ashes being returned to India.

Wanting the personal link with Welthy I represented, the Prime Minister, Indira Gandhi gave precedence to meeting me over a swarm of national and international dignitaries waiting in her outer office. The next day she wrote to me: "I think Mrs. Fisher aimed at something much wider than merely teaching the alphabet. Through literacy she tried to enrichen personality and also offered opportunities for employment."[4]

The Minister of Education of the Government of India, Sheila Kaul, who with her husband had been good friends of Welthy's, invited me to their home for a long, thoughtful talk about Welthy's life and the strenuous years of exacting work she devoted at the end of it to creating a base for literacy in India.

Dr. S.N. Saraf, head of the educational branch in the Planning Commission of the Government of India, said that there was money now for literacy, but lethargy in the Ministry of Education was the problem. He intended to push the bureaucrats before his retirement the following year. "We need a hundred more Welthy Fishers," he said, "and a Literacy House in every state."

The next year, 1982, Sheila Kaul announced that the Sixth Five Year Plan of the Government would allocate 128 crores of rupees (approximately one hundred thirty-three million U.S. dollars) for adult education, a quantum leap over previous Plans.[5]

In 1984, Mrs. Gandhi acknowledged that "an important part of our existing adult education programme includes Mrs. Fisher's ideas on integrated and functional education for adults."[6]

The same year Literacy House was named one of four regional resource centres serving the national network of *Nehru Yuva Kendras* (Youth Centres operating under the National Service Scheme of the State Universities, NSS) with training, information, evaluation and counselling for non-student youth in a wide variety of cultural, vocational and development efforts in villages. In addition to servicing sixty-five centres in five northern states, Literacy House is also the State Resource Agency for Youth Affairs for U.P., Welthy's strategic choice of location in that largest state in the nation (over one hundred and ten million population).

While publications, puppetry and silkscreen printing are still the backbone of communication and prime income generator, the focus of Literacy House training has shifted to the higher levels of responsibility and educational background of the emerging cadre of adult education workers, movement in the direction Welthy intended.[7]

The pioneer years of risk-taking over, Literacy House has become an integral part of the infrastructure being put in place throughout India to enhance all aspects of village life through literacy and adult education. Recognition of the rural people as the critical national resource has begun to be accepted, with the focus on young adults, exactly where Welthy targeted her efforts.

A former educator himself, *Acharya* Kripalani saw Welthy's approach as new in India, combining scientific experimentation and flexibility with a universally friendly attitude that flowed out from her House of Prayer. "Whoever thinks deeply of education will naturally think of Tagore's ideas," he said, giving Welthy full marks for that perception. Not noted for his charitable remarks, Kripalani considered Welthy to have none of the superiority feeling of other Europeans and Americans. She joined villagers in singing and dancing, language never a barrier. Most of all, he respected her power to make up her mind.[8]

As Literacy House began to look at its history, Girijapati Mukharji reflected on those transition years with the realization that the India Literacy Board had brought in "a succession of self-serving directors, intellectually inadequate and emotionally uncommitted."[9] Harsh judgment in the circumstances, for if Welthy had been less adequate and less committed, the gap would not weigh so heavily—nor would Literacy House exist.

In the resignation of his final years Bhagwan Sahay thought private support within India was unattainable and accepted the inevitable lessening of initiative as government support and bureaucracy increased.[10] There are younger minds in India today exploring ways of working upwards from the grassroots in self-sustaining endeavours, but such minds need more creative space than LH now permits in this period of consolidation. The matter has long been out of Welthy's hands, her gift to India theirs to shape for the twenty-first century.

The institution Welthy created has achieved full independence from its foreign cooperators, and literacy is finally on the government's priority agenda, with her strategic focus in place. The stairs of literacy are being built in painstaking articulation,[11] forward thrusts and disappointing fallbacks as individuals and institutions struggle to narrow the gap between their own privileged position and the injustice holding back the power of the non-literate.

In the literature of literacy, however, Welthy remains as invisible as the illiterate, their powerful human presence yet to be admitted into the club. At the intellectual level it is taken for granted that the human factor Welthy presented so eloquently is understood; in reality it is too painfully simple to recognize. The human imprint that Dr. Adiseshiah had taken as the lesson of Welthy's work will take time to come to full life in the various organizations with which she was associated.

Welthy's constant struggle to provide an environment for change and growth was essential to a pioneering effort, and she tenaciously defended an expandable, adjustable stance of the work as each new administrator tried to impose limits. In that spirit her refusal to delineate details of the future direction of Literacy House was her ultimate gift.

In her role as Chairman of the ILB and President of WE, Welthy's life was a living contradiction under which she did not collapse. The hard, practical, quantitative mindset of WE was pitted against the India Literacy Board's timeless tolerance of things good and bad in unresolved differences that she transcended, the peacemaker who kept the whole together.

Keeping the door of Literacy House open to all comers and the programme flexible was an extension of her own personal open-door policy. All of us who came to help Welthy walked through that door into the sunshine she created around us, making it possible to exercise our freedom. Many of us have floundered far from the nobility she accorded in treating us as if we were living our full potential. Still, we cannot forget. "The Gate that is Always Open" has become the Literacy House motto currently in use.

THE CHOICES OF A LIFETIME

Welthy did not fit within the established role for her times, but sought her own place beyond the system without creating enemies or feeling herself to be a victim of any kind. She understood that life is movement — change — choice.

Treasuring the spark of life within herself, Welthy made the lonely, difficult choices necessary for growth: when she let go of her operatic ambitions with its dependence on public acclaim; when she would not let Parla fashion her into a decorative wife; when she would not let the Methodists mould her into a stereotype missionary; when she would not let Cousin Dee lure her into the elite establishment; when she would not settle for a lover without total connection; when she would not sacrifice her potential for the association of Gandhi's ashram; when she would not be pulled down into despair by Einstein's negative outlook; when she would not be limited to blood relatives in her search for family; when she would not be confined to one exclusive, religious ideology; when she moved out from the influence of masculine authority into conscious acceptance of her own woman power; when she gave Literacy House its distinct, independent identity and location; when she insisted on listening to the village voice, refusing to depend on the limited public knowledge compiled by the British and their trained successors; when she moved beyond the concept of basic literacy to literacy as a fundamental human right affecting total human development; and when she chose to accept the experience of her years as her rightful opportunity to act.

* * *

Indira Gandhi had said that "the poor people of India are the wealth of Welthy Fisher."[12] No mere play on words to be dismissed as self-effacing charity at the expense of perpetuating the helplessness of others, Indira was speaking from her own awareness of powerfully conflicting forces demanding choice. For Welthy, the choice was to uncover the village mystique of poverty.

She had peeled back the accumulated layers of religions to carry their core with her. She placed herself at the living centre between rich and poor, educated and uneducated, East and West, freedom and responsibility. That movement between opposites was the essential rhythm of her life, the source of her energy and creative ideas, her recognition of reality. And in that fine balance she chiselled out the practical path of literacy.

By discipline and desire she transformed her pain at the loss of personal love into the broad depth of universal love. I know no way of measuring her gift of hope with any precision. But I do know with the certainty of the sun that Welthy Honsinger Fisher passed the spark from one century to another in her burning leap through the generations of her life.

Welthy dared to personalize her work, unafraid of identifying herself as a vital part of it. She never lectured; instead she offered the grand theatre of her whole personality. That enlivenment created an educational movement for adult literacy in India. The need she saw remains immense.

Taking positive action, announcing, not denouncing, she put individual responsibility before state responsibility. Being what you want others to be was her path to peace. As Dr. Bhola acknowledged: "When literacy work was an almost forgotten ideal, she provided the hope, the place, the visibility, the movement needed. She not only personalized a social concern . . . she powerfully influenced the literacy movement both at the national and international levels."[13]

While her own crisis-ridden Methodist Church debated in grand conference halls the relative merits of evangelical versus social needs,[14] Welthy, on the ground in India, offered clear signals of Christian tradition. It was not until her centennial year that she received full acceptance as a member of the flock, when the Methodists invited her to address their General Conference.[15]

When Henry Lacy was Executive Secretary for India and Nepal of the Methodist Global Board of Missions, he acknowledged that the secret of Welthy's success was in following her own concepts in seeking freedom for creative development.[16] The early disdain of some Methodists for her "excessive individualism" had changed to one of great pride and respect for her ability, even downright envy of the financial support she had achieved and her success in bridging the vast religious gaps. Lacy said it had always been the theologians, not the laity, who had been more critical.

Rev. Philip Gentile, who had planned the memorial service in Detroit, was moved to restore the nearly defunct Fisher Fund to its original intent, increasing its base tenfold with the help of a generous bequest from the Ford sisters' estate.[17]

THE AFFECTIVE PRINCIPLE

Welthy's method was love-based. She took the first step to let people know she liked them and reached out with long arms and hands to pull them in toward her. She wanted and needed people close to her. No slave to personal likes and dislikes, she took delight in each individual before sending them out refreshed by her hearty warmth.

In her study of eight older women it was only with regard to Welthy that Klaitz broke through the objectivity of her thesis to use subjective words such as "keen, sparkling, astonishing, attractive, looking twenty-five to thirty years younger" when she interviewed Welthy at ninety-eight, by far the oldest of the exceptional women she studied, admitting it was not easy to begin writing about someone as uncommon as Welthy.[18]

In the easy informality Welthy provided, genuine interaction took place spontaneously among people, creating a synthesis of thought and feeling. To take the life out of learning by insisting on objectivity and abstraction was a deadening split of mind and spirit that ignored the essence of human reality. Welthy could not do it. The pleasure principle was plain to see in her animated spark of learning.

* * *

Because she was eminently stable and vigilant in her quiet centering Welthy had the courage to live her life fully out in the open, able to withstand the inevitable criticism It was as if she carried the House of Prayer for All People with her, open to the love within to overcome fatigue, anxiety, and even illness. The wisdom of that love was apparent to all who would see. It was felt through her pen, her voice, her eyes, her laugh, the dignity of her bearing, and in her walk, bent knee knocking against knee, reminder of her own vulnerability.

In placing her priority on human qualities — and people invariably spoke of Welthy as being "so human", she cooly rejected any ambitions toward sainthood. "Why do I want followers?" she demanded. "I want leaders," individual people who themselves have been moved to reach beyond artificial limits.

She never thought of people working for her, but with her, by conscious choice and free to go at will. By stimulating awareness, offering ideas, creating an environment of freedom with money and tools, and then moving off centre, she allowed leaders to grow into their own shape. She needed that movement away herself in order to determine what was important and what was not, what was static and what was dynamic, the perspective that was her particular genius.

She took huge risks with people and projects, refusing to use narrow calipers in assessing them, in an open-ended operating style that made administrators shudder. As a leader she sparked creative energy — the erotic in each one reaching for connection to the whole — and provided opportunity. In that sense she was a real freedom fighter.

For Indians accustomed to the protective atmosphere of the joint family or the government, that was unfamiliar opportunity not always used well. That freedom was carefully cultivated by a sense of community radiating out from the House of Prayer in its classic, circular linking. For a moment under that thatched roof disparities fell away to reveal in symbolism their converse. For each one to catch the rhythm of that moment and live with it was Welthy's deepest desire.

Welthy created the capacity for leadership in others to a degree that is impossible to measure, as any educator knows. The impact of her recent work in India is partially discernible from existing records, but it is a monumental, if not impossible task to uncover its full extent by identifying all those in India and beyond who are building on the crude steps she carved. Our present awareness of illiteracy in modern society could trace a good part of its origins to the consciousness-raising Welthy began thirty-five years ago, which has touched so many. Is it possible to even guess at the reverberations on generations of mothers and daughters of Welthy's continual speaking tours through mainstream America for eight decades? Who can estimate Welthy's influence on a generation of young women and the men some of them married in Kiangsi province, spearhead of revolutionary thought in China?

* * *

Welthy was radical in choosing to keep herself free from the controlling limits of church, university, politics or business — organizations where she was offered opportunities that would have given her greater security and more visible success. Her life illuminates the perennial dichotomy of the individual versus the organization, and the great difficulty board-run organizations have in incorporating the human values of a leader such as Welthy, which their individual members of good will may honour highly and the organization may espouse.

Is it forever necessary to eliminate the vital force of a founder for an organization to survive? Can the necessary counterbalance to that extraordinary internal energy not be found in a less negative way than withdrawal to manageable externals?

For a century Welthy lived in the centre of that maelstrom and did not give up. She knew there were miles to go, and was where she wanted to be in the affirmative, authentic freedom of personal conviction. It gave her a lightness of touch in the most difficult, serious matters, the bright bounce so many spoke of. Others looked askance, finding it barely tolerable that Welthy could enjoy her difficult task so much.

In accepting illiteracy for what it is in the lives of millions of Indian villagers, Welthy approached it with the most practical, comprehensive programme ever devised in India. Her focus on the individuality of illiteracy — en masse — was an intensely political act. Many people leading today's global movement towards literacy-based development have been directly or indirectly influenced by Welthy and Literacy House, as it has attained full visibility in India with all its promises and pitfalls.

India's significant achievement of an overall literacy rate of forty percent is statistically overshadowed by a doubling of population since Welthy began her work. By far the greatest illiteracy remains with rural women, where the feminization of poverty is at its peak. Welthy knew that preoccupation with the statistics of illiteracy was a sure step towards numbing impossibility. When she said "sit where they sit" Welthy meant that equilibrium cannot be achieved with the weight of all the illiterates at the bottom. We too must move into the balance. She said it would take respect for the individual human right to be nourished and grow into her or his own stature, and knew it would take a century.

* * *

Welthy was in the forefront of those few twentieth-century women, in the period between the first and second waves of feminism, who built solid steps into the new era of conscious global living, striving for authentic interaction, pioneering the twenty-first century.

To Welthy the bound feet and veiled faces of the women of China and India symbolized bondage beyond their own lives into society as a whole. The freeing of women into informed living could magnify the "affective principle," the leaven Welthy believed necessary for growth at all levels of education and society."[19]

Seeing her own self-interest as part of the whole, Welthy kept her boundless heart responding to the proud strengths of the poor as well as their deprivations. She recognized the poor in spiritual wealth, as well as the poor in material wealth and knew her work was global.

Learning her own brand of feminism and motivation as she went, her method and action in India were intentionally fashioned to express in the most practical manner the essential unity of life on earth. Each one is part of the whole and we share a common destiny. Welthy said so with her life. She organized herself around the concrete issue of illiteracy, spoke clearly but without malice against the status quo of injustice and ignorance, and nurtured a partnership relationship with her co-workers without need to ridicule or crush those who differed with her.

As she had been doing throughout the decades of her life, she took herself and others seriously, a woman saying to the other half of the human race: "You'd better get used to us, brother, because we're here." No person or organization that ever dealt with Welthy had any doubt about that. Her lover's embrace with the world extended far beyond what any one man, one nation, one race or one religion could enfold.

As she had penetrated beyond the moongates of China, she found her way beyond the veil of India's mud walls to the heart and mind of the strong woman there, seeing in her a divine discontent that paralleled Nehru's anguish over India's century of submission to foreign power.

By stressing the importance of women and befriending people of all kinds, she built her own network of feminist cooperators, many of whom were men. Her support group was a vast global network of women, men and children of all races, as the widest possible base of connection. By dashing off letters daily she spun webs more complex than a giant spider's, some delicate, others determined, yet all within a beautiful structure of unity with clear purpose. When she needed support, she gave it. When she needed comfort, she gave it. When she needed understanding, she gave it. It was as clear as the law of gravity, that to receive, one gives. That Welthy received so much in life is testimony to the quality and abundance of her own giving.

* * *

In her respect for the accumulated, collective reality of both China and India as she observed them changing from continents to countries, Welthy showed an astute appreciation of history, both written and unwritten. From ancient self-governing communities based on the clan and caste, weakened through various forms of corruption and having lost the battle with modern political pressure for single central authority — the better to manage and defend — a part of her welcomed these new nations into the world.

If nationhood has been necessary for economic and political growth, as she who grew to proud womanhood in "the greatest nation in the world" understood, it was not the ultimate goal of humanity. Exclusive national loyalty had become cruelly limiting in two world wars and countless lesser ones. That wider allegiance Welthy had acknowledged on first arrival in China at the beginning of this century is only now coming within the realm of possibility. Along with extending her American pride to global patriotism Welthy had moved beyond the primacy of political history rooted in materialism and nationality. Education was her politics. Nor did she accord heaven or hell ultimate status. They were abstractions of the distant future, disconnected from the reality of visible human need.

Hopelessness, famine, poverty, and fear were not impossible abstractions to Welthy. She saw them in the faces of individual human beings and was able to act. As her ancestors had pioneered against harsh nature in the westward movement to open up America, Welthy pioneered on the front line of global living in her bold stride towards the new century.

She moved from the concept of the brotherhood of mankind, that excluded over half the human race, to the living practice of unity in the diversity of all people. That she chose to work for the last quarter century of her life away from the familiarity and comfortable affluence of her homeland was the strongest sign of the healing she hoped to generate.

In its utter simplicity the House of Prayer for All People is Welthy's definitive statement, where she rose above the prevailing morbid view of the twentieth century in the certainty of her own freedom to act. In actions emanating from her total personality, that responsive freedom took on an indefinable aspect of true art, her spoken words only a pulse away from singing. Out of her unwillingness to accept the injustice of illiteracy, Welthy gave life to her vision of peace with signals as clear as the temple bell ringing out over the century.

CHRONOLOGY

1879 Born September 18, Rome, New York.

1900 B.A., Syracuse University.

1903 Teacher, Haverstraw, N.Y. and Englewood, N.J.

1904 First trip abroad to France for summer.

1906 Methodist missionary, Principal, Bao-Lin School, Nanchang, China.

1918 Y.W.C.A. war worker in England and France. Lecturer in U.S. on women of the allies.

1920 First trip to India during world tour.

1921 Editor, Methodist magazine *World Neighbors*.

1924 Married Frederick Bohn Fisher, Methodist Bishop in India and Burma, friend of Gandhi and Tagore.

1938 Widowed at 59 by Fred Fisher's sudden death.

1939 Visited China and India as journalist, interviewed leaders.

1940's Travelled to South America and Middle East frequently, studying women and educational systems. Lectured throughout U.S. on women of the world and promoted Chinese Industrial Cooperatives.

1947 Visited China and India. Gandhi urged her to work in India.

1948 Chairman, World Day of Prayer.

1952 Returned to India to start literacy work.

1953 Founded Literacy House at Allahabad, India.

1956 Literacy House campus established at Lucknow, Uttar Pradesh.

1958 President, World Education, Inc., N.Y., initial sponsor of Literacy House.

1964 Welthy Fisher Comité established in Netherlands. "To Light a Candle", film produced by Santi Chowdhury for U.S. Information Service.

1966   Founded Young Farmers Institute of Literacy House.

        "Welthy Fisher", documentary produced by National Educational Television.

1969   Established Family Life Center at Literacy House.

        Key speaker at formative meeting of British Committee on Literacy, House of Commons, U.K.

1973   Visited China for first time since 1947.

1978   Visited Peking, oldest foreign guest of Government.

1979   Celebrated centennial year in United States.

        Television documentary on Welthy Fisher and Literacy House produced by All India Radio.

1980   Final trip to India as guest of Government, after previous 'farewell' visits in 1973 and 1977.

        Died December 16, Southbury, Connecticut.

HONOURS

1921   Hon. M.A. Syracuse University.

1938   Hon. Litt. D., Florida Southern College, Lakeland.

1948   George Arents Medal, Syracuse University.

1959   Hon. President, World Literacy of Canada, Toronto.

1961   Citation, Merrill-Palmer Institute, Detroit.

1962   Watumull Foundation Award, New Delhi, $1,000.

1963   Hon. International Member, Beta Sigma Phi.

        Hon. Ph. D., Western College for Women, Ohio.

1964   Ramon Magsaysay Award, Manila, $10,000.

        Librada Avelino Award, Centro Escolar Univ., Manila.

        Hon. International Member, Delta Kappa Gamma.

1965   Hon. Ph. D., Syracuse University.

1966   Women's National Farm & Garden Award.

1968   Ancient Scottish Rite Masons & Auxiliaries Award.

        Nehru Literacy Award (first recipient).

1970   Welthy Fisher Literacy House Endowment Fund, India.

        Humanitarian Award, Variety Clubs International.

1973	Hon. Chairman, World Education Inc., New York.
	Phi Beta Phi, Outstanding Achievement in Humanities.
1974	Pioneer Award, Adult Education Assoc'n. of U.S.A.
1975	Honour Award, India League of America.
1978	International Meditation Soc., Utica-Rome Chapter Award.
	Special Citation from U.S. Vice-President Mondale.
	UNESCO Pahlavi Prize, Honourable Mention.
1979	Rosicrucian Society Award.
1980	Hon. Litt. D., Delhi University, India.
	Commemorative postage stamp issued by Government of India.

FILMS

1965   "To Light a Candle", produced by Santi Chowdhury,Image India Films Private Ltd.,for U.S. Information Service. 16 m.m. B & W.

1967   "Welthy Fisher", produced by National Educational Television, N.Y., directed by James Beveridge, for Creative Persons Series, B & W, 30 min.

1973   "To Light a Candle", produced by White Tiger Productions, N.Y., directed by Tao Porchon. Colour, 45 min.

1979   Documentary on Literacy House, produced by All India Radio for centennial, in Hindi with some English. B & W videotape converted to American standard. 15 min.

        Informal videotape of Welthy Fisher at home and at her 100th birthday. (Highlights marked in index.)

Note: All films are in BU Collection

BOOKS AND ARTICLES PUBLISHED BY WHF

1922-3   "Twins Travelogues." Four stories for children about India, Korea, Japan and China. New York, Abingdon Press.

1923   "Shall Women 'Keep Silence' in the Churches?", *Christian Advocate*, Jun.21, 776-7.

1924   "Beyond the Moongate; being a diary of ten years in the interior of the Middle Kingdom. New York, Abingdon Press.

        "A String of Chinese Pearls." New York, The Woman's Press.

1926   "Top of the World." New York, Abingdon Pres.

1927   "Under the Southern Cross." Series of nine articles in *The Classmate*, Feb.-Mar.

         "Thinking Straight About China." *Indian Witness*, Apr. 6.

1929   "Missions True and False." *World Neighbors*, v.8, n.2, 51-3.

         "The Aunt Dorinda Letters." Series of eight articles in *The Classmate*.

1930   "An Appeal to Educated Woman." *Woman's Outlook*, Apr.

         "Freedom; a story of young India." New York, Friendship Press.

1935   "Harold Gray and his Social Experiment." *Christian Advocate*, Oct. 11, 829-31.

1938-9 "A Passage to India." Series of articles in *The Classmate*.

1941   "China has Changed her Mind." *The Classmate*.

1944   "Frederick Bohn Fisher; world citizen." New York, Macmillan.

1946   "Do Christians Really Want One World?" *The Church Woman*, Sept.

1948   "Gandhi as I Knew Him." *Unity*, May-June, 31-2.

1950   "Handbook for Ministers' Wives." New York, Woman's Press.

1962   "To Light a Candle." Autobiography. New York, McGraw-Hill.

1970   Introduction and Epilogue to reprint of "That Strange Little Brown Man Gandhi" by F.B. Fisher. New Delhi, Orient Longmans, xiii-xx, 233-46.

1971   Acceptance speech, Humanitarian Award, Variety Clubs International. *World Education Newsletter*, n. 17, spring, 1-7.

1973   "Women in the Changing Pattern of Society." in "Adult Education in India," ed. by Anil Bordia et al.

1979   "I Keep Inventing my Life." *World Education Reports*, n. 18, Jan.

GLOSSARY OF FOREIGN WORDS

Ahimsa .... Non-violence

Acharya .... Learned man

Bhoodan .... Land gift

Boorka .... Veil, including whole dress

Chawls .... Squatters' huts

Charpoy .... Wooden frame bed with webbing

Chota Hazri .... Little breakfast

Coolie .... Native porter

Dandy .... Open litter

Deepa .... Small light wick in oil

Dhobi .... Laundry man

Gaon Sathi .... Village companion

Gung Ho .... Working together

Gin Bao .... All clear

Gurkha .... Nepalese tribe of British army regiment

Gurudev .... Honourable teacher

Harijan .... Outcaste

Hazratganj .... Lucknow's main business street

Id .... Moslem holy day

Jumnapar Punarnirman .. Across the Jumna reconstruction

Khadi .... Homespun cotton

Kitabwala .... Bicycle fellow

Kumbh Mela .... Festival held every 12 years in Allahabad

Kutcha .... Raw, incomplete

Mahamandal .... Large group

Mahatma .... Great soul

Maidan	Open space, field
Mala	Garland
Mali	Gardener
Mataji	Respected mother
Mawari	Of an area in Rajasthan
Mela	Festival
Mullah	Muslim clergy
Naya Savera	New dawn
Paise	Penny in Indian currency
Pandal	Colourfully painted tent
Pathan	Tribe of NW Pakistan and SE Afghanistan
Pukka	Proper, definite
Punkah	Fan, suspended from ceiling or hand held
Purdah	Seclusion, woman's veil
Raj Bhavan	State governor's residence
Rashtrapati Bhavan	President's palace
Rishi	Sage
Sadhu	Holy man
Santiniketan	Abode of peace
Sanyasin	Woman who leaves behind worldly life
Sakshartaniketan	Abode of light (Literary House)
Shamiana	Marquee
Shangrila	Imaginary paradise on earth
Shum Chum	Deep ditch
Swaraj	Home Rule
Swadeshi	Own country
Tamasha	Spectacle
Tao	Way of life
Visvabharati	World knowledge
Zemindar	Landowner

LIST OF PHOTOGRAPHS

1. Welthy's mother.
2. Welthy's father.
3. Welthy, Mina, Mabel and Fred Honsinger.
4. Welthy and Bertha Deyo.
5. Welthy and her Pi Phi sisters.
6. Welthy at 21.
7. Welthy sailing for China.
8. Ilien Tang and Welthy.
9. Chinese scholars.
10. Bao-Lin School.
11. Gertrude Howe with Methodists.
12. The staff of Bao-Lin School.
13. Welthy the principal of Bao-Lin School.
14. Welthy in the YWCA.
15. Cousin Dee.
16. Betty.
17. Helen Krayer and Welthy.
18. Welthy on horseback.
19. Bishop and Mrs. Fisher.
20. Welthy and Fred with his parents.
21. The Fishers in Burma.
22. Welthy touring South African gold mine.
23. Welthy Honsinger Fisher.
24. Frederick Bohn Fisher.
25. Rabindranath Tagore.
26. Mira Behn and Welthy.
27. Welthy the lecturer.
28. Gandhi, Kasturba and Tagore.
29. Welthy the journalist.
30. Welthy with Frank Laubach.
31. The strong woman of Chillahwan.
32. A young man practising writing.
33. Literacy House staff welcoming Welthy.
34. House of Prayer for All People.
35. Dr. S. Radhakrishnan with Welthy.
36. The gate of Literacy House.
37. A Literacy House market mobile library.
38. The first Literacy House writers' workshop.

39. One of the first literacy classes.
40. A women's literacy class.
41. Welthy with Sucheta Kripalani and R. Mukherjee.
42. Indira Gandhi and Welthy in Assam.
43. Welthy greeting the Dalai Lama.
44. Nehru with Welthy.
45. Dr. Koshy and Welthy greeting Hadley Perrin.
46. Welthy and Dr. Koshy at education seminar.
47. National Study Group on Adult Literacy, 1964.
48. Literacy House puppets educate and entertain.
49. Dr. C.D. Deshmukh and Durgabai with Welthy.
50. Eleanor Roosevelt and Welthy.
51. Welthy and Mrs. S. Trivedi in village.
52. Ambassador and Mrs. J.K. Galbraith visit.
53. The staff of Literacy House.
54. Women greeting Welthy in Udaipur.
55. Welthy greeting the announcer puppet.
56. Welthy's family in America.
57. Welthy receiving Nehru Literacy Award.
58. Dr. James Draper talking with Welthy.
59. Inauguration of Young Farmers' Institute.
60. Coffee break with V.K.R.V. Rao and Tom Keehn.
61. Talking with village women.
62. Welthy off guard at 94.
63. In a Chinese commune.
64. With teacher trainees in Kwantung 1973.
65. With staff of Kwantung Teacher Training College.
66. With Soong Ching Ling, Peking 1978.
67. Doing her homework at 98.
68. Talitha Gerlach, Rewi Alley and Welthy.
69. Arriving at 100th birthday party.
70. Receiving honorary degree in Delhi, 1980.
71. Greeting Indira Gandhi.
72. Receiving flowers in Delhi.
73. With newly literate village women.
74. With Sally Swenson.
75. Her last summer.

Opposite title page: Welthy at 90 in New York.
Last page: Government of India's commemorative postage stamp.
Front cover: Arriving at Literacy House 1973.
Back cover: Lunch in a Chinese commune 1973.

NOTES

Many of the sources referred to in the Notes are unpublished materials in the Frederick Bohn and Welthy Fisher Collection (16C), Twentieth Century Archives, Boston University Libraries, and identified as "BU", followed by box and file number, where known. The most recent additions to the Collection had not been boxed or indexed at time of writing.

Welthy Fisher has been quoted extensively, and where not specifically noted, the quotations are from her own published and unpublished writings in the BU Collection, or made directly to the author.

IJAE is the abbreviation for the *Indian Journal of Adult Education.*

CHAPTER ONE – THE METHODIST ON LIBERTY STREET

1. Isaac F. Marcosson, "Industrial Main Street; the Story of Rome the Copper City" (New York, Dodd, Mead, 1953), 1.

2. The records of the First Methodist Episcopal Church, Rome, and the Women's Foreign Missionary Society of the Methodist Church at Drew University, Madison, New Jersey both show 1879 as Welthy Honsinger's date of birth. The 1880 date given in her autobiography is incorrect, as explained in Chapter Ten.

3. Robert M. Lake, "Prehistoric Rome and Romans" (Rome Historical Society, 1970).

4. Marcossan 1953.

5. Mignon Rittenhouse, "The Amazing Nellie Bly" (Freeport, New York, Books for Libraries Press, 1956).

6. Thos. J. McNamara, "The Twin Cities of the North; otherwise Rome and Saratoga; a brief historical sketch elucidating the flag sesquicentennial" (Rome, Citizens Press, 1927).

CHAPTER TWO – WHICH SONG TO SING?

1. U.S. Congressional Record, Jan. 9, 1900.

2. Reginald W. Wheeler, "A Man Sent from God; a biography of Robert E. Speer" (Westwood, New Jersey, Fleming H. Revell Co., 1956).

3. Ibid. 141.

4. Speer 1910.

5. Ibid.

6. Hunter 1984, 216.

7. WFMS Records. (BU)

8. Ibid.

9. Notebooks. (BU 3/2&5)

10. From Psalm 91.

CHAPTER THREE – LITTLE SISTER HAN AT BAO-LIN SCHOOL

1. Ross Terrill, "Flowers on an Iron Tree" (Boston, Little, Brown, 1975), 12.
2. Ezekiel 3:15, Westminster Study ed.
3. Nanchang Women & Children's Hospital, Annual Report to WFMS, Sept. 15, 1929. (BU 27/1)
4. It is unfortunate that Welthy did not write about Howe, because the Methodist archives had scant material on their pioneering women missionaries at the time of my research, a situation they are trying to recover now.
5. Suyin 1965, 67.
6. Bishop James W. Bashford, letter to Dr. Carroll, Board of Foreign Missions, Methodist Church, June 27, 1906. (BU)
7. Welthy Honsinger, letter to Henry and Emma Honsinger, February 25, 1907.
8. Hunter 1984, 81.
9. Margaret E. Burton, "The Education of Women in China" (New York, Fleming H. Revell Co., 1911), 19.
10. Bashford 1916, 122.
11. Arthur H. Smith, "The Uplift of China" (Boston, American Board of Commissioners for Foreign Missions, 1912), 48.
12. Suyin, 75.
13. Richard T. Baker, "Ten Thousand Years; the Story of Methodism's First Century in China" (New York, Methodist Episcopal Church, 1947).
14. Paul A. Cohen, in Foreward to Sidney A. Forsythe, "An American Missionary Community in China, 1895-1905" (Harvard East Asian Monograph 43, 1971), vii.
15. Welthy Honsinger, "End of an Era," draft manuscript. (BU)
16. Welthy Honsinger, draft manuscript.
17. George Richmond Grose, "James W. Bashford; Pastor, Educator, Bishop" (New York, Methodist Book Concern, 1922), 121.
18. Lady Tsao, "Instructions for Chinese Women and Girls," translated by Mrs. S.L. Baldwin (New York, 1900). (BU 32/4)
19. Pearl Chen Lin, "Songs of Another Spring," (Privately published poems of former Bao-Lin student, 1966), v.1, iii. (BU)
20. Welthy Honsinger, "1907 in China," draft manuscript. (BU)
21. Marya Backus Rankin, "The Emergence of Women at the End of the Ch'ing; the Case of Ch'iu Chin." In "Woman in Chinese Society," edited by Marjery Wolf and Roxane Witke, Stanford University Press, 1975, 39-66.
22. Welthy Honsinger, draft manuscript.
23. "China Centenary Mission Conference records; report of the great conference held at Shanghai Apr. 5 May 8, 1907" (New York, American Tract Society), 177.
24. Ibid.
25. Harrison S. Elliott, extracts from letters to his family, summer 1907. (BU)
26. Pearl S. Buck, as told to author, April 1969.
27. Welthy Honsinger, "China's Waiting Women," *Woman's Missionary Friend*, Mar. 1910, 78.
28. Notebook. (BU 3/2)
29. Hunter 1984, 64.
30. Speer 1910.

CHAPTER FOUR – THIRTY-FOUR THOUSAND BRICKS AND THE TEMPLE BELL

1. Hahn 1941, 65.
2. Zula Brown, Letter to author, Apr. 19, 1974.
3. Nanchang Women & Children's Hospital, Annual Report to WFMS, Sept 15, 1929. (BU 27/1)
4. Welthy Honsinger, "Dr. Sun Yat-sen Visits Dr. Ida Kahn's Hospital", *Woman's Missionary Friend*, Apr. 1913, 117.
5. Talitha Gerlach, "The Welthy Fisher I Know," notes to author, Jan. 15, 1974. (BU)
6. Mabel Honsinger, Journal of the 1st Session of the Kiangsi Woman's Mission of the Methodist Episcopal Church, Nanchang, Nov. 19-25, 1913.
7. Welthy Fisher in conversation with author.
8. Welthy Fisher referred to this student as "Delicate Orchid" in MG (p.25) and "Chang Tren" in TLC (p.111). The name Mai Lau is taken from a draft manuscript. (BU 31/4)
9. Dr. Ida Kahn, "Baldwin's First Commencement," *Woman's Missionary Friend*, Dec. 1913, 420.
10. Welthy Honsinger, "Flag of the Five Bars Waves Colorfully in China," *Springfield Sunday Republican*, Nov. 20, 1921.
11. Zula Brown, Letter to author, 1975.
12. Pearl Chen Lin, Letter to author, Nov. 6, 1973. (BU)
13. Wang Gwei-hsin, interview with author, T42.
14. Hubert S. Liang, letters to author, Dec. 28, 1974 and Feb. 24, 1975. (BU)
15. Hunter 1981, 33.
16. Varg 1958.
17. Helen Foster Snow, "Women in Modern China" (The Hague, Mouton, 1967), 71.
18. Walter N. Lacy, "A Hundred Years of China Methodism" (New York, Abingdon-Cokesbury Press, MCMXLVIII), 106.
19. Kelly 1983, 68.

CHAPTER FIVE – SHALL WOMEN KEEP SILENT?

1. *Palm Springs Life*, Aug. 1974.
2. Ibid.
3. D, 1917-1918, 51. (BU)
4. *YWCA War Work Bulletin*, 52, Dec. 20, 1918.
5. Ilien Tang, Letter to Welthy Honsinger, Apr. 20, 1919. (BU 42/10)
6. Dorothea Keeney, Letter to author, Feb. 25, 1974. (BU)
7. Welthy Honsinger, "Shall Women Keep Silence in the Churches?" *Christian Advocate*, Jun. 21, 1923, 776.
8. Kelly, 105.
9. Welthy Honsinger, "Where is She?", *The Arrow*, Pi Beta Phi, Mar. 1921.
10. Welthy Honsinger, "Young Japan at School," *American Review of Reviews*, Dec. 1921, 611. (BU 31/3)
11. "Christian Education in China; a study made by an educational commission representing the mission boards and societies conducting work in China," (New York, Committee of Reference and Counsel of the Foreign Missions Conference of North America, 1922), 12.

12. Hunter 1981, 365.

13. Welthy Honsinger Fisher, "The Force of India's Future: Her Village Women," Dec. 26, 1966. (BU) This article was submitted to *UNESCO Courier*, but never published.

14. *Cleveland Plain Dealer*, Sept. 28, 1919. (BU, FBF Life & Letters, 1/19)

15. Notebook 27. (BU 3)

16. Ibid.

17. Welthy Honsinger, "Shall Women Keep Silence?"

18. *Fort Worth Record*, Jun. 28, 1922. (BU, FBF Life & Letters, 2/105)

19. *Brooklyn Union*, Jul 9, 1922. (BU, FBF Life & Letters, 2/106)

20. *New York World*, Apr. 6, 1924. (BU 3/11)

21. "How an American Bishop has been Learning Christianity from Ghandi," *New York World*, Mar. 28, 1924. (BU 3/14)

22. Helen Krayer Schwartz, Interview with author, Oct. 21, 1972. T4.

23. Lillian Vogel, undated letter to author, c. 1978. (BU)

CHAPTER SIX — FELLOWSHIP, YES, FOLLOWSHIP, NO

1. H.E. Luccock, Letter to Fred Fisher, Sept. 27, 1924. (BU 18/2)

2. When an earthquake hit Santa Barbara the following year, Robert Bliss moved to a nearby apartment while repairs were made and never returned to his wife's castle, happy with a simpler life.

3. Welthy Honsinger Fisher, "Thinking Straight About China," *Indian Witness*, Apr. 6, 1927.

4. Dhanvanthi Rama Rau, "An Inheritance," (New York, Harper & Row, 1977), p. 119.

5. Isaacs 1958, 244.

6. Halford E. Luccock and Paul Hutchinson, "The Story of Methodism," (New York, Abingdon Press, 1949), 419.

7. Frances J. Baker, "The Story of the Woman's Foreign Missionary Society of the Methodist Episcopal Church, 1869-1895," (Cincinatti, Curts & Jennings, 1898).

8. S. Natarajan, "A century of social reform in India" (London, Asia Publishing House, 1959)

9. Quoted in *Sri Aurobindo's Action*, Pondicherry, Aug. 1984, 15.

10. Sam Higgenbottom, Letters to Fred Fisher, Dec. 28, 1925 and Apr. 8, 1926. (BU 18/2)

11. Dr. Ross M. Bradley to Welthy Fisher, Dec. 5, 1925. (BU 18/2)

12. Fred Fisher, Undated Letter to Welthy, Friday a.m., 10:30. (BU 42/7)

13. Fred Fisher, Undated Letter to Welthy, on train near Khandwa. (BU 42/7)

14. Notebook #12. (BU 3)

15. Chaturvedi & Sykes 1971, 209.

16. *Sidney Herald*, Jul. 13, 1925. (BU, FBF Life & Letters, 2, 166)

17. *Indian Witness*, Aug. 19, 1925. (BU, FBF Life & Letters, 2, 176)

18. *Leelong Advertiser*, Aug. 14, 1925. (BU, FBF Life & Letters, 2, 173)

19. "Aunt Dorinda Letters," *The Classmate*, Methodist Book Concern, v. 36. (BU 27/5)2

20. Frederick Fisher, "Indians in South Africa," (Calcutta, Association Press, 1925), reprinted from *The National Christian Council Review*, 15 pp.

21. *Calcutta Guardian*, Nov. 12, 1925. (BU 3/8)

22. Neera Desai, "Emergence and development of women's organizations in India," *Fireweed* (Toronto), Issue 20, 1985, 14-32.

23. For an overview of Indian women's lives, see "Indian Women," edited by Devaki Jain (New Delhi, Ministry of Information and Broadcasting, Government of India, 1975).

24. Welthy Honsinger Fisher, "Gandhi as I Knew Him," *Unity*, May-June, 1948, 31.

25. Fred Fisher, "Two Wise Men of the East," *Dearborn Independent*, Dec. 4, 1926. (BU 22/4)

26. Mohandas K, Gandhi, Letter to Fred Fisher, Nov. 2, 1926. (BU 20/20)

27. *Northwestern Christian Advocate*, Apr. 15, 1926. (BU, FBF Life & Letters, 2, 35)1.

28. D, 1927, Jun. 4.

29. Helen Krayer Schwartz, Interview with author, Oct. 21, 1972. T4.

30. Airey 1970. See also Alley, 1986.

31. Welthy Honsinger Fisher, "Thinking Straight About China," *Indian Witness*, Apr. 6, 1927.

32. Welthy Fisher, "The Day After Tomorrow, or The Quest of Youth," 22pp. (BU 31/1)

33. Isaacs 1958, 261.

34. "Four Men Stand Out," *Saratoga Methodist*, Jun 1, 1928. (BU, FBF Life & Letters, 3/32)

35. Helen Honsinger Halstead, Comment to author, Sept. 1975. T48

36. W.W. Bell, Letter to author, May 30, 1975. (BU)

37. Fred Fisher, Letter to Brother Neff, Apr. 29, 1929. (BU 20/16)

38. Welthy Honsinger Fisher, "Missions True and False," *World Neighbors*, v.8, 2, 1929, 513. (BU 27/7)

39. Mohandas K. Gandhi, Letter to Fred Fisher, Oct. 3, 1929. (Meth. 236/72)

40. Welthy Fisher, Speech to Cosmopolitan Club, Calcutta, 1930. (BU 27/7)

41. Isaacs, 298.

42. Fred took out personal insurance to cover the advances. After tolerating the unorthodox arrangement initially, the Board was unwilling to continue the precedent of assuming obligations taken on by Fisher, not for lack of trust but as a matter of administrative policy. Fred raised thousands of dollars and contributed personally to the fund. Believing he was acting responsibly, he refused to accept New York's view of the advances as his personal debt, though his payment of premiums on the insurance implied acceptance, and insisted on mutual responsibility with the Church in erasing it.

43. R.E. Diffendorfer, Letter to E.S. Johnson, Sept. 10, 1929. (BU 18/2)

44. The Bishops' meeting in New York decided not to answer or notice the pamphlet officially, observing that "it originated in an inter-racial marriage . . . without publishing banns, after strong opposition by Bishop Fisher and the women of the WFMS in the field." Mondol's friends wrote rabid articles in the Indian press, threatening to turn the American church against Fisher. Fred told them it might not be a hard job because missionary interest was easily killed in those days. The incident was blown out of all proportion, leading some to believe the rumour that it was the main reason Fisher left India, a view the Halsteads shared though they never discussed it with the Fishers.

45. Notes (BU 4/24), and Edgar D. Jones, "American Preachers of Today," (Indianapolis, Bobbs-Merrill, 1933), 184.

46. Malcolm Pitt, Interview with author, May 29, 1975. T47.

47. Fred Fisher, Letter to E.S. Johnson, Jul. 11, 1930. (BU 18/4)

48. Sheean 1949, 164.

49. Rabindranath Tagore, Letter to Fred Fisher, Dec. 5, 1930. (BU 20/21)

50. Sheean 1949, 160.

51. *New York Times Magazine*, Nov. 8, 1931. (BU 21/1)

52. Mohandas K. Gandhi, Letter to Fred Fisher, Oct. 9, 1931. (BU 20/20)

53. Mohandas K. Gandhi, Letter to Fred Fisher, Sept. 1, 1933. (BU 20/20)

54. Accepting Fisher hospitality only deepened the Halsteads' uneasy feelings. While grateful, they remained critical of the Fisher lifestyle and thought that if Fred preached about Gandhi's truth and simplicity, they should live like Gandhi. Gordon and Fred found themselves locked in battle over a minor administrative incident stemming from misunderstanding, a pattern that repeated itself in later years with Welthy.

55. T.S. (Ernest) Lauh, comment to author, 1972. T6.

56. J.B. Kripalani, Foreward to SBM, 1970 ed.

57. Wm. E. Bembridge, Letter to Fred Fisher, Nov. 25, 1934. (BU 18/5)

58. Wm. E. Kirby, Letter to Fred Fisher, Nov. 1934. (BU 18/5)

59. Mrs. E.A. Wooten, Letter to Fred Fisher, Mar. 13, 1935. (BU 18/5)

60. D. Dale Hughes, "Conscience of a City; the history of Central Methodist Church" (Detroit, Official Board, 1967), 59.

61. Angela Morgan, "Kinship", quoted by Fred Fisher in his 1934 book "Can I Know God?"

62. Angela Morgan, in her collection "Gold on Your Pillow", 1936.

63. Art Seidenbaum, "Retiring to a Grand Antique," *Los Angeles Times*, Apr.18, 1977. pt.4.

CHAPTER SEVEN — EXQUISITE LONELINESS

1. George Sutherland and E.M. Moffat, Letters to R.E. Diffendorfer, Dec. 19 and 22, 1939. (Meth. Film 12G/484)

2. Mohandas K. Gandhi, Letter to Welthy Fisher, Nov. 2, 1939. (BU 20/20)

3. Tagore 1917, 181.

4. Frances Shepard Healey, Interview with author, Mar. 13, 1974. T34.

5. Kelly, 161.

6. The Board held to the line that if Welthy settled the eighty thousand rupee debt through a payment to the Burma and Calcutta churches, they would pay the equivalent "personal" debts of the Fund to close the matter. E.M. Moffat, Letter to George Sutherland, Jan. 14, 1939. (Meth. Film 12G/484)

7. Edgar Snow, "Alley Teaching Guerilla Industry," *Saturday Evening Post*, Feb.8, 1941. (BU 23/2)

8. Alley, 128.

9. Rewi Alley, Interview with author, Peking, Oct.20, 1975.

10. Kelly, 166-70.

11. Welthy Honsinger Fisher, "Do Christians Really Want One World?" *The Church Woman*, Sept. 1946, 36.

12. "Twenty Years of the China Welfare Institute," (Shanghai, 1958).

13. Phoebe Hsia, Interview with author, Jun.22, 1974. T42.

14. Robert W. Lillard, "Mrs. Fisher foresees important future role for the Far East," *Syracuse Herald American*, Dec.10, 1939. (BU 23/2)

15. "Race problem study need declared urgent," *Los Angeles Times*, Mar.6, 1945. (BU 23/2)

16. Zeanette More, "Hope seen in attitude of Chinese," *Los Angeles Times*, Jan.17, 1945. (BU 23/2)

17. Fred Fisher's sermon notebooks are included in the Fisher collection at BU.

18. Nym Wales (pen name of Helen Foster Snow), unpublished "Notes on Beginning of Industrial Cooperation in China," 1961, 26. (BU)

19. Helen Foster Snow, Interview with author, Sept.19, 1975) T48

20. Soong Ching Ling, Letter to Welthy Fisher, Apr.1, 1978.

21. Welthy Fisher, "China Past and Present." (BU 31/4)

22. Ibid.

23. Soong Ching Ling, "Statement Urging Coalition Government and an Appeal to the American People to Stop Their Government from Militarily Aiding the Kuomintang," Shanghai, Jul.23, 1946. In "Struggle for New China) (Peking, Foreign Languages Press, 1952), 180.

24. Mahadev Desai, Letter to Welthy Fisher, Aug.5, 1940. (BU 19/9)

25. Mohandas K. Gandhi, Letter to Welthy Fisher, Dec.28, 1941. (BU 20/20)

26. Mohandas K. Gandhi, Postcard to Welthy Fisher, Oct.11, 1944. (BU 20/20)

27. Bishop F.J. McConnell's review in *Christendom*, 1944, 399-40.

28. Hsueh Cheng, Interview with author, Shanghai, Oct.30, 1975, and Letter Dec.28, 1975.

29. Mildred Sun, Interview with author, Hong Kong, Dec.27, 1972. T9.

30. Report on "Principalship in Baldwin School," Jan.2, 1948. (BU 27/4)

31. Graham Peck, "Two Kinds of Time" (Boston, 1950)

32. Anonymous article by A China Missionary, "First Thoughts on the Debacle of Christian Missions in China," *International Review of Missions*, 1951, 411.656

33. Gerald Tannebaum in "Twenty Years of the China Welfare Institute," 1968.

34. Rewi Alley, Letter to Welthy Fisher, Dec.15, 1975.

35. Rewi Alley, "Gung Ho" (Christchurch, New Zealand, Caxton Press, 1948), 58.

36. World Education has recently supported the reemerging Sandan School through the efforts of Rewi Alley (who died in Peking in December 1987), without acknowledging Welthy Fisher's earlier support of Rewi's work there.

37. Rewi Alley, Interview with author, Peking, Oct.20, 1975.

38. Rewi Alley, Letter to author, Mar.20, 1974.

39. Rewi Alley quoted by Graham Peck, "Two Kinds of Time," 2d ed (Boston, Houghton Mifflin, 1967), 176.

40. Padmini Sengupta, "Sarojini Naidu; a biography" (London, Asia Publishing House, 1966)

41. Welthy was 'chaplain' of the National Woman's Party in the U.S. As far as I know, it was wishful thinking on the part of Indian women who posted the notice re a World Women's Party.

42. Jawarharlal Nehru, "Discovery of India" (New York, John Day, 1946), 45.

43. Tagore 1966, verse 35, 27.

44. Welthy Honsinger Fisher, "Gandhi as I knew Him," *Unity*, May-June 1948, 21.

45. Valerie Fitzgerald, "Zemindar" (Toronto, McClelland & Stewart Bantam, 1982), 578.

46. Elisabeth Croll, "Feminism and Socialism in China" (Routledge & Kegan Paul, 1968)

47. Arthur Peacock, Letter to author, Oct. 1, 1977.

48. For the gathering momentum of Gandhi's influence, see Kelly, 180-88.

49. *Christian Science Monitor*, Jan.29, 1948. (BU 23/2)

50. *Leader*, 1953, 2 (BU 51/1)

51. *Des Moines Tribune*, Dec.15, 1948. (BU 23/2)

52. Open Letter to the President of the United States, August 1951, from the National Committee. See also "Group Opens Fight on M'Carran Act," *New York Times*, Dec. 27, 1950.

53. Talitha Gerlach, "The Welthy Fisher I Know," Notes to author, Jan.15, 1974, 8.

54. Welthy Fisher, "Meeting Einstein," unpublished article. (BU 32/2)

55. Albert Einstein, Letter to Welthy Fisher, Dec.18, 1950. (BU 20/19)

56. Albert Einstein, "Our Debt to Other Men; the Lure of the Mysterious," in "Living Philosophies" (New York, Simon & Schuster, 1937), 3.

57. Miriam Evans, Letters to author, Mar. & Apr. 1974.

58. Myrta Ross, Letter to author, Jul.14, 1974.

59. Pearl S. Buck, "A Great Good Spirit," *Unity*, May-June, 1948, 24.

60. Welthy Fisher, notes for speech "An American Woman Looks at her World," 1948. (BU 32/2)

CHAPTER EIGHT – BUILDING LITERACY HOUSE: 'MATAJI'

1. Welthy Fisher, "Call from the Cross," speech notes written after trip to Holy Land, 1950. (BU 33/4)

2. Isaacs 1958, 302.

3. Sir Benegal Narsing Rau quoted by Welthy Fisher in "People to People," unpublished article, 1954. (BU 32/2)

4. Nehru, 383-4.

5. Nehru, 567.

6. Robert Laubach, Interview with author. Syracuse, May 10, 1974. T37.

7. WLCL had recently been established in New York to receive non-sectarian funds, but was primarily supporting projects of the original literacy/literature arm (known as Lit-Lit) of American mission boards under the National Council of Churches.

8. David H. Eddy in "Preaching a New Gospel; the beginnings of World Education, Inc., 1950-1957." Paper in International Education, Boston Univ., Aug.6, 1982.

9. Frank C. Laubach, reported in World Literacy, Inc. minutes, Sept. 27, 1952.

10. Hess 1967.

11. J.C. Mathur, Letter written for Welthy's ninetieth birthday, Sept.2, 1969.

12. Alfred D. Moore, Letter to Welthy Fisher, Mar.31, 1953.

13. C.D. Deshmukh, Minister of Finance, Government of India, in Singh, 1973, 55.

14. Welthy Fisher speaking in the film "To Light a Candle." BU

15. Rashid Siddiqi, Interview with author, Lucknow, Jan.31, 1973. T13.

16. Iva Gorton Sprague, former World Literacy Trustee, Interview with author, Sept.18, 1974.

17. Bil Baird, American puppeteer, and former World Education trustee speaking on NBC "Today" show, c. 1969, and in informal discussion with author.

18. A.T. Mosher, Letter to author, Nov.16, 1974.

19. Extension Evaluation; report on the relation between worker performance and, (1) the level of education of extension workers, (2) the method of approach." (Allahabad, Leader Press, 1957). See also, "Experiment in Extension; the Gaon Sathi." (London, Oxford, 1956) Also Mayer, Albert et al. "Pilot Project, India; the story of rural development at Etawah" (Berkeley, Univ. of California Press, 1958).

20. Shanti Kabir, Letter to Marge Haggerty, Sept. 1954.

21. Ambassador Kenneth B. Keating, Telegram to Welthy's ninetieth birthday celebration, Sept.18, 1969.

22. Marge Haggerty, Letter to author, Mar.26, 1974.

23. In opting to side with World Literacy as her best hope for future support, Welthy was influenced by the fact that when she attended a WLCL meeting with Mrs. Laubach, neither of them were permitted to speak.

24. Frank Laubach, reported in World Literacy, Inc. minutes, Oct.16, 1955.

25. Ruth de Forest Stavola, Letter to Marge and Bill Haggerty, 1955.

26. Comfort Shaw, Interview with author, Lucknow, Feb.3, 1973. T15.

27. Isaacs 1958, 376.

28. Beatrice Pitney Lamb, Interview with author, Jan. 1974. T27.

29. William Haggerty, Interview with author, Southbury, Conn., Jan.1, 1974. T44.

30. Dr. Sarah Itty, Letter to author, Sept.2, 1974.

31. Radhakrishnan, 1960, 92.

32. Ibid.

33. Shaw continued to develop, refine and promote his plan for state library services, continuing after retiring from LH to produce several publications on libraries that have been used by U.P., the Central and other state governments.

34. Rinchen Dolma Taring, "Daughter of Tibet" (London, Murray, 1970), 266.

35. Harold S. Miner, former President of CARE and World Education trustee, Interview with author, March 1974. T33.

36. Leela Singh Steiner, Letter to author, Jul.7, 1975.

37. *Pittsburgh Press*, Dec. 16, 1959.

38. Eleanor Roosevelt, *New York Post*, Sun. Nov.16, 1958.

39. Kelly 1983.

40. P.L. 480 funds were the Indian *Rupee* equivalent of money owed to the U.S. for surplus wheat shipped to India on most favourable terms during years of famine.

41. Schlesinger Library, Radcliffe College, Mary Elisabeth Dreier papers, MC 309, folder 107.

CHAPTER NINE – THE LONGEST STRIDE

1. Lael Wertenbaker, Interview with author, Jun.6, 1974. T39.

2. *Rome Daily Sentinel*, Nov.5, 1963.

3. Pat Watters in *Atlanta Journal*, May 10, 1962. (BU 63/2)

4. *Honolulu Star Bulletin*, Dec.1, 1964. (BU 23/5)

5. Ellen Watumull, in conversation with author, Honolulu, Oct., 1968.

6. Welthy Fisher, quoted in *World Education Newsletter*, Fall 1962, 2.

7. Ellen Griffin, as noted in Welthy's 1964 diary notes.

8. Betty Brown Pinkstaff, Letter to author, Jan.7, 1975.

9. Nari Bajaj, in conversation with author, New York, 1967.

10. Anna Lord Strauss, in conversation with author, 1976. Also Mrs. Lucile Koshland, Letter to author Aug.20, 1976.

11. Rama Mehta in *Hindustan Times Weekly*, Apr.23, 1961. (BU 23/5)

12. Sterling Seagrave, "The Soong Dynasty," (New York, Harper, 1985), 446-8, 457-61.

13. Gordon Halstead, comments to author, Apr. 1974, T39. G. Halstead to Welthy Fisher, Letter Dec.5, 1961, and WF to GH Jan.8, 1962. Also Helen Krayer Schwartz, May 1974, and T.S. Lauh, June 1974, in conversation with author.

14. Richard McFadyen, World Education minutes, Jun.18, 1963,

15. Senator Kenneth Keating referred to his letter to President Kennedy in a letter to Viola Gaylord, Rome, N.Y. (BU 42/10). He also read into the *Congressional Record* of Apr.19 and July 14, 1961, that $151,000 (increased to $205,000) of PL 480 Funds would be made available to Welthy Fisher and Literacy House, and that Fulbright and Peace Corps people would participate in the publications and audio-visual programme. (BU 23/5)

16. Louise Leonard Wright, Interview with author, Feb.14, 1973. T16.

17. Richmond Mayo-Smith, Interview with author, Apr.1, 1974, T 34B.

18. T.A. Koshy, Interview with author, 1973. T12B.

19. For the development and testing of the first and second versions of *Naya Savera* see Ram Shankar, "A Comparative Study of Two Adult Literacy Primers," *IJAE*, v.38, n.1, Jan. 1977, 28-36.

20. Lisa Sergio in conversation with author, Southbury, Conn. 1973.

21. *Times of India*, Jul.4, 1964. (BU 63/3)

22. John Peters, Letter to WF, Aug.26, 1964. (BU 20/13)

23. Laurie Baker, Letter to WF Jul.15, 1964. (BU 20/13)

24. Marijke Geertsema, in Singh 1973, 30.

25. Dr. Seth Spaulding, Director, Dept. of School and Higher Education, UNESCO, Paris, in Singh 1973, 49-50.

26. Harbans S. Bhola, "The India Education Project; a case study of institution building and organizational conflict," (Bloomington, Indiana, Int. Dev. Research Center,n.d.[c.1974])

27. Harbans Bhola in conversation with author, Lucknow, 1968. Bhola left LH to work with UNESCO in Tanzania before taking up a position in international education at the University of Indiana.

28. Mushtaq Ahmed and others who remained connected to LH through the years in various capacities took exception to Bhola's published views, dismissing them as "pornography of social science," unworthy of professional criticism. Ten years later Ahmed gave me his profuse criticism in the form of pencilled notes throughout the publication. (BU) Also see his letter to author, Mar.29, 1977. This sustained difference in approach and attitude towards literacy work on the part of literacy experts points up the limitations of relying wholly on intellectual anaylsis. For Ahmed's approach see his "Eradication of Illiteracy; Can it be Done?" in *IJAE*, May 1977, 7-15.

29. Harbans S. Bhola, Letter to the Editor, *UNESCO Adult Education Information Notes*, n.3, 1984, 3.

30. Dr. Mari Bingham Wesche, Letter to author, Jan.4, 1981.

31. Dr. Eva Shipstone, conversation with author, Lucknow, Feb. 1977.

32. Lisa Sergio, ed., "Prayers of Women," (N.Y., Harper, 1965)

33. Malcolm Adiseshiah, speaking at IAEA reception for Welthy Fisher, India International Centre, New Delhi, Mar.8, 1980.

34. V.K.R.V. Rao, speaking at farewell reception for WH, New Delhi, Feb.21, 1973. T19.

35. While recovering from a fracture Welthy dictated several chapters for a book, but her own insistence on emphasizing active aspects of rural uplift were not what Virginia Baron of Dial Press had in mind. She wanted a general book on India dealing with such controversial subjects as caste and cows.

36. Stephen Blickenstaff, Letter to T.B. Keehn, September 14, 1966.

37. "Welthy Fisher", 1966. (BU)

38. Posted to Bonn, New York, Hanoi, and accompanied Lester B. Pearson, then Secretary of State for External Affairs, on his ground-breaking trip to Moscow in 1955.

39. Mrs. Grace Hampson, in *Sunday Gleaner*, Jamaica, Mar.21, 1982.
40. Chester Bowles in conversation with author, New Delhi, 1971.
41. Kelly 1983, 392, 404.
42. A.M. Rosenthal, Letter Aug.20, 1969 on occasion of WF's ninetieth birthday.
43. "Three Decades of World Literacy of Canada" (Toronto, WLC, 1988)
44. Stephen Blickenstaff, Letter to World Education, February 26, 1967.
45. For a summary of Mathur's contribution, see A.R. Deshpande, "JCM: A Creative Adult Educationist," *IJAE*, v.39, n.5-6, May-June 1978, 8-9. Also "Shri Jagdish Chandra Mathur No More," *IJAE*, Apr. 1978, 1-2.
46. Artur Isenberg, Letter to World Education, October 30, 1967.
47. J.C. Mathur, Letter to Welthy Fisher, June 10, 1967.
48. When it became clear that I was a trustee for check-signing purposes in the field only.
49. Report to the U.S. Agency for International Development on the Activities of Literacy House, Lucknow, India, July 1, 1964 June 30, 1969.
50. *National Herald*, Lucknow, Feb.9, 1970. (BU 47/1)
51. Kalidas Bhattacharya, Letter to Sudhakanta Roychoudhury, Jun.10, 1966. (BU 42/10)
52. Dr. Malcolm Adiseshiah, former Deputy Director General of UNESCO, speaking at IAEA Conference, Pondicherry, Dec.26, 1968.
53. Kenneth S. Keating, Letter to Welthy Fisher, June 17, 1969, states that he had told the President of the "fine work that you have done for India and for Indo-American relations."

CHAPTER 10 – ENDURING VISION

1. Erotic is defined as assertion of life-force, creative energy empowered, love in all its aspects, by Audre Lorde in "Uses of the Erotic: the Erotic as Power, Crossing Press, 1978."10 p.
2. Welthy's total income at that time was approximately $20,000 a year.
3. Welthy Fisher, Letter to Girijapati Mukarji, May 10, 1972.
4. Bhagwan Sahay's last post before retirement was as Governor of Kashmir.
5. Bhagwan Sahay in conversation with author, Bombay, January 1982.
6. C.D. Deshmukh in "Literacy and Development," New Delhi, 1973. (BU 64/3)
7. Six weeks after that fracture, Welthy was back on her feet in the San Diego Walk for Development, managing to walk two and a half miles altogether.
8. The Welthy Fisher Comite was established in the Netherlands in 1969, on the initiative of Maria Schroeder van-Gogh, Marijke Geertsema, and Siepie deJong. It raised and channelled funds for literacy work to Indian projects until operations ceased in 1987.
9. Speech quoted in full in *World Education Newsletter*, no. 17, Spring, 1971.
10. The phrase was used by Joel Lamstein, subsequent President of WE, in reporting new priorities, as told by R. Mayo-Smith to author, Boston, Nov. 1984. The capital of the fund was used to cover their administrative deficit as WE's global programme expanded. It has yet to be recovered.
11. U.S. State Department nomination in humanitarian category, 1977.
12. A. Deleon, Education Adviser to Government of India, Letter to Welthy Fisher, Jun.3, 1974.
13. Welthy Fisher quoted in "Adult Education in India; a book of readings," ed. by Anil Bordia, J.R. Kidd and J.A. Draper (New Delhi, IAEA, 1973).

14. Indira Gandhi, quoted in Mary C. Carras, "Indira Gandhi: in the crucible of leadership; a political biography" (Boston, Beacon Press, 1979) 237.

15. J.P. Naik, "The Functional Primary School", in *Literacy Discussion*, Summer 1975, 79-96, p.82.

16. Prem N. Kirpal, "New Concepts of Education," in *India International Centre Quarterly*, v.2, n.1, 1975, 21-34.

17. S.C. Dutta, "Adult Education in India," in *IJAE*, Aug. 1973, 2-6.

18. Guiseppe Bellucci, "Adult Education in India; an historical and critical analysis", Rome, 1972. An overview with reference to LH as one of a few endeavours offering encouragement.

19. V.V. Giri, President of India, in *National Herald*, and *New Statesman*, Feb.22, 1973. (BU)

20. For a full account of that visit see my "Welthy Fisher's Visit to The People's Republic of China March 1973."

21. UNESCO, Paris, Letter to WF, 1973. (BU)

22. Partial incontinence and constipation were constant problems in planning and managing Welthy's travel.

23. Welthy Fisher speaking at Literacy House South, Hyderabad, Mar.9, 1977, and quoted in the U.S. State Dept. recommendation for the Freedom Medal that year.

24. John G. Sommer, "Beyond charity; U.S. voluntary aid for a changing third world" (Washington, Overseas Development Council, 1977)

25. The matter was brought to Mrs. Gandhi's attention by Bhagwan Sahay, at the urging of Mrs. Lucile Kyle, Welthy's staunch supporter from Lake Placid, N.Y. and also a friend of Indira's. Welthy learned of this after the fact.

26. *IJAE*, March 1977.

27. For an account of that visit see my article "Centenarian Revisits Peking" in *Eastern Horizon*, May 1978, 29-33.

28. See Note 19, Chapter Seven.

29. Helen Foster Snow reported to the author after her 1979 trip to China that the Friendship Association had been extremely impressed by the fact of Welthy's visit under such difficult conditions for her.

30. Soong Ching Ling died in May 1981, five months after Welthy. From her own deathbed she asked her secretary to write to me expressing understanding and condolences on Welthy's passing.

31. Suyin 1972, 83-4. Also Sterling Seagrave, "The Soong Dynasty" (New York, Harper, 1985), 357-61.

32. Proceedings of the International Literacy Day Conference, Washington, D.C., Sept. 8, 1978, edited by Stuart Diamond. (National Endowment for the Humanities)

33. In arranging for that special citation from the Vice-President, World Education may have eclipsed the possibility of Welthy's nomination for the Freedom Medal that year.

34. Two observers strongly criticized WE's role, and Welthy's, with their projects in 50 countries which corresponded to the U.S. sphere of political and economic influence. WE was seen as trying to domesticate the illiterate to adapt to the status quo. Welthy was seen to have turned to India when opportunities for "corporate charity and welfare democracy" were no longer available to her in China. That cynical view is based on little knowledge of Welthy as an educator and a lack of facts as to her influence on WE's role, which my book attempts to rectify. See Ross Kidd and Krishna Kumar, "Co-opting Freire," in *Economic & Political Weekly*, Jan. 3-10, 1981, 27-30.

35. Iva Gorton Sprague, Marshall Clark, Louise Leonard Wright, Helen Rosenthal and others.

36. Kelly 1983 and Klaitz 1978.

37. Sculpted by Mico Kaufman from author's photo of Welthy in China in 1973, the medallion was produced by the Medallic Art Company as the gift of Donald Schwartz, son of Helen and Arthur Schwartz.

38. Against the better judgment of some WE people, I decided that we had every reason simply to celebrate Welthy's life, that for once it need not be a fund raising occasion. By then I did not have sufficient confidence in WE's financial management to ask her friends again for large sums of money when no account was given of their previous gifts to the Welthy Fisher Fund.

39. When Lisa Sergio had pressed the White House the day before to have the message, she was told it was too expensive to send personalized messages to centenarians. The actual message from President Jimmy Carter, in response to our request for a greeting to the gathering, was a form letter so embarrassingly inadequate to the occasion that Lael and Bramwell fabricated a few lines of personal recognition. We knew that Jimmy Carter considered his own mother's work in India, over a two year period, to be worthy of any media attention given, and that there was no political advantage to be gained in honouring Welthy's work in India.

40. Tripathi, Virenda. "Literacy Lady; 100 birth anniversary; Dr. (Mrs.) Welthy H. Fisher." Lucknow, Literacy House, 1980. 14 p., illus. Tripathi, Virendra. "The Story of Literacy House." Lucknow, Literacy House, 1980. 12 p., illus.

41. The undertaker at Munson Loveterre, Woodbury, Conn. said that Welthy's body looked like that of a woman aged seventy-five to eighty, her skin in amazing condition for someone who had been ill that long.

42. Bishop Ralph Ward, Jr., Letter to author, May 26, 1982.

EPILOGUE

1. Dr. Ira Mickenberg in conversation with author, Jan. 19, 1981.

2. It was suggested to Literacy House that a small plaque similar in size to the one in Detroit would be appropriate. Instead a large, traditional tombstone tablet had been prepared and was installed. Welthy was wary of any symbol in the House of Prayer and certainly did not wish to be worshipped. Work according to the best of each individual's convictions was the form of worship she sought to inspire.

3. Welthy's words in accepting the Magsaysay Award in Manila, 1965. 4.

Indira Gandhi, Letter to author, December 18, 1981

5. As reported in the *IJAE*, May 1982, p.31.

6. Indira Gandhi, Letter to author, February 1, 1984.

7. In thirteen one-day seminars held at LH for the Master Trainers of the NSS in 1986 over a third of the three hundred and fifty partcipants had doctorates, and over half had between ten and fifteen years' experience in formal education. Significantly, three quarters had less than five years in the emerging field of non-formal education. "The Achievements, 1986-87, Information Development and Resource Agency (IDARA)," Lucknow, Literacy House. 38 p. Also see Literacy House Annual Reports.

8. Dr. Colleen Kelly, Interview with J.B. Kripalani, New Delhi, Dec. 16, 1981.

9. Girijapati Mukharji, Letter to author, Mar. 22, 1985.

10. Bahgwan Sahay, Letter to author, c. 1982.

11. "The Udaipur Literacy Declaration" of the international seminar held at Udaipur, India, Jan. 1982, in *IJAE*, Mar. 1982, 8-9. T.A. Koshy's report in *IJAE*, Jan.-Feb. 1984,32-43. Working Paper of the Indian Adult Education Association on "Non-Formal Adult Education for Women" in *IJAE*, Dec. 1984, 12-19.

12. Indira Gandhi speaking at the reception given by the Ministry of Education for Welthy Fisher, Ahoka Hotel, New Delhi, March 21, 1980.

13. Harbans S. Bhola, in Singh 1973, p. 38.

14. Kenneth A. Briggs, "Methodists, in Search of a Coherent Identity, Acknowledge Crisis," *New York Times*, Apr.27, 1980.

15. Welthy was keen to accept the invitation but the timing and location of the Conference conflicted with previous arrangements.

16. Henry Lacy, Interview with author, New York, April 22, 1975. T-45A.

17. Philip Gentile, Letter to author, May 1, 1986. During lean years the principal of the fund had been invaded. Gentile recently built it up over the $500,000 mark.

18. Klaitz

19. Kelly, 1983, 411.

BIBLIOGRAPHY

"Adult education in India; a book of readings." Edited by Anil Bordia, J.R. Kidd and J.A. Draper. Bombay, Nachiketa Publications, 1973.

Airey, Willis. "A learner in China; a life of Rewi Alley." Christchurch, N.Z., Caxton Press, 1970.

Alley, Rewi. "At 90; memoirs of my China years. Peking, New World Press, 1986.

Andrews, Charles F. "Mahatma Gandhi's ideas; including selections from his writings." New York, Macmillan, 1930.

Banerjee, Hiranmay. "Rabindrinath Tagore." New Delhi, Gov't. of India, 1971.

Bashford, James W. "China; an interpretation." New York, Abingdon, 1916.

Chakravarty, Amiya, ed. "A Tagore reader." Boston, Beacon Press, 1961.

Chaturvedi, Benarsidas and Marjorie Sykes. "Charles Freer Andrews; a narrative." London, Allen & Unwin, 1949.

Cott, Nancy F. "The grounding of modern feminism." New Haven, Yale Univ. Press, 1987.

Fairbank, John K., ed. "The missionary enterprise in China and America." Cambridge, Harvard Univ. Press, 1974.

Fischer, Louis. "The life of Mahatma Gandhi." New York, Harper, 1950.

Fisher, Frederick Bohn. "India's silent revolution." New York, Macmillan, 1919.

— —"Personology; the art of creative living." New York, Abingdon Press, 1930.

— —"That strange little brown man Gandhi." New York, Ray Long and Richard R. Smith, 1932. Rev. ed. New Delhi, Orient Longmans, 1970.

— —"Can I know God?" New York, Harpers, 1934.

— —"The man that changed the world." Nashville, Cokesbury Press, 1937.

Gandhi, Mohandas K. "An autobiography; the story of my experiments with truth." Transl. by Mahadev Desai. Boston, Beacon Press, 1957.

— —"All men are brothers; autobiographical reflections." Comp. and ed. by Krishna Kripalani. New York, Continuum, 1984.

Hess, Gary R. "Sam Higginbottom of Allahabad; pioneer of Point Four to India." Charlottesville, Univ. Press of Virginia, 1967.

Hahn, Emily. "The Soong sisters." New York, Doubleday, 1941.

Hunter, Jane Harlow. "Imperial evangelism; American women missionaries in turn-of-the-century China." Ph.D. Thesis, Yale Univ., 1981. Published as "Gospel of gentility." New Haven, Yale Univ. Press, 1984.

Husain, Dr. Zakir. "Educational reconstruction in India." Gov't. of India, 1959.

Isaacs, Harold R. "Scratches on our minds; American images of China and India." New York, John Day, 1958.

Kelly, Colleen Adele. "The educational philosophy and work of Welthy Honsinger Fisher in China and India: 1906-1980." Ph.D. Thesis, Univ. of Connecticut, 1983.

Kripalani, J.B. "Gandhi, his life and thought." New Delhi, Gov't. of India, 1970.

Lannoy, Richard. "The speaking tree; a study of Indian culture and society." Oxford Univ. Pres, 1971.

Latourette, Kenneth Scott. "The development of China." Boston, Houghton Mifflin, 1917.

— —"A history of Christian missions in China." New York, Macmillan, 1929.

Laubach, Frank C. "Forty years with the silent billion; adventuring in literacy." Old Tappan, N.J., Fleming H. Revell, 1970.

McLoughlin, William G. "Revivals, awakenings, and reform; an essay on religion and social change in America, 1607-1977." Univ. of Chicago Press, 1978.

Mathur, J.C. "Adult education for farmers in a developing society." New Delhi, Indian Adult Education Association, 1972.

Mott, John R. "The decisive hour of Christian missions." New York, Student Volunteer Movement, 1910.

Mukerji, S.N. "Education in India; today and tomorrow." 4th ed. Baroda, Acharya Book Depot, 1960.

Nehru, Jawaharlal. Discovery of India. New York, John Day, 1946.

Oxenham, John. "Literacy; writing, reading and social organization." London, Routledge & Kegan Paul, 1980.

Radhakrishnan, S. "The Hindu view of life." London, Unwin, 1960.

Rao, U.S. Mohan, Comp. and ed. "The message of Mahatma Gandhi." New Delhi, Gov't. of India, 1968.

Rolland, Romain. "Mahatma Gandhi; the man who became one with the universal being." Transl. by Catherine D. Groth. New York, Garland, 1973. Reprint of 1924 ed. publ. by Century, New York.

Sheean, Vincent. "Personal history." New York, Garden City Publ., 1937.

— —"Lead kindly light." New York, Random, 1949.

Sheridan, James E. "China in disintegration; the Republican era in Chinese history, 1912-1949." New York, Free Press, 1975.

Speer, Robert E. "Christianity and the nations." New York, Fleming H. Revell, 1910.

Suyin, Han. "The crippled tree." London, Jonathon Cape, 1965.

— —A mortal flower." Bantam ed., 1972.

Tagore, Rabindranath. "Gitanjali" (song offerings). London, Macmillan, 1966. Reprint of 1912 ed. with introd. by W.B. Yeats.

— —"Personality." Macmillan Pocket Tagore, 1980. Reprint of 1917 ed.

— —"The religion of man; being the Hibbert lectures for 1930." Boston, Beacon Press, 1961.

Thomson, James C., Peter W. Stanley and John C. Perry. "Sentimental imperialists and the American experience in East Asia." New York, Harper, 1981.

Varg, Paul A. "Missionaries, Chinese and diplomats; the American Protestant missionary movement in China, 1890-1952." Princeton, 1958.

Vinoba. "Thoughts on education." 2nd ed. transl. by Marjorie Sykes. Varanasi, Sarva Seva Sangh Prakashan, 1964.

SELECTED ARTICLES ABOUT WELTHY HONSINGER FISHER

Scott, Barbara E. "Seventh Round-the-World Trip Uncovers New Progress in Orient to Mrs. Fisher." *Christian Science Monitor*, Jan. 29, 1948.

Harrison, Emma. "Woman Teaching Indians to Read." *New York Times*, June 30, 1957.

Lederer, William J. and Eugene Burdick. "Salute to Deeds of Non-Ugly Americans. *Life*, Dec. 7, 1959, 158-163.

Benegal, Som. "Light One Candle." *Kiwanis Magazine*, Dec. 1959-Jan. 1960, 23-29.

Grimes, Paul. "Literacy Village near Lucknow keeps Promise of aid to Gandhi." *New York Times*, Apr. 2, 1961, illus.

Spencer, John. "It is Better to Light one Candle than to Curse the Darkness." In "Workers for Humanity." London, Harrap, 1962.

Aichner, Josephine S. "Neighbor to the World." Syracuse University *Alumni News*, Winter 1966, 7-10.

Frazer, John and John Reddy. "She Lights the Lamp of Learning." *Together*, June 1967.

Swenson, Sally;. "Literacy brings new life to Indian villages." *Canadian Library*, Sept. 1967. 5 p.

"Born Welthy." Illus. booklet issued on occasion of 90th birthday. New York, World Education Inc., 1969.

Fosburgh, Lacey. "A Woman of 90 Combats Illiteracy in India." *New York Times*, Sept. 18, 1969, illus.

Petigura, Erike. "Lady with a Mission; at 91 Welthy Fisher still works for the poor." *Asia Magazine*, Jun. 27, 1971, 16-19. Also in *Imprint* (Bombay), Jun. 1971, 14-19.

Singh, Mrs. S. Mahendrajit, ed. "Abhinandan; homage to a world citizen." Literacy House, Lucknow, 1973. 94 p.

Johnston, Laurie. "Gandhi Gave her Start, Teacher of Indians recalls at 95." *New York Times*, Sept. 19, 1974, illus.

"Welthy Teaches Millions." In "Turning Point; a collection of short biographies." New York, Learning Trends, Globe Book Co., 1975.

Dumont, Tim. "Nonagenarian Views Old, New China; saw Republic's Birth." *Hartford Courant*, Oct. 24, 1975, 31, illus.

Mohan, Kusum. "Welthy Fisher; don't curse the darkness, light a candle." *Transindia*, Dec. 1976, 9-17, illus.

Vitullo, Ann. "The Rich Life of Welthy Honsinger Fisher; at 98 she still crosses the globe in the service of others." Syracuse University *Alumni News*, Fall 1977, 17-22, illus.

Johnson, Sharon. "Welthy Fisher; woman with a mission." *New York Times*, Apr. 2, 1978, 54, illus.

Klaitz, Linda. "An examination of the oral biographies of eight exceptional women." Ph.D. Thesis, Columbia Univ., 1978.

Swenson, Sally. "Centenarian Revisits Peking." *Eastern Horizon*, May 1978, 29-33, illus.

"There's no Stopping Welthy." *South China Morning Post*, Hong Kong, May 5, 1978.

Tandon, P.D. "Goddess of the Unlettered." *Imprint* (Bombay), July 1978, 21-26, illus.

Dempsey, Lotta. "Centenarian Carries on War on Illiteracy." *Toronto Star*, Jun. 13, 1979, C17.

John, V.V. "Lighting More than a Candle; Welthy Fisher's Memorable Work." *Times of India*, Sept. 18, 1979, editorial page.

"Welthy Honsinger Fisher; a purposeful life completes one hundred years." *Indian Journal of Adult Education*, Sept. 1979, 32-46.

Tripathi, Virendra. "Literacy Lady; 100 birth anniversary; Dr. (Mrs.) Welthy H. Fisher." Lucknow, Literacy House, 1980. 14 p., illus.

Schreiner, Samuel A., Jr. "Going Strong at 101." *Reader's Digest*, Dec. 1980, 139-143.

Nair, G.R. "The Legacy of Welthy Fisher; development through literacy." *Social Welfare* (India), Jan. 1981, 17-19, illus.

Keehn, Thomas B. "Welthy Honsinger Fisher." *Reports Magazine*, (World Education Inc., N.Y.) April 1981.

Kelly, Colleen Adele. "The Educational Philosophy of Welthy Honsinger Fisher in China and India 1906-1980; an intellectual biography." Ph.D. Thesis, Univ. of Connecticut, 1983. 475 p. U.M.83-19, 199.

See also "List of Published References and Articles on Welthy Honsinger Fisher, 1906-1983, Boston University Special Collection of 20th Century Personalities, 16C. 40 p.

INDEX

MAY 0 3 1989

LA
2317
.F58
S94
1988

16.G   0907943   1996 05 16

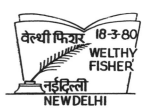

The design of the First Day Cancellation shows a book,
quill and ink-pot symbolizing adult literacy.